WORLDCOMP'13
July 22-25, 2013
Las Vegas Nevada, USA
www.world-academy-of-science.org

PROCEEDINGS OF THE 2013 INTERNATIONAL CONFERENCE ON E-LEARNING, E-BUSINESS, ENTERPRISE INFORMATION SYSTEMS, & E-GOVERNMENT

EEE 2013

Editors

Hamid R. Arabnia
Azita Bahrami
Fernando G. Tinetti

Associate Editors

Leonidas Deligiannidis
George Jandieri
Ashu M. G. Solo

(An Imprint of Laxmi Publications Pvt. Ltd.)
An ISO 9001:2008 Company

BENGALURU • CHENNAI • COCHIN • GUWAHATI • HYDERABAD
JALANDHAR • KOLKATA • LUCKNOW • MUMBAI • RANCHI • NEW DELHI
BOSTON (USA) • ACCRA (GHANA) • NAIROBI (KENYA)

This volume contains papers presented at The 2013 International Conference on e-Learning, e-Business, Enterprise Information Systems, & e-Government (EEE'13). Their inclusion in this publication does not necessarily constitute endorsements by editors or by the publisher.

Branches

Bengaluru	080-26 75 69 30	
Chennai	044-24 34 47 26,	24 35 95 07
Cochin	0484-237 70 04,	405 13 03
Guwahati	0361-254 36 69,	251 38 81
Hyderabad	040-27 55 53 83,	27 55 53 93
Jalandhar	0181-222 12 72	
Kolkata	033-22 27 43 84	
Lucknow	0522-220 99 16	
Mumbai	022-24 91 54 15,	24 92 78 69
Ranchi	0651-220 44 64	

Published in India by

An ISO 9001:2008 Company
113, GOLDEN HOUSE, DARYAGANJ,
NEW DELHI - 110002, INDIA
Telephone : 91-11-4353 2500, 4353 2501
Fax : 91-11-2325 2572, 4353 2528
www.laxmipublications.com info@laxmipublications.com

C—
Printed at:

Foreword

It gives us great pleasure to introduce this collection of papers to be presented at the 2013 International Conference on e-Learning, e-Business, Enterprise Information Systems, and e-Government (EEE), July 22 through 25, 2013, at The New Tropicana Hotel, Las Vegas, USA.

An important mission of the World Congress in Computer Science, Computer Engineering, and Applied Computing (a federated congress to which this conference is affiliated with) includes *"Providing a unique platform for a diverse community of constituents composed of scholars, researchers, developers, educators, and practitioners. The Congress makes concerted effort to reach out to participants affiliated with diverse entities (such as: universities, institutions, corporations, government agencies, and research centers/labs) from all over the world. The congress also attempts to connect participants from institutions that have* ***teaching*** *as their main mission with those who are affiliated with institutions that have* ***research*** *as their main mission. The congress uses a quota system to achieve its institution and geography diversity objectives."* By any definition of diversity, this congress is among the most diverse scientific meeting in USA. We are proud to report that this federated congress has authors and participants from 82 different nations representing variety of personal and scientific experiences that arise from differences in culture and values. As can be seen (see below), the program committee of this conference as well as the program committee of all other tracks of the federated congress are as diverse as its authors and participants.

The program committee would like to thank all those who submitted papers for consideration. About 65% of the submissions were from outside the United States. Each submitted paper was peer-reviewed by two experts in the field for originality, significance, clarity, impact, and soundness. In cases of contradictory recommendations, a member of the conference program committee was charged to make the final decision; often, this involved seeking help from additional referees. In addition, papers whose authors included a member of the conference program committee were evaluated using the double-blinded review process. One exception to the above evaluation process was for papers that were submitted directly to chairs/organizers of pre-approved sessions/workshops; in these cases, the chairs/organizers were responsible for the evaluation of such submissions. The overall paper acceptance rate for regular papers was 29%; 14% of the remaining papers were accepted as poster papers (at the time of this writing, we had not yet received the acceptance rate for a few individual tracks.)

We are very grateful to the many colleagues who offered their services in organizing the conference. In particular, we would like to thank the members of the Program Committee of EEE'13, members of the congress Steering Committee, and members of the committees of federated congress tracks that have topics within the scope of EEE. Many individuals listed below, will be requested after the conference to provide their expertise and services for selecting papers for publication (extended versions) in journal special issues as well as for publication in a set of research books (to be prepared for publishers including: Springer, Elsevier, BMC, and others).

- *Dr. Selim Aissi (World Congress Steering Committee); formerly, Chief Strategist - Security, Intel Corp., USA; Senior Business Leader & Head of Global Enterprise Security Architecture, Visa Corporation, USA*
- *Prof. Babak Akhgar (World Congress Steering Committee); Fellow of the British Computer Society, CITP; Professor of Informatics; Co-Director of CENTRIC (Centre of Excellence in Terrorism, Resilience, Intelligence & organised Crime research), Sheffield Hallam University, Sheffield, UK*
- *Dr. Fahad Al-Harby; The National Centre for Financial & Economic Information, Ministry of Finance, Riyadh, Saudi Arabia*
- *Prof. Nizar Al-Holou (World Congress Steering Committee); Professor and Chair, ECE Department; Vice Chair, IEEE/SEM-Computer Chapter; University of Detroit Mercy, Detroit, Michigan, USA*
- *Dr. Haider M. AlSabbagh (FECS); University of Basra, Iraq*
- *Prof. Hamid R. Arabnia (World Congress Steering Committee); Professor, Computer Science; Editor-in-Chief, The Journal of Supercomputing (Springer); Elected Fellow, Int'l Society of Intelligent Biological Medicine (ISIBM); The University of Georgia, Department of Computer Science, USA*
- *Peyman Arebi; Assistant Professor, Department of Computer Engineering, Technical and Vocational University, Bushehr, Iran*

- *Prof. Ezendu Ariwa (Publicity Vice-Chair); IEEE Consumer Electronics Chapter, UK&RI; Visiting Professor, Gulf University, Bahrain and University of Lagos and Kano State Polytechnic, Nigeria*
- *Dr. Azita Bahrami (Session Chair, EEE); President, IT Consult, USA*
- *Prof. Juan Jose Martinez Castillo; Director of The Acantelys Research Group and Coordinator of the Computer Engineering Department, Universidad Gran Mariscal de Ayacucho, Venezuela*
- *Prof. Juan Cuadrado-Gallego; Universidad de Alcala, Edificio Politecnico, Madrid, Spain; Ecole de technologie superieure, Canada*
- *Prof. Kevin Daimi (World Congress Steering Committee); Director, Computer Science and Software Engineering Programs; Department of Mathematics, Computer Science and Software Engineering; University of Detroit Mercy, Detroit, Michigan, USA*
- *Prof. Leonidas Deligiannidis; Professor, Computer Science, Wentworth Institute of Technology, MA, USA*
- *Somdip Dey (ICOMP); St. Xavier's College (Autonomous), India*
- *Prof. Houcine Hassan (FECS); Universitat Politecnica de Valencia, Spain*
- *Dr. Bing He (PDPTA); Cisco System Inc., USA*
- *Dr. K. S. S. Iyer (FECS); Symbiosis Institute of Telecom Management, India*
- *Prof. George Jandieri (World Congress Steering Committee); Georgian Technical University, Tbilisi, Georgia; Chief Scientist, The Institute of Cybernetics, Georgian Academy of Science, Georgia; Editorial Board Member: International Journal of Microwaves and Optical Technology, Georgia*
- *Prof. Seifedine Kadry (PDPTA); School of Engineering, American University of the Middle East, Kuwait*
- *Prof. Dong Hwa Kim; Hanbat National University, Korea; Visiting Professor, Budapest University of Technology and Economic, Hungary; International Einstein awardee for Scientific achievement (2010)*
- *Prof. Dattatraya V. Kodavade (World Congress Steering Committee); Head of Computer Science and Engineering, D.K.T.E Society's Textile & Engineering Institute, Ichalkaranji, Maharashtra State, India*
- *Prof. Raghu Korrapati; Elected Fellow, Walden University, Minneapolis, MN, USA*
- *Prof. B. Raja Sarath Kumar; Principal, Lenora College of Engineering, India*
- *Dr. Jong Kwan (Jake) Lee (MSV); Bowling Green State University, Ohio, USA*
- *Prof. Kun Chang Lee (World Congress Steering Committee); Professor of MIS and WCU Professor of Creativity Science, Business School and Department of Interaction Science, Sungkyunkwan University, Korea*
- *Prof. Zhongyu (Joan) Lu; University of Huddersfield, Huddersfield, UK*
- *Dr. Bala Krishna Maddali (GCA); GGS Indraprastha University, New Delhi, India*
- *Arshad Mansoor; Pakistan Aeronautical Complex, Pakistan*
- *Dr. Tao Mao (ICAI + GEM); Oracle America, Inc., USA*
- *Prof. George Markowsky (World Congress Steering Committee); Professor and Associate Director, School of Computing and Information Science; Chair International Advisory Board of IEEE IDAACS; Director 2013 Northeast Collegiate Cyber Defense Competition; Cooperating Professor Math and Statistics Department UMaine and School of Policy & International Affairs UMaine; University of Maine, Orono, Maine, USA*
- *Suzanne Kranjac McIntosh (SERP); Team Lead, IBM T. J. Watson Research Center, New York, USA*
- *Dr. Ali Mostafaeipour; Industrial Engineering Department, Yazd University, Iran*
- *Dr. Saurabh Mukherjee; Banasthali University, Banasthali, Rajasthan, India*
- *Prof. Prashant R. Nair; Vice-Chairman, Information Technology & Accreditation; Faculty, AMRITA-TIFAC Centre of Excellence in Cyber Security; India*
- *Dr. Asoke Nath; Department of Computer Science, St. Xavier's College, India*
- *Prof. G. N. Pandey (World Congress Steering Committee); Vice-Chancellor, Arunachal University of Studies, Arunachal Pradesh, India; Adjunct Professor, Indian Institute of Information Technology, India*
- *Prof. James J. (Jong Hyuk) Park (World Congress Steering Committee); Professor of Computer Science and Engineering, Seoul National University of Science and Technology (SeoulTech), Korea; President, KITCS; President, FTRA; Editor-in-Chiefs: HCIS, JoC and IJITCC Journals*
- *Prof. R. Ponalagusamy (MSV + PDPTA + SERP); National Institute of Technology, India*
- *Prof. Junfeng Qu; Clayton State University, Morrow, USA*
- *Prof. B. V. A. N. S. S. Prabhakar Rao (ICAI + SERP); VIT University, Chennai Campus, India*
- *Prof. Judy Ann Serwatka; Purdue University North Central, Indiana, USA*
- *Dr. Liang Shi; Senior Researcher, McAfee, USA*
- *Ashu M. G. Solo, (Publicity Chair); Fellow of British Computer Society, Principal/R&D Engineer, Maverick Technologies America Inc., USA*
- *Dr. Jiao Tao (ICAI); Oracle USA*
- *Prof. Fernando G. Tinetti (World Congress Steering Committee); School of Computer Science, Universidad Nacional de La Plata, La Plata, Argentina; Co-editor, Journal of CS and Technology (JCS&T)*
- *Dr. Predrag Tosic (World Congress Steering Committee); Microsoft, Washington, USA*
- *Prof. Ion Tutanescu (ICWN); University of Pitesti, Romania*

- *Prof. Vladimir Volkov (World Congress Steering Committee); The Bonch-Bruevich State University of Telecommunications, Saint-Petersburg, Russia*
- *Prof. Patrick Wang (IPCV + MSV + CGVR); Fellow of IAPR, ISIBM, WASE; Zijiang Chair Professor, ECNU, Shanghai and NTUST, Taipei, Taiwan; Founding President and CEO, Wang Teknowlogy Lab.; MIT Research Consultant; Harvard University, Adj. Faculty, USA; Northeastern University, Boston, MA, USA*
- *Dr. Wei Wei (GCA + ICOMP + ICWN); Xi'an University of Technology, Xi'an, P. R. China*
- *Dr. Alexander Wohrer (ICOMP + GCA); Program Manager ICT at Vienna Science and Technology Fund, Schlickgasse, Vienna, Austria*
- *Prof. Dr. Bernd E. Wolfinger (ICOMP + PDPTA); Telecommunications and Computer Networks Division, University of Hamburg, Germany*
- *Dr. Qiang Xu; Teesside University, England, UK*

As Sponsors-at-large, partners, and/or organizers each of the followings (separated by semicolons) provided help for at least one track of the World Congress: Aldebaran Robotics Inc., USA (http://www.aldebaran-robotics.com); Altera Corporation, USA (http://www.altera.com/); Computer Science Research, Education, and Applications Press (CSREA); Impulse Accelerated Technologies, Inc., USA (http://www.impulseaccelerated.com/); NVIDIA Corporation, USA (http://www.nvidia.com/object/about-nvidia.html); Parallella Community, Supercomputing for Everyone, USA (http://forums.parallella.org/); Pico Computing, Inc., USA (http://picocomputing.com/); SemiWiki.com, The Semiconductor Wiki Project, USA (http://www.semiwiki.com/); Solarflare Communications, Inc., USA (http://www.solarflare.com/); Stream Computing, Performance Engineers, The Netherlands (http://streamcomputing.eu/); Taylor & Francis, UK (http://www.taylorandfrancis.com/); US Chapter of World Academy of Science (http://www.world-academy-of-science.org/) ; and WEBestSOL & Webest Solutions Ltd, UK (http://webestsol.com/). In addition, a number of university faculty members and their staff (names appear on the cover of the set of proceedings), several publishers of computer science and computer engineering books and journals, chapters and/or task forces of computer science associations/organizations from 5 countries, and developers of high-performance machines and systems provided significant help in organizing the conference as well as providing some resources. We are grateful to them all.

We express our gratitude to keynote, invited, and individual conference/tracks and tutorial speakers - the list of speakers appears on the conference web site. We would also like to thank the followings: UCMSS (Universal Conference Management Systems & Support, California, USA) for managing all aspects of the conference; Dr. Tim Field of APC for managing the printing of the proceedings; and the staff of the New Tropicana Hotel in Las Vegas for the professional service they provided. Last but not least, we would like to thank the Co-Editors and Associate Co-Editors of EEE'13: Prof. Hamid R. Arabnia, Dr. Azita Bahrami, Prof. Leonidas Deligiannidis, Prof. George Jandieri, Ashu M. G. Solo, and Prof. Fernando G. Tinetti.

We present the proceedings of EEE'13.

Steering Committee, 2013
http://www.world-academy-of-science.org/

Contents

SESSION: LEARNING METHODS, E-LEARNING + EDUCATIONAL TOOLS, AND RELATED ISSUES

SESSION: E-GOVERNMENT AND ISSUES OF INTEREST TO GOVERNMENT, ELECTED OFFICIALS, AND RELEVANT AGENCIES

SESSION: E-BUSINESS, E-COMMERCE, E-BANKING, ENTERPRISE INFORMATION SYSTEMS, AND SECURITY

SESSION: MANAGEMENT, TOOLS, WEB, INFORMATION EXTRACTION + APPLICATIONS AND STANDARDS

SESSION: POSTERS AND SHORT PAPERS

SESSION: E-COMMERCE AND PRIVACY + EDUCATION AND LEARNING METHODS + KNOWLEDGE-BASED SYSTEMS

SESSION

LEARNING METHODS, E-LEARNING + EDUCATIONAL TOOLS, AND RELATED ISSUES

Chair(s)

TBA

Molly Open Source Online Lecture System

Ronald P. Vullo, Ph.D., Natallia Ivaniuk, M.S.I.T., and Sean Boyle, M.S.I.T.
Golisano College of Computing and Information Sciences
Rochester Institute of Technology
Rochester, New York 14623

Abstract – *For over 13 years, one of the authors has been developing and using a Web-based presentation tool for in-class and distance education. Recent advances in Web technology have made it possible to re-implement the system and incorporate the ability for educators to easily add a video track and synchronize their slides to it. We also added shared permissions multi-user editing capability and several other features. This new version of a time-tested Web-based lecture slide system provides distance learners a classroom-like experience via the Web and makes it easy for educators to develop, edit, share, and reuse presentations.*

Keywords: e-Learning, Distance Education, Video, Open Source, Web

1 Introduction

For over 13 years, one of the authors (Vullo) has been developing and using a Web-based presentation tool as part of the open source Molly Website development system. Although used primarily in the classroom, it was conceived of originally as a distance education tool, and has been used in the delivery of at least one complete distance education course. In the early days of the system, distance lectures were created with an integrated video of the lecturer that drove and synchronized the slides. This was accomplished via QuickTime's HREF Track mechanism, combined with JavaScript. While it worked, it was fussy and required considerable expertise, time, and effort to author such lectures. Security enhancements to JavaScript eventually broke the system and a second technique — again driven by a special QuickTime track — was used. While more reliable, it was still a complex and tedious process to author a lecture. With the release of the HTML5 standard came the incorporation of the <video> tag. With video now part of the Document Object Model (DOM), it became possible to control both the video and slides from JavaScript. More importantly, because the control codes and time codes no longer needed to be embedded in the video itself, it became possible to create a simple Web-based authoring environment. This finally made it possible to fulfill the original vision for the Molly system's distance learning component and was the genesis of this project. This paper describes the re-development and expansion of this lecture delivery system.

2 Project Overview

The Molly online lecture system emulates a real in-class environment and face-to-face communication with a professor by providing video lectures combined with automatic slide switching functionality. The main audiences for the system are students and faculty members. These user's groups have different business goals and needs that they wish to accomplish using our system.

During the design phase of the project, the requirements and expectations of the main intended audience were collected and analyzed. Students are interested in viewing any class materials online that will help them study their curriculum. Faculty members would like to use the system to share information with remote students as well as to make in-class presentations. The result of this analysis is presented in a form of use case diagrams.

There are two main actors in the system: Viewers and Editors. A Viewer is a user who is interested in viewing lecture content. It could be a remote student who is taking online class, as well as a professor who is presenting in class. An Editor is a user who is responsible for available lecture content and material (most typically the lecturer or professor). For these audiences, the system has two key components: a presentation portal and a management portal. The presentation portal is intended for the viewing audience, while the management portal is for content administration and management.

Figure 1 (below) shows a use case diagram for Viewers. Viewers would like the system to support two presentation modes:

- In-class presentation: for the in-class environment, the presentations are displayed without any video content and with manual slide switching.
- Online presentation: this mode includes video with automatic slide switching. Available lecture content includes slides and any additional notes from the professor. For easy navigation between slides, the user must have the ability to select the next and previous slides, as well as random access to any of the other slides. In addition, students can see other people's comments, suggestions and notes related to the slide content, and can post their own questions and comments for the whole community of users. In order to leave a comment and/or participate in forum discussions, a user must register themselves in the system. As far as the video, users have the ability to play, pause and seek. A print version is available containing all slide content and an additional notes section.

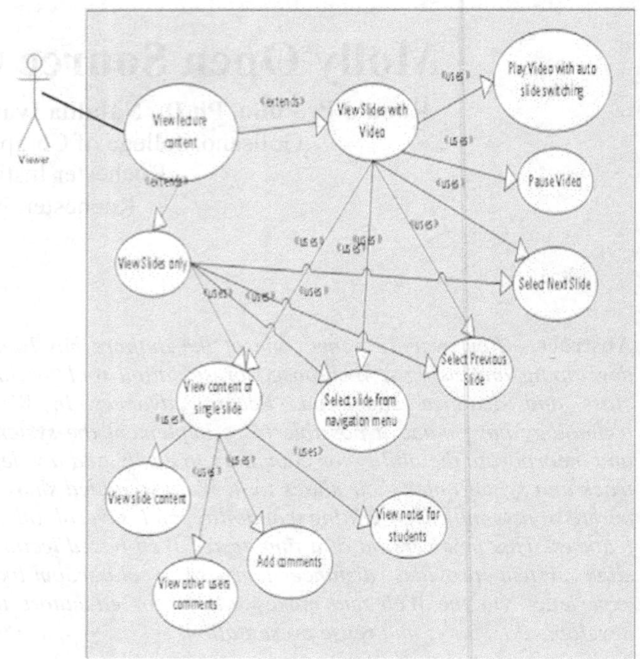

Figure 1: Use case diagram for viewers

Figure 2 (below) shows a use case diagram for Editors. Unlike Viewers, Editors are responsible for creating and managing lectures with all material required by the class curriculum. First, they need the ability to create lectures. The implemented solution provides two different ways of creating the context: either create a new lecture de novo or copy the content from an already existing lecture. The second approach is mainly suitable for classes with similar content; for example, classes that have versions taught to both graduate and undergraduate students. Editors must be able to see the list of all lectures that they have access to. They must be able to delete lectures, make lectures available online or take lectures offline.

The lecture content management functionality supports the capability to create, edit, delete, or reorder slides. Each lecture slide has an extra section for additional comments and notes regarding the slide content. Student notes are public and are available online for all viewers, while lecture notes are only available for Editors. The system provides the ability to upload pre-recorded video for the class with the video poster. It allows configuring automatic slide switching based on play position within the video content. For additional security, the owner of the lectures can grant and revoke Editor rights to other users of the system.

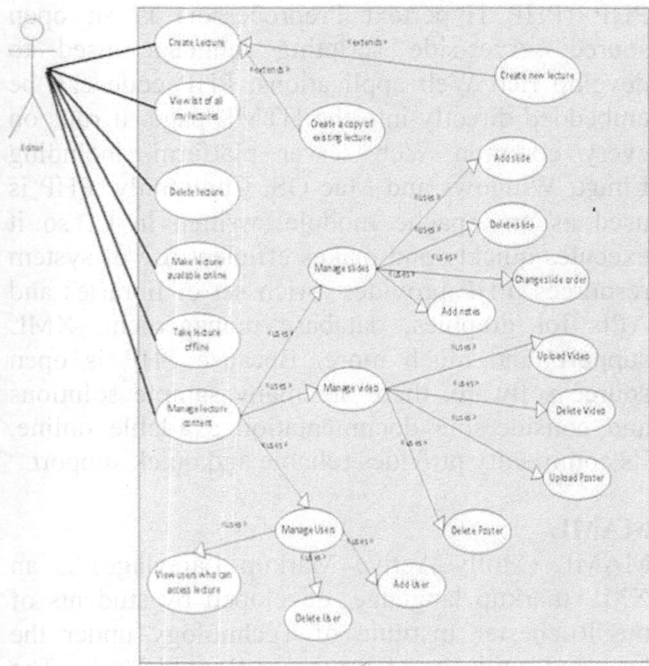

Figure 2: Use Case diagram for Editors

3 Application Architecture

The system has been developed using a standard three-tier architecture. In this model, the user interface, functional business logic, data storage and access are developed as independent components. This approach provides benefits such as reusability, flexibility, maintainability, and scalability.

Presentation Layer

This layer presents data to the user (Graphical User Interface). For the current implementation the latest web client-side technology, such as HTML5, CSS3, JavaScript and AJAX were used. The developed system is targeted to support the most common current browsers: Firefox, IE, Safari, Opera and Chrome.

Business Server Layer

This layer encapsulates the main business rules and services. This layer enforces required parameter validation, data dependencies and data integrity. For developing the service layer the server-side scripting language PHP5 and Molly middleware (molly.rit.edu) were used.

Data Layer

The data layer is responsible for data storage and interactions with persistent data. It combines both data sets and the database management system. A MySQL database was used as a backend for the current implemented solution, however Molly uses a database abstraction layer allowing other databases such as Oracle and PostgreSQL.

4 Technologies and Tools

The system is implemented using the latest Web technologies such as HTML5, CSS3, JavaScript and AJAX libraries with a MySQL backend. The server-side component had been built using PHP and MAML.

Hypertext Markup Language (HTML5, DOM)

HTML5 is a new version of HTML that is rapidly penetrating the Web market. HTML5 is a markup language developed for presenting content for web pages.

HTML5 was first presented in 2004 by the Web Hypertext Application Technology Working Group. In 2008, the first working draft of the specification was published. Since then, many browsers have started supporting HTML5 features.

HTML5 significantly improves standardization for browsers' behavior and presentation across different platforms. Compared to older HTML versions, it offers new features for easier Web application development and more sophisticated form handling. HTML5 was the driving reason for this new version of the Molly system due to its integrated support for graphics, video and audio. It provides APIs for embedding and controlling audio and video content. The new Canvas element provides support for 2D graphics animation without use of the Flash or Silverlight plug-ins.

Cascading Style Sheets (CSS)
Cascading Style Sheets are a set of rules that define how HTML elements are displayed and positioned on a web page. CSS styles can be defined in-line with HTML elements or imported from a separate style sheet. We used separate additional CSS files for this system, in addition to Molly's built in CSS, to simplify changing and configuring layout and styles of the page. As a result, in one of our future enhancements, users of the system will be able to select their own "skins" for the presentation of their slides.

Cascading Style Sheets were introduced 13 years ago, and are now ubiquitous on the Web. Style rules have significantly evolved over the years. The latest version, CSS3, offers very powerful features to make Web pages look cleaner and more sophisticated, such as rounded corners, multi-column layouts, borders for images, etc. CSS also allows slides to be formatted for printing automatically.

Cross-browser incompatibility in supporting different CSS styles, which leads to display differences, was a challenge for our design and implementation. In some cases, different attributes were used to support different browsers.

JavaScript
JavaScript is a lightweight, client-side scripting language. It is embedded in Web browsers in order to provide enhanced user interfaces and dynamic Web pages. JavaScript provides objects and classes to control the browser and its Document Object Model (DOM). It allows Web developers to place elements in an HTML form and respond to user events such as mouse clicks, form input and page navigation.

AJAX
The acronym AJAX stands for Asynchronous JavaScript and XML. It represents a set of web technologies used to create dynamic web pages by enabling asynchronous communication between the client and server. Using AJAX, the client makes asynchronous calls to the server to send and/or retrieve data without refreshing the whole Web page. It significantly reduces the user's wait time and provides a wider and richer range of possibilities for user interactions.

PHP
PHP (PHP Hypertext Preprocessor) is an open source server-side scripting language used to develop rich Web applications. PHP code can be embedded directly into the HTML page. It runs on every common Web server platform, including Linux, Windows and Mac OS. Commonly, PHP is used as an Apache module, written in C, so it executes quickly and makes efficient use of system resources. PHP provides a rich set of libraries and APIs for graphics, database management, XML support, and much more. Because PHP is open source software, there are many sample solutions and considerable documentation available online. Its community provides reliable and quick support.

MAML
MAML (Molly Active Markup Language) is an XML markup language, developed by students of the Rochester Institute of Technology under the lead and guidance of Professor Ronald Vullo. The idea behind MAML is to create a generic library of controls to help abstract complex server-side logic, including database access, and help developers focus on client-side functionality.

XML Molly tags are included in HTML mark-up. Upon page load, the Molly system parses included tags and replaces them with built-in functionality written in PHP. For this system, we relied on built-in user management functionality, such as login control, and database access from the MAML library.

JQuery Library
There are many JavaScript libraries available for Web developers. Designing any Web site, we need to carefully consider the choice of additional libraries. We must preserve a balance between

features that the library offers and its impact to the page size and performance. JQuery is a JavaScript open source library (developed by a student of Dr. Vullo's) that provides better interaction between HTML and JavaScript by simplifying existing DOM APIs and providing cross-browser transparency. JQuery was first released at the beginning of 2006. Today, the lead Web development companies, such as Google, Amazon, IBM, and Microsoft, are all using JQuery for Web applications. According toBuildWith.com, more than 50% of the top Web sites are using jQuery libraries. JQuery has a rich library of methods for AJAX development, which were used in developing our system. This library significantly simplified drag and drop functionality for slide reordering. We also took advantage of its rich API for displaying popups and navigation menus with animated sliding effects. Also, JQuery provides a minimized version for its code that helps reduce its impact on our pages' load times.

KineticJS

For implementing slides and video synchronization, we decided to use the KineticJS library. During our search for the most suitable library, we considered some of the most common HTML5 libraries, including Fabric, Paper, Easel and Kinetic.

The *Fabric* library is mostly focused on vector graphics tools. It provides an easy API for manipulating objects in the Canvas. It supports simple objects like circles, rectangles and polygons, as well as more complex shapes. It allows one to dynamically move, scale, rotate and group elements. The size of the library is 78-148kB.

Paper is an open source vector graphics scripting framework. It offers a Document Object Model for easy object access and manipulation, and a great deal of powerful functionality to create and work with vector graphics. However, there is no mention in its documentation of support for multi-touch devices. The library size is 219kB.

Easel is more suitable for building HTML5 interactive and animated graphics. It would be a good choice for a game project. It has nice and easy examples and documentation, as well as built-in support for touch devices. The library size is 65 kB. It seems that this library is a good choice for developers with Flash/ActionScript background.

KineticJS is a relatively new HTML5 library. However, thanks to its good documentation and support, it is quickly gaining popularity of the community. It is advertised to be very fast due to multiple canvases for speed. It allows one to draw shapes onto the stage, add event listeners to them, and move, scale and rotate them independently. The base code has good unit test coverage, which adds some confidence about its quality.

After some consideration, it was decided to go with KineticJS because it has all features needed for our purposes. It has good documentation and nice tutorials. It has very good event support, including support for mobile events and multiple browsers. The library is only 67kB. In addition, it shows very good performance.

TinyMCE is an open source JavaScript/HTML editor. It provides ability to convert HTML elements including text areas to editor instances. This editor offers a set of built in core HTML formatting tools, such as different font styles and decorations, formatted ordered and unordered lists, style alignments, etc. In addition to core functionality, there are many plugins available for TinyMCE to support additional features like image uploads. In our project, the JBImage plugin for TinyMCE was used to allow image upload.

The TinyMCE Editor supports multiple configuration options that allow customizing and controlling its behavior. TinyMCE was already integrated into Molly and so was a natural choice.

File Structure

Figure 3, below, indicates the file structure for our solution. The root folder of the solution contains the main Web pages. Since the solution is built on the top of the Molly framework, all Web pages have *.maml file extensions. These pages are processed by the MAML parser and all MAML tags are replaced with the results of built-in PHP code.

The *commands* folder contains PHP files with main server side logic and database access. Web pages are making AJAX calls to these PHP files to retrieve data or to perform operations on the data. These files are also responsible for data validation and error handling.

The *includes* folder contains files with code snippets that are shared between more than one page. For example, the login control in title, page headers. These files are added to the page using Molly's <maml:include> tag.

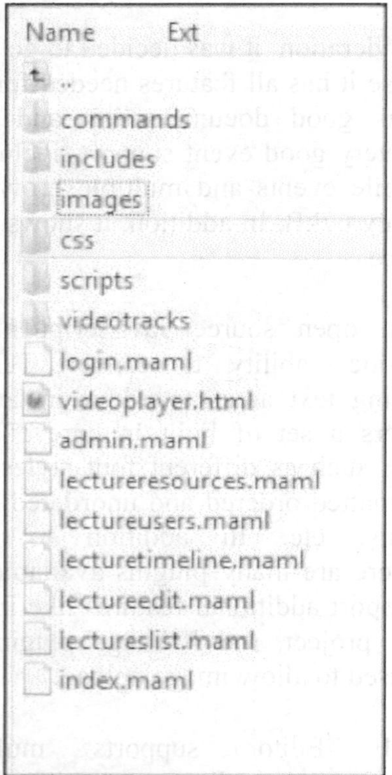

Figure 3: Project File Structure

The *scripts* folder contains JavaScript files. It has our custom scripts as well as third party libraries such as kinetic.js and jQuery scripts. In addition to such scripts, this folder also contains the TinyMCE controls with all required plugins.

The *css* folder contains files with CSS styling. JQuery CSS files are also located in this folder. Each Web page has its own style file with styles specific to this page. The standard styles used across all pages are combined in the *ipad.css* file. The MAML controls are using their own styling located in the *decor* folder of the framework.

The *images* folder contains images for Web pages and controls not included in Molly framework. In addition, any images uploaded by users for lecture slides are stored in this folder.

The *videotracks* folder is where lecture authors store their videos and poster images. Video and images for each lecture are located in their own folders inside *videotracks*. To preserve folders' unique names, lecture IDs are used as folder names.

5 Future Enhancements

The following features are being considered as part of ongoing development:

- Translation support for multiple languages
- Mobile device support
- Touch-screen support
- Lecture content versioning and the ability to revert to previous versions
- Automatic change-tracking and recording of change history
- Ability to customize the look and feel of individual lectures by providing different layout templates and skins (currently only possible for the entire site)

6 Conclusion

Our university, like many others, is looking to increase the use of technology to facilitate distance learning. This goal is all the more important as we continue to expand our international campuses around the world. The project described in this paper is one important piece of an online education strategy that has the potential to reach a vast number of students and does so with modest technology requirements.

7 References

B. Means, Y. Toyama, R. Mupphy, M. Bakia, K. Jones “Evaluation of Evidence-Based Practices in Online Learning: A Meta Analysis and Review of Online Learning Studies”.

Ed.gov. US. Department of Education. 2010. Web. 1 Sep 2012. http://www2.ed.gov/rschstat/eval/tech/evidence-based-practices/finalreport.pdf

D. Driscoll. Review of Moodle Course Management System. Purdue University. N.d. Web. 1 Sep 2012. http://www.bgsu.edu/cconline/Web_2_0_Reviews/Moodle_Driscoll/index.html

“Learning Management System (LMS) Review. Summary of Findings”. Dec 2009. Duke University. Web. 1 Sep 2012. http://elearning.duke.edu/wp-content/uploads/2010/02/LMS-Review-Report.pdf

“Premier Learning Unit Case Study”. RMD Studio. 2011. Web. 15 Sep 2012. http://www.rmdstudio.com/archived-projects/40-premier-learning-unit-case-study

Sakai. Longsight, Sakai Commercial Affiliate. N.d. Web. 10 Sep 2012. http://www.sakaiproject.org/about-sakai

http://support.apple.com/kb/TA25532

http://www.w3schools.com/html/html5_video.asp

Vullo, Ronald P., Ph.D.; Molly: Simplifying Development of Complex Web Apps, invited presentation to the Rochester Joint Chapters of the IEEE Computer and Computational Intel-ligence Society, Rochester, New York (June, 2012)

Vullo, Ronald P., Ph.D., Bogaard, Daniel S.; Better than HTML Web: XML for Program-ming-Free Dynamically Generated Web sites, WWW@10 (2004)

Vullo, Ronald P., Ph.D., Christopher A. Egert, Ph.D., Daniel S. Bogaard; Molly: Bringing Back Simplicity to Web Site Development and Web Research. White Paper, 2006

Vullo, R.P., et al. (October, 2000). Telemedicine initiatives in International Outreach at St. Jude Children's Research Hospital. Presentation at the American and European Associations for Cancer Education Joint Meeting.

Effective Implementation of e-Learning in Initial Learning Program: A Case Study

Soumya Hari

Corporate ILP Team, Tata Consultancy Services Limited, Trivandrum, Kerala, India

Abstract - *Case studies are effective in dealing with factors like creativity, innovation and context. This case study attempts to highlight the outcomes of introducing the concept of e-learning into teaching technical topics like Dotnet, Java, Mainframe and C++ of the Initial Learning Program at Tata Consultancy Services Limited in 2012-2013. These findings will be of interest to any organization that plans to implement e-learning methodologies to help its employees learn and remember the initial lessons of software development and the various programming languages with limited faculty support. The outcome of this case study indicates a stable and prominent increase in the use of e-learning strategies in consort with the traditional methods of training.*

Keywords: e-learning, strategy

1 Introduction

As the world gets more and more dependent on information technology systems, the leading organizations are beginning to realize the potential of information and communication technology (ICT) systems in developing the competencies of their employees. The knowledge of appropriate processes, effective strategies and procedures is essential to improvise the workforce capability through the implementation of e-learning techniques.

1.1 Objective of the case study

The aim of this case study (*Effective Implementation of e-Learning in Initial Learning Program*) is to establish the factors that affect e-learning in similar organizations and how best to leverage them and get the best results from e-learning. This paper is a research review which would increase the awareness in industry of the development, delivery and impact of cost-effective and instructionally sound e-learning.

2 Background

Tata Consultancy Services Limited (TCS) recruits thousands of engineering graduates every year from Computer Science and non- Computer Science engineering streams through campus recruitment programs from colleges all over India. These fresh recruits join in batches to one of the TCS ILP centres for their initial learning program. They are allocated to a technical stream like Java, Dotnet, C++, Mainframe, EIS, BIPM or Testing. During the initial learning program (ILP), these graduates are provided 60-day rigorous training on the key programming skills and concepts along with courses on Business Skills and professional etiquette.

2.1 The Challenges

Conducting the Initial Learning Program (ILP) entirely through traditional methods of teaching posed some challenges to the training managers. The challenges faced are as follows:

2.1.1 Number of learners

As many as 21,822 graduates joined the eight ILP centers in batches in 2011-2012, and the case has been similar for previous years as well. Among them, 50.4% were from Computer Science stream and 49.6% from non-Computer Science stream. 41.5% of them were allocated to Java, 17.7% to Mainframe, 14.4% to Dotnet, 13.5% to C++, 7.6% to BIPM and 5.2% to testing. There were around 400 faculties catering to them, thus resulting in a high student-faculty ratio. As a result, the faculties find it difficult to give individual attention to each student.

2.1.2 Fairness of faculties

Each technical and non-technical stream had faculties who were popular among the learners and had taken name as being the "best" because of the learning theories and teaching style they chose in teaching. It was not practical to engage them for every joining batch, and hence, the fairness and consistency in teaching could not be achieved.

2.1.3 Utilization of resources

The recruits included students from all engineering streams. So, the curriculum included even basic courses on computers and programming. The Computer Science students needed such sessions as a refresher course too. The faculties felt that if the sessions on basic programming topics were taken off their shoulders, they could save a lot of their valuable time and utilize it better in assisting the students with their lab sessions that certainly call for individual attention.

2.1.4 Learner Behavior

Age and behaviour of the learners are interdependent. Age is also an important characteristic that decides the effectiveness of learning. The faculties observed that young learners are more receptive to information from sources other than traditional classroom sessions. They are tech savvy and take interest in innovative methods of learning. They prefer learning through practxice than theory sessions. The faculties could make use of these aspects of young learners while designing learning videos for them. The use of learning videos and simulations to teach concepts could get the learners to think creatively and utilize their talents in a better way.

2.2 Approach to e-learning

In early 2012, the Corporate ILP team initiated the processes to create a series of video tutorials to teach the basic-level technical modules. The aim was to address the challenges in the existing system and improve the quality of learning and teaching. This could also seek solutions to problems associated with faculty crunches and logistics.

2.3 The project

A team of faculties from different technical streams was chosen to be involved in the project. They were briefed about the video creation project and their views on it were sought. After careful consideration, it was decided that e-learning can never replace traditional classrooms completely, but, can improve the quality of learning. It could be used in conjunction with traditional classroom sessions. The first step was to introduce e-learning into the organization's Initial Learning Program (ILP) by using video tutorials to teach the basic concepts in core technical courses.

3 Video Tutorial Creation

After deciding on the authoring tools and the platform for video hosting, the first step was to identify the topics in curriculum that could be moved as video topics. Since faculty-student interaction would be minimal in e-learning, it was decided to make videos to address the Level 1 or basic topics which are ideal for self-learning and do not require faculty intervention.

This was followed by train-the-trainer programs for the chosen faculties on the authoring and recording tools. The next step was to document the guidelines for video creation and to define the project activities systematically. A check-list was also put together and the faculties could use it to ensure consistency across streams in the application of learning theories and teaching styles.

3.1 Instructional Design Analysis

The instructional designer team analysed the following factors to design the course modules in each stream. The following are the observations of the audience and task analysis activity of the project:

3.1.1 Audience

Graduates (mostly of age-group 22-24) with diverse cultural background with varying levels of subject knowledge (The group consisted of both CS and non-CS graduates). Most of the audience population was well-versed in using computers.

3.1.2 Course goals

Each course is intended to improve the technical competencies of the learners in specific technical streams. So, the learners should be able to grasp the context of a problem and write code to address the basic programming requirements.

3.1.3 Details of learning environment

Each video will have appropriate graphics/images; on-screen text and audio integrated into it and is intended to be hosted in a video server. The modules will also be integrated with appropriate Check Your Understanding questions and assessments.

3.1.4 Number of videos

There were around 50 videos created on each topic. These videos addressed the Level 1 concepts in every technical stream. Some of these videos could be re-used as well, to address the same concepts across technical streams.

3.1.5 Video duration

Each video will be of 12 to 15 minutes duration.

3.1.6 Learning Objectives

The learning objectives are specific for each video.

3.1.7 Interactivity

The instructional designers tried adding scenarios into each video. These scenarios allow learners to select their options. Some of these were branching scenarios where the learners can choose a path to proceed based on their responses to specific problems.

3.2 Learning Pedagogies

E-Learning was used as a thread that deals with understanding the learning needs and ways of learning better with the best use of technology, and then designing the content to meet these needs. The courses were designed with the view that technology is not about giving the content on attractive templates and adding complex animations to it; it is not about introducing multiple "clicks" to make it user-interactive. It is about designing appropriate learning objects to teach different concepts making the best use of available technology. Each learning object carried the essence of classroom training in every possible way.

The term "pedagogy" refers to the activities that could be used to instruct a particular skill or the activities that impart learning. The faculties were as much involved in deciding on the right pedagogy as the instructional designers. These activities were designed based on the learning outcome that they should bring forth in terms of enhancing the learner's knowledge levels and motivating them to learn further. The faculties put forth a set of activities based on the learners' experience and the way they learn. Based on this preferred approach, the instructional designers helped to design each course, and this helped to make each course learner-friendly.

3.2.1 Gagne's Nine Events of Instruction

In addition to the training on new tools, the faculties were provided appropriate training on the instructional strategies and methods that foster effective learning. As a result, they have applied the nine events of instruction proposed by Robert Gagne in the development of each tutorial.

Figure 1: Gagne's nine events of instruction

3.2.2 Simulations

Full-motion recording of the screen and screen captures are used in software demos. For instance, the topic on *CRUD* in the *Application Understanding* module in Java uses simulations to demonstrate create, read, update and delete operations in a web-based application.

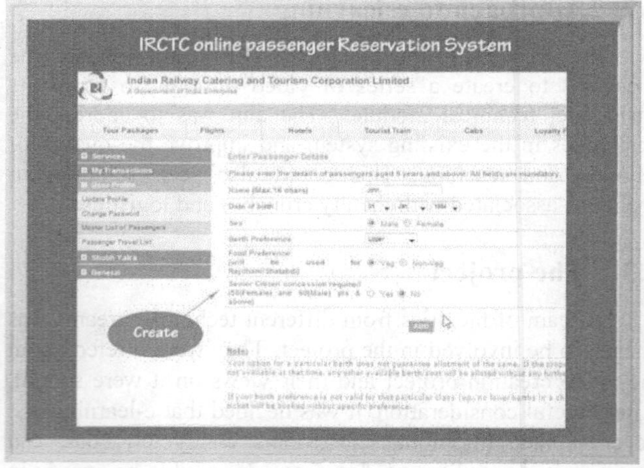

Figure 2: Simulation

3.2.3 Podcasts

A number of podcasts were recorded by experts in the particular topics and then included as a part of the video.

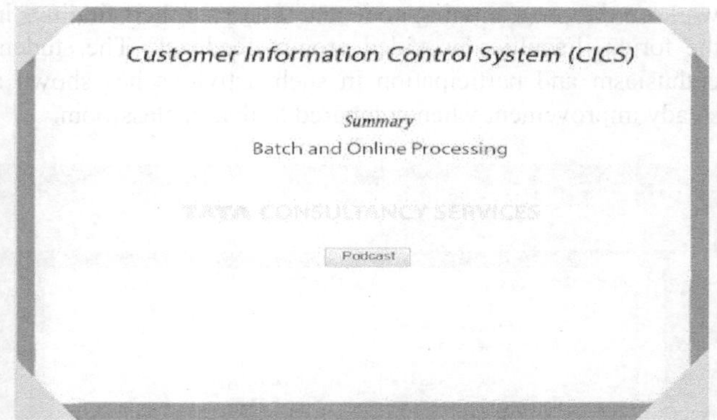

Figure 3: Podcast

3.2.4 Resources

Effective learning was ensured by making the best use of teaching resources available to the faculties. To teach the complex topics, they used tablet computers and interactive whiteboards. The screen capture is that of a C++ topic, where a tablet computer is used to teach the concept of pointers; this is also an example of how faculties have obtained a balance between e-learning and the traditional mode of training, while making use of the best options available in technology.

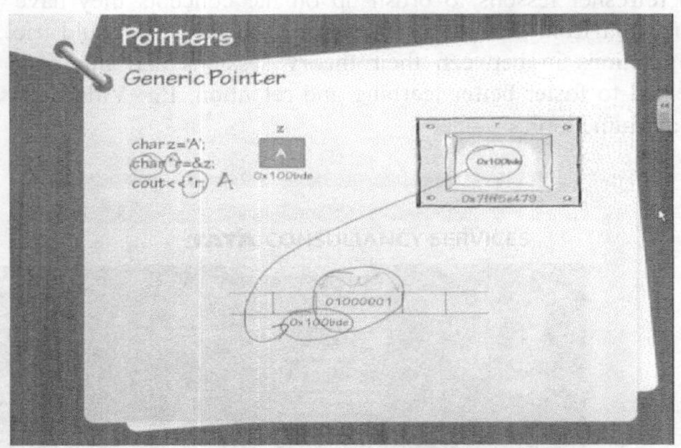

Figure 4: Resources

3.2.5 Examples and non-examples

The basic programming concepts were best explained using appropriate examples and non-examples. For instance, one of tutorials in the *User Interface* module in the Java stream points out that the nuclear disaster at the Three Mile Island Nuclear Power Plant was as a result of its highly complex and non-user friendly interface. The topic then goes on to discuss how user interface is a strong element in the design of efficient systems.

Figure 5: Examples and non-examples

3.3 Role of technology

3.3.1 Authoring tool

Adobe Captivate 6 was the authoring tool chosen to capture the videos. The videos were published with the following technical specifications: Resolution: 800*600, Maximum Bitrate: 2 Mbps, Quality: Youtube Widescreen SD, Format: mp4.

3.3.2 Learning Platform

These videos were hosted in a Learning Management Environment built on Sakai server. This made the tutorials easily available to the learners and they could access it from the labs and classrooms.

Figure 6: Learning Platform

3.3.3 Assessments and check your understandings

Assessments and Check Your Understanding questions are another feature of the learning modules.

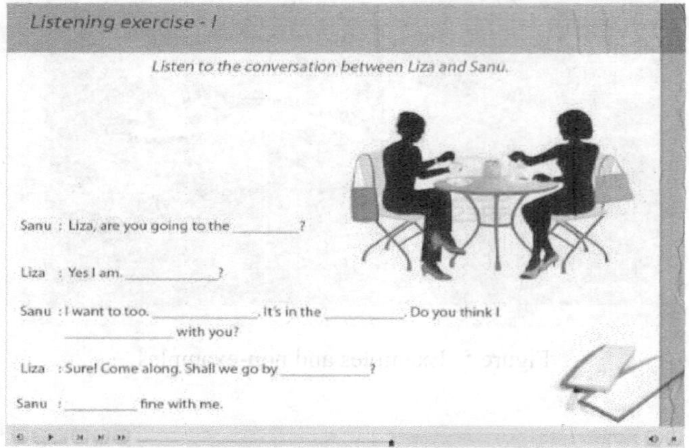

Figure 7: Assessments and CYUs

3.3.4 Discussion Forums

Another feature of the learning platform is the discussion forums that it offers. The learners use this to provide feedback to the faculties as well as to discuss concepts with other learners.

Figure 8: Discussion forum

3.4 Advantages of e-learning

3.4.1 Better student participation

The faculties succeeded in identifying the right kind of activities and teaching styles for most of the course modules, and that is the key to success in such projects.

For instance, most of the programming exercises followed "Show Me- Try Me" strategy. For example, simulations were used to explain a concept and then, the learner was provided with practice exercises. Some of these activities posed interesting challenges to the learners, and they were instilled to work on the programming code and then post their findings in the forum. Faculties provided prompt feedback. The student enthusiasm and participation in such activities has shown a steady improvement when compared to that in classroom.

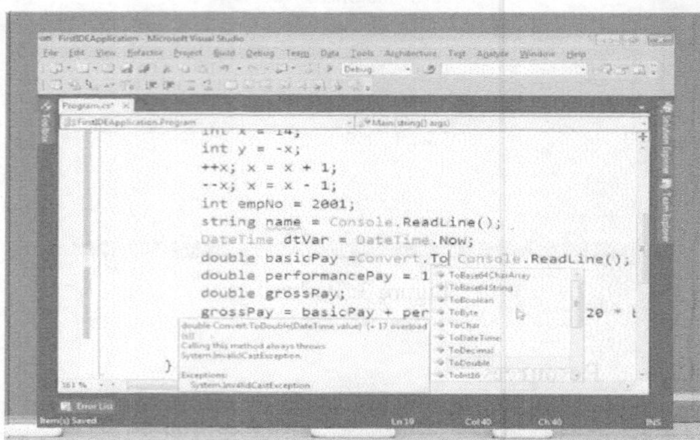

Figure 9: Ensuring learner participation

3.4.2 Improved Learning Retention

Viewing the video tutorials over and over again has helped the non-CS students to get a grasp on the basic topics. The recruits from the CS background could use these videos as refresher lessons to brush up on the concepts they have forgotten from their college classes. The faculties could use simulations in between their theory sessions and this also helped to foster better learning and retention. Eg: Videos on Mainframe topics

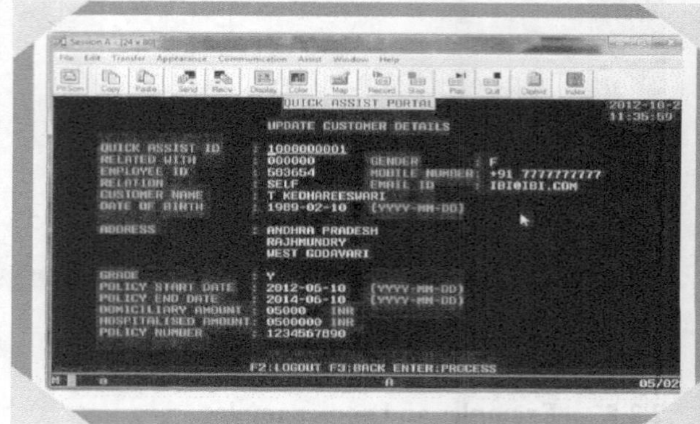

Figure 10: Mainframe example

3.4.3 Discussion Forums

The lack of class/group discussions initially posed a challenge to the faculties. The discussion forums included in the learning environment partially helped to solve this challenge. Soon, the learners started to make good use of these forums to discuss the technical aspects of the course as well as to share reference websites and to provide solutions to issues they face while working out the programs or codes. The faculties view this as improvement to the traditional classrooms, because, in traditional classrooms, the learners have always been discreet to discuss their views on a problem openly. But in the new scenario, the learners have started making better use of reference sites so as to be able to participate actively in discussions.

3.5 Challenges/ difficulties in e-learning

The introduction of video tutorials has successfully solved most of the challenges that existed in the system. However, the faculties encountered a few difficulties in their effort to create the video tutorials.

3.5.1 Changes to learning styles

Faculties had to adapt to new styles of teaching and make changes to the learning pedagogies that they followed to make better e-learning experience.

3.5.2 Challenges in conceptualization

The faculties encountered challenges with conceptualization of some of the videos and in creating them. The major difficulty was to keep the learners engaged without the luxury of face-to-face interaction or emotional connect with them.

3.5.3 Difficulties in getting feedback

Similarly, the faculties found it difficult to gauge the understanding of students, in spite of building in CYUs between modules. The feedback cycles also took longer than that in traditional training.

3.6 Results

3.6.1 Learner Feedback

The Corporate ILP team has collected feedback from 368 learners from the Java stream for whom video tutorials were used as primary mode of training. The tutorials were on the Information Management, Application Understanding, User Interface and Problem Solving modules. The feedback collected was on the effectiveness of video tutorials and their satisfaction levels.

25.54% of the learners have strongly agreed that the content presented in the video tutorials was clear and sufficient for them to understand the concept. 70.92% of the learners have agreed to it, while 3.5% have disagreed to it. These results indicate the interest of learners in taking up video tutorials.

3.6.2 Learning effectiveness

The effectiveness of video training can be measured by comparing the performance of a batch (Batch A) that had video tutorials as the primary mode of training to the performance of trainees in another batch (Batch B) that followed the traditional classroom method of training. The strength of Batch A and Batch B were 213 and 230 respectively. The assessment tests were taken as criteria to decide the learners' performances in both batches. There were no cases of training extension in Batch A (all of the participants scored the required average in the test), while 7 learners had to be extended in Batch B. This test result can be considered as a clear indicator of the effectiveness of video tutorial sessions.

4 Foreword

The following are the next steps planned in this direction:

4.1 For pre-ILP learners

Although it may not be possible to replace traditional classroom training completely with e-learning, blended learning has helped a lot to improve the quality of instruction and in highlighting independent learning. The advantages of video tutorials and their reception among learners have opened up more possibilities for these videos. The senior management has started to look into the possibility of using video tutorials on basic programming concepts to train the pre-ILP students; the students who have been recruited but yet to join TCS.

4.2 For post-ILP learners

Similarly, the possibility of using video tutorials as refresher courses for post-ILP batches (learners who have completed their Initial Learning Program but yet to be allocated to projects) is huge.

4.3 Hosting videos in TCS video channel

The hosting of ILP videos in the TCS video channel is the next step in technological advancement in this direction.

5 Conclusion

The introduction of video tutorials into the initial learning program at TCS has received mixed comments from learners and faculties. Most of the comments have held blended learning as learner-friendly mode of training. However, none of them has a completely negative comment to share about the project.

The learning group is more or less tech savvy and they readily accept blended learning as the future direction in learning. This mode of learning more or less meets their expectations in terms of how they should learn, the learning environments that best meet their training requirements, and how to leverage infrastructure to their best advantage.

When made use of in moderation and by interspersing them with lectures, video tutorials can improve the learner participation, retention and engagement. With the effective use of technology, it can be used as a powerful tool to be used in support of lectures.

6 References

[1] Center for Instructional Technology & Training: Gagne's Nine Events of Instruction, 2013.

[2] G. Conole, M. Dyke, M. Oliver, J. Seale: Mapping pedagogy and tools for effective learning design, 2004.

Improving Knowledge Management in e-Learning: A Contingent Framework for Efficient Knowledge Transfer

Dr. Anitha Chennamaneni[1] and Jayson G. Brown[1]
[1]Computer Information Systems, Texas A&M University – Central Texas, Killeen, TX, USA

Abstract - *Knowledge management (KM) is the top most important factor in e-Learning. This research paper explores the role of KM in e-Learning and develops a conceptual framework for successfully managing and transferring knowledge. We review different types of knowledge and discuss how varied KM techniques, e-Learning technologies, platforms and possible solutions improve KM and knowledge transfer in e-Learning programs. Our research framework is grounded theoretically in the knowledge creation theory and the media richness theory. This framework is extremely useful to the academicians and practitioners alike as it guides them in implementing a respectable pedagogy for effectively managing and transferring knowledge in the e-Learning environment.*

Keywords: Knowledge Management, Knowledge Transfer, Course Combination, Research Framework, Knowledge Management Systems

1 Introduction

E-Learning has become a well-known popular alternative to traditional education. Today, many colleges and universities around the world adopt it. Several universities are starting to teach online versions of their courses and new logical universities are coming to exist to include this demographic of the population. A number of trends such as developments in information and communication technologies, flexibility and convenience of distance education have accelerated the demand for e-Learning. Asynchronous online education allows individuals to achieve the ability to harness the power of the Internet or a local Intranet to obtain educational materials and services at any place or time with accessibility.

However, e-Learning poses some unique challenges as learning in this environment is distributed with students and instructors physically separated in space and time. In addition, the students exercise volitional control of learning rather than the instructor. The success or failure of learning in e-Learning courses depends not only on the course design and quality of the content, but also on how fruitful the knowledge transfer has been from the instructor to the students as well as from students to students. Therefore, knowledge management (KM) is the uppermost factor in any e-Learning environment.

This research paper explores the role of knowledge management in e-Learning and develops a conceptual framework for managing knowledge effectively in e-Learning programs. We discuss different types of knowledge and make an analysis of how varied KM techniques, e-Learning technologies, platforms and online solutions are usable in managing and disseminating the knowledge. Our research framework is grounded theoretically in the knowledge creation theory [1] and the media richness theory [2]. Our framework is extremely useful to the academicians and practitioners alike as it provides them the expertise to implement a respectable pedagogy to maximize the online students' learning curves with proper KM management. We will validate this framework through an assessment by a panel of experts as well as a lab experiment in a future study.

The rest of this research paper is organized as follows. The next section discusses the unique facets of learning in the environment of e-Learning. It will be followed by a review of KM literature on what constitutes knowledge, different types of knowledge and how knowledge is created. Following it, we describe the research framework for managing and transferring knowledge effectively. Finally, we conclude the paper with discussion on contributions to research and implications to practice.

2 The e-Learning environment

An important aspect of KM is the transferring and sharing of knowledge as opposed to dissemination of information. For the knowledge to be successfully transferred and shared there has to be a close interaction between the student, instructor, learning content and peers in the class. The e-Learning environment differs from traditional learning environment in many ways. First, the e-Learning environment allows both synchronous and asynchronous learning unlike traditional environment where synchronous learning is the most common form. The learning in the e-Learning context is generally self-paced, with zero to many virtual interactions using tools such as virtual lecture halls, Skype, chats, discussions and so forth. Second, students tend to be afraid to ask questions in traditional settings, which lowers participation, while students in online learning ask them easily [3]. Third, equal contributions from each learner can occur in the environment of e-Learning, while traditional methods must move on to the next lesson to accommodate their time periods which will leave out crucial contributions from students. Fourth, online education allows more time for the individuals to mediate about the situation and assert an effective meaningful response. Fifth, e-Learning environment requires the students to have access to technology and be competent in using the required technology to access the course content. Traditional methods will not need technology access and can press on without these types of amenities. The lack of this feature will create a technology access barrier against the student in the knowledge transfer of an e-Learning environment [4]. Several other differences exist between these two learning environments, but the above discussion facilitates crucial facets of e-Learning.

3 Knowledge

Knowledge is the accumulation and awareness of information, facts, ideas and principles. It can be acquired by study, investigation, observation and experience. Knowledge management is critical in harnessing these varieties of knowledge [6, 7]. Knowledge is the main capital of knowledge workers and exists in a variety of forms and media [5]. Knowledge can be explicit or tacit [1, 7]. The combination of explicit and tacit knowledge makes up the learning content in e-Learning. Knowledge management is critical in harnessing these types of knowledge [6, 7].

3.1 Explicit knowledge

Explicit knowledge is knowledge that is consciously understood and can be formally articulated, codified and documented [1]. Explicit knowledge exists in forms of words, documents, computer programs or other means [8]. Content management systems such as Blackboard and Web-CT support the creation, storage and distribution of explicit knowledge. The course administrator can upload the explicit knowledge content into the knowledge repository for the students to retrieve and review at any time during the lesson. Non-existence of this content material will lead the individuals to failure. In the environment of e-Learning, this is a crucial aspect since face-to-face meetings do not exist.

3.2 Tacit knowledge

Unlike explicit knowledge, tacit knowledge is subconsciously understood and applied. It is very difficult and challenging to articulate, share and leverage this type of knowledge. Generally speaking, tacit knowledge includes personal experiences, judgment, skills, individual expertise and integrates human factors such as beliefs, perspectives and culture that make it very difficult to interpret [4]. Because of "tacit-ness" in knowledge, it is not feasible to capture it in a report or a power point slide. In the e-Learning environment, articulation and sharing of tacit knowledge requires highly interactive conversations, shared experiences and the use of appropriate knowledge transfer techniques, such as storytelling, mentoring, content maps, tools and technologies that have the capability to support rich media.

The online environment can have sufficient explicit materials, but the lack of tacit knowledge will lead to confusion of the subject matter and the inability to complete the lesson. An example is in programming, the student might learn the syntax of the language that resembles the explicit knowledge but not the actual logic behind the coding, which is the tacit knowledge. Tacit knowledge is vital to increasing the learning and knowledge transfer [4]. Several instructors exhibits different levels of tacit knowledge due to their field experience and overall wisdom and it is important that this knowledge be shared with the students.

4 Knowledge transfer

Depending on the knowledge type, four different processes are involved in knowledge conversion and transfer [1]. These are socialization, externalization, combination and internalization [1]. Table 1 presents Nonaka and Takeuchi's KM model [1].

Table 1: Nonaka and Takeuchi's KM model [1]

	Nonaka and Takeuchi's KM model [1]		
	To		
From		Tacit	Explicit
	Tacit	Socialization	Externalization
	Explicit	Internalization	Combination

- Socialization involves transferring tacit knowledge from one person to another person through socializing and exchanging of ideas and experiences.
- Externalization involves articulating and translating tacit knowledge into explicit knowledge and storing it in a repository.
- Internalization involves acquiring explicit knowledge from repositories, books, Internet and other public sources and internalizing it, where upon it becomes tacit knowledge.
- Combination involves combining explicit knowledge from multiple sources to create new explicit knowledge.

4.1 Knowledge transfer in e-Learning

The current students' obtainment of knowledge requires a successful learning strategy from the instructor and an adequate feedback mechanism to determine the potency of the overall transfer of knowledge in each lesson. The feedback mechanism will serve to instill changes in the learning strategy and to fill in the voids that the students exhibit during the testing stage to achieve top optimization of overall knowledge transfer of the course material. Figure 1 presents the flow of knowledge during an e-Learning course, which facilitates the different stages and impediments to the knowledge transfer during the course's progress.

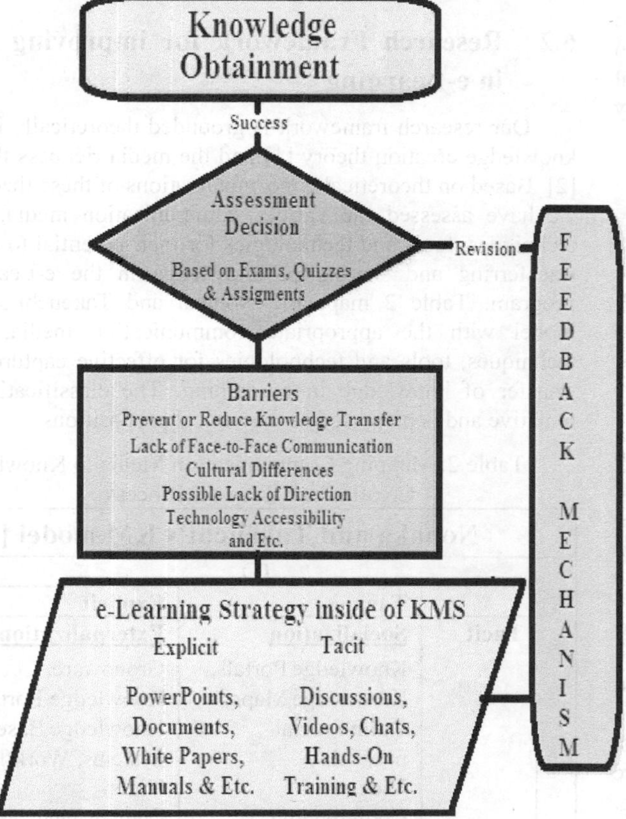

Figure 1: Knowledge transfer in an e-Learning environment

Communication technologies such as email, forums, chats and video conferencing support knowledge transfer [4]. Effective transfer of knowledge requires several prevention techniques to reduce barriers that will affect the learning of the online student(s) [4]. These barriers will include cultural differences, low computer literacy, lack of technology access, lack of trust and several impediments that affect the learning [4]. Online environments will have different types of barriers from traditional methods and will need proper adjustment to provide an excellent learning strategy.

5 KM in e-Learning

The management of knowledge is one of the key characteristics in achieving successful knowledge transfer in e-Learning [3]. The lack of efficient knowledge management will spark confusion among students, create impending barriers and lower the overall knowledge transfer of the lesson(s). These types of barriers need proper elimination or secession with a well-planned deterrence strategy to lessen the barriers' presence to achieve top optimization for the success of knowledge transfer in an e-Learning environment.

5.1 KM in traditional education

Traditional course delivery requires students to attend synchronous meetings in a physical classroom setting with the instructor presenting the lecture over the lesson's subject matter [10, 11]. There is not an online knowledge repository to provide explicit materials to the students in true traditional delivery. The students will need to take notes and uphold mental images of the lecture if the professor does not hand out hard copy material over the lecture. Explicit knowledge will come in the form of the course manual and the handouts. Other documentation from the instructor might be available depending on the learning strategy employed and the degree of active teaching involved. Much of the tacit knowledge that exists in the minds of individuals is transmitted through social group interaction and networks making knowledge management people-intensive [8]. Internship and mentoring exercises provide practical experiences to students. Upon externalization, the people-intensive knowledge becomes technology-intensive. The feedback mechanisms to determine the students' learning curves are crucial to achieve top optimization of the course's knowledge transfer. Hybrid courses have been emerging to instill an online knowledge repository. This hybrid development combines traditional and online functionalities [10]. Hybrid implementations need to analyze the material, determine the translation of this material to an online format and evaluate and change the strategy as issues emerge [10]. This functionality allows traditional settings to achieve several opportunities and lowers the course burden that might be present in traditional delivery.

5.2 Challenges of KM in e-Learning

The management of knowledge in e-Learning is a new ballgame in comparison to the traditional delivery. Students can set the learning at their own pace in most e-Learning instances [10]. The implementation of e-Learning is not hybrid and has several differences from traditional knowledge management. Explicit materials will be present in the online repository for downloading and studying. The lack of these materials and the absence of a procedure for advancing will present a barrier. There are no physical class meetings in e-Learning and the entire course is run in virtual reality [10].

Tacit knowledge becomes much harder to acquire from this standpoint due to the lack of observation and other tacit knowledge acquisition means that exist in the traditional setting. Therefore, it becomes critical to implement chats, discussions, wikis and video and audio conferences to raise the students' learning curves. Testing will come in the form of online quizzes and exams, but some institutions may require proctoring in these situations to reduce academic dishonesty. The results will provide the feedback mechanism to implement new materials in the knowledge repository that will help with the students' weaknesses. Another barrier in online setting is cultural differences. Online learning can harness worldwide or regional cultures that differ widely and may cause issues such as the ones with language and linguistics [4]. A last barrier in e-Learning is the lack of trust that appears in the online environment [4]. Students do not meet the instructor(s) and therefore may not establish an emotional bond that facilitates knowledge transfer. This can create distrust and cause the student(s) to create a mental block since these individuals are not sure over the legitimacy of the material or about bias presentation from the individual.

6 Improving KM in e-Learning

Knowledge management (KM) has various paths to establish sufficient knowledge transfer in e-Learning. A successful learning strategy or pedagogy with high degree of knowledge management in the online repository will raise knowledge transfer and the overall students' learning curves.

6.1 Media richness

A communication channel facilitates interaction and sharing of knowledge among individuals. Examples of few online communication channels include video conferencing, teleconferencing, chats and the use of social networking tools such as Web 2.0 technologies. Per media richness theory [2], each of these channels has its own advantages and disadvantages and as such is more suited to transfer particular type of knowledge over the other. The media richness is the ability of a medium to transfer information and has lean and rich implementations for each of the two types of knowledge [12]. Lean material will include electronic mails, documentation, asynchronous audio and discussions that are common in either learning methods. Video conferencing, face-to-face communication, and several other interactive tools facilitate rich media into an e-Learning environment. Any medium typically has two types of capacities to carry information. These are the data carrying capacity and the symbol carrying capacity [12]. The data carrying capacity is the ability to transmit overall information such as the throughput [12]. The symbol carrying capacity refers to the ability to carry metadata over the situation [12].

Media richness theory defines the richness of a medium as its capability to reduce uncertainty and equivocality in the information presented. It asserts that matching the richness of medium to the task improves the performance of the task. Further, it claims that richer media is better at supporting tasks that have both uncertainty and equivocality built into them. Rich media such as face to face interaction, video conferencing facilitates users to communicate effectively by allowing them to convey multiple cues (body language, facial expressions, voice tone etc.), immediate feedback, personalization and language variety, thus, improving the performance of the tasks. Alternatively, lean media is better suited to less equivocal tasks. The choice of media used to present contents in an e-Learning program influences how effectively knowledge is transferred and shared among the learners in the e-Learning course. For instance, lean media may be sufficient to transfer explicit knowledge. However, rich media is necessary to facilitate the effective transfer of tacit knowledge that requires high interactive conversations, shared experiences and use of knowledge transfer techniques.

6.2 Research Framework for improving KM in e-Learning

Our research framework is grounded theoretically in the knowledge creation theory [1] and the media richness theory [2]. Based on theoretical conceptualizations of these theories, we have assessed the various communication media, KM techniques, tools and technologies for their potential to allow transferring and sharing of knowledge in the e-Learning program. Table 2 maps the Nonaka and Takeuchi's KM model with the appropriate communication media, KM techniques, tools and technologies for effective capture and transfer of knowledge in e-Learning. The classification is tentative and is presented as theoretical propositions.

Table 2: Mapping Communication Media to Knowledge Creation and Transfer Process

	Nonaka and Takeuchi's KM model [1]		
		TO	
		Tacit	**Explicit**
FROM	**Tacit**	**Socialization** Knowledge Portals, Knowledge Maps, Online social networks, Video Conferencing, Web2.0 Technologies, Corporate Yellow Pages, Streaming, Audio/Video	**Externalization** Groupware, Knowledge Portals, Knowledge Based Systems, Workflow, Video Conferencing, Web2.0 technologies, Chat Rooms, Document Tagging
	Explicit	**Internalization** Innovation Support Tools, Web2.0 Technologies	**Combination** Document Management Systems, Document Tagging, Knowledge Portals, Intranet Based systems Discussion Forums, Chat Rooms

E-Learning technologies coupled with KM facilitate each of these different types of knowledge creation and conversion processes and allow a high level of knowledge transfer. Socialization requires the creation of a collaborative learning environment between the instructor and the students as well as among the students. Online social networks such as Facebook, Twitter, Web 2.0 technologies, knowledge portals and knowledge maps facilitate tacit to tacit knowledge transfer by identifying and promoting high interaction among students and instructors with special interests, shared experiences and knowledge. Online social networks often function as virtual lounges wherein instructor and students can converse with one-to-one, one-to-many, and many-to-many students and collaborate on their school work. Social networking sites such as KnowledgeBook, BookTag, and SlideShare are known to facilitate knowledge dissemination.

Externalization involves articulation and translation of tacit knowledge into explicit knowledge and storing it in a repository. The knowledge of instructors and other learners in the e-Learning course can be captured and represented using appropriate knowledge transfer mechanisms and can be made available for reuse by others. Some tools that externalize knowledge in e-Learning include content maps, knowledge portals, synchronous and asynchronous groupware, application sharing, instant messaging and learning management systems. Internalization involves acquiring explicit knowledge from repositories, books, the Internet and other public sources then internalizing it, where upon it becomes a tacit knowledge. Several e-Learning media such as Web 2.0 technologies, including wikis and blogs, foster an innovative learning environment. Finally, the combination technique creates new knowledge in the e-Learning course using knowledge portals, document management systems, document tagging and other means. Pedagogical techniques can also be included in this process.

6.3 Document tagging

E-Learning materials are exponentially rising in quantity causing difficulty to organize and disseminate materials with the abundant information [13]. Large collections of knowledge will become harder to sift through and can cause delays and confusion. Achieving the ability to index materials is crucial to the classification and the dissemination of knowledge in an online repository. Archiving knowledge will help with successful searching and rendering of information inside the knowledge repository and raise the efficiency of the overall knowledge transfer. Marking the documentation with descriptive tags becomes a common method of accomplishing efficient future searches [13]. Instilling this ability into the knowledge will allow efficient results during searching to the actual information that the user needed and eliminate false positives.

There is a great demand for knowledge and information causing information overload which is a serious issue [14]. Information overload is a critical barrier during a student's knowledge transfer and reduction of the said will prove vital to successful knowledge transfer. Adobe Acrobat, FileFold and several other knowledge control programs allow metadata tagging with certain versions for portable document formats or other documents with simple processes. Another example is Meta tags in HTML documentation that will permit the parser to optimize search engine results and the browser's behavior. A last method is document clustering, which help group documents and ensure effectiveness with the proper usage of algorithms to improve accuracy with similarity matrices and probabilistic methods [14]. Instilling these types of metadata functionalities in the material will improve overall knowledge management and benefit the courses' knowledge transfer in the e-Learning environment.

6.4 Yellow/White Pages

An expert directory is another managerial technique that exists to allow a source of obtainment for human capital and their respective knowledge. Yellow Pages, or sometimes referred to as White Pages, are essentially a list of available experts, expertise and contact information [15]. Yellow Pages foster knowledge communication between co- workers through the meta-knowledge of experts, but do not maintain the actual knowledge [15]. Tacit knowledge becomes highly available with this system and will help improve productivity and flexibility in these organizations. In the event of the necessity of knowledge to incur competitive advantage, then the recipient(s) can review the Yellow Pages and deduce possible knowledge sources over the particular topic for their specific issue. Large pools of employees from different geographical locations disallow the ability to personally know each of these individuals [15].

Keeping the system up-to-date is critical for efficient knowledge management. Personal ownership abilities to update their own respective instance will help eliminate the principles of neglect and ignorance with ensured participation. Initiating this directory into an easy to access area and reminding the users of its existence is another key aspect. The benefits from Yellow Pages are manifold. The institution will be able to identify who knows what and share the knowledge to gain competitive advantage [15]. The dissemination of knowledge is crucial for sufficient knowledge transfer to e-Learning students. Lack of expert directories such as yellow/white pages in the institution will incur a learning barrier and prevent successful student learning curves or development of pedagogies for instructors.

6.5 Combining course instances

Many universities generally have multiple sections for some of the courses taught each semester. Often, the instructors teaching different sections have different levels of tacit and explicit knowledge depending on their field experiences and other factors. Also, the teaching methods they employ are different. While some are proactive and provide all the content materials needed to maximize the student's learning, others may provide minimal content. This creates an impediment that will cause unfairness between these course sections and will cause few of the students not to achieve their full potential. A simple remedy is to store all the important content materials in a centralized repository and give students and instructors to access it.

The mandated learning objectives from the university system will remain the same in each section, but will have different delivery methods. Each instructor will still have his or her own pedagogy of teaching, but knowledge will be obtainable in every instance from the combined course area for the students. Discussions would achieve more responses from students, which raises the knowledge level and reduces bias of the subject. Other advantages remain and will raise the overall learning curve from the abundant material. The diagram below depicts this scenario to raise the efficiency of knowledge management and improve knowledge transfer in an e-Learning environment.

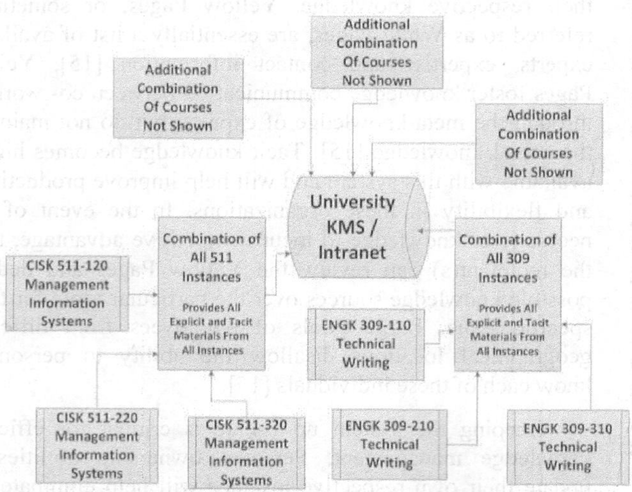

Figure 2: Knowledge Combination Inside of a KMS

7 Learning mgmt. & content systems

Implementation of efficient learning management with the previous research framework and the other facets exhibits a correct strategy to apply a successful e-Learning experience in an instructor's pedagogy. In traditional methods, knowledge creation and dissemination happens through lectures, face-to-face interactions, mentoring and practical hands-on experiences. E-Learning relies on learning management and content systems since both of these systems serve as repositories and medium of communication and collaboration during the entire course while synchronous actions are not present. The actual knowledge transfer is the most crucial aspect in learning and will require an efficient knowledge repository for the most successful dissemination capabilities.

Learning management systems can exist through intranets or extranets depending on the university's preference and funding. There are several operable database mediums to allow universities to harness this KM functionality. Moodle, Blackboard, WebCT and internal databases are a few examples of learning management systems. Each has a wide variety of available tools to implement successful management and dissemination of the course content. Several of these systems also allow communication, collaboration, group decision support and technical help. A crucial aspect of these systems is the interface's user friendly aspect and its functionality that it provides to the end user population. Management inside of these databases can be astounding, but the lack of navigability will cause user confusion causing a lower learning curve. Therefore, courses in the learning management system have to be carefully designed in order to optimize knowledge transfer.

8 Contributions & implications

This research article reviewed different types of knowledge and analyzed how usage of varied KM techniques, e-Learning technologies and platforms improve KM and knowledge transfer in e-Learning programs. We developed an extremely suitable framework for efficient knowledge management in e-Learning. The framework based on the knowledge creation theory and media richness theory utilizes a well-built pedagogy that minimizes barriers and raises the overall creation and transfer of knowledge. We will validate this framework through an assessment utilizing a panel of experts and a lab experiment in a future study.

Successful knowledge management in e-Learning begins with the implementation of explicit knowledge in the knowledge repositories, knowledge portals and learning management systems. However, it is important to note that managing and transferring tacit knowledge effectively is vital to increasing the overall learning of students. We assessed the various communication media, KM techniques, tools and technologies and contend that rich media is necessary for effectively managing and transferring tacit knowledge. Our framework and recommendations are extremely useful to the academicians and practitioners alike as they guide them in implementing a respectable pedagogy for effectively managing and transferring knowledge in any e-Learning program. Several other adjustments to help raise the adeptness of KM in e-Learning are also discussed. Instilling combination methods to reduce redundant materials will provide across the board information to all students. The use of document tagging and utilization of corporate yellow pages are other available methods to enhance learning.

9 References

[1] Ikujiro Nonaka and Hirotaka Takeuchi. "The Knowledge-Creating Company: How Japanese Companies Create the Dynamics of Innovation"; Oxford University Press Inc., May 1995

[2] Richard Daft and Robert Lengel. "Organizational Information Requirements, Media Richness and Structural Design"; Management Science, Vol. 32, No. 5, 554-571, 1986

[3] Md. Shiful Islam, Susumu Kunifuji, Motoki Miura and Tessai Hayama. "Adopting Knowledge Management in an E-learning System: Insights and Views of KM and EL Research Scholars"; Knowledge Management & E-Learning: An International Journal, Vol.3 No. 3, 375-398, 2011

[4] Nthaniel David Oye, Mazleena Salleh and N.A. Iahad. "E-Learning Barriers and Solutions to Knowledge Management and Transfer"; Information Management and Business Review, Vol. 3 No. 6, 366-372, Dec 2011

[5] Linh-Chi Vo. "Pragmatist Perspective on Knowledge and Knowledge Management in Organizations"; International Business Research (Canadian Center of Science and Education), Vol. 5 No. 9, 78-88, Aug 2012

[6] Rifat Shannak, Ra'ed Masa'deh, Zu'bi Al-Zu'bi, Bader Obeidat, Muhammad Alshurideh and Hamzah Altamony. "A Theoretical Perspective on the Relationship between Knowledge Management Systems, Customer Knowledge Management, and Firm Competitive Advantage"; European Journal Of Social Science, Vol. 32 No. 4, 520-532, Aug 2012

[7] Rana Geeta. "Knowledge Management and E-Learning Activities in the 21st Century to attain Competitive Advantage"; Advances In Management, Vol. 3 Issue 5, 54-56, May 2010

[8] William King. "Knowledge Management and Organizational Learning"; Annals of Information Systems (Springer-Verlag), Vol. 4, June 2009

[9] Samantha Murray and Joseph Peyrefitte. "Knowledge Type and Communication Media Choice in the Knowledge Transfer Process"; Journal of Managerial Issues Vol. 19 No. 1, 111-133, Mar 2007

[10] Genie Black. "A Comparison of Traditional, Online, and Hybrid Methods of Course Delivery"; Journal of Business Administration Online, Vol. 1 No. 1, 2002

[11] Roy Howsen and Stephen Lile. "A Comparison of Course Delivery Methods: An Exercise in Experimental Economics"; Journal of Economics and Finance Education, Vol. 7 No. 1, 21-28, Mar 2007

[12] Linda Trevino, Robert Lengel and Richard Daft. "Media Symbolism, Media Richness, and Media Choice in Organizations : A Symbolic Interactionist Perspective"; Communication Research: An International Quarterly, Vol 14 No. 5, 553-574, Oct 1987

[13] Daiga Bekere and Sarma Cakula. "Modeling of Collaborative Tagging Services for Sharing and Reusing E-learning Materials on the Web"; ICTE In Regional Development: 2008 Annual Proceedings, 65-72, 2008

[14] Kam-Fai Wong, Nam-Kiu Chan and Kam-Lai Wong. "Improving Document Clustering by Utilizing Meta-Data"; In Proceedings of the Sixth International Workshop on Information Retrieval with Asian Languages (Association for Computational Linguistics), Vol 11, 109-115, July 2003

[15] Stéphanie Gretsch, Heinz Mandl and Raphaela Schätz. "Implementation Process of a Knowledge Management Initiative: Yellow Pages"; New Research on Knowledge: Management Models and Methods, 311-332, Mar 2012

Design of Structured Syllabus and Subject Ontology for Adaptive Learning

Hyun-Sook Chung[1], **Jung-Min Kim**[2], **and Eun-Ok Baek**[2]
[1]Department of Computer Engineering, Chosun University, Gwangju, South Korea
[2]Department of Computer Engineering, Daejin University, Pocheon, South Korea
[3]Science, Math & Technology Education, CSU San Bernardino, San Bernardino, CA, USA

Abstract - *In this paper, we introduce our e-learning project that aims to make of creation, integration and interfacing of multiple ontologies on different layers, i.e. Curriculum ontology, Syllabus ontology, and Subject ontology. The primary objective of our project is to develop ontology-based e-learning support system which allows learners to build adaptive learning paths through understanding curriculum, syllabuses, and subjects of courses deeply. In this paper, we introduce our ontology model and propose an effective method for enhancing learning effect of students through construction of subject ontology. The subject ontology of a certain course is composed of an ontology made by a teacher and many ontologies made by students. It is used in discussion, visual presentation, and knowledge sharing between instructor and students. We used the subject ontology in two lectures in practice and found that the subject ontology enhances learning effect of students in according to the analysis of feedbacks of students.*

Keywords: curriculum, e-learning, learning path, ontology, syllabus

1 Introduction

Until now, ontology engineering has been applied in order to conceptualize knowledge of many different domains including education. Recently, lots of researches performed in order to apply Semantic Web technologies including ontology engineering to intelligent e-learning system development[1]. The researches applying ontology technology to education field are classified into curriculum or syllabus ontology creation[2],[3], ontology-based learning object organization, and ontology-based learning contents retrieval. The studies for education ontology creation include curriculum ontology creation[4] and personal subject ontology creation[5].

Mizoguchi[6],[7] proposed a ontology-based solution to solve several problems caused by intelligent instructional systems. Another works defined metadata of learning objects and learning path including curriculum based on ontology engineering technology[8],[9]. These works concentrated on management of learning objects and materials and performance enhancement of instructional systems. Ontology technology, however, can be used to make the knowledge structure, which improves the interaction among teachers and students and enables spontaneous learning of students, of teaching contents and learning materials of students based on semantic information[10].

Our e-learning project aims to make of creation, integration and interfacing of multiple ontologies on different layers, i.e. Curriculum ontology, Syllabus ontology, and Subject ontology. The primary objective of our project is to develop ontology-based e-learning support system which allows learners to build adaptive learning paths through understanding curriculum, syllabuses, and subjects of courses deeply. In this paper, we introduce our ontology model and propose an effective method for enhancing learning effect of students through constructing learner-based ontologies in which knowledge discovered by students is conceptualized and organized. Learner-based ontologies can be merged into teacher-based ontologies which conceptualize teaching contents in classes. Thus, our subject ontology is composed of teacher-based ontologies and learner-based ontologies. Teachers and students share and understand knowledge of learning materials based on learning ontologies.

This paper is structured as follows. Section 2 provides an overview of the layered structure of our learning ontologies. Section 3 represents the revised syllabus structure for supporting adaptive learning of students. We describe the hierarchical structure of subject ontology in Section 4. Section 5 shows the experimental result and in the end the paper presents our conclusion in Section 6.

2 The structure of learning ontologies

Commonly, a curriculum can be represented as a set of description of courses and syllabuses. A syllabus, which is identification and skeleton of a course, can be represented as a collection of several kinds of resources related to a certain course. We design the curriculum ontology in order to organize various semantic relationships, which include *hasSubtype*, *prerequisiteOf*, *basicOf*, *advancedOf*, *combinedOf*, and so on, existing between individual. The curriculum ontology conceptualizes the knowledge of curricula concepts, i.e. *ProgramOfStudy*, *Course*, *KeyConcept*,

AttainmentGoal, *AttainmentLevel*, and includes the direct semantic connections between courses and their syllabus ontologies.

The syllabus ontology conceptualizes the internal and external structures of syllabuses. A syllabus class, which is the core concept of syllabus ontology, has 9 data type properties, i.e. titleOfCourse, description, gradingPolicy, goalOfCourse, and 12 object type properties, i.e. oldVersionOf, hasInstructor, hasMaterial, hasSchedule, hasLectureRoom, to describe the contents and relationships extracted from traditional textual syllabus templates.

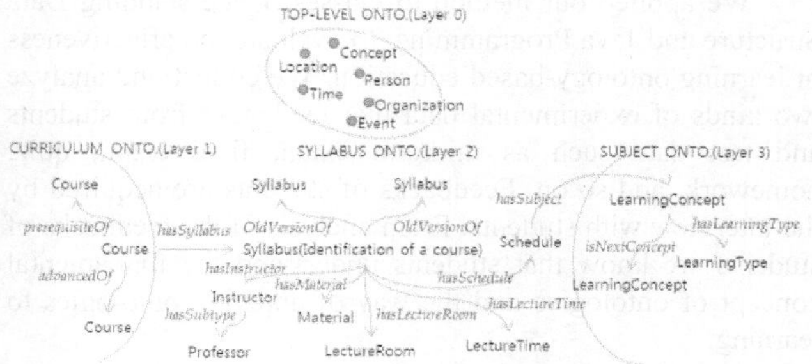

Figure 1. The layered structure of Top-level ontology, Curriculum ontology, Syllabus ontology, and Subject Ontology.

Figure 1 shows the relationships between syllabus ontology and each of other ontologies, top-level ontology, curriculum ontology, and subject ontology. Syllabus ontology has one or more subject ontologies because a conventional syllabus represents multiple concepts to be taught during a school semester. The *LearningConcept* class is top level concept in the subject ontology. The *LearningConcept* class has responsibilities to collect lower level topics and link to syllabus ontology. Following section 3 and 4 describe the detailed structure of the syllabus ontology and subject ontology.

3 Syllabus conceptualization

Adaptive learning path generation refers to the organization of learning objects in a proper order so that students can effectively study a subject area. In a learning graph a node denotes a learning object or learning element. However, effective assessment for learning activities of students is required in order to support adaptive learning of students. In other words, a node in a learning graph should be composed of lectures, learning goals, learning activities and assessment.

Thus, we have considered a syllabus as a node in a learning graph because it includes course description, learning goals, lectures, activities, and learning materials also. Figure 2 shows the syllabus-based learning graph in which learning graphs can be generated in two levels, i.e. course-level and concept-level. In this chapter, we define systematic models of learning goal, learning activity and assessment of a syllabus based on Bloom's taxonomy[11] which classifies behaviors of students to six cognitive levels of complexity. Table 1 shows cognitive, attitude, and skill domains of Bloom's taxonomy.

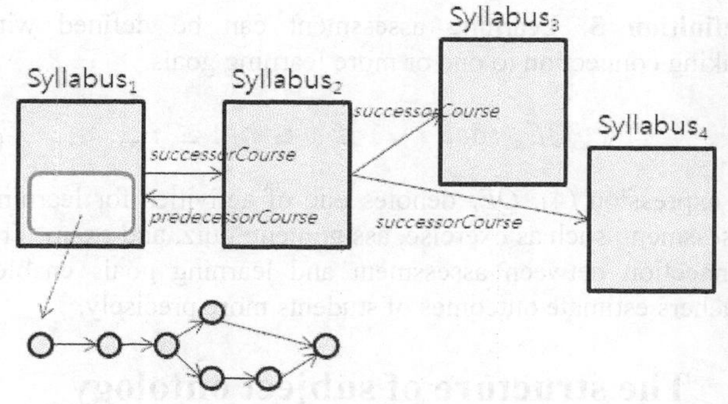

Figure. 2. The syllabus-based learning graph.

Table 1. Bloom's taxonomy

Levels	Cognitive	Attitude	Skill
1	Knowledge	Receiving	Imitation
2	Comprehension	Responding	Manipulation
3	Application	Valuing	Precision
4	Analysis	Organizing	Articulation
5	Synthesis	Characterizing	Naturalization
6	Evaluation		

Definition 1. Learning goal can be defined as a set of tuples in which each tuple is consisting of four items, learning goal, cognitive level, attitude level, and skill level.

$$\{< goal_p, C_i, A_j, S_k >\}, 1 \le p \le n, 1 \le i \le 6, 0 \le j \le 5, 0 \le k \le 5 \quad (1)$$

In expression (1), $goal_p$, C_i, A_j, and S_k denotes p-th learning goal, i-th cognitive complexity level, j-th attitude complexity level, and k-th skill complexity level respectively. For example, a teacher define a learning goal like as <"Understanding class inheritance in JAVA", C_3, A_3, S_2>.

Definition 2. Learning activity can be defined as a set of tuples in which each tuple is consisting of four items, learning activity, cognitive level, attitude level, and skill level. The types of learning activity performed by students defined as a set like as following expression (2).

$$LA = \{\text{READING}, \text{ESSAY}, \text{PRESENTATION}, \text{DISCUSSION}, \text{PRACTICE}, \text{EXERCISE}, \text{HOMEWORK}, \text{TEAM PROJECT}\} \quad (2)$$

$$\{< LA_p, C_i A_j S_k >\}, 1 \le p \le 9, 1 \le i \le 6, 0 \le j \le 5, 0 \le k \le 5 \quad (3)$$

In expression (3), LA_p denotes one of elements in a learning activity set. One or more learning activities should be mentioned in every week of lecture schedule in a syllabus.

Definition 3. Learning assessment can be defined with making connection to one or more learning goals.

$$\{\langle QE_p, goal_i \rangle\}, 1 \le p \le n, 1 \le i \le m \quad (4)$$

In expression (4), QE_p denotes one of activities for learning assessment, such as exercise, assignment, quiz, and exam. The connection between assessment and learning goals enables teachers estimate outcomes of students more precisely.

4 The structure of subject ontology

Subject ontology is composed of one or more of teacher-based ontology, several learner-based ontologies and learning materials. Teacher-based ontology contains learning concepts and knowledge structure to be studied in a class. Learner-based ontology contains concepts and knowledge structure created by students. When a teacher presents learning subjects, students investigate the subjects and extract meaningful concepts and knowledge structure to create a new learner-based ontology or extend existing learner-based ontology during their learning process.

Table 2. Classes, properties and relations defined in teacher-based ontology

Type	Name	Description
CLASS	LearningConcept	Root class
	FundamentalConcept	Conceptualization of fundamental topics of learning subjects
	AdvancedConcept	Conceptualization of advanced topics of learning subjects
	RelatedConcept	Conceptualization of additional topics of learning subjects
PROPERTY	Name	Concept name
	AuxiliaryName	Auxiliary name of concept name
	Definition	Definition of concept
	Description	Description of concept
RELATION	Fundamental-Concept-Of	A is fundamental class of B Reversed relation is Has-Fundamental-Concept
	Advanced-Concept-Of	A is advanced class of B
	Related-Concept-Of	A is related concept with B Reversed relation is Has-Related-Concept
	Example-Of	A is example class of B Reversed relation is Has-Example
	Exercise-Of	A is exercise class of B Reversed relation is Has-Exercise
	Same-Concept	Both concepts have same semantic

Subject ontology is described as following 5-tuples, $<C, P, I, R_H, R_C>$. The symbol C, P, I, R_H and R_C represent class, property, instance, hierarchy relation between classes and association between classes individually. Table 2 represents classes, properties, and relations defined in subject ontology.

5 Experiments

We applied our method to classes, Understanding Data Structure and Java Programming, to evaluate the effectiveness of learning ontology-based education. We collect and analyze two kinds of experimental data like feedbacks from students and test data such as midterm exam, final exam, quiz, homework, and so on. Feedbacks of students are acquired by the interview with students. From analysis of the feedbacks of students we know that students understand the fundamental concept of ontologies and the way of applying ontologies to learning.

However, creating of subject ontology is somewhat difficult work but it is useful to present, discuss, and share of studied subjects of students. The graph depicted in figure 3 shows the values of learning outcomes, which are understanding concepts(LO01), organizing relations(LO02), and so on, before and after applying learning ontologies to class. We compute the values of learning outcomes of students through evaluating of quiz, exams, homework, and so on.

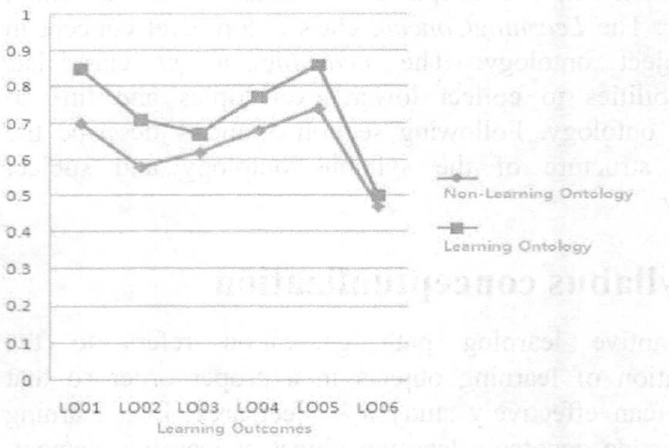

Figure 3. Learning outcomes before and after applying subject ontology to class.

Another experiment evaluates the retrieval performance of elements from syllabuses before and after transformation to our proposed syllabus template in section 3. Syllabus transformation and retrieval have been performed on 45 syllabuses of computer engineering field collected from the Web. As the result of our retrieval experiments, we know that precision, recall and f-measure averaged for 10 test sets is

0.78, 0.87 and 0.82 respectively. In addition, we know that our syllabus model is well structured and conceptualized than current syllabus formats from the result depicted in figure 4.

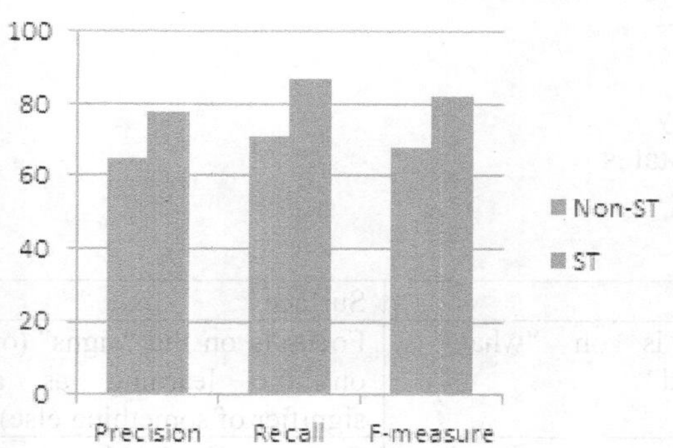

Figure 4. Comparison of retrieval performance between ST and Non-ST.

6 Conclusions

In this paper, we proposed the integrated and layered structure of learning ontologies for offline and online learning domains. Our ontology model's main entity is a syllabus because it is identification, definition, and contents of a course truly. We have designed curriculum ontology and subject ontology to be connected into syllabus ontology for supporting adaptive learning and knowledge sharing of students. In addition, our ontology model can be used as a knowledge base in intelligent e-learning management systems. Our future work will be adaptive learning path generation and recommendation based on the proposed learning ontology.

7 Acknowledgements

This work was supported by the Korea Research Foundation Grant funded by the Korean Government (No. 2013-027242).

8 References

[1] Yu D., Zhang W., and Chen X. New Generation of e-learning Technologies. In Proceedings of First International Multi-Symposiums on Computer and Computational Sciences(2006), pp.455-459.

[2] Chi, Y. Developing curriculum sequencing for managing multiple texts in e-learning system. In Proceedings of International Conference on Engineering Education, (2010).

[3] Libbrecht, P. Cross curriculum search through the Geoskills' Ontology. In Proceedings of SEAM'08, (2008), pp.38-50.

[4] Shackelford, R., McGettrick, A., Sloan, R., Topi, H., Davies, G., Kamali, R., Cross, J., Impagliazzo, J., LeBlanc, R., Lunt, B. Computing Curricula 2005: The Overview Report, ACM SIGCSE Bulletin, 38, 1, (2006).

[5] Apple W. P. F., Horace H. S. I. Educational Ontologies Construction for Personalized Learning on the Web. Studies in Computation Intelligence, 62, (2007), pp.47-82.

[6] Mizoguchi, R. Tutorial on ontological engineering-Part2: Ontology development, tools and languages. New Generation Computing, OhmSha&Springer, 22, 1, (2004).

[7] Mizoguguchi R., Bourdeau, J. Using Ontological Engineering to Overcome AI-ED Problems. International Journal of Artificial Intelligence in Education, 11, 2, (2000), pp.107-121.

[8] Marco R., Joseph S., Curriculum Management and Review - an ontology-based solution. Technical Report # DIT-07-021, University of Trento, (2007).

[9] Nilsson, M., Palmer, M., Brase, J. The LOM RDF binding - principles and implementation. In Proceedings of The 3rd Annual ARIDNE Conference, Lueven, Belgium, (2003).

[10] Sampson, D. G., Lytra, M. D., Wagner, G., Diaz, P. Guest Editorial: Ontologies and the Semantic Web for E-learning. Educational Technology and Society, 7, 4, (2004), pp.26-28.

Designing an online course to promote deep learning outcomes

B. Morgan
Western Oregon University
Monmouth, Oregon, United States

Abstract - *Online courses are seen as a means to deliver an educational experience to a wider audience. Often it is believed that face to face courses can simply be put online, in a plug and go model, and that will be sufficient to deliver deep learning outcomes. This paper first considers the difference between surface and deep learning then seeks to provide a pedagogical paradigm that promotes deep learning. The Communities of Inquiry (CoI) model for online course delivery models this paradigm and supports the assertion that deep learning is an obtainable objective, but is far more nuanced and requires far greater resources than the plug and go model suggests.*

Keywords: e-learning, online education model, Communities of Inquiry, deep learning outcomes, collaborative learning

1 Introduction

As the tertiary educational system continues to work to minimize expenses, many institutions are turning to distance education as a solution to their financial shortfalls [1]. However, there are still concerns about current technologies and their ability to deliver an educational experience that promotes deep learning [2], [3]. Given the current research into a successful pedagogical paradigm, it can be shown that online courses can be effective in delivering a deep learning experience.

This paper begins by defining deep learning followed by applying this definition to the theoretical framework of Communities of Inquiry (CoI), a theory that has been shown to actively engage learners and assist in designing online courses. Finally, an outline of a course model is given.

2 Definition of Deep Learning

Deep learning is often defined along with its contrasting outcome, surface learning. Table 1 is used to demonstrate perceived differences in the two distinct types of learning. Based on this information deep learning can be defined as knowledge that has been assimilated into previous knowledge and is applied to everyday experiences and interdisciplinary concepts. Students demonstrate this knowledge when they can argue or defend ideas broadly and coherently using knowledge and theory from multiple disciplines. Critical thinking is considered a precursor to deep learning.

Deep	Surface
Focus is on "what is signified"	Focus is on the "signs" (or on the learning as a signifier of something else)
Relates previous knowledge to new knowledge	Focus on unrelated parts of the task
Relates knowledge from different courses	Information for assessment is simply memorized
Relates theoretical ideas to everyday experience	Facts and concepts are associated unreflectively
Relates and distinguishes evidence and argument	Principles are not distinguished from examples
Organizes and structures content into coherent whole	Task is treated as an external imposition
Emphasis is internal, from within the student	Emphasis is external, from demands of assessment

Table 1. Comparison of Deep and Surface Learning [4]

Deep and surface learning are not attributes of the learner; an individual can demonstrate either trait depending on the situation [4]. Research has shown that a "deep strategic approach to studying is generally related to high levels of academic achievement, but only where the assessment procedures emphasize and reward personal understanding" [5, p. 4]. This establishes the necessity to design courses to provide support for and reward critical thinking and a deep approach to learning. Those outcomes may be demonstrated using Bloom's revised taxonomy [6] to operationalize deep learning by applying concepts 4.0 – 6.3 to student's communication on forums and written assignments:

Structure of the Cognitive Process
Dimension of the Revised Taxonomy [6]

4.0 Analyze – Breaking material into its constituent parts and detecting how the parts relate to one another and to an overall structure or purpose.

4.1 Differentiating
4.2 Organizing
4.3 Attributing

5.0 Evaluate – Making judgments based on criteria and standards.

5.1 Checking
5.2 Critiquing

6.0 Create – Putting elements together to form a novel,

coherent whole or make an original product.

6.1 Generating

6.2 Planning

6.3 Producing

In the next section a theoretical framework that research indicates is supportive of deep learning, as defined in this section, is examined.

3 Theoretical Framework – Community of Inquiry (CoI)

Recognizing the need for social interaction in online, asynchronous courses, Garrison et al. [7] developed a schema designed to promote communication. The three elements of this structure are defined by Garrison et al.[7] and are considered to be "crucial prerequisites for a successful higher educational experience" (p. 87). These elements are social presence, cognitive presence, and teaching presence. Figure 1 is the model depicting the interaction between these three elements.

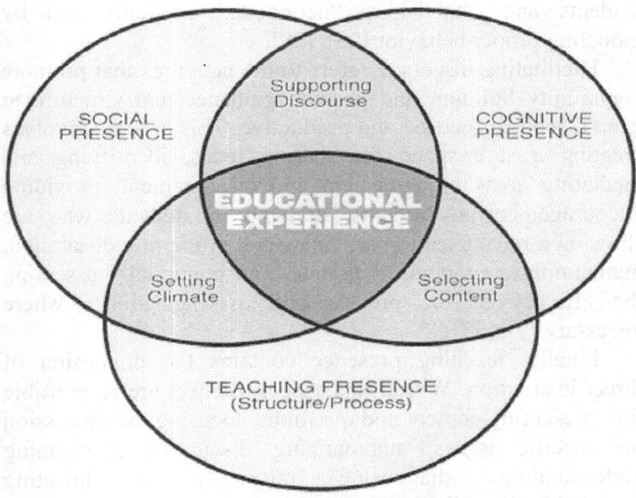

Figure 1. Model of the CoI Framework

Considering each of these elements separately allows reflection on their applicability to learning using computer-mediated communication.

3.1 Social presence

Learning theories support the premise that learning happens in community, through inquiry, and is socially constructed [8], [9], [10], [11]. Garrison et al.[7], who were inspired predominantly by the work of Dewey, used social construction of knowledge as the foundation for CoI, seeing social presence, guided by teaching presence, as support for cognitive presence. Social interaction historically has been seen as verbal interaction, however Garrison et al.[7] posited that, although oral communication is a rich medium, there are advantages to text based, asynchronous communication.

Nonverbal cues in face to face interactions were seen as necessary for more effective communication [12]. Without these nonverbal cues asynchronous, text-based communication was found to be more self-absorbed, and the relative status of participants largely unacknowledged compared to face to face communications [13]. Garrison et al. [7] asserted, however, that text-based, asynchronous communication had advantages over verbal communication and could assist in higher ordered learning objectives. They maintain, based on the work of Applebee [14], Fulwiler [15], and White [16], that verbal communication can be impulsive and fleeting. However, with text based communication, interchanges between people benefit from the ability to read and reread the issue being responded to and more time can be taken to form a response. Text based communication was seen to mediate the impulsivity sometimes associated with emotional outbursts [17].

Communication alone does not mean that deeper level learning is taking place. Social presence within the CoI framework is defined as "the ability of learners to project themselves socially and affectively into a community of inquiry" [18]. Although social presence has been shown to be based on student perception and is situational [19], the CoI framework provides the following indicators of social presence within an asynchronous communication medium: 1) emotional expression, 2) open communication, and 3) group cohesion [7].

As the CoI model shows, social presence is related to cognitive presence through discourse. Collaboration is essential for the construction of meaningful knowledge and cognitive development [7].

3.2 Cognitive presence

Cognitive presence is a product of communication and social presence that is facilitated to promote critical thinking [7]. The fact that students are interacting does not necessarily mean that they are interacting in ways that will promote the attainment of learning outcomes. Although social interaction as a quantitative measure can signal group cohesion, an important element of social presence, cognitive presence is reflected within the more qualitative measure of "purposeful and systematic discourse" [20]. Garrison et al. [7] developed the Practical Inquiry Model (PIM) to operationalize cognitive presence (Figure 2 on the next page).

Using the PIM to operationalize cognitive presence it can be seen that there is a correlation between cognitive presence and deep learning. Table 2 demonstrates cognitive presence through the lens of Bloom's revised taxonomy to make the case for cognitive presence supporting deep learning.

The discussion of cognitive presence highlights the critical need for the third element, teaching presence. Teaching presence is essential to guide, focus, and structure social interaction to achieve cognitive presence, which is fundamental for deep and meaningful learning outcomes. In fact research has shown that teaching presence is the most critical element of the CoI model [21], [20], [22], [23].

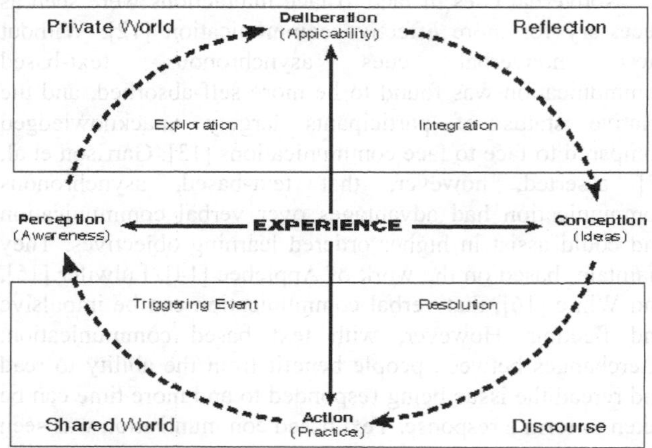

Figure 2. Practical Inquiry Model

Bloom's Structure of Cognitive Process		PIM Category	PIM Indicator
		Triggering events	Recognizing the problem
			Sense of puzzlement
Analyze	Differentiating	Exploration	Information exchange
	Organizing		Discussion of ambiguities
	Attributing	Integration	Connecting ideas
Create	Generating Planning		Create solutions
	Producing	Resolution	Vicariously apply new ideas
Evaluate	Checking		Critically assess solutions
	Critiquing		

Table 2. Correlating Bloom's Structure of Cognitive Process and Practical Inquiry Model

3.3 Teaching presence

The CoI model requires the interaction among all three elements as necessary for learning outcomes that are deep and meaningful. Research conducted on this model shows, however, that teaching presence is primarily responsible for the success or failure of outcomes [24], [25]. Garrison and Cleveland-Innes found that "teaching presence must be available, either from the facilitator or the other students, to transition from social to cognitive presence" [20, p. 143]. Additional research shows that it is important for teachers to model expected behaviors in order to create a community [26] and that high levels of interaction with instructors is significantly related to increased course satisfaction and perceived learning [27]. The teaching presence aspect of the CoI paradigm has three dimensions; design and organization, facilitating discourse, and direct instruction [7], [28].

The design and organization dimension of teaching presence includes selecting curriculum and technologies to be used, creating assignments and group activities with the technologies and medium in mind, creating a timeline for learning and communicating this information effectively with students and establishing "netiquette" explicitly and by modeling proper behavior [23], [29].

Facilitating discourse refers to the activities that promote community building and provide guidance and structure to keep discourse focused and productive. This process involves creating a safe space for sharing ideas, identifying and mediating areas of agreement and disagreement, providing encouragement to students, drawing in students who are showing a reluctance to participate and prompting discussion, maintaining a productive climate, and continually assessing the efficacy of the process and making adjusts where necessary [7], [23].

Finally, teaching presence contains the dimension of direct instruction. Within this aspect teachers are responsible for "presenting content and questions, focusing the discussion on specific issues, summarizing discussion, confirming understanding, diagnosing misperceptions, injecting knowledge from diverse sources, and responding to technical concerns" [23, p. 62].

4 COURSE MODEL

The theoretical framework outlined lays the foundation for the course paradigm detailed in Table 3.

	Teacher Role
Teacher Presence	
Pre-course setup	Creating Assignments: Assignments should move through the revised Bloom's taxonomy in order to facilitate deep learning. The first part of the assignment should be designed to analyze a problem – breaking it down into pieces and organizing the problem. The next step is to evaluate the possible solutions and the last step would be to put

<table>
<tr><td></td><td colspan="2">the pieces together to form a unique perspective on or solution to the given problem. The assignments should be created to include team projects and class discussions, requiring both synchronous and asynchronous forms of communication.

Choosing technology:
1. Synchronous communication – There are many options in this realm, but research has shown that in a synchronous, text-based form of communication it is important to have a system that shows who is online. Skype is an example of a technology that allows for instant messaging, with online visibility, as well as group voice interaction. This technology is also important to facilitate virtual office hours.
2. Asynchronous communication – The possibilities in this area can be forums, blogs, or wikis. Each of these provides students a means of communicating in a more formal arena, giving time to put thought into the communication. In asynchronous communication using notification tools helps students to participate more fully as they are informed when someone has responded to their post or the teacher has given feedback.
3. Learning Management Systems - Research has shown that LMS that provide all of the information for each week in one place and are navigated with the least number of clicks are preferred by students. Also listed as advantageous were having profile pictures next to discussion posts, the ability to add emoticons to posts and the WYSIWYG editors that allowed the transfer of formatting into posts when cut and pasted from another document [30].
The first week should be devoted to downloading and becoming familiar with technology, self introductions and getting to know each other. This supports developing relationships between students, forming social presence.</td></tr>
<tr><td>Direct Instruction</td><td colspan="2">• presenting content and questions,
• focusing the discussion on specific issues,
• summarizing discussion,
• confirming understanding,
• diagnosing misperceptions,
• injecting knowledge from diverse sources, and
• responding to technical concerns [23].</td></tr>
<tr><td></td><td>Teacher Role</td><td>Student Role</td></tr>
<tr><td>Social Presence</td><td>Activities that promote community building and providing guidance and structure to keep discourse focused and productive, including:
• creating a safe space for sharing ideas,
• identifying and mediating areas of agreement and disagreement,
• providing encouragement to students,
• drawing in students who are showing a reluctance to participate and prompting discussion,
• maintaining a productive climate, and
• continually assessing the efficacy of the process and making adjusts where necessary [7], [23].</td><td>Being responsible and respectful including:
• Completing individual work before the group meetings.
• Continuing participation in asynchronous discussions.
• Being on time for meetings using synchronous methods.
• Being respectful of others/ following the rules of netiquette. For example:
o Re-read your comments before you post them.
o Never make derogatory comments toward another person in the class.
o Do not make sexist, racist, homophobic, or victim-blaming comments.
o Do not demean others.
o Encourage others to develop and share their ideas.
• If problems arise, using the instructor as a mediator.</td></tr>
</table>

Cognitive Presence	Within the PIM model: • Provide a triggering event (e.g., an assignment or a question to focus discussion). • Provide adequate time in the course framework for student reflection. • Bring students back to the space of discourse, if needed provide scaffolding to assist in the integration of new ideas, and direct new discourse on the outcome of reflection. As this is an iterative model assignments should contain prompts that can be given to promote further iteration to obtain deeper levels of learning.	Within the PIM model: • Participate in the discussion and analysis with group members. • Take significant time and opportunities to contemplate the presented issue, putting it together with other concepts already learned. • Participate in the new discourse considering all new ideas each group member brings to the table. Share fully the ideas that came from individual reflection.

Table 3 – Course Model for teaching online

5 Conclusion

The issue concerning the possibility of engaging students online in a community of learners that promotes deep learning outcomes is a complex and multi-layered query. This paper provides support for the initial claim that deep learning in online course is possible. Additionally a model is outlined to facilitate the creation of online classes that provide the elements supported by the theoretical framework.

It should be noted that in order to create online environments that promote deep learning it must be taken into consideration that feedback from instructors is critical. This leads to the necessity for small classes. So the paradox exists that classes need to be larger to generate revenue, however they need to remain small to promote the elements that support deep learning. Teachers report that online classes require more preparation and more overall teaching time than face to face classes do [31].

In closing it is important to note that the CoI framework is dependent upon proper design and implementation. In order to promote critical thinking teachers must be prepared to guide and participate. The research shows that the ultimate success of an online course lies predominately with the instructor.

6 References

[1] D. Valentine, "Distance learning: Promises, problems, and possibilities," *Online Journal of Distance Learning Administration*, vol. 5, no. 3, 2002.

[2] J. M. Galusha, "Barriers to learning in distance education," *Interpersonal Computing and Technology*, vol. 5, no. 3–4, pp. 6–14, 1997.

[3] S. L. Howell, P. B. Williams, and N. K. Lindsay, "Thirty-two trends affecting distance education: An informed foundation for strategic planning," *Online Journal of Distance Learning Administration*, vol. 6, no. 3, 2003.

[4] J. S. Atherton, "Deep and Surface learning," *Learning and Teaching*, 2011. [Online]. Available: http://www.learningandteaching.info/learning/deepsurf.htm. [Accessed: 06-May-2011].

[5] N. Entwistle, "Promoting deep learning through teaching and assessment: conceptual frameworks and educational contexts," in *TLRP conference, Leicester*, 2000.

[6] D. R. Krathwohl, "A revision of Bloom's taxonomy: An overview," *Theory into practice*, vol. 41, no. 4, pp. 212–218, 2002.

[7] D. R. Garrison, T. Anderson, and W. Archer, "Critical inquiry in a text-based environment: Computer conferencing in higher education," *The Internet and Higher Education*, vol. 2, no. 2–3, pp. 87–105, 1999.

[8] J. Bruner, "The narrative construction of reality," *Critical inquiry*, vol. 18, no. 1, pp. 1–21, 1991.

[9] J. Dewey and A. W. Small, *My pedagogic creed*. E.L. Kellogg & co., 1897.

[10] J. Piaget, *Origins of intelligence in children*. International Universities Press, 1952.

[11] L. S. Vygotsky and others, *Mind in society*. Cambridge, MA: Harvard University Press, 1978.

[12] A. Mehrabian, "Some referents and measures of nonverbal behavior," *Behavior Research Methods*, vol. 1, no. 6, pp. 203–207, 1968.

[13] L. Sproull and S. Kiesler, "Reducing social context cues: Electronic mail in organizational communications," *Management science*, vol. 32, no. 11, pp. 1492–1512, 1986.

[14] A. N. Applebee, "Writing and reasoning," *Review of Educational Research*, vol. 54, no. 4, pp. 577–596, 1984.

[15] T. Fulwiler, *Teaching with writing*. Boynton/Cook Publishers, 1987.

[16] E. M. White, "Assessing higher-order thinking and communication skills in college graduates through writing," *The Journal of General Education*, pp. 105–122, 1993.

[17] D. Derks, A. H. Fischer, and A. E. R. Bos, "The role of emotion in computer-mediated communication: A review," *Computers in Human Behavior*, vol. 24, no. 3, pp. 766–785, May 2008.

[18] L. Rourke, T. Anderson, D. R. Garrison, and W. Archer, "Assessing social presence in asynchronous text-based computer conferencing," *The Journal of Distance Education / Revue de l'Éducation à Distance*, vol. 14, no. 2, Dec. 1999.

[19] A. G. Picciano, "Beyond student perceptions: Issues of interaction, presence, and performance in an online course," *Journal of Asynchronous learning networks*, vol. 6, no. 1, pp. 21–40, 2002.

[20] D. R. Garrison and M. Cleveland-Innes, "Facilitating cognitive presence in online learning: Interaction is not enough.," *American Journal of Distance Education*, vol. 19, no. 3, pp. 133–148, 2005.

[21] M. Cleveland-Innes, D. R. Garrison, and E. Kinsel, "The role of learner in an online Community of Inquiry: Responding to the challenges of first-time online learners," in in *Solutions and Innovations in Web-Based Technologies for Augmented Learning: Improved Platforms, Tools, and Applications*, N. Karacapilidis, Ed. 2009, pp. 1–14.

[22] J. C. Richardson and P. Ice, "Investigating students' level of critical thinking across instructional strategies in online discussions," *The Internet and Higher Education*, vol. 13, no. 1–2, pp. 52–59, 2010.

[23] P. Shea, C. S. Li, K. Swan, and A. Pickett, "Developing learning community in online asynchronous college courses: The role of teaching presence," *Journal of Asynchronous Learning Networks*, vol. 9, no. 4, pp. 59–82, 2005.

[24] C. N. Gunawardena, "Social presence theory and implications for interaction and collaborative learning in computer conferences," *International journal of educational telecommunications*, vol. 1, no. 2/3, pp. 147–166, 1995.

[25] S. R. Hiltz and M. Turoff, *The network nation: Human communication via computer*. MIT Press, 1993.

[26] R. E. Brown, "The process of community-building in distance learning classes," *Journal of Asynchronous Learning Networks*, vol. 5, no. 2, pp. 18–35, 2001.

[27] K. Swan, "Building learning communities in online courses: The importance of interaction," *Education Communication & Information*, vol. 2, no. 1, pp. 23–49, 2002.

[28] D. R. Garrison, T. Anderson, and W. Archer, "The first decade of the community of inquiry framework: A retrospective," *The Internet and Higher Education*, vol. 13, no. 1–2, pp. 5–9, 2010.

[29] T. Anderson, L. Rourke, D. R. Garrison, and W. Archer, "Assessing teaching presence in a computer conferencing context," *Journal of Asynchronous Learning Networks*, vol. 5, no. 2, pp. 1–17, 2001.

[30] Z. Unal and A. Unal, "A comparison of BlackBoard and Moodle for the teaching and learning of educational technology courses," 2010.

[31] S. Jones and C. Johnson-Yale, "Professors online," 05-Sep-2005. [Online]. Available: http://firstmonday.org/htbin/cgiwrap/bin/ojs/index.php/fm/article/viewArticle/1275/1195. [Accessed: 17-Apr-2011].

A Prototype Facilitators Dashboard: Assessing and visualizing dialogue quality in online deliberation for education and work

Tom Murray, Leah Wing[1], Beverly Park Woolf,
Alexander Wise, Shijun Wu, Lori Clarke, Lee Osterweil, Xiaoxi Xu
School of Computer Science, [1]Legal Studies Dept.
University of Massachusetts, Amherst, MA
Contact: tmurray@cs.umass.edu

Abstract: The emerging next generation ("Web 3.0") of socio-technological tool development is adding additional support for reflecting on and improving the *quality* of online information, communication, and action coordination. An important opportunity is that online systems can include tools that directly support participants in having higher quality and more skillful engagements. We are evaluating dialogue software features that support participants directly and "dashboard" tools that support third parties (mediators, teachers, facilitators, moderators, etc.) in supporting higher quality deliberation. In this paper we will focus on our work in educational settings (college classes) and on our development of a Facilitators Dashboard that visualizes dialogue quality indicators for use as facilitation tools or participant social awareness tools. We are particularly interested in supporting the "social deliberative skills" that interlocutors need to build mutual understanding and mutual regard in complex or contentious situations.

Keywords: Educational and Knowledge Building dialogue; deliberative skills; scaffolding; multiple representations; dashboards.

Introduction

As communication, collaboration, and knowledge building expand on the Internet the benefits and limitations of "Web 2.0" technologies become increasingly apparent [1]. The affordances of social networking, information sharing, and expansive search capabilities have lead to a dramatic increases in the *quantity* of information and connectivity without always supporting—and sometimes sacrificing—their *quality*. The emerging next generation ("Web 3.0") of socio-technological tool development adds additional support for reflecting on and improving the quality of online information, communication, and action coordination [2]. An important opportunity is that online systems can include tools that directly support participants in having higher quality and more skillful engagements. We are building and evaluating dialogue software features that support *participants* directly and "dashboard" tools that support *third parties* (mediators, teachers, facilitators, moderators, etc.) in supporting higher quality deliberation among participants. In this paper we will focus on our work in educational settings (college classes) and on our development of a Facilitators Dashboard that visualizes dialogue quality indicators for use by either third parties or participants. We are particularly interested in supporting the "social deliberative skills" that interlocutors need to build mutual understanding and mutual regard in complex or contentious situations [3][4].

Iandoli et al. [5] give examples of tools that provide visualizations and feedback about: the who, to-whom, when, and how-much (activity level) of conversation moves; show the structure and time-based evolution of topics and communication relationships; and provide meaning-making tools for relevance, importance, and summarization. They suggest that such tools "help people communicate in better and easier ways by reducing misunderstandings, facilitating the grounding process, and reducing its costs" (p. 73). Such tools not only compensate for some of what is lost in moving from face-to-face communication but can also provide novel means of visualizing, reflecting on, and improving collaborative processes that are not available in face-to-face communication. Bunder et al. [6] frame the issue in terms of "social and cognitive awareness tools" that "facilitate and institutionalize the natural processes of becoming aware about social and cognitive variables, thereby leading to adaptive behavior in collaboration" (p. 606). Third parties such as facilitators sometimes provide this type of structured support.

Communication, collaboration, and knowledge building have many facets, and we focus our research on a specific area: supporting the social deliberative skills and behaviors that allow interlocutors to build mutual understanding (or "negotiate meaning") in complex or contentious contexts. That is, when one is challenged to deeply consider and work with not just *an* idea or need, but *your* or *their* idea or need in relationship to *mine* or *ours*. These skills include social perspective taking, question asking, self-reflection, and meta-dialogue (see [7] [3]). Iandoli et al. describe a "debate dashboard" to enhance online knowledge sharing. Our focus on mutual understanding and meaning negotiation is different from, but overlapping with, those who focus on supporting debate or argumentation quality, problem solving, or knowledge building activities (including Iandoli et al., and also see [9]). Similar to Iandoli et al., we wish to provide visual feedback or mirroring tools about (1) individual users and aggregations of users; (2) the interaction process, and (3) the content of a dialogue.

Below we will describe the Dashboard tool, the discussion forum software that it interacts with, our initial formative evaluations of the Dashboard, and future plans. This research is part of a larger project that includes (1) testing whether special discussion forum features ("reflective tools") support social deliberative skills, and (2) using state of the art text analysis and machine learning algorithms to analyze social deliberative behavior in online communication. In Murray et al. [3] we report on experimental trials that show a significant impact and large effect size for the reflective tools in college classroom online dialogues. For every classroom or large group that uses our tools, there are only one or two facilitators, so our evaluations of the Dashboard will be more qualitative and case-based.

Recent advances in computational psycholinguistics allow for a more systematic and deeper analysis of dialogues, which is necessary to uncover subtle cues that might be diagnostic of critical deliberation characteristics. In [10] [11], we report on our work in developing computational methods to measure deliberative skills from online discussions, which have shown promising results. In this paper we will describe our progress and plans for displaying the results of such text analysis in the Dashboard.

Mediem Deep Deliberation Software

Before we describe the Dashboard software we will describe the enhanced discussion forum software that it interacts with. Our research indicates that simple scaffolding features can increase skillful deliberation online. In [3], we compared students using the reflective tools in Mediem with a control group not using these tools and found a large effect in social deliberative skill support due to the reflective tools. Mediem is an off-the-shelf application (developed by Idealogue Inc.[1]) that has been used (by others) in a number of dialogue contexts including interfaith discussions among college students.

The Mediem software was chosen for our study because it has a number of features designed to support deeper reflection and engagement. Mediem includes the three reflective tools. First is the Story feature, which gives participants a special place to say how the issue at hand relates to them personally, including relevant background information about themselves and "what is at stake" for them in the issue. Second is the Conversation Thermometer, a meta-dialogue tool that allows participants to rate (vote on) the quality of the conversation at any time. The choices can be customized by the administrator. Third is the Contribution Tag feature, which allows participants to give brief comments on other's contributions. It provides a fixed vocabulary similar to the sentence starters (or locution openers) used in other dialogue software, but the tags remain attached to the target post rather than starting a new post (see [12]).

Facilitators Dashboard Diagram Pane: Visualizing key indicators

Design considerations. We have prototyped a Facilitators Dashboard that provides third parties a "birds-eye view" of the state and flow of online engagements. We have piloted it with professional facilitators and also begun to pilot it as a feedback and "awareness tool" for participants. We built an API that allows the Dashboard to receive real-time updates on the dialogue state and posted text from the Mediem deep dialogue forum system. See Figure 1, which shows tools in the "Diagram" tab of the Dashboard. Similar to Iandoli et al., we aimed to visualize user, interaction, and content information, including participation levels, reply networks, and content or theme overviews—in both static and trend (timeline) visualizations. At a more ambitious level, we also aimed to use text and network analysis to identify skillful (or non-skillful) deliberation, emotional tone or sentiment. Further, we have made early forays into automatically identify dialogue phases (e.g. introductions, deliberation, impasses, persuasion) and turning/infection points or opportunities for intervention (e.g. silences or non-responsiveness, changes of phase or tone, sudden emotional tensions in multiple participants).

Unlike projects that help participants think logically or creatively, provide valid justifications, or design reasonable solutions (all of which are certainly important), and given our focus on social

[1] For more information about Mediem, which is Open Source software, see www.idealogueinc.com.

deliberative skills and meaning negotiation, we assumed that our facilitators would be most interested in supporting all voices being heard, participants acting respectfully, and encouraging reciprocal role taking, empathy, and self-reflection. Based on an informal analysis of the literature and our conversations with experts, Shrikant & Murray [13] identified a set of common problems encountered in online facilitation that facilitation tools might help monitor:

- Low or no participation of individuals or groups, or **silences** or lulls on the part of individuals, the entire group, or sub-groups (which can be due to disinterest/boredom in the discussion or discomfort/fear of speaking up);
- conversation **domination** by an individual or group;
- inappropriate or **disrespectful** behavior;
- **off-topic** conversation;
- tension-filled **disagreements**, or high emotional content;
- too much agreement or **politeness**;

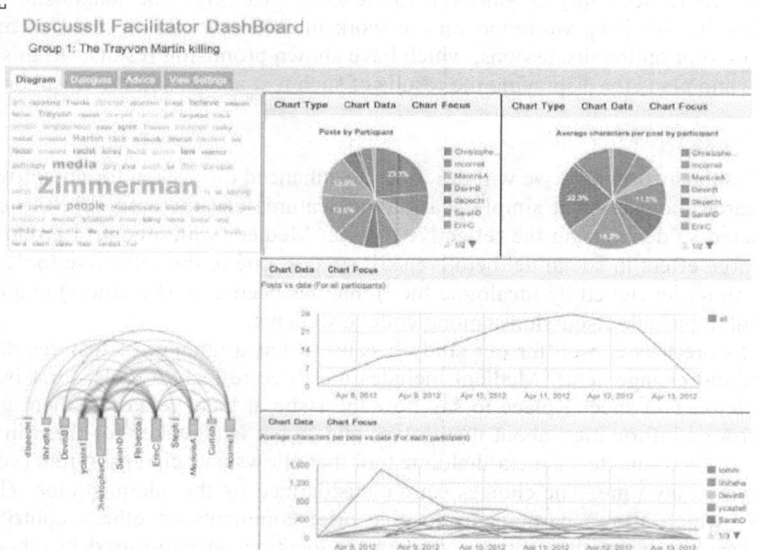

Figure 1: Facilitator Dashboard: Diagram Pane

We add to this list indicators of deliberative skillfulness that we would be interested in identifying and monitoring automatically (if possible): [2] social question asking and perspective-seeking behaviors; appreciation; social perspective taking; meta-dialogue (reflecting on the quality of the dialogue); proposing and weighing alternatives; systems or big picture thinking; peer mediation and facilitation; question answering and responsiveness; and topic initiation. The Diagram panel of the Dashboard shown in Figure 1 shows direct data displays that involve no analysis. Later we will discuss the Dialogue and Advice panels, which involve more in-depth processing. As the reader will note in the descriptions below, we have only begun to address all of these issues. But we feel that presenting the full list is a helpful indicator for where the field needs to go, and a map for our continued research.

Dashboard description: Diagram pane. Figure 1 shows data from a classroom discussion about the fatal shooting of Trayvon Martin by George Zimmerman which was a hot topic in the news during the time of this activity. When the facilitator begins using the Dashboard they select from a list of the deliberation projects, classes, or discussion groups registered with the Mediem software and the Dashboard (not shown in the Figure). Pie and bar charts show participation levels (number of participant posts and

[2] Note that in our research to measure the impact of reflective tools, we have a manual coding scheme for these items. In our text analysis and machine learning research we are also trying to create models to automatically recognize them.

average size of posts). Timelines show trends in these same metrics. A social network diagram shows who is replying to whom, with the thickness of the lines proportional to the number of replies. . A Word Cloud (see en.wikipedia.org/wiki/Word_cloud) graphically shows word frequencies through font sizes (the color and location of the words has no meaning in this representation).

When participants register on the Mediem site they have the option of entering demographic information, the structure of which is determined by the forum administrator. For the classroom trials we include gender and school grade level, but religious or political affiliation or other demographic information could also be captured and visualized. Figure 1 shows pie charts by individual. Figure 1 shows a view by gender. In this figure females are posting more often but males are posting longer posts. For the Trayvon Martin discussion shown in Figure 1, the class instructor was able to see that upper class students were more engaged and lowerclass students were more silent, which she found to be useful information.

At first glance the word cloud for our classroom discussion in Figure 3 may not seem particularly informative. It shows that in the discussion about the Trayvon Martin killing the students were, unsurprisingly, talking about the shooter, Zimmerman, quite a bit. In fact this pattern was common in all of the discussions we looked at—the words that stood out most were directly related to the topic at hand. One feature that we plan to add is the ability to add additional "stop words" that the Word Cloud will ignore (it already has standard stop words in the software). In this example, if Zimmerman were removed (temporarily) from the list then the differences between other terms would become more salient (as the font sizes would scale based on the range of most to least frequent words). However, one of our facilitators, trained in social justice issues, used the tool in a way that was unexpected to us. She was quick to point out that the conversation in this predominantly white classroom focused on Zimmerman, who is white, and there was surprisingly little mention of Martin, who is black. Each facilitator will draw their own conclusions from such observations, but we were encouraged to see that the tool supported insightful observations even in what seemed to be an unrevealing visualization to the untrained eye.

Dialogue and Advice Panes: Text Analysis

As mentioned above, one component of our project is researching automatic text analysis and machine learning algorithms (and soon also relationship networks) to identify deliberative skill, other indicators related to dialogue quality, and trends or opportunity points. Text analyses methods have advanced significantly in recent years. According to [14] the "increased use of automated text analysis tools can be attributed to landmark advances in such fields as computational linguistics, discourse processes... , cognitive science..., and corpus linguistics..." (p. 34). We are using three types of technologies. The first two, LIWC and Cohmetrix, are pre-existing text analysis tools that take text segments as inputs and output dozens of measurement or classification metrics. The third technology is a set of machine learning methods we are using that take text, reply and demographic information, and some of the LIWC and Cohmetrix outputs as input or training features, and output classification analysis (e.g. whether a segment of text demonstrates good "deliberative skill" or "self reflection").

In our work we are using the Cohmetrix multiple-level text analysis system [15], the LIWC "Linguistics Inquiry Word Count" application, and a variety of machine learning methods (see [4]). LIWC (Linguistic Inquiry Word Count [16]) is a well researched but "shallow" dictionary-matching text categorization system yielding about 80 linguistic categories (e.g. positive emotion words, pronouns, and causation words—some of the categories are defined by hundreds of words in the dictionary entry). CohMetrix [15] performs a series of deep-processing analysis (including semantic cohesion, latent semantic analysis, and reading complexity level) yielding about 100 metrics.

We have implemented the most straight-forward of these methods, LIWC-based dictionary-matching processing, into the Dashboard. An important thing about LIWC is that, though its dictionary-matching method is simple (like keyword-matching), hundreds of studies have been done using it (and contributed to its development) so many of the categories it uses are well researched in terms of how use of these linguistic categories correlate with important psychological or social phenomena. Other analysis methods will be incorporated into the Dashboard in the future (one of the constraints and unknowns is that some of the text processing methods will probably not run in real time, and thus, while useful in our deliberation analysis research, would not be appropriate for the Dashboard). The reader can look at the "common problems encountered in online facilitation" in the Design Considerations sub-section for an indication of the types of things we hope to eventually assess using automatic methods. We will sometimes refer to each metric or found category that our software evaluates in terms of an "agent" that that assesses and reports its findings, even though, depending on the feature, "agent" may be more a metaphor than an implementation description.

Kushal et al. [17] describe ForumReader, a dashboard tool for "large scale online discussion" that also uses some text analysis. Like other systems, ForumReader's text analysis is content-based, and is used to identify main topics of conversation, related topics, and topic clusters. It uses text-summarizing and clustering algorithms. Our interest is more in supporting reflection on the quality of a conversation than its content, which should be facilitated by LIWC and CohMetrix analysis. The Dashboard contains software agents that watch for patterns or categories in the dialogue, and flags occurrences that reach a certain threshold. The current version of the system matches a set of about 20 word categories found in the LIWC dictionaries. When the condition is met, the word is highlighted in the text and a line detailing the analysis is appended in yellow below the post. Of the 80 text categories LIWC classifies, the Dashboard is tagging these: first person singular & plural, second person singular & plural, swear, posemo, negemo, anx (anxiety/anxious), anger, sad, certain, sexual, assent, tentative, negate, and inclusive. There were arrived at through conversations with our facilitation experts, and the need to keep the number of categories manageable. LIWC was not conceived of as a system of analyzing deliberative dialogue, and our experts suggested three additional categories of interest that were implemented: always-never (always, every, never, none, all, never, everywhere, nowhere); should (should); and question-words (how, what, when, where, who, whom, whose, why).

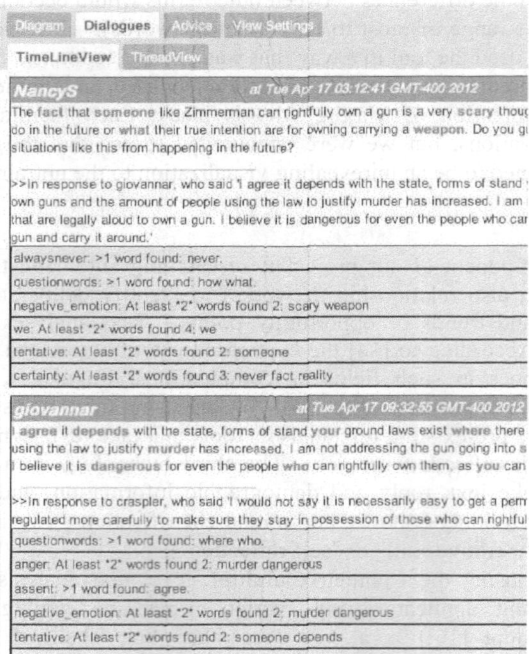

Figure 2: Dashboard: Dialogue Pane

As mentioned, this preliminary interface has proven, as expected, to be too busy and not graphically intuitive enough for facilitators to use easily. In the Next Steps section we describe our plans for improving it.

Formative Evaluation

We will not detail the numerous suggestions from our collaborators and advisors, many of which were implemented (and some of which are reflected in the design descriptions and rationale here). Recall that we worked closely with three professional mediator/facilitators over 18 months, and contracted feedback of 10 high-profile professional facilitator/mediators and leaders in that field, for a short-term consulting assessment. Overall the facilitators were very enthusiastic about the tools and their potential, finding the Dashboard "extremely helpful" and "extremely useful." In real-time classroom dialogue facilitation we instructed facilitators to take a very low-key role, motivating participation and supporting a safe space for all to contribute, but trying not to influence the conversation very much (thus we asked them to leave some of their facilitation skills unutilized). Therefore, most of the feedback on the Dashboard has been in noting what was interesting or potentially very useful to know about a group, but little of it lead to interventions in this phase of the formative evaluation. For example, a facilitator might note that males, or seniors, were slightly dominating a conversation. In these trials they did not try to remedy this, but noted how useful the tools would be if they did want to ameliorate such phenomena.

Peer facilitation and group auto-reflection. We mentioned above that we have a goal to test the Dashboard as a group-awareness (or group auto-reflection) tool with participants and peer-mediators or facilitators. Our early forays into this area have consisted of showing participants (college classes) the dashboard in follow-up focus group sessions after they have completed an online dialogue assignment. Verbal responses have been enthusiastic, but it is also clear that we will need a simpler version of the Dashboard for participants as compared with what we offer trained facilitators.

Next Steps

Our future plans include evaluating our tools in civic deliberation and online dispute resolution contexts and we have engaged potential collaborators in both of these areas. Above we mentioned our plans for further evaluation of the Dashboard, and noted that we have gathered many comments from facilitators on ways to improve and extend it. In this section we describe some of these design plans. We will add an Alert feature that will highlight high priority dialogue events and properties. As mentioned we plan to add other types of text analysis beyond the dictionary matching LIWC-style agents (as is possible for real-time analysis). These include: deeper structural linguistic properties of the sort measured by Cohmetrix, and agents that search for trends, patterns, or inflection points (facilitation opportunities) over time, and post Alerts. As noted, the "common problems encountered in online facilitation" in the Design Considerations sub-section shows the types of things we hope to eventually assess. Of the dialogue speech acts that we manually code for, which we are attempting to build machine models to recognize, we have noted several that might signal important turning points in a conversation: changes of mind, peer-initiated mediation, apologies, high emotional tone, and acknowledgments/appreciations.

We have mentioned that the information in the text Dialogue pane needs more graphical portrayal, which will include pie charts, bar charts, and trend lines for the deliberative properties identified by text analysis. In addition, the current analysis only tags *words* and annotates *posts* according to word categories found in the post. We plan to include visualization tools that show occurrences and frequencies of triggered agents at four levels: post, participant, sub-group, and whole-group. For example, a chart could illustrate how instances of Appreciation or Meta-dialogue compare between participants or groups, or how they trend over the course of a dialogue. A facilitator will be able to focus in on a particular individual (or group) and display all of the analysis for that person. We will also include Settings to toggle on and off particular analysis agents, to reduce clutter and allow facilitators to focus on dialogue properties relevant to the context. The parameters for agents (e.g. triggering threshold values) will be moved from an initialization text file to a user-friendly Settings interface.

We have begun work to include social network analysis in the Dashboard [18]). This will analyze reply or reference structure between participants to measure and visualize: mutuality/reciprocity, centrality/influence, density, cliques and selective responsiveness, and initiators vs. responders.

Conclusions

We have described a novel Facilitators Dashboard tool that visualizes dialogue quality indicators for use as facilitation tools or participant social awareness tools that includes textual analysis, and described our initial attempts to use it in educational settings. We are particularly interested in supporting the "social deliberative skills" that interlocutors need to build mutual understanding and mutual regard in complex or contentious situations. Developing methods to scaffold SD-skills in online deliberation, for participants and third parties, could have an impact in many online contexts, e.g. knowledge-building, situated learning, civic engagement, and dispute resolution.

One of the goals of education is to produce competent national and global citizens capable of participating in democratic self-governance and capable of wrestling with the difficult questions and dizzying array of information and opinion they face in our technologically advanced society. Students engaged in extended collaborative knowledge building, discussion, or problem solving eventually encounter moments of tension in which they are challenged to understand each other's perspectives and opinions. Engaging with others on complex topics requires not only learning the relevant facts and concepts and making logical inferences, but also engaging with the perspectives and opinions of others who may not share one's views or goals. Doing so requires skills that can be systematically supported. Our work points to how such skills can be supported in online deliberation, collaboration, and dispute resolution, in educational settings and beyond.

References

[1] O'Reilly, T. and Musser, J. "Web 2.0 principles and best practices", O'Reilly Radar, November, 2006

[2] Keen, A. The cult of the amateur: How the democratization of the digital world is assaulting our economy, our culture, and our values. NY: Doubleday Currency, 2007

[3] Murray, T., Xu, X. & Woolf, P.B.. An Exploration of Text Analysis Methods to Identify Social Deliberative Skills. In *Proceedings of 16th International Conference on Artificial Intelligence in Education* (AIED-2013). Memphis, TN, July 2013. K. Yacef et al. (Eds.): LNAI 7926, pp. 811–814, 2013.

[4] Murray, T., Stephens, A.L., Woolf, B.P., Wing, L., Xu, X. & Shrikant, N. Supporting Social Deliberative Skills Online: the Effects of Reflective Scaffolding Tools. Proceedings of 15th International Conference on Human-Computer Interaction (HCII-2013). Las Vegas, July 2013.

[5] Iandoli, L., Quinto, I., De Liddo, A. & Shum, S.B. A debate dashboard to enhance online knowledge sharing. VINE: The journal of information and knowledge management systems, Vol. 42 No. 1, 2012, pp. 67-93, 2012.

[6] Buder, J., Bodemer, D., Dehler, J., & Engelmann, T. SCAN tools for collaborative learning. In Proceedings of the 9th international conference on Computer supported collaborative learning-Volume 1 (pp. 606-615). International Society of the Learning Sciences, 2009.

[7] Murray, T., Woolf, B., Xu, X., Shipe, S., Howard, S. & Wing, L.. "Supporting social deliberative skills in online classroom dialogues: Preliminary results using automated text analysis." Proceedings of 11th International Conference on Intelligent Tutoring Systems (ITS-2012). S.A. Cerri and B. Clancey (Eds.). LNCS 7315, pp. 669–671, 2012. June 2012, Chania, Greece, 2012.

[9] Constantino-Gonzales, M. A., Suthers, D., & Escamilla, J. Coaching Web-based Collaborative Learning based on Problem Solution Differences and Participation. International Journal of Artificial Intelligence in Education, 13(2-4), 263-299, 2003.

[10] Xu, X., Murray, T. Woolf, B P. & Smith, D. Mining Social Deliberation in Online Communication -- If You Were Me and I Were You , In Proceedings of the 6th International Conference on Educational Data Mining (EDM), 2013.

[11] Xu, X., Murray, T. Woolf, B P, " Text Analysis of Deliberative Skills in Undergraduate Online Dialogue: Using L1 Regularized Logistic Regression with Psycholinguistic Features", In Proceedings of the 12th International Conference on e-Learning, e-Business, Enterprise Information Systems, and e-Government (EEE), 2013.

[12] Soller, A., Martinez, A., Jermann, P., & Muehlenbrock, M. From mirroring to guiding: A review of state of the art technology for supporting collaborative learning. International Journal of Artificial Intelligence in Education, 15, 261-290, 2005.

[13] Shrikant, N. & Murray, T. On Line Facilitation Guidelines for Supporting Social Deliberative Skills in Online Deliberation. Unpublished manuscript available from the authors. 2012.

[14] Graesser, A. C., McNamara, D. S., & Louwerse, M. M. 2 Methods of Automated Text Analysis. Handbook of Reading Research, 4, 34, 2010.

[15] Graesser, A. C., & McNamara, D. S. Computational analyses of multilevel discourse comprehension. Topics in Cognitive Science, 3, 371–398, 2011.

[16] Tausczik, Y. R. & Pennebaker, J. W. (2010). The psychological meaning of words: LIWC and computerized text analysis methods. Journal of Language and Social Psychology.

[17] Kushal Dave, Martin Wattenberg, Michael Muller. Flash forums and forumReader: navigating a new kind of large-scale online discussion. In CSCW '04: Proceedings of the 2004 ACM conference on Computer supported cooperative work (2004), pp. 232-241, 2004

[18] D'Andrea, A., Ferri, F. & Grifoni, P. "An Overview of Methods for Virtual Social Network Analysis". In Abraham, A. Hassanien, A. E., & Snášel, V. (Eds.) Computational Social Network Analysis: Trends, Tools and Research Advances. Springer. p. 8, 2009.

An Educational Java Applet for Understanding Principles of Synchronous BCD Counters

Dongsik KIM*, Jaeho CHA*, Seongyong LEE*, Saeron HAN*, Samjun SEO**

*Department of Electrical Engineering, Soonchunhyang University, KOREA

**Department of Electrical & Electronic Engineering, Anyang University, KOREA

Abstract – This paper presents web-based Java applet for understanding the concepts and principles of synchronous BCD counter. Through our educational Java applet, the learners will be capable of learning the concepts and theories related to digital experiments and how to operate the virtual experimental equipments.

The proposed educational Java applet is composed of three important components: Principle Classroom to explain the concepts and theories of synchronous BCD counters operations, Virtual Experiment Classroom to provide interactive Java applets about the syllabus of off-line laboratory class, Assessment Classroom and Management System. With the aid of the Management System every classroom is organically tied together collaborating to achieve maximum learning efficiency. We have obtained several affirmative effects such as high learning standard, reducing the total experimental hours and the damage rate for experimental equipments.

Keywords : Educational Java Applet, Synchronous BCD Counters, Web-based Virtual Experiments

1. INTRODUCTION

Recently, much interest has been drawn on the web-based solution for the experiments at universities with large number of students due to low cost. Teaching is no longer confined to a time and a place. The time and physical boundaries of the traditional classroom are stretched to a learning space. A growing number of universities worldwide are now offering virtual education problems. A simple search on the World Wide Web will result in hundreds of sites offering virtual courses or resources for developing and delivering such courses. Electrical and electronic experimental study is a very important component in engineering education. It not only acts as a bridge between theory and practice, but also solidifies the theoretical concepts presented in the classroom.[1]-[3]

Before the laboratory session, the learners should re-enforce basic concepts, prepare some design and simulation steps, and acquire a clear idea on what they should expect from the experimental work they will be carrying out in the laboratory. At the laboratory session, the learners are required to assemble the circuits, connect the equipment, make the measurements, compare the data to the expected behavior, and deliver a partial or complete report to the professor at the end of the session. This classical way of experimenting clearly has the following shortcomings.[4]-[6]

- The classroom lectures or the handouts are generally not sufficient for the learners to be fully prepared for a hands-on experiment or to appreciate the significance of the previously explained theory in the experiment to be performed.
- When the learners are passive observers or a semi-active part of an experiment, they will understand neither the correspondence nor the difference between theory and practice.

To cope with these difficulties, this paper presents methodology which can easily be used on the web by simple mouse manipulations. The methodology is to provide the learners with an educational Java applet which can enhance the multimedia capabilities of world-wide web. If the learners have access to the proposed Java applet through a typical web browser, they can make experiment on basic digital logic circuits through simple mouse clicks. Since this interactive educational Java applet is implemented to describe the actual on-campus laboratory, the learners can obtain similar experimental data through it.

In this paper, we implemented synchronous BCD counters by using Java applet as illustration. The implemented Java applet is composed of three important components: *Principle Classroom, Virtual Experiment Classroom, Assessment Classroom and Management System*. The proposed methodology can be used from elementary digital experiments to advanced electronic experiments included in the curriculum of the college of engineering. It has interactive multimedia contents to get the learners exact understanding of the concepts and theories of digital circuit operations, and the learners can build their own circuits and measure all information about the status of the circuits on the virtual space by simple mouse manipulation. Every activity done in the educational Java applet is recorded on database and provided to the learners as a printout form including experimental information and results. The educators check the submitted printout form to estimate how well the learners understand the experimental contents.

The implemented Java applet can be used in stand-alone fashion, but using as assistants of the actual on-campus laboratory class shows more encouraging results.

2. STRUCTURE OF PROPOSED JAVA APPLET

In Fig. 1, the structure diagram of our educational Java applet is shown. All of this can be achieved by the aid of Management System. The database connectivity is made by Professional HTML Preprocessor and the virtual laboratory environment is set up slightly differently for each learner.[7][8]

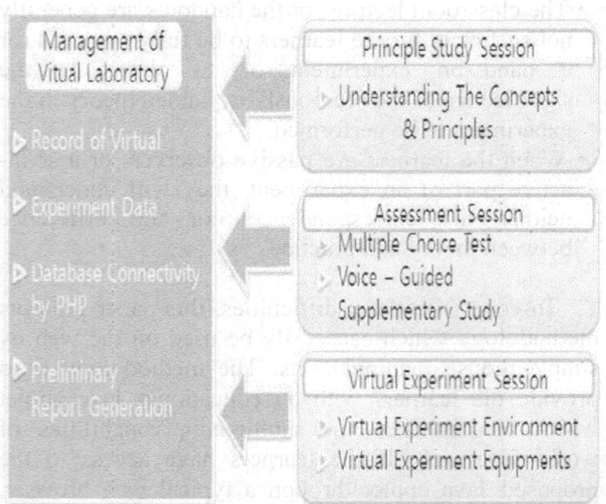

Fig. 1 Structure of our Educational Java Applet

2.1 Principle Classroom

The Principal Classroom is responsible for making the learners understand the concepts and theories of the circuit operations. Interactive Java applets with creative and intuitive ideas for each subject lead the learners to easily understand their operations.

Fig.2-Fig.3 show several important procedures from the educational Java applets for explaining the concepts of synchronous BCD counter. Using this Java applet, the learners can understand the wholes procedure that shows how the synchronous BCD counter will be designed. in addition, Fig. 2(a) shows the generation of initial and final state diagram for asynchronous BCD counter. When the learners click the decimal buttons, the corresponding binary codes will be displayed as shown in Fig. 2(b).

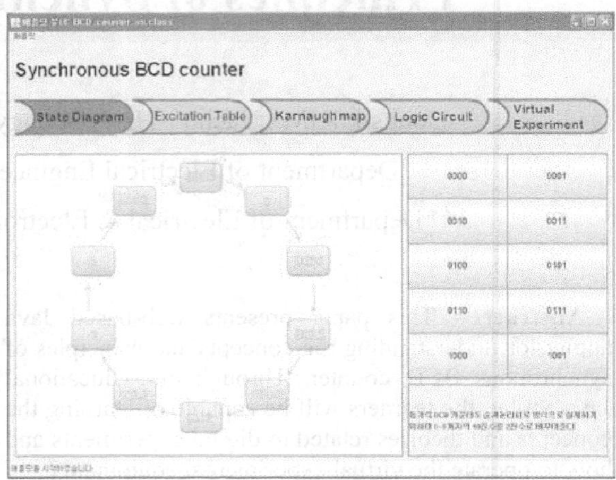

Fig. 2(a) The generation of initial sate diagram

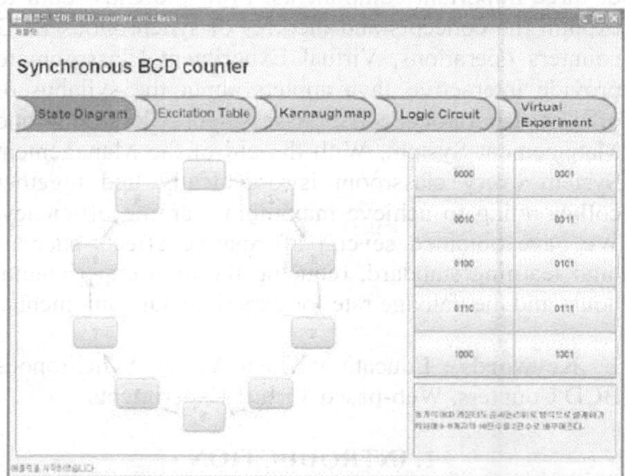

Fig.2 (b) The generation of final sate diagram

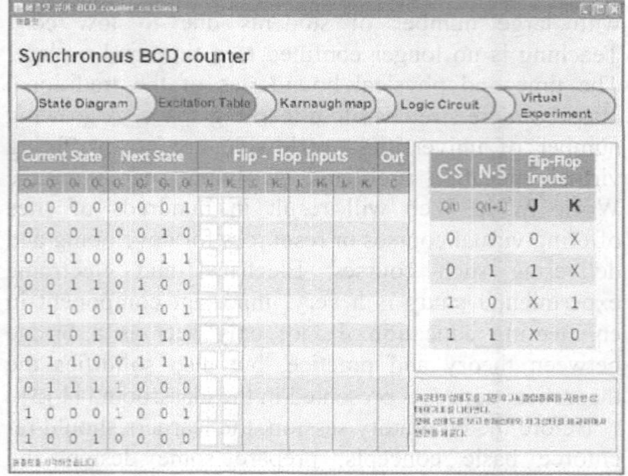

Fig.3 (a) Blank text fields for the inputs of JK flip-flops

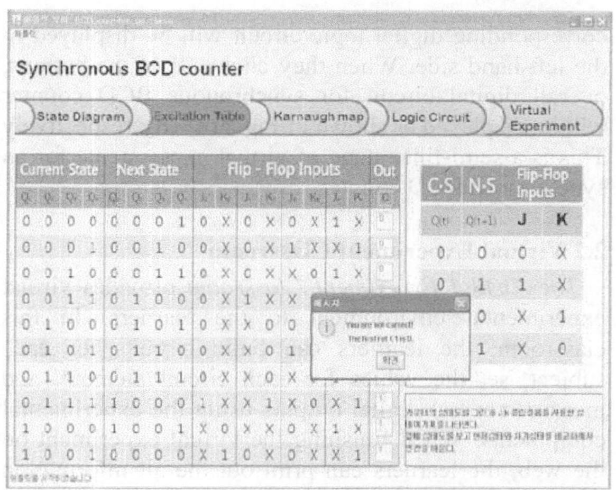

Fig.3 (b) Pop-up message in case of occurring mistakes

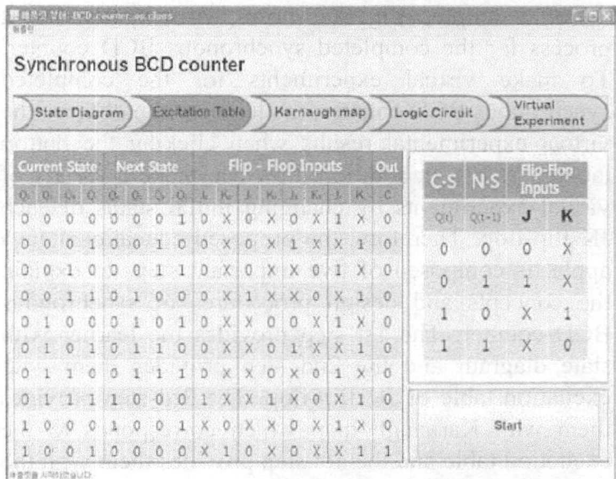

Fig.3 (c) Complete text fields for JK flip-flops

Fig. 3(a) shows the process that fills out the given text fields according to the excitation table of JK flip-flop. If the learners make mistakes when filling out text fields, the pop up message will be displayed promptly as shown in Fig. 3(b). Fig. 3(c) shows complete text fields for each input of JK Flip-Flops.

Fig. 4(a) shows the Karnaugh map that simplifies the Boolean algebra for each JK flip-flop. For example, if the third input of JK flip-flop is selected, corresponding Karnaugh map will be displayed in the right-hand side. The Karnaugh map simplifies the Boolean algebra when the learners clicks the button labeled 'next' as shown in Fig. 4(b). Therefore, they can easily understand the simplification process of Boolean algebra. Note that the learners are able to understand not the simple results but the overall procedure for simplification of Boolean algebra. Therefore, the higher learning efficiency can be improved than that of conventional approach for web-based education.

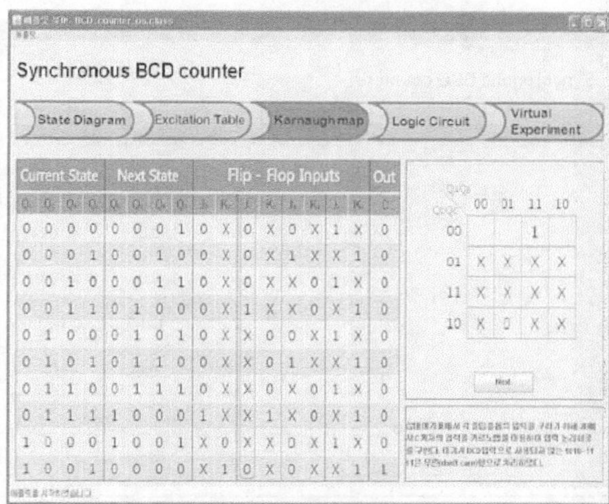

Fig.4 (a) Corresponding Karnaugh map for J_3

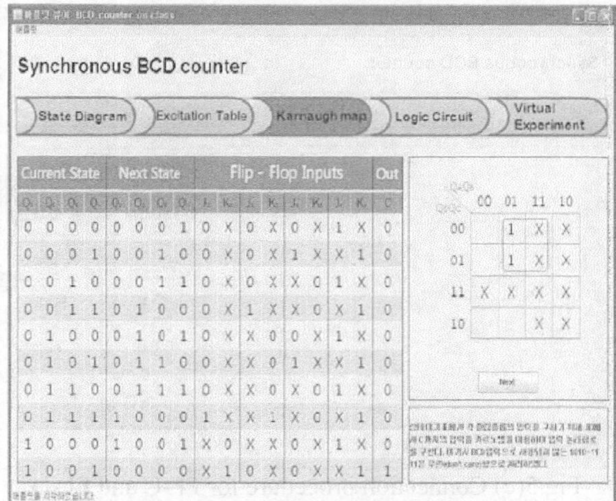

Fig.4 (b) Simplification process by using Karnaugh map

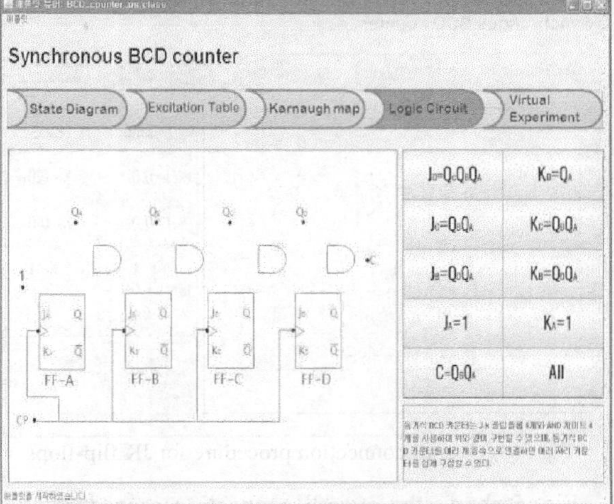

Fig.5(a) Connection procedure for each JK flip-flops

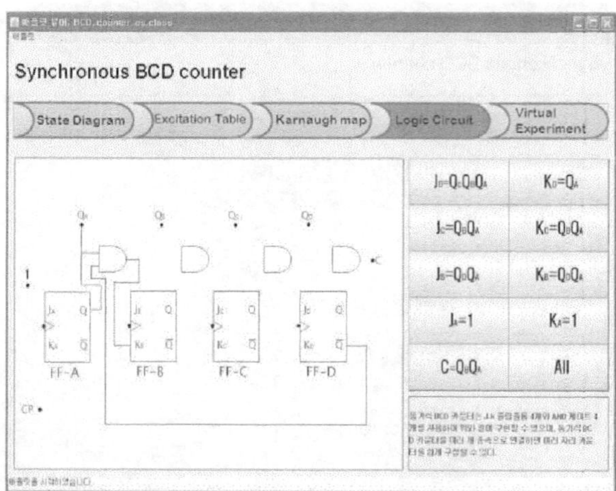

Fig.5(b) Connection procedure for FF-A

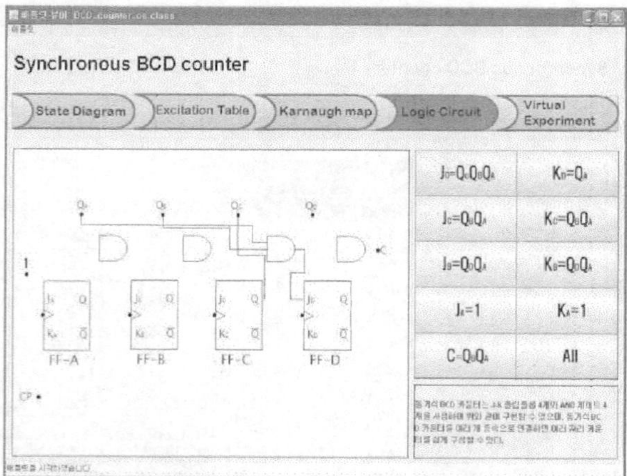

Fig.5(c) Connection procedure for FF-C and FF-D

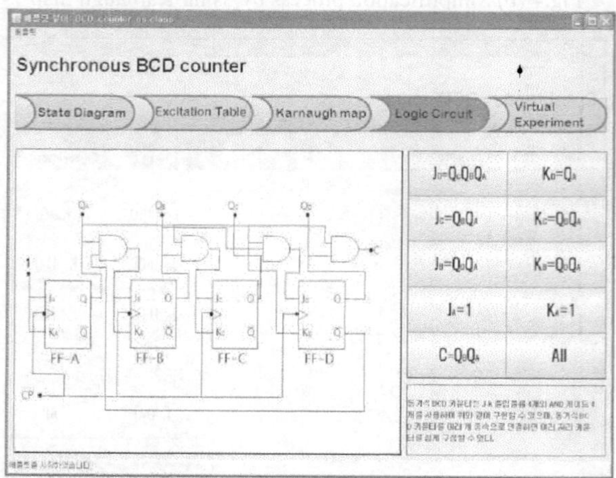

Fig.5(d) Overall connection procedure for JK flip-flops

Fig. 5 shows the overall connection procedure after simplification by Karnaugh map. For example, if the learners clicks each input button of JK flip-flops, corresponding digital logic circuit will be displayed in the left-hand side. When they clicks all of the buttons, overall digital circuit for synchronous BCD counter will be displayed as shown in Fig. 5(a)-(d), respectively. This is a semi-final stage of virtual experiments for an synchronous BCD counter.

2.2 Virtual Experiment Classroom

The Virtual Experiment Classroom provides virtual experimental environment to the learners. In this classroom, the learners can build circuits for each subject, set the values for each circuit element, and measure several digital outputs using the experimental equipments. When finishing the virtual experiment on the web, the learners can print out the all information related to the experiment which can be used as preliminary report for on-campus laboratory class

For example, Fig. 6 shows virtual experiment process for the completed synchronous BCD counter. To make virtual experiments for the completed synchronous BCD counter, the learners can observe the virtual experimental results when clicking the button labeled 'start' . In addition, they can make a variety of virtual experiments by changing initial states of each JK flip-flop. Therefore, the proposed educational Java applet is composed of five important steps to explain the concepts and design procedures of synchronous BCD counter. The 1st step provides the learner with state diagram and the 2nd step provides them with excitation table of JK flip-flop. The 3rd step provides them with Karnaugh map which corresponds to the excitation table and the 4th step provides them with the related circuit composition. Finally, they can observe the output waveforms of synchronous BCD counter for a variety of input conditions.

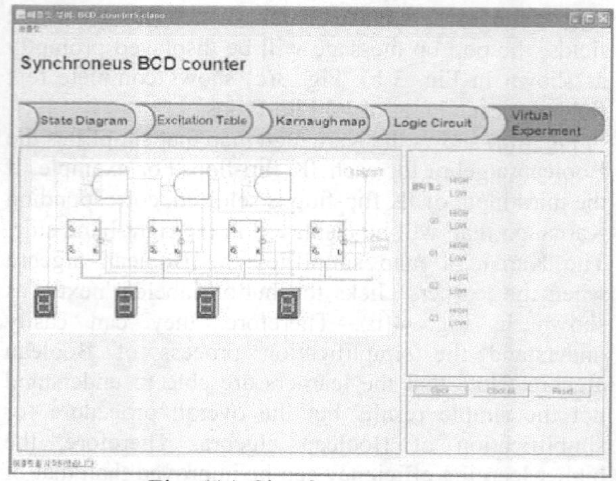

Fig. 6(a) Circuit composition

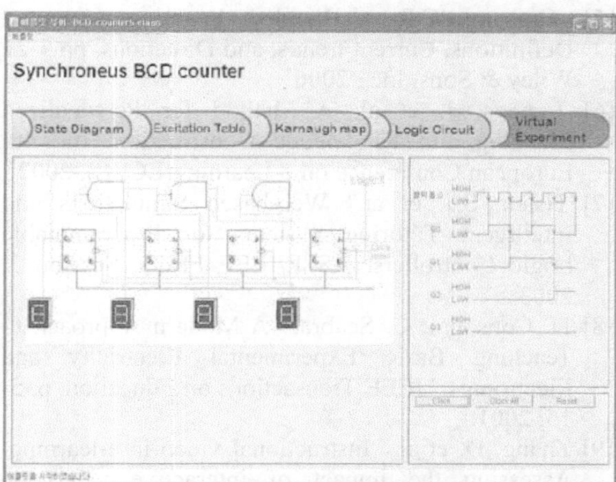

Fig. 6(b) Applying clock pulses

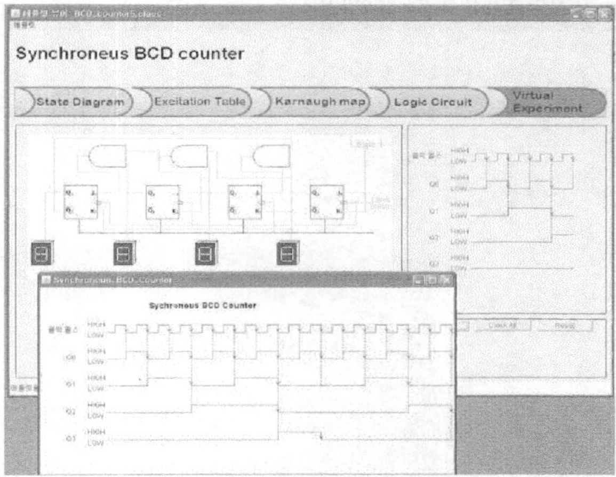

Fig. 6(c) Output measurements

In the virtual experiment classroom, every activity done there will be recorded on database and printed out as a preliminary report form. Once students fill in the text fields with the virtual experimental data and click the button 'SEND', the data will be transmitted and recorded on the database. The virtual experimental data recorded on the database can be retrieved to generate a preliminary report form by the Professional HTML Preprocessor (PHP) module program. Since the virtual experiment classroom is designed to provide students with slightly different environments, their preliminary reports will not be shared each other. If a student performs the same virtual experiments twice at different time, two experimental results might be different each other. Note that these situations in the virtual experiment classroom are similar to those in the on-campus laboratory. During the virtual experiment session, students obtain several virtual experimental data from their own circuits. They are required to fill in the truth tables with their own data they got from the virtual laboratory. Also, they press the button 'RESET' and restart if there are some mistakes with filling out the truth tables

Since the Virtual Experiment Classroom has an efficient virtual experiment applet with interactive multimedia contents, the quality of education and the learning efficiency can be improved.

2.3 Management System

Good instructional development is an iterative process by which the educators and learners perform formative assessments and summative evaluations to continually improve a course. Effective instructors use a variety of means, some formal and others informal, to determine how much and how well their students are learning.[9] Every activity occurred in the proposed Java applet will be recorded on database and printed out the preliminary report form. All of this can be achieved by the aid of Management System. The database connectivity is made by Professional HTML Preprocessor and the virtual laboratory environment is set up slightly differently for each learner. Fig. 7 shows database connectivity of *the Management System* using PHP.

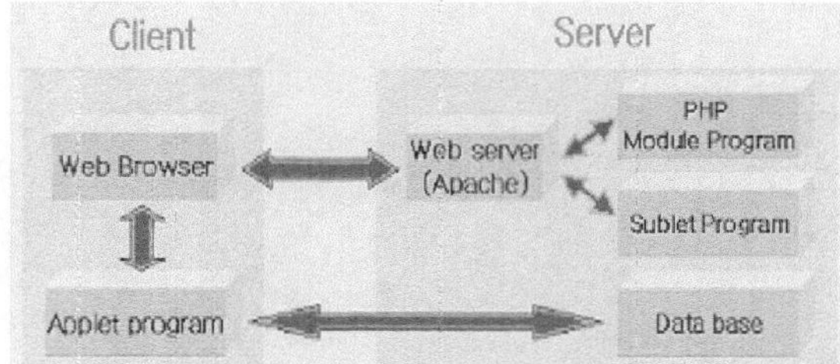

Fig. 7 Database connectivity of virtual laboratory

3. CONCLUSIONS

We implement an efficient educational Java applet with interactive multimedia contents, which can be used to enhance the quality of education in the area of digital circuit experiments.

Our educational Java applet shows that the difficult concepts, principles and theories related to the digital experiments can be conveyed to the learners effectively by interactive multimedia contents.

The proposed virtual experiment applet has brought several affirmative effects such as reducing the waste time and labor of both the educators and the learners, and the damage rate of real equipments, and increasing learning efficiency as well as faculty productivity.

Finally, our educational Java applet for digital circuits can be proved a viable, effective and cost-effective aid to the educational activities both for classes and for continuous education. We will challenge the advanced researches on the digital logic circuits in the near future.

REFERENCES

[1] Badrul, H. Khan, *Web-based Instruction: What is it and Why is it? Web-based Instruction*, 1997.

[2] M. Khalifa, R. Lam," Web-based Learning: Effect on Learning Process and Outcome," IEEE Transactions on Education, p.350-356, 2002.

[3] Burks Oakley, "A Virtual Classroom Approach to Teaching Circuit Analysis," IEEE Trans. on Education, 39, pp.287-296,1996.

[4] Dongsik Kim et al, "Implementation of a Web-based Virtual Laboratory System for Electronic Circuit Experiments," International Conference on Internet Computing, Las Vegas, USA, 2003.

[5] Graham, C.R : Blended Learning Systems-Definitions, Current trends, and Directions, pp.3-21, Wiley & Sons, Inc., 2006

[6] Lubega, J. et al, A Method for Personalized Tracking in Knowledge Construction, the 4th European Conference on e-Learning(ECEL), 2002

[7] Hsieh, S.J. et al," Web-based Simulations and Intelligent Tutoring Systems for Programmable Logic Controllers, ASSE/IEEE FECS, Session 3, 2003

[8] D. Consonni, C. Seabra," A Modern Approach to Teaching Basic Experimental Electricity and Electronics," IEEE Transactions on Education, p. 5-15, 2001.

[9] Zhang, D. et al, "Instructional video in e-learning: Assessing the impact of interactive video on learning effectiveness, Information & Management, Vol. 43, pp15-27, 2006

Android Exchange (AEx):
A Virtual Community for Students on eTeams

R. Shankar[1], F. McAfee[2], M. Harris[3], J. Folkes[4], and R. Behara[5]

[1] Department of CEECS, College of Engineering, Florida Atlantic University, Boca Raton, FL, USA
[2] SCMS, College of Arts and Letters, Florida Atlantic University, Davie, FL, USA
[3] Anthropology, College of Arts and Letters, Florida Atlantic University, Boca Raton, FL, USA
[4] Center for eLearning, Academic Affairs, Florida Atlantic University, Boca Raton, FL, USA
[5] ITOM, College of Business, Florida Atlantic University, Boca Raton, FL, USA

Abstract - *A group of faculty members from engineering, arts, anthropology, and business have jointly taught courses (for 3 years) on smart phone App development to undergraduate students. The students with academic background in these disciplines have come together to form teams and to develop unique smart phone Apps. Industry professionals from these disciplines evaluate these projects. An eLearning version of the joint course was taught recently. Android Exchange (AEx), a virtual community environment, is proposed here to build on that experience and on existing social and professional networks to connect participants with peers, mentors, professionals, and businesses for mutual benefits of learning, collaboration and jobs. This may also help with retention, motivation, recruitment, and scaling. AEx is enhanced by developing four other open source learning tools, for (1) learning and project asset annotation, (2) intelligent asset and web search, (3) video profiles of team partners, professionals and projects, and (4) team (learning, project and social) management skills.*

Keywords: *e-Learning, Design and Methodologies, Virtual Learning Environment, Team Projects, and Open-source Platform*

1. Background:

NSF defines cyberlearning as the use of networked computing and communications technologies to support learning [1]. They use the term 'cyberlearning' to evoke both cyber-infrastructure technologies and theoretical connections to cybernetics. This NSF taskforce poses the question: Why cyberlearning and why now. They conclude that few teaching innovations from the past have resulted in large-scale systemic changes in education. The perceived value is also shifting from products to solutions to experiences. "Today's learners live in that online experiential environment; today's schools do not." Design based research (DBR) , a practice-based research methodology, has come a long way in the past decade to address this [2]. We are integrating both the cyber-infrastructure and the learning sciences into a sustained and engaging environment. We mentor student teams across multiple disciplines that make up a typical authentic (or real-world) project team; this addresses yet another national need – to cut across various disciplines and educate students who can productively function in a 'multi-cultural' environment. Our team projects focus on the development of smart phone Apps, thus incorporating another global trend in the increasing use of smart phones and the consequent potential for jobs and business start-ups. We are also building similar infrastructures in other areas [3,4]. We almost exclusively use open source tools, thus providing for portability and scalability. App marketing in niche areas and the benefit of long-tail marketing [5] will aid program sustenance.

2. Infrastructure For Android Exchange (AEx):

Over the past three years, we have developed a mobile App development infrastructure at our university that spans multiple colleges and disciplines [6.7]. About 450 students from grade 10 to the graduate level (and beyond) have been involved in team projects in developing marketable Apps, with each team representing strengths in arts, engineering, business, and content as appropriate. Certification in eLearning and a joint summer eLearning course (with only arts and engineering students) has given the first two co-authors experience in managing such team efforts online. We have also identified areas for further improvement, with authentic learning [8], team management, peer networking, and tailored access to relevant material; these will be incorporated in our proposed socio-technological solution, as follows: we will develop a virtual community (a tool) called Android Exchange (AEx) of students, professionals, and small and large businesses, and connect them for mutual benefit of jobs, collaborations, and /or consulting. This has the potential to facilitate our eLearners in multiple ways. This will (1) improve learning effectiveness, (2) provide an opportunity for social and professional networking, and (3) address the issues of scalability, usability, sustenance, and portability, essential for widespread adoption.

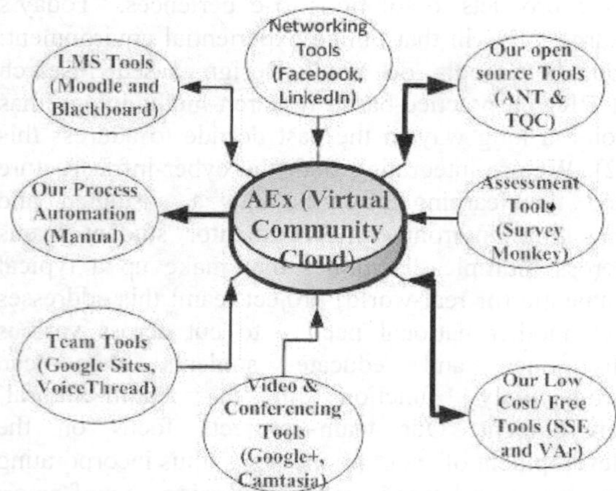

Figure 1: AEx and its associated tools (from others or our own).

Some of the AEx environment is built with loose coupling to existing tools for (1) Learning management systems (LMS), (2) Social and professional networking, (3) Team collaboration, (4) Assessment, and (5) Video Conferencing. Most tools are available free or at low cost. Our goal is to utilize these resources and supplement them with the missing pieces to help the eTeams thus: (1) Find information quickly at the right granular level, (2) Be motivated to achieve at a high level, and (3) To find partners, experts, mentors, and job providers, during the various phases of this course, program, or later as a professional. We will develop AEx as well as the following new open source tools and integrate them with AEx: (1) Annotator **(ANT)**, (2) Semantic search engine **(SSE)**, (3) Video archival **(VAr)** tool, and (4) Team Quality Control **(TQC)** plug-in. We will track the usage processes and automate later (with a Meta tool) to reduce costs. To develop our five tools, we will use open source tools, such as Eclipse for software development, Eclipse Modeling Framework for auto code generation [9], and Jena for semantic web [10, 11].

3. Current Teaching Flow:

We have taught joint courses (for engineering and arts students) since summer 2010, at high school, undergraduate, or graduate level. Here we document our recent efforts at wider collaborations, with undergraduate students and faculty from four disciplines of business, arts, sociology/anthropology, and engineering (BASE), and migration to eLearning. In spring and summer of 2012 we designed and taught these expanded courses. Each of us taught relevant material pertaining to our respective disciplines, then brought students together (after a mid-term summative exam to ensure that the students could contribute productively) to form cross-disciplinary teams to build mobile Apps. See the syllabi at [12]. The courses were on (1) software and system development for smart phones (for engineers), (2) animation and graphics for mobile applications (for artists), (3) App design and project management (for business majors), and (4) directed independent or research study (for anthropology majors). The first course emphasized a software component-based top-down system design approach for App development. The second course dealt with tools for asset (graphic and animation) buildup, and the aesthetic aspects in mobile application design. The third course focused on business theories, marketing strategies, project management, and work breakdown. The fourth course informed anthropology students on research methods to observe, document, and advise the project teams. Students met regularly, separated by disciplines, and a few times together, during the class hours. They were encouraged to meet outside the class with their team members from the paired courses. The hope was to mix visual artists, analytically minded engineers, and venture-oriented business students together in small teams to catalyze innovation, with anthropology students as ethnographers.

By mid-semester, the students presented their project ideas and got to work creating the applications. The combined team first had two week-long common project assignments: (1) story-boarding of their App, and (2) technical mockup. The student teams made presentations to the professors face-to-face (F2F) or online and were given feedback on technical, artistic, and marketing feasibility, similar Apps, and useful links. After that they had three additional week-long project assignments, on (3) discipline specific development, viz., of software components, graphic assets and marketing plan, (4) integration and testing, and finally (5) a portfolio presentation to BASE professionals to evaluate these Apps. The team presentations included a slide presentation, a marketing video, a live phone demo, etc. [13]. To sum it all, there was frustration and misunderstanding, but most teams managed to deliver a good App. To quote an anthropology student, *"oh, how the forced relationship can make a wonderful experience."*

3.1 eLearning Facilitator Certification:

The three teaching professors on this team have undergone an intensive semester long eLearning designer and facilitator certification at our Center for eLearning (CEL). This qualified us to teach the eLearning course last summer. CEL [14] fosters the "pedagogic integration of technology into the design of teaching and learning processes through collaborative efforts with faculty and other instructional technology personnel. It is where teaching, learning and technology intersect to meet the rapidly changing educational, social and economic environments in today's global society." The eLearning course used backward design of Wiggins and McTighe [15] and assessment techniques based on Angelo [16], Dunn [17] and Mueller [18]. It had us design our *summer joint course* as a class requirement and covered the following topics: manage the various LMS tools and functions; explain the basics of instructional design; apply policies and procedures appropriately; create learning objectives; create, manage, and maintain assessments; maintain standards and organization; manage course content and delivery; create, manage, and maintain learning activities and assessments; create, manage, and maintain communication; plan and facilitate active learning within a course when appropriate; evaluate an eLearning course based on a designated course evaluation rubric; and present to colleagues the key components of our designed course. Fowlkes [19], one of the co- authors on this paper designed and taught this course.

3.2 Role of Embedded Anthropology Students:

A central issue with regard to new pedagogical and workplace formations that count the web as their primary modality is: how are ordinary F2F interactions, upon which local culture is built, transformed and adapted to internet-based interaction? While the obvious social fact is the proliferation and active involvement of individuals in myriad social groups across the web [20], there appears to be a dearth of information concerning how individuals interact in the course of workplace team activities in the electronic realm [21].

During spring 2012, anthropology majors joined other undergraduate students to form BASE teams. Their role was that of social observers of team dynamics. They observed the team dynamics and cultural interactions, and also provided content. The research brought to light a number of hurdles to overcome in the formation of interdisciplinary teams. Foremost among them was the coordination of activities and this coordination ramified from the top level (the professors) to the bottom (the students). The creation of teams depended greatly on communication between the interdisciplinary professors, on coordinating activities in such a manner that each individual discipline was proceeding in a manner that recognized the parallel work of others. We now are actively developing a joint timetable to address this [12]. Especially problematic, though, were the types of activities that students themselves developed for working through application, process, and design issues. Each small group appeared to understand the end product and their role (as programmer, graphic designer, or marketer), but each was uniformly bereft of knowledge or skills for working together in a coordinated, team-centered manner. We are developing the TQC tool to address such issues.

The challenge is the resolution of these issues. The summer online course incorporated many of the recommendations from the embedded anthropology students; but more coordination problems ensued because of the eLearning dimension. For example, the student count dropped from 60 to 30 even before the first lecture. We may have overwhelmed the students with information at the Blackboard site. We will track such students now on and determine how to improve. The remaining 30 stayed with the course and completed their team Apps satisfactorily. Some advantages were also gained, for example via the 'lab' hour concept (see above).

4. Technology Implementation:

4.1 The AEx Tool (Figure 1):

It will loosely couple with many existing tools (that is, accept their outputs in a portable format), but will integrate well with our four other tools. The first author has earned a Sloan-C certificate on "Web 2.0 tools to improve learning." Bovard [22], the course teacher, cites at her site the following criteria in deciding on the right web 2.0 tools: (1) the tool should support your course's learning objectives; (2) Apply the following web 2.0 technology selection objectives to narrow the search space: access, usability, privacy & intellectual property, workload & time management, and fun factor; and (3) Apply one of the following to map the tools to the objectives: Sloan-C's Five Pillars [23], Swan's list on interactions and learning for online [24], or Chickering's Seven Principles [25]. Swan lists research findings and their implications for practice. We will present their mappings to AEx at the conference.

4.2 Semantic Search Engine (SSE):

An Internet search using any of today's popular search engines may return thousands or even millions of results for a given set of keywords, with only a few of them relevant. The user may have to repeat the search with different keywords. This wastes time and hinders productivity. We propose to develop a system that has the necessary intelligence to locate only those online documents that are relevant to a given user's needs. Students learning Android [26] App development will use SSE to customize searches for information related to their development projects. Google's Android site is Google-search based and lists every conceivable link, which is often daunting to search through. Further, there are other useful online sites (including ours). Our tool will integrate all such sites. No static search method will suffice, since this is an ever expanding field, with releases of new versions and technologies.

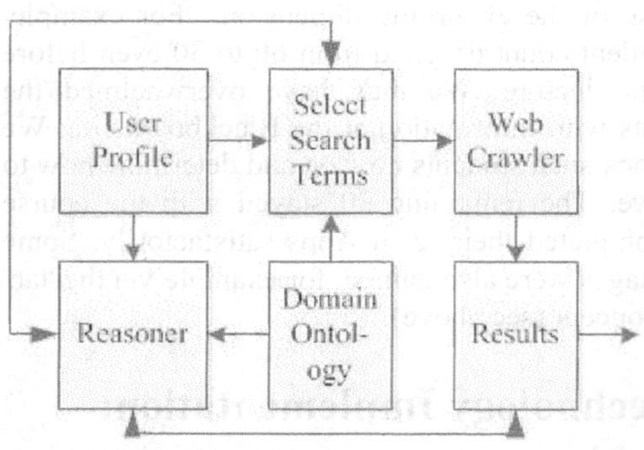

Figure 2: Search Methodolgy

Our search methodology addresses the limitations of conventional Internet searches through the use of domain ontologies, reasoners, user profiles and a web crawler. See Figure 2. An ontology is a graph of the relationships between terms that are relevant to a particular topic. A reasoner is a program which interprets these relationships to find terms related to a specified term. To assist in searches for information related to Android App development, the methodology defines domain ontology with terms of general interest to Android users and programmers. The user creates a user profile as a second ontology to help the search engine find the right type of information to meet the user's particular needs. The benefit of utilizing ontologies is that they are easy to customize. We have applied this methodology for a health App [10, 11].

4.3 Annotator (ANT) Tool :

Fishman et al., [27] develop a framework to address usability, scalability, and sustainability that is typically lacking in DBR studies. We add one more, that of portability, given that there are multiple learning management systems (**LMS**). diSessa and Cobb [28] recommend ontological innovation in which scientific terms must "cut nature at its joints," that is, they must make distinctions that truly make a difference, ignore the ones that are inconsequential, and enable explanations of interesting phenomenon. "We must develop theoretical constructs that empower us to see order, pattern, and regularity" in these complex settings of learning. Chi [29] provides an eight step objective and quantifiable segmentation process, for verbal data such as explanation, interviews and protocols. These can also be used for gestures and videotapes, as with our archived App videos and conferencing sessions. We will first develop a taxonomy for granular tagging of the App assets and artifacts that we have already accumulated over the past three years. All future student teams will be expected to submit their material with proper tagging. The tool will facilitate this process. The tool will provide an XML-based database for archiving and accessing all these entities.

4.4 Video Archival (VAr) Tool:

VAr will be developed to tag and search videos, created by student teams, professors, and professionals. The videos may be bio sketches, tutorials, lectures, App tear downs, business and professional profiles, team App presentations, App promotional videos, and interviews of teams and professional judges.

4.5 Team Quality Control (TQC) Tool:

Technological enhancements will require a strong backbone built from anthropological work. We call it "electronic ethnography" which is applied to undergraduate Android App development teams.

The primary role of anthropologist on the team is that of electronic participant observer (EPO). EPOs will focus their observations on communication strategies, the development of team member roles, and attempt to come to an understanding of the individual team dynamics. Traditional anthropological methods of participant observation [30] were developed in the context of personal F2F interaction; we will put them to use in the electronic domain. Textual interviews and communication between students will be the primary research modality; Skype, Google+ hangout, and Blackboard Collaborate tools for web-based meetings will also be used as opportunities for participant observation. Records of team interactions will also be tagged and archived for further research.

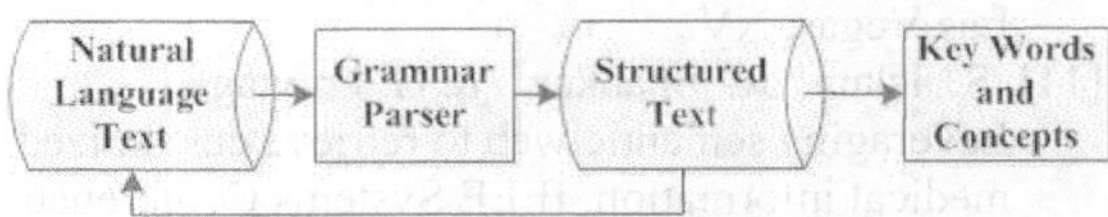

Figure 3: Natural Language Text Mining

Text mining research will be a top-down approach; it will complement the bottom-up approach cited above. This will involve the development of a text-analysis based solution to mine relevant unstructured (natural language text) data from the team. We will use existing open-source text mining tools. Similar to business information, much of team communications will be found in unstructured contexts in the form of natural language text, viz., blog and wiki postings, video conference notes, discussion forums, audio and email or text messages to teammates, and assignment submissions. This raw text is structured through patterns and trends such as statistical pattern learning. Some of the task are: classifying text documents, analyzing syntax, identifying relationships among documents, understanding questions expressed in natural language, extracting meaning and sentiment from messages, and summarizing them (Fig. 3).

We will apply text mining to develop the TQC tool where students can access related (and relevant) information to help in their specific project. We will build a database of Frequently Asked Questions (**FAQ**). TQC will search for such terms in student text (at their wiki site, emails to faculty members, etc.), search the FAQ database and send appropriate responses to the initiator. The tool will also generate alerts to professors for course queries/comments, or to the graduate students for any new terms, so appropriate action can be taken.

5. Discussion:

We discuss briefly the theoretical, technical, and big data perspectives. Expected outcomes and effectiveness metrics are not addressed due to lack of space.

5.1 Learning Theories:

DBR is a learning science that is interdisciplinary and draws on multiple theoretical perspectives and research paradigms which will potentially lead to understandings of the nature and conditions of learning, cognition, and development [31]. Learning, cognition, knowing, and context are irreducibly co-constituted and cannot be treated as isolated processes. DBR focuses on understanding the messiness of real-world practice, with context being a core part. Participants are not "subjects" assigned to treatments, but instead are co-participants in design and analysis. DBR is pragmatic. A systems engineering perspective is useful for developing an optimized framework for learning and evaluations [32].

5.2 Technological Solutions for Learning:

Sloan Consortium's effective practices site [33] show-cases technological approaches; these often lead to new tools that have proven effective in enhancing learning. Relevant tools from this site will be discussed at the conference. Outside of Sloan-C publications, Ko and Rossen [34] discuss solutions for online projects. Roberts [35] discusses self and peer assessment for eLearners.

5.3 Big Data Approaches:

Bienkowski et al. [36] have articulated the role of big data in terms of educational data mining (EDM) and learning analytics (LA). Over the next few years, much 'big data' will be collected from our collective experience and will be subject to conventional data mining techniques, to improve course pedagogy and the tool infrastructure. Our tools, however, will also provide dynamic real-time support. We list here such application areas [36] and their mapping to AEx: (1) User knowledge modeling - EDM from SSE queries; (2) User behavioral modeling - LA from TQC (and FAQ) queries; (3) User experience modeling - EDM from surveys and VAr; (4) User profiling - EDM and LA from judges' rubric-based scores and comments/feedback, respectively; (5) Domain modeling - From ANT; (6) Learning Component analysis and instructional principle analysis - EDM from AEx usage statistics (longer term); (7) Trend Analysis - EDM on App maturity and skill level from judges' comments/ feedback, and from App marketing successes (longer term); and (8) Adaptability and Personalization - LA from TQC (and FAQ), and personalization of SSE.

6. Conclusions:

We have developed an eLearning tool architecture that is ideal for facilitating eTeams. We believe that the following outcomes will be positively impacted: (a) sustenance, portability, scalability, and usability for LMS tools, and (b) retention, motivation, and recruitment of students. The tool infrastructure and potential for big data analytics provides for significant improvements in teaching and learning as the tools are deployed and used in our online courses.

7. References:

[1] NSF, Fostering learning in the networked world: The cyberlearning opportunity and challenge: A 21st century agenda for the National Science Foundation. A report of the NSF task Force on Cyberlearning. June 24, 2008, Christine L. Borgman (Chair), Retrieved from http://www.nsf.gov/

[2] T. Anderson and J. Shattuck, Design-based research: A decade of progress in education research?, Educational Researcher, Featured Article, 41(1), 16-25, Retrieved from http://edr.sagepub.com/content/current, 2012

[3] Robotics, Florida Atlantic University's website for robotics, http://robotics.fau.edu/ , 2011

[4] Semantic Web, Florida Atlantic University's website for Semantic Web Technologies, http://semanticweb.fau.edu/, 2011

[5] J.S. Brown & R.P Adler, Minds on fire: Open education, the long tail, and learning 2.0. EDUCAUSE Review, 43(1), 16–32, 2008

[6] Android, Florida Atlantic University's website for Android smart phones, http://android.fau.edu/, 2010

[7] R. Shankar, F. McAfee, & M. Harris, Smart phone app development: A multi-college approach, 2013 ASEE Annual Conf., June 2013, Atlanta, GA, accepted, See http://eteams.pbworks.com/

[8] M.M. Lombardi, Making the grade: The role of assessment in authentic learning, Educause Learning Initiative, ELI Paper 1: Retrieved from http://www.educause.edu/library/resources/making-grade-role-assessment-authentic-learning , 2008

[9] R. Shankar, J. Dickson, & C. Mozelny, A tool for ABET accreditation, 2013 ASEE Annual Conference, June 2013, Atlanta, GA, accepted. Available at http://eteams.pbworks.com/

[10] S. Islam, G. Freytag, & R. Shankar, Intelligent health information system to empower patient with chronic diseases, IEEE IRI Workshop on Health Informatics, August 2012, Las Vegas, NV.

[11] S. Islam, R. Shankar, & G. Freytag, Leveraging semantic web to retrieve customized medical information, IEEE Systems Conference, April 2013, Orlando, FL, paper presented. Draft available at http://eteams.pbworks.com/

[12] eTeams, FAU Professor's wiki site for joint course development. http://eteams.pbworks.com/w/page/61784805/FrontPage , 2012

[13] Videos, Florida Atlantic University webpage with links to all student marketing videos and media articles, http://faculty.eng.fau.edu/shankar/research/smart-phone-apps/, 2013

[14] CEL, Florida Atlantic University's website for Center for eLearning. http://www.fau.edu/cel/ , 2012

[15] G. Wiggins, & J. McTighe, Understanding by Design (2nd Edition). Pearson: Upper Saddle River, NJ, 2005

[16] T.A. Angelo, & K.P. Cross, Classroom Assessment Techniques: A Handbook for College Teachers (2nd Ed.), San Francisco, CA: Jossey-Bass, 1993

[17] L. Dunn, C. Morgan, M. O'Reilly, & S. Parry, The Student Assessment Handbook: New Directions in Traditional & Online Assessment, New York, NY: RoutledgeFalmer, 2004

[18] J. F. Mueller, (Authentic assessment toolbox [website], Retrieved from http://jfmueller.faculty.noctrl.edu/toolbox/, 2011

[19] J.K. Fowlkes, The Yin-yang of Learning, Education Partnership Conference, Sanford, FL, July 2010

[20] C. Kelty, Geeks, social imaginaries and recursive publics, Cultural Anthropology 20(X): 185-214, 2005

[21] T.P. Mackey & T.E. Jacobson, Reframing Information Literacy as a Metaliteracy, College & Research Libraries 72(1), 62-78, 2011

[22] B. Bovard, Web 2.0 Selection Criteria, Tek Trekker's blog. Retrieved from http://tektrek.wordpress.com/2009/03/02/web-20-selection-criteria/ 2012

[23] Sloan-C, The Five Pillars, Retrieved from http://sloanconsortium.org/5pillars, 2012

[24] K. Swan, Relationship between interactions and learning in online environments, The Sloan Consortium. Retrieved from sloanconsortium.org/publications/books/pdf/interactions.pdf , 2004

[25] A. Chickering, & S.C. Ehrmann, Implementing the seven principles: Technology as lever, AAHE Bulletin, October, 3-6, 1996

[26] Android developers website. Retrieved from http://developer.android.com/index.html, 2012

[27] B. Fishman, W. Marx, P. Blumenfeld, J. Krajcik, & E. Soloway, Creating a framework for research on systemic technology innovations, Journal of the Learning Sciences, 13(1), 43-46, 2004

[28] A.A. diSessa & P. Cobb, Ontological innovation and the role of theory in design experiments, Journal of the Learning Sciences, 13(1),77-103, 2004

[29] T.H. Chi, Quantifying qualitative analysis of verbal data: A practical guide. Journal of the Learning Sciences, 6(3), 271-315, 1997

[30] S. Schensul, J.J. Schensul, & M. LeCompte, Essential Ethnographic Methods, AltaMira Press, 1999

[31] S. Barab, & K. Squire, Design-based research: Putting a stake in the ground, Journal of the Learning Sciences, 13(1), 1-14. Retrieved from http://learnlab.org/research/wiki/images/a/ab/2004_Barab_Squire.pdf, 2004

[32] A. Collins, D. Joseph, & K. Bielaczyc, Design research: Theoretical and methodical issues, Journal of the Learning Sciences, 13(1), 15-42. Retrieved from http://treeves.coe.uga.edu/EDIT9990/Collins2004.pdf , 2004

[33] Sloan-C (2012a). Sloan-C Effective Practices site. http://sloanconsortium.org/effective 2012

[34] S. Ko, & S. Rossen, Teaching online: A practical guide, Boston, MA: Houghton Mifflin. 2001

[35] T.S. Roberts, Self, Peer, and Group Assessment in E-Learning: An Introduction. In T. S. Roberts' (Ed.) Self, Peer, and Group Assessment in E-Learning, Queensland, Australia: Central Queensland University. 2006

[36] M. Bienkowski, M. Feng, and B. Means, Enhancing Teaching and Learning Through Educational Data Mining and Learning Analytics, US Department of Education, October 2012, www.ed.gov

Recognizing Classroom Atmosphere with Good Attention to the Ongoing Lecture for Indexing its Archived Video

Koh KAKUSHO[1], **Yohei KOBAYASHI**[1], **Takeshi OKADOME**[1], **and Masayuki MURAKAMI**[2]
[1]School of Science and Technology, Kwansei Gakuin University, Sanda, Hyogo, Japan
[2]Research Center for Multi-Media Education, Kyoto University of Foreign Studies, Kyoto, Japan

Abstract - *This article discusses how to recognize the atmosphere in a classroom where the students show good attention on the ongoing lecture from its archived video as a novel video indexing technology for e-learning application. We first show that facial orientations of the students in the classroom can be used as a useful visual feature obtainable from archived videos in order to recognize the classroom atmosphere with good attention from the students to the lecture, based on our analysis on the relationship between the behavior of the students and the classroom atmosphere that our humans actually recognize by watching the videos. Second, we present a method of recognizing the classroom atmosphere by estimating facial orientations of the students in each image frame of the video. In our experiment with a real archived videos, the success rate (F-measure) of the recognition was about 70%.*

Keywords: lecture archiving, video indexing, classroom atmosphere, human behavior recognition, facial image processing

1 Introduction

With recent widespread of multimedia technologies to the field of higher education, it becomes quite usual for various universities to archive their lectures in the form including video streams accessible from the Internet[1]-[3]. Each student can watch these archives for review or self-learning of the archived lectures afterward. These lecture archives are also expected to be useful for faculty development of lecturers to improve their lectures.

Since it takes long time, which is actually as long as the amount of time spent for each lecture, to watch each archived lecture video completely, it is desirable that the video is indexed by various situations actually occurred during the lecture[4]. In order to cut down on labor for archiving each lecture by giving indices on the archived video by hand, it has been discussed in previous work how to recognize various kind of situations possible to occur in lectures by employing video image processing, for realizing automatic lecture archiving or video indexing[5]-[16].

We can consider various kinds of situations as those which are possible to occur in each lecture. Among those possible situations, most representative kinds of situations useful for searching scenes of the viewers' interests in the recorded video should be those concerning with the lecturer. Thus, most of the previous work has focused on recognizing those situations that include positions[5][6] and behaviors[7]-[12] of the lecturer, writing on the blackboard[8][11]-[13], pointed areas on the blackboard or slides[14], and so on.

In contrast to the work on recognizing situations of the lecturer described above, some other work focuses on those of the students: motion of each student[15] or making a question by one of the students[8][16], for example. When archived lecture videos are used for faculty development, in which lecturers are given the chance for reviewing their own lectures by watching the videos, situations of students concerning with their own behaviors during the lectures, their responses to the behavior of the lecturers, and so on are quite useful for considering how the lectures can be further improved afterwards.

Although above situations of the students are mainly concerned with the behavior of each individual student, it is also significant to consider situations of the students as a whole group. A group of students receiving the same lecture in the same classroom creates various kinds of atmosphere together at each moment of the lecture. Recognizing this atmosphere in the classroom should also be one of the important situations for indexing archived lecture videos for the purpose of faculty development. What the lecturers feel about whether they are successful or not are strongly affected by the atmosphere created by the students in the classroom during their lectures. If, for example, lecturers could feel the students are concentrating to their talks during the lectures, they would recognize their lectures are successful in attracting the interests of the students, and if not, they would think that their way of giving lectures or the contents of their lectures should further be improved to attract the interests of the students. These considerations could become possible if the archived lecture videos are given with the indices of the atmosphere of the students.

In the remainder of this article, we will discuss how to recognize the atmosphere created by a group of students from their behaviors observed in the archived lecture videos. Among the possible kinds of atmosphere, we focus on that with good attention from the students to the ongoing lecture. In section 2, we will first discuss the behaviors of the students useful for the visual feature to recognize our aimed classroom atmosphere with good attention based on our analysis of the archived video of a real seminar of a university. From the result of the analysis, we will propose to employ facial orientations of the students in the classroom as the behavioral feature for recognizing the atmosphere. In section 3, we will present a method of facial image processing and human behavior recognition for estimating the facial orientations of each student in the classroom from the archived video. In section 4, we will present our experimental results for evaluating the success rate of recognizing the atmosphere with good attention to the lecture. In section 5, we will give a summary of our work as well as some discussion on our future steps to extend our proposed method for recognizing other kinds of atmospheres, which are useful as the situations for indexing archived lecture videos.

2 Students' behavior for recognizing their atmosphere of attention

2.1 Recording a lecture video for analyzing students' behavior

Students could pay their attention to various things during the lecture: talk of the lecturer, notes that they are taking, emails coming in to their mobile phones, and so on. Among these things, we focus on the classroom atmosphere where the lecturer feels the whole students are paying their attention to the talk given by the lecturer, as described in section 1.

In order to realize recognition of this atmosphere from the archived videos by a computer, we first need to find the students' behavior that shows strong correlation with this atmosphere, as the visual clue observable in the videos for the recognition. For obtaining the archived video of a real lecture, we installed a camera in front of the classroom used for a seminar given by one of the authors and took a video of the students.

As a part of the seminar, each student is required to give a short talk about his/her own course work and comments on the talks by others. Due to this style of the seminar, all the students, except for the student who is giving a talk, are listening to the talk while taking notes for their comments during the class. Thus, what the students could pay attention at each moment of the class are the talk given by the speaker, the note they are taking for their comments, or other things, which include mobile phones for example. Moreover, the students could create relaxing and distracting atmosphere in the intervals between the talks by different students. As the result, various kind of atmosphere occurs with comparatively short periods of time during the class.

(A) "Paying attention to the talk"

(B) "Paying attention to the note"

(C) "Impossible to classify"

Figure 1: Sample image frames of the seminar with various atmospheres in the classroom.

We extract 30 image frames from the archived lecture video with 25 minutes in total length, so that the extracted image frames include the scenes with various atmospheres that actually occurred during the class. The atmosphere that the speaker could feel at the moment of each image frame is given by experimental participants. We asked six experimental participants to classify the atmosphere that they feel for each image frame into one of the following four categories:

(A) "Paying attention to the talk"
(B) "Paying attention to the notes"
(C) "Paying attention on other things"
(D) "Impossible to classify"

where (A) corresponds to the atmosphere aimed to recognize in this article. The atmosphere of each image frame is determined as the categories classified in the same way by more than four participants. The atmosphere of the image frames with less than all the four participants giving the same classification is determined as (D). Figure 1 shows sample image frames classified as (A), (B) and (D). In this experiment, there was actually no image frame to be classified as (C).

2.2 Correlation of the classroom atmosphere with students' behavior

In order to clarify visual clues for recognizing the classroom atmosphere with students' good attention to the talk, we analyze the correlation of the atmosphere with observable behaviors of the students. Since one of the most primal behaviors of the students observable in the video is facial orientation[17], we calculated by hand the rates of the students who are looking forward, downward, and either ways of right or left. Figure 2 illustrates those rates for each of the 30 image frames classified as one of the four atmospheres (A)-(D) in section 2.1.

In this result, the rate of the students looking forward seems to have strong correlation with atmosphere (A). For verifying this hypothesis, we calculated the coefficients of correlations of the rates of the students looking in the three kinds of directions with each atmosphere. Here, we only consider atmospheres (A), (B) and (D) for calculating the coefficients, because atmosphere (C) was not obtained in the classification described in section 2.1. By considering that atmosphere (D) represents the atmosphere intermediate between atmosphere (A) and (B), we assigned values 3, 1 and 2 to atmospheres (A), (B) and (D).

As the result, the calculated coefficients of correlation of atmosphere (A) with the rates of the students looking forward, backward and either ways of right or left is 0.73, -0.88 and -0.29, respectively. It implies that the rate of the students looking forward has strong correlation with atmosphere (A) . In the following discussion, based on the result above, we will focus on how to recognize atmosphere (A) by using the rate of the students looking forward as the visual clue.

2.3 Utility for the rate of students looking forward for recognition

If we think of employing the rate of the students looking forward as the visual clue for recognizing atmosphere (A), we first need to discuss whether this rate can actually be obtained from image frames of real archived lecture videos. In order to know in which direction each student is looking, we basically need to obtain facial orientation of the student. However, in general, it often fails to detect faces by facial image processing especially when the faces appear in small sizes in the image. For detecting the faces of the students in a stable manner, it is preferable to focus only on the faces close to the camera, which is installed in front of the classroom in the setting of our experiments.

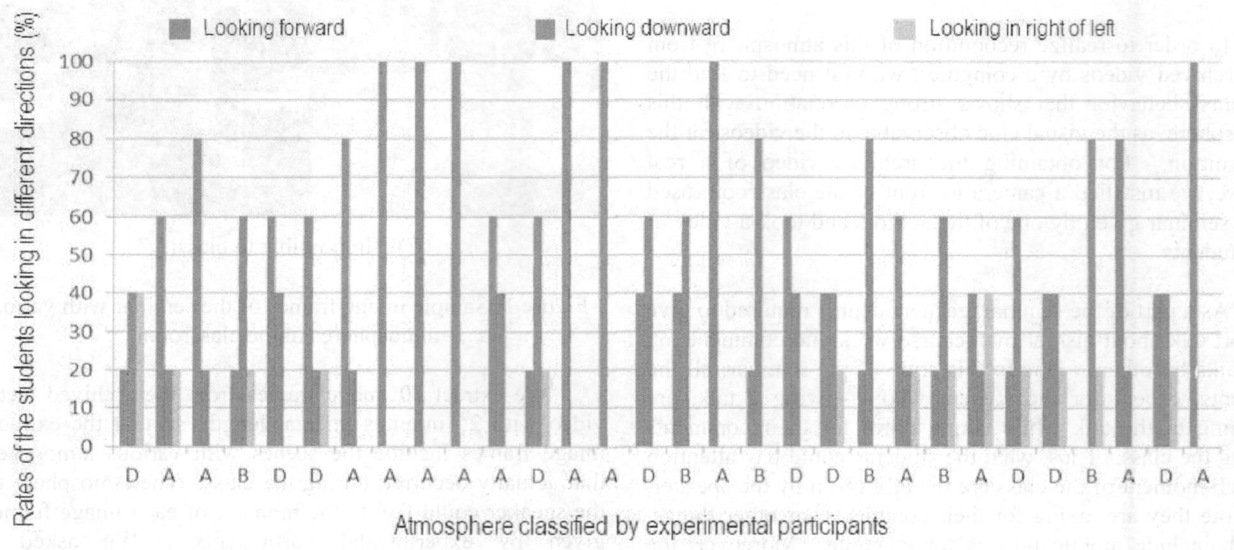

Figure 2: Rates of the students looking in different directions for each atmosphere.

In order to fulfill this requirement, we should employ facial orientations of the students sitting in the frontal area of the classroom for recognizing the atmosphere. We verified this possibility by calculating the coefficient of correlation of atmosphere (A) with the rate of the students looking forward only for representative five students sitting in the frontal area of the classroom. In the result, the value of the coefficient fortunately increases from 0.73 to 0.82. It would be because the behaviors of the students in the frontal area are more dominant for our humans to recognize the classroom atmosphere.

Finally, we calculated the precision rate and the recall rate expected in the recognition of atmosphere (A) based on the rate of the students looking forward in the frontal area. Both of these rates become maximum when we set the threshold value used as the criteria for evaluating the rate to 60%; the class is recognized to be in atmosphere (A) if the rate is more than 60% and not otherwise. For this threshold value, the precision rate and the recall rate for recognizing atmosphere (A) are 92.9% and 81.3% respectively, which result in 86.7% for the value of the F-measure.

For recognizing atmosphere (A) based on the rate of the students looking forward, we need to decide for each student in the frontal area of the classroom whether he/she is looking forward or not from the video images. We will propose a method for realizing it in the next section.

Figure 3: Result of face detection for an image frame of our archived lecture video.

3 Recognizing the atmosphere by facial image processing for lecture videos

3.1 Estimating the orientation of the face for each student in the classroom

The image region corresponding to the face of each student in each image frame is obtained by face detection of facial image processing as shown in Figure 3. For each facial region obtained by face detection, the orientation of the face to the camera can be recovered from the skew of the region. Although this orientation consists of the horizontal angle and the vertical angle from the direction towards the camera, we will only describe the face orientation within the horizontal plane obtained from the horizontal angle for simplicity in the following discussion. The face orientation within the vertical plane can also be obtained from the vertical angle in a similar manner.

We denote the above horizontal angle by α as illustrated in Figure 4. In order to decide whether the face is looking forward or not, we obtain its angle from the forward direction of the classroom. This angle denoted by θ is calculated from the two angles β and γ together with α as follows:

$$\theta = \alpha + \beta + \gamma \tag{1}$$

where β denotes the angle of the direction from the camera towards the face departing from the optical axis of the camera, and γ does the angle of the optical axis departing from the forward direction of the classroom, as illustrated in the figure. Please note that all of these angles are signed values which take positive values for counterclockwise rotations. Angle β can be obtained from the 2D position of the face in the image frame.

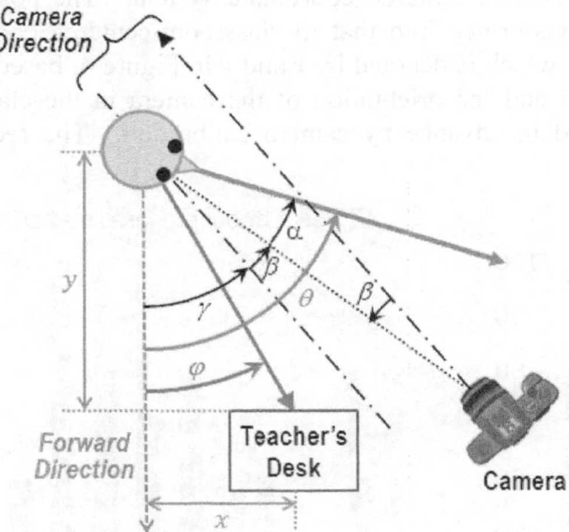

Figure 4: Angles for evaluating the orientation of the face of each student in the classroom.

3.2 Recovering the position of each student in the classroom

When a student looks forward for paying attention to the talk of the lecturer, his/her gaze is not purely directed to the frontal part of the classroom, but to the lecturer. In order to determine whether each student is looking forward for paying attention to the talk of the lecturer or not by considering the above issue, we employ the direction from the student towards the lecturer. The angle of this direction departing from the forward direction of the classroom is denoted by φ, as illustrated in Figure 4. By comparing the difference between θ and φ with a threshold value, we decide whether the student is gazing at the lecturer or not.

Angle φ is different for each student because it depends on the position of the student from the lecturer. We need to recover the position of each student in the classroom for comparing angle θ with φ. Assuming that the lecturer is standing around the teacher's desk located at the center of the frontal area of the classroom, we recover the position of each student in the classroom with the teacher's desk for the reference position.

Since the physical length between our eyes is known to be the same (6.3cm) without dependence on individuals, the 2D length between the eyes in the image is determined by the distance and the departure in the orientation of the face from the camera. Since the image region of the face has already been obtained together with its orientation to the camera in section 3.1, we can recover the position of the face with the camera as the reference position from the length between the eyes by further extracting their 2D positions in the facial region.

The position of the face recovered above is represented by the camera-centered coordinate system. The position is then transformed into that in classroom-centered coordinate system, which is denoted by x and y in Figure 4, based on the position and the orientation of the camera in the classroom obtained in advance by camera calibration. The recovered positions of the students, whose faces are detected in the image frame in Figure 3, are shown in Figure 5.

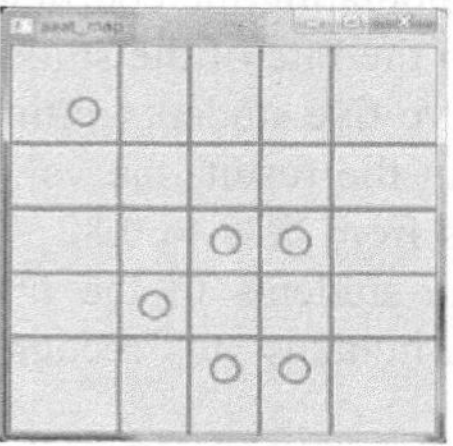

Figure 5: The recovered positions of the students whose faces are detected in Figure 3.

4 Experimental results

4.1 Evaluating the success rate for finding the students looking forward

In order to evaluate the success rate for the method described in section 3, we first evaluated the precision rate and the recall rate for deciding whether each student is looking forward or not by employing 30 image frames used for the experiment in section 2. We employed OKAO Vision, which is supplied by OMRON Corporation, for realizing facial image processing to detect faces and extract the 2D positions of the eyes in each image frame as well as estimation of the orientation of each face.

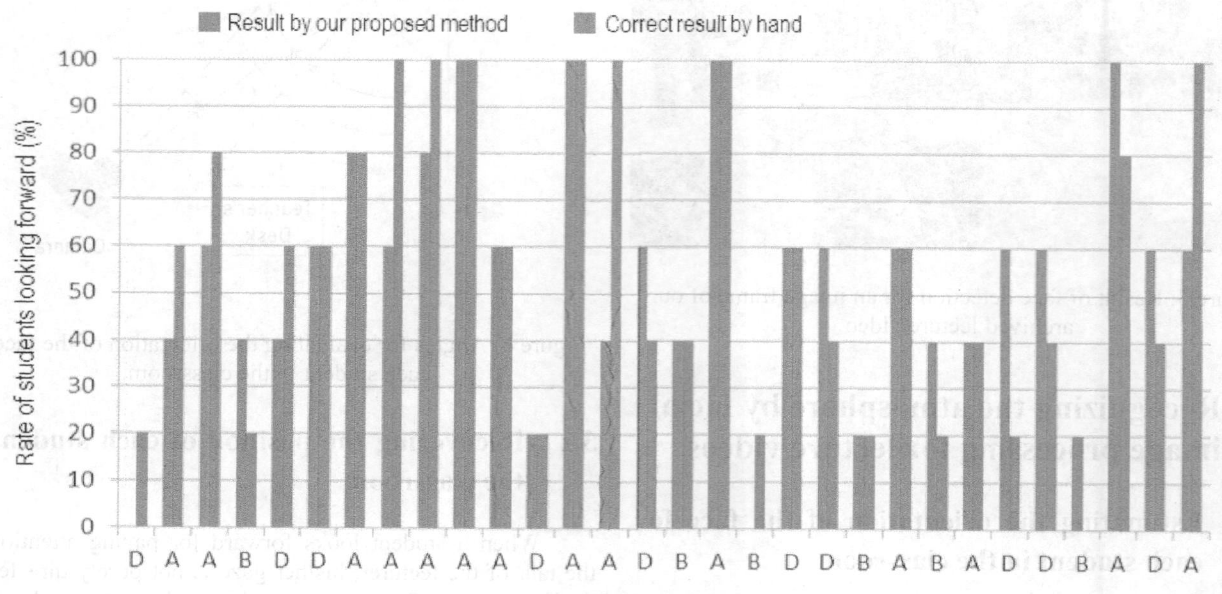

Figure 6: Results for estimating the rates of the students looking forward

Figure 6 shows the comparison between the results for estimating the rate of the students looking forward by our proposed method and by hand. In this comparison, the rates of precision and recall were 84.0% and 81.0% respectively, which attain 82.4% for the value of the F-measure.

4.2 Evaluating the success rate for recognizing the atmosphere

From the results in section 2.3 and 4.1, the F-measure for recognizing the classroom atmosphere with good attention to the talk of the lecture based on the rate of the students looking forward as the visual clue by deciding whether each student is looking forward or not using the method described in section 3 is expected to be 86.7%×82.4% = 71.4%. For verifying this expectation, we directly evaluate the result for recognition of the atmosphere from the archived lecture video by comparing it with the correct atmosphere classified by the experimental participants in the experiment in section 2.

The actual value of the F-measure obtained as the result of this evaluation was 68.8%, which is almost the same as the expected value above. It implies that the error in recognizing the atmosphere from the rate of the students looking forward and that in deciding whether each student is looking forward or not from the archived lecture video images occur almost independently without negative effect on each other. The above evaluation result can be seen as an average level among the success rates for recognizing various kinds of situations of lectures in previous works, which range from 50 to 90%, depending on the difficulty to recognize the aimed situation.

5 Conclusions

In this article, we discussed the possibility for recognizing classroom atmosphere created by a group of students from observable behaviors of the students. Among various kinds of atmosphere possible to occur during the lectures, we focused on the atmosphere where the lecturers could feel that the students are paying attention to their talks. As the process for attaining our research goal, we first clarified that the rate of the students looking forward is useful as a visual clue for recognizing the atmosphere from our analysis using an archived video of a real seminar of a university. Based on this result, we further proposed a method for estimating the rate of the students looking forward by deciding whether each student is looking forward or not using facial image processing for archived lecture videos. This method attains the success rate with an average level among the previous work on recognizing various kinds of situations of lectures.

Since our work described in this article is still at the early stage for recognizing various kinds of atmospheres of a group of students during the lecture, there are many things to do as our future steps. First of all, we need to verify the result in section 2 and 4 by employing more archived videos of more various kinds of lectures.

We also plan to apply our method for recognizing other kinds of atmospheres, especially the atmosphere where the students are paying attention to the note they are taking as another future step. From the experimental result in section 2, the atmosphere with students' attention to the notes seems to have correlation with the rate of the students looking downward, and our method for deciding whether the students are looking forward or not can also be applied for finding those who are looking downward, because both of those students can be found based on the orientations of their faces, which have already been estimated in our method. Thus, it would be comparatively easy to realize recognition of that atmosphere.

References

[1] M.Minoh, S.Nishiguchi: "Environmental Media - In the case of Lecture Archiving System - ," Knowkedge-Based Intelligent Information and Engineering Systems, PP.1070-1076 (2003).

[2] M.Murakami, S.Nishiguchi, Y.Kameda, M.Minoh: "Effect on Lecturer and Students by Multimedia Lecture Archive System," International Conference on Information Technology Based Higher Education and Traininig (ITHET), pp.377-380 (2003).

[3] M.Maharaj, A.de Lange: "The Impact of Podcasting on Student Lecture Attendance," IST-Africa Conference Proceedings (2010).

[4] T.Tuna, J.Subhlok, S.Shar: "Indexing and Keyword Search to Ease Navigation in Lecture Videos," Applied Imagery Pattern Recognition Workshop (AIPR) (2011).

[5] H-P.Chou, J-M.Wang, C-S.Fuh, S-C.Lin, S-W.Chen: "Automated Lecture Recording System," (2010).

[6] B.Wulff, R.Rolf: "OpenTrack - Automated Camera Control for Lecture Recording," IEEE International Symposium on Multimedia (ISM), pp.549-552 (2011).

[7] S.Tsuruoka, T.Yamaguchi, K.Kato, T. Yoshikawa, T.Shinogi: "A Camera Control Based Fuzzy Behaviour Recognition of Lecturer for Distance Lecture," IEEE International Conference on Fuzzy Systems, pp.940-943 (2001).

[8] T.Sakiyama, N.Ohno, M.Mukunoki, K.Ikeda: "Video stream selection according to lecture content in remote

lectures," Systems and Computers in Japan, 34(3), pp. 64-75 (2003).

[9] F.Wang, C-W.Ngo, T-C.Pong: "Gesture Traking and Recognition for Lecture Video Editing," International Conference on Pattern Recognition (ICPR), pp.934-937 (2004).

[10] A.Shimada, A.Suganuma, R.Taniguchi: "Automatic Camera Control System for a Distant Lecture based on Estimation of Teacher's Behavior," IASTED International Conference on Computers and Advanced Technology in Education, pp.106-111 (2004).

[11] M.Onishi, K.Fukunaga: "Shooting the Lecture Scene Using Computer-controlled Cameras Based on Situation Understanding and Evaluation of Video Images," International Conference on Pattern Recognition (ICPR), pp. 781-784 (2004).

[12] M.Onishi, M.Murakami, K.Fukunaga: "Intelligent autofilming of lectures based on interpretation of the scene environment and evaluating video footage," Systems and Computers in Japan, 37(11), pp.88-99 (2006).

[13] M.Onishi, M.Izumi, K.Fukunaga: "Blackboard Segmentation Using Video Image of Lecture and Its Applications," International Conference on Pattern Recognition (ICPR), pp.4615-4618 (2000).

[14] T.Sakiyama, M.Mukunoki, K.Ikeda: "Detection of the Indicated Area with an Indication Stick," International Conference on Multimodal Interface (ICMI), pp.480-487 (2000).

[15] S.Nishiguchi, Y.Kameda, K.Kakusho, M.Minoh, "Automatic video recording of lecture considering variety of motion and equability of scale for observing students," Journal of Advanced Computational Intelligence and Intelligent Informatics, 8(2), pp.180-188 (2004).

[16] M.Minoh, S.Nishiguchi, H.Higashi: "Recognition of dynamic situations in the classroom using multi-modal sensor information," Information Processing and Management of Uncertainty in Knowledge-based Systems (IPMU), pp.1757-1762 (2002).

[17] M.Murakami, K.Kakusho, M.Minoh: "Analysis of Students' Eye Movement in Relation to Contents of Multimedia Lecture," World Conference on E-Learning in Corporate, Government, Healthcare and Higher Education (E-Learn), pp.1965-1968 (2002).

Teaching Teams and Project Management in a Virtual Environment

C. Balch
Department of Business & Administration Northern Arizona University, Yuma, Arizona, USA

Abstract - *My signature class is a junior level Teams and Project Management learning experience. An important part of this class is crafting learning outcomes to address changing stakeholder needs, incorporating constantly changing tools for virtual team interaction and project management, and measuring outcomes. This paper provides a snapshot of the current evolution of this class as taught within the ACBSP accredited Northern Arizona University Business and Administration program. Paper content includes best practices in virtual team building; review of current technology to facilitate virtual teams; overcoming BlackBoard Learn limitations; and useful third-party associations. Synthesis of technologies is demonstrated and time-saving macros are described.*

Keywords: Virtual Teams, Team Building, Project Management

1 Introduction

With a nod to Six Sigma, TQM, MBO, etc., instructions to and activities for team participants are constantly evolving. An important part of the class is for students to actively critique their learning process during and after [1] The following is an adaption of a snapshot of an evolving scaffold students use as a framework as we cover each area in detail [2].

2 Best Virtual Team Practices

The following should be accomplished by all team members and receive special focus from team leader and project manager.

2.1 Define and contact your team

- Teams may be assigned or self-forming.
- Insure that you have current contact information for all team members.
- Confirm that everyone is aware they are a member of the team.

2.2 Define the goal

- Insure the team is focused on the same and correct goal.
    - If there is anything unclear about the specification, ask the person who defined the product for further specification.
    - Identify major stakeholders and consider their needs.
    - Each team member should state that they understand and agree upon the goal.
- If packaging of the results is unclear, confirm your understanding of what the deliverable should look like with the recipient.

2.3 Define communication tools, method(s), and protocols

Reach a consensus choice of communication tools and procedures. Insure that all team members agree to use the consensus tools and procedures.

- **Tools** Choice of tools depends on member resources including preferences and willingness to learn new communication tools.
    - Teams are likely to need both communication and file sharing tools.
    - It is often desirable to use multiple tools in each category.
    - The ideal tools for a task are not useful if team members cannot or will not use them. Thus, search for tools that all team members will use.
- **Methods** There are two major categories of communication. Most teams will use a combination of these.

- **Synchronous** communication occurs when all team members may interact at the same time. Phone calls and video conferencing are examples of tools for synchronous communication. Synchronous communication is particularly effective for rapid decisions but it requires that the team agree and follow up on a meeting time and method. Unless someone takes notes, typically there is little or no record of synchronous communication.
- **Asynchronous** communication occurs when team members communicate at different intervals. Email and Bulletin Boards are examples of tools for asynchronous communication. Asynchronous communication is particularly effective when team members have difficulty finding common times to meet. Typically asynchronous communication is automatically recorded for later review.

- **Protocols** are agreed upon team communication rules. Protocols include:
  - Agreed upon meeting times and tools for synchronous communication. Robert's Rules of Order [3] are a great way to organize a synchronous meeting. At the very least, a meeting should have and follow an agenda similar to agendas defined in Robert's Rules. Distribute the agenda with enough time for team comments before the meeting. Keep the discussion focused on the issue at hand (motion) and the agenda. There should be a review of assigned tasks at the end of the meeting.
  - Agreed upon tools and frequency of checking asynchronous communication. Asynchronous communication usually involves discussion threads where a topic is introduced and commented upon. For clarity, if you wish to start a new discussion topic, start a new thread.

2.4 Define, assign, and set deadlines for tasks. Confirm.

1. **Define** and assign operational tasks with outcomes to get from where the team is to the desired goal.
   a. Identify tasks that must be completed before tasks may begin and which tasks may be simultaneous.
   b. The detail of task description varies. Routine tasks are often grouped. Novel tasks may require a detailed breakout.
2. **Assign** team members to each task. Double check that every task has an associated team member.
3. **Set Deadlines** for every task. Pay special attention to when the team goal must be reached and tasks that must be accomplished before others may begin.
4. **Confirm** that all team members agree to and are willing and able to do their assigned tasks.

2.5 Monitor progress

- **Check** on team member progress at regular intervals.
- **Agree** on a common area where team members can post their progress, discuss obstacles, and report completed tasks.

2.6 Third Party Associations

In addition to stakeholder focus groups in which our content is reviewed by members of the business community, professional world companies have associations with the class. Many of these companies are probably not aware that our students use their products (see "Selected Resources for Virtual Teams" Balch, 2013c). Here are some notably useful alliances that require partnerships:

- Google Apps are essential to the success of this class. The combination of these applications provides strong team coordination and the ability to work on documents without change tracking concerns. *Google+*, *Google Drive*, and *Google Voice* are the most useful apps. Northern Arizona University subscribes to the free Google Apps for Education program.
- LinkedIn provides a professional networking area that allows our students and alumni to communicate in a moderated group. LinkedIn also allows us to track student success. Some recent events in our LinkedIn area are notable:
  - An alumni contacted me through the area to announce that he was now in a position of authority and would like an intern from our program.
  - In a recent Teams and Project management class assignment where students were strongly urged (but not required) to create a free LinkedIn account, three students received job offers within a day after creation of their profile.
- We are fortunate to have an alliance with Microsoft DreamSpark **[4]** where students receive a variety of Microsoft Applications at no cost. As a class requirement, students must install and use *Microsoft Project*. Use of *Microsoft Visio* is strongly encouraged.

3 Best Practices

Students complete six projects where they must create a web based presentation. All topics have a business focus. The first four projects have randomly assigned teams of about eight members. For the first four projects, I attempt to form teams composed of members who have not worked together before in the class. The last two projects follow a hiring hall format where leaders declare themselves, ask for team recruits, then leaders choose who they accept.

Parallel to the projects are discussions focused on various aspects of team building and project management. Discussion topics enhance class and departmental objectives. Common student comments include something like, "I recall covering this topic but we never really discussed it."

Upon completion of projects, students peer review their team members including themselves using a rubric (Balch, 2013d) based Google Form. Students also score and comment on all the projects using a rubric based (Balch, 2013e) . Reviews include a rubric based score and a comment area. Student feedback includes all the comments they made and all the scores and comments made about them for each project.

Lessons learned in Google Forms is to require students to login using their User Id which is automatically required and to require students to select the entity they are reviewing from a drop down list. Failure to force clear data selections creates a data set that needs much review and editing before it is usable.

Even with somewhat clean data, much automation is needed to provide complete feedback. I developed macros to remove duplicate entries and to group responses and package the results into email and web pages.

Students receive individual email after each project including their current class standing and peer comments and scores from the most recent project. Individual responses are shown without reference to the team member who made the comment.

4 References

[1] Antony, J. (2012) "A SWOT analysis on Six Sigma: some perspectives from leading academics and practitioners", International Journal of Productivity and Performance Management, Vol. 61 Iss: 6, pp.691 - 698

[2] Balch, C. 2013a. Building Virtual Teams. nau.edu. Retrieved March 2013 from http://oak.ucc.nau.edu/cvb23/handout/BuildngVirtualTeams.asp

[3] Roberts Rules of Order. Retrieved February 2013 from http://www.robertsrules.org/rulesintro.htm.

[4] DreamSpark. DreamSpark.com. Retrieved March 2013 from https://www.dreamspark.com/

[5] Balch, C. 2013c. Selected Resources for Virtual Teams. nau.edu. Retrieved March 2013 from http://oak.ucc.nau.edu/cvb23/hdoc/PresentationResources.htm

Balch, C. 2013b. On-line Scholarly Research. nau.edu. Retrieved March 2013 from http://oak.ucc.nau.edu/cvb23/handout/onlineresearch.asp

Balch, C. 2013d. Presentation Rubric. nau.edu. Retrieved March 2013 from http://oak.ucc.nau.edu/cvb23/hdoc/PresentationRubric.htm

Balch, C. 2013e. Peer Review Rubric. nau.edu. Retrieved March 2013 from http://oak.ucc.nau.edu/cvb23/hdoc/TeamMemberRubric.htm

Goldman, H. (2005) "The origins and development of quality initiatives in American business", The TQM Magazine, Vol. 17 Iss: 3, pp.217 - 225

Google Apps. Google.com. Retrieved March 2013 from http://www.google.com/apps/index1.html

LinkedIn. LinkedIn.com. Retrieved March 2013 from https://www.linkedin.com/

5 Appendix 1) Selected Technology to Facilitate Virtual Teams as of March 2013 [5]

The following sites represent the areas I currently find most useful in facilitating teams. This list is constantly evolving and my current preferred applications are found at: http://oak.ucc.nau.edu/cvb23/hdoc/PresentationResources.htm

5.1 Cloud Resource Collections

5.1.1 TechSupportAlert

(http://www.techsupportalert.com/content/best-free-online-applications-and-services.htm) Best Free Online Resources Yes

File Sharing / Synch on multiple computers

5.1.2 Box.net

(http://box.net) File sharing website. Allows you to upload very large files and provide a link that allows others to download them.

5.1.3 Dropbox

(http://db.tt/lqetUPA) Synchronize files on multiple computers. Creates a folder that is automatically synchronized with as many computers as you like. Simply add or update a file and the contents are update on all the other computers. Allows you to revert to earlier file versions. Sub folders can be shared with teams. PS: Use this link to install and we'll both get extra free storage.

5.1.4 Google Drive

(http://drive.google.com) Synchronize files on multiple computers. Creates a folder that is automatically synchronized with as many computers as you like. Simply add or update a file and the contents are update on all the other computers. Allows you to revert to earlier file versions. Sub folders can be shared with teams.

5.2 Gantt Charts

5.2.1 Clocking IT

(http://www.clockingit.com/) An online Gantt system with included communication tools. Note that this program outside the NAU domain and be cautious with your identity.

5.2.2 ViewPath

(http://viewpath.com) An online Gantt system with included communication tools. Note that this program outside the NAU domain and be cautious with your identity.

5.2.3 Gantter

(http://gantter.com/) An online Gantt system.

5.2.4 Gantt Chart

(http://www.youtube.com/watch?v=dp6J6Bw92d4)How to put a Gantt chart into a Google Doc. Note that this does not work with Google Chrome.

5.3 Meeting Scheduler

5.3.1 Doodle

(http://www.doodle.com/) Find times where everyone can meet.

5.3.2 NeedtoMeet

(http://needtomeet.com/) Simple way to finds that folks can meet.

5.3.3 ScheduleOnce

(http://www.scheduleonce.com/) Find times where everyone can meet. Works with Google calendar.

5.4 Development Tools

5.4.1 Audacity

(http://audacity.sourceforge.net/) Record, edit, mix, cut, etc Audio.

AuthorStream

(http://authorstream.com) Convert PowerPoint to video automatically.

5.4.2 Bitstrips

(http://www.bitstripsforschools.com/) Create online comics - 30 day free trial.

5.4.3 CamStudio

(http://camstudio.org/) CamStudio is a free video screen and audio capturing program. You might consider recording a PowerPoint on your computer as you talk your way through a presentation then polishing with Movie Maker.

5.4.4 DrupalGardens

(http://www.drupalgardens.com/) Create presentations online - also hosts.

5.4.5 Free Screen Cast

(http://freescreencast.com/) This screen capture program does not require that a program be installed on your computer. See Camtasia for reasons that you might want to do this.

Jing Screen Capture (http://www.techsmith.com/jing/) Another screen capture program that does not require program instillation. See Camtasia for reasons you might want to do this.

5.4.6 Know Case

(http://knowcase.com/) Brainstorming tool

5.4.7 Mind42

(http://www.mind42.com/) Collaborative Mind Mapping

5.4.8 Movie Maker

(http://www.microsoft.com/windowsxp/using/moviemaker/default.mspx) I suggest Movie Maker for creating and editing videos. There are many tutorials available on the web but this is a good start. You might consider having team members recording part of a presentation then using Movie Maker to combine and polish the final product. Do use transitions and titles, be careful with special effects.
Movie Maker download for Version 7 (http://explore.live.com/windows-live-essentials?os=win7)

This link shows how to get Movie Maker for Windows 7. Earlier versions of Windows have Movie Maker already installed.
PowerPoint simple slide to movie (http://www.youtube.com/watch?v=PK4XdJ-ywSs) How to convert a PowerPoint presentation suitable for upload to YouTube. Note: Powerpoint 2010 offers a variety of tools to convert content for the web. Another option for conversion is to do a screen capture.

5.4.9 Prezi

(http://prezi.com) Create and share presentations online - also hosts. Note: You could use one of the screen capture tools to make your Prezi presentation into a movie.

5.5 Webs.com

(http://webs.com) Create and share presentations online - also hosts.

5.5.1 Weebly

(http://weebly.com) Create and share presentations online - also hosts.

5.5.2 Wix

(http://wix.com) Create presentations online - also hosts.

5.6 Places to host your presentation

5.6.1 You Tube

(http://YouTube.com) You tube makes it very easy to share a video.
Request NAU Server Space (https://www4.nau.edu/its/webacct/index.aspx)NAU provides substantial space on their servers and they will increase your storage for class projects. You may upload your web resources here including pages and video.

5.6.2 Google Sites

(http://sites.google.com) Google provides free web space for projects.

5.6.3 SoundCloud.com

(http://soundcloud.com) Website to host sound

5.6.4 Vocaroo.com

(http://Vocaroo.com) Website to host sound

5.6.5 Wix

(http://wix.com) Create presentations online - also hosts.

5.6.6 Webs.com

(http://webs.com) Create presentations online - also hosts.

5.6.7 Collaboration Tools

5.6.8 Asana

(http://asana.com) Cloud based shared task list

5.6.9 AskClass

(http://askclass.net) Internet voting tool

5.6.10 Doodle

(http://doodle.com)Group scheduling tool.

5.6.11 Elluminate

(http://elluminate.nau.edu) Collaborate is NAU's adopted confercing system of choice. To use Elluminate in our class, follow the link and search for "Balch" then have your team login at the same time to your prepared team area. The passwords are BBA360. Be sure to try the various tools including WebCams, application sharing, webpage sharing, and the whiteboard. Try a review of your recording. Here is a link to Elluminate Help.

5.6.12 Free conference calls

(http://freeconferancecall.com) Free Conference Calls

5.6.13 Google Docs

(http://mail.nau.edu) NAU Google Docs
Google+ (https://plus.google.com/up/start/?et=ad&type=st) Sort of a combination of Skype and Facebook. Allows for multiple video feeds. "Start a Hangout" for a "Circle."

5.6.14 GotoMeeting

(http://gotomeeting.com) Another conferencing system.

5.6.15 Join.Me

(http://join.me) Share your screen with multiple viewers.

5.6.16 Second Life

(http://secondlife.com) A virtual reality.

5.6.17 Skype

(http://skype.com) Skype is a free application that allows you to have audio conferences, face-to-face video, and screen sharing. You can find me on Skype with my "NAUCharlie" handle. Yes

5.6.18 Zoho

(http://zoho.com) Document collaboration Yes

New Challenges in Teaching e-Forensics Online

Professor Eamon P. Doherty, CCE, CPP, SSCP
School of Administrative Science, Fairleigh Dickinson University, Teaneck, USA

Abstract *- This paper discusses how the topic of forensic imaging has changed because of the introduction of a new technology known as the solid state drive (SSD). The differences between the SSD and the magnetic disk hard drive are also discussed. This paper highlights the importance of online education for teaching e-forensics, how it is delivered, and why it is important for educating certain populations who cannot get to a traditional classrom. Lastly, this paper also discusses the need for a conference among many stakeholders to create a publically known standard, perhaps an ISO standard, for the SSD and why it would help for court cases involving the imaging and investigation of SSDs.*

Keywords: Computer Forensics, Cyber Forensics, Computer Security

1 Introduction

Teaching computer forensics online is very important since many policeman and National Guardsmen often have unpredictable work schedules and cannot attend and in person classes [1]. Online learning is also the only option for those students who want to study a very specialized topic such as e-forensics when they are deployed with the military and cannot travel freely. Creating a forensic image or a clone of a hard drive is considered by some authorities to be the most important task in computer forensics. The forensic image is a byte for byte copy of a suspect's hard drive. It includes both the used and unused space. A backup is only a subset of a forensic image because a backup only includes the files with data and not the unallocated space or "empty space" where remnants of evidence can be. Forensic examiners need to look at both allocated and unallocated space for exculpatory evidence to find someone innocent, not just guilty. If an examiner only has a backup, a defense attorney might create some doubt that some exculpatory evidence, finding his or her client innocent, resides in unallocated space. This is one concept that is important for new students of e-forensics to learn. There should also be an identical SHA-1 or MD5 hash of the forensic image and the suspect's hard drive or storage device which verifies that the image is a perfect clone of the suspect's drive. All experiments to produce evidence on the cloned image drive should also work on the suspect's drive. It should become obvious how important the forensic image has become in digital forensics. It is also common knowledge among people that hold a CCE (Certified Computer Examination) that some digital forensic examiners can have a career working for private investigators and lawyers while only specializing in the forensic imaging of hard drives. Therefore the forensic imaging of hard drives is a subject of great importance to anyone who teaches e-forensics. Two popular digital forensic tools that can be used to create a forensic image of a disk and provide a hash function for verification purposes are SMART from ASR Data Acquisition & Analysis and Winhex from X-Ways Software Technology AG [2].

This paper will discuss how one university has used online learning to teach the forensic imaging of hard drives in its computer forensics classes. In the last two decades the hard drives that have been encountered have been those with magnetic platters and read write heads. The methodology of forensically imaging these types of drives has been well established and has been accepted in many court cases. When an investigative technique and set of tools have been accepted by the legal community, the academic community, and practitioners, it is said to have passed the Frye Test.

The challenge to the established methodology of the forensically imaging of hard drives is the introduction of a new technology known as the solid state drive (SSD). These hard drives may have over twenty computer chips on their circuit board instead of platters with read write heads. Many of these drives also have proprietary algorithms and technology so that it is not possible to know where the data lies on the drive. The drive size or storage capacity is not constant and dynamically changes as blocks are labeled bad and no longer used by the operating system. There is also a garbage collection program that runs when the solid state drive is powered. This means that part of the drive may be deleting evidence while the computer forensic technician is simultaneously collecting evidence on another part of the hard drive. The challenge is further complicated by the various manufacturers of solid state drives who each have their own methods of storing and deleting data on the solid state drive. This means that computer forensic educators need to invite computer forensic practitioners, SSD manufacturers, and attorneys to create a national or international conference to discuss the framework of how to forensically image the solid state drive and have the image be accepted for use in a court case. If a set of tools and methodologies for imaging a solid state drive could be developed and accepted by the academic, legal, and practitioner communities, this would be a big breakthrough for computer forensics. It would also mean that computer forensic examiners would have a set of tools and methodologies to pass the Frye Test. "Citing Frye v. United States, 54 App. D.C. 46, 47, 293, F. 1013, 1014, (1923), the court stated that expert opinion based on scientific technique is inadmissible unless the technique is generally accepted as reliable in the relevant scientific community [3]." Having a set of standards for SSD technology would also mean that educators would be able to develop a new online lesson and allow students to learn how to image the solid state drive and get a MD5 hash that is the same for the suspect's drive and the newly created image for use in a computer forensic examination. This standard would have a high probability of passing the Frye Test and be useful to students who are eForensics practitioners.

2 Teaching Forensic Imaging Online

Fairleigh Dickinson University (FDU) has two classes that discuss the process of forensic imaging. One class is called MADS 6697 Current Issues in Cyber Forensics. The other class is called MADS 6637 Computer Seizure and Examination. Both classes are often taught in a traditional classroom, but are also taught online. Many students will self-identify themselves as policemen that live in rural areas and cannot easily attend the main campus. Some of these policemen and policewomen work the night shift or rotating shift thus making the online learning environment the only feasible solution to advance their education. Other students will self-identify themselves as national guardsman that were deployed in a place such as the green zone in Iraq or abroad. It becomes obvious that online learning is a feasible option for those in a war zone where commuting safely to a classroom is not possible. Some students in these classes often self-identify themselves as unemployed and seeking a career change. Online learning can be a good option for those who cannot afford the high price of gasoline for commuting to school faraway and for those who cannot take public transportation from their home to the university.

The students start by registering for their class, paying the tuition, and then getting their books. They are next given a username and password for a class such as computer seizure and examination. The class is conducted in FDU Webcampus and uses the online educational program known as Blackboard. Each week consists of activities such as textbook readings, reading course documents, and participating in a discussion board where students interact among themselves as well as with the professor. There are also course links where students can access video or Microsoft PowerPoint slides on topics such as forensic imaging. There are many YouTube videos on the subject of forensic imaging of hard drives. These films are produced by academics, practitioners, students, and commercial product vendors. These films show a variety of tools and techniques to forensically image a hard drive and verify the results. It is important to first verify which people, tools, and techniques are credible before presenting them to the students. The student will begin his or her knowledge of the hard drive by reading about the hardware such as the read-write heads and the platters that are used in the traditional magnetic platter hard drives. Chapter fourteen of the sixth edition of Operating System Concepts by Siberschatz, Galvin, and Gagne are a good source for teaching students the subject of mass storage structure and I/O scheduling [4]. The student then reads about the operating system and such concepts as the file directory, the file allocation table (FAT), clusters, and chaining. There is a body of literature that is well established about how magnetic platter hard drives store, retrieve, and delete information. The course documents for the class contain text, pictures, and links to vetted online videos. The education of how the hard drive works and how it can be forensically imaged applies to new hard drives as well as classic hard drives such as the Seagate Technology Model ST-412 with a capacity of ten megabytes. Figure 1 shows a full height ST412 hard drive on the right. It was partitioned into two logical drives of E and F. It is much bigger than a more modern common hard drive such as the Western Digital hard drive with an eighty gigabyte capacity which is also pictured in figure 1. It is important to teach students that evidence can appear in logical drives or in a hidden partition between the two drives.

Figure 1– Full Height and Modern Hard Drives

The next step is to teach the students how to create a forensic image of a magnetic platter hard drive. The simplest method is to start with a piece of hardware to wipe a hard drive and then duplicate the hard drive of a simulated suspect's hard drive to the wiped hard drive. Some hard drive duplicating equipment has an option for wiping a hard drive. This means that each byte of a hard drive is written with a pattern of zeroes so that there is no doubt about malware or evidence from another case being on a hard drive that will later contain the forensic image of the suspect's hard drive. The Logicube Solitaire Hard Drive Cloning Device Duplicator is one of many viable options for people with or without a technical backround. This device simplifies the forensic copy/imaging process. The suspect's hard drive is connected to the outside of the Logic Cube device and the wiped drive is connected inside the device [5]. Some menu buttons on the Logic Cube are selected and the process of forensic imaging begins until completion. A printer may be connected and a report about the MD5 hash can be printed.

Figure 2- The Logic Cube Equipment

Another method of teaching students to create a forensic image of a suspect's hard drive involves changing the bootup order of the devices in the bios. The bios settings can be changed so that the system first checks the CD drive, floppy diskette drive, or a flash drive for an operating system or bootable program. Then a CD with a program such as Helix 2 can be booted up so that a forensic imaging program is run. This will prevent the operating system on the subject's hard drive from booting up and changing access times and file dates thus potentially compromising the evidence and having it suppressed as possible evidence in court. Once a program such as Helix 2 or Access Data's FTK Imager is run, then the forensic image of the hard drive can be made through a USB storage device that is connected to the suspect's USB port. This technique is taught online by the use of text, PowerPoint slides, and a video. Once the forensic image of the simulated suspect's hard drive is created, the MD5 hash of the suspect's magnetic platter hard drive can be compared to the forensic image thus insuring a perfect match for examination purposes.

3 Issues Concerning a SSD

Scott Moultan, a computer forensic practitioner and speaker, says that the solid state drive (SSD) device is becoming more popular because it runs quietly and extends the time that one can run the laptop with only the battery as a power source [6]. He also says the device is popular because it weighs less and produces less heat than a conventional magnetic platter hard drive. It appears from the speech that there are not identical standards among all the various SSD makers and it may limit the forensic examiner's ability to get to all parts of the drive to access potential evidence. Scott also said that there are times when the SSD is powered on and quietly running, the garbage collection is moving data, and also zeroing out unallocated space [6]. He also discusses occasions on small consumer grade memory sticks when the device marks cells as bad and the storage capacity is not as large as it was [6]. Bell and Boddington, two writers for the Journal of Digital Forensics, Security, and Law, say, "Put simply: the SSD technology which is replacing magnetic hard drives is neither simple, well understood, nor homogenous; rather it is complex, poorly documented, and highly heterogenous. [7]" Bell and Boddington then further state,"Worst of all, it is active – that is to say, the SSD may act under its own initiative, and may undertake quite remarkable (and highly evidence-destructive) actions even in the absence of write commands from a computer, potentially regardless of efforts by police and forensic analysts to prevent invalidation of evidence [7]." From our previous discussions of forensics, it appears that this set of changes leaves a possibility that a defense lawyer might suggest that there is no guarantee that the tampering of evidence did not occur." It then becomes evident that manufactures should develop a set of standards about how data is stored, deleted, and repositioned on a SSD drive. The manufactures of SSDs may need to be approached by various governments and representatives of various legal systems to consider the redesign of these drives in the interests of the safety of the world community. Some attempts to add security features to technology to stop counterfeiting of US currency for example have been adopted whole heartedly by the printer industry. The color laser printer industry has added a technology that allows the serial number of the printer to be embedded in the paper. This feature when combined with a special purple light, allows the United States Secret Service the ability to know what printer a counterfeit United States currency note was printed on. However; other previous attempts by the United States government to change technology manufacturing for purposes for national security have not always been successful. The inclusion of a clipper chip in technology is one example of a good security precaution that failed miserably. In 1994, the New York Times reported this about the chipper chip, "The Administration's goal was to make it easier for law enforcement officials to conduct legal wiretaps on new generations of devices that send information over the telephone system, including wireless phones, computers and facsimile machines [8]."

4. Teach Best Practices of SSD Imaging

There is a possibility that the computer forensics community and legal community may have passed a golden age of forensics where it is consistently possible to get an exact forensic image of a solid state drive with MD5 verifiable results. If the manufactures do not disclose how their FTL Flash Translation Layer maps blocks of data from an abstract data structure to real SSD locations on the SSD, and how to cease the garbage collecting of data when performing a forensic image of a SSD, then a "best practices for SSD imaging" may be the best option that the e-forensics profession may obtain. A similar issue has arisen with some mobile devices that also compact space, reduce fragmentation, and do garbage collection. A best practices for SSD e-forensics may be to have a guideline for tampering such that if the possibility of tampering is suggested, the data in question may have to be verified by both parties in litigation.

Bell and Boddington wrote about a series of controlled experiments that measured the amount of data loss with SSDs [9]. The experiment that showed the least spoilage of data occured when the machine was immediately shut down after a destructive process and a Tableau write blocker was installed on the hard drive while it was turned off. The solid state drive was then turned on with the write blocker in place. A forensic investigation showed less than a one percent loss of data. Perhaps the installing on a write blocker on a dead system might be a consideration for a best practice.

5 Soliciting a Solution from the eForensics Student

The e-learner is very often an adult learner with many years of practical experience in law enforcement, the military or private security. He or she may only be in class to provide an audit trail for the knowledge that he or she gained informally in the work world. It would behoove the professor to use webex or another group conferencing technology to solicit a solution to obtaining a consistent verifiable forensic image of the SSD. Skype also has a group feature that allows multi-party VSee is a videoconference program that has had some success in Louisiana and could be considered for a small conference on the subject. It is possible that group discussions over time with various students could lead to a solution.

6 Encouraging the Use of Free or Low-Cost Tools

The e-learner may not always be able to afford many of the pricey eforensics tools that corporate investigators and law enforcement personnel may use. Rather than widen the digital divide, one should always provide an option for e-learners to use tools that can be downloaded and used for free such as Access Data's FTK Imager and some of the early versions of e-fense's Helix as shown in figure 3. Students can get practical experience and learn valuable new concepts by downloading free or low cost tools to practice the forensic imaging of hard drives, SD cards, and SSD drives. The practice may also enhance their confidence in using these tools and help convince a future employer of their abilities while discussing them in a job interview.

Some students have reported that they like using eFense's Helix because it comes on an ISO image that can be downloaded and put on a CD. Then that CD can be put in the CD drive of a simulated suspect's computer. If the bootup order in the BIOS starts with a CD, then the student can bootup without changing the hard drive and then use the 'Live Aquistion' tool to create a forensic image of the hard drive. The source is chosen. The destination drive such as a USB SSD drive can be selected after it is pluged in. Then a student can also name the image file and use a common file extension such as dd. The icon of a camera on the left side of figure three is an easy way for students to get information about the system's hardware and obtain any IP address if it is connected to a network. There is also documentation. Students who are comfortable with a tool can also seek newer versions of software that cost money when they have employment.

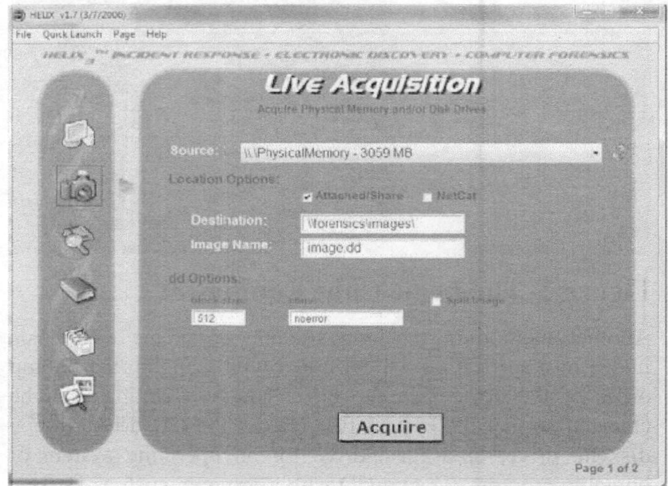

Figure 3- eFense's Helix Version 1.7

7 Conclusion

Magnetic hard disks are well understood and the forensic imaging and examination of these drives has become an established science that is accepted in court cases. The introduction of a new technology known as the solid state drive (SSD) has produced some concerns among digital forensic investigators, students, professors, attorneys, and the legal communities. These sets of heterogeneous devices behave in an unpredictable manner and have some aspects of their operations cloaked in a shroud of secrecy. This makes it difficult to consistently forensically image a solid state drive and get a MD5 hash that matches for both the suspect's drive and the imaged drive. Therefore it may be necessary to get the manufacturers, academics, practitioners, and the legal community together to create a series of best practices or modify the design of the device so that it may be forensically imagined with consistent results and examined easily for use in a digital forensics examination.

8 References

[1]. Doherty, E. P. (2011). Teaching Cell Phone Forensics and E-Learning, 2011 International Conference on e-Learning, e-Business, Enterprise Information Systems, and e-Government (EEE'11: July 18-21, 2011, Las Vegas, Nevada, USA). Conference Proceedings,Pages 161-5, ISBN 1-60132-176-7.

[2]. Solomon, M. G., Barrett, D., and Broom, N. (2005). Computer Forensics Jump Start. Alameda, CA: Sybex Inc. ISBN 0-7821-4375-X. p. 170-171.

[3]. Smith, F. C. and Bace, R. G. (2003). A Guide to Forensic Testimony, The Art and Practice of Presenting Testimony as an Expert Technical Witness. Boston, MA: Pearson Education, Inc. Addison Wesley. ISBN 0-201-75279-4. p. 407.

[4] Silberschatz, A., Galvin, P. B., and Gagne, G. (2003). Operating Systems Concepts, Sixth Edition. New York, NY: John Wiley & Sons, Inc. ISBN 0-471-25060-0. p. 491-536.

[5] Doherty, E. P., Stephenson, G., Liebesfeld, J., and Bruno, K. (2006). EForensics and Signal Intelligence for Everyone. Bloomington, IN: AuthorHouse. ISBN 978-1-4259-6861-8. p. 63-66.

[6] Moultan, S. (uploaded Jan. 24, 2009). Solid State Drives will ruin forensics part 1, 2 and 3. Presentation at Defcon 16. Youtube.com. Retrieved from: http://www.youtube.com/watch?v=WcO7xn0wJ2I&list=PLC337FACBF12BDCE2&index=1

[7] Bell, G. and Boddington, R. (2010). Solid State Drives: The Beginning of the End for Current Practice in Digital Forensic Recovery?. The Journal of Digital Forensics, Security and Law, volume 5, number 3, page 4. Retrieved From: http://www.jdfsl.org/subscriptions/JDFSL-V5N3-Bell.pdf

[8]. Lewis, P. H. (April 24, 1994). Of Privacy and Security: The Clipper Chip Debate. The New York Times, Technology Section. Retrieved from: http://www.nytimes.com/1994/04/24/business/of-privacy-and-security-the-clipper-chip-debate.html?pagewanted=all&src=pm

[9]. Bell, G. and Boddington, R. (2010). Solid State Drives: The Beginning of the End for Current Practice in Digital Forensic Recovery?. The Journal of Digital Forensics, Security and Law, volume 5, number 3, pages 7-12.

A Framework for the Development of Mobile Learning Resource: An Analysis of the Case "Reciting Chinese Ancient Poetry"

Yong Huang[1], **Qingchun Hu**[2]
[1] Shanghai Audio-video Education Center, Shanghai Distance Education Group
[2] School of Information Science & Engineering, East China University of Science and Technology, Shanghai, China

Abstract –*The paper analyzes our study on the project named "Reciting Chinese Ancient Poetry" which is implemented on smart phones and PDAs. It focuses on how to develop and assess effective and high quality mobile learning resource. A framework of the key factors we consider in the development is proposed. Especially, a multi-dimensions assessment approach is highlighted in the whole development process. Based on what we have done, some suggestions are put forward for the future research.*

Keywords: M-Learning Resource; Assessment; User Interface Design

1 Introduction

Mobile devices deeply impact our society currently, changing the way we communicate with another. Today's students have grown up with a new class of technologies that the previous generation might not have imagined, including smart phones and PDAs. Nevertheless, mobile devices are no longer simply a method of communication. They are changing the way we work and our everyday life, According to the Horizon Reports (www.nmc.org/horizon), experts have expected phones to have an impact on education. Some studies have reported that social web and mobile devices are the most important technologies for the near future in education [1].

Many studies on mobile learning (m-learning) have reported that students participating in m-learning can enhance their learning [2-4] .Currently, there it is not enough and high quality learning resource to establish m-learning for students in the outdoor education environment.

What we have done is to develop mobile learning resource to support primary students to learning Chinese Ancient Poetry through mobile devices, such as smart phones and PDAs. Our work is the pilot study and a sub part belongs to the project of "E-Bags". The project of "E-Bags" is organized and funded by Shanghai Municipal Education Commission. The main goal of "E-Bags" is to develop learning resource to support students' learning for K-12 in Shanghai. Currently, the project has launched [5-7]. In our work, one goal is to convert and integrate the existing e-learning resource into m-learning resource.

The major contribution of this study is the introduction of the assessment approaches when developing the m-learning resource. These suggestions and lessons come from our current work, which will contribute to the development of m-learning resource, including PDAs, smart phones for the researchers.

2 Highlighting Assessment Activities in the Development Process

Because m-learning is a relatively new and the m-learning resource is a relatively new pedagogical research field. The m-learning is characterized with not only its electrical and convenient, but also its pedagogical quality. The design, development and implementation of m-learning are very complex process.

There are many things we should to consider. First of all, not all learning contents are suitable for m-learning, how to choose the topics to develop, and what key points we should consider compared with the common education software used in the personal computer.

Currently, although existing e-learning resource is abundance all over the world, not all e-learning resource is suitable for m-learning. Thus, in our development framework, the first stage is to select appropriate topics which are suitable to be implemented in smart phones and PDAs.

Besides the selecting appropriate topics, another attention is how to improve the usability of m-learning resource. Some e-learning resources are "low usability and poor quality".

During the curriculum reform in China since 2005, a lot of educational software has been developed. For instance, in Shanghai, there has been an e-learning resource repository, (http://www.sherc.net/sherc/index/), which is funded and organized by Shanghai Municipal Education Commission. However, in the repository, some e-learning resource is seldom accessed since it was put into the repository. Based on the analysis of the infrequency access towards existing e-learning, we highlight the assessment activities in the whole development process (See Figure 1).

3 The Multi-Dimensions Assessment Approache

We proposed a multi-dimensions assessment approach to assess m-learning resource during the whole process, including pedagogical assessment, technology assessment, user assessment and publication assessment.

A. Pedagogical Assessment

Pedagogical assessment is executed by the pedagogical experts. The main goal is to analysis whether the instructional and learning theory is embedded. Pedagogical experts include teachers, instructional designer from the educational technology field.

B. Technology Assessment

Learning resource can be viewed as a kind of software. Technology assessment is defined from the view of software engineering to assess the software, including Requirements Analysis, Design, Implementation and Testing. We adopt the rapid prototype model. In every stage, technology assessment provides an assessment report before entering into the next stage.

C. User Assessment

User assessment is to assess the software form the usability. The attitude from users is very different from the experts. They view the software from different points, for instance, technologists pay attention to the module in the design, but as user, they don't care whether there is the module.

D. Publication assessment

Because the m-learning resource we developed will be issued with ISBN and used in K-12 school in Shanghai. In our work, the Publication assessment is defined as assessment by the General Administration of Press and Publication (www.gapp.gov.cn/). Based on the analysis of market report, and in order to improve the quality of the publication, three levels of edit assessment systems are carried out, which are abide by the rules of the General Administration of Press and Publication.

All these four dimensions support each other in the whole development process (See Figure 1).

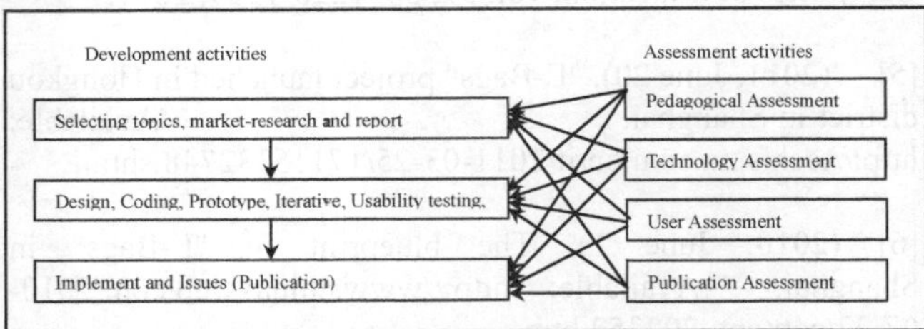

Figure 1. Highlighting assessment activities in the development process

The first stage: Selecting topics, market-research and report. This stage includes the analysis of user, feasibility. According to the users, the learning topic should be selected carefully and the feasibility is discussed and assessed.

The second stage: The rapid prototype development model. The main stage includes Design, Coding, Prototype, Iterative, Usability testing.

The third stage: The Implement and Issues (Publication).

In every stage, we arrange interview and questionnaires by the Multi-dimensions assessment approach.

The main goal of assessment is to improve the quality, the efficiency, the usability of the m-learning resource. In our project, the assessment is embedded in every stage. The main goal is to make the task have been negotiated and accomplished. In some condition, the development could be iterative and to-and-fro for several times. But, no matter how many times it iterates, the next stage launching is based on the previous stages that have been finished completed very well, and a report must be put forwards on every stage.

4 Discussion

A. Multi-dimensions assessment for selecting topics

In our work, Table 1 shows the outline of the rubrics for selecting topics, which is proposed to assess whether the topic is appropriate to be developed. The rubrics for selecting topics have been implemented in practice since last year. And the results show that it can improve the efficiency of the development in our work.

TABLE I. RUBRICS FOR SELECTING TOPICS

Criteria	Contents	Very satisfied---Not satisfied				
		5	4	3	2	1
Pedagogical Assessment	Teaching					
	Learning					
Technology Assessment	Requirements					
	Design					
	Implementation					
	Testing					
User Assessment	Usability					
Publication Assessment	Ideology					
Suggestions/Comments	□Yes □Revise □Re-assess □No □Other					

In 2010, we finished a project name "Excellent courseware for primary students in Shanghai". About 300 courseware were assessed, 72 courseware were selected to be published as CD-Rom. Our current work is based on the previous work to develop the corresponding learning resource for m-learning, including smart phones and PDAs. After the assessment activities base on above rubrics, from the 72 courseware, "Reciting Chinese Ancient Poetry" is selected as the first pilot study, which is used on the smart phones and PDAs.

B. Multi-dimensions assessment for the user interface design

Obviously, on the smart phones and PDAs, the user interface is so limited compared with the personal computer screen we use. Currently, the main stream size of user interface of smart phones is about 2.4 inches to 4 inches, for instance, Motorola, Nokia etc. Some screenshots of the "Reciting Chinese Ancient Poetry" are showed in the Figure 2.

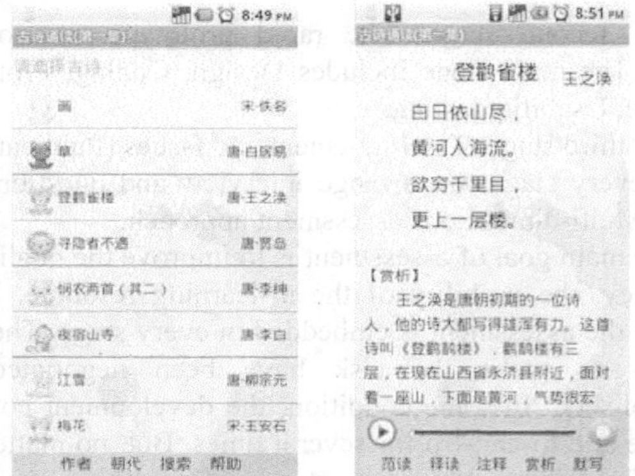

Figure 2. The user interface of the "Reciting Chinese Ancient Poetry"

The assessment for the user interface design is mainly usability evaluation. The usability means how to evaluate the quality of a user interface. The methods for usability evaluation are varied. One widely respected method among specialist is a collection of rules about user interface design. It is a set of heuristics proposed in a paper [8] and further developed in Nielsen's book Usability Engineering [9]. The revised version is Ten Usability Heuristics [10, 11] which are showed below.

(1) Visibility of system status.
(2) Match between system and the real world.
(3) Recognition rather than recall.
(4) Consistency and standards.
(5) User control and freedom.
(6) Flexibility and efficiency of use.
(7) Help users recognize, diagnose, and recover from errors.
(8) Error prevention.
(9) Aesthetic and minimalist design.
(10) Help and documentation

These ten usability heuristics give a guideline to design the detail questionnaires for usability evaluation. Most current usability evaluation questionnaires are derived from the ten usability heuristics [12]. Because of a number of advantages of heuristic evaluation, in our project, the usability heuristics are used to evaluate the design of user interface. The heuristic evaluation checklist is designed based on the ten principles from Nielsen. The goal is to see whether the technology could support students' interaction with the learning contents.

(1) Content: E-learning should not be the e-book, which directly copy from the paper-base textbook. We highlight the user interface for different devices. The font size is the very important element in m-learning, especially used in smart phones and PDAs. In our project, we enlarge row spacing, picture as background based on the analysis of users' questionnaires.

(2) Function: It is not easy for students to tape or write words on the mobile device. It is necessary to reduce the complexity for students to operate. In our design, learners are allowed to own their learning logs and their learning portfolio for them to browse and reflect their study.

5 Conclusion

In our framework of "Reciting Chinese Ancient Poetry", the assessment activities are executed five times, and the prototype is undergone the user assessments for about three months. Now, the fist version "Reciting Chinese Ancient Poetry" has been issued. The Table 2 shows some lessons and suggestions we derived from the Multi-dimensions assessment approach.

TABLE II. LESSONS AND SUGGESTIONS FROM THE MULTI-DIMENSIONS ASSESSMENT APPROACH

Tips	Analysis
Refine the contents	Make a scrutiny into the selected contents. .
Presentation style	Enlarge row spacing, picture as background.
Text, audio and video	Based on the learning requirements analysis, just text and video, no video, because of the type size of video is large.
Animation	Adding animation, such as flash, but no misapplication.

ACKNOWLEDGMENT

This research was supported by Research Innovation Program of Shanghai Municipal Education Commission under Grant No. 09YZ462 and 10YZ209.

6 References

[1] S. Martin, et al., "New technology trends in education: Seven years of forecasts and convergence " Computers & Education, vol. 57, pp.1893-1906 November 2011.

[2] N. Cavusa and H. Uzunboylu, "Improving critical thinking skills in mobile learning," Procedia Social and Behavioral Sciences, vol. 1, pp.434-438, 2009.

[3] T.-S. Chen, et al., "Context-aware writing in ubiquitous learning environments," Research and Practice in Technology Enhanced Learning, vol. 4, pp. 61-82, 2009.

[4] C.-S. Chang, et al., "The study on integrating WebQuest with mobile learning for environmental education " Computers & Education, vol. 57, pp. 1228-1239, 2011.

[5] (2011, June 20). "E-Bags" project launched in Hongkou district in Shanghai. Available: http://tech.sina.com.cn/it/2011-03-25/17115332748.shtml

[6] (2010, June 1). The blueprint of "E-Bags" in Shanghai. Available: http://www.chinaxwcb.com/2010-07/22/content_202352.htm

[7] (2011, June 20). The cooperation of "E-Bags" and Chinatelecom in Shanghai. Available: http://www.chinadaily.com.cn/micro-reading/tech/2011-05-24/content_2698569.html

[8] J. Nielsen and R. Molich, "Heuristic Evaluation of User Interfaces Methodology," in Proceedings of CHI'90 Conference on Human Factors in Computing Systems, 1990.

[9] J. Nielsen, Usability engineering. Boston: AP Professional, 1993.

[10] J. Nielsen, "Heuristic evaluation," in Usability Inspection Methods, J.Nielsen and R. L. Mack, Eds., ed: John Wiley & Sons, New York, NY,1994.

[11] J. Nielsen. (2013, Jan. 23). Heuristic Evaluation. Available:http://www.nngroup.com/topic/heuristic-evaluation/

[12] (2013, Jan. 30) The Usability Toolkit Available : http://www.stcsig.org/usability/resources/toolkit/toolkit.html

Text Analysis of Deliberative Skills in Undergraduate Online Dialogue: Using L1 Regularized Logistic Regression with Psycholinguistic Features

Xiaoxi Xu, Tom Murray and Beverly Park Woolf
School of Computer Science
University of Massachusetts, Amherst, MA
xiaoxi@, tmurray@, bev@cs.umass.edu

Abstract: We report on a text analysis and machine learning study of social deliberative skill using online dialogues on controversial topics from a college class. We report on our comparison between using the LIWC and Coh-Metrix text analysis feature sets, as well as demographic feature information in an L1 Regularized Logistic Regression machine learning algorithm.

Keywords: social deliberative skills, online dialogue and collaboration, machine learning, text classification

Introduction

Leaders, organizations, and nations are increasingly faced with complex issues requiring higher order thinking skills, and in particular what we call "social deliberative skills." King & Baxter [1] note that "in times of increased global interdependence, producing interculturally competent citizens who can engage in informed, ethical decision-making when confronted with problems that involve a diversity of perspectives is becoming an urgent educational priority…these skills; however, 'they are what corporations find in shortest supply among entry-level candidates' [2]." Jordan et al. [3] propose two important skill sets for skillfully addressing "complex societal issues, such as gang-related crime, deteriorating residential areas, environmental problems, long-term youth unemployment, [and] racist violence" (p. 34.) Jordan calls these skill sets "complexity awareness" and "perspective awareness," and they have significant overlap with social deliberative skills.[1] Ill-defined (or "wicked") social problems are defined as: have many interacting factors; have multiple stakeholders with heterogeneous viewpoints; are chronic and, while improvable, are not completely 'solvable' in any decisive sense; and require ongoing flexible attention because conditions evolve over time [3] [4]. Though these characteristics are used to describe intransigent social problems, they define many mundane situations as well. Parenting, perusing a career, maintaining intimate relationships, planning and managing a project, and "composing a life" in such a way as to balance one's many needs and constraints—these all present one with mini wicked problems on a regular basis. They require complexity awareness and perspective awareness to address the mental and moral demands of modern life [5]. It is important that we support the development of these skills in the educational systems.

Our overall research goals are to better *understand, assess, and support* SD-skills in online contexts. A prerequisite to researching how to support SD-skills is being able to *measure*, identify or assess them. This paper describes an aspect of our ongoing attempts to assess SD-skills using linguistic models. As part of our work investigating online support of SD-skills we have developed a hand-coding scheme for categorizing segments of online text. It has been used to evaluate software features in college classes, with encouraging results [6]. In parallel we are using text classification tools and machine learning to develop automated methods to categorize text to ascertain SD-skills and related indicators of deliberative dialogue quality, which we report on here. We are using automated assessment of SD-skills for two purposes: (1) to assess skill differences and correlations in our evaluative research [7] [8] [9], and (2) to display facets of

[1] According to Jordan: "Complexity awareness [is] a person's propensity to notice…that phenomena are compounded and variable, depend on varying conditions, are results of causal processes that may be…multivariate and systemic, and are embedded in processes [that involve non-simple information feedback loops]…If a person does not notice the complexity in which an issue is embedded, he or she will fail to consider many conditions, causes and consequences that may be significant for managing the issue (Kuhn, 1991)…Perspective awareness [is] the propensity to notice and operate with properties of one's own and others' perspectives" (Jordan, 2013, p. 41, italics added).

social deliberative skill in a Facilitators Dashboard that gives facilitators and teachers a birds-eye view of important deliberative properties of an online conversation [6].

We focus on the following social deliberative skills or capacities, which are seen repeatedly in the literature (described using a variety of terms):

- Social perspective taking (includes cognitive empathy, reciprocal role taking);
- Social perspective seeking (includes social inquiry, question asking skills);
- Social perspective monitoring (includes self-reflection, meta-dialogue); and
- Social perspective weighing (related to "reflective reasoning" and includes comparing and contrasting the available views, including those of participants and external sources and experts).

Capacities implied in the above include: tolerance for uncertainty, ambiguity, disagreement, paradox, and the ability to take first, second, and third-person perspectives on situations or issues (i.e. subjective, intersubjective (you/we/they), and objective).

Here we describe a continuation of prior work using the text analysis systems LIWC and Coh-Metrix to generate features for machine learning methods to assess SD-skills. In this paper we apply our methods to a new domain and add demographic data (gender and grade level) to the machine learning trials to assess the relative effectiveness of various methods in producing the most accurate machine learning model.

Background and Related Work

Automatic text analysis (including a wide variety of computational methods: supervised learning, latent semantic analysis, topic modeling, etc.) has been used successfully for a wide variety of purposes in educational contexts, including to: grade essays [10] [11], analyze content for conceptual understanding [12] [13], discover topics or themes , score text sophistication, writing quality, and reading grade level [14], detect off-topic behavior, assess learning styles [16], and score argumentative and question-answering quality [17] [18] [19] [20], identify dialogic moves and patterns, identify tutorial behaviors [21] [22]. As far as we know, we are the only ones researching text analysis to assess social deliberative skills such as perspective taking and meta-dialogue in educational contexts or in human dialogues of any sort. There has been related work in non-educational and non-dialogical contexts to identify psycho-linguistic and socio-linguistic phenomena such as emotional states and sentiment [21] [22], personality traits; and even to predict health improvement based on essay writing [23]. Text analysis methods have been used to classify speech acts (including dialogue moves, tutorial acts, argument moves, etc.). For example, Rosé et al. [17] achieved 53% accuracy on classifying "epistemic activity," 61% accuracy for "social modes of co-construction."

Our work uses the output of sophisticated text analysis systems (LIWC and Coh-Metrix) as feature inputs for machine learning algorithms. LIWC (Linguistic Inquiry Word Count, [23]) is a well researched but "shallow" dictionary-matching text categorization system yielding about 80 linguistic categories (e.g. positive emotion words, pronouns, and causation words). Coh-Metrix [22] [24] performs a series of deep-processing analysis (including semantic cohesion, latent semantic analysis, and reading complexity level) yielding about 100 metrics. A simplistic view of these systems is the LIWC categorizes speech acts based on *what* participants are saying, and Coh-Metrix produces measurements related to *how* participants are speaking. LIWC features are derived across topic domains and from people from all walks of life; Coh-Metrix features are generated across text genres from a wide spectrum of disciplines. Though LIWC's dictionary-matching method is simple (like keyword-matching), hundreds of studies have been done using it (and contributed to its development) so many of the categories it uses are well researched in terms of how use of these linguistic categories correlate with important psychological or social phenomena. LIWC and Coh-Metrix measurements are ideal for this study, where the discourse data comes from participants across a variety of topic domains and online contexts. Both LIWC and Coh-Metrix features have been shown to be valid and reliable markers of a variety of psycholinguistic phenomena.

In prior studies [9] we used text analysis in conjunction with multi-class machine learning methods to build models for individual deliberative skills. This proved to be challenging for the methods available to us at the time, and we shifted to the more tractable task of building models for a total or composite deliberative skill measure that was the aggregate of the individual sub-skills (later to return to individual skill modeling). A series of experiments, reported in several papers, refined our ability to automatically assess deliberative skill across multiple domains of online engagement. These experiments were conducted with a data corpus consisting of online interactions from three domains. Participant posts were first partitioned into segments if the type of speech act changed within a post (usually there were 1-4 segments per post). The domains were: an online civic engagement dialog (32 participants with 396 segments of text), two faculty communities engaged in logistical decision making (16 participants and 438 text segments), and, the largest set, college classroom online discussions of controversial topics (90 participants and 1783 text segments). Training was done based on human-rated assessment of deliberative skill, using a coding scheme that had shown inter-rater Cohen's Kappa statistics of 71% on average across the domains (average percent agreement of 76%), which is quite good for a scheme of its complexity [25].[2] Ten-fold cross validation over the data set was used in all cases.

Early work compared various machine learning methods including Naïve Bayes, Support Vector Machine, Topic Modeling, and Regularize Logistic Regression methods (experimenting with a number of parameters within each). We found L1 Regularized Logistic Regression to be the preferred model (though we continued to include comparison with other models though subsequent experiments to validate this finding). Next we compared the success of various feature sets including bag-of-words, LIWC, Coh-Metrix, and combinations of these. We found that using text analysis (LIWC or Coh-Metrix) outperformed bag-of-words methods, that LIWC features usually outperformed the Coh-Metrix features, and that combining these feature sets lead to worse performance that using them individually. Finally, we did cross-domain studies showing that superior models resulted from using certain domains as the training set [26]. Specifically, the model developed using the faculty community showed better performance on all three domains than either drawing training data from the entire corpus or drawing the training sample from the domain to be tested. It appears that this is because the faculty domain had the most balanced (least skewed) data, i.e. there was a sufficiently large percentage of text segments tagged as deliberative skills vs. others (about half).

We continue our research in the study reported here by: (1) applying methods developed previously to a new set of classroom online dialogue data and (2) adding demographic information, gender and grade level, to the models feature set. In this study we extend out prior research on building machine learning models to predict an aggregate (total) social deliberative skill measure.

Method

Data set. Twenty six students in a college Alternative Dispute Mediation class discussed two topics (the Trayvon Martin killing in Florida and Gun Control, one each week over two weeks) in using the Mediem deep dialogue discussion software. Students were randomly broken into three discussion groups of 8-9 members each, with all groups discussing these topics. There were 8 males and 14 females ranging in undergraduate grade level from sophomores to seniors, with one non-degree student. Each of the three groups used a different set of software features based on our protocol for an experimental study of the effects of tools to support social deliberative skills. In Murray et. al. [6] we discuss our findings that "reflective tools" showed a significant effect size in deliberative skills as measured by human coding, but for this paper we ignore the grouping of students as we are only interested in trying to model the human rating of total deliberative skill using computational methods. The data set consisting of 829 text segments from 369 posts. 43% of the segments were coded under the "deliberate skill" meta-category (vs. 57% "other").

Machine learning method. In this study, we used our highest performing machine learning method, L_1 regularized logistic regression (L_1RLR) [27] to model social deliberative behavior and predict its occurrences. L_1RLR is also preferred in this research because it not only works well with high dimension feature space and small data sets, but also is able to automatically select features and learn an easy-to-interpret (transparent) model. Being able to automatically select features mitigates the problem that little precedent research exists in this new area that is suggestive of features predictive of social deliberative behavior. Being able to yield an interpretable model presents fewer challenges for researchers in social science and communication science to understand the efficacy of a computational model for social deliberative behavior.

Before we describe L_1RLR, let us recall that the logistic loss function is defined as:

$$p(y|x; W) = \frac{1}{1+\exp(-\mathbf{W}^T x)}$$

[2] Our coding scheme has 42 categories, 17 of which indicate deliberative skills.

where x is the training data, y is the response variable, and W is the model we learn.

In regularized logistic regression, we solve the following optimization problem:

$$\underset{\mathbf{W}}{\mathrm{argmax}} \sum_i \log(p(y_i|x_i; \mathbf{W}) - \lambda * \Omega(\mathbf{W})$$

where Ω(W) is a regularization term used to penalize large weights.

In the case of L_1 regularized logistic regression, L_1 norm [27], or least absolute shrinkage and selection operator (Lasso) is used to induce the penalty. Previous research [28] has shown that L_1 regularization logistic regression requires the number of training examples that grows logarithmically with the number of features to learn well, which favors this study.

In our experiments, we used the l_1 regularized dual averaging algorithm [29] for solving l_1RLR. We trained l_1RLR (i.e., λ=1, γ=2) with various feature sets and carried out 10-fold stratified cross-validation.

Results and Discussion

We performed a set of experiments by exploring the effectiveness of different types of features on predictive accuracy, precision, recall, and F_2 measure (the harmonic mean of precision and recall that weights recall twice as high as precision). In Table 1, we report the average performance across cross-validation runs.

	LIWC features	Coh-Metrix features	LIWC+gender+gradLevel features
Accuracy	61.41	60.68	60.81
Precision	54.30	54.31	53.78
Recall	68.52	57.94	67.41
F_2 measure	65.11	57.18	64.16

Table 1: Predictive performance (in %) of L1 regularized logistic regression built using different type of features

Predictive performance and feature comparisons. As can be seen in Table 1, with computational models, we are able to predict social deliberative behavior with up to 61% accuracy, 54% precision, 68% recall, and 65% F_2 measure. LIWC features outperformed Coh-Metrix features by a slight margin overall, which confirms earlier findings (we did not model using combined LIWC and Coh-Metrix features as prior work suggested this would not help [26]). Surprisingly, adding the demographic information of gender and grade level as machine learning inputs did not improve performance (it degraded it slightly).[3] This suggests that variations due to grade and gender are already encoded in the text analysis features (of both LIWC and Coh-Metrix)—a hypothesis we will pursue in further research.

The performance of the L1-RLR on this data set outperformed the models reported en earlier studies of classroom data. In general, prior studies of multi-domains showed that prediction in the classroom domain was worse than in the other domains (civic engagement and faculty logistical decision-making). More specifically, the results reported here improved over previous results of classroom domains by 8% on precision and 64% on recall. We believe that this is mostly due to the newer data set having less data skew (43% deliberative skill on this set vs. 32% on the prior classroom data set). We are looking into methods to compensate for data skew, including training our models on the most robust data sets as opposed to the testing data sets [26].

In a larger sense, the results suggest that it may be feasible to train machine learning models to automatically analyze conversations in online communication to identify high-order communication skills such as social deliberative behavior.

Parameters in the learned model. As mentioned, one of the benefits of using L1-RLR is that the relative importance or weights of each feature can be inspected (they are related to the coefficients of the regression

[3] Indeed, when examining the learned feature space, we found that both gender and grade level features were shrunk by the L_1RLR model. In other words, both features were assigned zero weights in the final model.

model). The L_1 regularized logistic regression learned a model with 27 features in this domain. In other words, 55 out of the 82 LIWC features were shrunk by L_1RLR (which automatically prunes features, another advantage vs. other machine learning methods). In Table 2, we show the top 10 most salient features of the learned model. The rest of the 17 features have absolute feature weights less than 0.01 and are commented below.[4]

LIWC feature	Interpretation	Weight
assent	assent	0.335
WC	word counts	0.223
social	social processes	-0.051
Dic	dictionary words	-0.045
i	1st pers singular	0.028
funt	total function words	-0.024
posemo	positive emotion	0.023
AllPct	total punctuations	0.023
affect	affective processes	0.023
period	punctuation	0.022

Table 2: Top 10 LIWC features learnt by L1 regularized logistic regression

Next we summarize the characteristics of social deliberative behavior in the language of LIWC features. LIWC was not designed to measure deliberative skill or any sort of dialogue-quality related speech act categories, and predictive relationships between its categories and deliberative skill are expected to be secondary (i.e. resulting from more clearly relevant intermediate factors). Compared to "other speech acts", social deliberative behavior has: more assent words, longer messages, more 1st person pronouns, more positive emotions, more total punctuations, more affective processes, more certain words, more pronouns (i.e., personal pronouns and impersonal pronouns), more cognitive process, more auxiliary verbs, fewer social processes, fewer dictionary words, fewer functional words, fewer relative words, fewer words per sentence, fewer prepositions, fewer big words, fewer dashes, fewer words about time, fewer commas, fewer space words, fewer present tense, and fewer articles.

Assent-words (31 word stems including absolutely, agree, alright*, haha*, ok, yes, yup…) and the segment word count (WC) were by far the largest factors in this model. Pennebaker & King [30] say the following about assent and word count. Higher word count is related to better group performance. Lots of assents and questions stimulate better team performance. "Later in a group task, assents may signal consensus, early assents may indicate blind agreement by unmotivated group members" [31, p 33]; and "in a cooperative coordination context, higher total word count may signal better communication and agreement, whereas in a negotiation context it may signal a breakdown in agreement." (p. 35). Our related analysis of the faculty dialog also showed that word count was highly related to human assessment of deliberative skill, but, curiously assent was not so related [26]. Further work is ongoing to determining the domain-dependent aspects of deliberative behaviors.

Discussion and Conclusions

We have seen encouraging results in our attempts to model an aggregate classification for total social deliberative skill in a number of online deliberation domains, including in college classroom discussions. We believe that we will be able to improve the accuracy and recall values of the model substantially with additional research. We will continue to do research on modeling individual deliberative sub-skills and dialogue quality indicators, though it is not clear yet whether we will be successful with many of these (some, such as "appreciation", are not as difficult).

In future studies, we will perform similar tests on more domains and in various online contexts (e.g., collaborative problem-solving, negotiation, and disputation) to study the role that demographic features (e.g., gender, age, race) play in predicting social deliberative behavior.

---

[4] Note, the absolute value of the weights is meaningless and dependent on tuning parameters of the algorithm, and in general are not comparable from one model to the next. Only the relative sizes of the weights within a model are meaningful.

One of the most exciting applications of this work has been in the design and evaluation of a Facilitators Dashboard that shows a birds-eye view of certain dialogue parameters [6]. See Figure 1. We have begun to visualize some of the text analysis in this tool. Early comments from instructors and professional facilitators and mediators indicate that such analysis will be very useful for their work.

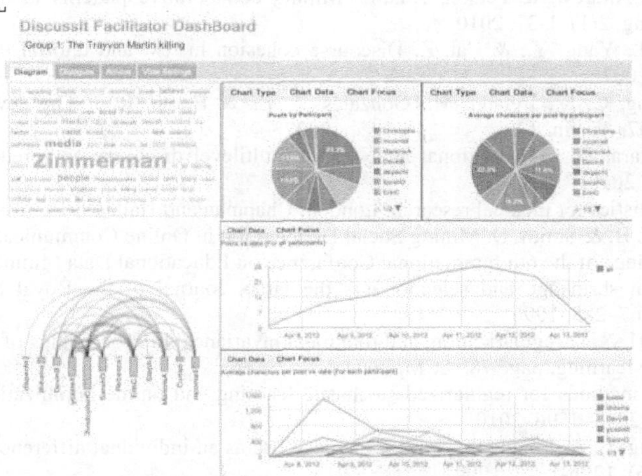

Figure 1. Facilitators Dashboard

References

[1] King, P. M. & Baxter Magolda, M. A developmental model of intercultural maturity. Journal of College Student Development, 46 (6), 571-592, 2005

[2] Bikson, T. K., & Law, S. A. Global preparedness and human resources. Rand Corporation, 1994.

[3] Jordan, T., Andersson, P. & Ringnér, H. The Spectrum of Responses to Complex Societal Issues: Reflections on Seven Years of Empirical Inquiry. Integral Review, February 2013, Vol. 9, No. 1, 2013

[4] Conklin, J. Wicked Problems & Social Complexity. Chapter 1 of Dialogue Mapping: Building Shared Understanding of Wicked Problems, Wiley, 2005

[5] Kegan, R. In over our heads: The mental demands of modern life. Cambridge, MA: Harvard University Press, 1994

[6] Murray, T., Wing, L., Woolf, B., Wise, A., Wu, S., Clark, L., Osterweil, L., Xu, X. A Prototype Facilitators Dashboard: Assessing and visualizing dialogue quality in online deliberations for education and work. International Conference on e-Learning, e-Business, Enterprise Information Systems, and e-Government, EEE-2013.

[7] Murray, T., Woolf, B., Xu, X., Shipe, S., Howard, S. & Wing, L. "Towards Supporting Social Deliberative Skills in Online Group Dialogues." Presented at The 7th Annual Interdisciplinary Network for Group Research Conference (InGroup). Chicago July 12-14, 2012.

[8] Murray, T., Stephens, A.L., Woolf, B.P., Wing, L., Xu, X., & Shrikant, N. Supporting Social Deliberative Skills Online: the Effects of Reflective Scaffolding Tools. Proceedings of HCI International 2013, July, 2013, Las Vegas, 2013

[9] Murray, T., Xu, X. & Woolf, P.B. An Exploration of Text Analysis Methods to Identify Social Deliberative Skills, In Proceedings of the 16th International Conference on Artificial Intelligence in Education (AIED), 2013

[10] Shermis, M. & J. Burstein (Eds.) Automated essay scoring: A cross-disciplinary perspective. Hillsdale, NJ: Erlbaum, 2003

[11] Dikli S. An overview of automated scoring of essays. The Journal of Technology, Learning and Assessment, 5(1), 2006

[12] Lintean, M., Rus, V., & Azevedo, R. Automatic Detection of Student Mental Models Based on Natural Language Student Input During Metacognitive Skill Training. International Journal of Artificial Intelligence in Education, 21(3), 169-190, 2011

[13] Azevedo, R., Guthrie, J.T., & Seibert, DThe role of self-regulated learning in fostering students' conceptual understanding of complex systems with hypermedia. Journal of Educational Computing Research, 30 (1), 87-111, 2004

[14] McNamara, D. S., Crossley, S. A., & McCarthy, P. M. Linguistic features of writing quality. Written Communication, 27(1), 57-86, 2010

[16] Ozpolat, E., & Akar, G.B. Automatic detection of learning styles for an e-learning system. Computers & Education, 53(2), 355-367, 2009

[17] Rosé, C., Wang, Y. C., Cui, Y., Arguello, J., Stegmann, K., Weinberger, A., & Fischer, F. (2008). Analyzing collaborative learning processes automatically: Exploiting the advances of computational linguistics in computer-supported collaborative learning. International journal of computer-supported collaborative learning, 3(3), 237-271.

[18] Kim, J., and Shaw, E. Pedagogical Discourse: Connecting students to past discussions and peer mentors within an online

discussion board, Innovative Applications of Artificial Intelligence, IAAAI 09, 2009

[19] Ravi, S., Kim, J. Profiling student interactions in threaded discussions with speech act classifiers. IOS Press, 2007

[20] Rus, V., Cai, Z., & Graesser, A. C. Evaluation in natural language generation: The question generation task. In Proceedings of the Workshop on Shared Tasks and Comparative Evaluation in Natural Language Generation (pp. 20-21), 2007

[21] D'Mello, Sidney, Olney, Andrew, & Person, Natalie. Mining collaborative patterns in tutorial dialogues. Journal of Educational Data Mining, 2(1), 1-37, 2010

[22] Graesser, A. C., Jeon, M., Yang, Y., & Cai, Z. Discourse cohesion in text and tutorial dialogue. Information Design Journal, 15, 199–213, 2007

[23] Pennebaker, J. W., Chung, C. K., Ireland, M., Gonzales, A. L., & Booth, R. J. The development and psychometric properties of LIWC2007. Austin, TX: www.LIWC.net, 2007

[24] Graesser, A., & McNamara, D. Computational analyses of multilevel discourse comprehension. Topics in Cognitive Science 3(2), 371–398. 2010.

[25] Altman, DG, Practical statistics for medical research. London: Chapman and Hall, 1991

[26] Xu, X., Murray, T. Woolf, B. & Smith, D. Mining Social Deliberation in Online Communication -- If You Were Me and I Were You , In Proceedings of the 6th International Conference on Educational Data Mining (EDM), 2013

[27] Tibshirani, R. Regression shrinkage and selection via the lasso. Journal of the Royal Statistical Society. Series B (Methodological) pp. 267–288, 1996

[28] Ng, A. Feature selection, l1 vs. l2 regularization, and rotational invariance. In Proceedings of the twenty-first international conference on Machine learning, page 78. ACM, 2004

[29] Xiao, L. Dual averaging methods for regularized stochastic learning and online optimization. The Journal of Machine Learning Research, 11:2543–2596, 2010

[30] Pennebaker, J. W., & King, L. A. Linguistic styles: Language use as an individual difference. Journal of personality and social psychology, 77(6), 1296-1312, 1999.

[31] Tausczik, Y. R. & Pennebaker, J. W. The psychological meaning of words: LIWC and computerized text analysis methods. Journal of Language and Social Psychology, 2010.

ByTE – A Flexible Binary Tree Editor

A. Chan[1]

[1]Dept. of Math. and Computer Science, Fayetteville State University, Fayetteville, North Carolina, USA

Abstract - *We describe the development of ByTE, a flexible Binary Tree Editor that is aimed at academic usage. The software allows easy incorporation of the created trees into other documents, and hence is beneficial to instructors for preparing presentation material. The files created by the software are saved as text files in XML format, allowing instructors to perform automated grading and/or manual inspection/modification of the trees. The software will be released free for non-profit use.*

Keywords: Online learning; Binary tree; Data structures; Algorithms, Online tools; Software application.

1 Introduction

In this article, we describe the development of ByTE, a flexible Binary Tree Editor. Binary trees are important data structures in computer science education, especially in data structures and algorithms courses. They also occur in higher-level courses and can be used to implement many other high-level algorithms such as AVL trees, red-black trees, etc. It is important that students understand how binary trees operate in order to master the course material. There are many software packages available on the Internet. These software packages allow the users to create/manipulate/experiment with binary trees. However, many of these software packages are written as course projects and/or for demonstrating the operations of certain specialized data structures implemented with binary trees, and therefore have limitations that hinder their usages as academic tools. Furthermore, many of these software packages are written as Java applets [3] that operate directly inside the Internet browsers and have no access to the local file systems (and consequently, will not allow the users to save/load work to/from files). We were looking for tools that could create binary trees with (almost) no restrictions and allow easy incorporation of the created trees into presentation for class use. Unfortunately, we could not find any existing software package that fit our requirements. Therefore, we decided to create our own software.

The structure of this article is as follows. We review some of the existing and related work in Section 2. In Section 3, we list some of the driving requirements of ByTE. Section 4 discusses the design and implementation of ByTE. We discuss how ByTE is packaged and distributed in Section 5; and Section 6 concludes our discussion.

2 Related Work

There are many interactive binary trees builders available on the Internet; most of them appear in the form of Java applets; and many of them are designed for specialized binary trees.

Gustafson and Kjensli [6] have created a Java applet named Binary Treesome. This applet started as a course project. In addition to normal binary trees, the applet can handle specialized binary trees, including binary search trees and AVL trees. The applet restricts the labels in the nodes to be non-duplicated integers between 1 and 99 inclusive, and it allows binary trees of up to a height of 7. The applet automatically adjusts the width between nodes. However, when the tree becomes too wide for the applet window, part of the tree will run off the applet window and some of the nodes become inaccessible. We note that the limitation on node labels gives a natural restriction on the size of the trees created (that is, 99 nodes at most).

On his web page, Kloss hosts an animated binary tree applet [10]. Like the Binary Treesome applet, it restricts the labels in the nodes to be non-duplicated integers between 1 and 99 inclusive, and the binary trees will be configured into binary search trees automatically. There seems to be no limit on the height of the trees. However, when the tree becomes too large, part of the tree will run off the applet window and that part of the tree will be inaccessible to users.

Ierardi hosts on his web page another animated binary search tree applet [9]. In this applet, the users have no control over the labels of the nodes. The node labels are assigned automatically and are not visible to the users. There seems to be no limit on the height of the trees, and the applet makes an effort to keep all nodes inside the applet window. However, when the tree becomes too large, nodes start to overlap each other and become indistinguishable to the users.

Gogeshvili created an applet that is very similar (in functionality) to the Binary Treesome applet mentioned above [7]. In addition to binary search trees and AVL trees, it also supports red-black trees and splay trees, but it seems that there is no support for vanilla plain binary trees. Like the Binary Treesome applet, node labels are restricted to be non-duplicated integers between 1 and 99 inclusive. However, there seems to be no limit on the height of the trees, and when the tree becomes too large for the applet window, controls are available to adjust the spacing of the nodes to make the tree fit inside the applet windows (with the possibility of overlapping nodes).

Kováè's applet is a little different. It supports many data structures that can be used to implement search trees [12][13]. Supported data structures include the binary search trees, AVL trees, B trees, red-black trees, AA trees, skiplists, maximum heaps, minimum heaps, treaps, scapegoat trees, and splay trees. Like almost all other applets discussed, it restricts labels to be non-negative integers less than 100, but it also allows the numeral zero to be a label. Also like almost all other applets, once the tree becomes too large for the applet window, part of the tree will run off the window and become inaccessible. A more interesting feature is that the applet provides statistical data so the user can see how efficient a particular data structure is on implementing the search trees.

Baker et al. implemented a data structure visualizer and tester [1]. This visualizer/tester is intended to be used with the textbook by Goodrich [8]. It supports binary trees as one of the many data structures it can visualize and test. The package is designed based on abstract data types (ADT) and hence requires the users to have a good understanding in the programming details about the data structures they want to deal with.

3 Software Requirement

The reasons that we developed ByTE were twofold. First, students need a convenient way to create binary trees for electronic assignment submission. The binary trees created must not have any restrictions (other than the basic requirement that they must be binary trees) so that students are allowed to make mistakes. Second, faculty members need to be able to create visually attractive binary trees for presentation.

The following lists some of the requirements [17] we have developed for ByTE:

- The binary tree created by ByTE can be of any size. If the binary tree is too large to fit inside the window, scroll bars will be provided.
- The users can put any label (up to a reasonable length) on a tree node.
- The labels can consist of any printable characters supported by the operating system.
- The users can easily append new nodes to an existing tree.
- The users can easily remove an existing node when the deletion is possible.
- The layout will be adjusted automatically to avoid clustering.
- The users can zoom in and out.
- The users can load and save the binary tree from and to a file.
- There will be safeguards to prevent accidentally closing the software without saving the work in a file.
- The users can save the binary tree as an image.
- The users can print the binary tree to any printer supported by the operating system and take advantage of the high print quality of modern printers.
- The users can capture the binary tree as an image onto the system clipboard (so that it can be pasted into other applications such as PowerPoint presentations and Word documents).
- The users can change the interface to their own native languages (if supported).

4 Design and Implementation

4.1 Definition of Binary Trees

We define the binary tree based on Goodrich [8]. A binary tree is a set of nodes connected by edges. The edges define a parent-child relationship among nodes. Each node can be a parent and have zero to two children. All but one node in the tree has a single parent. The only node that has no parent is a special node designated as the root of the tree and placed at the top of the tree. The tree is traditionally drawn in a way such that parents appear above their children. Figure 1 shows a typical binary tree.

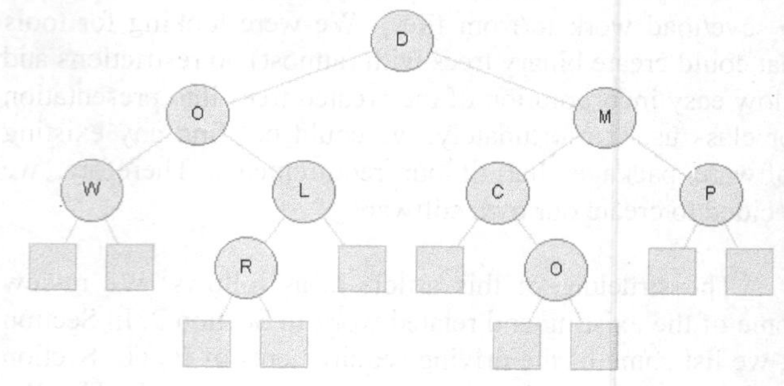

Figure 1. A typical binary tree

The binary trees, as defined by Goodrich, are proper binary trees; that is, each node has either no child (an external node) or two children (an internal node). Nodes with only a single child are NOT allowed. The advantage of using a proper binary tree is that the manipulation of tree nodes is much simpler. For example, since we do not have single-child nodes, we do not have to worry whether a single node is a left child or a right child. This is important since most definitions of binary trees insist on maintaining order within the children. A more important benefit of using proper binary trees is that it becomes easier to identify removable nodes. As Goodrich pointed out, a node is removable if and only if it is an internal node and it has at least one external child. If an internal node has both children being internal, it cannot be removed without some complicated (and sometimes ambiguous) manipulation. External nodes are clearly non-removable since the removal of an external node creates a non-proper binary tree.

Although data can be put in external nodes, we suggest not doing so, as recommended by Goodrich. In this way, the trees created can easily be converted to those used in other textbooks that allow internal nodes to have a single child (for example, see [14]). All we have to do is to enable the users to hide the external nodes. The external nodes, when hidden, will still be visible on screen; they are only grayed out. This is necessary since, as described later, some of the operations depend on the accessibility of the external nodes. However, the external nodes, when hidden, will not show up in the printout or in the captured image, nor in the saved image file. We note that data assigned in hidden external nodes (if existed) will not be captured in the saved-as image, copied-to-clipboard image, or printer output.

4.2 Tree Manipulation

The binary trees, as defined here, can never be empty. Therefore, we always generate an external node automatically in a newly created tree, as shown in Figure 2.

Figure 2. A newly created binary tree

We define several operations to manipulate the tree. Clicking a node will select the node, with the effect that the node will be outlined in red color (when a hidden external node is selected, it is outlined in black color). Double clicking an external node or pressing CTRL-E when an external node is selected will convert it into an internal node – by appending two external nodes as its children. This is done by applying an "expand external" operation as described in Goodrich.

Double clicking an internal node or pressing CTRL-D when an internal node is selected allows the users to enter and/or modify the label associated with the internal node. The label will always be centered in the node. The spaces in an internal node can accommodate approximately 5 to 6 English characters without going outside the node boundary. The same also applies to external nodes, with the exception that double-clicking an external node is reserved for expanding the node; and the spaces in an external node can accommodate 3 to 4 characters.

Finally, selecting an internal node with at least one external child will allow the user to delete the node by pressing the DELETE key. This corresponds to the "remove above external" operation in Goodrich.

All of these operations (and most that will be discussed) can also be carried out by using menu selection, tool bar icons, and/or the context-sensitive menu.

4.3 Tree Layout

The binary tree is laid out in the application window using a simple algorithm. First, all external nodes are placed in a rectangular grid. The way these external nodes are placed ensures no two external nodes are put in the same vertical grid (that is, each external node will have a distinct x-coordinate value), while the depth of the external node determines its horizontal grid (the y-coordinate value). Once the external nodes are in place, the locations for internal nodes can easily be determined. All parents are positioned one level above their children, while their x-coordinate value is calculated to be the average of their children. This ensures the appearance of the tree to be neither too crowded nor too sparse.

The tree edges are drawn from the center of the children to the center of their corresponding parent. However, edges are always drawn first so that the nodes can cover the supposedly invisible portion of the edges.

In general, the nodes are drawn in a bottom up order, from external nodes, propagating up to the root (that is, the root is the last node to be drawn). This will ensure that the tree will be drawn nicely, with proper spacing between nodes. We note that the tree is redrawn completely whenever a change is made to the tree or when the user performs any action that will affect the appearance of the tree (e.g. selecting a different node and/or choosing to show or hide external nodes). Figure 3 shows a typical binary tree. Figure 4 shows the same tree with all external nodes "hidden".

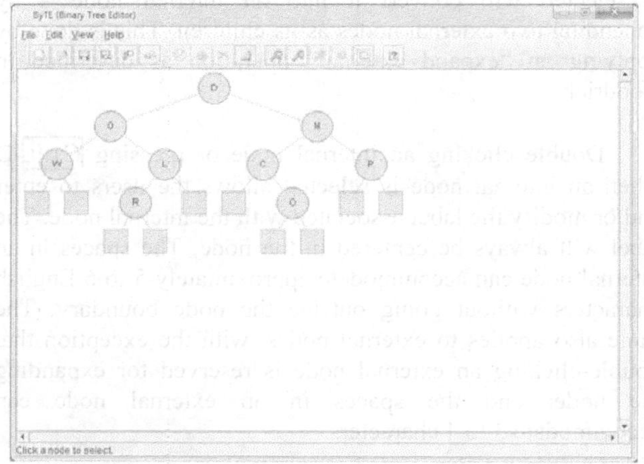

Figure 3. A binary tree in ByTE

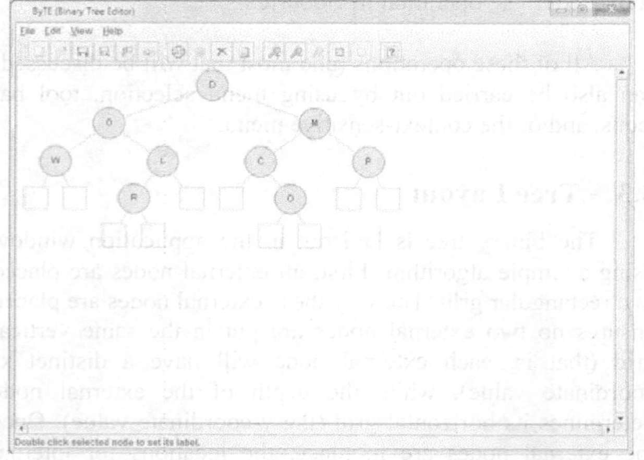

Figure 4. The example tree with external nodes "hidden"

4.4 File Operations

The software supports 4 file operations. The users can open an existing tree file; they can save the loaded tree back into the same file; they can save the loaded tree (or a newly created tree) into a file with a different name; or they can save the tree as an image file in a PNG (Portable Network Graphics) format. We note that if the tree has been saved as an image, it becomes impossible to load the tree back from the image file; however, it is always possible to reload the tree from the saved tree file. Also, when the tree is saved as an image, external nodes will not show if they are set to be hidden.

ByTE is implemented in Java. Java has native supports for at least 3 graphics formats: GIF, JPG, and PNG [3]. We choose PNG as the only supported format for several reasons: PNG is an open format [16] (GIF is proprietary) and it supports lossless compression (JPG is lossy). Although PNG does not support animation, this feature is not required for our purpose. Also, PNG is supported by almost all major productivity software. Finally, if the users wish, they can easily convert the PNG images to other formats (there are numerous free or commercial tools for this task). The image is saved using screen resolution.

On loading and saving the tree from and to a file, our first approach is to use Java's native support for object serialization. Object serialization is easy to use, but it also has several limitations. The files created by object serialization are binary files. It will be difficult for human users to inspect the file, not to mention to modify the file (when necessary). A more serious problem is that Java's development team has explicitly claimed that there will be no guarantee that the file created by object serialization with one version of JRE (Java Runtime Environment) will be recognizable by another version of JRE; and the serialization will change if the class definition changes. This will make long-term support very difficult, if not impossible.

To avoid the problems associated with object serialization, we developed a simple XML schema to represent the trees. Now, the trees are saved as text files and can be inspected by human users. If necessary, the users can also make minor changes using any text editor. Instructors can even write simple scripts to compare trees and hence enabling automatic grading of student assignments. Figure 5 shows the tree file produced by the sample tree in Figure 1.

4.5 Interaction with the Operating System

Other than the file operations, the software still has several mechanisms to interact with the operating system.

Printing is an important feature for software applications that are aimed at academic usage. Students may need to print a draft of their work for studies, discussion, or continuation of the work. If required, the printing feature will produce a neat output for submission purpose. The printing will use vector graphics provided by Java2D [11] in order to produce high quality graphics on the printed paper. If necessary, the tree will be scaled to fit on one page. This does not work well for very large trees, but the situation may not be applicable in the academic environment.

In our opinion, a more important feature is to allow the users to copy the tree onto the system clipboard. The users will then be able to paste the copied tree into other applications such as Word documents or PowerPoint presentations. The tree is copied on the system clipboard as a bitmap image.

```
<?xml version="1.0" encoding="UTF-
8"?>
<tree version="1.0">
    <internal>
        <data>D</data>
        <internal>
            <data>O</data>
            <internal>
                <data>W</data>
                <external/>
                <external/>
            </internal>
            <internal>
                <data>L</data>
                <internal>
                    <data>R</data>
                    <external/>
                    <external/>
                </internal>
                <external/>
            </internal>
        </internal>
        <internal>
            <data>M</data>
            <internal>
                <data>C</data>
                <external/>
                <internal>
                    <data>O</data>
                    <external/>
                    <external/>
                </internal>
            </internal>
            <internal>
                <data>P</data>
                <external/>
                <external/>
            </internal>
        </internal>
    </internal>
</tree>
```

Figure 5. XML file created by ByTE

Like the "Save As Image" feature mentioned before, both the printing and the copy-to-clipboard features will not print or copy the external nodes if they are set to be hidden. Figure 6 shows a copied image of the sample tree we have been using throughout the article.

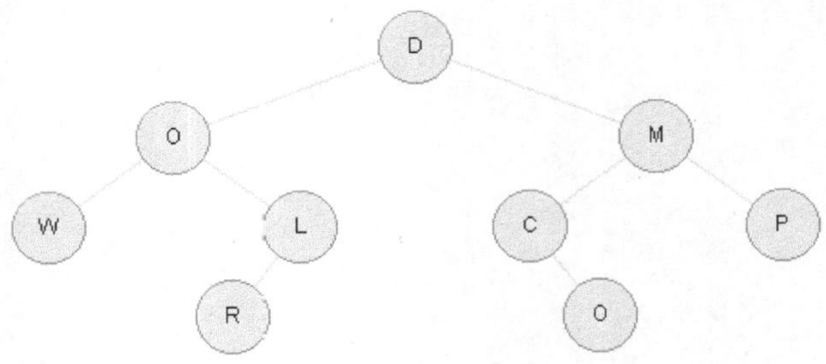

Figure 6. The sample tree when copied onto the clipboard

4.6 Internationalization and Localization

The initial implementation of the software supported only English user interface. However, we considered the effect of globalization on e-Learning and carefully re-implemented the user interface to support internationalization (i18n) and localization (l10n) based on Java's guideline [2][5]. Currently, the software supports English, Spanish, and French, as well as Simplified and Traditional Chinese. Other languages may be supported in the future. The users' choice of language is persistent across sessions of software invocation.

5 Packaging and Distribution

Although ByTE is implemented in Java, it is packaged as a WIN32 application using JSMOOTH [15]. JSMOOTH is a freeware package that provides a WIN32 wrapper around the jarred class files. Providing the software as a WIN32 application has the advantage that it will be easy to use the software on a Windows platform. The software will be downloaded as a single executable file. No installation is required. Hence, even students without administrator privileges on campus machines can easily use the software. However, JSMOOTH is only a wrapper to provide an easy startup of the program. It does not have support for the JRE, so the users still need to have access to a working JRE (which should be installed on most Windows system already). If the application is executed on a machine where no working JRE can be found, the user will be notified and given an option to download and install a suitable JRE version. We note that installing JRE does require administrator privileges.

The software is also packaged as a MAC OS X application, using the Mac OS X built-in JAR Bundler utility.

ByTE will be released as a freeware for non-profit use. It will be available at the author's web site [4].

6 Conclusions

We have developed ByTE, a flexible Binary Tree Editor, which is intended for academic use. Much effort was put into the development to ensure quality comparable to commercial software. It allows easy incorporation of the created trees into other documents, and therefore is beneficial to instructors for preparing presentation material. The created trees can be saved to files and reloaded into the software later, allowing electronic assignment submission. We used XML to save the created trees into files, allowing instructors to write scripts for performing automated grading as well as manual inspection/modification of the trees. The software will be released as freeware for non-profit use.

7 References

[1] R. Baker, M. Boilen, M. Goodrich, R. Tamassia, and B. Stibel. "Testers and Visualizers for Teaching Data Structures", in Proceedings of the Thirtieth SIGCSE Technical Symposium on Computer Science Education, Page 261-265, 1999.

[2] J. Bloch. "Effective Java", 2nd edition. Prentice Hall, 2008.

[3] M. Campione and K. Walrath. "The Java Tutorial: Object-Oriented Programming for the Internet", 2nd Edition, Addison Wesley, 1998.

[4] A. Chan, ByTE Web Site, http://faculty.uncfsu.edu/achan/software/ByTE as of May 2013.

[5] A. Deitsch and D. Czarnecki. "Java Internationalization". O'Reilly Media, 2001.

[6] B. Gustafson and J. Kjensli. Binary Treesome Web Site, http://www.iu.hio.no/~ulfu/AlgDat/applet/binarytreesome as of May 2013.

[7] A. Gogeshvili. Java Models Web Site, http://webdiis.unizar.es/asignaturas/EDA/AVLTree/avltree.html as of May 2013.

[8] M. Goodrich and R. Tamassia. "Data Structures and Algorithms in Java", 5th edition. John Wiley, 2010.

[9] D. Ierardi. Standard Binary Search Tree Web Page, http://aleph0.clarku.edu/~achou/cs102/examples/bst_animation/BST-Example.html as of May 2013.

[10] J. Kloss. Animated Binary Tree Web Page, http://www.cs.jhu.edu/~goodrich/dsa/trees/btree.html as of May 2013.

[11] J. Knudsen. "Java 2D Graphics. O'Reilly Media, 1999.

[12] J. Kováè, J. "Vyhµadávacie stromy a ich vizualizácia" (Tree Data Structures and their Visualization), Bachelor's thesis, Comenius University, Bratislava, 2007.

[13] J. Kováè. Binary Search Tree Web Site, http://people.ksp.sk/~kuko/bak as of May 2013.

[14] M. Main. "Data Structures and Other Objects Using Java", 2nd Edition. Addison Wesley, 2003.

[15] R. Reyes. JSmooth Web Site, http://jsmooth.sourceforge.net as of May 2013.

[16] G. Roelofs. "PNG: The Definitive Guide". O'Reilly & Associates, 1999.

[17] S. Schach. "Object-Oriented and Classical Software Engineering", 8th Edition. McGraw Hill, 2010.

Technological Gap: The Education Case of the State of Puebla, Mexico

Juan Carlos Botello[1], Martin Dávila[2]
[1] Escuela de Negocios, Universidad Popular Autónoma del Estado de Puebla, Puebla, Puebla, Mexico
[2] Departamento de Ciencias Sociales, Universidad Popular Autónoma del Estado de Puebla, Puebla, Puebla, Mexico

Abstract - *The teaching-learning process may have several obstacles; one of those would be a cultural situation of students but also the ICT (information and communication technologies) resource distribution per children. When we refer to cultural situation, we mean the language or dialect that they speak. In the state of Puebla, Mexico, there are primary schools in which courses are taught to students who do not speak Spanish and they only speak their own dialect. On the other hand, the use of information and communication technologies in primary schools in Puebla is a fact but a main concern in schools is that the languages in which are operated is Spanish. The present article will also deal with the distribution of enciclomedia sets per children population in the 217 communities of the state of Puebla. To analyze this situation, we find that turns out to be very important and with a negative effect on both the implementation and acceptance of a multimedia program in these schools, generating a technological gap between students. The government efforts are being decimated because of this cultural divide prevalent in many communities in the state of Puebla, Mexico.*

Keywords: Primary schools, information technology, resource distribution, cultural gap, technological gap.

1 Introduction

Various studies have demonstrated the importance and the impact of diverse material resources and equipment of different types [1] to improve efficiency, the learning process and teaching results [2]. According to the Director of UNESCO, Mr. Koichiro Matsura, in his discourse delivered on the 19th of December 2007, "...the information and communication technologies have the power to increase learning access, especially for vulnerable communities in remote areas...", additionally,"...these new technologies can help governments to monitor, manage and apportion educational services in a more efficient way..." he acknowledges information and communication technologies as a basic tool to close the digital divide [3] between cities and countryside, as defined by Inclán [3] as well as between nations.

The basic public educational sector in Mexico is one of the least favored with respect to the use of information technologies which is unacceptable if the digital divide is to be closed [4]. It is undeniable that in a nation of well-educated citizens there is a profound contribution to the development of a knowledge-based society [5], of a more just and participative society. However, insufficient availability and utilization of information and communication technologies, the low budget increases in educational resources [6] and the inefficient use of available resources [7] are characteristic for the Mexico educational system, which still has not completely manage to appropriate ICT in spite of the presence of approved programs by the UNESCO as in the case of the enciclomedia system, the program of Physics Education with Technology and the Program of Mathematics Education with Technology whose objective is to incorporate the use of information and communication technologies in the teaching of physics and mathematics in secondary public schools.

This paper will try to portrait the current situation in Puebla´s primary school system with respect to the inclusion and use of the information and communication technologies as an educational tool in teaching and learning process, especially the use of the enciclomedia system in the 5th and 6th grades of primary schools since very few publications have touched on the problem and have seldom taken it into consideration as a factor in educational quality improvement. Consequently, there has been negative impact on productive tasks and the creation of new forms of social interaction in Mexico which could be the foundation of understanding the importance which ICT has in today´s education [8].

The initial step of this paper is to offer an exploration of the operation of the Mexico educational system, thereafter information related to the enciclomedia program, the equipping of classrooms for the 5th and 6th primary grades between the 217 counties of the State of Puebla with this tool will be presented. A model will be developed with the objective of analyzing the impact of the number of systems in relation to the localization of primary schools, according to total indian population numbers per county, per school modality (state, federal, indigenous and indigenous shelter) and the number of enciclomedia sets according to children population in the state of Puebla. Finally, conclusions will be offered.

2 Literature review

The Mexico educational system is based on the General Educational Law which, in turn, is based upon Article 3 of the Mexican Constitution. In it are established the general provisions, organization and general structure of the Mexico educational system. In the institutional framework are basic education, middle schools and higher education, each with its different levels and modalities.

In primary education, three modalities are recognized: the General Primary School (urban and rural), the Indigenous Primary School and the Community Primary School. Primary education consists of a 6 year cycle and is obligatory for all mexicans. For purposes of this paper, general state, federal state, indigenous and indigenous shelter schools in the 217 counties of the state of Puebla will be dealt with.

During the schoolyear 2005-2006, approximately 32 million students were enrolled in the Mexico School System in all of its different levels, types and modalities in 230 000 education centers. The largest number of students, nearly 25 million, were enrolled in basic education (secondary and primary schools) this also includes secondary schools for the working population. This level represents 80.4% of total student enrolment in 92.3% of the school installations (214,394).

14,548,194 students were enrolled in primary education (13,371,543 in public schools and 1,176,651 in private schools) in 98,045 schools (90,896 public schools and 7,149 private schools). 5,979,256 students were enrolled in the secondary education system, (5,531,111 in public schools and 448,145 in private schools) in a total of 31,667 schools (28,246 public and 3,766 private). At the high school level a total of 3,658,754 students (2,924,529 in public schools and 743,225 in private schools) attended 12,841 schools (7,590 public and 5,257 private).

The efforts to create a wide infrastructure coverage at the different education levels has been impressive but still not sufficient during various federal administrative periods [9]. For example; 90% of the recourses destined for the education sector in 2006 were for current operation costs and only the small remainder went forward investment and innovation.

Various studies offer information with respect to the impact of the quantity and quality of educational recourses used [10]. In this context, in a study covering the year 2004 education inequalities in Mexico [11] it is pointed out that the use of some inputs are related with the yield, as was the case of the use of computers in spanish and mathematics courses where the impact was positive.

In Mexico´s National Development Plan for 2007-2012 it is acknowledged as well that there are still lags in the educational system such as the lack of opportunities to access to quality education as well as in advances in technology and information. Therefore, the Plan establishes a collection of objectives and strategies to foment development. Objective number nine: "Elevating the quality of education postulates a series of considerations to achieve this objective which is designed to comply with a combination of strategies. Strategy 9.3 recognizes that educational methodologies must adapt themselves to a changing world to assure the integration of knowledge through new information technologies. Respectively, strategy 9.4, objective 10 and strategy 10.1 describe the importance of the apportionment of resources in an efficient and equitable manner (through our model we will demonstrate that the apportionment of resources in the State of Puebla for equipping classrooms with the enciclomedia system is done differently) to reduce regional inequalities, modernizing and broadering educational infrastructure.

The stated objective of the National Development Plan recognizes the necessity of spurring development and utilization of new technologies in the educational system to permit the integration of the students into the knowledge society. Therefore, strategy 11.1 has been designed specifically to reinforce the use of new technologies in the teaching process and in the development of abilities in the use of information and communication technologies starting at the basic education level.

In this same context, the State Plan for the Development of the State of Puebla 2005-2011, recognizes the necessity to broaden educational infrastructure to guarantee equal opportunity of access to and continuance in the system for all Puebla citizens. Consequently, at the administrative level effective deconcentration is fundamental in establishing an integral administrative modernization program which contemplates efficiency in planning structure and the operation of the department. In the diagnosis of the Primary educational level it was established that deteriorating infrastructure still prevails and that there is scarcity of resources. In that sense, if students or children find out that conditions of ICT in schools are not appropriate for educational purposes, then they will have to solve their problem by using home computers. From 2001 through 2004, there has been a substantial increase in the use of computers in Mexico by children above 6 years old [12] at home, which means that more than 25% of the total of children population uses a computer at home. In 2011, 33.5% of total population of the state of Puebla was considered as a computer user [13]; below national mean (41.9%).

For its part, the National Institute for the evaluation of education (INEE), an organization created in Mexico for the evaluation of quality in the Mexico educational system has conducted various studies [26] [27] [28] [29], which reveal the state of school resources available in the matter of information and communication technologies for primary and secondary schools, plus physical space, teaching aids (which includes the availability of computer science teachers) the number of computers and/or other electronic devices, study programs and financial resources.

In the context of the above, we acknowledge that the current educational policy of the Mexican government has evolved, passing from being an indicator of social welfare to being a product adapted to serving that which determines the new political and economic order [14]. As shown, the technological revolution is an element which has obliged nations to adapt their public policies [15] in light of this factor and educational policy [16] it cannot and must not be disregarded in this context that the educational context has changed [17]. The democratization of education, for its part, appears to be part of the objective of the new economic policy with the eagerness to reduce social inequalities by bringing education to all corners of nation [18].

Emphazing just how much attention must be paid to the incorporation of information and communication technologies in education, various programs of Mexico´s federal government (Ernesto Zedillo, Vicente Fox and Felipe Calderón) have acknowledged its importance and consequently programs like enciclomedia (during the administration of Vicente Fox) were created for basic education. That is to say, the investment which the government must make in order to adopt new information technologies in the educational sector is essential [15] and not to be delayed [19]. The assignment of this resource must be made in such a way, that it does not contribute to the broadering of social inequalities. In that, special care must be taken in deciding which order and how the government will employ this resource and where it will come from [18].

The focus of this paper is the primary school and the incorporation of information and communication technologies through the enciclomedia program in the classroom. Information and communication technologies have been incorporated in the primary school in different ways around the world as well as in its different levels [20] [21]. Some schools have established laboratories and/or computer rooms, multi-media rooms and/or audiovisual rooms, computers and/or audiovisual equipment in the classrooms [22] with the intent to have equipment which could help the educational community to develop abilities to compete in the marketplace and have better working conditions in the future [18] but, people might choose not to use them for reasons other than the lack of technological skills [23]. Therefore, the digital divide can also be expressed in terms of the abilities needed to take advantage of the information and communication technologies [24] such as the use of English language as the most common used in the internet. In this sense, there are countries that the official spoken language is not English but dialects are or something between an official language and dialects.

Enciclomedia is an educational strategy which originated in 1998 and consists of a system of articulated resources which, through digitalization of textbooks and the incorporation of various multimedia resources like videos, photos, maps, graphs, encyclopedias [3] and electronic blackboards [20]. Enciclomedia has linked its lessons in order to contribute to the qualitative improvement of education in public schools in Mexico and is now totally linked to fulfill the educational objectives. It is an innovative way of using technology in the school and thereby can contribute to overcome current issues in education in Mexico. For example, teachers can consult ENCARTA to disspel any doubts that may have arisen among the students during class or the teachers can flesh out the information they are imparting to the students about pre-hispanic cultures with videos of the principal archaeological zones, students can also find interactive excercises on mathematics among others.

The gradual incorporation of information and communication technologies into the classroom, the modernization of pedagogical practice, the production of new educational materials are characteristic of this system.

Enciclomedia began to be used in classrooms of the 5th and 6th grades of primary schools of the 2003-2004 schoolyear and has still not reached its end. At present, it consists of two stages: in the first stage (school year 2004-2005) 21,434 electronic blackboards were installed in classrooms in 7,211 schools as well as in 548 teacher training centers. 670,062 students in the general primary system, 15649 in the indigenous primary system and about 25,000 teachers have benefitted from the enciclomedia system. In its 2nd phase, school years 2005-2007, 150,000 electronic blackboards have been installed in the same number of schoolrooms in Mexico [25].

3 Objectives, variables, hypotheses and data

3.1 Objectives

Some factors affect the broadening of the digital gap in developing countries. One of those factors is the way in which educational resources are distributed in public schools but also the social access. The objective of this paper is to analyze the relationship between the equipping of classrooms with Enciclomedia in public primary schools in the State of Puebla and its geographic location, its modality, the size, the type of indian population in every county in the state of Puebla and distribution of Enciclomedia sets per children population.

3.2 Variables

3.2.1 numeq (Number of classrooms equipped with Enciclomedia)

Numeq has been selected as a dependent variable relative to the number of classrooms of the 5th and 6th grades of Primary Schools in the State of Puebla equipped with Enciclomedia. The independent variables in their different modalities which will be considered are:

3.2.2 primest (State Primary School)

This variable refers to the State Primary modality in the State of Puebla. It is a dummy type of variable because the presence of the State Primary in the database is expressed with a 1 and the other modalities with a 0.

3.2.3 primfed (Federal Primary School)

This variable refers to the Federal Primary modality in the State of Puebla. It is a dummy type of variable because the existence of Federal Primary in the database is expressed with a 1 and the other modalities with a 0.

3.2.4 primindi (Indigenous Primary School)

This variable refers to the Indigenous Primary modality in the State of Puebla. It is a dummy type of variable because the existence of the Indigenous Primary in the database is expressed with a 1 and the other modalities with a 0.

3.2.5 Dist (Distance in km. Between the City of Puebla and the surroundings counties)

This variable refers to the existing distance in kilometers between the Capital City of the State Puebla and its counties.

3.2.6 habindi (Indian Inhabitants)

This variable refers to the total of Indian inhabitants for all the municipalities of the State of Puebla.

3.2.7 numdial (number of dialects spoken in State of Puebla)

This variable refers to the total number of dialects spoken in all the municipalities of the State of Puebla.

3.2.8 popinf (number of children population)

This variable refers to the total number of children population in all the municipalities of the State of Puebla.

3.3 Hypotheses

H_1 = The number of Enciclomedia sets depends on the distance between the capital city of Puebla State and the municipalities.

H_2= The number of Enciclomedia sets depends on the total of Indian inhabitants for all the counties of the State of Puebla.

H_3 = The number of Enciclomedia sets depend on the distance, Indian inhabitants, federal primary school, state primary school and indigenous primary school.

H_4 = The number of Enciclomedia sets depend on the number of dialects spoken in the State of Puebla.

H_5 = The number of Enciclomedia sets depend on the number of children population in the State of Puebla.

3.4 Data

The State Coordination of Distance Education of the Ministry of Public Education of the State of Puebla in Mexico (CETE-SEP) provided us with a database which contained the following information of the State of Puebla: County name and its localities (these data had to be verified individually to correct errors with respect to names and number of localities referred to), the number of classrooms equipped with Enciclomedia in the fifth and sixth grades of Primary School (2532 school rooms is the total of the sample), school modality (Federal Primary, State Primary, Indigenous Primary).

Herby item, this database displays 3 levels of Enciclomedia classroom equipment. The two first levels contain the information of equipment in Enciclomedia classrooms for fifth and sixth grades of Primary School in different stages (I and II) and the third level (III) has information of equipment for the first grade of Secondary. In this paper only level II of equipment for fifth and sixth grades of Primary School for the years 2005 and 2006 will be dealt with.

Added to the database mentioned above, are four more variables. The first variable is the distance in kilometers existing between the capital of the State of Puebla and the 216 counties in the rest of the State, the second variable is the number of Indian inhabitants in each county of the State of Puebla, the third variable is the number of dialects spoken in the State of Puebla. The dialects are: Náhuatl, totonaco, mixteco, mazateco, zapoteco, popolaca, chocho, otomí, tlapaneco, tepehua and the last variable includes the total number of children in the 217 municipalities of Puebla.

4 Descriptive Statistics

4.1 Research variables

Table 1 shows descriptive statistics for the research variables used in this paper. The number of observations is 217 that correspond to the total number of municipalities. The maximum classrooms equipped with enciclomedia systems are 650 and the mean corresponds to 27.68 enciclomedia sets per county. The major distance from the City of Puebla is 300 km. the average of distance is 120.27 km. The maximum Indian inhabitants in one municipality are 47,199. The mean of Indian inhabitants in all counties is 2,772 and the standard deviation is 5,591. The mean of children population in all the counties is 8,894.

Variable	Mean	Std. Dev.	Min	Max
numeq	27.68	48.81	1	650
dist	120.27	66.04	1	300
habindi	2,772	5,591	0	47,199
popinf	8,894	28,289	132	400,228

Table 1 Descriptive statistics for variables listed above

4.2 School modality

In table 2 is shown the descriptive statistics of the school modality variables used in this work. The average of state primary schools equipped with enciclomedia sets per county is 2.36 while in the federal primary schools are 6.51.Finally, there are more federal primary schools than state primary schools or indigenous primary schools.

Variable	Mean	Std. Dev.	Min	Max
primest	2.36	4.85	0	66
primfed	6.51	8.39	0	78
primin	2.61	5.34	0	38

Table 2 Descriptive statistics for modality

4.3 Dialects spoken

In table 3 is shown the percentages for each dialect spoken in the State of Puebla. The most spoken dialect is Nahuatl as shown in the table. The less spoken dialect spoken is Tepehua.

Dialect	percentage	Dialect	percentage
náhuatl	62.42%	popoloca	2.68%
totonaco	16.44%	zapoteco	2.01%
mixteco	8.39%	Chocho	0.67%
otomí	3.36%	tlapaneco	0.67%
mazateco	3.02%	tepehua	0.34%

Table 3 Dialects spoken in the State of Puebla

5 Models, methodology and results

5.1 Models

The following equations are the proposal models to prove the hypotheses postulated earlier:

$$\text{Model} \quad numeq = \beta_0 + \beta_1 dist \tag{1}$$

$$\text{Model} \quad numeq = \beta_0 + \beta_1 habindi \tag{2}$$

$$\text{Model} \quad numeq = \beta_0 + \beta_1 dist + \beta_2 habindi + \beta_3 primest + \beta_4 primfed + \beta_5 primind \tag{3}$$

$$\text{Model} \quad numeq = \beta_0 + \beta_1 numdial \tag{4}$$

$$\text{Model} \quad numeq = \beta_0 + \beta_1 popinf \tag{5}$$

5.2 Methodology

The methodology that we follow is with a linear regression by ordinary least squares was utilized in such form as to permit arriving at the relationships.

5.3 Results

5.3.1 Hypothesis 1

In table A1, there is a relationship between the number of enciclomedia sets and the distance between Puebla City and the remaining municipalities. The furthest (300 km far away from Puebla city) the less primary school equipped with the enciclomedia system.

5.3.2 Hypothesis 2

In table A2, we can demonstrate that the municipalities with more inhabitants deserve more equipped classrooms with enciclomedia system.

5.3.3 Hypothesis 3

The number of Enciclomedia sets is related to the distance, the number of Indian inhabitants and the school modality (Table A3).

5.3.4 Hypothesis 4

In table A4, we can demonstrate that the municipalities with most spoken dialect deserve more enciclomedia sets.

5.3.5 Hypothesis 5

Findings in table A5 show that the more children population in municipalities the more enciclomedia sets they get.

6 Conclusions

The National Development Action Plan of México has included within its action iniciatives, the incorporation and use of information and communication technologies in the education sector, particularly for the basic education, with the proposal of introducing the student to the Knowledge society. In table 2 it can be seen that there are a larger number of Federal Primary Schools equipped with Enciclomedia in the State of Puebla with 78, while in the Puebla State Plan for Development no mention is made of information and communication technology in the education sector and it can be seen that only 66 State Primary Schools are equipped with Enciclomedia. As Stiglitz [22] has indicated, the assignation of this resource must be made in such a way as to not contribute to the widening of the social inequalities, wherefore special care must be taken in deciding which order the government apply this resource, as well as from which sources it will come, so that the way in which this resource is distributed to primary schools in the State of Puebla does not contribute to the broadening of the digital gap between Federal Primary Schools and State Primary Schools. Apparently, results from hypothesis 5, indicate that children deserve more enciclomedia sets but the bad resource distribution is a fact in the state of Puebla.
It can be said in Table A1, that the farther away any of the 216 municipalities are from the State Capital, the lower the number of Primary Schools with Enciclomedia equipment, this point is particularly important for decision makers in so far as in equipping classrooms with Enciclomedia [30], without regard as to what might be the motive for why the most distant Primary Schools are less equipped, the end result is that these areas have less access to information and communication technology, and from that we can conclude the State Plan for Development in Education and the National Plan for Development in Education are not pursuing the same objective, at least in the incorporation of information and communication technology in Primary Schools. In Table A2 we show that the number of Indian inhabitants with respect to the number of equipment sets have a positive relationship, this means that a major number of Indian inhabitants the government provides more enciclomedia sets for that kind of population. But at the same time, government realizes that municipalities with more Indian population should have more enciclomedia sets.
Finally, the municipalities with more than two spoken dialects are the most favored with enciclomedia sets, in order to reduce the cultural and technological gap.

7 References

[1] Ruiz Cuellar, Guadalupe. (2006). La calidad de la educación básica en México. Capítulo 3. Docentes, infraestructura y equipamiento de las escuelas. p.p. 117. México. INEE

[2] Fernández, T., Banegas, I., Blanco, E. (2004). Sistema de Cuestionarios de Contexto INEE 2005 – 2008. Fundamentos teóricos de los conceptos propuestos a ser observados en los módulos permanentes del Sistema de Cuestionarios de Contexto para el ciclo de evaluaciones 2005 – 2008. México: INEE

[3] Reimers, Fernando. (2006). Aprender mas y mejor. Fondo de Cultura Económica.

[4] Quéau, Philippe, Governing the Global Knowledge Society, citado en "Desarrollo de la Sociedad de la Información en América Latina y el Caribe". Menezes, Claudio, Consejero Regional, División de la Sociedad de la Información, UNESCO-Montevideo

[5] Vilaseca, Jordi. (2002). La economía del conocimiento: paradigma tecnológico y cambio estructural. Working Paper Series WP02-003. UOC.

[6] Cárdenas, Oscar. "El gasto educativo: una propuesta de financiamiento a la educación básica". Volumen XVI. Número 2. II Semestre de 2007. Gestión y Política Pública.

[7] Bracho, Teresa. "Perfil nacional encargado para el Informe de Seguimiento de la EPT en el mundo 2008, Educación para Todos en 2015 - ¿Alcanzaremos la meta?". México. Estudio de Caso. UNESCO, 2007.

[8] Botello, Juan Carlos (2008). "Las Tic´s y el Sistema Educativo Mexicano". Working paper. Congreso Internacional de Investigación en Ciencias Administrativas. Tijuana, México.

[9] Alcántara, Armando. (2006). 25 años de políticas educativas en México. IISUE-UNAM.

[10] Schmelkes, S. (1997). La calidad de la educación primaria: Un estudio de caso. México: Fondo de Cultura Económica.

[11] Treviño, E. y Treviño, G. (2004). Estudio sobre las desigualdades educativas en México: la incidencia de la escuela en el desempeño académico de los alumnos y el rol

de los docentes. Colección Cuadernos de Investigación México: INEE.

[12] Disponibilidad y Uso de Tecnologías de Información en los Hogares en México (2004). México. INEGI

[13] Estadísticas sobre disponibilidad y uso de tecnología de información y comunicaciones en los Hogares (2011). México. INEGI

[14] Infraestructura Escolar en las Primarias y Secundarias de México (2007). México. INEE

[15] Panorama Educativo de México 2007. (2007). México. INEE

[16] La calidad de la Educación Básica en México 2006. (2006). México. INEE.

[17] Instituto Nacional para la evaluación de la educación. Artículo: El estado que guardan nuestras escuelas. (2007). Fundación Este País. México. INEE

[18] Valle Cruz, Maximiliano. (1999). Modernización Educativa o Reconstrucción de la legitimidad del Estado en México. Papeles de Población, abril-junio, número 020. Universidad Autónoma del Estado de México.

[19] Carty, Anthony., Phelan, Pat. (2006). The nature and provision of technology education in Ireland. Journal of Technology Education. Vol. 18 No. 1

[20] Young, Shelley S.C. (2008). A study of uses of ICT in Primary Education through Four Winning School cases in the Taiwan schools cyberfair. Vol. 11, Issue 3. Educational technology & society. Bassin, Colin. (2006). ICT integration in schools. Where are we now and what comes next?

[21] Tejada Fernández, José. (2000). La educación en el marco de una sociedad global: algunos principios y nuevas exigencias. Profesorado. Revista de currículo y formación de profesores. Año/vol 4, Universidad de Granada. Granada, España.

[22] Stiglitz, Joseph E. (2000). Economics of the public sector.

[23] Lam, J.C. Y. & Lee, M.K.O. (2006). Digital inclusiveness-longitudinal study of internet adoption by older adults. Journal of management information systems, 22(4), 177-206

[24] Huerta, E. & Sandoval-Almazan, E. (2007). Digital literacy: Problems faced by telecenter users in Mexico. Journal of information technology for development, 13(3), 217-232

[25] Andere, Eduardo. (2007). ¿Cómo es la mejor educación en el mundo?. Políticas educativas y escuelas en 19 países. Ed. Santillana

[26] Jenson, Jennifer. (2006). Finding space for technology: pedagogical observations on the organization of computers school environments. Volume 32(1). Canadian Journal of Learning and Technology

[27] Passey, Don. (2006). Technology enhancing learning: analysing uses of information and communication Technologies by primary and secondary schools pupils with learning frameworks. Vol. 17, No. 2. The Curriculum Journal.

[28] Wang, Qiyun, Woo, Huay Lit. (2007). Systematic planning for ICT integration in topic learning. Vol. 10, Issue 1. Educational technology & society.

[29] Información estadística de Enciclomedia. Extraída el 28 de Enero de 2008, desde (http://www.enciclomedia.edu.mx/Conoce_Enciclomedia/Numeralia.htm)

[30] Botello & Davila, (2012). Equipping the public primary schools in Puebla: The case of the Enciclomedia System in the State of Puebla, Mexico. Journal of Computer Technology and Application, 3(10), 668-677

Appendix

Table A1. Stata's results for model 1.

numeq	Coef.	Std. Err.	t	P>t	[95% Conf.	Interval]
dist	-0.080403	0.050112 3	-1.6	0.11	-0.1791773	0.018371 3
_cons	37.34764	6.872129	5.43	0	23.80227	50.89301

Table A2. Stata's results for model 2.

numeq	Coef.	Std. Err.	t	P>t	[95% Conf.	Interval]
habindi	0.0058843	0.000439 8	13.38	0	0.005017 3	0.0067512
_cons	11.36197	2.739836	4.15	0	5.96159	16.76235

Table A3. Stata's results for model 3.

numeq	Coef.	Std. Err.	t	P>t	[95% Conf.	Interval]
dist	- 0.064067 5	0.0118168	-5.42	0	- 0.087361 6	-0.0407734
habindi	0.001575 3	0.0002016	7.81	0	0.001177 8	0.0019727
primest	5.233161	0.2128716	24.58	0	4.813534	5.652789
primfed	2.278273	0.1175275	19.39	0	2.046595	2.509952
primindi	0.892540 3	0.1830616	4.88	0	0.531676 3	1.253404
_cons	1.515214	1.682382	0.9	0.369	-1.801216	4.831645

Table A4. Stata's results for model 4.

numeq	Coef.	Std. Err.	t	P>t	[95% Conf.	Interval]
numdial	15.42128	5.638245	2.74	0.00 7	4.307964	26.53459
_cons	6.49981	8.403063	0.77	0.44	-10.06312	23.06274

Table A5. Stata's results for model 5.

numeq	Coef.	Std. Err.	t	P>t	[95% Conf.	Interval]
popinf	0.0016445	0.0000356	46.16	0.000	0.0015742	0.0017147
_cons	14.03861	1.048015	13.40	0.000	11.97291	16.10431

Proposal of the Integrative Class Assistance System Using Smart Phone

Kazuya Murata, Takayuki Fujimoto
Graduate School of Engineering, Toyo University
Kujirai2100, Kawagoe-City, Saitama, Japan
murata@medianation.jp, me@fujimotokyo.com

Abstract – *In recent years, cellular phone and smart phone spread regardless of an age group and inflect as a convenient tool. Particularly, as for the modern university student, most students possess cellular phone or smart phone. Also about the E-mail, the student uses "The E-mail of cellular phone or smart phone" not "The E-mail of computer". In this way, cellular phone and smart phone are utilized widely. It is no exception by the school education. There is really the example teaching using cellular phone or smart phone. Form this, it is admitted that the class using cellular phone or smart phone is useful. However, the class using cellular phone or smart phone has a big problem. It is a problem called "Inappropriate use" such as games. This "Inappropriate use" is the most serious obstacle in the present. For this problem, the practical use of class use of cellular phone or smart phone is very difficult. Therefore, in this study, we build environment limiting "Inappropriate use" of smart phone. Furthermore, we implement class assistance contents application to realize a class using smart phone. By this environment system, we build environment enabling class assistance while limiting "Inappropriate use".*

Keywords: Smart phone, Inappropriate use, Class use, Class assistance,

1 Introduction

Currently, The cellular phone grew up to the electronic equipment that anyone possessed. Now in particular, the cellular phone users of a businessman and student increase. With it, the diffusion rate of the cellular phone increases, too. As one of its background, there is the development of high-performance cellular phone called "Smart phone". Particularly, Smart phone spread mainly on 20s. From this, as for the modern university student, almost students possess a cellular phone or smart phone. In addition, cellular phone or smart phone is used in every scene of the life. It is no exception in the field of education. The student is utilizing cellular phone or smart phone as substitution of a dictionary, ad a tool that investigates what is not understood. In other words many students utilize a cellular phone or smart phone as the "class use". Actually, with a cellular phone or smart phone, the class using "Twitter" exists, and there is the example of the use of an interactive class. Thus, it is thought that the usefulness is recognized as for the class using a cellular phone or smart phone. However, there are many problems for the realization of class using such a mobile device.

The particularly most problem is "Inappropriate use". When we really assume a class using mobile device, "Inappropriate use" such as games is most problems. Furthermore, by such a class, it is assumed that all students use a cellular phone or smart phone. Therefore, it is assumed that it is very difficult that the teacher finds "Inappropriate use" and warns. In this way, as for the class using a cell-phone or a smartphone, there are a great many problems for the realization. Therefore, the realization of the class using mobile device is extremely difficult now. So, in this study, we develop environment and system to solve such a problems.

2 Purpose of Study

The purpose of this study is development of the environmental system that can utilize high-performance mobile device such as smart phone with a class positively. Therefore, in this study, we develop an integrated learning environment system to realize active class use of the smart phone. By this environmental system, we build environment limiting "Inappropriate use". In addition, we develop application for the class assistance that student can participate in class with smart phone positively.

3 Integration System

In this study, we develop a learning environment system to realize a class using a smart phone. As a method, at first we build environment limiting "Inappropriate use". In addition, we develop the contents that a student can participate in class with smart phone positively.

In order to build this integrative environment, we need to build the environment that "Inappropriate use" is restricted.

As a method to build environment limiting "Inappropriate use", we build this environment by three following structure. And we show this summary in figure 1.

(1) Blocking and control of mobile device communication environment in classroom

(2) Wireless LAN access restrictions limit set class

(3) Construction of class contents and assistance tool system

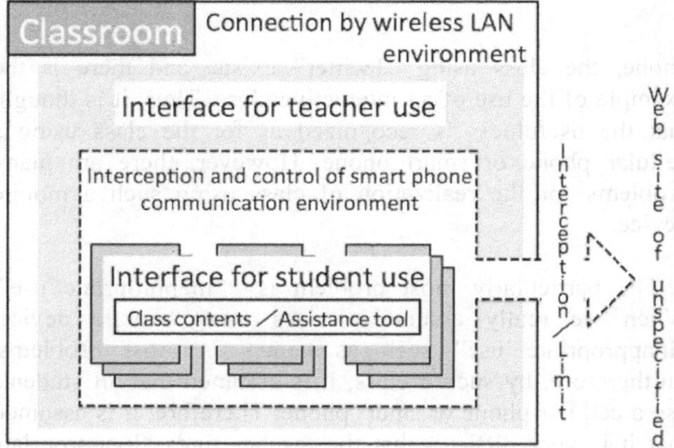

Figure 1. Summary of system

3.1 System Constitution (1) Interception and control of cellular phone and smart phone communication environment in classroom

We perform interception and control of the communication environment of smart phone in classroom to limit "Inappropriate use" as the first stage of environment construction. By this environment, we limit "Inappropriate use" using the cellular radio wave of smart phone.

In this study, as a method to build interception and controlling of the communication of smart phone, we use cellular radio wave jamming device called "Super Keita DCX1000MK2".

3.1.1 Summary of cellular radio wave jamming device

"Super Keita DCX1000MK2" is a device to send radio wave that can interfere with cellular radio wave to.

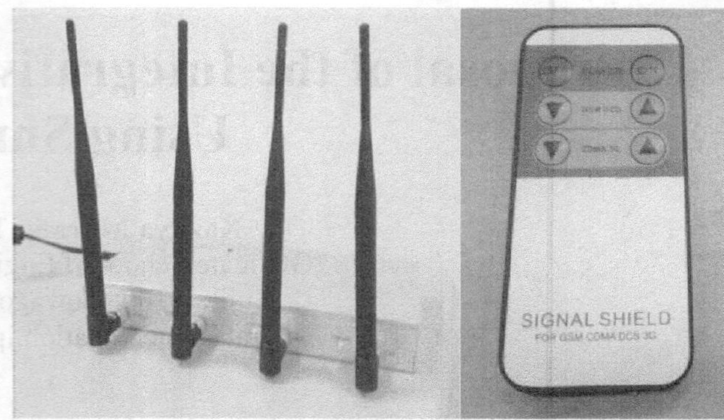

Figure 2. "Super Keita DCX1000MK2" and Remote Control device

"Super Keita DCX1000MK2" is an improved model of "Super Keita DCX1000" that is a previous version. In "Super Keita DCX1000MK2" of the previous version, there was a problem of heat radiation processing. Therefore, heat radiation was not enough, and was not able to use the long time. However, in "Super Keita DCX1000MK2" of the improved model, heat radiation processing is improved. Therefore, "Super Keita DCX1000MK2" is used for along time becomes possible. From this, when we used environment of "Inappropriate use" with class, we thought that it was device which could show an effect enough.

"Super Keita DCX1000MK2" can interfere with cellular radio wave in range of approximately 20m, and can make the carrier of all cellular radio wave the "outside". In addition, this device has its own antenna included. By this antenna, this device can stabilize the interference of cellular radio wave.

In "Super Keita DCX1000MK2", the interception of cellular radio wave of 3G type used in 96% of Japanese cellular phone and smart phone is possible. Furthermore, this device can interrupt the cellular radio wave of GSM type used in 82% of world mobile device. From these, this interference device has very high versatility.

In addition, this device using a remote control device operation is possible. By this remote control device, a switch of on/off of power supply is possible, and can change the strength of the jammer, too. In this way, also in class in a narrow classroom, it becomes possible to demonstrate an effect only in classroom.

Figure 3. Strength of jamming device

From these, in this study, we build environment limiting "Inappropriate use" with this device.

3.2 System Constitution (2) Wireless LAN environment that set the access restriction of class limitation

As the second stage to limit "Inappropriate use", we build environment enabling the connection of smart phone using wireless LAN.

In this study, we use class assistance environment using the Internet connection by wireless LAN. In this case as environment necessary first, it is necessary to interrupt the Internet connection using cellular radio wave of smart phone. However, this problem is settled by using cellular radio wave jamming device of system constitution (1).

Next, it is setting of wireless LAN for exclusive use of class. The student cannot connect smart phone to Internet using cellular radio wave as far as an interference device starts. However, as for the high-performance mobile devices such as smart phone, WiFi function is possessed basically. Using this WiFi function, Internet connection is enabled without needing cellular radio wave of smart phone by being connected to wireless LAN. Furthermore, we set the limit to be accessible only on a website of the specific address or domain that we appointed in this wireless LAN By this setting, we build connection environment where use only for class purposes is possible.

3.2.1 Setting and construction of access limit environment

H This study is realized as a method to limit the connection except the address that we appointed using "Squid" of proxy server software. "Squid" is the proxy server software that broadcast and cache perform of communication such as HTTP and HTTPS, FTP, SSL, etc. It is free software, and can get anyone.

This study permits connection of only the specified address or domain using "Squid", and restricts the other connection. As the setting method, at first a file called "squid.conf" is installed when we install "Squid". In "Squid", various setting is possible by editing a file called "squid.conf". As a setting method, we define the access control list (Whitelist) of the address or domain that permits connection to "squid.conf" And we set an address or domain that wants to admit access in a whitelist. By this setting, only the address or domain that we set becomes accessible to a whitelist. The website with an address or domain that are not described in a whitelist becomes the access refusal. By this setting, we limit the connection except the address or domain that the teacher appointed.

3.3 System Constitution (3) Class Contents and Assistance Tool

By environment of system constitution(1) and system constitution(2), we build the environment that enabled class assistance using wireless LAN while limiting "Inappropriate use".

The next system constitution, to enable a class using smart phone, contents to assist class are necessary. Using WiFi function of smart phone and contents for class assistance, the student is connected to class limited wireless LAN and uses it. In this method, this study enables class assistance using smart phone while limiting "Inappropriate use". In this study, we build space providing three class contents and assistance tools.

(1) Acquisition and reading of the teaching materials or documents to use in class

(2) Communication tool to ask questions about class

(3) Reaction tool answered to question or questionnaire from a teacher

3.3.1 Acquisition and reading of teaching materials to use for class

Assuming a recent class, class only textbook was very low. The current class has many classes using print document or PowerPoint for class understanding in addition to a textbook. In other words it is thought that this comes to often use a document for class assistance. In this study, we build system providing the contents or assistance tool that can acquire document or PowerPoint for exclusive use of class by Internet connection.

3.3.2 Communication tool that performs question about a class

In recent years, "Remark of the student in class" such as a student's opinion and question is decreasing. However it is not same as they're not being an opinion and a question that there are few remarks of student. However, it does not mean that student does not have a question. Rather, it is thought that there are also many students who want to ask a question among students.

Therefore in this study, as class assistance contents, we implement contents for question contributions that can ask a question about the class to a teacher. In addition, all students can share the answer with the question of the student by these contents. By this structure, the student can watch a question anytime, and smooth class assistance is become possible.

3.3.3 Reaction tool to reply for question or questionnaire from a teacher

The question of student is enabled with question contribution tool and becomes the system that can get an answer. However, there are many scenes of "Questions from a student to a teacher" as well as "Questions from a teacher to a student" in class. Therefore, we implement the question answer form from a teacher as a class assistance tool. By this tool, the teacher can easily perform the question to a student and simple questionnaire. In addition, the student of respondent can easily reply it with "Yes" or "No". By this system, the teacher can perform a smooth the class.

4 Development of Prototype System

In this study, we build the environment that enables class assistance while limiting "Inappropriate use". Therefore, we develop the prototype system of three contents and assistance tools for a class, "Acquisition and reading of teaching materials", "Contribution and share of question", and "Answer to question or questionnaire from a teacher". This chapter describes a system development environment and practice example of prototype system.

4.1 Development Environment of System

When the class using environment system proposed by this study is assumed, class contents or assistance tool need to be systems in which flexible use is possible. From this, prototype system has a desirable system that does not limit a platform and career.

This prototype system is built as CGI by a Perl language for mounting of the server portion that bears preservation and processing of information. The interface portion that a teacher and a student use is mounted by HTML and Javascript so that difference in use environment by apparatus may not occur. This summary is shown in Figure 4.

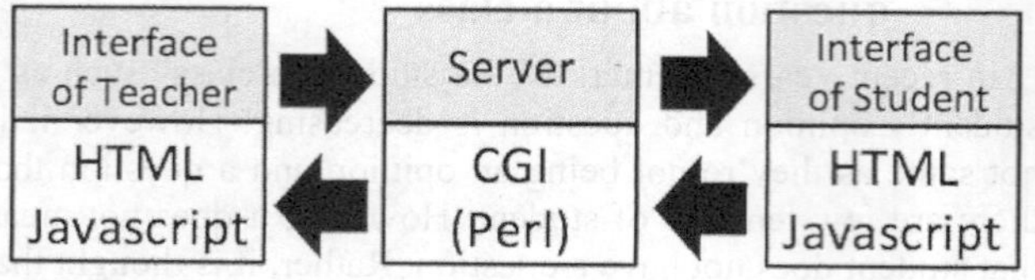

Figure 4. Summary of development envrionment of system

4.2 Summary of Prototype System

This section describes the example of execution of operation by smart phone of a prototype system. As a premise, it is the environment that restricted "Inappropriate use" by the jamming device of cellular radio wave of smart phone, and wireless LAN of access restriction. This system moves to the top page of figure 5 when connected to the address that admitted access.

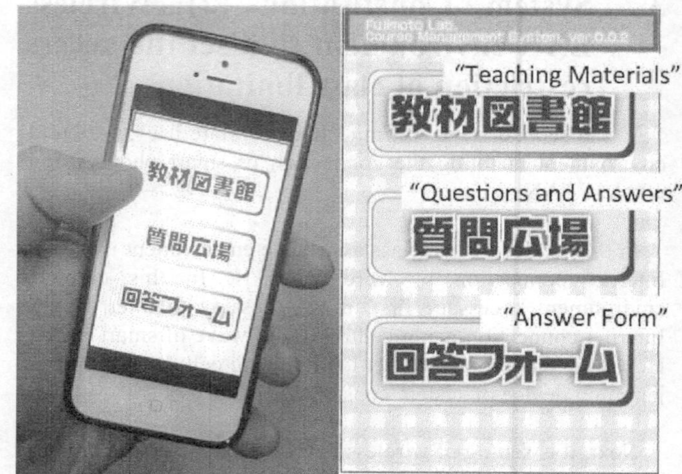

Figure 5. Top page of system

4.2.1 Acquisition and reading of teaching materials

When acquisition and reading of teaching materials tap a top button of "Teaching Materials" established in the top page, student move to page of figure 6.

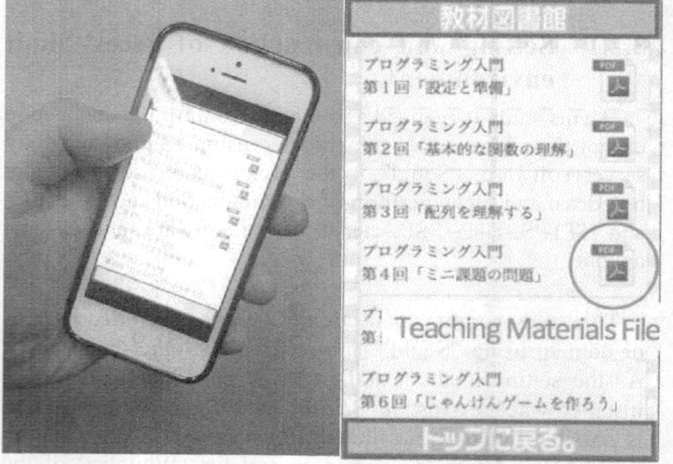

Figure 6. Page of acquisition of teaching materials

The file of teaching materials is installed in this page by the file of PDF form. The student can acquire the teaching materials of PDF file by tapping an icon of PDF.

4.2.2 Contribution and share of question

When contribution and sharing of question tap "Questions And Answers" of middle button of the top page, student move to the page of figure 7.

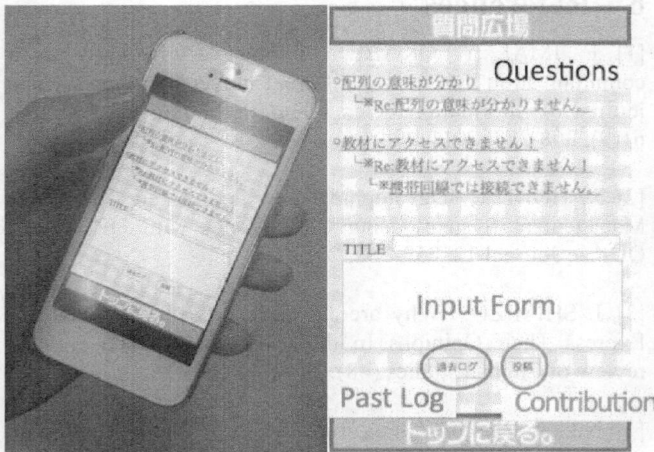

Figure 7. Page of qestion contribution

First, when a student contributes a question, it is necessary for the student to input a question into an input form of the lower of figure 7. Next, when the tap of the contribution button is carried out, the student is the specification that can add a question to the upper part.

The sharing of a question and answer taps "Past log" button installed beside a contribution button, the student move to the page of figure 8. This page can read a past question and answer. In addition, all these pages are the specifications that reading is possible.

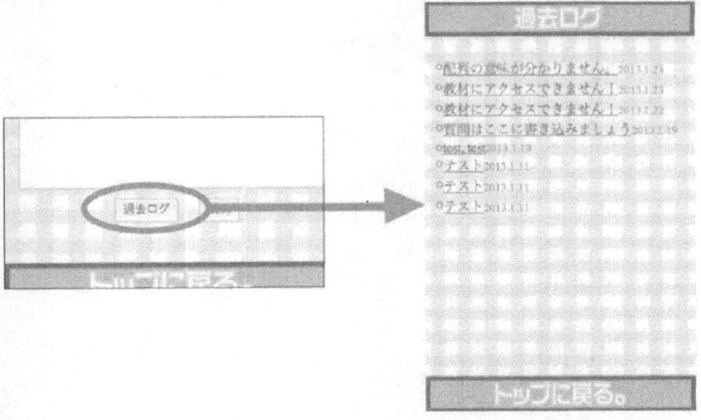

Figure 8. Question share

4.2.3 Answer to question or questionnaire from a teacher

The page that answers the question or questionnaire from a teacher is the same as other contents, and moves from a top page. A student moves to an exclusive page by carrying out the tap of "Answer form" of lower button.

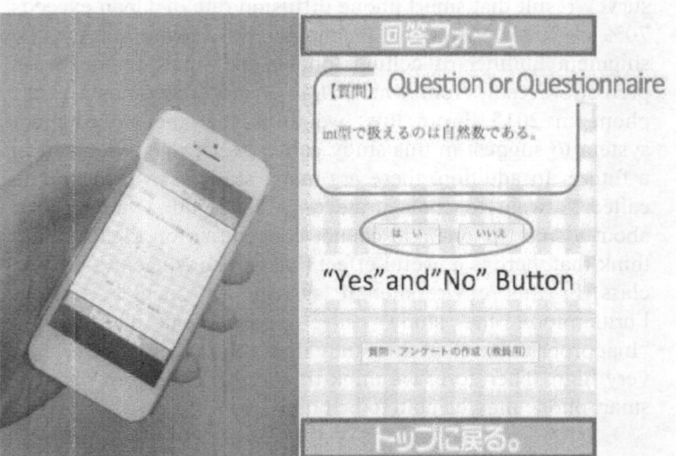

Figure 9. Question and questionnaire reply form from a teacher

The question or questionnaire from a teacher is listed in this page. The student can easily reply it with a button of "Yes" or "No" installed in the page for the question or questionnaire.

4.3 Consideration and Problem of Prototype System

As a prototype system of the system that enables class assistance, this study developed the system that offers three class contents or assistance tools, "Acquisition of teaching materials", "Contribution and share of question", and "Reply of question or questionnaire from teacher". This system is still a prototype system, but thinks that it can be established as class assistance contents even if we use it with class. Moreover, we think that positive class participation can be promoted from the convenience that this system can be used with an individual smart phone.

However, a problem has been left in this prototype system. It is a difference by the operating system of smart phone. When we used this system, a difference has occurred for reading of the system with a smart phone of iOS of Android. As a future examination matter, it is necessary to carry out the design that a difference of iOS or Android does not produce thoroughly.

5 Conclusion and Consideration

In this study, we were intended to build the environment that enabled class assistance while limiting "Inappropriate use". As a method, we developed the prototype system in various structure such as "jamming device of cellular radio wave", "Wireless LAN that set connection restrictions", and "Class contents and assistance tools". And we think that the purpose of this study has been achieved by this environment and system. Although the diffusion rate of smart phone in the world is very high now, but diffusion rate of smart phone of Japan is as low as about 20%. However, these is a forecasting survey result that smart phone diffusion rate of Japan exceeds 70% in 2016. Moreover, in another forecasting survey, the shipment number of cellular phone and smart phone has a prediction result from which 70% or more becomes a smart phone in 2015. From this, we think that the environment system to suggest in this study can expect enough demand in a future. In addition, there are many students with a trouble called "I want to concentrate on a class, but I am worried about a smart phone and cannot concentrate on a class". We think that there is a useful effect that can be concentrated on a class in this environmental system for such a student. Furthermore, the study using environment that limited "Inappropriate use" of this study does not exist, and novelty is very high. Therefore, we think that a new class form using a smart phone may be able to be built.

Today, there are many students suffering from "cellular phone poisoning" to use a cellular phone or smart phone in spite of the whole class. "Cellular phone poisoning" becomes a kind of social problem. It is thought that such a student can promote forward class participation as for the environment system that enables class assistance while limiting "Inappropriate use" to suggest in this study. From these, we think that integrated environmental system to suggest in this study is very high in a future.

6 References

[1] F. IMAI, Y. OKABE, "A practice of twitter as a communication tool in two different university classes", The journal of Information Science and Technology Association 61(9), 368-373, 2011-09-01

[2] N. HONDA, "Development and Trial of an Attendance Management System Using Cell Phones with QR Code", Otemae Journal 12, 253-262, 2011

[3] J. SHIMIZU, "Why are Japanese Students Reluctant to Express Their Opinions In the Classroom?", The Hiyoshi review of English studies (48), 33-45, 2006

[4] Nikkei BP consulting, Inc. "Feature Phone and Smart Phone "Personal Use" Fact-Finding, http://consult.nikkeibp.co.jp/consult/news/2012/0726sp/, 2012-7-25

[5] Seed Planning, Inc. "Prediction Survey of Diffusion of Smartphone",http://www.seedpLANning.co.jp/press/2012/2012072601.html, 2012-7-26

Integration of Massive Open Online Education (MOOC) System with in-Classroom Interaction and Assessment and Accreditation: An extensive report from a pilot study

A. I. Maria Joseph [1], B. Asoke Nath[2]

[1,2]Department of Computer Science, St. Xavier's College (Autonomous), Kolkata, India

e-mail: [1]mariajoe29@hotmail.com, [2]asokejoy1@gmail.com

Abstract : *The advent of Massive Open Online Course (MOOC) in the arena of online education in the recent years has catapulted several novel ventures, both commercial and non-commercial, offering access to quality online courses at higher education level. MOOC, by its very definition, throws open the door of knowledge to any motivated individual learners anytime and anywhere for free, but having no formal accreditation attached to it. The new MOOC wave into the sea of higher education has obviously attracted an incredible number of individual learners in tens of thousands globally. Contrary to the notion of MOOC courses having no formal accreditation, the authors propose a clear purpose of participation and accreditation by transferring 'credits' of successful students towards completion of undergraduate degree program. This paper explores a possibility of integrating Winter 2013 DB Course, a MOOC course by Stanford University, for a group of students within a formal higher education institution in India combining classroom interaction, proctored evaluation of this online course and a clear purpose of transfer of credits towards completion of the home institution's "An Introduction to Database Management System Course". This paper presents a study of this experiment and its opportunities and challenges, and suggests recommendations for its effective implementation in the future.*

Key Words: Massive Open Online Education (MOOC), Open Educational Resources (OER), Technology Enabled Teaching Learning, academic credentialing, Blended learning

1. Introduction

Modern digital and web technologies have opened up a plethora of revolutionary opportunities to enhance online teaching and learning experience. They redefine the domain of higher education. These developments have spawned new online 'disruptive' models to educate large number of students at college degree levels at no cost. One such disruptive model is Massive Open Online Course (MOOC), not so surprisingly termed by Forbes as the "Next Big Profitable Thing – the $1 Trillion Opportunity"[2], which has a huge potential to usher in new learning models, methods, and learners as a significant change agent in the current traditional education system. A survey by Babson Survey Research Group, Massachusetts, USA, in 2012, reveals the rate of growth in online education is significantly increased by ten times as against the 2 per cent growth rate in the overall all higher education student population. The survey further indicates that in USA alone over 6.7 million students are taking at least one online course as compared to previous year and 65 per cent of higher education institutions view that online learning is a critical part of their long term strategy[2]. This online revolution can benefit people who had previously no access to quality higher education at low cost. Interestingly, it is observed that almost one third of these massive online students are from non-US countries such as India, China and Brazil [9,10,16].

MOOC's amazing features are the large enrolment of thousands of motivated global learners, its efforts to make available free academic courses, and its scalability[9,13]. Though there is a huge rush in tens of thousands of people registering for MOOCs, the completion rate is rather dismal to mere 10 or less per cent.[9,10,13,22]. Though there are various factors contributing to this 'low' result, lack of time and formal accreditation as incentive for completion of MOOC courses are cited excuses [7]. In this context one of the authors (MJ) blended, on an experimental basis, the Stanford's Winter 2013 DB Course with campus classroom instruction in St., Xavier's College, Kolkata, with a clear purpose of deeper participation and transferring of credits towards the completion of a course titled "An Introduction to Database Management System" As part of this pilot study, the author(MJ) conducted key quizzes, assignment and exams of this MOOC course together with home institution's required exams in a proctored manner ensuring authenticity of students engaged in online learning which is one of the key contentions related to MOOC courses [9,16]. This paper presents the pilot study and its opportunities and challenges. This paper first introduces the concept of MOOC and its characteristics, then explores related works implementing a hybrid model using MOOC, then highlights the details of pilot study and its opportunities and challenges, and finally draws conclusion and future scope.

2. Overview of Massive Open Online Education (MOOC)

The term MOOC stands for Massive Open Online Course. *Massive* refers to scale giving opportunity for connections among participants, *Open* doesn't mean just free but refers to open access, open syllabi and self-directed learning outcomes, *Online* points to making materials available on internet in abundance, and *Course* referring to structure of the online course[22, Dave Cromier in an MOOC and Business Plan discussion]. In other words, it is meant to "integrate the connectivity of social networking, the facilitation of an acknowledged expert in a field of study, and a collection of freely accessible online resources" [22]. A key characteristics of a MOOC is flexibility so that students can choose their level of participation in an "a la carte" manner without fees and any prerequisites other than internet access and interest, no predefined expectations for participation including no formal accreditation"[9,22].

The first MOOC was a course on "Connectivism and Connective Knowledge(CCK08)" in 2008 by George Siemens and Stephen Downes and is distinguished from other MOOCs as cMOOC. cMOOC means Connectivist-MOOC emphasizing on its distributed participatory networked learning [13,22, 23]. As MOOC is transitioning from "free education resources" to "scalable free courses" [9], many popular higher education institution ventured into MOOC such as MIT, Harvard, Stanford, UC Berkeley Princeton, University of Pennsylvania, Duke University, to name a few. MITx, edX (a joint initiative of MIT and Harvard), Coursera, Udacity and Udemy are platforms whose courses are termed as xMOOC. It provides typical instruction oriented online courses. Some of the other prominent MOOCs offered by Stanford faculty in fall 2011-courses were in Artificial Intelligence, Databases and Machine Learning. These trio courses attracted several hundreds of thousands of students crossing 300,000 together[10,32, 33].

It is further classified as network-based, Task-based and Content-based[21]. Network-based relies on connectivist-style methods of connection, constructing knowledge distributed on the open web platforms. While Task-based MOOCs focus on developing skills by emphasizing on completion of a set of outlined activities, Content-based MOOCs, offered by big universities and non/commercial entities for a large number of students with automated testing with a goal of acquisition of specific content.

As there are a large number of students taking MOOCs, there are varieties of student archetypes as well. They could be broadly categorized into four major types[7,17]. First, "lurkers/indifferent students" – they do not engage with others. Most of these students are registered with MOOC just to observe and watch a few videos and learning materials. Second, "passive students"- they view the course as a source of information and are expected 'to be taught' as in traditional in-classroom model and do not actively participate in activities such as class / forum discussions. Third, "partially engaged /Drop-In students" - they are interested in specific topics and direct most of their active participation within the course for that topic and do not complete the course. Fourth, "active/memorably engaged students"- set goals for themselves, get connected with others, peer grade others works and get engaged with materials in personal learning network especially using social media such as discussion forums, blogs, twitter, flickr, YouTube, etc.

However these archetypes are not static. Students may move from one to the other within a course or change over time from being passive to active participants or drop out and leave the course. Therefore, level and completion of MOOC courses largely depends on their motivation level, self-discipline and learning styles. There is no external pressure on them to complete courses. So the rate of completion of MOOC courses is at 10 per cent or less [10]. Some cited reasons include lack of time and other commitments in life, but importantly lack of incentives or recognition in terms of certificates and employment opportunities on completion [7].

The authors are concerned that all students should be encouraged to stay active at least through the entire duration of course by incorporating it within one's classroom environment as well as to integrate it within its assessment and grading system of the home institution. An experiment was carried out to test this idea into formal teaching-learning environment and is described in the following sections.

3. Some similar work as MOOC :

MOOC, by its definition, charges no fee and offers no certificates. Departing from this position, since the first ever MOOC was offered, it was informally practiced that a higher education institution which offers MOOCs is free to accept the credits of its successful students enrolled in a MOOC course. The first instance took place in the University of Manitoba, Canada, for 25 of its students enrolled in the CCK08 facilitated by George Siemens and Stephen Downes[22]. But it was also reported that a higher education institute which was not an organiser of a MOOC Course evaluated and accepted the credits of one of its student who took CCK08 [15]. Similarly the University of Freiburg, Germany, accepted credits of successful students of Stanford's CS221 Artificial Intelligence course and transferred the credits towards the completion of its course on Artificial Intelligence at the Department of Computer Science of the same university, after its own internal evaluation of its students [35]. The University of Helsinki, Finland, used the credits of a MOOC Course offered by itself, as part of admission process in their university in 2012 by acknowledging formal credits of CS1 Computer Science Course and admitting them into their own university[35].

In another interesting development in March 2012, Tony Hyun Kim[29] integrated edX's online materials with face-to-face teaching for a group of 20 teenagers in Ulan Bator, the capital of Mongolia, who were a tiny part of a huge 155,000 participants from 160 countries mainly from the US, India, UK, Columbia, Spain, Pakistan, Canada, Brazil, Greece and Mexico. The course was MIT's 6.002x on "Circuits and Electronics" and the results were amazing. Of these 20 students, 12 earned certificates of completion and 1 fifteen year old teen aced the course, that was, one of 320 students worldwide.

In a major variation from the traditional practices of credentialing of MOOC courses, in September 2012, edX[28] announced that students enrolled in its MOOC courses will have a choice of getting their learning validated with a proctored final exam administered by a third party. edX has named Pearson VUE Service for this purpose. This third party will charge a nominal fee for final academic evaluation service. However there is no evidence as to whether it is implemented. In yet another milestone move in the U.S., Colorado State University-Global Campus[24] has announced that it will transfer academic credits towards completion of a Bachelor's degree at the Global Campus for a Udacity course on "Introduction to Computer Science: Building a Search Engine". Apart from this, several universities in Austria and Germany[24] such as the University of Salzburg, the University of Freiburg, the Free University of Berlin, and the Technical University of Munich, have begun implementing transfer of credits for courses offered by Udacity. It should be noted that Udacity charges a nominal fee per course for issuing a certificate of completion which could be used in some of these universities for transfer of credits towards Bachelor degree[24].

The novelty of this pilot study is to make another leap towards integrating free quality online courses offered by xMOOC platforms into the academic system of traditional Universities and Colleges which will facilitate the evaluation and acceptance of such credits of their successful students within the home institution. This paper evaluates such an attempt in the next section of the paper.

3.1 The context and rationale of pilot study

The structure and method of offering MOOC could really benefit students learning in difficult situations where there is no access to consistent high quality higher education due to lack of qualified faculty, infrastructure and academic facilities, and high cost of higher education. This is a typical situation in the developing world. There is greater need for quality higher education in the developing world. Therefore it is obvious that one third of student population of many of the popular courses of MITx, edX, Udacity and Coursera, is from the developing world[16]. As against this reception of MOOC, there is a strong criticism on the low completion rate and the negative perception of the media hype about MOOC. In an interesting survey of 103 professors who taught a MOOC by the Chronicle of Higher Education[18] in March 2013, indicate only 28 per cent believe that students who succeed in their MOOC deserve a formal credit from their home institutions though 79 per cent believe that MOOC is 'worth the hype'. In a similar survey of Chief Academic Officers by Babson Survey Research Group[2], the recent estimate in 2012 stands at 30 per cent "accept the value and legitimacy of online education"

It is in this context, the authors propose to approach MOOC, not as a replacement of traditional in-class instruction, but rather to integrate selectively those courses which are in line with the academic courses of home institutions which are not organisers of any MOOC. This pilot study attempts to test the following research questions:

- Can students in traditional in-class instruction benefit from a new form of blended online learning by mixing local instruction together with MOOC content?
- What are the attitudes of students towards informal online learning as part of regular academic course?
- Can a higher education institution integrate quality MOOC courses and accept credits of successful online students towards completion of their bachelor's degree and to build a case to this end?

This study collected data from two surveys - a pre-MOOC and a post-MOOC survey. The pre-MOOC survey contained a series of 9 questions and was conducted prior to the start of Stanford's Winter 2013 DB Course to determine their initial attitude and readiness to take this MOOC course. The post-MOOC survey was carried out after the completion of the MOOC course with a series of 17 questions to primarily decipher the students' actual level of satisfaction, participation, performance, its impact and attitude towards transferring of their MOOC's marks to formal credits of a DBMS course in their home institution.

3.2 A Pilot Study made in-classroom environment:

Table 1 Some Statistics of the Pilot Study

Statistics	Informal[1]		Formal[2]	
	Participants	Percentage	Participants	Percentage
Total Participants	64127	-	35	-
Partial Assignment Completion	20836	32.5 %	35	100%
Receipt of Statement of Accomplishment	4854	7.6%	25	71.4 %
Receipt of Statement of Accomplishment with Distinction	1927	3.0%	2	5.7%

A pilot study was conducted incorporating the Stanford's Winter 2013 Databases Course (Winter2013 DB) in a traditional in-classroom environment in St. Xavier's College, Kolkata, a higher education institute in India. This winter 2013 DB is the second offering of Stanford, from January to March 2013, on Database Management Systems (DBMS) after the success of its first offer in fall 2011. A group of 35 students were formally registered for a course on Database Management System (DBMS). As a requirement, these students were also requested to register for Stanford's Winter 2013 DB course which could be used to complete an introductory course on DBMS of St. Xavier's College. Incidentally, Winter2013 DB online course's timeline aligned with the home institution's

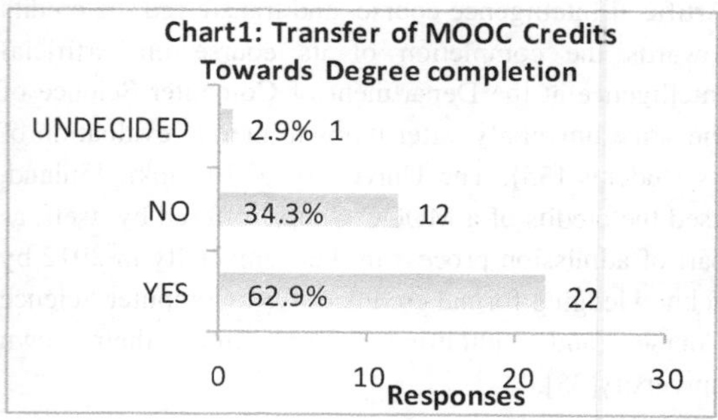

course exactly in the same semester.

Therefore it was easy to integrate Stanford's Winter 2013 DB course with the traditional classroom environment. Instead of the lecture format, the students and course teacher met every week for 2 hours to discuss on the Stanford's material that was due every week. Since the students were asked to go through the materials outside class hours, spending at least 2-3 hours a week, some spent even longer than 10 hours, relevant topics were discussed in a kind of "flipped classroom" set up. This enabled students to delve deeper into the depth of topics. This avoided presenting course

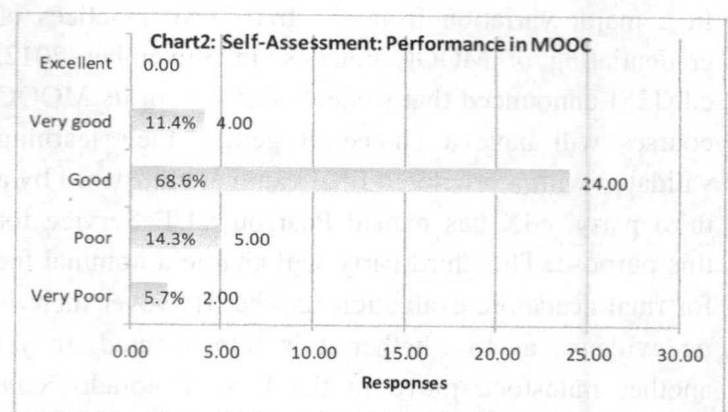

material in lecture format, except for a few hours on teaching prescribed topics which were not covered in the Winter 2013 DB course. As most of the students had already read up and watched video materials for the week, it was much easier to explain and discuss issues which were not clear.

It is interesting to note the big difference under the "Turning in assignments" category, Informal Students (34.5%) as against Formal Students (100%) turning in some work in the Winter 2013 DB Course. The authors believe that the noticeable difference due to the expectation of students and the clear incentive system of transferring credits of this MOOC towards their completion of home institution's DBMS course, as indicated in the chart1 above on "Transfer of MOOC Credits to Academic Degree Completion". The other reason could be personal mentoring and guidance provided to the formal students during the entire duration of the Winter 2013 DB Online Course.

The chart3 below reveals that many students were satisfied with course content and the feature of online interaction with the other participants globally.

Chart3: What is your overall impression of the Winter 2013 DB Course?

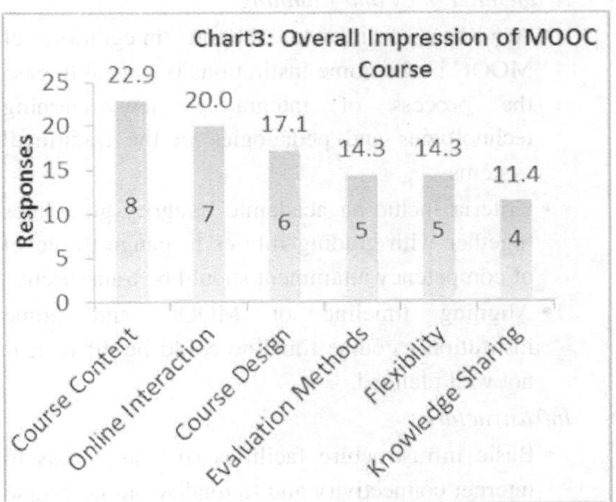

3.3 Opportunities and Challenges

From the perspective of participants of this pilot study, the authors briefly examine the opportunities and challenges of this pilot study. They are dealt with under these headings: Size of participants, Credentialing, Commitment, authenticity and personalization. They are briefly discussed below:

i. Number of participants:

A MOOC course is open to anyone. Anyone can take it anywhere. It provides an opportunity to go beyond one's class room, region, country and continent, out into global level of "borderless education" hearing global voice. If one is keen on getting connected with a diverse people, they are almost present virtually right there via various web platforms. On the other hand, the sheer size of people, 64127 registered learners in the Winter 2013 DB Course, could be very intimidating. Some students of this pilot study wondered how to get connected to so many thousands of students. More importantly, there is no scope for instructors to pay personal attention to anyone, no individual student get feedback from instructor either.

ii. Credentialing:

The content of the course is free for anyone's access. Departing from the initial notion of MOOC, a formal certificate could be offered to students who complete additional evaluation and are willing to make payment for administrative services [24,28]. The contention of the authors is that non-organizers of MOOC courses should be encouraged to adapt suitable MOOC courses and conduct necessary assessments of formal students and accordingly transfer credits towards completion of degree program. In this pilot study, it is towards the completion of the home institution's DBMS course. It is exciting to note in chart 1 that 62.9 per cent of students strongly agree to this proposal, while 34.2 per cent disagrees and 2.8 per cent is undecided on this issue. However one must keep in mind that currently there aren't many courses available which could fit into the existing curriculum structure of the home institution. Even those few MOOC courses may not match with the prescribed syllabi of non-organizers of MOOC courses.

iii. Commitment:

Table 2 Time Commitment for MOOC Course

1-2 hours	3-4 hours	5-6 hours	7-8 hours	10-12 hours
10	15	6	2	2
29%	43%	17%	6%	6%

This table presents the commitment of formal students in terms of number of hours. It indicates their weekly hours spent on this Winter 2013 DB course apart from the regular class hours on DBMS in the home institution. The authors believe that participating in a MOOC for a reward such as a formal certificate or credit transfer will enable students to be committed. It will help them to be committed to the course in terms of longer hours of learning and completing all assignments and timely participation in most online activities. The above table indicate that some students have put in as much as 10-12 hours. But there are students who get overwhelmed by the amount of energy and time it takes to get connected to open course. The survey data also shows that the self-assessment of the formal students on their participation in the Winter 2013 DB Course in terms of following all the study materials is at 60 per cent, and on performance meaning completing all assignments and activities 68.5 per cent.

iv. Authenticity:

A MOOC provides a mechanism to record all the activities of students online and they are free to do what and how they want. At the same time, it is difficult to monitor all activities of students as they are free to access materials and perform assignments "anywhere and anytime". This is one of the majors concerns of MOOC's critiques. In this case study, key quizzes and exams were conducted proctored in the home institution. This assisted in ensuring the authenticity of students' activities and their academic performance.

v. Personalization:

In MOOC, students are encouraged to do learning at their own space selecting what is appropriate to them. Even though the online course could be exactly same course in the home institution, but the depth and breadth of subject, the learning style of learners and their contexts may be obstacles preventing them from taking any online course. It is really difficult to tailor the content to each individual student. However in this case study, topics which were not included in the online DB course was adequately discussed, while scaffolding students to learn materials provided in the online DB Course. Since the number of students was small, it was easy to mentor them individually. This, in turn, enhanced teacher-leaner personal relations as well as more active participation in the course.

vi. Attitudinal Change:

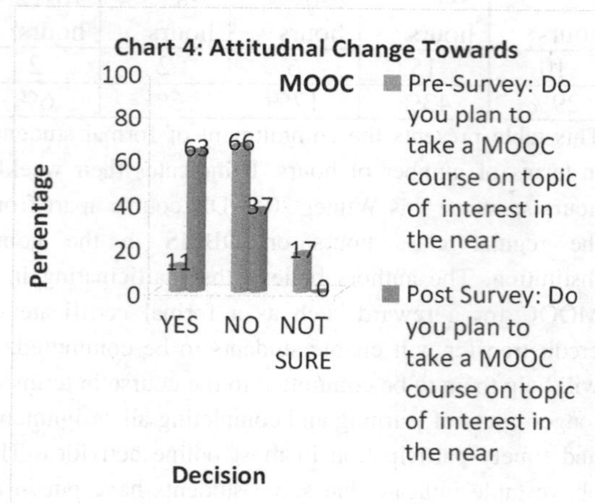

A key result of this pilot is that there has been a tremendous change in formal students' attitudes towards online learning, especially to MOOC courses. In the pre-survey which was conducted prior to the starting of the Winter 2013 DB MOOC course, it was noticed that 66 per cent expressed the opinion that they don't plan to take a MOOC course/online course. This is contrary to the general notion that youngsters are enthusiastic online learners.

In the post-survey, response to the same question on attitudinal change, 60.per cent plans to take a MOOC course for personal learning in the near future. A 66 per cent strongly suggests that the home institution should offer MOOC courses at the earliest in the college campus.

4. Issues to be considered for formal MOOC integration

Based on the lessons learnt from this pilot study, the authors suggest the following.to fit a MOOC course into the context of higher education institution, especially in the developing world. Due to the brevity of this paper, they are briefly outlined below:

- *Academic Policy and Planning*
  - Academic policy to support integration of MOOC in the home institutions is crucial to ease the process of integrating new learning technologies and pedagogies in the traditional systems.
  - Criteria including academic integrity guidelines together with grading rubrics to gauge the level of competency attainment should be transparent.
  - Aligning timeline of MOOC and home institution's course timeline could be difficult if not well planned.
- *Infrastructure*
  - Basic infrastructure facilities such as access to internet connectivity and to quality online course materials are basic requirements.
- *Attitude*
  - Attitudes of students and staff to online learning teaching should be positive and be motivated to make use of existing MOOC courses.
- *ICT Skills*
  - Sufficient ICT Skills of both students and staff are required to do online activities, assignments and exams.
- *Assisting Students*
  - Effective mentoring and guidance is important to help students to actively engage in online courses.
  - A continuous positive feedback on the progress students is recommended.
  - Provide sufficient time to students to complete the tests/quizzes conducted by MOOC, as it

might require more time than proposed timeframe of MOOC course calendar.

- Providing learning materials in languages and cultures which are relevant to local context is highly encouraged.

4.1 Some recommendations:

The authors make a few recommendations which will aid non-MOOC organizers planning to integrate MOOC courses with their academic systems. Based on the experiment of this pilot study, the following recommendations highlight key aspects like facilitation, the role of teachers and assessment. These are briefly discussed below:

- **Facilitation**: The home institution must facilitate in two ways: infrastructure facility and instructors' role.
  - *Facilitation by the home institution*: The home institution should be committed to enhance infrastructure facilities such as PCs, robust network, internet access and library resources which will aid in the integration of a MOOC course within the campus.
  - *Instructors' Role:* This refers to the changed role of the teachers who will use MOOC courses within his/her academic course. The teachers should take on the role of mentor and guide, rather than instructor. This will help build healthy relationship among the teachers and students in online learning.

- **Flipped Classroom:** When appropriately MOOC courses are integrated, there will be extra class hours gained especially by avoiding lecture format classes. The extra class hours could be utilised positively for more interaction and in depth discussion of relevant topics. Activities like project or research work or creating knowledge artefacts could be introduced. Robert Beichner's "SCALE-UP" and Eric Mazur's[14] "peer instruction" could be of some help in this process of 'flipped classroom' scenario. This implies that teachers should participate in the 'flipped classroom' approach as learners so that they genuinely facilitate enriched learning in the classroom.

- **Proctored Assessment:** As discussed in the section 'Similar work on MOOC' in this paper, there are several ways of integrating MOOC courses within a home institution. The authors suggest a method in which a home institution integrates a MOOC course equivalent to its academic course. The home institution allows its students to get registered for these MOOC courses and assist them to engage with the online course materials and other participants globally. At the same time, the home institution can conduct important online quizzes and exams proctored manner so that it could be used for transferring of credits towards completion of specific courses. This also implies that formal students are not burdened with external evaluations and monetary payment. This however does not prevent capable students to take any external evaluation of MOOC course done by an external institution like Udacity.

5. Conclusion and Future Scope

Digital advancement provides many opportunities for enhancing online teaching and learning experiences. MOOC has brought in lots of innovative changes in the realm of higher education. MOOC provides access to quality online courses to anyone and anywhere at no cost. As MOOC continues to gain currency, many take up self-spaced online learning. However higher education institutions remain sceptical of MOOC's legitimacy as formal academic credit, as there is lack of authenticity of online leaners. To address this issue, this pilot study was conducted. It explored a new method of integrating MOOC in a higher education institution. In this method, a home institute combines face-to-face interaction as well as monitoring of key online quizzes and exams of MOOC courses. This will assist in establishing the authenticity of students' academic works which can be further assessed by the home institution's evaluation method. As a result, MOOC's credits of successful students could be counted towards completion of a specific home institution's course.

However there are challenges which need to be addressed such as infrastructure facilities, academic policy for accreditation of MOOC course, the role of teachers as mentor and guide, staff and students' attitudes towards online learning, specific plans to flip the classroom with learning activities, and proper assessment systems. An initial experiment could be cumbersome, but it is worth the effort to get a positive result. One such positive result is the change of attitudes of students to online learning. Now many students feel confident that they can take MOOC courses for their personal learning. They even suggest that the home institution should move in the direction of offering MOOC courses. It is important to have more evidences to build a case for this approach. Therefore the authors intend to continue similar experiments on other MOOC courses to augment more data evidence and apply it in an innovative blended learning in higher education.

6. Acknowledgement

The authors are very grateful to the Department of Computer Science, St. Xavier's College (Autonomous), Kolkata, for allowing do research work on MOOC and emerging online teaching methodologies. The authors are very much grateful to Fr. Dr J. Felix Raj, Principal, St. Xavier's College (Autonomous), Kolkata, for his constant encouragement in research work.

7. References

[1] Agariya, A. K. & Singh, D. (2012). e-Learning quality: Scale development and validation in Indian context. An International Journal of Knowledge Management and E-Learning. 4(4). 500-517. Retrieved form www.kmel-journal.org/ojs/index.php/online-publication

[2] Allen, I. E.,&Seaman, J.(2013 January). Changing Course – Ten Years of Tracking Online Education in the United States, Babson Survey Research Group, Massachusetts, USA

[3] Anderson, T., &Dron, J. (2012 September). Learning technologies through three generations of technology enhanced distance education pedagogy. European Journal of Open Distance and E-Learning. Retrieved from http://www.eurodl.org/

[4] Bacow, L. S., Bowen, W. G., Guthrie, K.M., Lack, K. A. & Lon, M. P. (2012 May). Barriers to adoption of online learning systems in U.S. Higher Education. ITHAKA S+R. Retrieved from http://www.sr.ithaka.org/research-publications/

[5] Bregar, L., Bavdoz, M., Orgrajensek, I. Papic, M., & Bester, J. (1999 December). On-line course: From experimental use to integration into a university programme. Retrieved from www.eurodl.org

[6] Bowen, W. G., Chingos, M. M., Lack, K. A., & Nygren, T.I. (2012 May). Interactive Learning Online at Public Universities: Evidence from Randomized Trails. ITHAKA S+R

[7] Chamberlin, L., &T. Parish, MOOCs: Massive Open Online Courses or Massive and Often Obtuse Courses?

[8] Christensen, C. M., Horn M. B., & Johnson, C. W. (2008). Disrupting Class – How disruptive innovation will change the way the world learns. MGraw Hill. New York

[9] Cooper, S., & Sahami, M. (2013 February). Reflections on Stanford's Moocs. Communication of ACM 56(2), 28-30

[10] Daniel, J. (2012 September). Making Sense of MOOCs: Musings in a Maze of Myth, Paradox and Possibility, KNOU

[11] Davidson, N. (2012, Dec 10). Size isn't everything, The Chronicle Review - The chronicle of Education, retrieved from http://chronicle.com

[12] Day, J., & Foley, J. (2006 November). Evaluating a web lecture intervention in a human-computer interaction course, IEEE Transactions on Education, 49(4)

[13] Educause. (2011 November). Seven Things you should know about MOOCs

[14] Fagen, A. P., C.H. Crouch, & E. Mazur. (2012). Peer Instruction: Results from a range of classrooms, The Physics Teacher, 40

[15] Fini, A. (2009 November). The technological dimension of a Massive Open Online course: The case of the CCK08course tools. The International Review of Research in Open and Distnace Learning. Retrieved from http://www.irrodl.org/index.php/irrodl/article/view/643/1402

[16] Hayman, P. (2012 December). In the year of Disruptive Education, Communication of the ACM 55(12), 20-22

[17] Hill, P. (2013 March). The four student archetypes emerging in MOOCs. E-Literate [Web log blog].Retrieved from http://mfeldstein.com/

[18] Kolowich, S. (2013, Mar 18). The minds behind the MOOCs. The Chronicle of Higher Education. Retrieved from http://chronicle.com

[19] Jahng, N., Krug, D., & Zhang, Z. (2007 January). Student Achievement in Online Distance Education Compared to Face-to-Face Education. European Journal of Open Distance and E-Learning. Retrieved from http://www.eurodl.org/

[20] Jung, M. L., Loria, K., Saha, R.M.P (2008). E-Learning: Investigating University Student's Acceptance of Technology. European Journal of Open Distance and E-Learning. Retrieved from http://www.eurodl.org/

[21] Lane, L. M. (2012). Three Classification of MOOCs, retrieved from http://lisahistory.net

[22] McAuley, A., Stewart, B., Siemens, G., &Cormier, D. (2010).The MOOC Model for Digital Practice.Retrieved from http://www.elearnspace.org

[23] Machun, P. A., & Wang, M. (2012). MOOCs: Is There An App For That?-Expanding Mobilegogy Through An Analysis Of MOOCs And iTunes University

[24] Mangan, K. (2012, Sep 6). A First for Udacity: a U.S. University will accept transfer credit for one of its courses, The Chronicle of Education, 6 September 2012 – retrieved from http://chronicle.com/article/

[25] Martin, F. G. (2012 August). Will massive open online courses change how we teach? Communications of the ACM 55(8)

[26] Morrison, D. (2013 March). A Tale of Two MOOCs @ Coursera: Divided by Pedagogy. Online Learning Insights [Web log blog]. Retrieved from http://onlinelearninginsights.wordpress.com

[27] Pantò E., Comas-Quinn A. (2013), The Challenge of Open Education, Journal of e-Learning and Knowledge Society, v.9, n.1, 11-22.

[28] Parry, M. (2013, Mar 20) edX Offers Proctored Exams for Open Online Course, http://chronicle.com

[29] Parry, M. (2012, Oct 1). 5 ways that edX could change education, The Chronicle of Higher Education, Retrieved from http://chronicle.com

[30] Piech, C., Sahami, M., Koller, D., Cooper, S. and Blikstein, P. (2012). Modeling how students learn to program. In Proceedings of the 43rd ACM Technical Symposium on Computer Science Education (SIGCSE '12). ACM. New York. 153–160

[31] Rajasingham, L. (2011 June). New Challenges Facing Universities in the Internet-Driven global Environment. European Journal of Open Distance and E-Learning. Retrieved from http://www.eurodl.org/

[32] Rodriguez, C. O. (2012 July). MOOCs and the AI-Stanford like courses: Two successful and distinct course format for Massive Open Online Courses. Retrieved from http://www.eurodl.org/

[33] Sahami, M., Martin, F. G., Guzial, M., &Parlante, N. (2013 March). The Revolution will be Televised: Perspectives on Massive Open Online Education. SIGCSE of ACM, 457-458.doi: 978-1-4503-1868-6/13/3

[34] Vardi, M.Y. (2012 Noember). Will MOOCs destroy academia? Commun. ACM 55(11), 5.

[35] Vihavainen, a., Luukkainen, & Kurhila, J. (2012 October). Multifacted support for MOOC in Programming. SIGITE'12 of ACM. 171-176. doi: 978-1-4503-1464-0

A Programmer Self-training System with Programming Skill Evaluation and Personalized Task Recommendation

Shu Lin, Qinjian Zhang, and Wenxin Li
Department of Computer Science, Peking University, Beijing, P.R.China

Abstract— *Thanks to the widespread use of computers, the basic programming ability is becoming an essential skill for almost all the college students. Although many current online judge systems provide stable and efficient services in automated programs testing [1], it seems that there is limited help to the learners since few study suggestions is given to them. In this case, learners may feel disoriented during their studies. This paper aims to solve this problem by implementing a system based on one existing platform – Bailian, which will evaluate the learner's programming skills by combining three scores from different perspectives separately, and then recommend some suitable tasks to them according to the grades of both learners and problems. The system also includes an automatic contest generator to generate contests for self-testing. The quality of these contests is guaranteed since the grades as well as the categories of problems are considered during generating.*

Keywords: Online judge system, Bailian, programming skill evaluation, personalized task recommendation, automatic contest generation

1. Introduction

With the advent of information era and the popularization of computers, programming is no longer a peculiar skill of programmers. Almost all subjects requires programming skills – for example, we need to process large data sets or solve complex formulas in mathematics and physics, tabulate statistics data or predict the developing trade of some object in social science, design and produce fantastic animations in arts, and so on. Without programming, these jobs would become tall orders.

Nowadays, there are many kinds of platforms designed for helping learning programming, and the most efficient one is called Online Judge System, or "OJ" for short. An online judge system may contain hundreds of thousands of problems which demand diverse ideas and techniques to solve. A learner can practice his programming skills by registering a new account, opening one problem and reading its description, coding a program which does exactly what the problems demand, and submitting the solution to the online judge system. Because the online judge system uses robot judges instead of humans, it will return an objective verdict in mere fractions of seconds just after the submission. Thus the learner is able to know whether his solution is correct or not, and may correct the errors according to the result [2].

However, it is far from enough for learners. Since most of online judge systems are initially designed for programming contests, beginners will be completely flummoxed by the sea of problems – in another word, the green hands have no idea where to begin. Even old hands may lose their positions if they are not aware of their actual grades. It happens occasionally when a learner

- Tries to solve hard problems which beyond his ability, or
- Has solved many similar problems redundantly, which he should not have to.

Both of them are wasting learner's precious time.

Another flaw in most of the current online judge systems is the utilization rate of problems is quite low. Learners prefer to solve "famous" problems, because these problems have been solved many times, and proved to be good ones. Also it is easy to find lots of reference solutions for these problems, which is really helpful once a learner is getting into trouble. If things continue in this way, the "famous" will become more "famous", fewer and fewer learners show their interest in other "infamous" problems, even some of those "infamous" ones may be good.

In this paper, we are going to design and implement a system that

- Evaluates programming skill of learners;
- Gives some personalized study advices (by task recommendations) to learners;
- Generates contests for testing learner's programming ability.

The system is based on OpenJudge, an existing online judge system maintained by Peking University.

In order to provide a better programming learning platform, at first we have graded all problems according to the levels of difficulty. We have also classified them by what algorithm is used during solving. Then for each learner, we determine the grade of his programming skill by the grades as well as the classifications of solved problems. After that, we can recommend some proper problems to the learner. Finally, we provide a service that generates contests individually for each learner, which will test learner's programming skill in a more effective way.

The next section describes the current online judge systems in detail. From Section 3 to Section 7 shows the current implementation of our system. Section 8 introduces how to use our system. Finally, we draw a conclusion in Section 9.

2. Brief Introduction to Online Judge Systems

2.1 General View

In a general online judge system, users need to solve problems in the problem set. Two kinds of problem sets are available:

- Practices: Users can solve the problems whenever they want;
- Contests: Users need to solve the problems within the limited time.

While solving a problem, the user reads the problem description, picks one of his favorite programming languages and writes a program which does exactly what the problem demands, then submits it to the online judge system. Once the robot judge on the system receives a program from the user, it will test the program by some test cases to see if it runs normally, and produces the right answer under the problem requirements[1]. It takes only a few seconds. Then the user will receive a verdict indicating the result of the judgment.

The rules of scoring the solution vary in different systems. Many of them use the ACM International Collegiate Programming Contest (ACM/ICPC) rules. The user gets full score if and only if the solution produces right answers in all test cases, otherwise, no score points received. The submitted time and the penalty time (twenty minutes for every previously wrong solution for that problem) is also considered in the contests [3]. Other systems use rules that the solution gets score points of each right answers. Some systems even use more complicated method to calculate the score, for example, TopCoder [4].

2.2 POJ

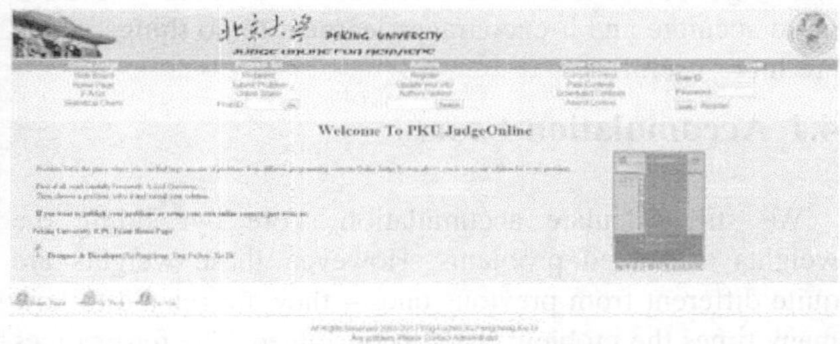

Fig. 1: POJ Home Page

Figure 1 shows the home page of Peking University Online Judge System (POJ [5]). It is developed by Artificial Intelligence Lab of Peking University in 2003. POJ used to be an ACM/ICPC training platform for Peking University students only. Today, POJ is a platform not only for contest training but also for daily practice, and it is providing services to learners around the world.

POJ is a typical "ACM/ICPC-style" online judge system. Most of the problems are selected from ACM/ICPC and the ACM/ICPC rules are applied in scoring users' solutions. As a result, the problems might be too hard for the beginners to start with.

2.3 OpenJudge

Fig. 2: OpenJudge Home Page

Several years ago, the POJ development team had released a free version POJ, so that everyone can build their own judge systems for programming related courses. However, due to the difficulties of system configuration and lack powerful servers to support, it does not work out fine. Therefore, a new online judge system – OpenJudge [6] is built for this application. Teachers or coaches can create their own private groups on OpenJudge, and use their own problem sets for teaching or training [7].

At present, there are over 180 active groups on OpenJudge, including middle school hobby groups, collegiate teaching groups, as well as many on-job programmer groups.

The problems in OpenJudge are from many different sources: ACM/ICPC, Olympiad in Informatics for high school students, homework of academic courses, etc. So that learners in any grade can find suitable problems for themselves in OpenJudge.

3. Preparation

We choose the largest public group – Bailian [8] (Means "Hundreds of Practices" in English) group as the basic platform to implement our system. That is because:

- This group contains the most learners among all groups;
- Everyone can join this group without any limitation;
- All problems in the problem set are public to everybody;

[1]Each problem has a time limit as well as a memory limit for the programs.

- There are many easy as well as hard problems in the problem set, meeting the needs of both beginners and expert programmers.

So far, there are up to 2267 problems in the problem set of Bailian. It takes nearly half a year grading and classifying these problems manually.

3.1 Grading Problems

We have graded all problems in our system from Grade 1 to 5 according to the levels of difficulty, Grade 1 is the easiest and Grade 5 is the hardest.

Table 1: The result of problem grading.

Grade	Count	Level of Difficulty
Grade 1	288	Basic programming training
Grade 2	368	Simple but fallible process
Grade 3	429	Data structures and algorithms
Grade 4	418	Algorithm analysis
Grade 5	641	Challenges for contestants
Other	123	Do not recommend

Table 1 shows the number of problems and the levels of difficulty on each grade.

We also suggest that:

- On Grade 1, learners are going to get familiar with programming languages as well as our system.
- On Grade 2, learners are facing problems which may be simple but required a lot of patience. These problems will make the learners realize that how important a clean coding style is – nobody enjoys finding bugs in a mess.
- On Grade 3, learners start to learn some basic algorithms as well as data structures, which are important in increasing performance of programs.
- On Grade 4, learners need to know how to analyze advanced algorithms, for example, discuss the time complexity and space complexity of them, or do some mathematical deductions before solving problems.
- On Grade 5, these problems are so hard that only recommended to the expert programmers.
- For other ungraded programs, we will not recommend them to anyone because they are not worth solving[2].

3.2 Classifying Problems

Another preparation before evaluating learner's programming skill is classifying problems by the algorithms used in the standard solutions.

We roughly classify the problems into ten categories [9], which are listed in Table 2.

[2]Sometimes the description of a problem is ambiguous, or there is something wrong in the test data, or the problem is almost the same as another one.

Table 2: Categories of problems.

Categories	Count
Basic Practice	382
Divide-and-conquer	49
Greedy Algorithms	86
Dynamic Programming	335
Search Algorithms	306
Simulation	237
Data Structures	130
Graph Algorithms	236
Computational Geometry	131
Number-Theoretic Algorithms	252

4. Programming Skill Evaluation through Different Perspectives

Almost every online judge system is using the same method for calculating user's rank: just sort the users in a decrease order of their scores.

Though this method is quite simple, it has some disadvantages:

- The weight gap between easy problems and hard problems is too small, especially in ACM/ICPC scoring rules (no difference at all). In this case, many users will prefer to solve easier problems in order to raise their rank quickly. There is no benefit to improving their programming skill.
- Some users practice hard and have solved a lot of problems, but always get bad scores in contests; other users seldom practice programming on the system, but often perform well during contests. In this method, the previous ones are better, but apparently the truth is to the contrary.
- Users only need to concentrate on solving their problems, though helping others is also a good way to improve their programming skill. There is no reward mechanism for contribution.

In our evaluation system, we evaluate learner's programming skill in three independent perspectives: accumulation, challenge, and contribution. The result of evaluation is much more accurate and it encourages learners to do things which are more useful.

4.1 Accumulation Score

We still calculate accumulation score by adding the weights of solved problems. However, these weights are quite different from previous ones – they are related to how many times the problems have been solved. The fewer times a problem has been solved, the higher weight it will have, and vice versa. In addition, we want to enlarge the weight gap between easy problems and hard problems. Then the learners may be led to challenge harder ones.

The problem weights are calculated by Function 1.

$$W(x) = \max(100 - 10\log_2(x), 1) \tag{1}$$

Where x is the times the problem has been solved. The image of it is shown in Figure 3.

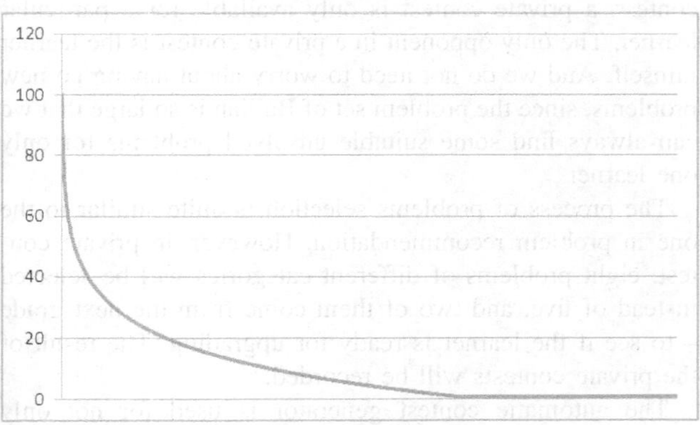

Fig. 3: The Image of W(x)

4.2 Challenge Score

Challenge score is designed for evaluating learner's performance during the contests. It can also make the contests more competitive, and contestants will gain more experience from it.

In our system, learner's challenge score gained in a contest can be calculated as follow:

```
CALCULATE-SCORE(CONTEST)
1  user ← {users joined in contest ordered by rank}
2  N ← length(user)
3  for i ← 1 to N
4      do score[i] ← previous score of user[i]
5  ▷ Discard contests which few users join in
6  if N < 10
7      do exit
8  for i ← 1 to N
9      do point[i] ← (−99i+100N−1)/(N−1)
10 for i ← 1 to N
11     do for j ← 1 to i − 1
12         do if score[i] > score[j]
13             do point[i] ← point[i] − 1
14 sum ← 0
15 for i ← 1 to N
16     do sum ← sum + point[i]
17 for i ← 1 to N
18     do score[i] ← score[i] + (10·N·point[i])/sum
```

The function for calculating *point* on Line 9 is linearly related to the rank of contestants, and the champion will get 100 points, the last one will get only one point.

For each contestant, his *point* will decrease by the number of players who perform better than him in this contest but have lower challenge score before this contest. The code from Line 10 to Line 13 is dealing with the process.

The final challenge score a contestant received is calculated on Line 18. It ensures that the total challenge scores received in a contest is ten times of the number of contestants. Notice that someone may "gain" negative challenge score due to his extremely awful performance during the contest.

To avoid losing challenge score, contestants will pay more attentions in contest. Everyone will try his best to compete, making the contest becomes a rat race, which is good for every contestants.

4.3 Contribution Score

We also encourage programming learners to help others or even make contributions to the development of our system by giving them contribution score. It gives the learners a sense of accomplishment, which will push them to study harder. We always believe that, only when a learner can be able to teach or test others, does he really mastery the knowledge.

We provide three different ways of contribution, from easy to hard:

1) Write short but critical hints for the solved problems;
2) Share the studying experience with others by giving a public lecture;
3) Set some new problems for coming contests.

5. Grading Programming Ability

We make use of the result of problems grading and classifying to grade the learners' programming ability. The accumulation, challenge, and contribution scores are also take into account.

We divide the learning process into three phases:

1) The main task at Phase 1 is practicing more, and learning new skills.
2) Once the learner holds lots of knowledge in hand, he may start to join contests frequently, in order to raise the ability of programming under pressure.
3) After programming for several years, the learner may become an expert. Then he is encouraged to show his talent in helping others.

6. Personalized Task Recommendation

The other important service provided by our system is personalized task recommendation, which can be important study advices for learners.

Before recommend problems to a learner, we first examine into the problems solved by him to determine which grade he is on. On each grade, a learner is required to solve enough number of problems of the same grade for each category. Once the requirement is met, the learner will upgrade.

After determined the learner's grade, we find some suitable tasks for recommendation using the algorithm:

```
TASK-RECOMMENDATION(USER)
1  solved ← {problems solved by user}
2  grade ← previous grade of user
3  recommended ← {previous recommendation}
4  while solved meets the requirement on grade
5       do grade ← grade + 1
6          recommended ← {}
7  recommended ← recommended − solved
8  while length(recommended) < 5
9       do problem ← select(grade, recommended)
10         Insert problem into recommended
```

The function "select(grade, recommended)" on Line 9 will select a problem randomly from problem set which:

- It has not been solved by the learner yet;
- Its grade is equal to the learner's grade;
- Its category is not appeared in previous recommended problems.

These limitations ensure that, the recommended problems are suitable for the learner according to their difficultness, and we will not give two or more similar problems to the learner at the same time.

In addition, we put the recommended problems on a striking position – on the right side of Bailian home page (see Figure 4). Thus, it will remind the learners to solve these problems all the time.

Fig. 4: Bailian Home Page

7. Automatic Contest Generator

A regular contest provides a platform for contestants to enjoy competing with each other. However, it requires new problems, which is hard to get. And the result of the contest contains no useful guideline for testing what learners have already learned, because at most time, the problems are either too easy or too hard for them.

We also implement an automatic contest generator for generating private contests for learners. Unlike a regular contest, a private contest is only available for a particular learner. The only opponent in a private contest is the learner himself. And we do not need to worry about having no new problems, since the problem set of Bailian is so large that we can always find some suitable unsolved problems for only one learner.

The process of problems selection is quite similar to the one in problem recommendation. However, in private contest, eight problems of different categories will be selected instead of five, and two of them come from the next grade – to see if the learner is ready for upgrading. The result of the private contests will be recorded.

The automatic contest generator is used for not only testing oneself but also generating examinations for course teaching. Teachers may simply input the expected number of problems, the average difficultness of problems, and then press "OK" – a suitable exam is born. It will save teacher's time from problem selection, and make the resource of problems be fully used.

8. Directions for Using Our System

At present, our system provides 2267 problems for users. Thousands of active users and hundreds of active groups are using our system for programming learning or teaching or something related.

We are pleased to give some brief instructions to both learners and teachers who want to experience the services on our system.

8.1 Directions for Learners

As a learner who is going to start your way of programming learning on our system, you need to

1) Register a new account on OpenJudge [10].
2) Join in Bailian group by clicking "Join in" on the home page of Bailian [8].

After that, you are able to see the "My Status" column on the right side of the page, including evaluation scores of your programming skill as well as recommendations. Now you can practice yourself by solving recommended problems, or generate a contest for self-testing.

8.2 Directions for Teachers

As a teacher who decides to use our system on your course, you are required to

1) Register a new account on OpenJudge.
2) Send a Request for creating a new group to the webmaster of OpenJudge [11]. You will received a reply from the webmaster soon.
3) If your request is accepted by OpenJudge, you will see a new private group under your full control. You can arrange the problem set, contests, and users in this

group freely. And you can use the automatic contest generator as many times as you want.

4) You need to ask your students to join in this group first, or they will have no access permissions on the resource in it.

9. Conclusion

The evaluation and recommendation system and the automatic contest generator we have implemented make a great improvement on the original Bailian group. The purpose is to provide a more suitable programming learning platform for learners at all levels. Learners can be able to studying programming on our system by themselves. As well, they are encouraged to exchange their experience and ideas during learning. And the system can be applied in any programming related courses.

There is still room for improvement in our system. For example, grade problems in an automatic way. Although the result of classifying a problem's category is quite unanimous among most experienced programmers, the grade of the problem may be controversial. That is because the difficulty of the problem depends on subjective judgments from different people. In this case, we need to do more research on automatic problem grading to make the grades more objective and forcible.

We also plan to evaluate the actual effectiveness of our system by tracking learner's behavior. We will collect the feedbacks from learners as well as the records of learner's actions, in order to figure out how much has the system changed in learner's programming learning.

We are welcoming programming learners from all over the world into our system for studying programming. And we are also looking forward to seeing more and more teachers are using our system in their courses.

References

[1] Wikipedia. (2013) Online judge - Wikipedia, the free encyclopedia. [Online]. Available: http://en.wikipedia.org/wiki/Online_judge

[2] S. S. Skiena, M. A. Revilla, *Programming Challenges*, 2003 ed. New York, USA: Springer, 2003.

[3] ACM/ICPC. (2013) World Finals Rules. [Online]. Available: http://icpc.baylor.edu/worldfinals/rules

[4] Topcoder. (2012) Algorithm Competition Rating System. [Online]. Available: http://apps.topcoder.com/wiki/display/tc/Algorithm+Competition+Rating+System

[5] (2013) The POJ website. [Online]. Available: http://poj.org/

[6] (2013) The OpenJudge website. [Online]. Available: http://openjudge.cn/

[7] OpenJudge. (2013) About. [Online]. Available: http://openjudge.cn/about.html

[8] (2013) The Bailian website. [Online]. Available: http://poj.grids.cn/

[9] T. H. Cormen, C. E. Leiserson, R. L. Rivest, C. Stein, *Introduction to Algorithms*, 3rd ed. Cambridge, USA: MIT Press, 2009.

[10] OpenJudge. (2013) Register. [Online]. Available: http://openjudge.cn/register/

[11] OpenJudge. (2013) Create New Group. [Online]. Available: http://openjudge.cn/groups/new

An Online Methodology For Individualized Education

Daniel D. Gajski[1], **Quoc-Viet Dang**[1], **and WenLiang He**[2]
[1]Henry Samueli School of Engineering, University of California, Irvine, CA, United States
[2]School of Education, University of California, Irvine, CA, United States

Abstract - *Online courses have been debated by various sources, including Governor Jerry Brown, the UC regents, and numerous college administrators, faculty, and students. The motivation behind such discussion is varied. Since there is no standard in online education, it has produced erratic results in terms of student performance and costs to students as well as administration. Online tools, if managed and prepared for properly, have the opportunity to provide the highly regarded individualized learning experience of the small classroom with the lower costs of large lecture halls while decreasing overall overhead costs. This article presents tools and a methodology to provide the small classroom experience in a much larger setting while keeping overall costs and time commitment down as well as improve overall student performance.*

Keywords: Online Methodology, In-Class Improvement, Flipping Classroom

1 Introduction

Online courses, the latest hot topic in education, have been debated by various sources, including Governor Jerry Brown [1], the UC regents, and numerous college administrators, faculty, and students. The motivation behind such discussion is varied. Administrators see offering online courses as a way to increase the number of students despite the shortage of large lecture halls, while generating some financial savings. Faculty and students are more skeptical, fearing they will miss the face to face student-lecturer interaction in and out of the classroom. Of course, with some traditional in-class courses, having hundreds of students with varying backgrounds and motivation, the student-lecturer interaction has already been severely diminished from smaller classroom sizes, which are no longer feasible due to the shrinking educational budget. Since there is no standard in online education, it has produced erratic results in terms of student performance and costs to students as well as administration.

However, online tools, if managed and prepared for properly, have the opportunity to provide the highly regarded individualized learning experience of the small classroom with the lower costs of large lecture halls while decreasing overall overhead costs. In fact, the tools used for online courses can be utilized to improve the existing traditional classroom dynamic. Students are trained from high school to prepare for testing by memorizing as many facts and examples as possible in order to answer each question. On the other hand, college professors tend to follow a top-down approach in teaching where they cover concepts, some math or algorithms, and methods or processes of finding proper solutions. These processes, especially in Engineering, must be understood and not just memorized because they have many steps involved: specification, analysis, design and synthesis, optimization, verification, implementation, and testing. In a small college classroom of 20-30 students, lecturers can help students who fall behind individually by expending their out-of-class time. In a larger class of 150 students or more, the small classroom teaching style doesn't work as well since the time commitment for both the lecturer and students are dramatically increased for the same duration of time.

The tools and methodology presented in this article aid in providing the small classroom experience in a much larger setting while keeping overall costs and time commitment down. Such tools and methodology can be applied to any learning environment, not just online, to better prepare students for learning concepts and solving problems. It must cover

a) Lectures
b) Sample problems with solutions
c) Questions and answers
d) Homework
e) Tests

2 Improving the In-Class Environment

We will compare the typical teaching methodology for a large classroom with a modified methodology that utilizes online tools to provide a richer learning environment for students. Our initial research compares two groups of students (Group A & Group B) taking a Digital Logic Design Engineering course during two separate quarters. Online course material consisted of custom content developed specifically for this Digital Design course as well as existing UCI tools through EEE (Electronic Educational Environment). We compare the students across 3 exams:

Exam 1: Both groups are taught based on a typical teaching methodology (overviewed below). Online lecture videos are available but no special emphasis is given to them. All material is covered in lecture and/or discussion sections. This exam is used to normalize the results for the following two exams.

Exam 2: Group A continues to be taught using the typical teaching methodology. Group B is presented with a typical Online course methodology. All lectures & samples are to be reviewed online via online videos. In-class lecture & discussion sections are now treated like online meetings; the professor and teaching assistants only cover questions asked and do not repeat any lectures.

Exam 3: Group A continues to be taught the typical teaching methodology. Group B is presented with a hybrid methodology based on in-class and online processes. A general lecture is given per topic each classroom session. Students are expected to review specific details and caveats that are covered by online videos & submit questions before the next classroom session. In the following lecture or discussion, specific questions are answered that are submitted by students, similar to an online course web meeting.

c) many students are not prepared and have no questions, exacerbating the above situations. Much of the information the students need is presented once in a lecture and/or discussion. If they miss the lecture or get lost on a concept taught, they fall further and further behind as the class progresses.

Therefore, the presentation is general and not helpful to many students with weak backgrounds or insufficient skills while leaving other students bored and non-attentive. To help alleviate some of these issues, sample problems can be covered in discussion sections with fewer students, but the above situation still applies, just on a smaller scale. Weekly homework is assigned to keep students on track; however, due to learning habits from students' past educational experiences, assignments are generally completed to gain points rather than understanding the concept from the material.

In the typical in-class environment with ever increasing classroom size and varying student skill levels, most of the lecture and discussion time available is used to cover examples, go over homework solutions, and prepare for testing. There is simply not enough time available to

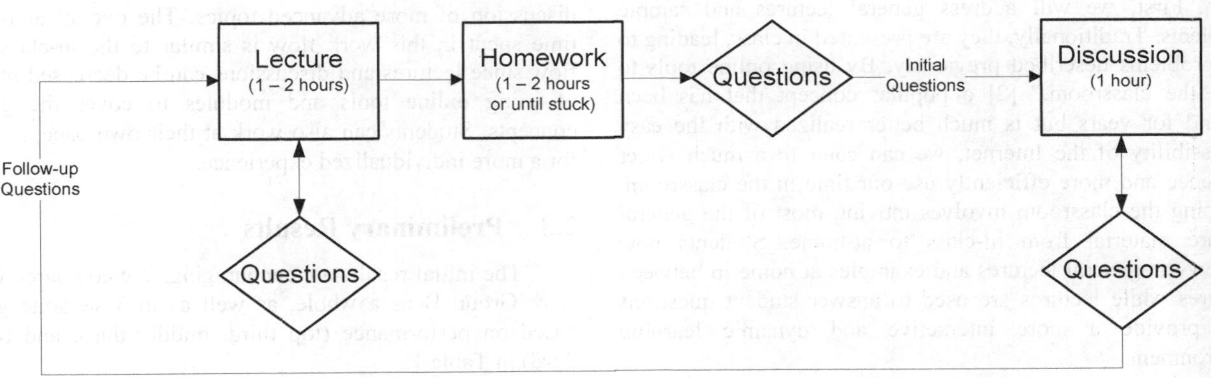

Figure 1: A Typical In-Class Methodology Work Flow.

2.1 A Typical In-Class Learning Environment

The in-class teaching environment was originally developed for small classes (20-40 students). However, enrollment in many college courses has grown to over 100 students per class. Lectures for a couple hundred students in a large lecture hall for 1-2 hours are very difficult because

a) schedulers have problems with room sizes and cannot schedule too many short lectures or discussions.

b) a single presentation needs to cater to the varying skill levels and knowledge of all 100-200 students.

individualize the learning experience for many students with the current teaching methodology.

In Figure 1, a typical in-class methodology is presented. Students are given a 1-2 hour lecture, which may cover several concepts. During this time, general questions are covered. Follow-up questions are not typically asked since students need to think about the material, read more references, or do some homework before they have additional questions. When they attempt the homework, they may have initial questions. These are answered during the discussion section, along with some follow-up questions from the lecture. This method is not efficient since it moves at the rate of the slowest students and much of the time is spent answering

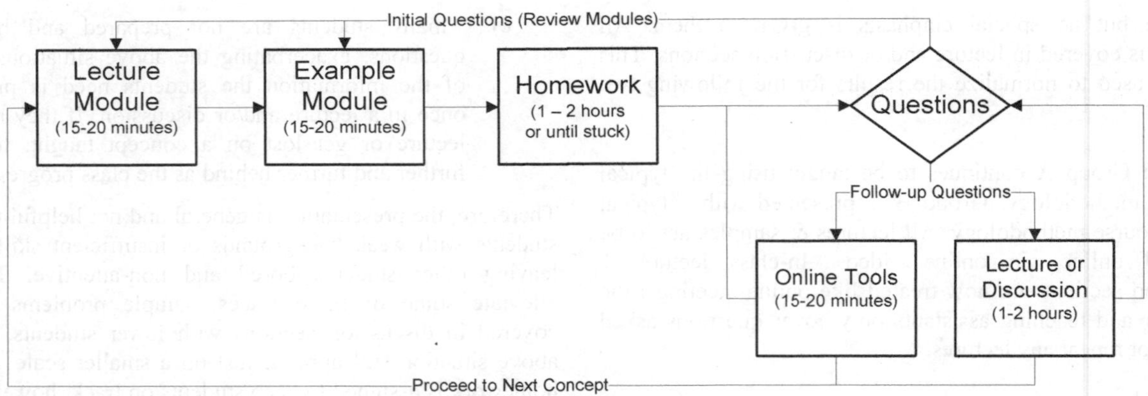

Figure 2: A Typical Online Methodology Work Flow.

general questions since follow-up questions require additional review of the material.

2.2 Adding an Online Methodology

In order to have more advanced discussion and cover concepts that help struggling students as well as advanced students in a large class, the "what, where, when, and how" of information to be presented and consumed must be improved upon. First, we will address general lectures and sample problems. Traditionally, they are presented in class, leading to the problems described previously. By using online tools to "flip the classroom," [2] a popular concept that has been around for years but is much better realized with the easy accessibility of the Internet, we can cater to a much wider audience and more efficiently use our time in the classroom. Flipping the classroom involves moving most of the general lecture material from in-class to at-home. Students now review the general lectures and examples at home in between lectures while lectures are used to answer student questions and provide a more interactive and dynamic learning environment.

Lectures can be succinct and split into individual modules or concepts instead of a weekly 1-2 hour lecture session which usually covers several topics. Students can review the material multiple times, refer to references at their own pace, and discuss with classmates, teaching assistants, and the professor regarding the material presented. Classroom time can now be utilized for more advanced discussion and better targeted toward student skill levels based on the content they discuss through available online tools, such as the course mailing lists and message boards.

In the Online methodology work flow, shown in Figure 2, students begin by reviewing 15-20 minute lecture and/or example modules. Any initial questions regarding the lecture, example, or homework can typically be answered by reviewing the module again in more detail, which is not typically possible with a traditional in-class environment. If there are follow-up questions, they can be answered using online tools, such as message boards or mailing lists.

The turn-around time per concept is much quicker than a typical in-class work flow and can happen multiple times throughout any given week. An in-class or streaming lecture and discussion can still take place; however, note that the majority of questions asked now are follow-up questions, which allows for more efficient use of interaction time and discussion of more advanced topics. The overall amount of time spent in this work flow is similar to the in-class work flow since lectures and discussions can be decreased in favor of using online tools and modules to cover the general concepts. Students can also work at their own pace, allowing for a more individualized experience.

2.3 Preliminary Results

The initial results are encouraging. We compared Group A & Group B as a whole, as well as in 3 separate groups based on performance (top third, middle third, and bottom third) in Table 1.

As stated earlier, we will be using Exam 1 as the normalization factor. Students in Group A & Group B received the same typical in-class teaching methodology for material leading up to Exam 1. On average, students from Group B score between 4-8% lower than students in Group A. All other factors being equal, we expect this performance to stay in that range. Since we change the teaching and learning methodology for Exam 2 & 3, we expect some changes in performance as well.

For the material covered in Exam 2, a typical online methodology was used, which just moved lectures from in-class to online videos. This can help address in-class problems like scheduling of large lecture halls, being able to present to students of varying skill levels by allowing them to choose the appropriate videos, and keep overhead costs down in a general sense. There is a minor improvement in allowing the lecturer to reach out to students of different skill levels

Table 1: Group A vs. Group B Performance.

Exam 1:	Group A	Group B	Difference	Improvement
All Students:	81.31%	75.07%	-6.24%	n/a
Top 1/3:	90.24%	85.76%	-4.47%	n/a
Middle 1/3:	80.63%	74.58%	-6.05%	n/a
Bottom 1/3:	72.85%	64.86%	-7.98%	n/a
All Students:	65.28%	60.42%	-4.86%	1.37%
Top 1/3:	79.37%	79.44%	0.08%	4.55%
Middle 1/3:	64.92%	60.14%	-4.78%	1.27%
Bottom 1/3:	51.22%	41.67%	-9.55%	-1.57%
All Students:	53.52%	54.72%	1.20%	7.44%
Top 1/3:	70.77%	72.53%	1.76%	6.24%
Middle 1/3:	54.23%	55.31%	1.09%	7.14%
Bottom 1/3:	35.12%	36.32%	1.20%	9.18%

through the videos and online message boards; much of this effectiveness depends on the students' willingness to and frequency of which they use the technology. Since some material is offloaded outside the classroom, there is more time to spend on individual student questions during the classroom session. Similar to the video and online message board issue, this also depends on the students' motivation to take advantage of these opportunities.

As a whole, students in Group B showed a marginal improvement over students in Group A (1.37%). When split into three separate groups based on performance, the top third of students in Group B outperformed the top third of students in Group A by approximately 4.55% after normalization is considered, the middle third of Group B did 1.27% better, and the bottom third did 1.57% worse than Group A.

In an attempt to bring learning to a more individual level using online tools, Group B students were taught using an online hybrid methodology that goes beyond the typical in-class or online methodologies for Exam 3. Students in Group A continued to receive a traditional in-class teaching educational environment.

In the hybrid methodology, we combine the advantages of in-class and online environments. The classroom is still "flipped," where much of the learning is done outside of the classroom through online videos, mailing lists, and discussion on message boards in between scheduled class sessions. However, we help guide students with introductory lectures and answer general questions during an early classroom session. Since a significant portion of the material is covered outside of the classroom, there is more time for individualized help and advanced discussion in the classroom itself. From there, students are required to go through online lecture and sample videos. Finally, they must take notes and submit questions on concepts they wish to be discussed in following lectures.

Using this method, students in Group B performed significantly better than students in Group A as a whole and as smaller groups. After the normalization factor, Group B averaged 7.44% higher on the exam, with the top third performing 6.24% better in Group B, middle third 7.14% better, and bottom third 9.18% better than Group A.

2.4 Student Feedback

Student feedback regarding the traditional, online, and hybrid methodologies have shown that online videos and tools

Table 2: Helpfulness of Different Formats of Instruction for Students in Group B.

Helpfulness:	1 (least)	2	3	4	5	6 (most)
Reading Textbooks:	24.09%	21.90%	20.44%	13.87%	10.95%	8.76%
Watching Online Lecture Videos:	3.65%	6.57%	11.68%	30.66%	32.12%	15.33%
In-Class Lectures:	12.50%	16.18%	19.12%	19.85%	19.85%	12.50%
Watching Online TA Example Videos:	0.73%	2.19%	3.65%	13.87%	28.47%	51.09%
In-Class TA Examples:	2.92%	5.84%	15.33%	22.63%	30.66%	22.63%

Table 3: Study Habits of Students in Group B after Class.

Study Habits:	1 (never)	2	3	4	5 (very often)
Reading Textbooks:	18.71%	27.34%	27.34%	17.27%	9.35%
Watching Online Lecture Videos:	2.90%	5.07%	20.29%	32.61%	39.13%
Watching Online TA Example Videos:	2.90%	4.35%	18.12%	26.81%	47.83%

are aiding in improving their overall performance.

First, we review how students ranked each format of instruction in terms of helpfulness in understanding the course content in Table 2.

In general, online lecture and TA example videos are preferred to in-class lectures and examples. Reading the textbook is the least preferred of the 5 learning formats. As mentioned earlier, lectures were not formatted as traditional lectures, but were handled similar to Q&A type sessions; therefore, the basic knowledge required for the class is presented in the videos. More time is spent discussing deeper concepts in-class, which was more useful to students who were studying more often or participating more often in-class. TA examples were more popular than concept lectures since they are given similar homework problems and solutions to review.

Next, we look at how students are spending their time studying outside of the classroom in Table 3.

Again, students in our Digital Design Logic course preferred watching online lecture and TA example videos over reading textbooks. The videos were able to better target varying skill levels of students and could be updated throughout or between the quarters. Since students receive a general overview and more detailed example in short concise videos, they can more efficiently prepare for the next lecture or homework as well as discuss problems rather than reading long chapters in a textbook.

Lastly, we review how much time is actually spent studying for this course compared to other courses in Table 4.

Considering 3-4 classes is a typical full-time course load, students are studying more for this course than any other single course in their curriculum. This is due to the more rigorous studying methodology required for the Digital Design course including studying online videos, completing homework based on the videos, and submitting questions for lectures based on each set of online lecture and example videos. However, they are still studying well under the 40 hours total that is typical of a full-time course load. A typical course requires about 10 hours per week of total studying; with more students studying in the 6-10 hour range, we would expect the performance of the students to be even higher.

3 Conclusions

This modest sampling of using online teaching methods to improve an existing large in-class environment has been shown to be effective. Overall, students have varying amounts of motivation to ensure they do well and get the most out of their learning experience. Initial feedback suggests that the online videos are well received once they are presented with our hybrid teaching methodology. By using online tools, making small changes to how in-class sessions are utilized, and adjusting how students learn inside and outside the classroom, student performance can be increased without impacting factors such as cost and quality of education. In fact, by utilizing new technology and spending time to find effective means of conveying concepts and materials like that of the hybrid online methodology we can provide a more individualized experience for larger student classes in this time of increased enrollment, with a small increase in the number of TAs, and some initial online investment.

4 References

[1] David Siders. "Jerry Brown carries the day on online classes at UC, CSU"; *The Sacramento Bee* 17 January 2013. http://www.sacbee.com/2013/01/17/5120340/jerry-brown-carries-the-day-on.html

[2] J.W. Baker, "The 'Classroom Flip': Using Web Course Management Tools to Become the Guide on the Side." 11th Conference on College Teaching and Learning, Jacksonville, FL, 12-15 April 2000.

Table 4: Study Frequency of Students in Group B Outside of Class.

Studying Frequency:	0 - 2h	2 - 4h	4 - 6h	6 - 8h	8 - 10h	> 10h
Preparing and Studying for This Class:	24.09%	21.90%	20.44%	13.87%	10.95%	8.76%
Preparing and Studying for Other Classes:	3.65%	6.57%	11.68%	30.66%	32.12%	15.33%

Applying a Developed Conceptual Framework for Testing the Suitability of Four Dynamic Platforms for Teaching Web Applications Development

J. Dehinbo[1]

[1]Department of Web & Multimedia Computing, Tshwane University of Technology, Pretoria, South Africa

Abstract - *Developing intellectual capital in web application development necessitates enabling students to perform at their best capacity level when the platform chosen by the institution is suitable for learning the relevant concepts. However, the various platforms for developing dynamic Web applications suggest the existence of the problem of choosing the most suitable platform for learning the concepts of web applications development in tertiary institutions towards enhancing learning. This study tests a framework by Dehinbo [16] to determine suitable platform for teaching Web application development in tertiary institutions by evaluating four platforms namely Java Servlets, Java Server Pages, Active Server Pages and PHP using various research methods including descriptive inquiry, document analysis, observations and programming tests. While PHP emerges as a suitable platform, the significance of the study lies in the establishment of a comprehensive but specific set of criteria that can be used as a scientific basis for selection.*

Keywords: Web applications development platforms, Internet and Web, programming languages, web techniques, comparison frameworks, evaluation

1 Introduction and background

This study tests a framework developed in previous studies which establish various criteria that can be used to evaluate dynamic Web platforms to determine a suitable platform for teaching Web applications development in tertiary institutions in order to contribute towards enhancing learning in developing intellectual capital in web development. The framework, Dehinbo [16] includes components to ensure suitability for teaching structured basic programming concepts [13], object oriented programming concepts [8], file processing [7], exception handling [9], database processing [10], Web techniques [14] and XML processing [15]. Other components are to ensure latency and speed of processing [4], portability [11] and ease of use [12].

The study is necessitated by the existence of the problem of choosing the most suitable platform among various platforms for teaching the concepts of web applications development by undergraduate students in tertiary institutions.

Vinoski [24] indicates that the many platforms and vendors from which one can choose does not make easy the task of choosing the one that would best solve one's problem. Which of these platforms would be most suitable for teaching Web application development? Lim [19] states that information systems departments need to reexamine their curricula in order to prepare students to face the challenge of being productive in a computing world swamped with web technologies. The use of various programming and scripting languages could also lead to elements of repetition and confusion. Yet, comprehension is very important in undergraduate studies [25]. The comprehension of relevant concepts by students may be affected by the choice of platform because according to Sebesta [23], the language in which programmers develop software places various limits on the development efforts. Thus, the choice of dynamic web application development platform should involve critical evaluation:

> "Web development tools need to be analyzed in terms of its purpose (what it is designed to do), technology (ease of use, robustness, scalability, security, performance, etc.), support (portability, cost, ISP support), and how well it works in the real world [2:105]".

Thus, we apply a developed comprehensive framework to evaluate the suitability of four specified platforms. This involves analyzing the platforms according to a variety of features and characteristics.

2 Literature review

Wiedenbeck *et al.* [25] observe that evaluating programming languages, development platforms and tools is very important for understanding the effects on novice programmers, but is difficult to carry out. This possibly supports the view of Apte et al. [1] that a study of existing literature showed varying conclusions about the superiority of one dynamic Web platform over another. Also, Prechelt [22] indicates that programmers usually hold varied strong opinions on development platforms' suitability.

To reduce varied opinions on development platforms' suitability, it is important to establish clear criteria for evaluation. The most important criterion for evaluating a tool is the suitability for doing the job for which the tool is needed. In this regard, Ashenfelter [2:105] emphasize that web development tools need to be analyzed in terms of their purpose. Thus, for choosing a language or platform that is suitable for learning introductory programming, Holt *et al.* [17] use the criteria that it should be appropriate for introducing programming concepts used in the real world such as in business, science and government; and it should encourage systematic problem solving. Similarly, Kolling and Rosenberg [18] suggest enabling useful concepts from theoretical model and avoidance of conceptual redundancy, as achieving the same thing in a variety of ways can mean flexibility to the expert, but usually confuses beginners.

For more information on related literature review, Dehinbo [14] presents a summarized view. A key point observed is that choosing a suitable platform should involve exhaustive evaluations of various options based on various relevant criteria that are backed by scientific facts and results. These studies relating to the established framework fill this gap in the body of knowledge by being unique in the following ways: The advantages and strengths of platforms should be examined and ranked in the light of certain desired qualities relevant to specific use such as the suitability for teaching Web techniques. This is just as for example, the ease of teaching increases productivity in institutions than platform's flexibility which could be preferable in industries. This informs our identification of desirable concepts of Web application development before establishing the criteria used for the evaluations.

3 Research Design and Methodology

An interpretive research design is used involving elements of descriptive, analytical and comparative studies. McMillan and Schumacher [20:33] state that while a descriptive study describes a system with the aim of characterizing it as it is, by using numbers, comparative study investigates the differences, thereby taking descriptive study a step further. Therefore, a descriptive approach is used to characterize desirable features of the platforms towards establishing a set of criteria [16]. In applying the established criteria, an analytical approach is used to analyze and evaluate platforms to determine the level of satisfaction of the criteria for learning Web concepts. Also, an experimental approach is used to estimate the latency of the platforms.

a) The descriptive method used in establishing the framework involves document review and study of various manuals and textbooks for different platforms from various sources and established body of knowledge, including those written by the designers and originators of the platforms as well as various websites for the applicable web servers such as Microsoft Internet Information Server (IIS) and Apache tomcat. This is to identify features that could enhance the teaching of techniques in Web applications development. These features were characterized to establish criteria for evaluating the suitability of platforms for learning Web techniques. The established criteria serve as a model. Bowling [3:141] describes models as abstract representations of the essential characteristics of phenomena of interest that make explicit, the relationships and comparison between the characteristics. The model for this study presented in [16] is hereby applied for analyzing, evaluating and comparing specific platforms.

In testing the framework, the analytical method is aimed at evaluating specific platforms to ascertain their level of satisfaction of the established criteria. Therefore, documents were reviewed for the specific platforms to be evaluated and compared, and answers were sought to the questions and the availability of features that serve as the criteria.

Moreover, experience was used to physically observe the support for various Web techniques by the platforms. Bowling [3:358] describes observation as a research method in which the investigator systematically watches, listens to and records the phenomenon of interest. Scores were then assigned to each platform based on the availability of desired features, the level of support enabled on specific tasks or the inherent characteristics of the platform

Using close-ended "Yes/No" questions, the measuring tool has values on a scale of 1 to 3, where:

3 = "Yes"; 2 = "Not quite or with minor workaround", and 1= "No".

Establishing reliability: As a way of increasing validity, answers to the criteria questions were sought from established and recognized sources. The accompanying references are provided for verification or for more information. This is supplemented with practical experiences and programming tests confirming the satisfaction of some of the criteria established. Also, to increase reliability, the quantitative characterization and evaluation using numbers would enhance clarity in the choice of platform with the highest score. This is unlike just using qualitative sentences to evaluate the platforms, at the end of which it could be difficult to say which platform is really more suitable. Furthermore, reliability is enhanced with the scale of 1 and 3 thereby avoiding subjective situations of distinguishing between, say, a score of 3 or 4 on a scale of 1 to 5.

b) The latency experiment aims to estimate the execution speed for programs written using each of the dynamic Web platforms in order to gain information on the suitability of these platforms for recurrent program testing in a practical laboratory session. Dehinbo [4] presents the full details of this experiment and then ranks the performance of the platforms. It should be pointed out that users of the framework can conduct their own latency experiment, as long as a ranking of the platforms eventually emerges.

Data analysis: The data analysis was done using simple statistical parametric analysis, such as sums and means. The scores for all the criteria were summed up for each web based dynamic platform to obtain a total score from which the platform with the highest overall score can be identified.

Limitations: As an interpretive study, a particular limitation is that of the subjective view of the researcher. However, users can add/remove certain criteria or change their weights.

4 Developed framework applied

The developed framework as presented and published in Dehinbo [16] consists of a series of criteria for evaluating the platforms, as well as a programming experiment for ranking the platforms in order of their performances. The various categories and subdivision of the criteria and experiment are provided in table 1 below:

Table 1. Summary of the developed framework applied Source: (Dehinbo [16]).

Criteria to measure the overall suitability for the teaching of Web application development concepts:
Basic/structured programming concepts Lexical Structures; Data types; Expressions and Operators; Control Structures; Functions and modularizations (Dehinbo [13]) **Other Web development concepts** Object-oriented programming (Dehinbo [8]) Web techniques (Dehinbo [14]) Database handling capabilities (Dehinbo [10]) File processing capabilities (Dehinbo [7]) Exception handling capabilities (Dehinbo [9]) Extensible Markup Language (XML) support (Dehinbo [15])
Criteria to measure the ease of use and speed of use Availability of smart Integrated Development Environment (Dehinbo [12]) Features to simplify execution and increase latency (Dehinbo [6])
Latency experiment to measure the speed of execution of program (Dehinbo [4])
Criteria to measure the affordability of the platforms and related components Evaluating the cost of acquiring the platform and related software (Dehinbo [6])
Criteria to measure the portability of the platforms Evaluating the architectural neutrality, portability, generality and the familiarity of the operating environment of the platform (Dehinbo [11])
Survey (Included to informally document the experience of past students taught using the platforms and see how it relates to the results of testing the framework)

The first set of criteria aims to measure the suitability for teaching the Web application development concepts. This is subdivided into criteria to measure suitability for teaching basic programming concepts, object-oriented programming concepts and those for teaching other Web application development concepts. The basic programming concepts [13] include lexical structures, data types, expressions and operators, control structures, and functional modularizations, while the other programming and Web development concepts include object-oriented programming [8], Web techniques such as HTTP support, session and application state management; Obtaining server information; Form processing and Validation [14], database handling capabilities [10], file processing capabilities [7], exception handling capabilities [9] and XML support [15]. These are to establish that the platform is actually capable of satisfying the purpose of teaching Web application development concepts. An important assumption made here is that, for undergraduates, factors that could enhance readability of the code would enhance comprehension of the code. Our priority here is to get the students started enthusiastically, and as they progress in their studies, other standards of software developments can be phased in. Otherwise students could become disillusioned with dynamic Web applications development, create a low self-esteem and achieve low pass rates.

The second set of criteria aims to measure the ease of use [12] and the speed of use of the platforms. This involves the criteria to measure the availability of desirable features of smart IDEs and features to simplify execution and decrease latency [4]. To supplement the features that decrease latency, the latency experiment is included to rank the platforms in order of their latency. It is important to note, however, that users of the framework can conduct their own latency experiment, as long as it ranks the platforms. The platform with the lowest latency is given a high score while that with the highest latency is given a low score. Users can then multiply these scores with weights as they find necessary. Using the platform and its applicable IDE that is user-friendly and fast to use is the goal here. Fast execution and speedy operations would ease the recurrent compiling-testing-debugging activities in students' laboratory sessions.

The third set of criteria measures the cost [6]) and portability of the platforms [11]. The cost criteria ensure a chosen platform's affordability by students such that they can install it easily on their PC at home and practice extensively. A freely downloadable platform would definitely be within the reach of many students. Portability criteria ensure compatibility across major hardware specifications and operating systems. This increases the likelihood that work started in the laboratory can be continued on their home PC or even be continued on their future office computer in workplace after graduation. Minimum hardware requirements for such platforms, as well as portability across major operating systems, would make the platform available to a greater number of students. The next section presents the results of testing our framework using evaluations to arrive at our final choice.

5 Summary of the results of applying the developed framework

In summarizing the published results of the various subcomponents of the framework, table 2 below presents the overall developed framework as well as the results of testing the framework as published in various articles and combined in the overall results given in the table to determine the platform with the overall best score. Figure 1 also gives a pictorial chart showing the overall scores of the platforms.

Looking more critically at the framework's components and their results in table 2, the first component contains the results of the criteria to evaluate the suitability of platforms for teaching the basic concepts of programming and object-oriented programming as well as other Web application development concepts. This is followed by the criteria established to evaluate the ease of use, speed of use, as well as affordability and portability of the platform.

Table 2. Summary of the developed framework and the overall result of its testing.

Criteria categories	Servlet	JSP	ASP	PHP
Basic concepts				
Lexical Structures	19	21	28	24
Data types	13	13	22	27
Expressions and Operators	18	18	25	26
Control Structures	11	11	23	19
Functions and modularizations	13	11	9	12
TOTAL SCORE	**74**	**74**	**107**	**108**
Other Web development concepts				
Object-oriented programming	33	33	21	33
Web techniques	29	29	33	31
Database handling capabilities	11	11	15	16
File processing capabilities	25	25	25	30
Exception handling capabilities	19	19	19	24
XML support	15	15	15	15
TOTAL SCORE	**132**	**132**	**128**	**149**
Overall suitability score for teaching Web dev. concepts	**206**	**206**	**235**	**257**
Ease of use, latency, affordability and portability				
Availability of smart Integrated Development Environment (IDE)	64	63	58	58
Features to simplify execution and increase latency	37	38	45	47
Cost of the platform and related software	12	12	10	14
Architectural neutrality and portability of the platform	24	24	11	22
TOTAL SCORE	**137**	**137**	**124**	**141**
Assigned Latency score	**4**	**2**	**6**	**8**
OVERALL SCORE	**347**	**345**	**365**	**406**

Lastly, the latency experiment component measures the speed of execution of Web programs. The testing of the developed framework was conducted using four selected platforms namely Java Servlet and JavaServer Pages, Active Server Pages and PHP. From the results in table 2, it is evident that PHP is considered most suitable in each result category namely;

- ☑ the category for the suitability for teaching Web development concepts,
- ☑ the category for the ease of use, latency, affordability and portability,
- ☑ the category for the latency experiment.

Java Servlet and JSP are considered least suitable based on all the criteria, though, when the latency result is added, JSP becomes the most unsuitable. However, Java Servlet is ranked equal to PHP in suitability for teaching object-oriented programming concepts.

Taking a closer look at Java Servlet and JSP, JSP had the least score on the whole, although in some cases it ranked the same as Java Servlets while in other cases it ranked the same as ASP. This is to be expected given the fact that JSP shares the same background language with Java Servlet, and also shares logic similar to ASP's way of embedding code within HTML tags. This suggests that while JSP gained from the simplicity of its structure by simply embedding code in HTML, this same simplicity requires later translation into Servlet thereby obstructing high latency.

JSP ranked second along with Java Servlet in the category of the *ease of use*, latency, affordability and portability. This could be explained as due to the background power of the Java Programming language, the fact that it is free and open source, its matured and free IDEs as well as the interoperability of the Java environment with other technologies such as various DBMS, middleware such as RMI, CORBA and the recent mobile technologies.

While ASP ranked second most suitable on the whole, it ranked lowest in the category of suitability for teaching object-oriented programming concepts. This is an area that Windows.NET is likely to address. ASP's ranking higher than JSP could be explained by the familiarity with Microsoft's look and feel in many related products.

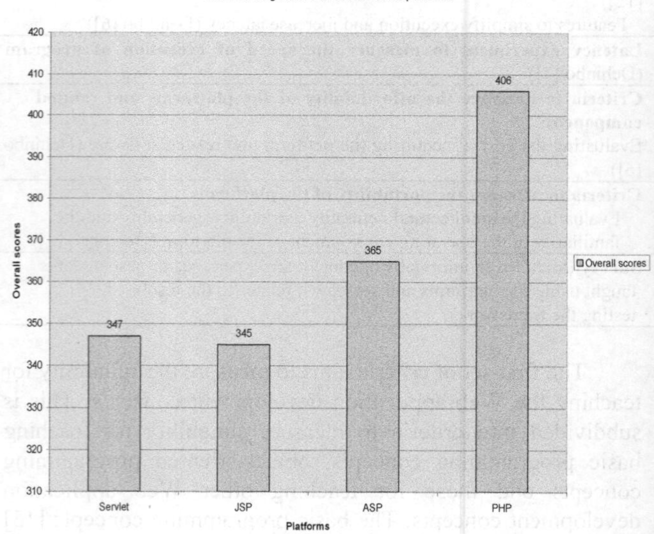

Figure 1. Chart showing the total scores for all the platforms

Pedagogically, ASP and PHP, from experience, seem to be more suitable for teaching and learning Web techniques due to the simplicity of their commands and functions. In summary, applying the established criteria reveals that PHP has the highest score followed by ASP and then the Java-based platforms. It should however be noted that the scores are subjectively based on the author's knowledge and experience as well as the current design version of the platforms. They are thus subject to change.

Therefore, the emphasis of this study is on the establishment of the criteria that enables the selection among the platforms. Users can thus adapt these criteria to their own taste and can also test or apply the criteria on other platforms.

Finally, it is worthy to note that the ranking of the overall results, as shown in figure 1 above, differs slightly from the trend in the rankings in the results of the survey. The difference is that the survey results for JSP are higher than those for Java Servlets. This could be because students are interested in the simplicity of structure in JSP and have little regard for other important criteria. This highlights the relevance of the study as it considers results using various criteria and looks at the research problem from different angles.

6 Conclusions

We applied a conceptual framework that can be used to determine a suitable platform for teaching dynamic Web applications development in tertiary institutions. The framework has taken into consideration the need to satisfy certain requirements that are considered important to the effective comprehension of Web application development concepts. These are aimed at ensuring: effective teaching of dynamic Web applications development concepts; suitability for real life programming that students will be exposed to as they graduate; affordability to allow for individual ownership of the chosen platform by students, so that they can practice on their own.

Other requirements that are considered important are: to enhance comprehension by using commands that have a reasonable number of unique basic syntactical components with syntax, semantics and meanings that make commands easy to remember; allowing an efficient teaching environment by ensuring suitability for completing tasks within a reasonable time period with features that promote good readability of code, tracing and debugging aids with useful and smart integrated editing environments equipped with context sensitive helps.

Further affordability is ensured through the requirements for the use of minimum disk space and memory resources, with simpler architecture to facilitate speedy operations, and simpler execution steps because of higher-level commands as well as ensuring portability among major operating systems through the affordability, architectural neutrality, generality and familiarity of the operating environment.

The results of applying the framework indicate that out of the four dynamic Web platforms evaluated, PHP is considered most suitable. This could probably be due to the fact that it is suitable for teaching structured programming, object oriented programming as well as web application development concepts. Moreover, it is a Free and Open Source Software (FOSS) that is free both in cost and license's freedom to modify source code. Furthermore, PHP is portable and equipped with a free easy-to-use IDE as well as free DBMS (MySQL). It also supports various Web servers, DBMS and interoperates with other technologies.

7 Recommendations

Based on the essence of this study, it is recommended that comparisons of platforms be done with specific uses and criteria in mind. Rather than merely listing the advantages and strengths of each platform in a comparison, the advantages and strengths of each platform should be examined and ranked in the light of certain desired qualities relevant to specific "context of use". This is because certain strengths may be of highest priority to specific "context of use" only. For example, at the University of Technologies, the ease of learning a programming language increases our productivity more than the flexibility of the programming language or platform.

8 Research contributions

While not aimed at persuading readers that one dynamic Web platform is better than another, the main contribution of the research is to help readers make a more informed decision on which platform is more suitable for teaching Web application development in tertiary institutions. This implies that the framework ensures that although the chosen platform may or may not be the most powerful or most common in the market, it is the one that has features that contribute to the accomplishment of Web application development expertise by students in tertiary institutions. Further contributions emanate from the insights provided into the analysis of various features of specified platforms.

We need no longer have to rely only on features promised by the platform development teams, since according to Olivier [21:41], such might contain marketing or publicity hype. Neither do we have to rely simply on general comparisons. The choice of a platform using our developed framework provides a level of certainty with a systematic way of choosing a suitable dynamic Web platform to enhance teaching of Web application development in tertiary institutions. This provides the possibility of increasing the learners' potential in such a way that could lead to developed intellectual capital and higher productivity.

9 References

[1] Apte, V., Hansen, T. and Reeser, P. (2003) "Performance comparison of dynamic Web platforms." Computer Communications. Vol. 26, No. 8, pp. 888 – 898.

[2] Ashenfelter, J.P. (1999). "Choosing a Database for Your Web Site", USA : Wiley Computer Publishing.

[3] Bowling, A. (2002). *"Research methods in health"*. 2nd edition. UK: Open University Press.

[4] Dehinbo, J. (2005). "The performance of web-based 2-tier middleware systems". *Journal of Issues in Informing Science and Information Technology*. Vol. 2, No. 2005, pp. 757-769. Online. Available from http://2005papers.iisit.org/I59f23dehin.pdf Retrieved 13/05/05.

[5] Dehinbo. J. (2006a). "Determining a suitable programming language for the B.Tech. degree in Computer studies dept, TNG.", In: *Proceedings of the Information Systems Education conference (ISECON)*. Held in Dallas, TX. USA. 2-5 November 2006. Online. Available from http://isedj.org/isecon/2006/3144/ISECON.2006.Dehinbo.pdf

[6] Dehinbo, J. (2006b). "Towards a framework for determining a platform for teaching Web application development in tertiary institutions in South Africa". *MSc Dissertation*. Unpublished. School of Computing, UNISA, Pretoria.

[7] Dehinbo. J. (2007). *"Evaluating the suitability of dynamic Web platforms for teaching File Information processing"*. In: R. Carlsen et al. (Eds.), *Proceedings of Society for Information Technology and Teacher Education International Conference (SITE). ISBN: 1-880094-51-4*. Vol. 2007, No. 1, pp. 2985-2992. Chesapeake, VA: AACE. Held in San Antonio, Texas. USA. 27-31 March 2007. Online. Available from: http://www.editlib.org/p/25060

[8] Dehinbo. J. (2008). *"Evaluating the suitability of dynamic Web platforms for teaching object-oriented programming"*. In: K. McFerrin et al. (Eds.), *Proceedings of Society for Information Technology and Teacher Education International Conference (SITE). ISBN: 1-880094-51-4*. Vol. 2008, No. 1, pp. 3729-3735. Chesapeake, VA: AACE. Held in Las Vegas, NV. 3-7 March 2008. Online. http://www.editlib.org/p/27828.

[9] Dehinbo. J. (2009a). "Evaluating the suitability of dynamic Web platforms for teaching Exception handling". *Information Systems Education Journal.* Vol. 7, No. 12, pp. 1-13. ISSN: 1545-679X. Available online. http://isedj.org/7/12/ISEDJ.7(12).Dehinbo.pdf Retrieved 24/03/09.

[10] Dehinbo. J. (2009b). *"Establishing and applying the criteria for evaluating the suitability of dynamic Web platforms for teaching Database processing concepts"*. In: *Proceedings of the Information Systems Education conference (ISECON).* Held in Crystal City/Washington, DC. USA. 5-8 November 2009. Online. http://proc.isecon.org/2009/3752/ISECON.2009.Dehinbo.pdf

[11] Dehinbo. J. (2010). "Establishing and applying criteria for evaluating the portability of dynamic e-learning development platforms in tertiary institutions". In J. Sanchez & K. Zhang (Eds.), *Proceedings of World Conference on E-Learning in Corporate, Government, Healthcare, and Higher Education* Vol. 2010, No. 1, pp. 467-474. Chesapeake, VA: AACE. Held in Orlando, FL. 18-22 October, 2010. Online. http://www.editlib.org/p/35589

[12] Dehinbo. J. (2011a). "Establishing and Applying Criteria for Evaluating the Ease of Use of Dynamic Platforms for Teaching Web Application Development". *Information Systems Education Journal.* Vol. 9, No. 5, pp. 86-96. October 2011. Available online. http://isedj.org/2011-9/N5/ISEDJVol9No5.pdf ISSN: 1545-679X Retrieved 24/07/2011.

[13] Dehinbo. J. (2011b). "Establishing criteria for evaluating the suitability of Web application development platforms for teaching basic programming concepts". In: M. Koehler & P. Mishra (Eds.), *Proceedings of Society for Information Technology & Teacher Education International Conference,* Vol. 2011, No. 1, pp. 1795-1802. Chesapeake, VA: AACE. Held in Nashville, TN. USA. 7-11 March 2011. Online. http://www.editlib.org/p/36558

[14] Dehinbo. J. (2011c). "Establishing the suitability of dynamic Web application development platforms for learning Web techniques". In: *Proceedings of the* 2nd International Conference on Information Management and Evaluation (ICIME 2011), Held in Toronto, Canada, 27-28 April 2011. Online. Available from http://www.academic-conferences.org/icime/icime2011/icime11-proceedings.htm

[15] Dehinbo. J. (2012). "Suitability for teaching Extensible Markup Language (XML) processing in selecting dynamic Web platform for teaching Web application development". In P. Resta (Ed.), *Proceedings of Society for Information Technology & Teacher Education International Conference,* pp. 1722-1728. Chesapeake, VA: AACE. Held in Austin, TX. USA. 5-9 March 2012. Online. Available from http://www.editlib.org/p/39837

[16] Dehinbo. J. (2013). "A comprehensive framework for establishing dynamic Web platform for teaching Web application development in tertiary institutions". In: R. McBride & M. Searson (Eds.), *Proceedings of Society for Information Technology & Teacher Education International Conference (SITE 2013)*, pp. 2063-2069. Chesapeake, VA:

AACE. Held in New Orleans. USA. 25-29 March 2013. Online. Available from http://www.editlib.org/p/48407

[17] Holt, R., Wortman, D., Barnard, D. and Cordy, J.R. (1977) "SP/k: a system for teaching computer programming.", Communications of the ACM. Vol. 20, No. 5, pp. 301-309.

[18] Kolling, M. and Rosenberg, A. (1996) "Blue: A language for teaching object-oriented programming." In : Proceedings of the 27th SIGCSE Technical Symposium on Computer Science Education, Philadelphia. New York. pp.190-194.

[19] Lim, B.L. (2002). "Teaching web development technologies: Past, present, and (near) future". *Journal of Information Systems Education*. Vol. 13, No. 2, pp. 117-123.

[20] McMillan, J.H. and Schumacher, S. (2001). "*Research in education*". 5th edition. USA: Addison Wesley Longman, Inc.

[21] Olivier, M.S. (1999). "*Information Technology Research: A Practical Guide*", 2nd edition. Pretoria: Van Schaik.

[22] Prechelt, L. (2000). "An Empirical Comparison of Seven Programming Languages". *Computer*. Vol. 33, No. 10, pp. 23-29.

[23] Sebesta, R.W. 1996. "*Concepts of Programming Languages*", 3rd ed. USA: Addison-Wesley Publishing Company.

[24] Vinoski, S. (2003). "The performance presumption", IEEE Internet Computing. Vol. 7, No. 2, pp. 88-90.

[25] Wiedenbeck, S., Ramalingam, V., Sarasamma, S. and Corritore, C.L. (1999). "A comparison of the comprehension of object-oriented and procedural programs by novice programmers". *Interacting with Computers*. Vol. 11, No. 3, pp. 252-282.

An Investigation in the Impact of Mobile Learning on today's Educational Environment

Faisal Manga, Joan Lu
Department of Informatics, University of Huddersfield, Huddersfield, West Yorkshire, United Kingdom

Abstract - *Integrating mobile learning with pervasive learning may change the education environment and open new doors to possible opportunities in the coming years. This paper will consist of a literature review, mobile education, technologies used to deliver content, present findings, discussions, and an evaluation. It concludes that technology-enhanced learning encourages student engagement. However, the limitations of current mobile technologies do cause the barriers on the adoption of the new technology in a wide range of classrooms and learning environments.*

Keywords: Audience Response Systems, e-Learning, m-Learning, Individual Response System, Pervasive Mobile Learning

1 Introduction

The 21st Century has seen a vast growth in technologies [20]. Introducing new technologies has transformed education in terms of learning and teaching [6]. It has transformed the way in which people are able to share and access information with the introduction of social networking sites and various sharing platforms that allow users to share the information over the Internet.

Having the latest technologies such as Smartphone and tablets allows learners to learn from any location at any given time. Web based learning tends to be an integration of e-Learning and m-Learning together. The idea of introducing mobile devices has enriched student experiences and enhances their educational environment. Various tools and technologies allow students to adapt themselves into new learning environments.

Technology has advanced over the years. New technologies are being introduced to the market on a regular basis but customers are finding it hard to stay with the current trends, because the technology market has changed rapidly with the introduction of touch screen Smartphone and tablets [17]. Having introduced these devices, they are turning out to be more popular than desktops seen as more consumers are buying tablets, as they are easy to carry around wherever you go.

The way in which lessons used to be taught before has been changed [6]. The days when staff used to educate students with text books and blackboards are possibly no longer apparent [3]. Back then the technology was limited [3], because nowadays staff are integrating technology and learning together, however some staff feel that using too much technology may have a negative impact on the students, academia and the educational environment.

This paper presents some investigation in the impact of Mobile Learning on today's Educational Environment. Due to the rapid increase in technologies, learners are able to learn at any place at any given time as long as they have an Internet connection. With pervasive learning, the learner is able to access information based on their location, and learning materials can be accessed on their smart phone devices.

2 Background

As there is no single definition of mobile learning, IADIS [8] define mobile learning as:

"Any educational provision where the sole or dominant technologies are handheld or palmtop devices."

The above definition states that mobile learning can be done via smartphones, tablets and other mobile technologies.

The history of mobile learning dates back to the 1990s where Apple Classrooms of Tomorrow (ACOT) were in partnership with Orange Grove Middle school, who are based in Arizona [4]. The name of the project was "Wireless Coyote"; the aim of this project was to see how staff and students would use mobile computers that were connected by Wireless Local Area Network (WLAN) and Wide Area Network (WAN) [4]. The study consisted of different people ranging from 6th grade students, teachers and research personnel who were from Apple Computer [4]. The group created their own program where real time data was shared, as well as having voice-activated walkie-talkies so students were able to discuss their findings [4].

In the mid 2002 – 2003 there was a project where 150 teachers from 30 schools in England took part in [14]. The teachers were asked to evaluate different devices such as PDAs, laptops and mobile phones. Part of the test was to see that would help support staff in their teaching. Some of the advantages from the project were how portable the devices were, and the cost was cheaper for PDAs compared to using laptops. There were some disadvantages such as the screen was small, not enough technical support, and problems occurred when connecting with the networks [14].

Two other projects were conducted one focused on "Learning2Go" which was conducted in Wolverhampton (UK) and the other one was "Hand-e-Learning" which was carried out in Bristol (UK) [14]. Both the projects ensured that both the staff and the students carried a mobile device with them [14]. Funding and support were provided by the parents for these projects to be tested out [14]. Project was re-launched again after undergoing some changes, the study found that the students could carry the portable devices where ever they went, large amount of data could be stored such as notes from the lesson and maybe tasks which needed to be completed [14].

3 Mobile Education

There still isn't one single definition of mobile learning that is something which will be determined in the future when mobile learning becomes more evolved and effective in everyday practice.

Who would have thought that technology would have moved at a rapid pace, especially if you look at the Internet which was developed in the 1960s? [12].

A quote once said by a former US President [16], was:

"*You're talking about the Internet, you're talking about cell phones, and you're talking about computers.*"

The quote was mentioned in 2001, since then the field of technology has vastly improved. A newspaper article mentioned in the Guardian stated that mobile learning has the potential to improve education and the way it is accessed in developing countries [16]. Allowing mobile learning in developing countries allows young students to explore the life of education and face the employment challenges [16]. By introducing mobile learning it improves not only for the student but also benefits staff and the way which education is looked at from a different perspective [16] [9].

3.1 Introducing mobile education at Colleges & Universities

If mobile learning was introduced at College/Universities it would be a better opportunity due the size of some classes [19]. Especially for top Universities where there are a few hundred students. With the infrastructure and the money, which is spent at a University, compared to a College it would benefit students, seen as they would move around the campus but still be connected to the University Wi-Fi [19].

Mobile learning (m-Learning) is when a learner isn't in a specific location, the user can be anywhere at any time. Many people nowadays carry the latest gadgets ranging from smart mobile phones to the latest tablets, whether they are using 3G networks or even the latest 4G Network [7].

In this day and age it's possible for students to communicate through the FaceTime feature which is available on the iPhone, or even the latest form of video calling Skype [18]. As of January, statistics show that there are over 31 million users worldwide who use this service [18]. You can be at any side of the world but as long as you have an Internet connection you can talk to family and friends. You can discuss your work with your friends and have discussion on certain topics [18].

3.2 Mobile Education Frame Model

A model for framing mobile learning has been created by Koole [1] [13]. The model looks at the technical aspects of mobile devices as well as the social and the personal aspects of learning. The FRAME model looks at the learning experiences using a mobile device. Information is consumed whether it's done individually or done collectively [1].

Below Table 1, Table 2 shows the different characteristics of mobile learning and the different suitable devices for mobile learning.

Table 1
Characteristics of Mobile Learning

Mobile learning characteristics	Implications for mobile learning design
Ubiquitous	Content on mobile can be accessed from anywhere [5].
On demand	Mobiles are always on [5]
Location	Mobile offer the service of delivering content via Global Positioning System (GPS); also the user can allow to receive push notifications [5]

Table 2
Suitable DEVICES for MOBILE LEARNING

Devices	Types
Smart phones	Blackberry, Microsoft phones
Digital phones	IPhones, Samsung, Nokia, Sony Ericsson, all available with 3G connectivity, handsets have bigger screens, has video, audio flash and java capabilities, delivering richer mobile leaning content
Non – telephone mobile devices	MP3 players, Applied IPod

In order to deliver content in mobile learning there are different technologies which are available, these can be read [5].

4 Impact of Mobile Learning for teachers and students

Attewell et.al [2] discusses the impact of mobile learning for teachers and students. Having mobile technologies in classrooms can be useful as they promote interactivity between the staff and the students. Attewell et.al [2] also states that having mobile devices promotes collaborative learning in classrooms. Students tend to work with one another on exercises. Also students become more alert and more interactive and willing to participate in exercises and discussions.

Mobile learning is used outside the classrooms; students can use devices such as the tablets and smart phones to conduct their work. They have e-book readers such as the kindle where they can read books.

4.1 From Online Survey

Below are the responses which the researcher has gained over the period when the survey was conducted online.

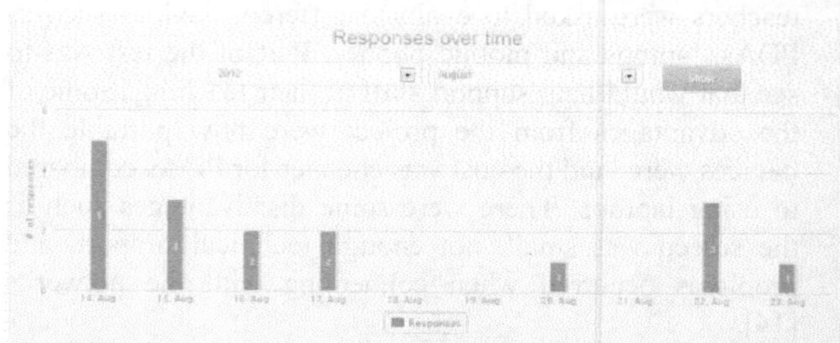

Figure 1: Online feedback numbers

Since the survey was online for a few days, the researcher received 17 feedbacks in total. The number was important to see how many users participated in the survey and on which days the survey was completed.

4.2 Highest Level of Education

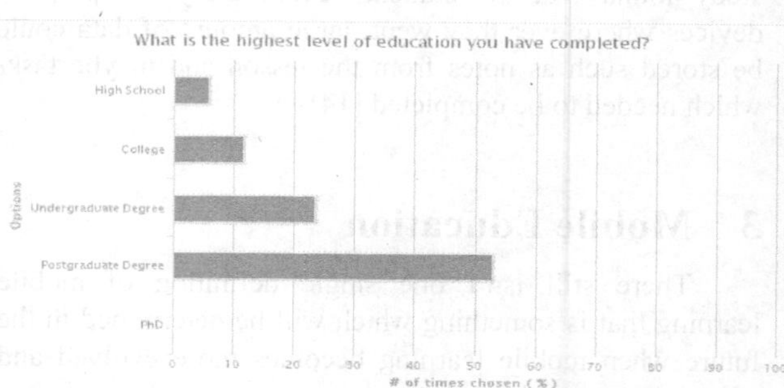

Figure 2: The results show various level of education which the participants have

The results show that majority of people who participated in the survey were postgraduate students. 9 out of the 17 were postgraduate students, 4 were undergraduate students, 2 were from college, and 1 from high school and 1 had a teaching degree as their highest qualification.

4.3 Access to Wi-Fi on your phone

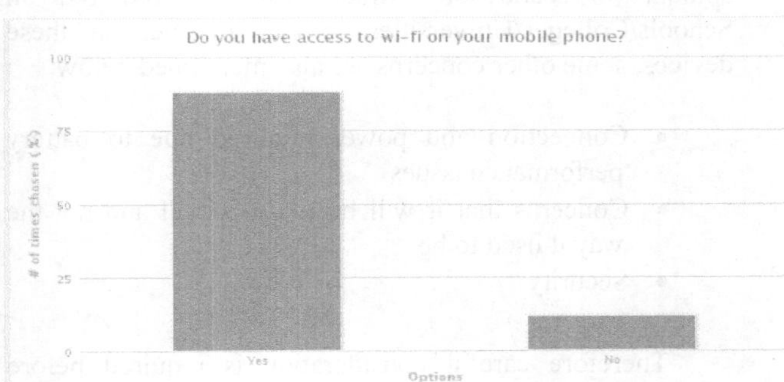

Figure 3: The results show people who have access to Wi-Fi on their phone

This question focused on whether the participants had a Wi-Fi connection on their mobile phones. If they said no to have a cellular network with data enabled, they could access materials if they had Wi-Fi on their mobile and were within range of a free Wi-Fi hotspot. However 2 people (11.8%) stated that they didn't have Wi-Fi on their phones which would mean that they have basic mobile phones, not the smart new ones which have so many features. Some people are old fashioned and like to keep it simple, they may only use mobile phones for calling and texting purposes.

4.4 University of Huddersfield Project

The University of Huddersfield are working on a large scale project which is led by Professor Joan Lu. The project is focused on Student Response Systems [10-11] [15] and funded by the European Commission (EC). The group have created a Wireless Response System (WRS) shown in Figure 4. The application can be used on smartphones as long as the user is connected to the Wi-Fi. The system is designed to be user friendly and doesn't require you to be an expert in the field.

The SRS work by the tutor initiating the question, the student responds, results can be viewed by the tutor instantly [10, 15]. Other functionalities on the program include audio, timer and pause.

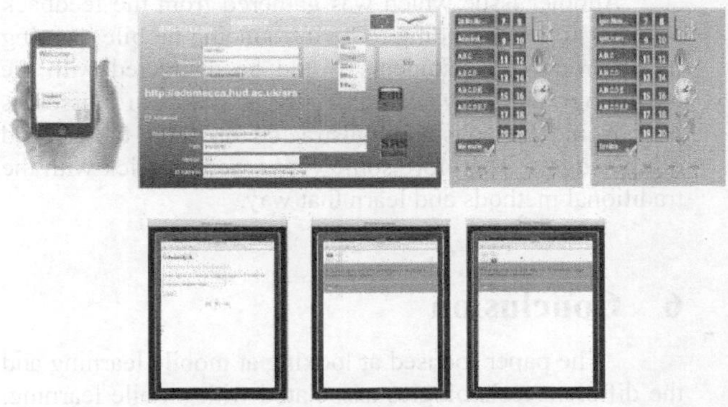

Figure 4: Student Response System with Multilingual languages [9]

Having a WRS allows you to have an enhanced learning experience and ensure that you have an open conversational framework which is responsive [11, 15].

Figure 5: Wireless Response System with multimedia functions [11]

5 Discussion and Analysis

To summarise on this section it can be said that from the responses which people have given on this survey, mainly it has been positive. People like the idea of introducing mobile learning into classrooms as they believe it will transform the way which tutors teach and the way which students learn. Especially for people who have learning difficulties it can be useful for them to introduce such technologies which can help them. It doesn't have to apply to University students, it can be useful small kids as they begin to interact while using the tablets and using the education apps to learn.

Some negative feedback surround mobile learning would be security, some people are worried how secure will it be seen as people would be logging in and registering their details. Will there be some secure features which will relax the minds of those who are worried.

Another issue which was gathered from the feedback was that if you are going to be introducing mobile learning in classrooms, the students would be distracted with the technology and they wouldn't pay attention in classes as they would be constantly distracted on their tablets and other gadgets. Therefore some views were to stick with the traditional methods and learn that way.

6 Conclusion

The paper focused at looking at mobile learning and the different technologies associated with mobile learning. The paper looked at the characteristics of mobile learning, along with suitable devices for mobile learning. The paper looked into how mobile learning has an impact on today's educational environment. The paper discussed how introducing mobile learning at Colleges and Universities would have a positive impact with regards to their education and how their acquire information and learn new skills.

It would be ideal to have mobile learning at schools from an early age, in this day and age technology is vastly improving and new technologies are introduced on a regular basis. Having children engaged in technologies at early would allow them to acquire knowledge in a fun and interactive way whilst using tablets and other suitable devices.

Tutors will find it easy by using different form of technologies and integrating them into their teaching. It will allow them to plan their lessons out more effectively and ensure that students are engaged in classrooms. This will ensure that the students receive a high level of education, and hopefully learn more and enjoy their lessons.

The paper discussed the benefits of how mobile learning allows you to learn at any location as long as you are connected to a WI-FI, you can learn at your own space in your own time. As mentioned in the paper the interactivity between the staff and students improves as the students are more engaged in classrooms and are willing to take part, rather than shying away, it brings a new element of interaction but at the same time focuses on learning.

The studies show that people are willing to try new things and willing to accept the form of mobile learning in their day to day activities. They are willing to do their exams on mobile devices and embrace the fact that the future of education is all down to mobile learning. Overall the results from the study are positive and they would like to see mobile learning introduced into their classrooms on a regular basis.

There are some issues which need to be taken into consideration such as the cost of the devices, the huge amount of bandwidth which will be required in Schools/Colleges/Universities to run Internet on these devices, some other concerns are also mentioned below:

- Connection and power required due to battery performance issues
- Concerns that it will be too practical and not the way it used to be
- Security

Therefore careful consideration is required before making a decision whether it's the right move to introduce mobile learning into classrooms or whether to stick with the traditional method.

Acknowledgements

The authors would like to thank for all the support provided by EU Lifelong Learning Programme, University of Huddersfield, all members of XDIR research group, especially, for Zhaozong Meng, Guo Wei, Gehao Lu, Pascal Pein, Lan Wang, David Parker, and Robin Sissons.

7 References

[1] Ally, M. (2009) *Mobile Learning Transforming the delivery of education and training.* 1st ed. Edmonton: Athabasca University.

[2] Attewell. J, Smith S. C, Douch. R, (2009) *The impact of mobile learning*. 1st ed. London: LSN.

[3] Corbeil, G. (2007) *Can PowerPoint Presentations Effectively Replace Textbooks and Blackboards for Teaching Grammar? Do Students Find Them an Effective Learning Tool?* CALICO Journal, 24 (3), p-p 631-656.

[4] Grant, C. W. (1993) *Wireless Coyote: A computer-supported field trip* [online pdf] Available at: <http://encore.oise.utoronto.ca/download/attachments/37758/Wireless+Coyote+a+computer-supported+field+trip.pdf> [Accessed 5 July 2012].

[5] Guy. R, (2009) *The evolution of mobile teaching and learning.* California: Informing Science Press.

[6] Halverson, R. Smith, A. (2009) *How new technologies have (and have not) changed teaching and leaning in schools.* Journal of Computing in Teacher Education. 26 (2).

[7] HT Media Ltd. (2012) 'Airtel introduces 4G network' *General Interest Periodicals-India.*

[8] IADIS (2005) *Defining Mobile Learning.* International Conference Mobile Learning.

[9] Lu, J (2012) *Learning with Mobile Technologies, Handheld Devices, and Smart Phones: Innovative Methods.* IGI Global, Hershey, PA , USA.

[10] Lu, J. Pein, P R, Hansen, G. Nielsen, KL. (2010) *User Centred Mobile Aided Learning System: Student Response System (SRS)*, Technology (CIT), Bradford, UK.

[11] Lua, J. Meng, Z. Lu, G. Stav, B, J. (2010) *A new approach in improving operational efficiency of wireless response system.* This paper appears in: Computer and Information Technology (CIT), 2010 IEEE 10th International Conference. Braford, UK.

[12] Leiner. B, Cerf. V, Clark. D, Kahn. R, Kleinrock. L, Lynch.D, Postel. J, Roberts.L, Wolff. S. (2012) *Brief history of the Internet* [online] Available at: <http://www.internetsociety.org/internet/internet-51/history-internet/brief-history-internet> [Accessed 7 July 2012].

[13] Mobileben, (2009) *A model for mobile learning* [online] Available at: <http://mobileben.wordpress.com/2009/04/15/a-model-for-mobile-learning/> [Accessed 9 July 2012].

[14] Pachler, N., Bachmair, B., Cook, J. (2010) *Mobile Learning: Structures, Agencies, Practices.* 1st ed. New York: Springer.

[15] Pein R. P., Lu J. and Stav J. B. (2009) (2009) *Integrating Mobile Computing Solutions into Distance Learning Environments.* In: International Conference on Mobile Communications and Pervasive Computing (MCPC 2009), 23rd-25th March 2009, Leipzig, Germany.

[16] Roopanarine, L. (2012) *Mobile phone boom in developing world could boost e-learning* [online] Available at: <http://www.guardian.co.uk/global-development/2012/may/30/mobile-phone-developing-world-elearning> [Accessed 8 July 2012].

[17] Smarttech. (2012) *SMART board 800 series interactive whiteboard* [online] Available at: <http://smarttech.com/us/Solutions/Higher+Education+Solutions/Products+for+higher+education/Interactive+whiteboards+and+displays/SMART+Board+interactive+whiteboards/SMART+Board+800> [Accessed 5 August 2012].

[18] Statistic Brain. (2012) *Skype Statistics* [online] Available at: <http://www.statisticbrain.com/skype-statistics/> [Accessed 10 July 2012].

[19] Traxler. J, (2007) *Defining, discussing and evaluating mobile learning: the moving finger writes and having writ....* IRRODL, 8 (2).

[20] Vinu P. V, Sherimon P. C, Krishanan. R, (2011) *'Towards pervasive mobile learning – the vision of 21st century' Procedia Social and Behavioral Sciences.* 15, pp. 3067-3073.

Problems of Establishing Effective Development for E-Learning Academic Staff at Universities in Developing Countries

N. Moussa[1]
[1]Advisor to the president and Mathematics Professor, Ahlia University, Al Manama, Bahrain

Abstract - *In this paper some problems of the establishment of e-learning academic staff development at Universities in developing countries are given. The current situation of academic staff development in many universities in developing countries is illustrated. A set of measures to achieve an effective e-learning academic staff development are proposed. Those measures include an action plan and a follow-up plan. Some recommendations and conclusion are stated.*

Keywords: E-Learning, Academic Staff Development, Developing Countries, Problems, Action Plan, Follow-up Plan.

1. Introduction

The current situation of academic staff development in general at many universities in developing country is illustrated in section 2. Some problems of establishing an effective e-learning academic staff development are discussed in section 3. In section 4 a comprehensive set of measures to be considered in the process of establishing an effective e-learning academic staff development including an action plan and a follow-up plan is proposed. Some recommendations are given in section 5. Finally a conclusion is then stated in section 6

2. Current Situation

Among other aspects, the academic staff development in general at universities in several developing countries is not effective in almost all aspects, e.g. for faculty, students and communities (see [1], [2], [3], [4]).

3. Problems

Applying internationally acknowledged measures for academic staff development is highly recommended for universities in developing countries (see [5], [6], [7]). Unfortunately the following typical problems in developing countries hinder this process:

- Heavy teaching load for all faculty.
- Very crowded classes even at private universities.
- Attending many long meetings,
- Poor IT facilities and poor skills of faculty.
- Assigning unsuitable slots for workshops and/or seminars.
- Assigning unsuitable slots for workshops and/or seminars.
- Less acknowledgement for attendees of the workshops and/or seminars.
- Assigning limited budget for e-learning academic staff development.
- Little exchange with internationally acknowledged universities.
- More interest of faculty in doing research.
- More interest of faculty in doing consultation for higher living standards.
- Bad coordination between different colleges and directorates.
- Cultural problems for expatriate faculty

4. Measures

4.1 Action plan

The proposed action plan is as follows (see [8], [9], [10], [11], [12]):

- Reducing the normal teaching load and restricting extra teaching loads.
- Reducing the number of students in all courses..
- Updating the IT facilities.
- Enhancing the IT skills of the e-learning academic staff.
- Offering helpful workshops and seminars.
- Assigning suitable slots for workshops and seminars.
- Accommodating those slots into the university teaching schedule.
- Advising the administration to avoid numerous long meetings.
- Advising the administration to avoid numerous long meetings
- Requesting the administration to acknowledge attendance of faculty of offered workshops and seminars.
- Advising the administration to assure good coordination between colleges and directorates.
- Requesting the administration to enhance exchange with international acknowledged universities in this field.
- Encouraging faculty to including development in their interests beside doing research and consultations
- Assigning certain budget for development.

4.2 Follow-up plan

The members of the standing e-learning academic staff development committee should do the following actions:

- Holding general lecture each semester to motivate faculty to attend offered workshops and seminars.
- Visiting faculty individually and responding to their needs.
- Meeting with department chairs and responding to their needs.
- Visiting Deans and responding to their comments and proposals.
- Getting individual feedback from the faculty after attending workshops and/or seminars.
- Publishing the committee recommendations.

5. Recommendations

To solve the problems given in section #3 towards establishing effective development for e-learning academic staff at universities in developing countries successfully we recommend to:

- Decreasing the teaching load and restricting extra course for all faculty, especially the junior ones.
- Limiting the number of enrolled students in all sections.
- Updating IT facilities and Enhancing IT skills of faculty.
- Assigning suitable slots for workshops and seminars and allocating them in the schedule.
- Acknowledging workshops' and seminars' attendees moralic and financial through assigning a special budget for e-learning academic staff development (salary, increment, and promotion).
- Encouraging faculty to devote time and effort beside doing research and consultations.
- Increase exchange with internationally acknowledged universities in the field.

6. Conclusion

Solving problems for establishing an effective development for e-learning academic staff needs a huge effort from the administration, the standing development committee, and faculty at universities in developing countries. This goal could be achieved through a practical action plan and an effective follow-up plan. Also enhancing exchanging knowledge with international acknowledged universities is highly recommended

7. REFERENCES

[1] Moussa, N., Saleh, D., "Optimizing the Process of Internal Quality Assurance of E-Learning in Developing Countries", for presentation and publication in the Proceedings of the WORLDCOM11 International Conference on e-Learning, e-Business, Enterprise Information Systems, e-Government & Outsourcing (EEE'11) , Las Vegas, Nevada, U.S.A., July 2011 pp 141- 147.

[2] Moussa, N., "Internal Quality Assurance of E-Learning in Developing Countries", Proceedings of the WORLDCOM10 International Conference on e-Learning, e-Business, Enterprise Information Systems, e-Government & Outsourcing (EEE'10) , Las Vegas, Nevada, U.S.A. July 2010, pp. 114-120

[3] Moussa, N., Moussa, S., "Quality Assurance of E-Learning in Developing Countries", Journal of Nonlinear Analysis, Volume 71, December 2009, pp e32-e34.

[4] Moussa, N., Moussa, S., "Economical and Social Impacts of E-Learning in Developing Countries", Proceedings of the WORLDCOM09 International Conference on e-Learning, e-Business, Enterprise Information Systems, e-Government & Outsourcing (EEE'09) , Las Vegas, Nevada, U.S.A. July 2009, pp. 155-161

[5] Nabil Moussa, "Quality of Education in Developing Countries", A Chapter in the Book : "Higher Education in the Twenty-First Century: Issues and Challenges -Al-Hawaj, Elali & Twizell (eds)", Taylor & Francis Group, London, ISBN 978-0-415- 48000-0, pp. 109 – 112.

[6] Mohamed, A., "Accreditation of Higher Learning Institution", A Chapter in the Book : "Higher Education in the Twenty-First Century: Issues and Challenges – Al-Hawaj, Elali & Twizell (eds)", Taylor & Francis Group, London, ISBN 978-0-415-48000-0, pp. 85-94.

[7] UNESCO's Centre of Higher Education in Europe, 2007.

[8] Karin Crawford, "Influences on Academics' Approaches to Development: Voices from Below", International Journal for Academic Development, Volume 15, Issue 3, 2010, pp 189-202.

[9] Academics' Perceptions of their Professional Development Needs Related to Leadership and Management: What Can we

[10] Tony Harland, David Staniforthb, "Academic Development as Academic Work", International Journal for Academic Development, Volume 8, Issue 1-2, 2003, pp 25-35.

[11] Barbaraington-Miller, "Developing New Academic Developers: Doing before Being", International Journal for Academic Development, Volume 17, Issue 2, 2012, pp 121-133.

[12] Moussa, N., "Academic Staff Development at Universities in Developing Countries", Proceedings of the 6th International Conference on Power Control Optimization (PCO2012), Volume 1, 2012, pp 1-2

Some Issues and Challenges in E-learning Methodologies and E-assessment System

Maria Joseph Israel[1] **and Asoke Nath**[2]
Email: joseph.maria@sxccal.edu asokejoy1@gmail.com

[1,2] Department of Computer Science, St. Xavier's College (Autonomous), Kolkata, India

Abstract - *E-Learning, or Computer Assisted Learning is now one prime research area of computer science as well as in Education Science. E-learning can be defined as learning through the new Information and Communication Technologies or ICT. In Education we have various types of teaching learning methodologies such as conventional educational system or face to face interaction, postal coaching based on printed study materials, distance education system where teaching learning process has two major components one is study material and the second is counseling sessions and now after year 2001 we have added one more education system called e-learning methodologies. E-learning is assisted by e-assessment or Computer Assisted Assessment (CAA). The CAA has an important role to issue certificates to the successful candidates in e-learning. The e-learning will not be a successful method if it is not supplemented by proper computer assisted evaluation process. In the present paper we have made a thorough study on different aspects of e-learning methodologies, Learning Objects(LO) and Computer Assisted Assessment. The CAA platform is called as eWorkbook. The system can be used for evaluating a learner's knowledge by conducting learner on-line tests. The time is coming when e-learning will be the best possible method of transmitting education among people located far away from any academic institution. Moreover due to flexible time policy in e-learning the busy people can also take the advantage of it. The authors have tried to explore different features of e-learning methodologies and also the e-testing mechanism.*

Keywords: e-learning, Computer assisted learning, ICT, Computer assisted assessment

1 Introduction

e-learning may be defined as "learning through the new Information and Communication Technologies or ICT. The word e-learning is a combination of two fields one is Distance Education and the other is Computer Based Training(CBT). In CBT Computer is used as the main tool for learning process. The CBT software and the materials are now available in different media such as CD, Internet website etc. Normally the software is made in such a way that anyone can learn the subject using self-learning instructional material.

Distance Education or Distance Learning is not a new teaching learning methodology. The distance education slowly developed due to the requirement of the learners those who reside in remote places and cannot come to take education from a reputed institute which may be far away from him/her. The distance education can be thought of three generations. The first generation is the nineteenth-century native teaching through postal communication. The second generation starts in the 70s and makes use of TV, Radio and satellites. The third generation based on data networks. The word E-learning came when the CBT was combined with the collaborative use of data networks. This event coincides with the time in which hypermedia resources started to be distributed through the Internet, that is, with the introduction of the World Wide Web. E-Learning is an interdisciplinary area of scientific research. To make E-Learning successful the researchers from education science and computer science have to apply their mind together. The education scientists have to give more interests in pedagogical aspects of e-learning and the computer scientists have to give more interest on the technology part of the e-learning process. To design e-learning system one has to design the intelligent tutoring systems, to standardize e-learning system, to design e-testing methodology, use of Web Technology including usability and accessibility etc. The use of e-learning in education has implied a transition from an institution–centered model to a learner-centered model. In e-learning sometimes one has to mix traditional instructional materials with newer technology based material. This approach, called blended learning method and it is more suitable in those environments in which the pedagogical aspect prevails over the mere competency transfer one. Blended learning forecasts that the normal lessons are integrated with on-line lessons and with the availability of instructors and learners of synchronous (chat, videoconference) and asynchronous (e-mail, forum) communication tools. In any academic institution the blended learning approach is commonly used e-learning methodology.

A piece of e-learning material, of any granularity, is commonly referred to as Learning Object (LO). According to IEEE Learning Technology Standard Committee (IEEE LTSC, 2007), the Learning Object (LO) is any entity, digital or non-digital, that may be used for teaching and learning process. According to ADL SCORM (ADL, 2007) LOs in the minimal form of teaching learning objects are called assets. An aggregation of LOs, which can be distributed in a content package, is a Content Aggregation. Another important characteristic of LOs, according to SCORM's classification, is their capacity of being launched in the learning environment and of establishing a communication with it. A LO equipped with a module which gives such functionalities to it is called a Sharable Content Object (SCO). The software system for the production of LOs is the LO authoring tool, while the software system for administering LOs to learners and for creating a collaborative learning environment is commonly called Learning Management System (LMS).

One important aspect of e-learning is the standardization of e-learning systems. Standardization in e-learning methodology is mainly aimed at achieving interoperability among Learning Management Systems (LMSs) and Learning Object (LO) authoring tools. The term Computer Managed Instruction (CMI) or SCORM Run-Time Environment often refers to a set of functionalities which allow LOs to be launched in the LMS and to exchange data with it. Their adoption is crucial in the achievement of full interoperability among LMSs and LO authoring tools. Even desirable, standard compliancy and guideline adoption are difficult to obtain for LMS producers. In the present work the authors have presented a thorough study on adoption of CMI functionalities in Object-Oriented and Message-Oriented LMS systems, respectively. The former is framework, named CMIFramework, which allows LMS developers to rapidly adopt CMI functionalities in Object-Oriented systems. The latter is a Service Oriented Architecture (SOA)-based reference model for offering the CMI functionalities as a service, external to the LMS.

2 What is E-Learning?

E-learning is not just about training and instruction but also about learning that is made for individuals. There are different terminologies which have been used to define on-line teaching and learning process. There is no straight forward definition of e-learning is available till now. To define e-learning the commonly used terms are Internet learning, distributed learning, networked learning, tele-learning , virtual learning, computer-assisted learning, Web-based learning, and distance learning. E-learning also includes the delivery of learning material through Internet, satellite broadcast, audio-video tape/CD, interactive TV program and CD-ROM. All of these terms mean that the learner is at a distance from the tutor or instructor, and the learner uses some form of technology (usually a computer) to access the learning material, and that the learner uses technology to interact with the tutor or instructor and other learners, and that some form of support is provided to learners. E-learning refers to the use of information and communication technology (ICT) to enhance and/or support learning in tertiary education. However this encompasses an ample array of systems, from students using e-mail and accessing course materials online while following a course on campus to programs delivered entirely online. E-learning can be different types, a campus-based institution may be offering courses, but using E-learning is tied to the Internet or other online network. So we can say that E-learning is an education process or system via the Internet, network, or standalone computer. E-learning processes include Web-based training, computer-based training, virtual classrooms and digital collaboration. E-learning means the teaching material is delivered via the Internet, intranet, audio or video tape, satellite TV, and CD-ROM. So one can define e-learning is basically Internet-Based training or Web-Based training. Today you will still find these terms being used, along with variations of E-learning (EL). EL is not only about training and instruction but also about learning that is tailored to individual. Different terminologies have been used to define learning that takes place online.

3 Different Components of E-Learning System:

E-learning system can be broadly categorized into the following:

3.1 E-Learning Courses:

The most important component of e-learning is to prepare educational courses. Educational course materials or courseware are usually modified and added with various different media and are uploaded to a networked environment for online accessing. There are several popular learning management systems such as WebCT and Blackboard which are commonly used by educational institutions to introduce e-learning education system. In achieving a more motivating courseware, courseware designers have began to add innovative presentation such as simulations, storytelling and various other innovative materials. E-learning is very similar to classroom teaching environment whereby both of the learners and the instructors are together related to the common course arrangement and flow.

3.2 Blended Learning

Blended learning or Integrated Learning provides a good transition from classroom learning to e-learning. Blended learning is a combination of a face to face teaching and online learning. This method is most effective for any higher education where both face to face and on-line training is required. It encourages educational and information review beyond the classroom settings. It combines several different delivery methods, such as collaboration software, web-based courses and computer communication practices with face to face instruction. Integrated learning utilizes the best of classrooms with the best of online learning.

3.3 Informal Learning

Information learning can be said to be one of the most dynamic and adaptable features of learning but it is least recognized. To get any new information we use some search Engine like Google. Each search Engine is coupled with information storage tools, personal management tools. That is why we get any information so fast from Google search engine. Sometimes we get more information during break time than in formal learning environment. We progress more in our jobs through informal learning, sometimes using trial and error and other times through conversations.

3.4 Collaborative Teaching and Study

It is very old style but very effective. This method enables learners to learn something in a small group, then to find similar type of group and then interact with them about one's doubts. This way one can learn a new subject very fast. Collaborative teaching is a teaching method by a group composed of teachers.

To implement this method teacher should focus on the plans he/she put together, teaching, appraisal and making detailed discussions and arrangements of the course outline and content. Collaborative teaching as an innovative teaching method makes use of two or more teachers and assistants contributing their talents in one or several classes and curricula. Collaborative teaching changed the traditional teaching style. With each teacher's academic specialty being employed more diversified learning directions and boundless thought space can be provided for students. Collaborative teaching research was conducted on the core "introduction to design" courses hoping that the teachers could contribute their talents, gain more professional knowledge and form a long-term collaborative group amongst themselves. This is the first motivation. Moreover, the learning motivation is an important factor for effective learning. The teachers should adopt various teaching methods and stimulate students' learning motivation.

3.5 Knowledge Management

Globalization is focused on e-learning because e-learning technology has the potential to bring improved learning opportunities to a larger audience than has ever previously been possible. Knowledge management is an essential process which is concerned with how to create atmosphere for people to share knowledge on distribution, adoption and information exchange activities in an organization. The impression of knowledge management and the theory of e-learning reveal powerful relationship which is causing disarray between the two fields.

3.6 Networks of Learning

Learning network is a procedure of developing and preserving relationship with people and information and communicating to support each other's learning. Therefore Learning network is enhanced and offers chances to its members to engage online with each other, sharing knowledge and expertise. Now the use of pen and paper in our educational system today is producing inadequacy and challenges in the digital era that we are in today where subject matter is changing speedily. The application of personal learning networks will create connections and develop knowledge for workers to remain current in their field.

4 E-Learning Methodologies

E-learning exploits Web technology as its basic technical infrastructure to deliver knowledge. The current trend in any academic or industry is to increase the use of e- learning and in the near future a higher demand of technology support is expected.

4.1 Interaction in Learning

Learner(s) and Tutors(s) Interaction, then Learner(s) and Learner(s) Interaction are two types of interactions are among humans. We are familiar with these types of interactions. Most of the research studies are based on these two types of interaction, especially in the research of Computer Assisted Collaborative Learning (CACL). If collaborative type of study is used in an online class then students should be more motivated to actively participate in online social interactions. This increased active group interaction and participation in the online course, hence, resulted in higher perceptions of self-reported learning. Whereas individuals working alone online tended to be less motivated, perceive lower levels of learning, and score lower on the test of mastery.

In CACL, researchers usually distinguish two types of interactions. One is called synchronous interaction, requires that all participants of interaction are online at the same time. Examples of synchronous interaction include Internet voice telephone, video teleconferencing, text-based chat systems, instant messaging systems, text-based virtual learning environments, graphical virtual reality environments, and net based virtual auditorium or lecture room systems. Synchronous interaction promotes faster problem solving, scheduling and decision making, and provides increased opportunities for developing. However, the cost of synchronous interaction is usually very high, and synchronous interaction is more constricted due to time differences. The second method is asynchronous interaction, in which learners or tutors have freedom of time and location to participate in the interaction, examples including interaction using e-mail, discussion forums, and bulletin board systems. It has been reported that by extending interactions to times outside of classes, more persistent interaction and closer interpersonal bonds among students can occur. Thus, while one cannot totally simulate a real classroom with synchronous interaction, one can offer asynchronous interaction that provides time for better reflection, and allows global communication un-bounded by time zone constraints. Asynchronous interaction thus is more commonly provided in CACL systems than the costly synchronous interaction.

4.2 Self-paced e-Learning

Learners are offered e-learning courseware (also called Web based training (WBT)), which can be complemented by supplemental resources and assessments. Courseware is usually housed on a Web server, and learners can access it from an online learning platform or on CDROM. Learners are free to learn at their own pace and to define personal learning paths based on their individual needs and interests. E-learning providers do not have to schedule, manage or track learners through a process. E-learning content is developed according to a set of learning objectives and is delivered using different media elements, such as text, graphics, audio and video. It must provide as much learning support as possible (through explanations, examples, interactivity, feedback, glossaries, etc.), in order to make learners self sufficient. However, some kind of support, such as e-mail based technical support or e-tutoring, is normally offered to learners. When self paced e-learning is offered through an Internet connection, there is the potential to track learners' actions in a central database.

5 E-Assessment System

E-Assessment, also known as Computer Assisted Assessment (CAA), is a sector of e-learning aimed at assessing learner's knowledge through e-learning means. The reduced human contact between the instructor and the learner, due to distance, besides the necessity of evaluating a big mass of learners in strict times, affects assessment. Therefore, the means for knowledge evaluation had to evolve to satisfy the new necessities. To conduct structured tests, more rapidly assessable method started gaining a heavier weight in the determination of learners' results. Multiple Choice question type is extremely popular in structured tests, since, among other advantages, a large number of its outcomes can be easily corrected automatically. Each question contains multiple options. The only correct answer is called the "key". Several commercial and open source e-assessment systems are available for administering tests based on it. Furthermore, being still actual the necessities of measuring learner's participation to the class, some metrics and tools have been developed to measure it. A state of the art analysis allowed us to identify the following important requirements for an effective environment for developing and using assessment tests:

(1) High reusability of the authored content.

(2) The courses and classes must be well organized.

(3) There must be flexible access control system to the tests.

(4) The authored content should have quality tracking.

(5) The reporting section should be well planned.

The e-assessment system can be used for evaluating a learner's knowledge by creating (the tutor) and taking (the learner) on-line tests based on multiple choice question types. The questions are kept in a hierarchical repository, that is, it is tree-structured, in the same way as the file system of an operating system. In such a structure, the files can be thought of as questions, whether the directories can be thought of as macroareas, which are containers of questions usually focused on the same subject. A macro area can still contain other macroareas. The tutors are free to organize the tree as they wish, e.g. keeping the questions of the same course in a macroarea and further splitting it according to the chapters they cover. Every item (a macro area or a question) has an owner, which is the tutor that authored it. The tutors can choose whether to share their questions or not, assigning a value to the permissions associated to each item. Permissions are for reading, writing and using the items. Some other information about the questions is present in the repository, such as: difficulty (selected by the tutor), language, keywords, number of times the question was selected for a test and expected time for a learner to answer. The tests are composed of one or more sections. This structure facilitates the selection of the questions from the repository, but it is still useful for the assessment, where it can be important to establish if one section is more important than another to determine the final grade for the test. There are two kinds of sections: static and dynamic. The difference between them is in the way they allow question selection. For both the static and the dynamic sections, a macroarea in the question repository must be specified. For a static section, the questions are chosen directly from the sub-tree located by the specified macroarea. For a dynamic section, some selection parameters must be further specified, leaving the system to choose the questions randomly across the sub-tree located by the specified macroarea whenever a learner takes a test.

6 E-learning Tools

There are three types of e-learning tools:

(i) Curriculum tools,
(ii) Digital library tools and
(iii) Knowledge representation tools.

We can generally say that each type of tool emphasizes different aspects of the e-learning process. Curriculum tools provide a systematic and standard environment to support classroom learning; their functions are particularly helpful in the initiation and selection stages. Digital library tools facilitate effective and efficient access to resources to support exploration and collection. Knowledge representation tools focus on formulation and representation. Now we will discuss these three tools in detail.

6.1 Curriculum Tools

Curriculum tools are widely used in high school and college of education. Materials are selected and organized to facilitate class activities. Additional tools, such as discussion forums and online quizzes, are integrated to support collaboration and evaluation. A typical commercial curriculum tool includes three integrated parts: instructional tools, administration tools, and student tools. Instructional tools include curriculum design and online quizzes with automated grading. Administration tools include file management authentication, and authorization. Student tool functions include:

(a) Browsing class material: readings, assignments, projects, other resources

(b) Collaboration and sharing: asynchronous and synchronous bulletin boards and discussion forums.

(c) Learning progress scheduling and tracking: assignment reminders and submission, personal calendars, and activity logs.

(d) Self-testing and evaluation: tests designed by instructors to evaluate student performance

WebCT and Blackboard are the most popular commercial curriculum tools. A review comparing these two tools suggests that Blackboard's flexible content management and group work support [3] make it more suitable for independent and collaborative learning. WebCT's tighter structure and fully embedded support tools make it more appropriate for guided, less independent learning. In general, these tools are tailored more to support class activities than independent research or self-study.

6.2 Digital Library Tool

The curriculum tools support class functions, while digital library tools focus on locating resources. These functions support the exploration and collection phases of information search. Digital library tools help users find the right information. Digital library features usually include search, browsing, and discovering special collections or exhibits. Search and browsing are used to locate resources and explore related topics. Special collections or exhibits contain organized materials representing a unique treasure for interested users.

6.3 Knowledge Representation Tool

Knowledge representation tool help learners to visually review, capture, or develop knowledge. Curriculum tools rely primarily on a text-based, syllabus approach to describing course content. This approach often fails to describe the relationship of concepts and skills covered in one course to those covered in another. It also fails to show the knowledge base that a learner will have acquired at the end of his/her course of study. A visualization tool can engage both learners and instructors in an active learning process when they construct spatial semantic displays of the knowledge, concepts, and skills that the learner possesses and acquires. The e-Learning evolution proposes a good number of tools assisting the instructional designer during the analysis, design, implementation, and delivery of instruction via the Web. If on one side an automated support should be provided by authoring tools on the other side these tools should implement suitable e-learning process design methodologies.

7 Conclusion and Future Scope

In modern education system E-learning is one of the best methods for exchanging knowledge between teacher and the taught. The rapid growth in internet technology has made E-learning so useful for everyone in the globe. Unlike conventional educational system it allows us to gather knowledge and education both by synchronous and asynchronous mode. E-learning delivers content through electronic information and communications technologies (ICTs). The use of these facilities, involves various methods which includes systematized feedback system, computer-based operation network, video conferencing and audio conferencing, internet worldwide websites and computer assisted instruction. This delivery method increases the possibilities for how, where and when employees can engage in lifelong learning. E-learning has opened the door for learning lifetime. The major success of e-learning depends on its e-evaluation system. In the present work we have given some idea how the evaluation process may be done in e-learning process. But there is a lot of scope to improve it. Finally we conclude that synchronous tools should be integrated into asynchronous environments to allow for education "anywhere" and "any-time". This environment would be primarily asynchronous with background discussion, assignments and assessment taking place and managed through synchronous tools that integrate into the asynchronous environment. There is lot of scope to work on e-assessment system and in Mobile Learning or m-Learning. The authors are presently working on that.

8 Acknowledgement

The authors are very grateful to Department of Computer Science, St. Xavier's College (Autonomous), Kolkata for allowing to do research work on e-learning. The authors are very much grateful to Fr. Dr. J. Felix Raj, Principal, St. Xavier's College (Autonomous), Kolkata for constant encouragement in research work.

9 References:

[1] Douglas, I.(2001). “Instructional Design Based on Reusable Learning Object: Applying Lessons of Object-Oriented Software Engineering to Learning System Design”. In Proceeding ASEE/IEEE Frontiers in Education Conference, Reno, NV, 2001. Vol. 3. pp.: F4E1-F4E5.

[2] N.D. Oye , M. Salleh, and N.A. Iahad, “Challenges of E-learning in Nigerian University Education Based on the Experience of Developed Countries,” International Journal of Managing Information Technology, vol. 3, no. 2, 2011, pp. 39-48.

[3] M. Lorrain, “Strategies to Engage Online students and Reduce Attrition Rates.,” The Journal of Educator Online.2007.

[4] Haythornthwaite, C.(1999). "Collaborative Work Networks among Distributed Learners,"Proceedings of the 32nd Hawaii International Conference on System Sciences, IEEE Computer Society Press, 1999.

[5] Li, T., Sambasivam, S.E. (2003). Question Difficulty Assessment in Intelligent Tutor Systems for Computer Architecture. Information Systems Education Journal, Vol. 1 (51)

[6] Lin, N.H., Shih, T.K., Hui-huang, H., Chang, H. P., Chang, H. B., Ko, W. C.; Lin, L.J. (2004), Pocket SCORM, Proceedings of 24th International Conference on Distributed Computing Systems Workshops, Tokyo, Japan, pp. 274-279

[7] Oye N.D, Mazleena Salleh, N.A. Iahad, E-Learning Methodologies and Tools, IJACSA, Vol.3, No.2,2012

[8] Xiaofei L., El Saddik, A., Georganas, N.D. (2003), An implementable architecture of an elearning system, Proceedings of IEEE Canadian Conference on Electrical and Computer Engineering, pp. 717 - 720 vol.2Advanced Distributed Learning (ADL) Initiative. Available at: http://www.adlnet.org, 2004.

[9] Antelmo, D., Costagliola, G., Ferrucci, F., Fuccella, V. (2005), A Web-based Computer Aided Assessment Tool Supporting Question Quality Improvement, Proceedings of IADIS International ConferenceWWW/Internet 2005, pp. 77-84

[10] Costagliola, G., Ferrucci, F., Fuccella, V., Gioviale, F. (2004b), eWorkbook: a Web Based Tool for Assessment and Self-Assessment, Atti di DIDAMATICA, pp. 621-630

[11] Ausburn, L.J. (2004) ‘Course design elements most valued by adult learners in blended online education environments: An American perspective’, Educational Media International, vol. 41, no. 4, pp. 328-337.

[12] Baker, C. (1992). Attitudes and Language. Clevedon: Multilingual Matters.

[13] Cooner, T. S. (2005) ‘Dialectical constructivism: Reflections on creating a Web-mediated enquiry-based learning environment’, Social Work Education, vol. 24, no. 4, pp. 375-390.

[14] Garnham, C., & Kaleta, R. (2002). Introduction to Hybrid Courses.
Teaching with Technology Today, 8(6).

[15] Oye , N.D, Mazleena Salleh, N.A. Iahad, E-Learning Methodologies and Tools, International Journal of Advanced Computer Science and Applications, Vol.3, No.2, Ppp. 49-52(2012)

[16] N.D. Oye , M. Salleh, and N.A. Iahad, “Challenges of E-learning in Nigerian University Education Based on the Experience of Developed Countries,” International Journal of Managing Information Technology, vol. 3, no. 2, 2011, pp. 39-48.

E-Learning Factors and Definitions

Abdullah Abdulaziz AlShoshan

[1] 1000 FANER Drive 2125-4511
Southern Illinois University
Carbondale Illinois 62901
[2] Technical and Vocational Training Corporation - Saudi Arabia
shoshan@siu.edu

Mehdi Zargham

1000 FANER Drive 2125-4511
Southern Illinois University
Carbondale Illinois 62901
mehdi@cs.siu.edu

Contact author: AlShoshan

EEE '13

Abstract - This research has focused on the key factors that affect e-learning. These factors have been grouped into four broad categories of instructor, student, interface design and resource support. In terms of the instructors, this mainly refers to the ability of the teacher to provide different e-learning activities and facilitate the learning process. The student perspective involves the ability and willingness of students to collaborate in the teaching/learning process, as well as his/her ability to give feedback relating to the e-learning experience. Other influential factors relate to the interface design that refers to the appearance of the learning environment. Under this, consideration is given to the availability and security of the system, user-friendliness and the content that is delivered. The final category relates to resource support encompassing the availability and speed of the systems. Online help'and support are also critical elements in enhancing learners' experience.

Key words: e-Learning, e-Learning plans, e-Learning resources, e-Instructor, e-Student

INTRODUCTION

Volery and Lord [1] address e-learning within three frame works: technology, instructor and student knowledge of technology. Slime [2] has, however, grouped e-learning into four categories: instructor, student, information technology and university support. Ozkan [3] suggests areas to be: system quality, service quality, content quality, learner perspective, and instructor attitudes. Others studies have partitioned and categorized e-learning in different circles: human part, technical part and course part. This study is going to measure an efficacy of e-learning models for comparative purposes. From the review of variety of sources, we believe and have surmised the best development and deployment of e-learning into four dimensions: Instructor, Student, Interface Design and Resource Support. The rest of this paper defines and provide examples for each of the dimensions. At the end of the paper a summery is provided.

INSTRUCTOR

Educational environment through e-learning relies on several factors to obtain high quality of learning and each plays an important role for the learning outcomes. Volery highlights three areas while defining traditional instructor "instructor technical competence, attitudes towards students and classroom interaction"[1]. Gillette [4] notes "teaching through the web requires instructors to reconsider their previous assumptions about the nature of teaching, lecture, testing, and student/teacher interaction". E-instruction is "instruction delivered via an electronic network such as the Internet"[5]. E-learning instructor, sometimes called e-instructor, is the person who chooses suitable technology materials for clarifying and explaining course contents. The instructor is responsible to evaluate students and give the qualification assessments. An instructor in e-learning could use technology as part of the course or the course completely works via technology support. Instructor's evaluation is a result for determining characteristics related to instructor responses, teaching aims and students' knowledge. Instructor's characteristics [6] are "Instructor attitude towards student, Instructor attitude towards e-learning and Computer skill". Puri [7] mentions many factors related to instructor in e-learning including: alternative submission of assignments, interactive course, teacher as facilitator and pedagogy. Nathan [8] mentions learning styles as an important element for instructor efficiency, and Volery and Lord [1] state the same idea. In summary, we can assert the important factors for e-instructor as following: provide online activities, teaching styles, teacher as facilitator, familiarity with different technologies tools, computer skills, feedback, and pedagogy.

A. Provide Online Activates

Note: here we assume most of the activities are provided by organization or can be accessed free on the internet.

Khan [9] presented some web-based activities that support learners to understand course like, discussion forum, chat room, email and mailing list, online resources and tutorials. Similarly, Selim [2] addresses discussion group, blackboard and e-mail as a means of measuring the instructor's effort and enthusiasm in the e-learning course. The instructor should encourage student-student and student-instructor interaction by web tools in alternative ways either for optional or required assignments.

B. Provide Different Teaching Styles

"Instructors should adopt interactive teaching style" [2]. Kanninen [10] thinks that Felder-Silverman learning style model supports e-learning where this model has four dimensions: sensory/intuitive, visual/verbal, active/reflective and sequential/global. Also, this paper suggests that students should have a choice to pick the appropriate way for e-learning. We can say that the teacher has to diversify ways of delivering information to students where that gives a greater opportunity to understand and interact with the course. The instructor should be aware that he/she has students with different skills: kinesthetic, auditory and visual.

C. As Facilitator

According to Sunnarborg [11], there are four tips for an instructor to be a facilitator. He/she has to know student's background, knowledge and experience in subject. Next, the instructor presents topics slowly and clearly, and makes the information applicable by connecting content to real environment. Finally, allow students to act as instructors by presenting their suggested explanation methods and supporting students to teach each other. Sengupta et al. [12] in a paper titled designing a scaffolding for supporting personalized synchronous e-learning states that students aid instructors and organizations in solving e-learning problems. In brief, the e-learning instructor has to include students' experiences and suggestions in teaching.

D. Familiarity with multimedia and technology tools.

A traditional instructor uses their voice and blackboard for transferring information to students while an e-instructor environment needs computer and internet capability for expounding materials. Not all instructors have these ability and skills. Most times tools are provided by organization or free at internet. The e-instructor who has good experience with technology and multimedia tools can choose the suitable way for any subject. Most of the programs are patterns and the instructor has to be experienced in them to be used. Organization provided training for facilities as well as the ability and qualification of using these tools are the cornerstone. Baylor and Ritchie [13] emphasizes on the importance of relation between technology and instructor several times. Once, they say that instructor computer use outside school as one of the criteria for successful e-learning. On other part, they note that instructor's technology competency and instructor's technology integration are elementary characteristics in e-instructor. Also, Mehregan et al. [14] mention that the third important factor for achieving success e-learning is instructor's computer skill.

E. Give feedbacks

Not only the role for instructor to use the tools and methods available in e-learning system in the organization, he has to take the initiative ideas and tools to improve and develop e-learning system. Also, e-instructor has to discover errors and weaknesses in the system and he should state any points need to develop, add, modify or delete. This special role of e-instructor can be done by an experienced instructor that has familiarity with media education beside how to direct tools to become useful for the learning process. The instructor feedback characteristic has been mentioned by Barron [15], he said that meaningful feedback is a factor out of ten factors to succeed in academic online learning. Similarly, participants' feedback addressed as a tool for developing global e-learning by Nathan [8]. Finally, why feedback? The answer is that "Learning, although at a distance, should be treated as an activity that involves all participants in the system, and as an activity in which monitoring, review and feedback are regularly used to enhance all components of teaching, learning and the system of delivery."[16]

F. Pedagogy

In e-learning pedagogy, Sengupta et al. [12] define effective pedagogy as synchronous student-facilitator collaboration for enhancement of the learning quality. Similarly, Frimpon [17] explains that modern pedagogy known as e-learning that delivered via all electronic media for the purposes of effective learning process. Also, Nathan [8] states "identified technology and pedagogy issues, and corporate culture as factors that contribute as barriers to the successful use of e-learning". We can define e-instructor pedagogy is the instructor effort through technology tools by innovating methods for fruitful e-learning.

STUDENT

Student is any person who studies and is engaged in learning (dictionary.com). Student can be: learner, pupil, trainee, and anyone who is improving his knowledge through any kind of educational system. The e-learning system is affected by student skills and background. According to Musa and Othman [18], student characteristics have been classified in three types: students computing competency, student collaboration activities, and course contents and design. Mehregan et al. [14] consider that computer skill, motivation, commitment and learning speed are student characteristics that should measure to evaluate e-learning. Selim [2] emphasized that students need to have time management in e-learning. Frimpon [17] mentions students' (discipline, computer competency, attitude towards, participation and involvement) as critical success factors for e-learning. In my view, I consider student characteristics that effect on e-learning are collaboration (participation and involvement), learning speed, discipline (commitment), computer skill, motivation, and giving feedback. Let's define them one by one:

A. Collaboration (participation and involvement)

As reported by Musa & Othman [18], collaboration is an involvement of students and the instructor in e-discussion groups. Students' participation in e-learning consists of reading messages in the course discussion group and interacting with messages. Discussion groups could be live chat discussion, discussion forums, or any unrestricted online tool for discussion. Learning community and ease interaction with others are foundations for participation. Also, the e-learning could fail if students do not participate in working groups [17]. We can say that e-teacher has to encourage, create and be involved with internet activities along side e-students for successful e-learning courses.

B. Learning speed

Student learning speed counted as a significant issue in e-learning [14]. Learning speed compared to the traditional learning is what we try to explain here. Students can understand and deal with course materials through e-learning tools, and feel it is equal or more advantages than face-to-face learning. Learning speed can be defined by student satisfaction on e-learning which is measured by: student enjoyment, comfortable, not intimidate and absorption to the course [2].

C. Discipline (commitment)

The e-learning environment depends on online interaction. In regular courses students have to attend and participate in classroom. E-learning environment gives flexibility in location and time for courses participation. We should note that flexibility could be generating negligent students, if the students do not have enough skills in "time management". Student's discipline is indicated by involvement in discussions, assignments, quizzes, tests and other online activities.

D. Computer skills

"Student prior IT experience such as having a computer at home and attitude towards e-learning is critical to e-learning success."[2] Student who enrolled in e-learning course should have basic abilities for using hardware and software (computer literacy) like, typing, using the Internet, installing programs, downloading and browsing files. The computer skills are required because all of e-learning undertakings are in virtual environment that need computer as a tool in between.

E. Motivation

Keller [19] defined motivation as "the choices people make to what experiences they will approach or avoid, and the degree of effort they will exert in that respect". Nathan [8] stated that "successful e-learning depends largely on the self-motivation of individuals to study effectively. Tampa Bay Times released an article "Success of Florida Virtual School is difficult to measure" [20] that pointed out that motivation is a significant driver impacting a student's aptitude to success in e-learning. E-student who has dissatisfaction on e-learning mostly would not accept its tools and would not reach its goals. Motivation depends on intrinsic characteristics and some extrinsic characteristics of the student. Smith [21] gave four factors to raise motivation. First, engage students in e-course by attracting their attention. Second, organization or course advisor clarifies the goals for students and makes the course consistent to student's experiences. Third, give confidence by forwarding attribution that student "is capable of performing in a certain manner to attain certain goals". Finally, inspire positive feeling to student that creates satisfaction state to e-learning.

F. Giving feedbacks

Feedbacks are student's evaluations for course content, instructor, design, facilities and any related topics, and suggestions to improve course inputs, outputs and outcomes.

INTERFACE DESIGN

Puri [7] defines "interface design" as a concern with the look and feel of e-learning environment. The interface design is the intermediate atmosphere for the e-learning environment. Ignoring principles of ease of use, and quality of "interface design" would negatively effect outcomes of e-learning. Here we talk about website features that are designed to support interaction and the quality of the users' experience and include: website reliability, website speed, website backup, error tracking, website friendliness, course platform, web security, and update.

A. Internet connection

Bandwidth of a website on e-learning is a very important issue because slow website gives a negative sense to the users (students and teachers). Also, speed of website related to time at tasks, like chat or online exam, can prove frustrating for users. The bandwidth could limit contents of a course because contents take long time in upload and download. The content types like videos may be avoided if speed is not suitable to the case. The internet bandwidth depends on the number of connections to a website and speed of the connections.

B. *System Reliability and Availability*

This is one of the most important technological factors in e-learning. Without access to e-learning facilities, the learning cannot take place. Therefore, before choosing a given type of media for e-learning or engaging in any e-learning activities, it is important to consider the technological barriers that may affect the availability and reliability of the system. According to Mungania [22], organizations which target international students need to focus on the language, infrastructural and geographical barriers that can affect access to the e-learning system. The size of graphic images and the sizes of files which may be downloaded need to be limited. This may also involve limiting the number of items that can be downloaded. Such measures help to guarantee the availability of the system [22].

The availability of services may also be improved by making use of redundant hardware/software such as servers and routers [23]. Periodic assessment of the performance and loading of the system by the administrators helps to ensure that services are uninterrupted, which ensures that student satisfaction with e-learning is enhanced. Such assessments help to identify those critical areas that need to be attended to in order to enhance efficiency and availability of the system.

C. *System Backup Procedures*

Backup procedures help to address technological concerns where measures should be put in place to avoid loss of data and critical information. E-learning involves a variety of materials such as journals and books online, and it is important that such material is accessed unaltered. Regular backups of data are an essential element in analyzing risk. In addition, students need to back up their courses/materials periodically or as soon as changes are made to them [23]. The learning institution needs to develop a backup procedure by following certain guidelines.

First, the personnel to be involved in the backup procedure need to be identified. Secondly, the learning institution needs to consider the frequency with which the backing procedure will be carried out. Thirdly, it is important to understand who is to be notified in the event that a backup problem occurs. This involves understanding the support that can be obtained from the vendors of hardware and software components in the event of such a problem. For instance, if copies of data are stored on stored media, it is important to consider the exact location of such media.

D. *System Error Tracking*

Bugs are a common occurrence in the development of many systems. These errors usually occur during the technical design phase. In e-learning, this is a major concern that needs to be addressed in order to guarantee the security of the e-learning system. During an e-learning project life cycle, there are various bugs that will be identified. It is therefore important to develop a tool that tracks such bugs and ensure that these bugs are resolved after the project is completed. This may involve using a simple tool such as a simple database [24].

For instance, an excel spread sheet may be used to record these errors by having columns that clearly show the item, the type of error, the owner and priority [24]. In addition, a variety of server tools exist which may be used to enable the users enter the comments directly into the database and allow the managers of the project run the bug reports once. This helps to avoid running error databases separately which may be time consuming. In addition, tracking software can help to manage the development process, and this is mainly achieved through reusable templates. Such templates can be used for a variety of purposes, including testing and debugging [24].

E. *User Friendly Learning System*

Some of the pedagogical features of a virtual learning environment involve easy and structured methods of finding and sharing information, as well as communicating with the tutors and peers. This means that the technical infrastructure needs to be robust and user-friendly [16]. Therefore, navigation within the learning environment needs to be easy where it is easy for the students to get course content. It should take a short time to get to the required course content, easy downloading of files and well-constructed websites that are easily navigated [22].

This is one of the technological barriers that can limit how an e-learning system is used. The selection of the tools and the Learning Management Systems greatly affects the interaction between the students and the teachers [16]. The choice of the learning systems should be based on the pedagogical requirements and the technical environment of the learning institution. In a learning institution where technology is widely used, it is likely that most of the learners and teachers will find the e-learning system user-friendly. However, for those institutions that do not heavily employ technology, the choice of the learning system should be based on ease of use. It is important that the e-learning system is stable enough to serve the needs of the diverse learners, content creators and administrators. This requires that the access and delivery of material must be prepared in a manner that is easy to use and should be highly intuitive. This helps to guarantee usability of the e-learning system [25].

F. *Courses (Content, Maintenance and Platform)*

The amount of material that is produced for e-learning is enormous. The main issue regarding this aspect relates to the selection and the sequencing of the learning materials, and the quality of material produced and used in a course [25]. Although the content may involve printed material, it is highly digital and hence very diverse. In this case, the content used in e-learning is not entirely produced by the teachers. With e-learning, students have become producers of the learning materials, and this makes quality a major concern issue when examining content [16]. The development of this content should extend into consideration of the materials that will be downloaded and those that will be presented on screen.

In addition, the institution should focus on the learning support needs for the teachers and students, especially if such material is to be used by others [26]. The learning platform is also a critical factor as far as e-learning courses are concerned. The e-learning platform forms the core of the e-learning systems which is supposed to meet for main functions: management of students, the dissemination of knowledge, testing and facilitation of communication. The use of these platforms allows the learning institution to leverage the available resources efficiently so as to enhance the learning and teaching processes. These platforms are supposed to ensure that students interact with course material in an engaging and efficient manner. In addition, these platforms have functionalities that allow students to perform self-test in order to check their own level of knowledge [25]. Other aspects of the courses such as multimedia presentations and virtual labs are launched from these platforms.

G. *Network Security*

E-learning highly depends on information and communication technologies. It is based on: updating, storage, distribution and sharing of information via the internet; and delivery of content to the end user via a network. This makes the concept of network security a major consideration in e-learning [23]. Network security in e-learning should thus focus on user authentication, protection of information from unauthorized access and maintenance of data integrity.

There are a number of approaches that have been adopted to address the problem of network society. First, a firewall may be used to control access. This is a combination of software and hardware security systems which help to prevent unauthorized persons from accessing an institution's network from outside that institution. In this case, traffic that flows from outside the institution has to pass through the firewall and this is achieved by blocking access of the local network and only permitting access via the firewall. Secondly, digital right management may be employed which might help to protect the assets stored over the internet such as pdf files [23].

One of the approaches used is cryptography where secret and public key algorithms are used to protect the information. For instance, in public key algorithm, one key is used in the encryption of messages or data and another key is used to decrypt these messages. In addition, other authentication techniques such as passwords, digital signatures and digital certificates may be used in order to limit unauthorized access to the network. This can also be enhanced by biometric authentication which helps to give more enhanced security [23].

H. Evaluate and Update

Evaluation in e-learning involves the assessment of learners as well as an evaluation of the learning and instruction environment. Assessment of students is classified into two broad categories: the summative assessment which grades students to demonstrate their achievement, and these judgments are made based on the set objectives. Secondly, formative assessment is employed as a diagnostic tool for teachers and students in order to identify the weak areas that require improvement.

By undertaking formative evaluation, the learning product can be improved during the development phase. The designers consider the leaner's feedback and thus communicate with the producers to make the necessary updates [27]. There are several elements that are considered during the evaluation stage. First, in terms of pedagogy, consideration is given as to how the contents are presented and how they support the learning activities.

Secondly, technological evaluations involve understanding the effectiveness of the learning management systems in delivery the online content as well as how it manages this content [27]. Furthermore, this stage involves considering how well the learning materials are managed and maintained. In terms of the institution, an evaluation has to be made regarding how the content is aligned with the desired academic quality of the institution [27]. Finally, this evaluation seeks to identify how the learners perceive the look and feel of the content that is governed [27]. In general, these evaluations are important in identifying those areas that need to be updated in order to enhance the efficiency of the e-learning system.

RESOURCE SUPPORT

A. Staff Qualifications and Experiences

This is one of the dimensions that affect the quality of a give e-learning program. The staff members are involved in a variety of activities that are crucial to the success of the e-learning program. First, the staff should be able to design, produce and test new learning materials. Having qualified and experienced staff will ensure that the content produced meets the required standards as set by the institution, staff members are required to test these materials before dispatching them to the students.

Secondly, it is the responsibility of the staff to ensure that the materials are stored and dispatched as required. There is a need to have qualified personnel who manage the learning materials and protect it against loss or damage. Third, it is the responsibility of the staff to ensure that the learners are well arranged in order to facilitate their access to the learning materials. For instance, the learners could be arranged in learning centers in order to ensure that they access the learning materials with ease. Fourth, it is important to have qualified and experienced staff members who monitor the progress of the learners. This also involves assessing as well as accrediting the learners depending on their qualifications.

Finally, in order to maintain an effective learning system, it is important to have an evaluating team who will periodically evaluate the learning systems. This may comprise of network administrators and IT experts. In general, the qualifications and experiences of the staff members involved affect the distribution of the materials and the efficiency of the learning system.

B. Online Help System and Online Chat

One of the important aspects in e-learning is interactivity. This relates to how students interact with their teachers, peers and the learning materials. In broad terms, this interaction relates to the interactions students have with the content and with people. This interaction might be via asynchronous modes of communication, commonly known as chat [28]. There are four main advantages of having an online help and support system in e-learning. First, it helps to facilitate student assessment as well as collecting feedback from learners. This may involve the use of quizzes and peer reviews [28]. Secondly, students are able to engage in discussions with either of their peers and/or their teachers. This helps to enhance their experiences in e-learning. Thirdly, such systems help in the enrichment of content where resources are made to be more interactive. As noted earlier, these students are not only users of learning materials, but also actively engage in the creation of such materials. Students and teachers engage in the process of enhancing the content through online communications. Finally, such systems enable for skill support through the use of various resources such lecture notes [28]. The use of online help systems and chat has the advantage of extending the reach where remote audiences actively take part in the learning process simultaneously. This helps to extend education to those persons who could not attend at a given time.

C. Speed and Availability

Availability is one of the confidence building requirements in an e-learning environment. For e-learning to be successfully adopted, it is important that network based applications remain available all the time in order to enhance the productivity of users. For instance, if a learning system is too slow because of a denial of service attack, the users end up taking more time to access materials and complete their work, and this greatly affects their productivity. Speed and availability are critical components that help students achieve their desired educational goals [29]. For example, students are required in getting critical information at the beginning of a course relating to the subjects, lecturers, assignment schedules and material required [29]. Such information needs to be available to the learners in a form that is concise and understandable whenever and where ever it is accessed.

The availability of the e-learning system is thus affected by its design. For instance, if the site has too much content or too complicated, availability is affected. It is therefore important for such considerations to be made when designing the e-learning systems [29]. In addition, for those sites that have a high volume of material, there is the need to have a high speed internet connection to effectively load pages [29]. These two aspects also affect the efficiency of the systems where if a system is unavailable, it will be inefficient and students find it difficult to complete the required tasks. It is crucial for users of such systems to ensure that the devices they use have the necessary capabilities to guarantee high speed connection and availability.

D. *Training for Students and Staff*

The adoption of e-learning requires that both the teachers and students acquire new skills in order to effectively embrace it. This is because the education shifts from being purely teacher centered to one that is more collaborative where teachers become facilitators and act as the intermediaries between the students and the materials [30]. Lack of adequate training for both staff and students can lead to lack of engagement in the e-learning activities. The training of these two groups should mainly focus on the use of modern ICT tools in learning and teaching.

Some of these technologies include social media, computers and teleconferencing tools. In addition, this training needs to focus on their attitudes towards ICT and other educational technologies. For instance, staff members are likely to experience many problems when their institutions adopt flexible and open learning and make use of ideas that they do not fully understand or are not in accord with their traditional practices [30]. Therefore, training of staff and students is a step taken in ensuring all stakeholders fully engage in e-learning. In addition, this also ensures that the benefits of e-learning are realized through full exploitation of communication and education technologies.

REFERENCE

[1] T. Volery and D. Lord, "Critical success factors in online education," *International Journal of Educational Management*, vol. 14(5), pp. 216-223, 2000

[2] H. M Selim "Critical success factors for e-learning acceptance: Confirmatory factor models," *Computers & Education*, vol. 49(2), pp. 396-413, 2007.

[3] S. Ozkan and R. Koseler, "Multi-dimentional students evaluation of e-learning systems in the higher education context: An empirical investigation," *Computer & Education*, vol. 53, pp. 1285-1296, 2009.

[4] D. Gillette, "Pedagogy, architecture, and the virtual classroom," *Technical Communication Quarterly*, vol. 8(1), pp. 21-36, 1999.

[5] G. Gregory, "Academic senate of California polytechnic state university,"[online] in *Academic Senate*, 2012. http://www.academicsenate.calpoly.edu/sites/academicsenate.wcms.calpoly.edu/files/agendas/12-13_agendas/sa111312.pdf (Accessed: 11 January 2013)

[6] M. Momeni, M Jamporazmey, and F. Bahadori, "Comprehensive framework for evaluating e-learning systems: Using BSC framework," *International Journal on E-Learning*, vol. 12(1), pp. 81-98, 2013.

[7] G. Puri, "Critical success Factors in e-Learning– An empirical study," *International Journal of Multidisciplinary Research*, vol. 2(1), pp. 149-161, 2012.

[8] E. P. Nathan, Critical success factors: How one multinational company develops global e-learning," Ph.D. dissertation, Ithaca College, New York, 2009.

[9] B. H. Khan, "A framework for e-learning," [online] *LTI magazine*, 2001. http://lomo.kyberia.net/diplomovka/webdownload/partial/elearningmag.com/E-Learning%20-%20A%20Framework%20for%20E-learning.pdf (Accessed: 15 May 2013)

[10] E. Kanninen, "Learning styles and e-learning," M.S. thesis, Science, Tampere University of Technology, Tampere, Finland, 2008.

[11] M. Sunnarborg, "From teacher to facilitator," [online] *Learning Solutions Magazine*, 2008. http://www.learningsolutionsmag.com/articles/74/from-teacher-to-facilitator (Accessed: 27 January 2013)

[12] S. Sengupta, B. Mukherjee and S. Bhattacharya, "Designing a scaffolding for supporting personalized synchronous e-learning," CS & IT-CSCP, vol. 6, pp. 505-511, 2012.

[13] A. L. Baylor and D. Ritchie, "What factors facilitate teacher skill, teacher morale, and perceived student learning in technology-using classrooms?," *Computers & Education,* vol. *39*(4), pp. 395-414, 2002.

[14] M. R. Mehregan, M. Jamporazmey and M. Mehrafrouz, "Application of fuzzy analytic hierarchy process in ranking modern educational systems' success criteria," *International Journal of e-Education, e-Business, e-Management and e-Learning*, vol. 1(4), pp. 299-304, 2011.

[15] B. Barron, "Interest and self-sustained learning as catalysts of development: A learning ecology perspective," *Human Development*, vol. *49*(4), pp. 193-224, 2006.

[16] Swedish national agency for higher education , " E-learning quality: Aspects and criteria for evaluation of e-learning in higher education,". *in 45 Tryckeri AB*, Solna, pp. 1-91, 2008.

[17] M. Frimpon, "A re-structuring of the critical success factors for e-learning deployment," *American International Journal of Contemporary Research*, vol. *2*(3), pp. 115-127, 2012.

[18] M. A. Musa and M. S. Othman "Critical success factor in e-Learning: an examination of technology and student factors," *International Journal of Advances in Engineering & Technology,* vol. 3(2), pp. 140-148, 2012.

[19] J. M. Keller, "Motivational design of instruction." *Instructional Design Theories and Models:* 3860433, Hillsdale, NJ, 1983.

[20] R. Catalanello and M. Sokol, "Success of Florida virtual school is difficult to measure," [online] *Tampa Bay Times,* 2012. http://www.tampabay.com/news/education/k12/success-of-florida-virtual-school-is-difficult-to-measure/1209497 (Accessed: 29 October 2012)

[21] R. Smith, "Motivational factors in e-learning," [online] George Washington University, 2008. http://www.ruthcsmith.com/ (Accessed: 15 January 2013)

[22] P. Mungania, "The seven e-learning barriers facing employees," [online] *the Masie Center*, pp. 1-80, 2003. http://aerckenya.org/docs/ElearningReport.pdf (Accessed: 25 February 2013)

[23] N. Barik and S. Karforma, "Risks and Remedies in E-learning System," *International Journal of Network Security & Its Applications (IJNSA)*, vol. 4(1). Pp.51-59, 2012.

[24] M. Harrison, "Four technology tips for e-learning project managers," *Kineo Insight,* pp. 1-22, 2007.

[25] A. Al-Dahoud and T. Walkowiak, "Dependable e-learning systems," *E-Learning, Experiences and Future,* Safeeullah Soomro, Ed, Rijeka, Croatia, InTech, 2010, pp. 295-304.

[26] Backroad Connections Pty Ltd, "Developing e-learning content," *Australian Flexible Learning Framework Quick Guides series*, Australian National Training Authority, pp. 1-16, 2003.

[27] B. Khan "Program Evaluation in E-Learning," [online] 2008. http://asianvu.com/bk/elearning_evaluation_article.pdf (Accessed: 25 February 2013)

[28] C. McNaught.,P. Lam, C. Keing and K. F. Cheng, "Improving e-learning support and infrastructure: An evidence-based," in *Technology Supported Learning and Teaching: A Staff Perspective*, Hershey, PA, Information Science Publishing, Idea Group Inc. pp. 71-89, 2006.

[29] A. Y. Alsabawy and A. Cater-Steel, "Identifying the Determinants of E-learning Service Delivery Quality," *23rd Australasian Conference on Information Systems,* 2012, pp. 1-10.

[30] V. Vrana et al, "Analyzing academic staff and students' attitudes towards the adoption of e-learning," [online] http://asiapacific-odl.oum.edu.my/C70/F275.pdf (Accessed: 25 February 2013)

SESSION

E-GOVERNMENT AND ISSUES OF INTEREST TO GOVERNMENT, ELECTED OFFICIALS, AND RELEVANT AGENCIES

Chair(s)

TBA

Personal information systems usability and contents tailoring by users

C. Detraux [1] and D. L. Scapin [1]
[1] INRIA, Domaine de Voluceau, 78153, Le Chesnay Cedex, France

Abstract - *This paper describes an experiment on the usability of a new personal information management system on internet (PIMI). The goals are to evaluate its usability, and to assess user tailoring as an evaluation technique. Thirty users participated to the study : a first part consisted in a standard user test (SUT) and a second part was a usability test with tailoring by users (UTT). Overall, a total of 51 usability problems were diagnosed. Among those, 32 resulted from SUT, and 19 from UTT. Part of the latter (11) are additional to the ones identified during SUT, and to those diagnosed previously by usability inspection (UI with Ergonomic Criteria). The active involvement of users through customization scenarios appear to provide additional cues for usability assessment, and for design (new generic usability recommendations).*

Keywords: Usability evaluation; evaluation methods; user tailoring; personal information systems; e-gov.

1 Introduction

Personal information management systems (PIMs) and tools are now widely offered on internet and smartphones to support our daily lives, as citizen, employees, stakeholders, family members, friends, etc. Such novel systems and tools need to be usable, especially for reaching the goal of various government initiatives for "paperless" administrative procedures. The study presented here has been conducted with that goal, in a ANR-PIMI project which aims at developing a Personal Information Space on Internet for supporting remote e-procedures (getting a passport, paying taxes, obtaining social services, etc.). This study follows up on previous work that contributed to the iterative design of the current prototype. An initial research [1] carried out several usability studies: 1 administrative forms analysis; 3 "focus groups" on information storage, and on sharing; 1 online questionnaire on the same topics for a wider range of audience; 1 "card-sorting" study to validate categories created by users and to organize their information. All the design/ evaluation iterative steps led to a PIMI mock-up, taking into account users' needs as they were collected. Another research [2] complemented the approach through an experiment to validate the information content and structure of the mock-up that was partly modifiable. The results allowed to validate the item structure for the future personal space, and started assessing user modifications as evaluation cues, and provided usability recommendations. Going further, in the current study, the goal is twofold: evaluate the usability of the advanced PIMI prototype (in terms of contents and structure), and investigate the role of various methods in usability problems diagnosis. In the experiment, a standard user test (SUT) and a test with tailoring (UTT) are compared. The results are then compared to a previous usability inspection (UI). This paper first reviews some aspects of the literature on PIMs, on user tailoring, and on usability methods comparisons. Then, the experiment method, procedure, material, participants, and main results are presented. The conclusion discusses lessons learned and directions for future work.

2 Other Work

Personal Information Management Systems (PIMs) refers to studies on how users manage their data and personal documents. From a usability point of view, the literature is not yet very rich. Some are partly covered in CSCW conferences [3], of course mainly on cooperation, groups, social interactions; and on societal aspects in [4]. Other papers are more directly concerned with usability for individuals, such as « user's personal digital ecosystem » in [5], or about the evolution of usage with tablets in [6], or on privacy in [7], and [8]. Also contributions concerned facilitated form-filling in [9], web search in [10], and supporting flexibility between devices in [11]. Some studies attempted, through longitudinal studies, to understand how people make notes and archive their information in [12], or looked at mobile practices in [13]. However, very little can be found on usability assessment, as reported in [2, op.cit.], in which, besides a review of 15 PIM tools, highlights are provided about the organization and information retrieval aspects among which hierarchical structures seem still to be the most widespread and users favorite [14] [15] [16] [17], but that also show users difficulties in creating consistent and meaningful hierarchical structures, and in naming categories/items. Our current experiment attempts to go further on those issues of personal information structure and naming.

User tailoring. Previous work [2, op.cit.] reviewed the literature on tailoring and personalization. No real novel contributions were found beyond [18] [19] [20] [21] on user modifications in systems design/development, its usability and impact on usability measurements. On the other hand, many papers relate to other issues, such as recommender systems [22], social networks [23], games [24], physical environments [25], e-learning [26], etc. In short, very few experimental results exist about user modifications as a means of usability evaluation. This study on a prototype intends to complement this by providing new empirical results.

Usability evaluation methods (UEMs) are numerous (see [27]). Comparing them is very complex and lengthy, especially when following guidelines and criteria such as in [28] [29]. In a thorough literature review [30] issues were reported (see [31] [28 & 29, op.cit] [32]), such as using appropriate metrics, problem severity, whether putative usability problems extracted in analyses are genuine, thoroughness, problem similarity, and usability problem interpretation. In the current study, we attempted to alleviate these difficulties through a thorough problem coding. However, while we used a rather large set of participants in the experiment, the usability inspection carried out was only co-conducted by 2 experts, unlike the above study [30, op.cit.].

3 Experiment

The goal of the experiment is to evaluate the PIMI prototype through information on the intuitive user behavior. The specific objectives are to verify: the usability of the user interface when entering/ filling information; finding items; modifying contents (categories/ sections names, items display order, deactivating items); the understandability of current naming of categories, sections, and items; the appropriateness of the information structure; and the level of tailoring that users intuitively perform; and its role on usability problems diagnosis.

3.1 Method and procedure

The sessions were conducted individually and supervised by the experimenter. They were conducted in the participants' own working or study environment (offices for researchers and administrative staff; computer room for students). This allowed easy access to their personal belongings (bags, wallets, diaries, personal or work computers) for the tasks required. The prototype was presented on a laptop computer and sessions recorded with a screen capture software (video and sound). A pilot test was conducted with one subject to assess the experimenter's discourse and to calibrate scenarios duration (in order, for the experiment to last less than one hour). The sessions were conducted in three main phases:

- **Initially**: presentation of the project, of the experiment objectives, and of the prototype (how to navigate, enter, save and modify the PIMI). The participants were encouraged to think aloud about their difficulties in relation to the task scenarios, the tool, the data.

- A phase of **work on the tasks and scenarios**: in a **first part**, 4 task scenarios were proposed consecutively: <u>Scenario 1</u>: personal identification tasks (e.g., enter name, identity card information, address, phone); <u>Scenario 2</u>: tasks about professional contacts and student curriculum.; <u>Scenario 3</u>: data entry tasks on two types of forms; <u>Scenario 4</u>: to verify whether proposed redundancies are understood, accepted and the path(s) followed to find them. In a **second part**, two steps were proposed: a **first step** where a scenario required to make changes according to the instructions (function "Custom PIMI" or "Customization Options" to "Enter and View Information"). A **second step** required the participants to browse the entire prototype structure to make the changes they wished.

- **Finally**, a questionnaire allowed the participants to comment on the prototype, and on the difficulties they had. The questions were "closed" (yes-no or list of options). However, the experimenter encouraged the participants to justify their answers orally (audio recording) or in writing.

3.2 Material

Information items. The latest results from a previous study [2] resulted in a structure of information items with 10 categories, with 35 sub-categories : Identity (personal identity, ID papers, family); Work (current work/ affiliation details, career, student curriculum, and professional contacts); Papers (ID papers, salary sheets, social security card); Contacts (personal & professional); Agenda (personal & professional); Transportation (private, public); Codes (entry codes, locks, phones, passwords, websites, credit cards); Finance (income and benefits, investments, loans, bank accounts); Taxes (income tax reference, tax deductions, tax bracket, property tax, housing tax); Health (social security & health insurance, physicians, medical records, emergency contact person), for a total of 73 information items.

Prototype. The PIMI prototype (PC V0.3) was available locally with a Firefox browser on a Windows platform. Figure 1 shows a screen shot of the prototype.

Experimenter's equipment : video screen capture software: NCH Software : it allows recording the entire sessions through video capture of the screen, as well as all the user comments (with the participants' authorization). Observation checklists cards are also completed by the experimenter during the sessions to gather the most relevant information on various aspects explained in the scenario descriptions.

Participants' equipment : laptop with prototype and capture software installed. Description sheets with scenarios and tasks to perform. Additional forms: when participants did not have expected data, the experimenter provided them with business cards of a specialist doctor, of a colleague, etc. Uploadable files required in the scenarios are installed (e.g., fictitious identity card.jpg, academic career.pdf). Final questionnaire with questions about the prototype, its use and opinions on such personal information systems, with a specific part on tailoring and associated involvement of participants.

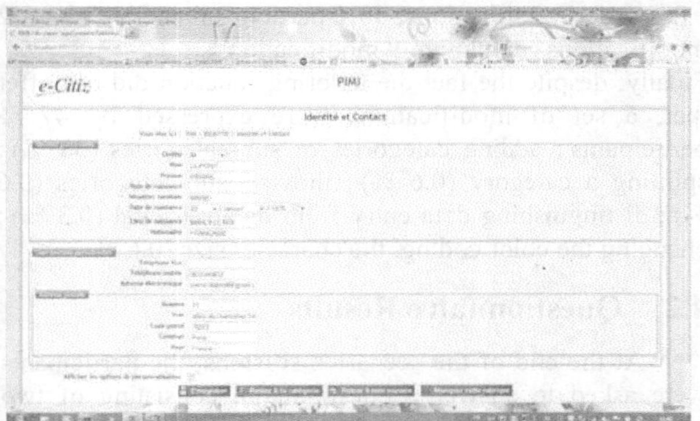

Figure 1. A Screenshot of PIMI Prototype

3.3 Participants

The sessions were conducted with 30 participants: 10 researchers (computer science institute); 10 administrative staff (computer science institute and university); and 10 university students. They were 16 male (53.3%) and 14 female (46.6%). The average age was 36.06 years (s.d. 16.8 y). For researchers, 8 were male (80%) and 2 female (20%). Age average was 47.5 years (s.d. 17.48 y). For administrative staff, 9 were female (90%) and 1 male (10%). Age average was 41.2 years (s.d 11.4 y). For students, 7 were male (70%) and 3 female (30%). Age average was 19.5 years (s.d. 1.17 y).

4 Results

Session duration averaged 46.93 mn. (s.d. 10.16). In the category researchers, it was 46.3 mn. (s.d. 8.38). For "administrative staff", it was 51.9 mn. (s.d 11.76). For "students", it was 42.6 mn. (s.d. 8.69).

Analyses are based on observed difficulties and errors, as well as participants comments. **Difficulties** include delays finding information, idle time, messy navigation; **Errors** include wrong or unsyntactical actions; **Comments** are expressed by participants during sessions, or in a questionnaire. Most comments reinforce the observed difficulties or errors. It is noticeable that the problems were diagnosed from: observed errors and difficulties (33%), participants' comments (27%), and 40% from both.

Concerning **participants groups**, no differences were found in terms of errors for SUT (students: 43/124, administratives: 42/124, researchers: 39/124). On the other hand, for UTT, students modified much more (90 modifications, i.e., 19 naming, 37 masking, and 34 order), while 75 for the administratives (i.e., 16, naming, 32 masking, and 34 order), and 50 for the researchers (i.e., 7 naming, 34 masking, and 9 order). Noticeably, answers to the questionnaire showed that the 5 participant's negative opinion on tailoring easiness are 3 researchers and 2 administratives. Overall, it seems that younger users (students) incline more at suggesting and tailoring.

Difficulties in finding information. In Scenario 1, 16,1% participants had difficulties finding the item « Parents ». In Scenario 2, only 3,2% had difficulties finding the item « Professional Contacts ». In Scenario 3, 58,1% could not find the items « Social Security» and « Specialized Physician », and 19,4% had trouble finding them. In Scenario 4, 33,3% had trouble finding « I.D.» (attached file), and 3,3% could not find it at all. In other words, accessing categories and sub-categories is not a problem, unlike finding individual items.

Naming issues. The terms participants had a few understanding difficulties with are : *(in personal identifications)* family situation (6/30), birth name (3/30), birth location (1/8) ; *(in colleagues' information)* number (11/30) ; *(in student curriculum)* university curriculum and courses (2/30) ; *(in social security)* beneficiary (8/30), coverage period (25/30), number (11/30) ; *(in other health specialists)* personalized name (28/30). To summarize, a few terms are either not well chosen, or lack precision, or are not presented in a sufficient context.

Navigation difficulties : 19/30 participants had least 1 difficulty (only one had 4 (total 33, average 1,1 ; s.d. 1,15). Some difficulties led to errors : in Scenario 1, 7/30 had difficulties, and 3 errors ; in Scenario 2, 5/30 difficulties, and 2 errors ; in Scenario 3, 4/30 difficulties, and 2 errors ; in Scenario 4, 5/30 difficulties, and 1 error ; in Scenario 5.1 (modification) 7/30 difficulties, and 3 errors ; in Scenario 5.2 (modification) 5/30 difficulties, and 4 errors. Usability problems are mainly related to navigation buttons, and lack of short-cuts.

Saving forms led to 30 difficulties : 70% participants had at least 1 difficulty, and 3 participants with 3 difficulties. They concerned : scenario 1 (13 difficulties including 2 that led to error) ; scenario 2 (7 difficulties including 4 that led to error) ; scenario 3 (9 difficulties including 2 that led to error) ; scenario 4 was not concerned by the save function ; scenario 5.1. (none); scenario 5.2. led to 1 error. The issues here relate to lack of feedback, and naming confusions.

Errors confirm the issues above. A total of 124 errors was observed through the experiment (average 4,13 per participant ; sd 2,17) : Scenario 1 : average 1,13 ; sd 1,25, with at least 1 error for 18 participants, and 5 for 1 participant ; Scenario 2 : average 1,3 ; sd 1,2, with at least 1 error for 20 participants, and 4 for 1 participant ; Scenario 3 : average 1,3 ; sd 1,05, with at least 1 error for 23 participants, and 5 for 1 participant ; Scenario 4 : only 1 error ; Scenario 5.1 : 3 errors for 3 participants (1 each) ; Scenario 5.2 : 8 errors (average 0,26 ; sd. 0,69), with at least 1 error for 5 participants, and 3 for 1.

4.1 Personalization

To study the way people modify their personal information content and structure, 2 scenarios were proposed along 2 distinct steps : **Step 1** followed a set of modification instructions the participants completed. The goal was to familiarize the participants with the tailoring functions, and to observe their potential difficulties. **Step 2** was at the participants' initiative : they were asked to modify the PIMI content and structure as they wished.

4.1.1 Modifications by instructions

Paths followed **:** For **naming**, 63,3 % participants went directly to the tailoring function, while 6,7% went to each category; the other 30% chose to start first with categories, then concluded with the tailoring function. For **masking** categories, 86,7 % participants went directly to the tailoring function, while 13,3% participants used both ways.

Difficulties : For **naming changes**, 90 % participants had no trouble ; only 6,7% took a little time and only 3,3% did not succeed. For **masking** categories, 56,7 % had no trouble ; 36,7% took a little time and only 6,7% did not succeed. For **order** modification 43,3 % had no trouble ; **36,7%** took a little time. For **reinitializing the default structure**, there was no major difficulty, 96,7 % did it easily, only 3,3% took a bit more time.

4.1.2 User initiative modifications

Table 1 shows a total de 222 modifications (researchers C1 to C10, administrative A1 to A10, students (E1 to E10), with an average of 7,4 per participant (sd: 4,79).

Table 1 : User Initiative Modifications

	Naming Categories	Naming Sub-categories	Masking Categories	Masking Sub-categories	Masking Items	Ordering Categories	Total	
C1	0	3	1	1	1	0	6	Total: 50
C2	1	0	1	0	0	0	2	
C3	0	0	2	3	0	0	5	
C4	0	2	1	2	0	4	9	
C5	0	0	5	2	0	3	10	
C6	0	1	0	0	0	0	1	
C7	0	0	2	0	5	0	7	
C8	0	0	1	0	0	0	1	
C9	0	0	3	1	0	2	6	
C10	0	0	2	1	0	0	3	
A1	0	0	0	0	0	5	5	Total: 75
A2	4	1	4	2	0	0	11	
A3	1	2	3	2	0	9	17	
A4	0	0	1	0	0	4	5	
A5	2	0	3	0	0	8	13	
A6	2	1	1	0	0	4	8	
A7	0	0	4	0	0	0	4	
A8	2	1	1	0	0	4	8	
A9	0	0	1	0	0	0	1	
A10	0	0	4	0	6	0	10	
E1	1	0	2	0	5	0	8	Total: 90
E2	3	2	1	1	0	0	7	
E3	2	0	1	1	0	2	6	
E4	0	0	1	0	0	0	1	
E5	0	0	1	0	0	8	9	
E6	1	1	2	2	6	4	16	
E7	0	0	1	0	0	4	5	
E8	0	1	3	1	0	0	5	
E9	2	3	5	2	0	7	19	
E10	1	2	1	1	0	9	14	
TOTAL	22	20	58	22	23	77	222	
Average	0,73333333	0,66666667	1,93333333	0,73333333	0,76666667	2,56666667	7,4	
S.D.	1,0806554	0,9589266	1,38796138	0,90718714	1,90613046	3,10376116	4,79655048	

All participants made modifications: from just 1 by 4 participants, up to 17 by 1 participant. Table 1 also shows the most common modifications (103 masking modifications, 77 categories order modifications, and 42 naming modifications).

- for Naming, 22 modifications concerned categories (40 % participants), and 20 sub-categories (40 % participants).
- for Masking, 58 modifications concerned categories (93,3 % participants), 22 sub-categories (14,3 % participants), and 23 items (3,2 % participants).
- for Order modifications, 50% participants made at least 2 modifications (maximum 9 modifications).

Finally, despite the fact the tailoring function did not offer that, a set of modifications were expressed by 47 % participants : adding categories or sub-categories (33 %) ; splitting a category (0.6 %) ; moving sub-categories (0.6 %) ; distinguishing data entry from data retrieval (0.3 %) ; changing the color coding, the character size (0.6 %).

4.2 Questionnaire Results

At the end of the scenarios sessions, the participants were asked to answer a questionnaire consisting of two parts: a first part with specific questions about tailoring, and a second part with more general questions about the PIMI prototype, and improvements they would like to see.

Part 1 : questions on tailoring

Most participants (83.3%) liked the capability of modifying the structure of their personal Information space. Most participants (93.3%) also found it easy for categories naming modifications, and for sub-categories naming modifications (80%). It was also easy for masking categories and sub-categories (93.3%). It was judged much less easy for modifying categories order (36.7%). In addition, the participants suggested other types of modifications that were not implemented in the prototype, such as : adding new categories and sub-categories (9/20) ; changing the visual design, e.g., colors, formats (4/30) ; and providing forms horizontally (2/30).

Part 2 : general questions and improvements

A slight majority of the participants (60%) feel ready to use a system like the PIMI prototype. Their motivation is mainly the capability of centralizing all their data, and limit paper use. For those who felt less ready (33.3%) and those not ready at all (6.7%), their main concern are security and trust. Most participants (80%) said they did nor experience difficulties in using the prototype. Only a few expressed difficulties either moderate (16.7%) or strong (3.3%). In addition, 25/30 participants (86,2%) made suggestions for improvement, basically attempting to alleviate some of the usability problems found earlier.

From a more methodological point of view, it is noticeable that, overall, the various usability evaluations conducted in this study led to the diagnosis of a larger set of usability problems than simply asking users through a questionnaire.

However, the participants' answers, particularly through their suggestions confirmed part of the problems identified.

5 Discussion

User tailoring: The active participation in that session was strong: a total of 222 modifications were made, and all participants made at least one change with a maximum of 17 for one participant (average 7,4 modifications per participant, sd. 4,79).

The modifications can be characterized by 4 main goals: to simplify (through masking and changing names); to clarify (through the change of names); to facilitate access (through the change order categories); to secure (through masking).

Some methodological lessons can be learned:

- participants' modifications help identify additional usability problems.
- the participants felt having a more important role, express themselves more, provide criticisms, advice and express their preferences. In short, they take ownership of the system, even strengthening their opinion on some usability issues that did not seem too "troublesome" initially.
- considering the need for today's systems being used for a wider audience, varying in terms of age, sex, occupation, skills, and contexts, it is effective to provide tailoring functions for the users (e.g., for vocabulary, techniques, navigation needs).

In short, facilitating users' role as "actors" rather than "passive" participants has strong merits.

Usability Methods comparison: Figure 1 shows the number of usability problems diagnosed through the 3 usability methods (Standard Usability Testing (SUT), Usability Testing with Tailoring (UTT), and Usability Inspection (UI).

Overall, there are no real significant differences in the usability problems nature, except the obvious different interaction states in which they occurred, due to the task scenarios (modification states for UTT, and data entry states for SUT). However:

- There is about the same number of specific usability problems for each evaluation technique : 9 for UI (26% of total) ; 11 for SUT (34% of total) ; 11 for UTT (58% of total). In percentage though, UTT has the highest score of specific problems.
- There are many (highest score) problems common to UI and SUT (21, i.e., 62% of UI and 66% of SUT).
- There are much less problems common to UI and UTT (8, i.e., 24% of UI and 42% of UTT).
- There are even less problems common to SUT and UTT (4, i.e., 12% of SUT. and 21% of UTT).
- There are very few problems common 3 ways to UI, SUT and UTT (4, i.e., 12% of UI, 12% of SUT and 21% of UTT).

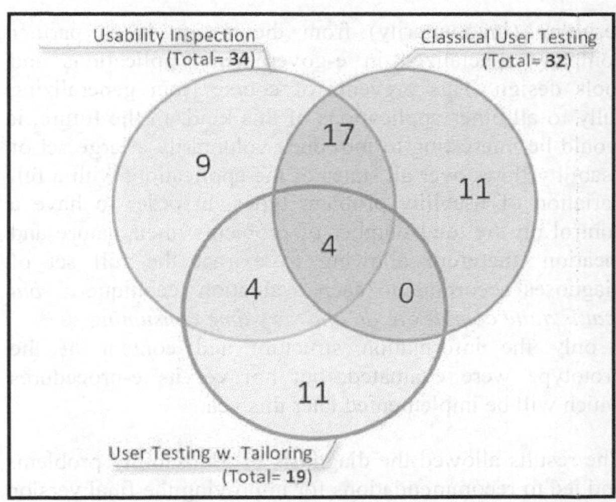

Figure 1 – Usability problems per evaluation method

Also, it can be noticed that :

- (for their 4 common ones) there is no problem common to SUT and UTT that is not also diagnosed with UI.
- (for their 21 common ones) 17 problems have been diagnosed with both SUT and UI, but only 4 also diagnosed with UTT.
- (for their 8 common ones) 4 problems have been diagnosed with both UTT and UI, and 4 also diagnosed with SUT.

Unlike previous findings in [25, op.cit.], SUT and UTT do not seem to lead to more problem diversity than UI. However, it shows that SUT and UTT seems particularly efficient for the diagnosis of problems that require a particular state of interaction to be detectable. On the other hand, UI supports the identification of problems directly observable, often related to learnability and basic usability.

6 Conclusion

This paper reported research work associated with the usability evaluation of a prototype for personal information management. The experiment, with 30 participants (researchers, administrative, and students), followed 4 classical task scenarios for user testing, and 1 scenario allowing participants' tailoring of the prototype information structure and content.

First some limits should be pointed out, such as:

- For both SUT and UTT, the experimenter's presence may have hindered access to some prototype functions (e.g., on-line help) as it was just simpler to ask the experimenter.
- Also, except in the modification scenario, participants remained focused on the tasks, not exploring further. User monitoring through time may be useful.
- A varied set of usability problems has been diagnosed. However, there was no control on the usability flaws,

resulting (involuntarily) from the design by a partner company specialized in e-government applications and tools design. This prevents of course from generalizing fully to all other applications of this kind. In the future, it would be interesting to introduce voluntarily a large set of usability flaws over all states of the application, with a full variation of usability problem types, in order to have a control on the total number of problems, their nature and location, therefore allowing to extract the full set of diagnoses according to each evaluation technique ... *but that is quite complex to do and very time consuming.*
- only the information structure and content of the prototype were evaluated, but not yet its e-procedures which will be implemented later this year.

The results allowed the diagnosis of 51 usability problems and led to recommendations for improving the final version of the prototype.
From a methodological point of view, we investigated the relative role of the two evaluation methods used in the experiment (standard user test (SUT) and user test with tailoring (UTT)). Additionally, the results were also compared to results from a usability inspection (UI).
The three evaluation techniques are quite complementary, but direct involvement of the users through a tailoring scenario enriches the evaluation, pointing at unexpected paths, function use, understanding of concepts, etc.

While usability inspection based on Ergonomic Criteria allowed to make a general diagnosis for usability problems (several types and in many states of the interface), user test allowed to identify similar types of problems, but with a more detailed focus, despite only on a fewer interaction states.

Using tailoring scenarios allows users to 'express themselves more about the system by showing their preferences and thus promoting a more collaborative design and evaluation process.

Overall, the active and direct participation of users by providing new structures, terms, pathways, and functions lead to very rich usability cues for evaluation and design.

For future research work, several issues seem worth investigating:
- security and trust is still an issue, even though a positive perception seems facilitated by user involvement in tailoring structure and content, but little is known yet about the full picture, with e-procedures.
- real usage: one must find ways of actually evaluating real use through innovative and intelligent tools for collecting real-time user data, including on evolutionary tailoring.
- mobility: PIMs, such as the prototype evaluated in our study with a PC, will obviously need to be used on smartphones and other tablets. A mobile PIMI version is being developed, but its usability, and compatibility with PC version, including its plasticity will need to be assessed.

Acknowledgement: This research was supported by the ANR project PIMI.

7 References

[1] D. L. Scapin, P. Marie-Dessoude , M. Winckler, C. Detraux. Personal Information Systems: User Views and Information Categorization, in "Proc. Centric2011-4th. Intl. Conf. on Advances in Human-oriented and Personalized Mechanisms, Technologies, and Services", Barcelona, Spain, 2011.

[2] C. Detraux, D. L. Scapin. User Modifications as Usability Evaluation Cues for a Personal Information Space, in EEE2012, Intl. Conf. on e-Learning, e-Business, Enterprise Information Systems, and e-Government", Las Vegas, USA, 2012.

[3] CSCW13-1. Proc. of the 2013 ACM Conference on Computer Supported Cooperative Work v.1 / Amy Bruckman / Scott Counts / Cliff Lampe / Loren Terveen San Antonio, Texas 2013-02-23 2013-02-27 2013 ACM n.141 p.1566

[4] Oakley, R. L. and Salam, A. F. Cyber Citizens and Cyber Deviance: Exploring Social and Technical Factors as Antecedents to Cyber Deviance and the Implications for Cyber Citizenship. Proc. of the 2012 AIS SIGHCI Workshop on HCI Research in MIS 2012-12-16 p.7.

[5] Kay, J., Kummerfeld, B. Creating personalized systems that people can scrutinize and control: Drivers, principles and experience. ACM Transactions on Interactive Intelligent Systems 2012-12 v.2 n.4 p.24

[6] Buttfield-Addison, P., Lueg, C., Ellis, C., and Manning, J, "Everything goes into or out of the iPad": the iPad, information scraps and personal information management. Proc. of 2012 Australian CHI Conference 2012-11-26 p.61-67.

[7] Ploderer, B. Smith, W., Howard, S., Pearce, J., and Borland, R.. Things you don't want to know about yourself: ambivalence about tracking and sharing personal information for behaviour change. Proc. of 2012 Australian Computer-Human Interaction Conference 2012-11-26 p.489-492

[8] Rawassizadeh, R. Towards sharing life-log information with society / Behaviour and Information Technology 2012-11 v.31 n.11 p.1057-1067.

[9] Winckler, M., Gaits, V., Vo, D.-B., Firmenich, S., and Rossi, G. An approach and tool support for assisting users to fill-in web forms with personal information New frontiers in documentation II / ACM 29th Intl. Conf. on Design of Communication 2011-10-03 p.195-202.

[10] Nitsche, M., and Nuernberger, A. InFrame-Browsing: Enhancing Standard Web Search Poster Papers. Proc. of Symposium on HCI and Information Retrieval 2012-10-04 p.16

[11] Ardito, C., Costabile, M. F., Desolda, G., Matera, M. Piccinno, A., and Picozzi, M. Composition of situational

interactive spaces by end users: a case for cultural heritage Living history Proc. 7th Nordic Conference on HCI 2012-10-14 p.79-88.

[12] Van Kleek, Max G., Styke, W., Schraefel, M. C., Karger, D. Finders/keepers: a longitudinal study of people managing information scraps in a micro-note tool Reading & writing / Proc. ACM CHI 2011 2011-05-07 v.1 p.2907-2916

[13] Lindroth, T., and Bergquist, M. Breadcrumbs of interaction: situating personal information management Proc. Fifth Nordic Conference on HCI 2008-10-10 p.266-273.

[14] F. Evequoz and D. Lalanne, "I thought you would show me how to do it - studying and supporting PIM strategy changes". PIM Workshop, ASIS&T 2009, 35-42.

[15] S. Henderson. and A. Srinivasan, "An empirical analysis of personal digital document structures", Proc. HCI International 2009, Berlin, Heidelberg: Springer-Verlag, 2009, pp. 394–403.

[16] S. Henderson, "Guidelines for the design of personal document management user interfaces". PIM Workshop, ASIS&T 2009, 2009, pp. 65-72.

[17] K. Voit, K. Andrews and W. Slany, "Why personal information management (PIM) technologies are not widespread". PIM Workshop, ASIS&T 2009. (2009) 60-64.

[18] A. I. Mørch and N. D. Mehandjiev, "Tailoring as collaboration: the mediating tole of multiple representations and application units". Computer Supported Cooperative Work. 9(1) (2000): 75-100.

[19] L. Zhu, I. Vaghi, B. R. Barriceli, "A meta-reflective wiki for collaborative design". Proc. of the 7th International Symposium on Wikis and Open Collaboration (WikiSym'11).ACM, (2011), 53-62.

[20] R. Demunieux, V. Ganneau, G. Calvary and E. Gegovska, "Les interfaces plastiques : premiers retours utilisateurs, évaluations en laboratoire" .Ergo-IA 2008. 117-124.

[21] C. Dörner, F. Yetim, V. Pipek and V. Wulf, "Supporting business process experts in tailoring business processes". Interact. Comput. 23, 3 (2011), 226-238.

[22] Heung-Nam, K., Majdi, R., and El Saddik, A. Tailoring recommendations to groups of users: a graph walk-based approach. Proc. of the 2013 International Conference on Intelligent User Interfaces 2013-03-19 v.1 p.15-24

[23] Zimmerman, A., And Lorentz, A. LISTEN: a user-adaptive audio-augmented museum guide Special issue on Personalizing Cultural Heritage Exploration. User Modeling and User-Adapted Interaction 2008-11 v.18 n.5 p.389-416

[24] Gamberini, L., Spagnolli, A., Carradi, N., Jacucci, G., Tusa, G., Mikkola, T., Zamboni, L., and Hoggan, E. Tailoring Feedback to Users' Actions in a Persuasive Game for Household Electricity Conservation. Proc. of the 2012 International Conference on Persuasive Technology 2012-06-06 p.100-111.

[25] Mirri, S., Salomoni, P., and Prandi, C. Augment browsing and standard profiling for enhancing web accessibility. Proc. of the 2011 International Cross-Disciplinary Conference on Web Accessibility (W4A) 2011-03-28 v.2 p.5.

[26] Kolås, L. & Staupe, A. (2007). A Personalized E-learning Interface. In: The Proceedings of the international IEEE Conference on Computer as a tool. Eurocon 2007 (pp. 2670-2675). Poland: IEEE Computer Society.

[27] D. L. Scapin, E. Law, Nigel Bevan, and the WG1 contributors (2008). Final Report MAUSE COST 294 WG 1 :Critical Review and Analysis of Individual UEMs. COST-294 Project MAUSE (December 2008)

[28] Gray, W. D. and Salzman, M. C., 1998, Damaged merchandise? A review of experiments that compare usability evaluation methods. Human-Computer Interaction, 13, pp. 203-261.

[29] Hartson, H. R., Andre, T. S. and Williges, R. C., 2001, Criteria for evaluating usability evaluation methods. International Journal of Human-Computer Interaction, 13, pp. 373-410.

[30] Bach, C. and Scapin, D. L.. Comparing Inspections and User Testing for the Evaluation of Virtual Environments, in "International Journal of Human-Computer Interaction", 2010, vol. 26, no 8, p. 786-824

[31] Cockton, G., Woolrych, A., Hall, L., and Hidemarch, M., 2003, Changing Analysts' Tunes: The Surprising Impact of a New Instrument for Usability Inspection Method Assessment. In Proc. of People and Computers XVII: Designing for Society, Springer Verlag, pp. 145-162.

[32] Hornbæk, K. and Frøkjær, E., 2005, Comparing usability problems and redesign proposals as input to practical systems development. In Proc. of ACM Conference on Human Factors in Computing Systems, (New York, NY: ACM Press), pp. 391-400.

A Strategic Framework for E-Democracy Development

Ayo[1] C.K., *Oni[1] A.A. and Mbarika[2] V.W.
[1]Department of Computer and Information Sciences, Covenant University, Ota, Nigeria,
[2]Department of Marketing and E-Business, Southern University, Baton Rouge, USA

Abstract - *There are several e-participation projects initiated by different actors around the world but sustainability and citizens' acceptance of online public participation remains a difficult task. Examples of good practice are extremely rare in e-democracy implementation. Most government particularly, in the developing countries, do not have detailed and well established strategy for e-democracy realization, sustainability and citizens acceptance. This work argues that e-democracy implementation, especially in the resource poor countries, should be driven by a strategic approach guided by quality designs that will enhance sustainability and make tools for online engagement accessible to all segments of the society. This work adopts a qualitative approach using Grounded Theory Method (GTM) to develop a strategic framework for e-democracy development, which is largely missing from most national e-democracy strategies. The work introduces a strategic framework which serves as a generic abstraction of existing e-democracy strategies, implementation and best practices.*

Keywords: e-democracy, strategy, best practice, strategic, framework,

1 Introduction

Most government have achieved substantial progress in using ICT to connect with citizens. Most government have developed e-government strategy to increase transparency, and efficiency in public administration. However, the potential of ICT in governance is yet to be fully drawn. What is most available around the world is provision of e-services. Only few countries have advanced their policies and strategy for ICT enabled governance to participatory e-democracy stage. Several authors have worked on having a lasting e-democracy implementation, but no effort have produced a generic and structured framework that integrates the most fundamental elements of a successful implementation.

A strategy is the basic directional decisions for purposes and missions. It can also be referred to as what top management does that is of great importance to the organization. Strategy helps management to identify what to do and outcomes to expect [15]. We define e-democracy strategy as a plan for e-democracy systems, their supporting infrastructure, people and process which maximise government's ability to achieve an informed and engaged citizenry.

This work aims at developing a strategic framework which will serve as generic abstraction of e-democracy strategies and implementation. This study adopts a systematic literature review based on Grounded Theory Method (GTM) to develop the strategic framework. Choice of literature was based on the availability of published documents on e-democracy strategies, implementation and practices of countries within the top 20 position in e-participation ranking according UN e-government report [20]. Materials were sourced from academic database, international development organisations (EU, UN, UNPAN, OECD), research institutions (Demo-net, Hansard Society, Democracies Online Newswire), and countries specific Web sites.
This diversity provides a comprehensive view of strategies, implementation and good practices in e-democracy implementation from different domains.

2 Related Works

One of the key issues in e-democracy development is the acquisition of system that considerably meet government's needs and the needs of the citizens to participate in the democratic process. Different scholars have worked on having a lasting e-democracy implementation, such notable efforts are found in [1] [4] [12] [9] [6].

Critical keys and potential barriers to the success of e-democracy development must be considered to achieve a successful development [1]. They therefore, identified six key issues to be considered in e-democracy development which include investment, leadership, training, technological flexibility, access and digital divide, and privacy and security.

Similarly, Clift in his approach to e-democracy development, proposed a "top ten e-democracy: to do list" that will help government jumpstart the use of ICT in improving their democratic process [4]. These include among others announcing all public meetings online in a systematic and reliable way, putting "Democracy Button" on site's top page, holding government sponsored online consultations, developing e-democracy legislation, Internet education for elected officials, and etc.

Furthermore, a framework for sustainable e-Democracy development based on governance development standard called COBIT 4.1 was presented by [6]. The framework presented a 4 + 1 construct of e-democracy development process comprising: Stakeholders and policy; Information and Communication Technology; Development methodology; Process and project management; Environment and e-Democracy components.

A framework for e-Democracy development based on a promising relationship between e-Democracy and spatial dimension was proposed by [9]. The system presents an extensive use of the spatial dimension in a wiki collaboration environment to capture and integrate e-democracy information.

Strategic e-democracy framework which includes directional plan and basic component of e-democracy programme is still missing both in literature and in government strategies.

3.0 Research Methodology

This research adopts a systematic literature review involves a rigorous and well defined procedure applies to an existing literature [17]. Review methodologies in Information Systems research include: the eight steps for systematic literature review [17], systematic approach to literature review [11], writing a literature review [21], grounded theory method for literature review [23] and structured case [3]. We considered grounded theory approach as an appropriate method for framework development in this research because it support development of concepts and constructs that are grounded in data.

Grounded theory is an inductive method of analysing data with the aim of generating concepts, themes or theory that is grounded in qualitative data [19]. Grounded theory method has a set of principles and techniques which makes it suitable for quality qualitative research. These include principle of emergence, constant comparative analysis and theoretical sampling. Analysis of data to develop concepts, themes, and theory using grounded theory approach employs three analytical techniques. The three techniques are open coding, axial coding and selective coding [7]. Open coding involves identifying concepts, categories and their properties in a corpus [7]. Axial coding involves establishing relationships of identified categories and sub-categories of concepts or themes focusing on answering why, where, when, and how about the categories [14]. Selective coding involves selection of core variables of the emerging theory or concept. Table 1.0 summarized how GTM was used to review literature beginning with domain identification.

Previous studies were used as data so that concepts for the strategic framework could emerge. The sample composed of secondary data drawn from materials sourced from Information Systems centric publications and e-democracy strategy and implementation report documents. Electronic databases were searched for peer-reviewed journal articles, book chapters and conference proceedings on e-democracy. The Web sites of government agencies and those of international organisation and academic institution dealing with piloting and reporting e-practices were searched for relevant data. This includes OECD and Demo.net, and public.net.

4.0 The Proposed E-democracy Framework

The analysis of the major contents/focal points of e-democracy strategies, research and practice in literature was the starting point in developing the framework. These major contents which we referred to as constructs spelled out directional plan for the component strategic framework. We examined each of these components from our sample literatures in detail with an effort to structure the emerging strategic framework of e-democracy. It is important to understand the basic elements of each of these components as well as the relationships among them. Going through this process enables us to determine why and when relationship between the components [7] This also enables further classification of the components of the framework and in turn makes it very simple and clear. The next section presents some of the components and Figure 1.0 presents the strategic framework.

Table 1.0: Summary of Steps for Applying GTM to Literature Review

Steps	Tasks	Application in this study
1. Define	1.1 Define criteria for inclusion and exclusion	Studies conducted on e-democracy implementation from top countries in e-participation ranking
	1.2 Identify the field of research	Information Systems, e-democracy, e-government and online participation research
	1.3 Determine sources	- Peer reviewed journals, conference papers, book chapters; - Leading international development organizations e-library (e.g.: EU, UN, OECD), - Research institutions sites; and - Search Engines
	1.4 Specify search terms	e-democracy strategy, e-government strategy, e-engagement, e-participation, online participation strategy, online participation, e-politics, digital democracy,
2. Search	Search articles	Conduct the search in identified sources
3. Select	Select articles	Select articles using the criteria. Articles were selected for the analysis based on their focus on e-democracy.
4. Analyze	Open coding	Identify concepts and categories with their dimensions
	Axial coding	Relating categories and their subcategories
	Selective coding	Refining categories and their relationships
5.Presentation	Presenting results	Reporting insights from the review

4.1 Component of E-democracy Framework

Policy Framework

E-democracy policy framework captures the technological, legal and political process to back e-democracy implementation. It can be described as outlined strategy with respect to the purpose, structure and course of action laid down for achieving a set goal or agenda of e-democracy. The policy document should detail the strategic vision, strategic aim and objective, strategic policy, mode of implementation and overseeing body. Though the elements are the least mentioned components in literature their importance cannot be overemphasized.

i **Specific Strategic Policy:** policy content is largely missing in most e-democracy strategy at both conceptual and implementation stage. The overview of e-government and e-democracy by United Nations Department for Economic and Social Affairs (2003) reported that only 13 (8%) out of 190 member countries have direct/clear statements or policy encouraging citizen participation. High level policy direction serves to accelerate and deepen second and third generation ICT applications. "A strong e-democracy policy with specific measurable goals is essential to promote long-term progress in implementation" [22].

ii **Vision:** vision is another element that is rarely mentioned in e-democracy implementation. Inclusion of strategic vision in strategic document for e-democracy will set direction for implementation. Queensland government Government's e-democracy agenda classified e-democracy vision as one of the strategic dimensions towards desired outcome. Vision will set the focus for activities and serves as motto of the e-democracy governing body [8].

iii **Strategic Aim and Objectives:** each government implementing e-democracy is trying to achieve certain objectives. Objectives are extremely important. They justify the huge investment committed to e-democracy and help to measure the outcome of e-democracy. Strategic objective provides an overview of what the government is going to achieve therefore they must be defined in coherent manner and backed with appropriate choice of tools and technology for it to be accomplished.

iv **Guiding principles:** are rules, procedures, guidelines, and laws that must be followed in order to achieve a desired objectives. They help conformity to standard. Table 2.0 shows a list of guiding principles and from Queensland and OECD

Level of Engagement: This component of e-democracy considers the levels of citizens' engagement [13]. Different bodies of knowledge have defined various levels of citizens participation however any level of participation chosen must match the vision and objective of e-democracy and implementation with appropriate tools.

Table 2: Guiding Principles and from Queensland and OECD

Guiding Principles	
accessibility, Clarity, Simplicity, Accountability, active citizenship, mutual respect, early involvement, responsiveness	Queensland
early planning, implement to fit target group, integrate e-method with traditional ones, Test and adapt your tools, promotion, analyse result, provide feedback,	OECD
Privacy, commitment, evaluation (process and impact)	Queensland and OECD

Technology and Tools: a number of tools exist to facilitate online participation. The choice of tools to engage should be informed by the level of engagement sought, the objective sought to achieve by the government and the accessibility of the tools to the citizen. The choice of a wrong tool for a particular set of objective would be a waste of investment.

Stage in policy making: this dimension considers when to engage citizens and the tools and technologies that the capacity to facilitate the level of engagement required. This dimension also demands taking a close look at the objective in order to achieve the desires outcome.

Stakeholders: E-democracy is about people, technology and democratic process. This dimension considers who should be engaged and by whom [13]. There are different categories of stakeholders in e-participation such as elected representatives, government employees responsible for implementing policy, policy-makers, businesses, civil society organizations (CSOs), ordinary citizens, journalist, multi-disciplinary team to support the socio-technical nature of e-participation, etc. Each group should be specifically identified and their respective roles clarified. Identifying and clarifying the responsibilities of stakeholders is useful in characterizing e-democracy initiatives and reducing the complexity in ownership.

Rule of Engagement: the conduct of stakeholders is important in online participation. Rule of engagement among others include a clear statement on the conditions of use of the site, and the extent of usage of personal data.

Critical Success Factors: important issues pertinent to the success of e-democracy project were explored. They are key issues to be considered in making participatory e-democracy user-friendly and effective. These are technological, social and political, social, technological issues that makes for good success in e-democracy implementation. These are beyond the traditional concerns of the digital divide.

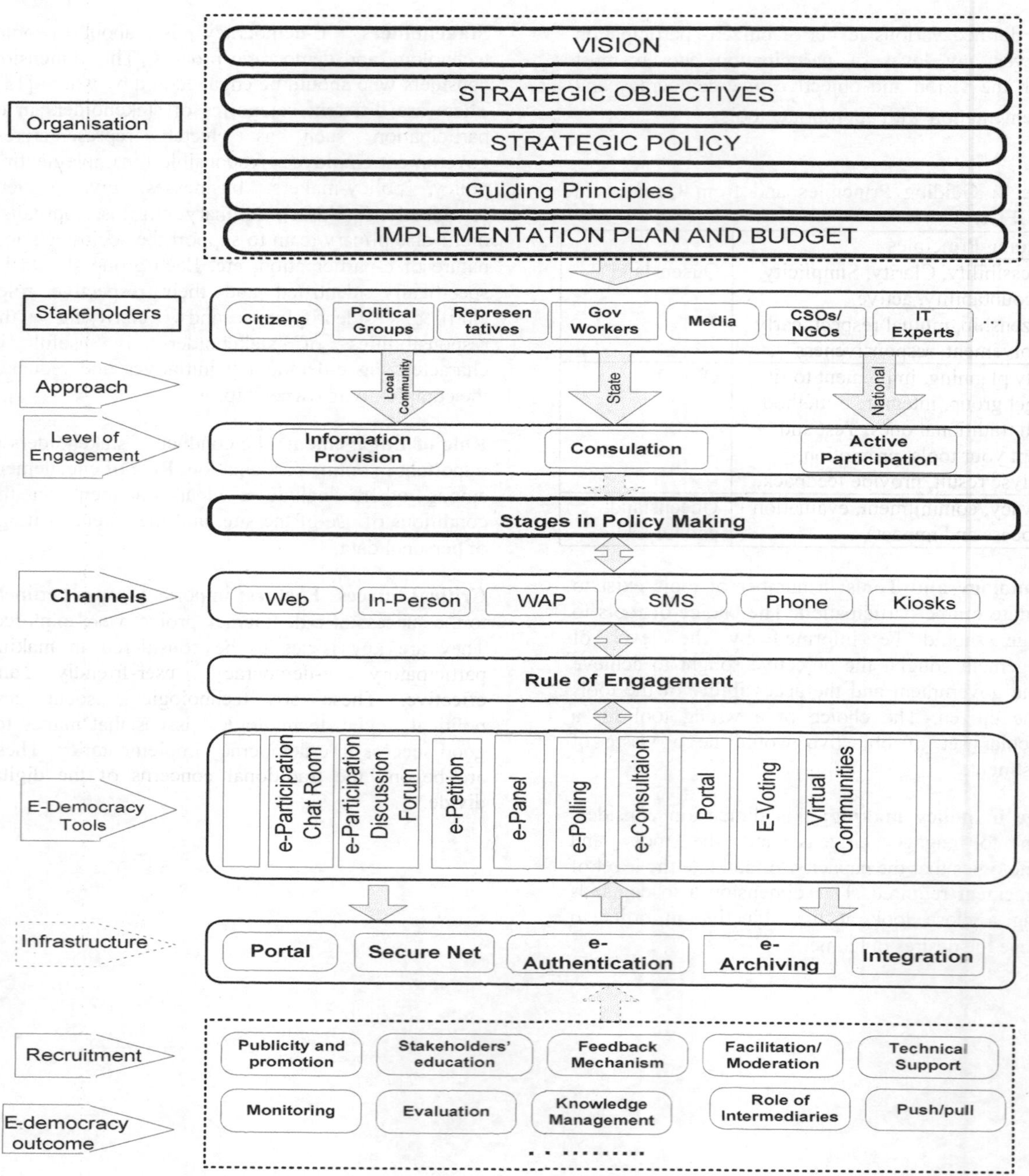

Figure 1: The proposed Strategic Framework of E-democracy

5 Discussion and Conclusion

Figure 1 presents the proposed strategic framework of e-democracy. It is a comprehensive, best practice based and generic framework. The reason for this strategic framework gives a simplified and comprehensive conceptualisation of e-democracy strategy. It could serve as first point of call when discussing e-democracy implementation. It shows how different basic components required for e-democracy implementation fit together. The framework is designed to be modular for the sake of flexibility. Each component of the framework is a module in itself and its interaction with other modules can be depicted from the diagram. It is an extensible generic framework and requires local customization. It is thus easy to add a new module or update a module. The strategic framework is meant to add value to detailed textual strategy where available or to serve as a quick alternative in the absence of textual strategy.

In conclusion, this framework is a result of comprehensive study of e-democracy strategy and implementation report produced by (34) cutting-edge research across different countries among the top 20 countries in e-participation implementation. Framework is a top-level documentation of strategic directions, goals, components, principles and implementation guidelines. Framework serves as a generic abstraction of an e-democracy implementation. This graphical representation gives a lot of information at a glance, makes planning and foreseeing of discrepancies a lot easier at the early stage of e-democracy implementation. It would save governments a lot of time, research, money and disappointments. It helps to identify contradiction, misalignment and out of orchestration with the general policies early.

5 References

[1] Black, A. and Noble, P. "E-Democracy around the World: A Survey for the Bertlesmann Foundation"; Phil Noble and Associate, Charleston, SC, pp. 1-88, 2001.

[2] Blumler, J.G. and Coleman, S. "*Realizing Democracy Online: A Civic Commons in Cyberspace";* Institute for Public policy Research, London, 2001.

[3] Carroll, J. M. and Swatman, P. A. "Structured-case: A methodological framework for building theory in information systems research"; *Proc of ECIS*, Vienna, Austria, 2000.

[4] Clift, S. L. "E-government and Democracy: Representation and Citizen Engagement in the Information Age"; 2004. Retrieved Nov., 2010, [www.publicus.net]

[5] Coleman, S. and Gotze, J. "Bowling Together: Online Public Engagement in Policy Deliberation". Hansard Society. 2001. Retrieved 8th Oct., 2010 [www.hansardsociety.org.uk]

[6] Funilkul, S. and Chutimaskul W. "The Framework for Sustainable eDemocracy Development,"; *Transforming People, Process and Policy, Vol 3 No 1, pp 16-31,* 2009.

[7] Glaser, B. "Basics of Grounded Theory Analysis. Mill Valley"; Sociology Press, 1992.

[8] Hogan, M., Cook, N., and Henderson, M. "The Queensland Government's e-democracy Agenda"; Australian Electronic Government Conference, Centre for Public Policy, University of Melbourne, 2004.

[9] Jayasena, G.N. and Karunaratna, D.D. "Towards an Enabling Framework for eDemocracy through the Integration of Citizen Participation along the Spatial Dimension Using Free and Open Source Technologies"; Proceedings of the 24th South East Asia Regional Computer Conference, November 18-19, 2007, Bangkok, Thailand.

[10] Kotsiopoulos, I. "Bringing Together and Accelerating e-Government Research in the EU"; ICT for Government and Public Service Unit, European Commission, 2009.

[11] Levy, Y. and Ellis, T. A Systems Approach to conduct an effective literature review in support of information systems research. Informing Science Journal, 9, pp 181-212, 2006.

[12] Local E-Democracy National Project. "Deeper and Wider Community Engagement: e-Democracy and its Benefits for Local Authorities, Councilors, and Communities"; NorthLincsNet, Improvement and Development Agency, London, pp. 1-38, 2006.

[13] Macintosh, A. "Characterizing E-Participation in Policy-Making". Proceedings of the 37th Hawaii International Conference on System Sciences, Computer Society Press, 2004.

[14] Matavire, R. and Brown, I. "Profiling grounded theory approaches in Information Systems research. European Journal of Information Systems"; 1-11, 2011.

[15] Mintzberg, H. "The Rise and Fall of Strategic Planning"; New York: Free Press, 1994.

[16] OECD, "Promise and Problems of E-Democracy: Challenges of Online Citizen Engagement"' 2003. [Online], Retrieved Dec., 2010 [www.oecd.org/dataoecd/9/11/35176328 .pdf]

[17] Okoli, C. and Schabram, K. "*A guide to conducting a systematic literature review of information systems research*"; Sprouts: Working Papers on Information Systems, 10(26), 2010. http://sprouts.aisnet.org/10-26.

[18] Rabaiah, A. & Vandijct, E. "A Strategic Framework of e-Government: Generic and best Practice"; In Les Worrall (ed) Leading Issues in e-Government Research, Academic Publishing International Ltd. Pp 1-32, 2011.

[19] Strauss, A. and Corbin, J. "The Basics of Qualitative Research: Techniques and Procedures for Developing Grounded Theory"; London: Sage 1998.

[20] UN E-Government Survey. "Leveraging E-government at a Time of Financial and Economic Crisis"; UN Economic and Social Affairs, 2010.

[21] Webster, J. and Watson, R. "Analyzing the past to prepare for the future: Writing a literature review"; MIS Quarterly, 26(2), xxi-xxii, 2002.

[22] Henderson, M., Hogarth, F. and Jeans, D. "E-Democracy Policy in Queensland"; Encyclopaedia of Digital Government. IGI Global, 2007. 455-461. Web. 3 Jun. 2013. doi:10.4018/978-1-59140-789-8.ch069

[23] Wolfswinkel, J., Furtmueller, E. and Wilderom, C. "Using grounded theory as a method for rigorously reviewing literature"; European Journal of Information Systems, 1-11, 2011.

Information Quality Assessment for E-Government Systems

Mona A. Alkhattabi
Assistant Professor
College of Computer Sciences and Information
Imam Mohammad Bin Saud University
P.O.Box 92309 Riyadh11653 Saudi Arabia
Monaalkhattabi@ccis.imamu.edu.sa
Mkhattabi@imamu.edu.sa

Abstract. *E-government systems offer a promising solution as an information exchanging channel. Enhanced technology could signify faster and easier access to information but does not of necessity guarantee the quality of this information. Hence it is crucial to develop valid and consistent methods of quality measurement and accomplish careful information quality assessments. Information quality frameworks are developed to appraise the quality of information systems, in general from the designers' perspective. The latest proliferation of e-services and e-government mainly, rises the require for a new quality framework in the context of e-government systems. The major contribution of this research is to propose a new information quality framework, we will report the results based on original survey data and factor analysis. Furthermore, we will validate the anticipated framework using an empirical approach on the basis of data from an original questionnaire and structural equation modelling (SEM) analysis, confirmatory factor analysis (CFA) in particular. Nevertheless, it is complicated to evaluate information quality in an e-government context since the perception of information quality is difficult and it is expected that the measurements will be multidimensional in nature.. Reliable measures need to be achieving in a systematic approach, whilst considering the reason of the measurement. Hence, we will adopt a Goal Question Metrics (GQM) approach to expand a set of quality metrics for the identified quality attributes within the anticipated framework. We then will identify an assessment model and measurement proposal, based on a multi element analysis technique.*

Keywords: E-government, Information quality, Information system, Information extraction, Quality framework, Quality metrics.

1 Introduction

This research focuses on the assessment of IQ (Information quality) in the context of e-government systems, particularly, on identifying the key dimensions for IQ from the users' point of view, in order to build a framework for IQ in e-government systems. The research will classify a set of quality metrics to measure the quality of the information. This will be based on the anticipated framework and will eventually facilitate the evaluation, allow comparison, and investigation of IQ. Moreover, it will examine the opportunity of incorporating a web mining approach, information extraction method, in order to mechanize the appraisal process. The purpose of this paper is to present an indication of the research problem, the rationale, and the organisational perspective for the study.

E-government services and technologies present users with distributive, collaborative, and interactive features which facilitate to overcome the limitations of space and time, this authorize information to be distributed. In fact, e-government has improvement from basically a delivery tool to a fundamental mechanism for a wide range of government services. However, the lack of direct contact among users, which is considered to be an important barrier in shaping the efficiency of the entire process, raises many issues on the overall quality of the presented services. In this field, literature examines the quality of the published resources in two ways: firstly, focusing on the content of these materials and secondly investigative the technique in which such content will be delivered to the users.

The majorities of methodologies which are used to appraise the quality of the distributed materials are qualitative and are in general user oriented since they depend on linguistic proposals from the students. Furthermore, the measurement procedure is based on the user's viewpoint, while the particular criteria are required to be simply comprehensible by the user. Therefore, the measurement methods are user centred because they generate linguistic recommendations of the material, these are based on the user's linguistic opinion judgments. The major problem with these traditional measurement methods is that they rely on human judgment, this can be doubtful and inaccurate, and in addition involves huge amounts of effort and time. It as a result appears logical to acquire advantage of web mining techniques to computerize the retrieval methods of the information required in the quality measurement.

2 Objective

This study will focus on proposing measures for the quality of the content provided by e-government systems by identifying the main quality standards. The major issue in measuring the quality for any online distributed systems is identifying the criteria of the quality, as the quality in distributed online systems, such as e-government systems, is considered to be a multidimensional and interdependent subject that is dependent on the objectives and context of the system. Moreover, because web quality is a complex concept, its measurement is neither simple task nor straightforward in fact it expected to be multidimensional in nature [1,2]. This research will present quality evaluation metrics to measure the content of the materials distributed via e-government systems. Furthermore, it will also focus on the practicability of integrating web mining techniques as a means of gathering the essential information to perform the assessment measurement. In addition, it will focus on the expansion of the assessment scheme.

3 Research Approach and Methodology

In order to attain the research objectives, the study was prepared in the following phases: 1) improvement and validation of an IQ framework for e-government systems;

2) develop quality metrics and identify an appropriate assessment method; 3) examine the framework, quality metrics and the measurement method via a case study. The first phase concerned developing and validating a framework which would represent potential factors and attributes that might impact ahead IQ in e-government systems. The previous proposed frameworks, from the related literature, will be used jointly with a user questionnaire in order to construct the framework. The questionnaire will be designed according to the methods launched by Churchill [3], and implicated a cross-sectional survey. The aim was to determine the users' view of the relative significance of the quality dimensions for information available in e-government systems. The collected data will be used along with factor analysis and linear regression to build the quality framework.

For the validation methods, a more focused and purpose-driven survey will be carry out. A sample will be collected from e-government users and developers in Saudi Arabia. The anticipated framework will be validated using a confirmatory factor analysis (CFA) approach [4] as a mean of structural equation modelling (SEM) goodness-of-fit test [5]. After that, a goal question metric (GQM) approach [6] will be used in the metric identification, to compute the quality of the information. The GQM approach is based ahead the assumption that to achieve a focused measurement, first the project's goals should be specified. hence, the final measurement can be analysed to decide whether the goals were actually achieved [7,8,9]. Figure 1 showed the GQM model.

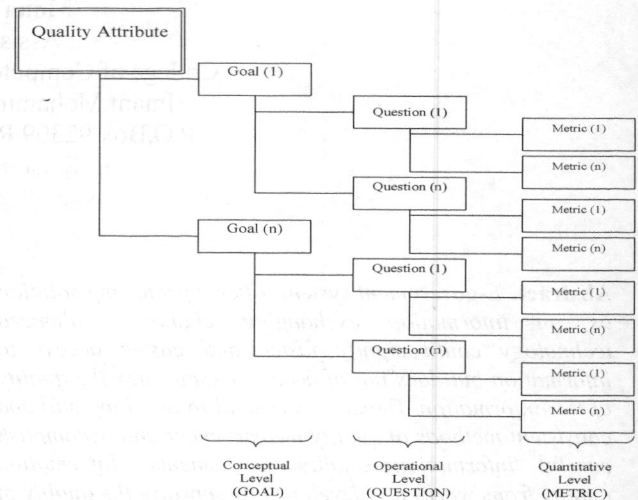

Figure1. The hierarchical structure for the GQM model[1]

4 Conclusion

The aim of this paper is to propose a study to build quality standards for the content presented by e-government systems, with defining the major dimensions of the information quality. Further that, the research will focuses on identifying a set of metrics to measure the quality of the information, in order to facilitate the evaluation and analysis of information quality. In addition, since human judgment is fallible, this research expected to study the viability of incorporating web mining techniques as a means of gathering the required information to carry out the assessment measurement.

5 References

[1] A. M. Aladwani and P. C. Palvia, "Developing and validating an instrument for measuring user-perceived web quality" Information & Management, vol. 39, pp. 467-476, May, 2002.

[2] M. Alkhattabi, D. Neagu, and A. Cullen, "Information quality framework for e-learning systems"

[1] Source: M. Alkhattabi, *Information Quality Assessment in E-learning System,* PhD Thesis, Informatics Research Institute, School of Computing, Informatics and Media, University of Bradford.2010

Knowledge Management & E-Learning: An International Journal (KM&EL), 2010, Vol 2, No 4

[3] J. Churchill, Marketing research: Methodological foundation (7th .ed), Hinsdale, IL: The Dryden Press, 1999.

[4] D. Harrington, Confirmatory factor analysis, (1st .ed), New York: Oxford University Press, 2009.

[5] B. Byrne, Structural equation modeling with amos: Basic concepts, applications and programming (1st .ed), Mahawa, New Jersey: Psychology Press, 2001.

[6] H. Koziolek, "Goal, question, metric" chapter in: Dependability metrics: Advanced lectures, I. Eusgeld, F.C. Freiling, and R. Reussner, Berlin: Springer-Verlag Berlin, 2008, pp. 39-42.

[7] V. Basili, G. Caldiera, and D. H. Rombach, 1994, The goal question metric approach [Online]. Available: https://docweb.lrz-muenchen.de/cgi-bin/doc/nph-webdoc.cgi/000110A/http/scholar.google.de/scholar=3fhl=3dde&lr=3d&cluster=3d4068380033007143449

[8] K. M. Khan, "Assessing quality of web based systems" in proceedings of International Conference on Computer Systems and Applications (IEEE/ACS), pp. 763-769, Doha, Qatar, March 31-April 04, 2008

[9] F. Alfonso, L. Luigi, M. Sandro, C. Stefano, O. Giandomenico, and O. Elena, "Applying gqm in an industrial software factory" ACM Transactions on Software Engineering and Methodology (TOSEM) vol. 7, pp. 411-448, 1998.

[10] K. Buvaneswari, W. A. Venkataraman, and J. Ward, "An introduction to software quality" US Army Corps of Engineers, Waterways Experiment Station (WES), Washington, DC, Technical Report, no. ITL-99-4, June, 1999.

[11] K. Kahn and M. Ramakrishnan, "Assessment model for software maintenance tools: A conceptual framework" in proceedings of Pasific Asia conference on Information systems (PACIS), pp. 527-536, Brisbane, Australia, 1997

[12] M. Alkhattabi, D. Neagu, and A. Cullen, Assessing information quality of e-learning systems, Computers in Human Behavior, Elsevier,2011, 27 (2): 862-873.

An E Governance model using cloud computing technology for Developing Countries

Manoj Kumar
IIIT Allahabad
ise2012020@iiita.ac.in

Manish Shukla
IIIT Allahabad
ise2012008@iiita.ac.in

Sonali Agarwal
IIIT Allahabad
sonali@iiita.ac.in

G.N. Pandey
IIIT Allahabad
pandey63@gmail.com

Abstract— **Information and communication technology (ICT) is an emerging era of present decade and playing a vital role for the advancement of our global society. As the popularity of ICT enabled application is increasing E-Governance has been established as a revolution not only in developed country but also in developing nations. E-Governance is a way to achieve good governance through ICT in order to have better citizen participation. The sole aim of E-Governance is to establish strong and transparent relationship between citizens, government organization and business organization so that a faith could be developed among all. This could also ensure improved services, optimized Government process and an ideal democratic environment for government operations. The cloud computing is a vibrant application development which provide solution for all E-Governance infrastructure development at lower cost and less time requirements. In this paper, the significance of cloud computing in present scenario has been described. An E-Governance model framework which utilizes the potential of cloud computing is presented. The various aspects and infrastructure requirements for typical Governance cloud has been discussed in this paper. A detail investigation about merits and demerits of the proposed solution has been done on the basis of SWOT analysis and concluding remark has been presented at the end of this paper.**

Keywords — **Information and Communication Technologies (ICT), E Governance, Cloud Computing.**

I. Introduction

Information and communication technology (ICT) is an emerging era of present decade and playing a vital role for the advancement of our global society for getting timely information and making communication faster. As the popularity of ICT enabled application is increasing, E-Governance has been established as a revolution not only in developed countries but also in developing nations. So E-Governance is the necessity of time for not only in developed countries but also developing nations. As internet reachability increases, demand of E-Governance is also increases. So, E-Governance is an essential requirement to any nation for providing better citizens participation and intergovernmental relationship. The sole aim of E-Governance is to establish strong and transparent relationship between citizens, government organization and business organization so that a faith could be developed among all. Selection of technology for E-Governance is a critical task because of ever increasing demand of cost, security; reliability and confidentiality are associated with E-Governance. The cloud computing is a vibrant application development which provides solution for all E-Governance infrastructure development at lower cost and less time requirements.

The first part of this paper explores the e-governance concept and implementation requirements. Second part of this paper highlights the significance of the cloud computing technology in E-Governance implementation. The various aspects and infrastructure requirements for typical E-Governance cloud has been discussed and a cloud computing based E-Governance model has been presented. A **SWOT** analysis is performed to highlight advantages and drawbacks of proposed model.

II. E GOVERNANCE

E-Governance provides an automation of all government functionalities and enhances organizational efficiency and citizen participation. [2] The effective e-governance involves e-governance requirements and components of the e-governance. These terms are explored below.

E-Governance Requirements

E-Governance provides a way to improve government work and make easy sharing of information with the citizens. For practical implementation of E-Governance it is important to identify certain factors which are going to play key role during deployment of E-Governance.

The e-governance requirements are divided into three parts for proper investigation which is shown in fig 1:

1. **Government to Government:** The need of government to government functionality is fully related to administration, inter government control and monitor on the government. It focuses on the inter communication between two governments and other aspects of the government to government communication.
2. **Government to Business:** Business organizations are important for any country and contributing substantially for the development. Government also keep an eye on these organization for enforcing the policies ,standards and accountability .here it essentially required to automate government to business interaction such as tender management, contract management ,tax payments etc.
3. **Government to Citizen:** Basically, the prime responsibility of any government is citizen service. Government to citizens interface is required to facilitate them basic emanates, proper education,

health care and a quality life. A single window government solution could help to achieve citizens satisfaction required in E-Governance. Fig 1 is representing the typical requirement of E-Governance.

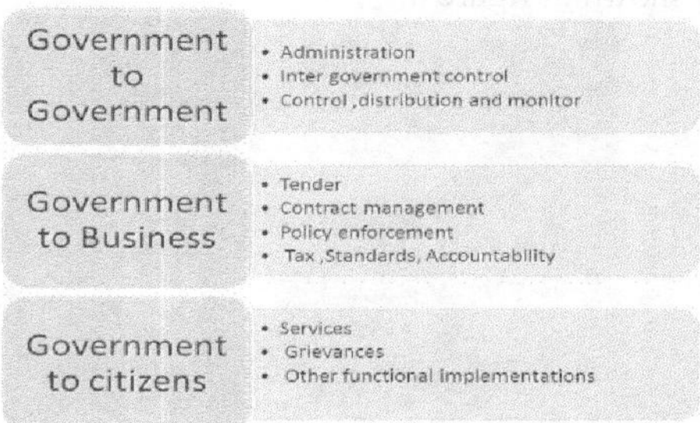

Figure 1: Typical requirements of e-governance

Components of a typical E-Governance Application

Three tier architecture for E-Governance is shown below in **figure 2**. The architecture consists three layers of the system. In the data storage layer, proper schema for data storage has been defined for e-governance. It provides foundation for storage for data which is coming from different processes and serves the request of the any process which demands the data. Application layer works between user layer and data layer. It facilitates the connection between user process and data layer. The upper layer or user layer has a Graphical User Interface for the user interaction with the system. In E-Governance system, a user can interact with the help of upper layer (GUI) and can get information from the system. The government officials and legislatures can update the information of the system with the help of upper layer .This architecture has following advantages in context of E-Governance [3]:

• **Heterogeneous System**: E-governance application support different platforms, different hardware and different working software. It integrates all these heterogeneous systems to fulfill the requirements of t E-Governance.

• **Modifiability**: In 3-tier architecture, responsibility of each tier is fixed. Segregation of responsibilities makes it easy to modify and code at any tier.

• **Scalability to handle many clients**: Clients communicate with the system by using application layer. This application layer provides database connections to clients. The strength of client deploying several servers on application layer.

• **Integrated Data Access**: Most of the applications use data from different sources. Application layer provide facility of managing the connection to database. Application is used to connect all these data sources. Figure 2 explains the architecture of E-Governance with three layers.

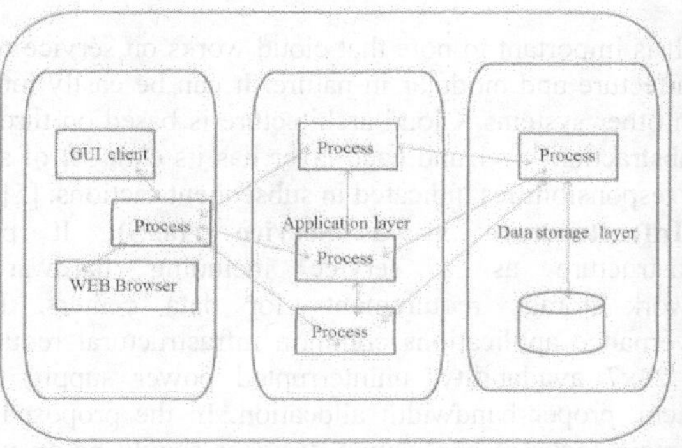

Figure 2: Typical architecture for an E-Governance application

III. CLOUD COMPUTING

Cloud computing is upcoming area with three main features namely service availability, pay as per services, scalable feature [4]. It is based on service oriented architecture and the model could be categorized as follows:

a) **Public Cloud** – it is a type of cloud where third party will provide services to client via internet. Each user will have its access mechanism provided by the third party. Public cloud is a cost effective method to provide services.
b) **Private Cloud** – private cloud has many benefits over public cloud depending upon the service required. In addition in private cloud data and processes are managed by organization itself. It provides better and controlled infrastructure for security.
c) **Community Cloud** – Community cloud provides services to a community within organization. Members of community can access data on community cloud. Communities are formed by grouping of people with shared interest.
d) **Hybrid Cloud** –it is a combination of private, public and community cloud. It has maximum functionalities as compared to all cloud and non critical information is handled by public cloud while critical information and processing is done on organization controlled private cloud. Figure 3 illustrates the different layers of cloud computing for E-Governance.

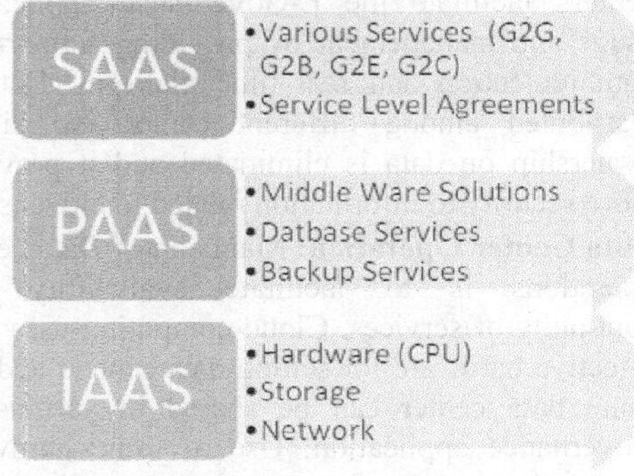

Figure 3: Layers of cloud computing for e-governance

It is important to note that cloud works on service oriented architecture and modular in nature. It can be easily integrated with other systems. Cloud architecture is based on three types of abstraction layer and each layer has its own set of services and responsibilities indicated in subsequent sections: [5].

Infrastructure as a Service (IaaS): It provides infrastructure as a service including hardware and networks/storage requirements for data centers. For E-Governance applications common infrastructural requirement are 24x7 availability, uninterrupted power supply to data centers, proper bandwidth allocation. In the proposed model the main focus of application designer should be on usability and functionalities of E-Governance system.

Platform as a Service (PaaS): Cloud provides different type of platforms as a service such as OS provisioning, middleware support services, database support services and workflow management. In e-governance with cloud advantages departments can get resources whenever they need them as compared to traditional methods.

Software as a Service (SaaS): It provides all application requirnment for success full implementation of E-Governance .For example , Suppose an E-Governance plan decides to extend their area at district level Than no software is required to purchase at district level but cloud provider will provide required software along with additional standards services such as employee management system, district management solutions; call center service etc. in this manner cloud can provide best solution as per requirement, Hence cloud reduces cost of E-Governance.

Cloud Vision for E-Governance:

This section performs a selection of elements for the cloud which is useful for implementing the cloud based E-Governance.

- **Internet over Cloud:** Most of services on internet are dependent on cloud 70% of the internet users are also using cloud in various applications.
- **Distributed Data Centers:** Individual information systems are vulnerable to risks such as outside attacks, intruders, environmental risks etc. Distributed data centers provide protection from these types of threats [5]. Distributed data centers facilitate the E-Governance application usage and management by providing support for communication and real time platform. Data is distributed among different centers so single ownership on data is eliminated and it provides more security to information related to citizens.
- **Data Center Operation:** Main aim of Data center operations is to facilitate availability and continuity of services. Cloud computing uses cost effective hardware for setting data centers and the same data center can be shared in various E-Governance application. Use of same hardware setup is used for various e-government applications. It increases the resource utilization and provides scalability to the E-Governance system. On the basis of resource consumption future plan could be built for e-governance applications. The key features of data center are shown in figure 4.

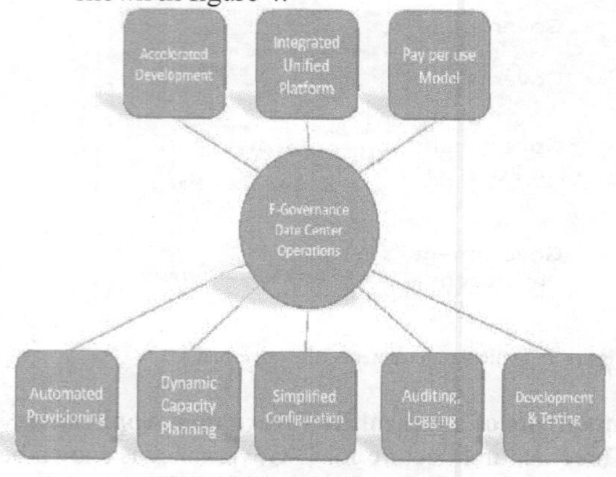

Fig 4: Data center operation for e-governance and cloud computing

IV. INDIAN E- GOVERNANCE CLOUD STRATEGY:

The proposed E- Governmental cloud provides a complete infrastructure for the implementation of government services including administrate and regulatory and social welfare [6]. Each cloud model has its own benefits and level of assurance for implementing the e-governance in India. The cloud strategy for e-governance in India is based on dedicated cloud for their specific services designed for E-Governance. The figurer 5 indicates the presence of dedicated clouds with their specific tasks:

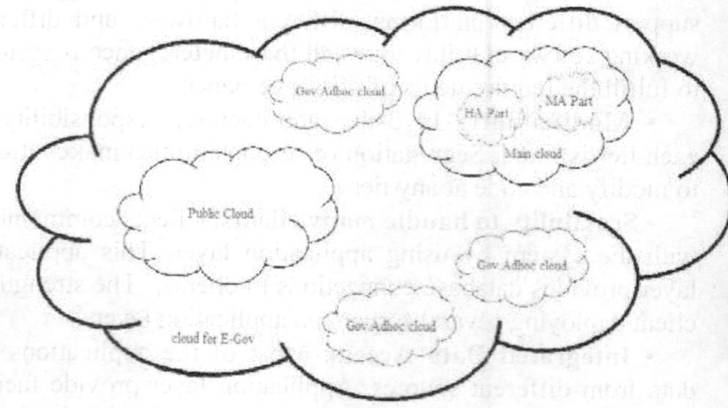

Fig 5: Cloud computing model for e-governance with high, medium and low assurance

The above mentioned cloud model offers the low cost computing resources which are suitable for implementation of E-Governance. Here in the figure, the cloud structure for E-Governance is divided into high assurance and medium assurance parts. This is because whole e-governance requirement cannot meet with the public cloud. These two categories of cloud are different in security and other requirements required. There is also some agency cloud exists in the E-Governance so that required interoperability between Governmental cloud and agency government cloud could be maintained as per standards. These standards will provide efficient and scalable cloud computing for governmental cloud .This also provides different level of security as well as other governmental requirements [7].

The three categories of cloud such as high assurance and medium assurance parts are described as follows:

- **High Assurance part** –Here, a physically devoted computing resources group is dedicated for governance. These resources are only used by government to provide its high assurance requirements.
- **Medium Assurance part** – A resource pool for cloud computing which will be collectively used by non-government cloud users .It provide a lower cost of resources for cloud computing. There is also a security control in the hands of the government.
- **Basic Assurance part** – this is a computing resource group of cloud computing based on public cloud offerings.

The figure 6 presenting layered implementation of Cloud computing model for E-Governance in India.

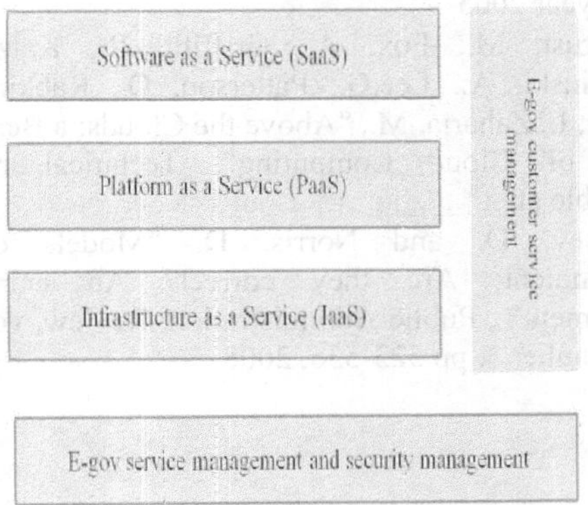

Fig 6: layered implementation of Cloud computing model for e-Gov in India

The configuration of layers for E-Governance is shown in below table 1.

Table 1: configuration of layers of e-Governance

Layer of cloud	Configuration of layers for e-governance	
Infrastructure as a Service (IaaS):	• Server hosting • Internet access • LAN/WAN • DNS	• Web servers • Storage • Data management • Computing hardware
Platform as a Service (PaaS):	• Knowledge management • Data mart	• Content management • Instrument and testing
Software as a Service (SaaS):	• Web applications • Meta data management • Portal services • Enterprise services • Workflow • Human management	• Human resource • Groupware • Collaboration • Digital asset management • Digital signature • Communication

Government will provide citizens services and other facilities like customer relationship, web management and business support through its government cloud. In this way, the government cloud is also responsible for standardization of the services [8] .This cloud model will provide a cost saving cloud computing structure for the e-governance [9]. These services are given below which will be implemented in the cloud computing model for perfect e- governance which is shown in fig 6. The other services required for customers and other e-governance management aspects are shown in the table 2 below:

Table 2: other e-governance management aspect and its services

Other service	Configuration of services	
Customer services	• Personalization • Customer assistance	• Reporting tools • Online help
E-govt. service management and security management	• Call centers • Billing and accounting • Quality of service management • Backups • ID authentication	• Firewall and network security • Intrusion prevention • Cryptography • Virus protection

V. SWOT ANALYSIS OF PROPOSED MODEL OF E-GOVERNANCE

SWOT study focuses on four main points: Strength, Weakness, Opportunity and Threat analysis of e-governance application. Nowadays internet is an integral part of our life [10] [11]. Government also applies these methods to handle their operations and communicate with their citizens for making public confidence for them. Cloud computing provides a cost effective method to implement e-governance applications for any developing country. The SWOT analysis of this model is done below:

Strength:

E-government projects utilize capabilities of internet technologies which are very advanced these days. Mobile telephony provides a way for providing services on mobile phones. Ability of cloud computing to scale up services at any instance gives strength to e-governance application. Cloud offers the ability to handle time related computing. Suppose an organization handles homogenous load throughout year but in specific month they need more resources. In this situation cloud computing provides solution by providing more resources. Cloud reduces the maintenance cost, infrastructure cost and energy consumption. Maintenance cost mainly due to technology up gradation. Time to time up gradation of server configuration, with proper security mechanism and data management comes under maintenance phase. Cloud computing provide full control over access mechanism. It provides different access mechanism for different type of users.

Weakness:

The major problem of implementing e-governance application is low level of literacy and shortage of skilled employee for development of e-government projects. E-governance applications have no usefulness in low level areas such daily use applications because of bandwidth shortage. Organization worried about losing physical control over data and information. Cloud service providers are also unable to give information about data servers and location data to the client. It creates situation of confusion in mind of clients. Cloud providers continuously try to resolve these issues. But due to this weakness large organizations do not rely on cloud based systems for critical applications.

Opportunities:

The main part of providing e-governance services is to provide hardware setup at low cost. Availability of e-governance in rural areas is achieved by providing services on cheap mobile phones. Mobile technology can be used to provide services at government level. Media can play important role in spreading awareness about e-government services. Public private partnership will also be useful in e-gov application.

Developing countries can use the information and communication technologies with the cloud computing and could allow the business organizations and citizens to benefit from these technologies.

Threats:

Some basic threats in cloud e-governance are associated with increasing manpower cost, increment in the broadband cost and no reachability of internet. Without support of legislators, cloud e-governance cannot be implemented. There is also a regional language factor in the success of the cloud e-governance. A major threat is associated with the security of the cloud based governmental data which may be hacked. PPP model may make impact on the partnership with the private sector so it may be a threat to the private sector. There is a big threat from the entrenched incumbents. There are some threats from the lack of standards in cloud technology. So it may create a problem in the implementation of the e-governance with the help of the cloud computing. Basically, cloud computing based e-governance is most interoperable so there should be enough support from the legislators.

VI. CONCLUSIONS

Cloud provides a better way to offer services to clients related to different regions. Cloud follow service oriented architecture and provide low cost hardware/software resources. E-governance could use both service oriented architecture and cloud architecture and can provide services to citizens and governments at low operating cost. In this paper, a novel cloud computing based E-Governance model has been presented .A SWOT analysis is also performed to highlight the strength and challenges of the proposed model. The paper also suggesting three tier cloud architecture especially for Indian scenario which could transform the nation into information society.

REFERENCES:

1. Minqi Zhou, Rong Zhang, Dadan Zeng, Weining Qian; Services in the Cloud Computing era: A survey, IEEE Software, p40-46, Oct. 2010.
2. Marawar, T, Kale, S, Araspure, K., E-Governance,IEEE Software, p183-186, Feb. 2010.
3. Nataraja, P, Raju, G.T, A novel approach towards proliferation of E-Learning in India through the analysis of existing ICT scenario, IEEE Software, p1298 – 1302, 2011.
4. Gong Zhang, Chiu, L, Ling Liu, Adaptive Data Migration in Multi-tiered Storage Based Cloud Environment, IEEE software, p148 – 155, 2010.
5. Department of Information Technologyhttp://www.mit.gov.in
6. Poonam R Gupta, D K Jain, Road map for E-Governance.
7. Arun Chandrasekaran & Mayank Kapoor,State of Cloud Computing in the Public Sector – A Strategic analysis of the business case and overview of initiatives across Asia Pacific. http://www.frost.com/prod/servlet/cio/232651119.pdf.
8. White paper on cloud computing for e-governance.
9. Grant, G., and Chau, D., "Developing a Generic Framework for E-Government", Journal of Global Information Management, Volume 13, Number 1, pp 1-30, year 2005
10. Armbrust, M., Fox, A., Griffith, R., Katz, R., Konwinski, A., Lee,G., Patterson, D., Rabkin, A., Stoika, I., Zaharia, M., "Above the Clouds: a Berkeley view of Cloud Computing", Technical report, available at http://abovetheclouds.cs.berkeley.edu
11. Coursey, D. and Norris, D. "Models of e-Government; Are they correct? An empirical assessment" , Public Administration, Review, volume 68, Number 3, pp 523-536, 2008

A Statistical and Simulation Model for Environmental Sustainability

John Wang, Montclair State University, 1 Normal Ave., USA

ARTICLE INFO

Keywords:
Sustainability
Economic sustainability
Health sustainability
Social sustainability
Environmental sustainability
Simulation

ABSTRACT

Sustainability is the key to finding solutions to problems facing the Earth such as insufficient access to food, environmental degradation, declining natural resources, vanishing forests and deteriorating communities. Sustainable development is a common challenge for the global community, which has become a widely recognized goal for human society. This paper compares the sustainability of U.S. with other twenty countries. The mathematical comparison was completed using a statistical and simulation model to compare and analyze the five categories across each country.

1. Introduction

Global sustainability is development that meets the needs of the present without compromising the ability of future generations to meet their own needs [4] [1]. Without sustainability, we will see a rapid deterioration in our quality of life. In order to maintain or improve the quality of life, we must find innovative ways to improve our ways without increasing the use of natural and physical resources beyond the capacity of the environment to supply them indefinitely [27]. Each and every day, we are faced with decisions that affect the environment. Decisions such as using a plastic water bottle, unnecessarily printing papers, cutting down trees, or abusing electric and gas consumption lead to a deterioration in the sustainability of the Earth.

It's hard not to notice the shift in tone of political leaders, the media, and many people over the past decade when it comes to the preservation of our planet. With "green" initiatives such as reducing carbon footprints to growing organic foods, people are more conscious of how they treat the Earth and also how they treat their bodies. People want to live longer and enjoy a quality of life that can be passed down to future generations. This is called sustainability - to keep up or keep going, as an action or process [35] [17]. In order for us to maintain a presence on this planet we have to learn how to manage our natural resources wisely. In order to manage something you must first be able to measure it. There are a many indicators that help us to identify problematic areas of sustainable development; these measures are expressed in numerical form. With this information in hand, it will be easy to compare sustainability standards of different countries.

In our opinion, sustainable development can be divided into four categories: economic sustainability, health sustainability, social sustainability, and environmental sustainability. People, corporations, and governments need to work to establish policies, standards, and guidelines to work towards short and long term goals in order to achieve high sustainability. A high level of sustainability is not easy to achieve since the complex factors and every day issues that arise affecting the results, as well as the decisions made by people on a daily basis throughout the world.

The purpose of this paper is to analyze a number of elements within each category in order to compare the relevance of each against the level of sustainability among twenty-one countries. For each category, three to five subcategories have been identified and defined. Data has been collected and analyzed for each subcategory. We will create an index that measures each country's sustainability relative to one another and rank them accordingly.

This paper is structured as follows. In the next section, we begin with discussion of the relevant literature. This is followed by our model development. Using a statistical and simulation model, it is shown that mathematical evaluation can be performed in the collected dataset. Next, a theoretical foundation has been provided. The paper concludes with a discussion of current ranking and potential research directions.

2. Model development

2.1 Economic indicators

The measurement of welfare and sustainability is a fundamental aspect in assessing a nation's development and quality of life. Economic growth is a major component in measuring a countries level of sustainability [2]. Macroeconomic data presentation has become internationally standardized which has established a coherent, consistent and integrated set of macroeconomic accounts, balance sheets and tables based on a set of internationally agreed concepts, definitions and classifications. A comprehensive economic framework within which data can be compiled and presented in a format that is designed for purposes of economic analysis and policy-making [24]. It also serves as a basis for the calculation of key indicators of economic performance including GDP, net national savings, unemployment and investment.

2.1.1 Gross domestic product (GDP)

The GDP is one of the primary indicators used to gauge the health of a country's economy. It represents the total dollar value of all goods and services produced over a specific time period. GDP is expressed as a comparison to the previous quarter or year. The addition of consumption, investment, government spending and net exports is the more commonly used approach at deriving at GDP. A high GDP typically indicates a nation with healthy economic production and growth [6].

GDP is in many ways the central measure of an economy's growth. The faster the growth in the real GDP for that nation, the faster the growth in jobs will soon occur. Although the relationship between the measure and inflation is more tenuous, it is generally acknowledged that if the level of real GDP exceeds that of potential real GDP, inflation will increase. GDP's high correlation with unemployment and inflation make it a key measure of a country's economic stability [13].

2.1.2 Unemployment

According to United Nations Statistic division, the adult unemployment rate refers to the proportion of the adult (aged 15 years and older) labour force that is unemployed, unless otherwise specified. The unemployed are persons who are currently without work, who are currently available for work, and who are seeking or have sought work recently. The base for these statistics is the labour force (that is, the economically active portion of the population), not the total population [32].

The national definitions used vary from one country to another as regards inter alia age limits, reference periods, criteria for seeking work, treatment of persons temporarily laid off and of persons seeking work for the first time. Inter-country comparisons are further hampered by the variety of types of source used to obtain information on unemployment and the differences in the scope and coverage of such sources [14].

2.1.3 Gross national income

Gross national income (GNI) is the sum of value added by all resident producers plus any product taxes (less subsidies) not included in the valuation of output plus net receipts of primary income (compensation of employees and property income) from abroad. In other words, GNI measures the total income of all people who are citizens of a particular country while GDP (gross domestic product) measures the total output of all persons living in that particular country's borders [28].

Gross national savings is equal to gross domestic savings (gross domestic product minus final consumption) plus net income and net current transfers from abroad. The United Nations system of national accounts defines gross national income as "the aggregate value of the balances of gross primary incomes for all sectors; (gross national income is identical to gross national product (GNP) as hitherto understood in national accounts generally)" [32].

2.1.4 Foreign direct investment

Foreign direct investment is net inflows of investment to acquire a lasting management interest (10 percent or more of voting stock) in an enterprise operating in an economy other than that of the investor. It is the sum of equity capital, reinvestment of earnings, other long-term capital, and short term capital, as shown in the balance of payments [3].

2.2 Health indicators

Over the past 50 years data relating to health indicators have significantly improved. The world has seen considerable health gains, and childhood mortality has been decreasing due to control and prevention of diseases. Advancement in technology and medicine has increased life expectancy rates around the world. Health and sustainable development are closely connected. Development in countries cannot be achieved or sustained when the population is suffering from poor health conditions and inadequate access to healthcare. Economic growth and a clean environment contribute to improved health and an individual's well-being [23].

2.2.1 Health expenditure per capita (PPP)

Total health expenditure per capita is the per capita amount of the total public and private health expenditure. Health expenditure includes health services, family planning activities, and nutrition activities, but excludes the provision of water and sanitation. Purchasing Power Parity (PPP), known as the international dollar, are rates of currency conversion constructed to account for differences in price levels between countries [34]. Per capita spending is directly associated with the quantity of resources purchased to benefit an individual's health to provide effective healthcare.

2.2.2 Health expenditure (% of GDP)

Total expenditure on health in the country given as a percentage of its GDP is rising more rapidly than overall economic growth in countries around the world. Data from the Organization for Economic Cooperation and Development (OECD) show that over the past 50 years healthcare spending has increased by an average of 2 percentage points higher than the growth of GDP. Healthcare spending in 40 years is predicted to be more than 10% of the GDP for most countries [7]. The United States, not only spends much more per capita on health care, but has also had one of the highest spending growth rates. The share of GDP devoted to health care spending was 17.3% in 2009, which is a 7 percentage point increase in health spending within the past thirty years and is one of the largest among other countries [9].

There have been several independent studies carried out in different countries researching the reason behind the increasing numbers in healthcare spending. These studies took place during various time periods and used different researching techniques, but all came to similar conclusions. The aging of the population accounts for about 20% of the increase in spending. Technological change, described as the enhanced capabilities of medicine, accounts for 50% of the increase. Growth in real incomes, an aging population and technological change are the primary cause of increased healthcare spending [7]. In addition, history shows during recessions many countries experienced an increase in health spending share of GDP [10].

2.2.3 Measles immunization

Measles are one of the most highly contagious human diseases. In 1980, prior to the use of the vaccine, an estimated 2.6 million deaths occurred worldwide due to measles. It was the leading cause of high infant mortality rates during the pre-vaccine era with 90 percent of children having measles by the age of 15. One of the Millennium Development Goals set by the United Nations is to reduce the overall deaths among children by two-thirds, by 2015. Spreading the measles vaccination to areas around the world to reduce mortality among children is used as an indicator towards the progress of this goal. The improvement of living conditions, better nutrition status, and areas where vaccinations have been instituted have decreased the spread of measles significantly [29].

2.2.4 Life expectancy at birth

Life expectancy at birth is frequently used as a component of demographic data for countries around the world. It represents the average lifespan of a newborn, and is an indicator of the overall health and quality of life in a country. Less developed regions that suffer from famine and disease result in lower life expectancies. During the twentieth century life expectancy grew rapidly due to improvements in public health, nutrition and the availability of medicine for curable illnesses. Global life expectancy reached 68 years within 2005-2010. High-income developed countries rose to 80 years, compared to 67 years decades ago. Over the same time period, low-income countries rose from 38 to 60 years [11].

Communicable diseases, mainly infections, were the cause of 31% of all deaths in the world. Non-communicable diseases, such as cancer and heart attacks, are responsible for 60%, and injuries for 10%. These totals varied significantly by geographic area, but there is one common factor in life expectancy throughout the world and within all income groups, women almost always live longer than men. Globally, females have a life expectancy of 70 years, compared to 65 for males. This discrepancy is highest in Europe by 13 years and lowest in Africa by two years. Overall, Africa has the world's lowest life expectancies due to the unfortunate AIDS epidemic [21].

2.3 Social indicators

The extensive range of social indicators includes many measures towards a country's sustainable development. Social indicators provide information regarding the conditions in which people live, and the actions taken by governments to improve and preserve them without compromising the future generations' ability to meet their own needs. Many social indicators assess the availability and ability for an individual to access opportunities, which will enhance their quality of life. Over the years literacy rates have increased, education has improved and there have been more opportunities available, indicating progress towards international sustainability [28].

2.3.1 Literacy rates

Literacy, the percentage of people who are able to read and write, is the root to human development and economic growth. According to the latest data, 793 million adults, two-thirds of them being women, continue to lack basic literacy skills. Globally, literacy rates are on the rise, up 2.3% in the past 10 years, and 10.6% in the past 20 years. More than half of the global illiterate population is in the region of South and West Asia where there are growing populations, internal conflict, gender inequality, and inadequate funding for basic education [31].

Literacy is one of the key steps towards improving the economic, health and social indicators of sustainability development. It is a means for development, the key to communication, and enables learning of all kinds improving the quality of life. Poor literacy skills result in a lack of participation in education, employment, and community life and the inability to capitalize on basic skills needed to improve the standard of living. Literacy is also linked with poverty reduction, economic growth and wealth creation and it is the start to lifelong learning [19].

2.3.2 School life expectancy

School life expectancy is defined as the total number of years of schooling a child can expect to receive. When using this indicator in international comparisons the education structure in the different countries must be taken into consideration. A year or grade completed in one country is not necessarily the same in terms of educational content or quality as a year or grade completed in another country.

According to United Nations statistics, around 67 million children do not attend primary school, and 72 million adolescents are missing out on their right to secondary education. If these current trends continue, it is projected that there could be more children out of school in 2015 than there are today, resulting in lower levels of literacy rates [32].

2.3.3 Internet users

Worldwide, the total number of Internet user will grow from 2 billion in 2010 to 2.7 billion in 2015, when 40% of the world's population will have access to its vast resources. The McKinsey Global Institute constructed a study in May 2011, which aimed to estimate the extent of the impact the Internet has on numerous countries and the world economy. It's evident that the use of the Internet is and has been changing lives, and many still debate about the effect the Internet has, and how to control its power for the common good. However, this report finds that the Internet has delivered substantial economic growth and created jobs on a large scale. It contributes to GDP more than the agriculture and energy sectors combined. Developed countries experienced a 21% growth in GDP linked to the increasing number of users over the past 5 years. The study concluded that the Internet correlates with wealth creation, and is one of the largest contributors to global economic growth and sustainability [12].

2.3.4 Human Development Index (HDI)

The United Nations Development Program designed the Human Development Index in 1990 as a measure of the quality of life through the availability of essential choices needed for human development. An individual should have the option to acquire knowledge, access resources needed for a decent standard of living, and the opportunity to lead a long and healthy life [22].

The 2011 Human Development Report states that global challenges of sustainability and equity must be addressed together to improve human development. There has been remarkable progress in living standards for decades within most countries. Continuous efforts towards ending social inequalities and reducing environmental risks must be made for the benefit of future generations as well as for those living today. "Promoting human development requires addressing sustainability—locally, nationally and globally—and this can and should be done in ways that are equitable and empowering" [30].

2.4 Environmental indicators (pollution)

2.4.1 Industrial greenhouse gas (GHG) emissions

The “greenhouse effect” occurs naturally, making life as we know it possible. During the past century, however, human activities have substantially increased the amount of greenhouse gases in the atmosphere, changing the composition of the atmosphere and influencing climate. Some greenhouse gases are almost entirely man-made. Other greenhouse gases come from a combination of natural sources and human activities.

Greenhouse gas emission is an extremely important sub-category in our report. The excessive amounts of greenhouse gas emission modify the greenhouse effect process in a harmful way. Moreover, the negatively modified greenhouse effect causes high amounts of global warming, which directly interferes with future generations' survivability and the sustainability of the environment respectively. The major greenhouse gases emitted into the atmosphere through human activities are carbon dioxide, methane, nitrous oxide, and fluorinated gases. Many of these gases can remain in the atmosphere for tens to hundreds of years after being released [33].

2.4.2 Fresh water pollution

Fresh water is a strategic resource for humans as well as for nature. It is a source of energy, an avenue for transportation, habitat for organisms, and absolutely essential for life. Water resource developments have substantially changed freshwater flow and inundation regimes, and are fundamentally altering the life histories - thereby threatening the long-term survival - of thousands of species, including humans. We consider human and environmental wellbeing to be congruent with sustained disease resistance (or avoidance), good nutrition, and persistence of species-appropriate population dynamics. Quality fresh waters are increasingly scarce throughout most of the world, and fresh waters environments are experiencing declines in biodiversity far greater than those in the most impacted terrestrial and marine ecosystems. If trends in human demands for water remain unaltered, and if species losses continue at current rates, the opportunity to maintain much of the remaining biodiversity will soon vanish. The human crisis associated with pollution and declining water quality is already severe, with perhaps 40% of the Earth's population lacking clean water or adequate sanitation [16].

2.5 Environmental indicators (natural resources)

2.5.1 Arable land (% of total land)

The first subcategory is the arable lands. This subcategory represents the measure on the potential food production. The potential food production gives an idea about how a country is sustaining the use of its lands for the future generations. For the food industry, the depletion of arable land and a growing world population demand controlling the sustainability of agricultural inputs to the industry. Controlling the sustainability of these supplies means controlling the economic, social, and environmental performance of the supply chain [5].

2.5.2 Protected areas - areas managed for sustainable use and natural reserves

The second category is the Protected Areas. We thought this is an important subcategory because it is represents a country's concern on how much it cares to protect the basic habitat which started it all. This care shows a country's dedication to expertise on how to balance the sustainability via protecting species and creating a clean economy out of it.

2.5.3 Forests (% of total land)

Forests, which are an integral component of the biosphere, cover about 30% of the world's total land area. Forests provide many significant resources and functions including wood products, habitat for wildlife, water and soil conservation and serve as a filter for pollutants. Forests thus support employment and biodiversity. The larger the forest area the better, healthier and more sustainable is the country. It also implies that the government is working on forest growth and regeneration [26].

3. Mathematical evaluation

After collecting the data for each sub-category, and organizing each in a table (see table 1), we altered the data to value each factor similarly for comparison purposes. In order to do so, we utilized a ranking system on a scale from 0 to 9, with 0 being the lowest and 9 being the highest. The ranked data is displayed in a table (see table 2) for comparison and analysis.

The ranking was automatically completed utilizing a computer simulation built in excel. The simulation ranked the data elements on the scale of 0 to 9. The values were ranked based on whether a higher or lower value was better. For example, GDP is usually ranked from highest to lowest, with the highest values typically indicating a healthy economic climate with in the country. On the other hand, the unemployment rate is usually ranked from lowest to highest, with the lower values indicating a high job placement or number of jobs available within in that country. Our group used our judgment and the definition of each sub-category to decide whether or not each would be ranked on a high or low scale. Regardless of whether the values were ranked on a high or low scale, 0 remains the lowest and 9 remains the highest across all sub-categories.

Once all data has been ranked on the same scale, we can now analyze the data in order to compare the sustainability among the twenty-one countries based on the five indicators: Economic, Health, Social, Pollution, and Natural Resources. Using Pareto Optimization, the simulation built in excel converted the ranked sub-category data and translated it to scores out of 100 for each of the five categories (see table 3). The higher the score, the better the country ranked in sustainability, with zero being the lowest and one hundred being the highest. Due to the various real life diverse factors, issues, and situations that affect each indicator, it is not easily determined which solution will optimize the sustainability for one country.

Once the categories for each country were scored on a scale of 0 to 100, we calculated the overall scores across all countries and then sorted highest to lowest based on the countries average (see analysis). This was done to compare all five indicators as one variable across all countries in order to rank the countries based on their sustainability. The results are described in the conclusion section.

4. Conclusions

For the analysis of the sustainability of various countries, we collected data of key indicators, which combined and evaluated give an overall picture of sustainability. Note that differences such as political environments and types of government have not been included. Instead we evaluated each country on the same scale and scored them accordingly to their performance. The model analyzes and scores the countries in following four areas: Economic, Social, Health, and Environment. Environment consists of two categories: natural resources and pollution. Within these five categories we have included a total of 20 subcategories to analyze the performance of these areas for different indicators. By keeping other things equal, we can set aside many arguable differences and focus on the results of the data, which are represented by an average of the five categories; all populations are dependents of for their long term sustainability.

From evaluating our model and sorting the scored averages in descending order, interestingly eight of the ten countries are in the continent of. The United States is ranked as ninth out of twenty one. The reason for the moderate performance is due to the not strong environmental score, whereas all other categories performed quite well. This is an indication of the importance of a balanced score between the variables, and no sector can be neglected if long-term sustainability is the objective since all sectors are interdependent of each other.

References

1. Abbott, K.W. (2012) 'Engaging the public and the private in global sustainability governance', *International Affairs*, Vol. 88, No. 3, pp.543-564. DOI: 10.1111/j.1468-2346.2012.01088.x.
2. Beça, P. and Santos, R. (2010) 'Measuring sustainable welfare: a new approach to the ISEW', *Ecological Economics*, Vol. 69, No. 4, pp.810-819.
3. Daily, G. and Ehrlich, P. (1992) 'Population, sustainability, and earth's carrying capacity', *BioScience*, Vol. 42, No. 10, pp. 761-771.
4. Faucheux, S., Muir, E. and O'Connor, M. (1997) 'Neoclassical natural capital theory and "weak" indicators for sustainability', *Land Economics*, Vol. 73, No. 4, pp.528-552.
5. Hamprecht, J., Corsten, D., Noll, M. and Meier, E. (2005) 'Controlling the sustainability of food supply chains', *Supply Chain Management,* Vol. 10, No. 1, pp.7-10.
6. Hobijn, B. and Steindel, C. (2009) 'Do alternative measures of GDP affect its interpretation?', *Economics and Finance*, Vol.15, No. 7, pp.1-7.
7. Jackson, M. P. (2009) 'Debate: we just do not know: healthcare expenditure trends', *Public Money and Management,* Vol. 29, No., 3, pp.9-10.
8. Kao, C. (1994) 'Evaluation of junior colleges of technology: the Taiwan case', *European Journal of Operational Research*, Vol. 72, No., 1, pp.43-51.
9. Kaiser Family Foundation. (2011) 'Health care costs: health care spending in the United States and selected OECD countries', available at http://www.kff.org/insurance/snapshot/OECD042111.cfm (accessed on June 16, 2012).
10. Kemp, R. and Martens, P. (2007) 'How to manage sustainable development', *Sustainability: Science, Practice, & Policy*, Vol. 3, No. 2, pp.5-14.
11. Kondro, W. (2010) 'Global life expectancy rises', *Canadian Medical Association Journal,* Vol. 182, No. 6, pp.E342-E343.
12. Manyika, J., Hazan, E., Bughin, J., Chui, M., Pélissié du Rausas M. and Said, E. (2011) 'Internet matters: the net's sweeping impact on growth, jobs, and prosperity', McKinsey Global Institute, available at http://www.mckinsey.com/Insights/MGI/Research/Te

chnology_and_Innovation/Internet_matters (accessed on June 16, 2012).
13. Menon, A. and Welsh, J. (2011) 'Understanding NATO's sustainability: the limits of institutionalist theory', *Global Governance*, Vol. 17, No. 1, pp.81-94.
14. Michelon, G. (2011) 'Sustainability disclosure and reputation: a comparative study', *Corporate Reputation Review*, Summer, Vol. 14, pp.79-96.
15. Moldan, B., Hák, T., Kovanda, J., Havránek, M. and Kušková, P. (2004) 'Composite indicators of environmental sustainability', *Statistics, Knowledge and Policy*, Vol. 1, No. 2, pp.1-10.
16. Naiman, R. J. and Dudgeon, D. (2011) 'Global alteration of freshwaters: influences on human and environmental well-being', *Ecological Research*, Vol. 26, No., 5, pp.865-873.
17. Nierenberg, D. (2012) 'World watch presents: growing solutions', *Harvard International Review*, April, Vol. 33, pp.72-75.
18. OECD. (2011) 'Health at a glance, health expenditure and financing', available at http://www.oecdilibrary.org/docserver/download/ (accessed on June 16, 2012).
19. Richmond, M., Robinson, C. and Sachs-Israel, M. (2008) 'The global literacy challenge; a profile of youth and adult literacy at the mid-point of the United Nations literacy decade 2003 – 2012', available at http://unesdoc.unesco.org/images/0016/001631/163170e.pdf (accessed on June 16, 2012).
20. Roca, L.C., and Searcy, C. (2012) 'An analysis of indicators disclosed in corporate sustainability reports', *Journal of Cleaner Production*, Vol. 20, No., 1, pp.103-118.
21. Rosenberg, M. (2010) 'Overview of life expectancy', available at http://geography.about.com/od/populationgeography/a/lifeexpectancy.htm (accessed on June 16, 2012).
22. Roy, M. and Fink, N. (2010) "Healthy" human development indices', *Social Indicators Research*. Vol. 99, No. 1, pp.61-80.
23. Schirnding, Y. (2011) 'Health in sustainable development: the role of indicators', World Summit on Sustainable Development, World Health Organization, available at http://www.who.int/wssd/resources/indicators/en/ (accessed on June 16, 2012).
24. Schneidewind, U. and Augenstein, K. (2012) 'Analyzing a transition to a sustainability-oriented science system in Germany', *Environmental Innovation and Societal Transitions*, In Press, Corrected Proof, Available online 24 May 2012.
25. Searcy, C., & Elkhawas, D. (2012) 'Corporate sustainability ratings: an investigation into how corporations use the Dow Jones sustainability', *Journal of Cleaner Production*, Vol. 35, pp.79-92.
26. Sharma, N. and Rowe, R. (1992) 'Managing the world's forests', *Finance & Development,* Vol. 29, No. 2, p.31.
27. Spence, M., Ben Boubaker Gherib, J. and Ondoua Biwolé, V. (2011) 'Sustainable entrepreneurship: is entrepreneurial will enough? A north-south comparison', *Journal of Business Ethics*, Vol. 99, No. 3, pp.335-367. DOI: 10.1007/s10551-010-0656-1.
28. Stevens, C. (2005) 'Measuring sustainable development', *Statistics Brief*, No. 10, September, OECD, Paris.
29. Strebel, P., Cochi, S., Hoekstra, E., Rota, P., Featherstone, D., Bellini, W. and Katz, S. (2011) 'The journal of infectious diseases, A world without measles', *Oxford Journal of Medicine,* Vol. 204, Suppl. 1, pp.S1-S3.
30. United Nations Development Program (UNDP). (2011) 'Human development report 2011, sustainability and equity: a better future for all', available athttp://hdr.undp.org/en/reports/global/hdr2011/ (accessed on June 16, 2012).
31. UNESCO. (2009) 'Rates are rising, but progress is slow', available at http://www.uis.unesco.org/literacy/Pages/Literacy-adult-youth-2011.aspx (accessed on June 16, 2012).
32. United Nations Statistics Division. (2011) 'Demographic and social statistics', *United Nations Statistics Division*, available at http://unstats.un.org/unsd/demographic/ (accessed on June 16, 2012).
33. Vong, S., Boruff, B.J. and Morrison-Saunders, A. (2011) 'Addressing climate change through environmental impact assessment: International perspectives from a survey of IAIA members', *Impact Assessment & Project Appraisal*, Vol. 29, No. 4, pp.317-326. DOI: 10.3152/146155111X12959673796001.
34. World Health Organization. (2011) 'World health indicators', available at http://apps.who.int/whosis/database/country/compare.cfm?country=CUB&indicator=PcTotEOHinIntD&language=english (accessed on June 16, 2012).
35. Warner, K. (2011) 'Environmental change and migration: methodological considerations from ground-breaking global survey', *Population & Environment*, Vol. 33, pp.3-27. DOI: 10.1007/s11111-011-015.

On the Implementation of one Registration, one Vote in South African Elections

Bassey Isong[1], **Ndwamato Netshipise**[1], **Gilbert Dzawo**[1] **and Munienge Mbodila**[2]
[1]Department of Computer Science & Information Systems, University of Venda, Thohoyandou, South Africa
[2] Science Foundation - Computer Science Unit, University of Venda, Thohoyandou, South Africa

Abstract - In any democratic setting, having regular free and fair elections is very critical to the stability of the nation as building trust and confidence is to promoting citizen's participation. In South Africa (SA) elections, though free and fair as seen, technically the system does not guarantee one man with one registration and one vote. Consequently, voter's fraud are not exception, though remains "closed". The system needs to be improved in order to protect the integrity of the elections. Therefore, the objective of this paper is to implement a new approach for SA elections based on real-time voter registration and identification. As part of the implementation, a novel system prototype called VOTEX System is presented.

Keywords: vote, elections, registration, real-time, identification.

1 Introduction

The explosion of information and communication technologies (ICTs) recently, especially the internet has been valuable and yielding positive impacts. In today's e-society, the impact of ICT have been felt in various aspects of life via e-services and e-practices [1,2]. In the perspective of e-services, ICT has brought about e-government which is more open, democratic, and efficient [3, 4]. E-government improves e-democracy that engages citizens support for democratic decision-making processes and strengthen representative democracy through the use of ICTs tools. In particular, ICTs application on electoral processes have be quiet remarkable especially in most developed nations such as the US, UK, Japan, Brazil and so on [5,6].

In a healthy democratic setting, trust and confidence building is very important especially when the electoral system process is transparent and allows for the participation of all electoral stakeholders [3]. Studies have shown that when citizens lack the full confidence that their elections are free and fair, a decline in levels of voter participation is always the end results [4, 7]. Thus, for democracy to be established and thrived, elections should be organized and conducted in an unbiased manner and free of voter's frauds [2]. Confidence in electoral processes is perhaps a precondition and South Africa (SA) is not an exception. One way of achieving such level of confidence is through the incorporation of e-democracy via the use of ICT tools into the electoral processes that is not only limited to the communications of policies, but also to the protection of the elections integrity.

Generally, in Africa, e-democracy and ICTs application has been limited to the communication of information and service, participation promotion and trust building where much has not been done to protect the integrity of the elections. In SA elections point of view, though employed some ICTs in its electoral process, relevant tools are not effectively employed during voter registration and voting that aim at ensuring its integrity. Consequently, it is difficult, if not impossible to track down voter's frauds. By implication, one man with one registration and one vote is not guaranteed. To this end, voter's frauds in the form of multiple registrations, multiple voting, figure falsification and impersonation, remains at large though unnoticed.

It is indisputable that when electoral systems surrounded by unnoticed irregularities exist, the trustworthiness and the integrity of the elections can be compromised and corruption of democracy or failures is inevitable [8]. Therefore, a new approach that is more trustworthy, cost-effective and reusable is important to protect the integrity of the SA elections. The approach addresses voter's fraud originating from registration and identification of voters. Our objective in this paper is to analyse and implement a new approach of voter registration and identification during elections in SA. This implementation is an extension of the work published by [9,10]. The proposed approach is the real-time registration and identification that utilizes biometric technologies. Accordingly, a novel system prototype called VOTEX System is implemented. With our proposed system, eligible voters will only have the opportunity to register once and vote once.

The paper is organized as follows: section 1 is the introduction, section 2 gives an overview of SA elections issues, section 3 describes the requirements specification and section 4 provides the proposed system structure. Section 5 presents the implementation of the system while sections 6 and 7 are the paper discussions and conclusion respectively.

2 Why South African Elections?

SA is a multi-party democratic nation with elections performed at three levels: National, Provincial elections and the Local elections [11]. SA elections have been free and fair despite the rated flaws in the world Democracy Index survey carried out by Economist [11] since the inception of democracy. However, from the technical point of view, system used does not completely guarantees election's integrity and, thus, requires to be improved.

One issue with SA electoral system is that the voter registration technique employed does not completely protect the integrity of the elections. This is important because voter registration can make or break an election [12]. Irrespective of the fact that SA election is believed to be free and fair, the registration system do not technically guarantee that one man only register once. For instance, the zip-zip barcode reading machines employed for capturing voter's information is only concerned with the automatic recording and matching of voter's information with no visible verification and identification that is transparent to every voter [13]. In this way, possible avenues for voter's frauds may be created and be exploited. With the technique, it is possible for a voter to register twice or more in same or different locations if he/she has more than one ID book in possession or even impersonate. This may exist because no stronger security measures are in place to track down these forms of frauds.

In the same vein, the nature of identification done at the voting station on Election Day lacks security strength. The measure employed neither guarantee that one man only vote once nor ensures that the vote is cast by an authentic person. With such technique, a voter may only vote if his/her name and ID number is found on the voter's roll or has any proof of registration. Going by the case of multiple registrations, it is also possible for voter having more than one ID book and registration to vote as many times as registered because no stronger security measures is in place to track them down. In addition, the ink on voter's thumbs after voting can easily be washed with strong chemicals with no trace. If this continues, the integrity of SA elections will not be upheld and may lead to failure of democracy one day. Hence, it is important to employ an approach that is strong enough to ensure that one man registers and vote only once irrespective of the location or the documents at hand. This requires that SA election has to be conducted in a real-time mode.

3 Requirements Analysis

3.1 System requirements

The first task is to specify the underlying requirements for designing and developing the system. The two basic system requirements that are expected to be satisfied by the proposed system are as follows:
*R1: the system shall allow one man to register **only** once for an election, and*
*R2: the system shall allow one man to vote **only** once during election.*

R1 is the key requirement that implements one man, one registration, while R2 implements one man, one vote. Details are discussed as follows.

1) *General:* In all cases, only authorized users can have access to the system. Two users are identified: election officials (EO) and system administrator (Admin).

Requirement Name: Login
Description: This feature enables authorized user to have access to the system.
Justification: Only authorized EO and Admin having valid credential can access the system.

2) *Voter Registration:* The basic functionalities that are required of the system are:

Requirement Name: Check Registration Status
Description: This feature enables user to check if a voter has registered before or not.
Justification: A voter is only allowed to register once.

Requirement Name: Register Voter
Description: This feature enables user to register voter's information if not in the database
Justification: Every eligible voter's information must be stored in the central database.

Requirement Name: Update/Delete Voter
Description: This feature enables user to update/delete voter's information already in the database
Justification: registered information in the database has to be maintained regularly.

3) Voter Identification: The basic functionalities that are required of the system are:

Requirement Name: Identify Voter
Description: This feature enables user to check if a voter is actually the registered and authentic one.
Justification: only registered voter is only allowed to vote and vote only once.

Requirement Name: Check Vote Status
Description: This feature enables user to check identified voter against voted or *not_voted.*
Justification: only registered voter not already voted are allowed to vote.

Requirement Name: Register Vote
Description: This feature enables user to register vote cast by the voter into the database
Justification: vote cast figures have to be recorded to check falsification of result figure.

3.2 Use cases analysis

As part of the requirements analysis and modeling, this section presents the representation system actors, their roles and the overall system use case for both voter registration and identification process. These are discussed as follows:

1) *Actors:* The system actors are shown in Fig. 1.

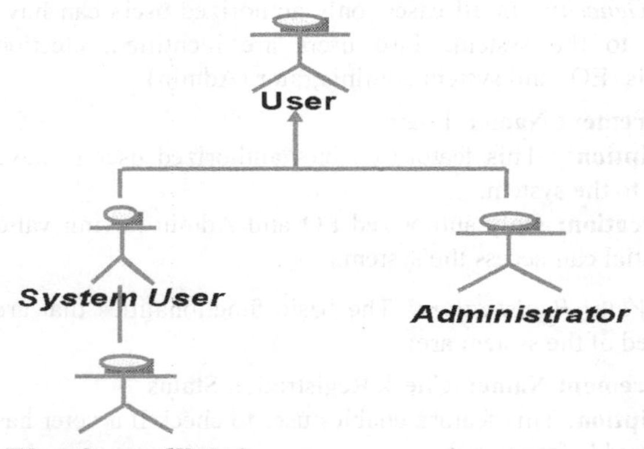

Figure 1: System Actors

The roles of each actor are stated below:
Election Official:
The role of the election officials are:

- Check Registration Status
- Register voters
- Update/Delete Voter
- Identify Voter
- Check Vote Status
- Register Vote

Administrator:
The administrator roles are:

- Create User's Account
- Create database
- Delete database
- Print database information

In this paper, we shall only discuss the roles of the EO.

2) ***System Use Case Model***

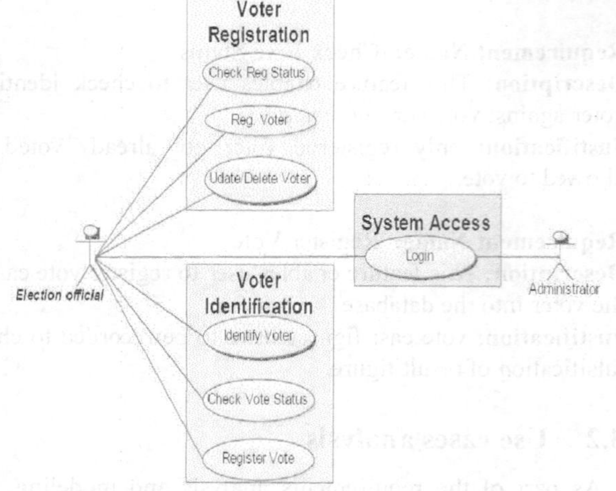

Figure 2: VOTEX System use case

Fig.2 provides the general use case model of the entire system, showing actors, features and their interactions.

3.3 Use cases descriptions

This section provides detailed description of the process involve in the use case analysis of the requirements. Table 1 gives a description of the general system access, Table 2 gives a description of the voter registration process while Table 3 provides description for the voter identification process. In all cases, the use case name, actor, pre-condition, main scenarios and alternative scenarios are provided. Consequently, the details are as follows:

1) Login Sequence

Table 1. General Login Sequence

Use Case Name	Login
Actor	EO, Admin
Pre-condition	Both users should have valid user id and password to have access to the system
Main Scenarios	1. To have access to the system, the EO or admin must first login 2. for successful login (EOl), a page is display to either perform *registration* or *identification* 3. for successful login (Admin), a page is display to perform database creation, deletion and printing
Alternative Scenarios	1. unsuccessful login ▪ the system inform the user of incorrect credentials ▪ step 1 in the main flow 2. not a valid or authorize user

2) Registration Sequence

Table 2. Registration Sequence

Use Case Name	Register Voter
Actor	EO
Pre-condition	The EO should first check the registration status and the voter should have a valid ID book and proof of residence
Main Scenarios	1. To register a voter, the EO must first login 2. If given access, he/she must first check if the voter's status is *not_registered* or *registered* 3. if the status is *not_registered*, the official must register the voter with the following information: Name, ID_Number, Sex, Date_of Birth, City, Municipal, Province, Photo and Finger_print 4. A voter is issued proof of registration
Alternative Scenarios	1. #status - *Registered* ▪ Registration is denied ▪ The voter is issued proof of registration 2. the voter is eligible to vote

3) Identification Sequence

Table 3. Identification Sequence

Use Case Name	Identify Voter
Actor	EO
Pre-condition	The EO should first check the *vote_status* and the voter may have a valid proof of registration
Main Scenarios	1. To identify a voter, the official must first login 2. If given access, he/she must first check if the voter is the real person using fingerprint 3. if he/she is the real voter, the official should then check if the *voter_status* is either *not_voted* or *voted.* 4. if the status is *not_voted,* the voter is allow to vote 5. after voting, the official registers the vote
Alternative Scenarios	1. #not a valid voter ▪ voter is sent a way 2.# vote status - *voted* ▪ voting is denied ▪ voter sent away ▪ voter arrested

4 Proposed System Design

4.1 System components

The various components that are required for the system to meet the objectives of voter's registration and identification have already been discussed in [9,10]. These include the central database, a secured wireless network, mobile PCs, fingerprint scanners, cameras, and mobile printers during both exercises for effective and real-time registration and identification of voter. (Fig. 1)

4.2 System Architecture

Fig.1. shows the architecture of the proposed system. The architecture consists of system components relevant at both registration and voting stations as well as their interactions. Details of the components working in achieving the overall goal are explained in subsequent sections.

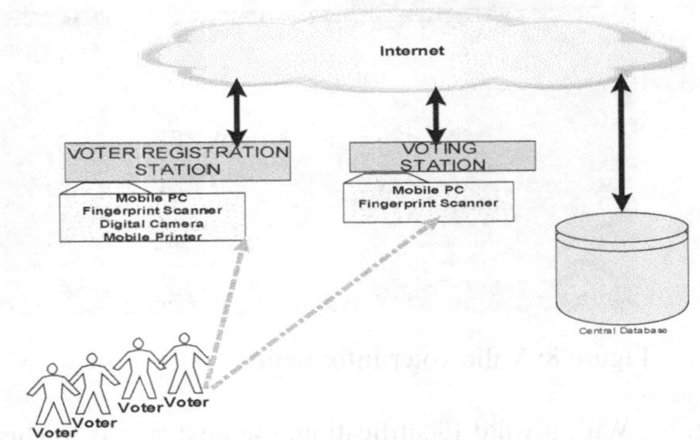

Figure 3: Simple system architecture

5 System Implementation

This section provides the implementation phase which shows how the requirements stated earlier are realized during the election. Details are discussed below:

5.1 The VOTEX system

Our proposed system is called VOTEX and is a web-based application developed to provide two services of voter registration and identification on a real-time basis. VOTEX is not a voting system or party related system but a system to protect election's integrity. It is a prototype implemented with the requirements described in the above use cases in section 3 of this work. Fig. 4 shows the home page of the system and we proposed it to be the official website of the independent electoral commission (IEC) of SA.

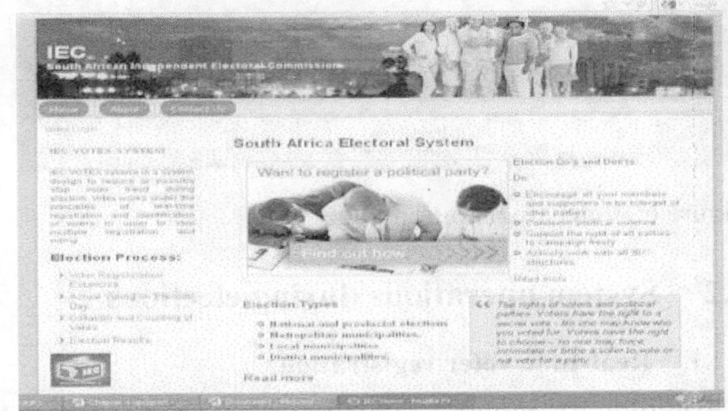

Figure 4: IEC home page

1) User Login

At the left hand side of the home page is the VOTEX Login where access can be granted to only authorize users. With VOTEX, only two types of users are allowed access to the system: *Admin* and *EO*. When an EO logon to VOTEX, he/she is redirected to a page where applicable operations can be chosen: ***VoterRegistration*** and ***VoterIdentification*** (see Fig. 5)

Figure 5: IEC Welcome Page

For instance, when the button ***VoterRegistration*** is clicked, a voter registration page is displayed (see Fig. 6.) For security reasons, the ***VoterRegistration*** button is only enabled during voter registration exercise and is disabled during Election Day. Accordingly, ***VoterIdentification*** button is only enabled during Election Day and is disabled during voter registration exercise.

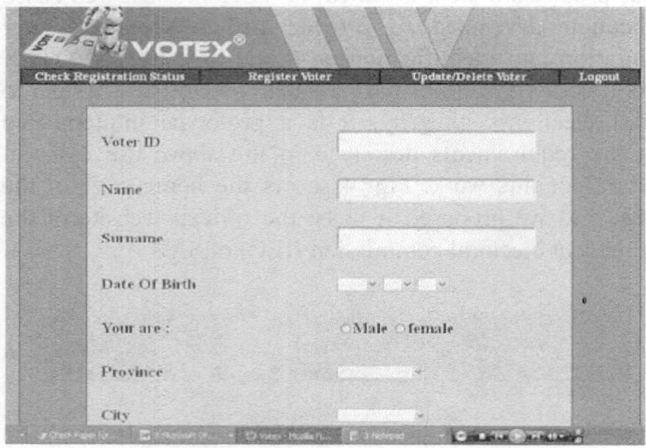

Figure 6: Voter Registration Page

5.2 System operations during elections

5.2.1 Real-time voter registration

Real-time registration is the exercise towards ensuring the integrity of the elections and to guard against voter's frauds. The rationale behind the real-time registration is to ensure that one man register only once. This is achieved through the following procedures: (See Fig. 3)

i. At the registration station on a public registration day, Voters need to show their bar-coded green ID book or a temporary ID document and proof of residence to validate their residential area.

ii. After verification, the registration status of the person is checked with VOTEX using the fingerprint as input by clicking button ***VoterRegistration*** on VOTEX (see Fig.5). If the voter has already registered in another location, the system will display all the registered information and will not be allowed to register again. (See Fig. 7).

iii. If the voter hasn't register yet, VOTEX will return "***Voter not found***" and then proceed to the next stage which is the actual registration. At this point, the entire voter's information as stated in the registration use case of section 3 will be captured and stored into the central database in a real-time mode. With VOTEX, voters' information can be collected, recorded, updated, deleted and stored. The mobile printer will be used to print out temporal proof of registration to all registered voters.

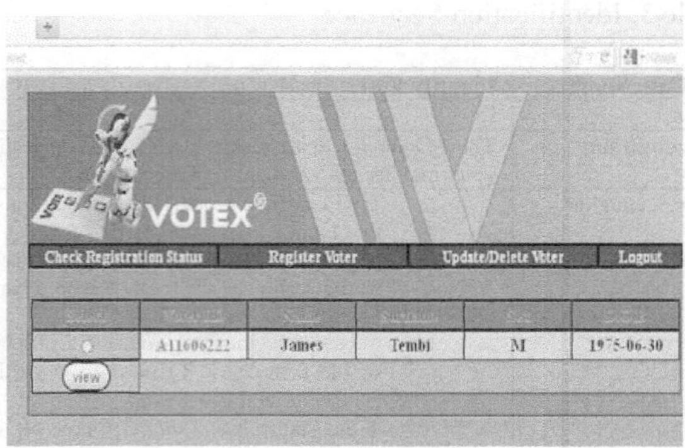

Figure 7: Registration status

5.2.2 Real-time voter's identification

This approach is employ on the actual Election Day. During this process, each voter will be individually identified against the information stored in the central database on a real-time approach via VOTEX system before allowed to vote. The rationale is to ensure that one man has only one vote and he/she is a real voter. The procedures are as follows:

i. On Election Day, as a voter enters the voting station, his or her finger is scanned with the fingerprint reader by the electoral official. The output of the operation is then used to automatically query the central database directly in order to identify the voter. (see Fig. 3). This is done by clicking ***VoterIdentification*** button on VOTEX (see Fig.5)

(a) Upon valid identification, specific stored information about the voter is display by VOTEX (see Fig. 8)

(b) Upon invalid match, VOTEX will return "**Voter not found**" and he/she will not be allowed to vote, meaning he/she is not a valid or registered voter. The voter is then sent out of the voting station.

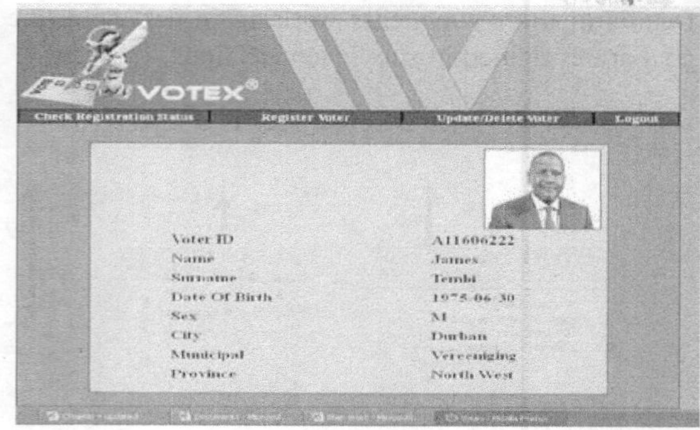

Figure 8: Valid voter information

ii. With a valid Identification, the next step is to check the Voting Status of the voter. That is, checking if he or she has ***voted***, ***not_voted*** or ***disqualified*** using the ID No. or the first/surname where necessary.

(a) If the status is ***voted***, the system will display the page shown in Fig. 9 and will not be allowed vote again. The page will display the voter ID, the city where voting takes place, the vote_status and the exact time he or she voted.

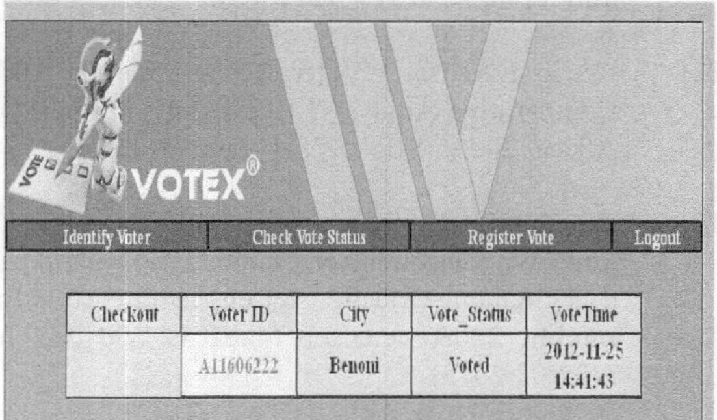

Figure 9: Voter's vote status

(b) If the voter hasn't voted before or the status is ***Not_Voted,*** VOTEX will return **"Voter not found"** which signifies that the voter be allowed to vote. After voting, the Vote Status is immediately changed to **Voted**.

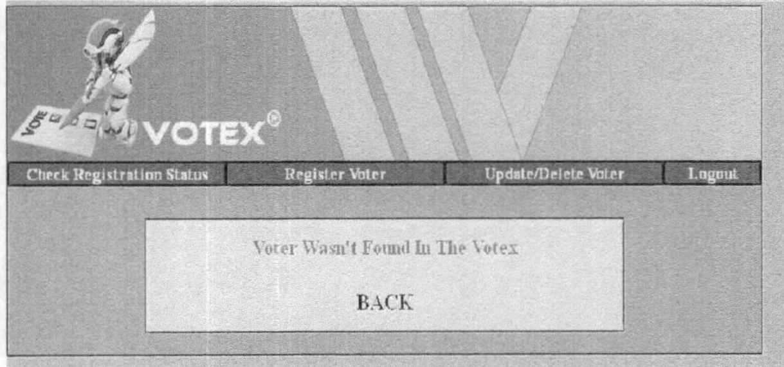

Figure 10: Unregistered voter status

With VOTEX, the actual voting can take any strategy or form either by traditional approach or through the use of voting machine as long as the voter's privacy is preserved.

6 Discussions

Trust and confidence in democracy can be promoted as well as the electoral process transparent and open to all electoral stakeholders especially when basic ICT tools are utilized. Most importantly is when the integrity of the elections is protected. As an objective of this work, SA elections have to adopt a new approach aim at protecting elections integrity. With the system's operations, it is apparent that our proposed system shall set a simple and clear standard for protecting the integrity of the elections if adopted for use. The approach will not only be beneficial to the SA government, but also to other developing countries in Africa where voter's fraud is the order of the elections. This is important because, where such situations thrived, failure of democracy is imminent. Therefore, VOTEX idea is designed to close the security gaps that exist in the current election process used in SA as discussed in section 2 of this work. With this proposed system, regardless of the location or number of green ID books a voter has, it is not only difficult but impossible to register or vote more that once in an election.

Other aspect of VOTEX is its associated benefits. Firstly, with VOTEX, voter's ID may not be necessary during voting since identification will be done in a real-time mode. Implementing this will in turn saves the cost of producing and issuing voter's ID card or trying to win parliamentary support for its approval in a nature. This is possible through use of fingerprint coupled with its known security strength. Accordingly, with VOTEX the falsifications of election results figures or other irregularities as common among many developing nations will be put under control by registering every vote cast in the polling station in a real-time mode. Lastly, with this proposed method, a central database can be implemented and maintained regularly especially where it never existed. This will in turn save the cost of creating new ones and will also provide supports to other sectors of the government and the NGOs where identification is required.

Security is another important aspect of the proposed system. Due to its web-based operation coupled with the exponential growth of Internet threats, we have implemented an intrusion detection system (IDS) simply called VOTEX IDS or VIDS. VIDS is designed to repel and deny immediate access to any malicious attack or input thrown against the system. Because of space constraint, we excluded the security part in this paper. For more information about VIDS, refer to [9]. Other issues that could adversely affect the operation of the system include resistance to change and other issues not identified in this paper. However, giving due attention to these impediments can create a significant impact aimed at enhancing the operations of VOTEX which in turn will ensures the integrity of the elections at large.

7 Conclusions

The impact of ICT on today's e-society and elections in particular, has been quite beneficial. In this paper, we have presented a proposed approach aimed at ensuring the integrity of elections in SA. The approach is in the form of real-time voter registration and identification. The proposed approach is to ensure that one man has only one registration and one vote during elections. In addition, we implemented the approach by designing, developing and presenting a novel system prototype called VOTEX. With its operation, based on its operational mode in terms of efficiency, we therefore conclude that by taking advantage of relevant ICT tools in electoral processes, it can go a long way to rid fraudulent practices that is engulfing our elections and uphold its integrity.

8 References

[1] Welch, E. W and Hinnant, C.C., "Internet Use, Transparency, and Interactivity Effects on Trust in Government" Proceedings of the 36th Hawaii International Conference on System Sciences (HICSS'03) IEEE, 2003

[2] Gronlund, A. Democracy in an IT-framed society. Communications of the ACM, January 2001, Vol.44

[3] Yanqing, G., "Analysis on How to Enhance E-Democracy through E-Government", Proceedings of 2011 IEEE International Conference on Management and Service Science (MASS), August, 2011

[4] E-Democracy: Putting Down Global Roots, Janet Caldow, IBM Institute for Electronic Government, January 2004

[5] Dill, D. L: Electronic Voting: An Overview of the Problems, Computer Science, Stanford University, 2004.

[6] Simons, B: Electronic voting systems: the good, the bad, and the stupid, Communications of the ACM, October 2004, Vol. 2 Issue 7

[7] Deeping Democracy through E-Governance, Pippa Norris, Harvard University, The other e-participation-related article commissioned by the UN as an input into their World Public Sector Report, May 2003

[8] Isong, B. E. Ekabua, O. O. and Mbodila, M. "Towards One Person, One Vote via Real-Time Voter's Registration and Identification". Proceedings of the 11th International Conference on e-Learning, e-Business, Enterprise Information Systems, and e-Government (EEE'12). WORLDCOMP'12, Las Vega, Nevada, USA, July 16-19.

[9] Isong, B., Netshipise, N. and Dzawo, G.: A New Approach for Protecting Elections Integrity in South Africa. *International Journal of Computer Applications* 62(20):10-18, January 2013. Foundation of Computer Science, New York, USA. 28th January, 2013

[10] Isong, B. and Netshipise, N.: "Extending E-Democracy to Enhance Voter Registration and Identification: South Africa Elections Perspective" *International Journal of Computer Science & Engineering Technology (IJCSET),* Vol. 4 No. 01 Jan 2013, pp. 35-43, ISSN: 2229-3345

[11] "Elections in South Africa". http://www.etu.org.za/toolbox/docs/govern/elections.html (18/02/2013)

[12] Astrid Evrensel: "Voter Registration in Africa: A Comparative Analysis" EISA, Johannesburg -South Africa, 2006. ISBN: 978-1-920095-93-2

[13] "South African Election Types" http://www.elections.org.za/content/Dynamic.aspx?id=575&name=Elections&LeftMenuId=100&BreadCrumbId=220&ekmensel=14ae2c49_100_252_btnlink . (28/02/2013)

[14] Gil, Y., Moon, D., Pan, S. and Chung, Y., Fingerprint Verification System Involving Smart Card, InformationSecurity and Cryptology - ICISC 2002 (LNCS 2587), Nov. 2002, Seoul, Korea.

[15] Diaz, Raul. "Biometrics: Security Vs Convenience". SecurityWorld Magazine. 30 August, 2010

Antecedents of E-trust: A Study among Taxpayers in Malaysia

Moein Mayeh[1], T. Ramayah[2], and Sureswaran Ramadass[1]
[1]National Advanced IPv6 Center, Universiti Sains Malaysia, 11800 USM. Penang, Malaysia
[2]School of Management, Universiti Sains Malaysia, 11800 USM, Penang, Malaysia

Abstract - *In recent years, Malaysian government has increasingly benefited from information technology to enhance their services, known as electronic government (e-government). However, despite considerable investment, citizens' adoption rate is still not as expected. Tax e-filing system is one of the critical e-government services, which assists taxpayers in filing their tax returns electronically each year. Since citizens' acceptance of tax e-filing system is influenced by their trust to this system, there is a need to understand the factors that predict the users' trust on tax e-filing system. This study, conducted a survey among taxpayers in Malaysia, aims to investigate the role of perceived security, perceived privacy, and perceived service quality as antecedents of E-trust. A total of 290 responses were analyzed in SmartPLS using Structural Equation Modeling (SEM). The findings of this study indicate that the above factors are important predictors of users' e-trust in tax e-filing context.*

Keywords: E-government; Tax e-filing; E-trust; Perceived Security; Perceived Privacy

1 Introduction

Scholars define e-government as the use of information and communication technology in government services; and particularly, the utilization of internet in order to facilitate the access and delivery of government's information, operations and services [1]. The main objectives of e-government initiatives are to build services with main focus on citizens' needs and to provide ease of access to the government services [2]. As a result, e-government services improve convenience that matters for both government as a service provider and citizens as the service recipients. These services include but not limited to asking a simple question by citizens, paying bills and taxes, receiving payments, downloading documents and many other services.

In this study, we focus on tax e-filling system as one of the important e-government services which is particularly of governments' interest because taxes form critical sources of the governments' revenue. E-filing system enables taxpayers to submit their tax returns electronically to the tax authorities (government). In addition, e-filing helps to prevent many mistakes which might occur by taxpayers in manual filing [3].

Tax e-filing system has been introduced and implemented in Malaysia since 2006. According to the latest report which appeared in the Sun newspaper on December 20th, 2012, around 2.8 million people had filed their tax returns online in Malaysia in 2012 [4]. Although, this indicates a growth from 2.3 million participants in 2011 [4], 1.25 million participants in 2009 [5], 874,841 participants in 2007 and 186,343 participants in 2006, the acceptance rate of this system is still low in Malaysia and there are rooms to improve (there were 6.4 million eligible taxpayers in Malaysia in 2009 [6] which shows that the users' percentage rate was almost 19%). In another study conducted by United Nations, it is reported that Malaysia ranked 8th in e-government development index in Asia in 2012 and is also taken the 40th slot in the world e-government ranking which shows a fall from 2010 [7]. So far, several studies such as Fatimah and Lai [8] and Lai and Choong [9] emphasized that tax e-filing system is far behind its target in Malaysia.

Issues such as lack of privacy, security, and service quality have been reported to influence users' trust in e-government systems [7]. This research, conducting a survey study, will investigate the role of these factors on predicting citizens' trust to tax e-filling system among taxpayers in Malaysia. This study also provides critical understanding of the factors that influence taxpayers' trust on tax e-filing system in Malaysia.

2 Research model and hypotheses

2.1 E-trust

Trust as a complex and abstract concept has different meanings across variety of fields. Mayer, Davis, & Schoorman [10] defined trust as "The willingness of a party to be vulnerable to the actions of another party based on the expectation that the other party will perform a particular action important to the trustor, irrespective of the ability to monitor or control that other party". Moreover, P. A. Pavlou [11] trust as ''a belief that one may rely upon a promise made by another.''

Trust plays important role in online business context which there is lack of control, lack of inefficiencies and potential opportunism, anonymity, and lack of proximity in such transactions. In other words, transactions in online context appears to be more of mechanical interactions and different than in traditional way where it occurs in person [12]. The role of trust in online context has been investigated in different studies so far [13]. This study is concerned with the role of trust in tax e-filing systems.

Lack of trustworthiness to the online system providers will increase customers' unwillingness to adopt online systems. The importance of trust in online interactions is becoming more critical due to the expansion of online services in recent years [14]. The role of trust also has been studied in e-government context. It is argued that building trust is a major factor in e-government adoption [15]. Given the fact that this study investigates the role of trust in online systems, it follows the notion of e-trust which is mainly used by researchers in online systems' context [14, 16]. This study also follows the definition of Gefen [17] in e-commerce environment which says: "general belief in an online seller that brings about behavioral intention."

In the context of usage and adoption of the e-government system, trust has categorized under two main dimensions in different studies; "trust on the government" and "trust on internet" [18]. Following this classification, in order to trust online government services, citizens need to believe that government has recreated adequate technical and managerial resources to fully secure and implement the system. Along with these requirements and perceptions, for adopting e-government services, citizens also need to trust the online channels in terms of legal protection [19], security and safety [20].

From technology perspective, trust in technology means that the online tasks or transactions will be accomplished successfully without any error [1]. Another aspect of trust can be viewed from the citizens' concerns about the credibility of internet infrastructure. Trust in reliability of the technology is mainly about the level of security and suitability of internet as an online channel. Risks of privacy and security which threaten citizens in online transactions have been discussed in previous studies [14]. This study follows above classification of trust. Therefore, the trust has two dimensions in this study; Trust on government and trust on internet which has been extracted from [18].

2.2 Perceived security

In the virtual World that internet is an open network without any control by human over individual transactions; people are reluctant to file their tax returns electronically [21]. There is also the possibility that financial and personal information being misused for fraudulent purposes which make taxpayers to hesitate to reveal their information.

Examples of security dangers include potential threads to data or network resources in the form of destruction, disclosures, modification of data, denial of service, and/or fraud [22]. These issues reduce the level of customers' trust and discouraging them to disclose their personal information in online transactions. Thus, security mechanisms make consumers believe that online transactions and payments are safe [22].

Therefore, perceived security is one of the main barriers to the acceptance of online-based systems [17, 23]. Relation between security and trust can be further explained as the belief about the safety of information system toward system hacking, malware or introduction of viruses. For instance, a user who trusts on the security of the system will expect to use the system hassle free without any crash from unsafe software or introducing viruses in their machine [24]. As discussed, this study will be examined relationship between perceived security and e-trust in tax e-filing system. Scholars [21, 22, 25, 26] studied security and privacy as key antecedents of trust in different environment such as online trading system, online retailing, and online banking. As such, to investigate the impact users' perceived security on e-trust, the following hypothesis is proposed:

H1: Perceived security has a positive effect on e-trust.

2.3 Perceived privacy

In online environment where users have to share their personal information to perform online transactions, privacy issues on how service provider obtains, stores and reuses information become critical. Hence, service providers need to ensure them of how personal information is protected by them. As a result, privacy emerged as an important issue by the move of government toward a higher level of online interactions with citizens, including transfer of private information such as tax returns and medical records.

As such, Yousafzai et al. [16] defines privacy as customers' perception about their ability in controlling and monitoring their own information. Privacy is mainly concerned with the issue of protection of identifiable information of individuals (on the internet) and involves the adaptation and implementation of a privacy policy, disclosure, choice or consent of consumers [27]. This study, concerning the tax e-filing system, follows McLeod and Pippin's [24] definition of privacy which says personal tax information of users will not be revealed to any unauthorized individuals or companies.

Although perceived privacy and perceived security seems similar concept, they are two different concepts. As discussed in recent two sections, perceived security emphasizes on technical prevention for hackers' attacks which cause system break down (to steal information). On the other hand, perceived privacy is more concerned about legal requirements and good practices to protect users' personal information by online service provider [26].

Scholars discuss the role of perceived privacy as a critical determinant of users' acceptance of online services [25, 28]. The study by Lean, et al. [29] have found positive relationship between perception of privacy protection and trust in the context of e-government services in Malaysia, while Roca, et al. [22] did not find the significant relationship between perceived security and perceived trust in the context of online trading systems in Spain. To further explore the relationship between users' perceived privacy and e-trust in online environment, this study will develop and test the following hypothesis:

H2: Perceived privacy has a positive effect on e-trust.

2.4 Perceived service quality

For the last few years, "Quality" was one of the most important issues in the business world [30]. Service quality in information systems generally introduced in order to evaluate the quality of services of IT departments in organizations. Service quality reflects the subjective evaluation of consumers between the actual quality of service they received and what they expect [31]. Since in online electronic environment, customers might not meet service provider prior to their transactions at all, perceived service quality plays an important role to build customers' trust to their provider [32].

Most of the information systems attract customers by offering excellent services. Therefore, service quality becomes a proper mean to increase the success of services (services such as e-government services) [31]. As such, scholars have identified service quality as one of the fundamental criteria of information systems success [33]. As such, this study will investigate the role of perceived service quality on e-trust and consequently on intention to use of tax e-filing system.

Scholars discuss service quality as one of the important determinants of online trust [34, 35]. This study particularly will investigate the effect of perceived service quality of users on e-trust in the context of tax e-filing system. As such the following hypothesis is proposed to be tested:

H3: Perceived service quality has a positive effect on e-trust.

Based on this comprehensive literature review, the proposed research model is presented in Figure 1.

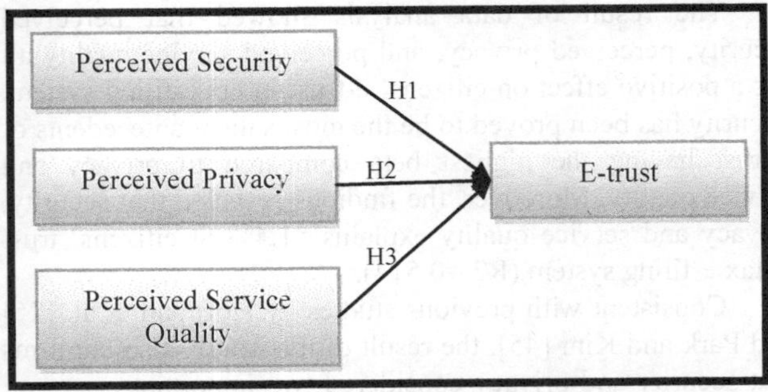

Figure 1 Research Framework

3 Research method

This research is a quantitative research which is also known as hypothesis-testing. A field survey was employed to evaluate and test the research hypothesis in this research. Survey of this study was constructed using mail questionnaire along with the paper-based questionnaire. The unit of analysis for this study is individuals (citizens of Malaysia) who use tax e-filling system. The population of this study focuses on all citizens of Malaysia who used tax e-filing system at least once before. Data were collected from the five cities in Malaysia such as Penang, Selangor, Terengganu, Johor Bahru, and Pahang due to their considerable population in compare to the other cities. Totally, 290 questionnaires were used for the analysis.

For this study, Partial Least Squares (PLS) [36, 37] as component-based SEM has been adopted to analyze the survey dataset. To be specific, the researcher used MPLS Smart Version 2.0.M3 [38].

4 Data analysis

The first step in the PLS analysis procedure is to test the measurement model (outer model) for construct validity. It investigates the fundamental relationships between the indicators (items or observed variables) and the theoretically defined constructs [39]. In the first step, we tested individual item reliabilities by looking at their loadings to their related constructs and their cross loadings with other constructs. As mentioned by Hair et al. [40], the factor loading of .50 and above on a specific factor has been considered standardized and acceptable. Three items with loadings below the accepted value that loaded weakly on the hypothesized factors were removed from the scale. Table 1 shows the item loadings and cross loadings from the analysis of the theoretical model. As such, checking the cross loadings, it can be seen that all items, measuring a construct, loaded highly on their specific constructs while loaded lower on other constructs on the same row. This result indicates the constructs validity.

Table 1 Factor loadings and cross loading

	E-trust	Perceived Privacy	Perceived Security	Perceived Service Quality
ETR3	**0.750**	0.344	0.502	0.436
ETR4	**0.808**	0.386	0.520	0.492
ETR5	**0.859**	0.466	0.560	0.559
ETR6	**0.847**	0.427	0.559	0.485
ETR7	**0.772**	0.365	0.480	0.476
PRI1	0.363	**0.769**	0.386	0.400
PRI2	0.388	**0.841**	0.397	0.368
PRI3	0.416	**0.871**	0.414	0.384
PRI4	0.463	**0.834**	0.535	0.439
SEQ1	0.496	0.423	**0.800**	0.494
SEQ2	0.500	0.417	**0.832**	0.429
SEQ3	0.602	0.480	**0.889**	0.558
SEQ4	0.551	0.430	**0.802**	0.441
SQU1	0.393	0.373	0.451	**0.670**

SQU2	0.295	0.248	0.360	**0.669**
SQU3	0.417	0.299	0.367	**0.763**
SQU4	0.399	0.337	0.356	**0.713**
SQU5	0.540	0.383	0.482	**0.771**
SQU6	0.469	0.371	0.422	**0.655**

Bold values are loadings for items which are above the recommended value of 0.5

4.1 Convergent Validity

In the next step, the researcher tested the measurement model for convergent validity in order to check to what extent the multiple items of a concept are in agreement [41]. As suggested by Hair et al. [42], convergent validity was assessed by employing factor loadings, composite reliability (CR) and the average variance extracted (AVE).

Composite reliability (refer to Table 2), indicates the degree to which the variable indicators demonstrates the latent variable. In this study, composite reliability of each variable exceeded the acceptable value of 0.7. In addition to that, the average variance extracted (AVE) which measures the variance captured by the items related to measurement error. AVE should be higher than 0.5 [42]. The results indicate that all constructs' items (indicators) are valid measures for their constructs based on their value and statistical significance.

Table 2 Results of measurement model

Model construct	Measurement item	Loading	CR[1]	AVE[2]
E-trust	ETR3	0.750	0.904	0.653
	ETR4	0.808		
	ETR5	0.859		
	ETR6	0.847		
	ETR7	0.772		
Perceived privacy	PRI1	0.769	0.898	0.689
	PRI2	0.841		
	PRI3	0.871		
	PRI4	0.834		
Perceived Security	SEQ1	0.800	0.900	0.692
	SEQ2	0.832		
	SEQ3	0.889		
	SEQ4	0.802		
Perceived Service Quality	SQU1	0.670	0.858	0.502
	SQU2	0.669		
	SQU3	0.763		
	SQU4	0.713		
	SQU5	0.771		
	SQU6	0.655		

4.2 Discriminant validity

In this step, we test the discriminant validity of the measures which are defined as the extent to which items of a construct are distinct from other construct (concepts) [43]. To evaluate the discriminant validity the average variance extracted for each construct should be greater than the squares of the correlations between the construct and all other constructs [44]. The result is depicted in Table 3 which indicates adequate discriminant validity.

Table 3 Discriminant validity of constructs

	ETR	PRI	SEQ	SQU
ETR[3]	**0.808**			
PRI[4]	0.494	**0.830**		
SEQ[5]	0.649	0.527	**0.832**	
SQU[6]	0.607	0.481	0.580	**0.708**

Finally, Table 4 presents the results of path coefficients (β) and significance for the structural model. A Close look at the t-value shows that all hypotheses in this study were supported.

Table 4 Path coefficients for structural Model

	Hypotheses	β	SE	T-value	Supported
H1	Privacy → E-trust	0.135	0.053	2.529	Yes
H2	Security → E-trust	0.397	0.061	6.494	Yes
H3	Service Quality → E-trust	0.312	0.054	5.824	Yes

5 Discussion

The result of data analysis showed that perceived security, perceived privacy, and perceived service quality all has a positive effect on citizens' e-trust in tax e-filing system. Security has been proved to be the most salient antecedents of e-trust having the highest beta compared to privacy and service quality. Moreover, the findings revealed that security, privacy and service quality explains 51.4% of citizens' trust in tax e-filing system ($R2 = 0.514$).

Consistent with previous studies by Hoffman et al. [25] and Park and Kim [45], the result of this study, also confirms that security and privacy considered two important issues on the users' trust in the online-based system in comparison with

1 Composite reliability (CR) = (square of the summation of the factor loadings)/{(square of the summation of the factor loadings) + (square of the summation of the error variances)}

2 Average variance extracted (AVE) = (summation of the square of the factor loadings)/{(summation of the square of the factor loadings) + (Summation of the error variances)}

3 E-trust

4 Perceived Privacy

5 Perceived Security

6 Perceived Service Quality

the conventional systems. Unlike general perceptions about privacy and security that views security and privacy as similar concepts, the result of this study reveals that they are separate constructs which are measured by different items. The result also indicates that perceived security and service quality have the strongest positive effect on e-trust.

The direct positive relationship of security toward e-trust is consistent with some prior studies [22,26]. As discussed by Shon et al. [46], security issues in online transactions are considered as the primary concern of online users. In order to switch from traditional paper-based tax filing to online systems, users need be convinced about online security protection of their service providers. However, the result of Novak et al. [47], which says that security has the least effect on trust in online environment, is in contrast with this study.

In this case, government agencies can provide services with the high security such as utilizing multiple firewalls and secure socket layers (SSL) in all their internet transmissions. In addition, for making this process transparent to citizens, they need to explain the process of security infrastructure through posting it online in the website and in instructions document which mailed to the citizens.

In the consistent of the study by Lean, et al. [29], this study also found that perceived privacy has a positive effect on e-trust. Lean, et al. [29] conducted their study in the context of e-government in Malaysia which is very similar to this study. In contrast, Roca, et al. [22], did not find significant relationship between perceived privacy and perceived trust in the context of online trading systems. This indicates that the more private information (such as financial income information in tax e-filing system) is shared, the more people are concerned about privacy issues (in online trading system, only information about transaction and few personal information will be collected from service provider).

In addition to the security and privacy, this study has found positive effect of service quality on users' e-trust. This is consistent with some previous studies [34, 48]. K. Jones and Leonard [32] discussed the significant impact of the quality of website in users' trust in electronic commerce. Service quality of online systems can be maintained by providing services error free and on time, having online customer service, and responding to the system failures quickly [49].

This study has several implications for practitioners (government). This research also helps government to extend its understandings of citizens' adaption factors. As a result, they would be able to execute better strategies to increase adoption rate and success of tax e-filing systems.

Moreover, government agencies need to ensure that proper privacy practices are in place. This also needs to be well communicated to the citizens. For example, government can put their privacy practices in their website. Similarly, this also applies to security issues. Government need to inform citizens of its security protection practices. Providing this information to the citizens, would help to increase the level of trust among Malaysian citizens which eventually lead to higher acceptance rate of tax e-filing system.

In addition to privacy and security which are very important to build trust in online environment, the quality of online service is also critical. Since in online electronic environment, customers might not meet service provider prior to their transactions at all, perceived service quality plays an important role to build customers' trust to their provider [32]. In this regard, government needs to provide accurate, timely and dependable services [18]. Having a positive and error free experience with online tax filing, not only increase users' trust but also encourage them to spread the words and invite other friends to use this system.

We examined the construct of e-trust in tax e-filing system environment. Moreover, it was found that e-trust in tax e-filing system which in this study was defined in two dimension; trust to government and trust to technology (internet) can be considered as one component (based on factor analysis). Thus, future research can use this construct as a measurement for e-trust in tax e-filing context.

6 Limitations and future studies

There are several limitations which can be addressed in future research. First this study is a cross-sectional research and data were collected at one point of time whereas it is believed that people's behaviors might change over the time. Therefore, this study suggests that longitudinal study can give more insights about factors that affect users' behaviors. This study only focuses on the factors that are important to predict users' E-trust. But it did not investigate why these factors are important. As a result, a qualitative study can be appropriate to explore if there are other factors affecting E-trust.

The respondents in this study are chosen from five selected cities in Malaysia. The e-filers in these cities might have different perceptions on tax e-filing system from other cities. Separate study is suggested to be conducted in rural areas since the factors might be different from urban areas (where we selected our responses from). Thus, it is suggested that future studies select their responses from wider geographical locations.

7 Conclusion

This study has investigated the role of perceived security, perceived privacy, and perceived service quality on the e-trust of the citizens. The relationship between these variables were hypothesized and empirically tested in tax e-filing system environment in Malaysia. Data were collected from those who had experience using tax e-filing system. A total of 290 responses were analyzed using structural equation modeling exploiting SmartPLS.

The result reveals that perceived security, perceived privacy, and perceived service quality are important determinants of e-trust. These variables together explained 51.4% of the variance of E-trust. The study also examined the role of antecedent variables in predicting e-trust of online taxpayers. It is also found that e-trust in tax e-filing system context is unidimensional (unlike what previous studies found). Moreover, we have found out that security and privacy are two different concepts in tax e-filing environment. Finally, understanding these factors would help government to adopt proper strategies which eventually increase the acceptance of tax e-filing system.

8 References

[1] Teo, Srivastava, and Jiang, *Trust and electronic government success: an empirical study.* Journal of Management Information Systems, 2008. **25**(3): p. 99-132.

[2] Sahu, G.P. and M. Gupta, *Users' acceptance of e-government: A study of Indian Central Excise.* 2008.

[3] Berdykhanova, D., A. Dehghantanha, and K. Hariraj. *Trust challenges and issues of e-government: E-tax prospective.* in *Information Technology (ITSim), 2010 International Symposium in.* 2010.

[4] Loo, C. (2012, Dec 20), *E-filing of 2011 tax returns ends on Dec 31*, in *thesundaily*. Retreived from http://www.thesundaily.my/news/5659747.

[5] Azmi, A.C. and N.L. Bee, *The Acceptance of the e-Filing System by Malaysian Taxpayers: A Simplified Model.* Electronic Journal of e-Government, 2010. **8**(1): p. 13-22.

[6] Bernama. *IRB Notes 30 Per Cent Increase In E-Filing.* 2009 [cited 2011 31 May]; Available from: http://www.bernama.com/bernama//v3/news_lite.php?id=408209.

[7] Nations, U., *United Nations E-Government Survey 2012.* 2012, Department of Economic and Social Affairs: New york.

[8] Fatimah bt Alwi and L.M. Ling. *Embracing Electronic Tax Filing: Survey Evidence from Members of Malaysian Institute of Taxation.* in *International Accounting and Business Conference 2008.* 2008. Johor: Faculty of Business Management and Faculty of Accountancy, UiTM Johor.

[9] Lai, M.L. and K.F. Choong, *Motivators, Barriers and Concerns in Adoption of Electronic Filing System: Survey Evidence from Malaysian Professional Accountants.* American Journal of Applied Sciences, 2010. **7**(4): p. 562-567.

[10] Mayer, R.C., J.H. Davis, and F.D. Schoorman, *An integrative model of organizational trust.* The Academy of Management Review, 1995. **20**(3): p. 709-734.

[11] Pavlou, P.A., *Consumer acceptance of electronic commerce: Integrating trust and risk with the technology acceptance model.* International Journal of Electronic Commerce, 2003. **7**(3): p. 101-134.

[12] Hsu, L.C. and C.H. Wang, *A study of e-trust in online auctions.* Journal of Electronic Commerce Research, 2008. **9**(4): p. 310-321.

[13] Kim, D. and I. Benbasat, *Trust-related arguments in Internet stores: A framework for evaluation.* Journal of Electronic Commerce Research, 2003. **4**(2): p. 49-64.

[14] Belanger, F., J.S. Hiller, and W.J. Smith, *Trustworthiness in electronic commerce: the role of privacy, security, and site attributes.* The Journal of Strategic Information Systems, 2002. **11**(3): p. 245-270.

[15] Srivastava, S.C. and T. Teo. *Citizen trust development for e-government adoption: Case of Singapore.* in *Pacific Asia Conference on Information Systems (PACIS).* 2005: AIS Electronic Library (AISeL).

[16] Yousafzai, S.Y., J.G. Pallister, and G.R. Foxall, *A proposed model of e-trust for electronic banking.* Technovation, 2003. **23**(11): p. 847-860.

[17] Gefen, D., *E-commerce: the role of familiarity and trust.* The International Journal of Management Science 2000. **28**: p. 725-737.

[18] Carter, L. and F. Bélanger, *The utilization of e government services: citizen trust, innovation and acceptance factors**. Information Systems Journal, 2005. **15**(1): p. 5-25.

[19] Felix B. Tan and P. Sutherland, *Online Consumer Trust: A Multi-Dimensional Model.* Journal of Electronic Commerce in Organizations, 2004. **2**(3).

[20] McKnight, D.H., V. Choudhury, and C. Kacmar, *Developing and validating trust measures for e-commerce: An integrative typology.* Information systems research, 2003. **13**(3): p. 334-359.

[21] Mukherjee, A. and P. Nath, *Role of electronic trust in online retailing: a re-examination of the commitment-trust theory.* European Journal of Marketing, 2007. **41**(9/10): p. 1173-1202.

[22] Roca, J.C., J.J. García, and J.J. de la Vega, *The importance of perceived trust, security and privacy in online trading systems.* Information Management & Computer Security, 2009. **17**(2): p. 96-113.

[23] Jarvenpaa, S.L., N. Tractinsky, and L. Saarinen, *Consumer Trust in an Internet Store: A Cross-Cultural Validation.* Journal of Computer-Mediated Communication, 1999. **5**(2).

[24] McLeod, A. and S.E. Pippin. *Security and Privacy Trust in E-Government: Understanding System and Relationship Trust Antecedents.* in *42nd Hawaii International Conference on System Sciences.* 2009. Hawaii: IEEE.

[25] Hoffman, D.L., T.P. Novak, and M. Peralta, *Building consumer trust online.* Communications of the ACM, 1999. **42**(4): p. 80-85.

[26] Casaló, L.V., C. Flavián, and M. Guinalíu, *The role of security, privacy, usability and reputation in the development of online banking.* Online Information Review, 2007. **31**(5): p. 583-603.

[27] Yakov Bart, V.S., Fareena Sultan, & Glen L. Urban, *Are the drivers and role of online trust the same for all web sites and consumers? A large-scale exploratory*

empirical study. Journal of Marketing, 2005. **69**: p. 133-152.

[28] Poon, W.C., *Users' adoption of e-banking services: the Malaysian perspective.* Journal of Business & Industrial Marketing, 2007. **23**(1): p. 59-69.

[29] Lean, O.K., et al., *Factors influencing intention to use e-government services among citizens in Malaysia.* International Journal of Information Management, 2009. **29**(6): p. 458-475.

[30] Chang, I., *An empirical study on the impact of quality antecedents on tax payers' acceptance of Internet tax-filing systems.* Government Information Quarterly, 2005. **22**(3): p. 389-410.

[31] Pitt, L.F., R.T. Watson, and C.B. Kavan, *Service quality: a measure of information systems effectiveness.* MIS quarterly, 1995. **19**(2): p. 173-187.

[32] Jones, K. and L.N.K. Leonard, *Trust in consumer-to-consumer electronic commerce.* Information & Management, 2008. **45**(2): p. 88-95.

[33] Rai, A., S.S. Lang, and R.B. Welker, *Assessing the validity of IS success models: An empirical test and theoretical analysis.* Information systems research, 2002. **13**(1): p. 50.

[34] Chee-Wee, T., I. Benbasat, and R.T. Cenfetelli. *Building citizen trust towards e-government services: do high quality websites matter?* in *Hawaii International Conference on System Sciences, Proceedings of the 41st Annual.* 2008: IEEE.

[35] Islam, M.D.A., et al., *Factors affecting user satisfaction in the Malaysian income tax e-filing system.* African Journal of Business Management, 2012. **6**(21): p. 6447-6455.

[36] Wold, H., *Causal flows with latent variables: partings of the ways in the light of NIPALS modelling.* European Economic Review, 1974. **5**(1): p. 67-86.

[37] Wold, H., *Systems analysis by partial least squares.* Measuring the unmeasurable, 1985: p. 221-252.

[38] Ringle, C.M., S. Wende, and A. Will, *SmartPLS 2.0 M3.* University of Hamburg, 2005.

[39] Lim, K., et al., *Do I Trust You Online, and If So, Will I Buy? An Empirical Study of Two Trust-Building Strategies.* J. Manage. Inf. Syst., 2006. **23**(2): p. 233-266.

[40] Jarvenpaa, S.L., N. Tractinsky, and M. Vitale, *Consumer trust in an Internet store.* Inf. Technol. and Management, 2000. **1**(1-2): p. 45-71.

[41] Schurr, P.H. and J.L. Ozanne, *Influences on exchange processes: Buyers' preconceptions of a seller's trustworthiness and bargaining toughness.* Journal of Consumer Research, 1985: p. 939-953.

[42] Hair, J.F. and R.E. Anderson, *Multivariate data analysis.* 2010: Prentice Hall.

[43] Ramayah, T., J.W.C. Lee, and J.B.C. In, *Network collaboration and performance in the tourism sector.* Service Business, 2011: p. 1-18.

[44] Fornell, C. and D.F. Larcker, *Evaluating structural equation models with unobservable variables and measurement error.* Journal of Marketing Research, 1981: p. 39-50.

[45] Park, C.H. and Y.G. Kim, *Identifying key factors affecting consumer purchase behavior in an online shopping context.* International Journal of Retail & Distribution Management, 2003. **31**(1): p. 16-29.

[46] Shon, Z.-Y., F.-Y. Chen, and Y.-H. Chang, *Airline e-commerce: the revolution in ticketing channels.* Journal of Air Transport Management, 2003. **9**(5): p. 325-331.

[47] Novak, T.P., D.L. Hoffman, and Y.F. Yung, *Measuring the customer experience in online environments: A structural modeling approach.* Marketing Science, 2000. **19**(1): p. 22-42.

[48] MD. Aminul Islam, D.H.M.Y., Wan Sallha Yusoff and Atikah Nor Binti Johari, *Factors affecting user satisfaction in the Malaysian income tax e-filing system.* African Journal of Business Management, 2012. **6**(21): p. 6447-6455.

[49] Parasuraman, A., V.A. Zeithaml, and A. Malhotra, *ES-QUAL: a multiple-item scale for assessing electronic service quality.* Journal of Service Research, 2005. **7**(3): p. 213-233.

Automated Quickly Extracting Special Chemical Words for Food Security Problem

Liu Jinshuo[1], Yang Nanhai[2], Sun Chaonan[2!], Zhang Zhi[1], Yang wei[3], Zhang Yulong[1]

1. Computer Science School, Wuhan University, P. R. China

2. International School of Software, Wuhan University, P. R. China

3. Hu Bei Institute of Standardization, P. R. China

Abstract: Automated extracting Special Chemical Words (SCWs), is a key procedure of determining the food security problem. This paper proposes an approach combining statistical and our rule-based method, to automatically quickly extract the Special Chemical Words (SCWs) crawled from the internet. The method includes Chinese naming rule, pairwise rule, word segmentation, and statistics for Frequency of Likely-Token Comparison (FOLTC). The performance of the approach is evaluated by the real data set crawled from 5 the food-concerned websites. The accuracy is 89%.

Keywords: FOLTC; Chinese naming rule; Food safety;

1 Introduction

Currently, food safety issues have been more and more vital to Chinese people. Quickly discovering the food safety problem has become the challenging problem to regulatory authorities. With the rapid development of the internet, more information is disseminated online, so how to quickly determine the emerging new problem is very important from the massive data of the internet.

The basic procedure of our method of discovering the food security problems includes:

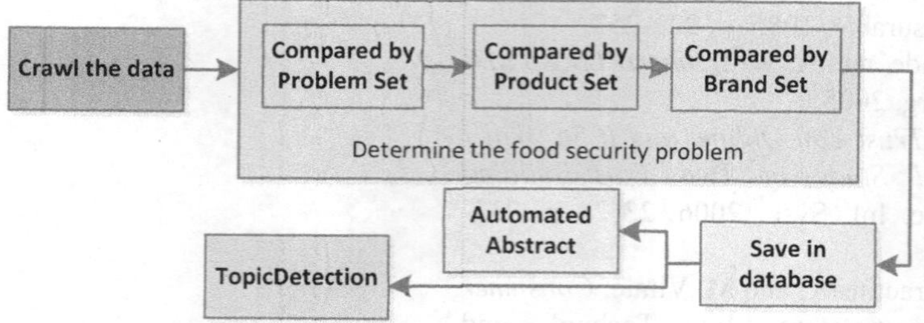

Figure 1. basic steps of food security problem discovering and summarizing

Firstly, crawl the target related data, and save as the file system; secondly, determine which saved files are food security problem concerned; thirdly, save the distilled data into database; fourthly, utilize the incremental cluster method to do the topic detection; finally, use the automated abstract technique to summarize and demonstrate the food security problem information. For determining the food security problem, we compare the crawled data by problems, products, and brands. The

This paper is supported project of Local defects in design and product management mechanism and information platform Funded by General Administration of Quality Supervision, Inspection and Quarantine of the People's Republic of China HBQTS_2011QK280

Correspondence author should be Sun Chaonan

problems are partially manually collected and partially automated extracted by our model. Automated quickly extracting SCWs are one part of expanding the problem dataset. But in general, SCWs are very hard to automatically quickly and correctly distill, as proper nouns include Chinese person names, place names and brand names etc.

At present, the United States, India, Japan and most of the advanced Europe countries have already done quantities of related researches aimed at Named Entity Recognition. MuktaMajumder[1], proposed a novel technique using the feature set and active learning to train the conditional random filed model, then corrected the low confident annotations by human supervision. The selected candidate features include word feature, affix feature, capitalization information, numerical feature and parts-of-speech information. Prof Jianhan Zhu[2], Victoria Uren and Enrico Motta presented a adapting method, developed a browser plug-in called ESpotter, which recognizes entities of various types on Web pages and highlights them. The plug-in can addresses the problem of certain domains by self-adapting lexicon and patterns to these domains. The Japanese expert TomoyaIwakura[3] used NE-related labels of words repeatedly from unlabeled data. It used the method's priority NEs—IREX to do the experiment. Recently, the domestic researches about Named-Entity extraction come to a booming period. Ying Chen[4] developed a robust web personal name information extraction system. Its main task is clustering and then extracting the attributions of the focus web person. Lin and Mei[5] applied their theory of Named-Entity extraction in TaoBao, based in the supervised method of product name entity recognition, the conditional random filed model, hidden markov model and maximum entropy mode have been utilized separately, and successfully recognized the proper name of products.

Previous approaches either built a name entity database, or only used static information from the published word segmentation. We built up the unsafe problems database with 2182 names. After matching real texts against this database, we found out that this approach cannot achieve a plausible result because of the following two reasons: (1) Current Chinese word segmentation system, is unable to update its database in time which leads to inappropriate segmentation. For example, "苯并芘" which English name is 'benzopyrene' , is splited into "苯", "并", and "芘" , when processed by word segmentation. This case has nothing to do with food safety. (2) The existing created problems databases need to be updated continuously as new things come out at any time on the Internet. As updating database demands a great deal of work, it will be unrealistic if operated manually.

Our method of automated extract the SCWs includes: ①. The problems database is built up based on the official food safety website. ②. Analyze the SCWs among the training set, then obtain the probability. ③. Construct a rule base, which contains the rules based on Chinese naming rule. ④. Select the candidates based upon the probability estimation token. ⑤. Confirm the candidates by applying Chinese naming rules. The system is tested on a real news corpus. The recall and precision are 11% and 91% respectively.

The structure of this paper: part 1 introduce the FOLTC; part 2 is the theoretical basis; part 3 gives the elaboration of our algorithm—FOLTC; part 4 demonstrate the result and analysis of the experiments; part 5 is the conclusion.

2. Backgrounds

2.1 Basic Concept

Concept 1: In any articles, we use "! ",", ","? ","。","; "Etc. as identifiers to split texts into sentences, and we define every sentence as **S**. If a text is represented as **T**, so $T=S_1S_2\cdots\cdots S_i\cdots\cdots S_n$[6,7]

Concept 2: In any sentences, we use FOLTC to split every sentence into tokens, and we define every token as Token. If a sentence is represented as **S**, so $S=Token_1Token_2\cdots\cdots Token_i\cdots\cdots Token_n$

Concept 3: In any Corpus, we call the times of a token presents as frequency, which can be expressed by a function ***f(token).***

Concept 4: Updating problem database automatically by adding emerging things which leads to unsafe food problems, using the FOLTC algorithm, which is defined as **Auto-Expanding Problem Database.**

3. The FOLTC Model

3.1. Automatically discovering the SWCs according to Chinese Name Rule

According to Chinese naming rules, in most cases, the similar of name entity is named by the same suffix. For example: ①Define "what "+ "**token including**"剂" as a kind of special chemistry word. ②Segment the Chinese word, and select the adjacent words from right to left starting with **'token including '剂' "**, which is called "**Token**"（Refer to fig 2）. ③Put the recognized unsafe problems into database. ④Analyze the sentence including '**Token**' in the database which has nothing to do with food safety at the end of the first round. If the only string "**Token**" is split, and count the consecutive tokens in front of the "**Token**", and count its number as **n**. It comes out three expressions.

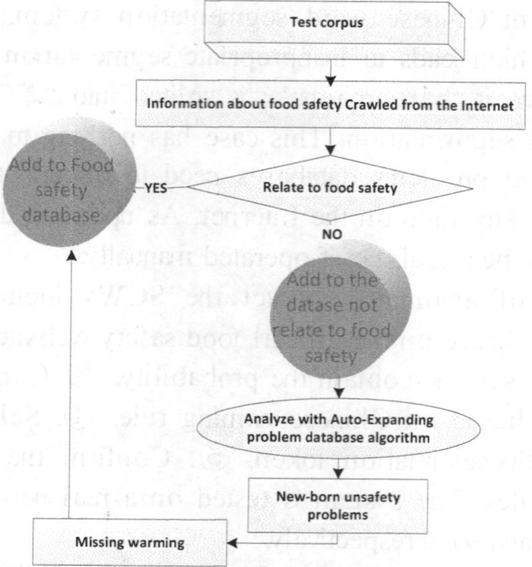

Figure 2: Statistics-based and Rules-based Algorithm Flow Chart

$$S=\{Token_n, Token_{n-1}, Toke_{n-2}, \cdots\cdots, Token_1\} \quad (3.1)$$
$$NewToken_1=Token+Token_1 \quad (3.2)$$
$$NewToken_n=NewToken_{n-1}+Token_{.n}(n>1) \quad (3.3)$$

Takee the first token "$Token_1$" adjacent to the token "**Token**", if ***f(Token)*** equals ***f(NewToken₁)***, then take the second token "$Token_2$" adjacent to the token "$Token_1$", and compare the value of $\boldsymbol{f(NewToken_1)}$ and $\boldsymbol{f(NewToken_2)}$. If $\boldsymbol{f(NewToken_1)}$ equals $\boldsymbol{f(NewToken_2}$, then keep extracting the previous token and comparing the value of $\boldsymbol{f(NewToken_{j-1})}$ and $\boldsymbol{f(NewToken_j)}$. If the value of $\boldsymbol{f(NewToken_{j-1})}$and $\boldsymbol{f(NewToken_j)}$ **are not equal,** then we think that " $NewToken_{j-1}$ "is a new-born food which need to be added into the database.

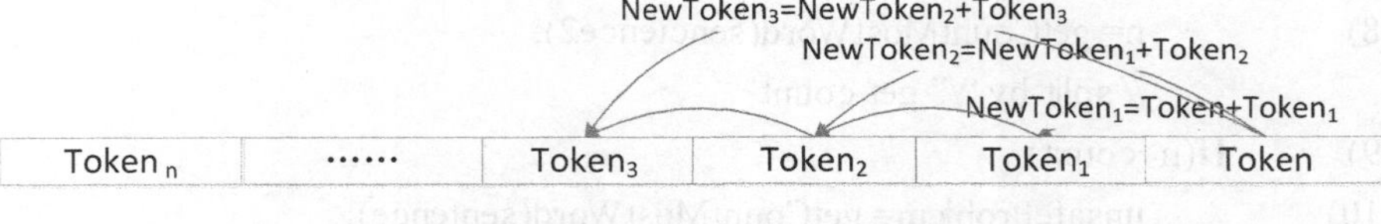

Figure3: Example of Name Entity Parsing

Function AutoAddProblems1(T)

(1) foodName=null;

(2) count=0;

(3)**FOR** each sentence S_i in the T **DO**

(4) **IF** food token is contained in the sentence **DO**

(5) n= getCountMostWord(senctence); //split by "/" get count

(6) **If**(n>count)

(7) foodName= getCountMostWord(sentence);//split by "/" get Name

(8)**ENDFOR**

(9)**Return** foodName+food token;

3.2. Compensated with Pairwise Rule

Extract sentences which including tokens from the unsafe problems database, which means that there are probably unsafe tokens such as harmful chemicals. So it comes out that if a word split into several tokens, every two adjacent token's times present in the article is absolutely equal. Take two tokens which are adjacent to each other as a new token.

$$S=\{Token_1, Token_2, Token_3, \cdots\cdots, Token_n\} \quad (3.2)$$
$$NewToken_{m-1}=Token_{m-1}+Token_m \quad (3.3)$$

Figure out $\boldsymbol{f(NewToken_{m-1})}$, which are compared in pairwise comparison. If $\boldsymbol{f(NewToken_{m-1})}$, $\boldsymbol{f(NewToken_m)}$ are two equal terms, and $\boldsymbol{f(NewToken_{j-1})}$ equals $\boldsymbol{f(NewToken_j)}$**,but** $\boldsymbol{f(NewToken_{m-1})}$ bigger than $\boldsymbol{f(NewToken_i)}$, then we take the biggest value. (See fig 3)

$$(Token_{m-1}+Token_m+Token_{m+1}) \quad (3.4)$$

One new unsafe problem token should be added into the unsafe problems database.

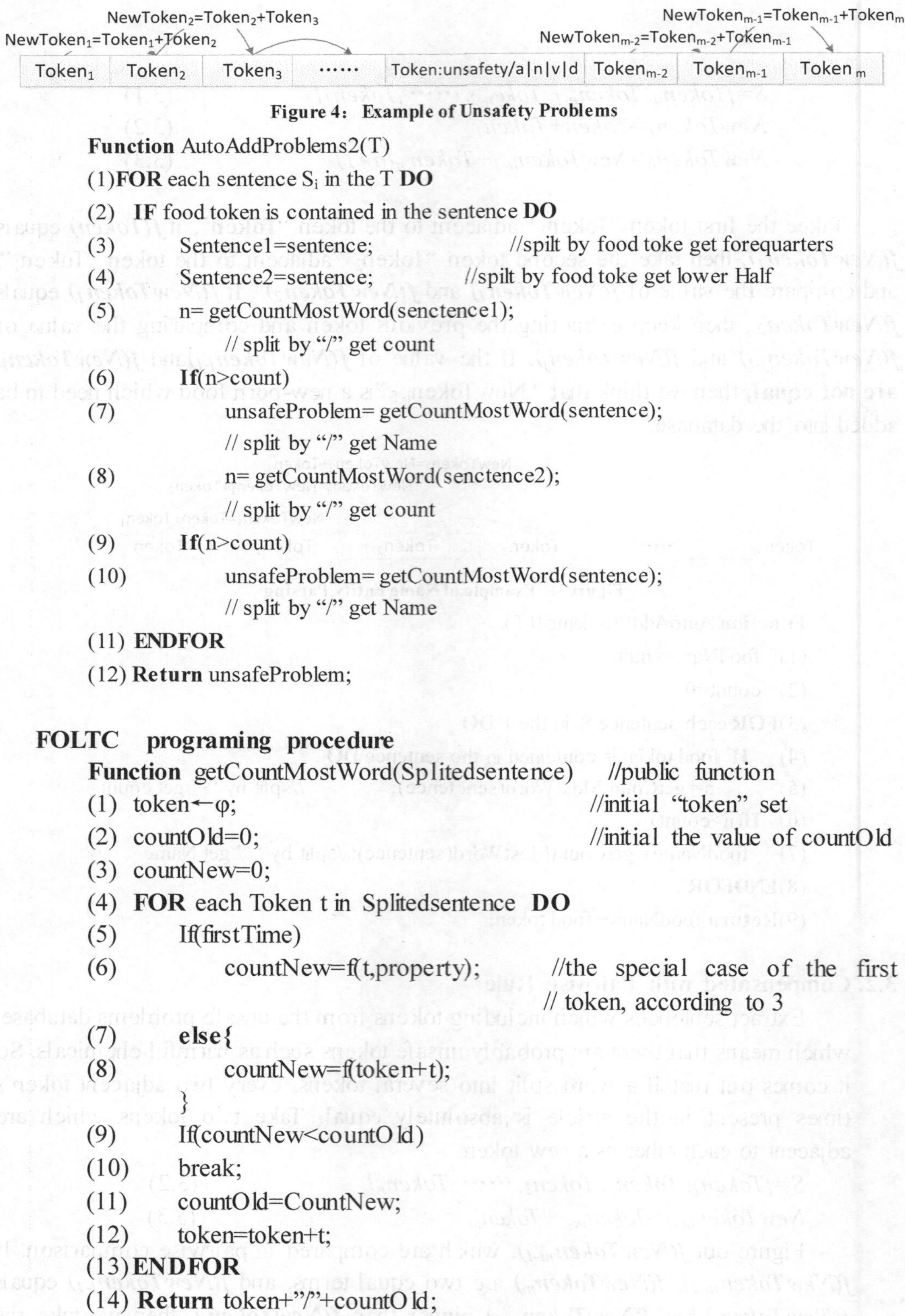

Figure 4: Example of Unsafety Problems

```
Function AutoAddProblems2(T)
FOR each sentence Si in the T DO
  IF food token is contained in the sentence DO
     Sentence1=sentence;          //spilt by food toke get forequarters
     Sentence2=sentence;       //spilt by food toke get lower Half
     n= getCountMostWord(senctence1);
          // split by "/" get count
     If(n>count)
          unsafeProblem= getCountMostWord(sentence);
          // split by "/" get Name
          n= getCountMostWord(senctence2);
          // split by "/" get count
     If(n>count)
          unsafeProblem= getCountMostWord(sentence);
          // split by "/" get Name
ENDFOR
Return unsafeProblem;
```

FOLTC programing procedure

```
Function getCountMostWord(Splitedsentence)   //public function
token←φ;                                     //initial "token" set
countOld=0;                                  //initial the value of countOld
countNew=0;
FOR each Token t in Splitedsentence DO
     If(firstTime)
          countNew=f(t,property);      //the special case of the first
                                       // token, according to 3
     else{
          countNew=f(token+t);
     }
     If(countNew<countOld)
     break;
     countOld=CountNew;
     token=token+t;
ENDFOR
Return token+"/"+countOld;
```

4. Experiments

①Firstly, utilize the database having nothing to do with food safety. ②Then, filter out sentences about food safety in the database after processed by the FOLTC which proves the missing warning. ③Count the number of the sentences of database concerned with food safety. ④Figure out the Remedial rate. Remedial rate is the core parameter of the FOLTC's function. The lager the value of the Remedial rate, the more efficient the FOLTC is.

The following is an example of automatic recognition of unsafe problems token:

- **Original text:** 被检验出致癌物质苯并芘。
- **Segmented text:** 被($Token_1$)/ 检验($Token_2$)/ 出($Token_3$)/ 致癌($Token_4$)/ 物质($Token_5$)/ 苯($Token_6$)/ 并($Token_8$)/ 芘($Token_9$)
- **New combined token:** 被检验($NewToken_1$)/检验出($NewToken_2$)/物质苯($NewToken_3$)/苯并($NewToken_4$)/并芘($NewToken_5$)

Table 1: Automatic Recognition of Unsafe Problems Token in Real News

Unsafe problems token(Token)	Frequency of the $NewToken_1$	Frequency of the $NewToken_2$	Frequency of the $NewToken_3$	Frequency of the $NewToken_4$	Frequency of the $NewToken_5$
致癌	1	1	2	6	6

Because the value of $f(NewToken_4)$ equals $f(NewToken_5)$, as described in the 3.2 .so we can figure out that ($Token_4$+ $Token_5$ +$Token_6$) which is namely "苯并芘" in this example, is new unsafe problem which should be added into Unsafe Problem database.

The testing corpus consists of the articles are crawled from the official food safety websites: http://www.xinhuanet.com/food/, http://www.cfqn.com.cn/, http://shipin.people.com.cn/, http://pc.39.net/sp/ (websites), http://t.qq.com/zhangwuji9/ (twitter). After the corpus is tagged by initial recognition module, 17436 food news, 789 brand names and 173 unsafe problems are recognized, among which 718 brand names are correct, boundary-error are 12%, entirely incorrect 51, meanwhile there are 20 names cannot be recognized. Then, we apply the FOLTC to process these unrecognized names, and 16 names are recognized. Finally, the recall and precision obtained are 89%and 12% respectively.

Some errors cannot be overcome by the system. We ignore the special cases because of the unfamiliar naming way. The proposed proposal is based on statistics. We may take normal tokens as candidates, such as automatic recognition of unsafe problems. We count two groups with same value, which one holds a new-born unsafe problem, while the other does not. The latter case may lead to information redundancy warning.

5. Conclusion

This paper introduces FOLTC's application background, algorithm's content, and test analysis. The experimental results show that the combination of statistical and rule-based techniques is effective and efficient in the automatic recognition of SCWs for unsafe problems. As updating database manually demands a great deal of work and is inefficient. In addition, imperfect statistics may cause low accuracy. So FOLTC will win popularity. The FOLTC is not only oriented for SWCs of food safety test, but also for auto field such as garment industry etc. According to special Chinese naming rules, imperfect Chinese word segmentation, and continuously updated database, FOLTC will be developed into any auto-update database. To increase the accuracy of recognizing candidates and develop rules with word similarity will be our future work.

6. References

[1] MuktaMajumder*, Utsav Barman, Rahul Prasad, Kumar Saurabh, Sujan Kumar Saha.A Novel Technique for Name Identification from HomeopathyDiagnosis Discussion Forum.2nd International Conference on Communication, Computing & Security [ICCCS-2012]

[2] Jianhan Zhu, Victoria Uren, Enrico Motta.Espotter:adaptive named entity recognition for web browing. Professional Knowledge Management :Lecture Notes in Computer Science Volume 3782, 2005, pp 518-529

[3] TomoyaIwakura. A Named Entity Extraction Using Word Information Repeatedly Collected from Unlabeled Data.Computational Linguistics and Intelligent Text Processing. Lecture Notes in Computer Science Volume 6008, 2010, pp 212-223.

[4] Ying Chen, Sophia Yat Mei Lee, Chu-Ren Huang.A robust web personal name information extraction system .Expert Systems with Applications Volume 39, Issue 3, 15 February 2012, Pages 2690 – 2699

[5] Feng Mei, Researches of product name entity recognition and normalization. Master's thesis, Language technology processing center of Harbin Institute of Technology, 2011.

[6] Weisong Zuo. Studies on Sentiment Analysis of Chapter Based on Rule and Statistics. *Computer Software and Theory College of Information and Engineering.* 2010.5

[7] ZHU Yan-lan, MIN Jin, ZHOU Ya-qian, HUANG Xuan-jing,WU Li-de. Semantic Orientation Computing Based on HowNet. *Department of Computer Science and Technology , Fudan University.* 2005.5

SESSION

E-BUSINESS, E-COMMERCE, E-BANKING, ENTERPRISE INFORMATION SYSTEMS, AND SECURITY

Chair(s)

TBA

Consumers' knowledge acquisition through eWOM: from social networks to retailing

Eleonora Pantano
Department of Mechanical, Energetics and Management Engineering
University of Calabria
Arcavacata di Rende (CS), Italy
eleonora.pantano@unical.it

Piero Migliarese
Department of Mechanical, Energetics and Management Engineering
University of Calabria
Arcavacata di Rende (CS), Italy
piero.migliarese@unical.it

Vincenzo Corvello
Department of Mechanical, Energetics and Management Engineering
University of Calabria
Arcavacara di Rende (CS), Italy
vincenzo.corvello@unical.it

Abstract—**Due to the large diffusion of social networks, these media offer a huge platform where users share judgements, comments and opinions that organization could exploit for achieving information on consumers' preferences and market trends, with benefits for the development of more effective marketing strategies. In particular, this paper focuses on the use of Facebook among youth, with emphasis on consumers' knowledge of social network as influencing factor on their interest towards others' posts and on the use of the medium for directly interacting with the firms. Hence, this work aims at deeply understanding how this medium can be used for acquiring knowledge on clients emerging from both the consumer-to-consumer and consumer-to-business interactions, and transferring this knowledge in products/services.**

Keywords—knowledge acquisition, knowledge management, eWOM (e-word of mouth communication), social networks, retailing

I. INTRODUCTION

Past studies identified the critical role of knowledge acquisition for the success of an organization [1]. Similarly, the knowledge acquisition of consumers is a fundamental factor for business profitability, by developing new and effective retail strategies. In this scenario, previous researches highlighted the pervasive impact of social networks like Facebook by affecting organizational and marketing strategies, social and educational process, research, etc. [2], due to their ability to provide efficient e-business platforms, research and education networks, direct channel between client and vendors, social communities, etc. [2].

From a consumers' perspective, they use this interactive channel for expressing opinions, accessing others' comments, asking suggestions and recommendations. Due to the extensive use of this channel for retrieving information and posting observations and judgements especially by youth [3], organizations might exploit social networks like Facebook for acquiring knowledge on consumers' preferences and market trends. For instance, this channel is dramatically changing the tourism industry, which usually involves the purchase of intangible (e.g. tourism packages) and unknown products (e.g. possible future tourism destinations), by proposing new way for promoting localities and supporting cultural heritage [3].

Hence, on the one hand the online posts show the popularity level of products and brands, on the other these comments represent a review of the current marketing strategies and the level of consumers' satisfaction. In this way, the online consumer-to-consumer interactions provide recommendations and advise on a huge number of current firms/services/products, while the consumer-to-business interaction shows clients' evaluations of the current firm's product/service [4] [5] [6]. In particular, these interactions are part of the eWOM (electronic word of mouth communication) and represent an informal way of communication through the electronic channel, which consumers perceive as more trustworthy and persuasive than traditional media such as television or newspapers [7] [8] [9].

Since the information retrieved online support the decision-making process held offline [10], the interactions among consumers are able to influence consumers' buying decision and purchasing behaviour also while consumers are physically in the point of sale, by affecting especially client' confidence with the recommended product [7] [11]. For these reasons, many firms solicit consumers' positive reviews to encourage other users. Although consumers take into account the rate of the products available online, they pay attention more to the full comments posted by others to collect more detailed information before the choice [7].

The aim of this paper is to investigate how social networks like Facebook may be considered a powerful source for acquiring knowledge on consumers' behaviours for the development of more efficient strategies, and how this knowledge can be transferred in retail strategies. To achieve this goal, the research focuses on consumers' knowledge of social network as influencing factor on their interest towards others' posts, and on the use of the medium for directly interact with firms, with emphasis on the contents of consumers' posts. In this way, it is possible to deeply understand to what extent this medium can be used for acquiring knowledge on clients emerging from both the consumer-to-consumer and consumer-to-business interactions.

In particular, the first part of the paper is devoted to the use of eWOM (electronic word of mouth communication) as knowledge source for business purposes, while the second one employs a qualitative research involving consumers' knowledge of social networks, their attitude towards posting online judgements and complains for firms, their interest towards others' posts, and their specific attention towards such elements of the comments.

II. Theoretical Background

Consumers' needs have been largely recognized as a driver for the efficient product innovation. Thus, consumers' knowledge acquisition plays a critical role especially for developing new successful strategies [12]. Despite the important role of knowledge sharing in innovation process, developers' and consumers' viewpoint may be different. For this reason, efficient methods and technologies for measuring and achieving information on customers' preferences are compulsory for business profitability. Despite the large usage of questionnaires for this purpose [13], many current studies are focusing on the adoption of new and more efficient techniques for acquiring a large amount of helpful users' creative contribution [14] [15] [16]. In this context, different and more interactive methods might be able to solicit consumers' ideas and access also to a so-called tacit knowledge, which has a critical importance for achieving competitive advantages.

Social networks offer a new platform able to provide data on consumers' behaviour and preferences constantly updated and detailed. In fact, consumers take care of updating their profile, sharing their preferences or the new experiences, creating lists of interests, and suggesting products and brands. Hence, this media brings together large communities of consumers, who spontaneously exchange knowledge [17]. Users' comments are intended to communicate pieces of information to other individuals. However, they are available in a written form that firms can exploit for learning about users' interests, opinions and behaviours, as well as for predicting market trends. In fact, existing literature has often focused on the possibility to exploit users comments, reviews and discussions as a source of knowledge on products and brands [18] [19] [20]. This information can be then converted into knowledge on market for developing customized products and marketing campaigns, targeting extant products and services, etc. [20]. Furthermore, from social networks also consumers can obtain knowledge on products and on the business that produces them [21]. On the one hand, they seek knowledge from other consumers, which are perceived as a more reliable source compared to vendors [6] [22]; on the other one, they seek firm's news concerning launching new product, services, reward campaigns, etc..

The role of eWOM has been found to be growing in the Internet shopping sector [23]. Although eWOM can be considered a sort of word-of-mouth communication held online, it has peculiarities that go beyond the potentialities of traditional word-of-mouth: it is quicker, involves larger numbers of people and can be stored, aggregated and analysed more efficiently [3] [8]. For instance, concerning consumer-to-consumer know-how exchanges, it has been found that this interaction has a direct relationship with loyalty intentions, as well as an indirect relationship with the overall value of firm's offering [24]. The number of available comments can be very large and their quality variable, in terms of quality and quantity of the posts (i.e. some opinion are expressed with more words, others with just a couple, others with a rate, etc.), and presence of provocative suggestions or insult [25] [26]. For instance, customers exploit the eWOM to acquire knowledge and information especially when they want to purchase risky, intangible products or unknown items, such as in the case of booking a hotel or choosing the destination of the next holiday [3]. Other studies have found that low involvement users tends to conform to eWOM both when it is negative and positive, while high involvement users tend to conform only in the case of negative reviews [27]. Negative eWOM can be considered as a negative statement concerning a certain product or organization widely available through Internet [28] [29] [30]. Consumers usually pay more attention to negative reviews than to positive ones, because they consider the negative ones more informative [29] [31]. Since negative eWOM provides valuable information [32], it can be considered a further opportunity for organizations to acquire knowledge made available on social networks for improving the current products/strategies, and achieve an evaluation on the current products and strategies. Hence, while positive eWOM collects consumers' positive considerations of product/firm characteristics and desires for developing new products, negative eWOM provides a detailed evaluation of the existing ones for improving the actual offer.

From a marketing and management perspective, extant research has studied eWOM from several points of view: motivation to post online, information searching and sharing process and decision-making process. The point of view of organizations and vendors, instead, is still under-investigated. The literature still misses detailed studies on the impact of social networks from an organizational perspective. Although some authors have found that an organization's experience with social media influences its attitude towards eWOM and negative eWOM [8], there is still a gap in literature concerning firms' behaviours, perceptions and reaction towards consumers' reviews [33]. Despite the growing body of literature on social networks like Facebook and on eWOM, the point of view of organizations' with emphasis on the eWOM as a source of knowledge on costumers has not been addressed in previous studies, as well as the research on the use of eWOM for extracting knowledge on consumers is still in progress.

III. Methodology of Research

This paper aims at investigating how to acquire knowledge on consumers' needs and opinions for marketing purposes through their interaction within social networks like Facebook. To achieve this goal, we evaluated consumers' interest towards others' posts and their attitude towards posting comments directed to firms with personal judgements on products and services, with emphasis on the contents of these posts. In particular, the research involved 507 subjects randomly recruited in Italy between November and December 2012 (242 male and 265 female). Participants were asked to fill an anonymous questionnaire concerning their usage of social networks. We chose a qualitative approach because it is particularly effective in exploring the consumers' attitude, experiences and responses by identifying the issues that are the most meaningful for consumers [34].

The age group is composed of 217 respondents younger than 25 years, 200 between 26 and 35 years old, and 91 respondents older than 36 years. 294 of them got a secondary school qualification, while 174 fort a Master Degree and 37 a PhD or a post-degree qualification.

Each interview has been coded and performed through the MaxQda software for a content analysis, which allowed evaluating users' response. This investigation is mainly based on consumers' knowledge of social networks as factor influencing their usage of the media for retrieving and sharing information. In particular, we consider this aspect as an influencing factor of both consumers-to-consumers interaction and consumers-to-business interaction through Facebook.

IV. KEY RESULTS

The analysis identifies how consumers consider their knowledge of social networks including Facebook, Twitter, Instagram, etc.. The first analysis aims at investigating the knowledge of social networks and their usage for sharing experiences, posting comments, accessing information from others' judgments, and directly complaining/interacting with firms on services and products. 37 respondents stated to have a scarce knowledge of web 2.0, 190 a sufficient knowledge and 280 a good knowledge; 107 never used social networks for directly interacting with firms, by complaining or suggesting improvements about a certain product/service; 316 used these channels for these purposes at least once, and 84 used more than 5 times; 116 had a scarce interest towards others' comments, 232 had a sufficient interest towards others' comments and 159 had a good interest towards others' comments. Furthermore, the findings indicate that 32 respondents have no knowledge of social networks, 190 have a sufficient knowledge, and 280 have a good knowledge.

A subsequent contingent analysis investigates the evaluation of association structure between consumers' knowledge of these media and their attitude to use the media for directly interacting with firms (Table 1); and the association between the knowledge of social networks and consumers' interest towards others' comments (Table 2), which occurred in each interview.

TABLE I. CONSUMER-TO-BUSINESS INTERACTION THROUGH SOCIAL NETWORKS BY KNOWLEDGE OF SOCIAL NETWORKS (IN ONE YEAR)

	At least once	More than 5 times
No knowledge	2%	1%
Sufficient knowledge	25%	4%
Good knowledge	32%	11%

TABLE II. CONSUMER-TO-CONSUMER INTERACTION THROUGH SOCIAL NETWORKS BY KNOWLEDGE OF SOCIAL NETWORKS

	No interest in others' post	Sufficient interest	Good interest
No knowledge	4%	-	7%
Sufficient knowledge	-	20%	1%
Good knowledge	-	24%	22%

V. DISCUSSION AND CONCLUSIONS

Since past studies demonstrated the possibility to influence consumers' purchasing decisions especially for people who make an extensive use of the media [3], this study enlarges these results, by providing important insights for deeply understanding to what extent social networks like Facebook may be considered a powerful source for acquiring knowledge on consumers behaviours that could be transferred in retailing. The central question of this work is whether firms can learn about market and future trends (on the basis of consumers' characteristics and preferences) when a large amount of information is available, and use this knowledge to evolve a successful direct-marketing strategy, with emphasis on retail aspects (e.g. how and what distributes, end-users, etc.).To achieve this goal, the research involved 507 subjects, by focusing on a questionnaire devoted to investigate consumers' knowledge of social network as influencing factor, their interest towards others' posts, and the use of the medium for directly interact with firms.

In particular, our findings show the large use of experienced consumers' social networks as (i) source of knowledge on products/brands/firms by taking note of others' comments, and (ii) tool for sharing knowledge with other potential consumers, in accordance with past studies that identified the important role of consumers' behaviour while interacting with an online social platform [3] [4] [5] [6]. These results suggest to what extent the previous knowledge of the media influences' consumers' effective usage for retrieving information. Noteworthy finding concerns the usage of social networks also by users with a scarce knowledge from a consumer-to-business point of view, by showing that the usage increases with the experience with the social network, but also people with a scarce experience used the medium for commenting products/brands on the firm/product page: the 2% of users with no knowledge used at least once and the 1% used more than 5 times. Similarly, from a consumer-to-consumer perspective, also people with no experience shows a good interest in others' posts (7%), even if this interest changes with the experience with the medium. The findings are consistent with Pantano and Corvello [8] who demonstrated that the experience changes the firm's reaction towards online comments/posts, in the context of negative eWOM.

Hence, these results show that, even if consumers have a scarce knowledge of social networks, they use the medium and this usage increases with the increasing of knowledge. The presence of comments of experiences and not-experienced users would prompt firms to pay more attention to comments posted online, both in case of consumer-to-consumer interaction and in case of consumer-to-business interaction. Furthermore, we expect that the usage of this medium for this purpose will increase with the diffusion of Internet ubiquitous access (i.e. the reducing cost of smartphone and internet connection increases the Internet access anywhere and anytime).

Hence, our results provide some useful indications on the content of the knowledge shared during the consumer-to-business interactions. In fact, consumers' post directed to firms contain mainly complaining, which consists of a detailed judgement related to (i) a malfunctioning of the service, (ii) a malfunctioning of the product, (iii) a wrong (broken) service/product, (iv) dissatisfaction concerning firm's behaviour, and (v) request for a different service/product. Since the social networks allow storing consumers' comments, firms are able to collect a large amount of comments (by focusing on the most recent ones) and investigating through content analysis software for achieving a detailed evaluation of the current product/service, and of their expectations. In fact, the current client's dissatisfaction includes the expectation of a different (better) product/service, which can become the starting point for developing a new product/service or enhancing the existing one.

For these reasons, in the one hand firms should take into account all the comments posted on their *virtual walls* for understanding both the elements that consumers like more and the ones that they dislike; in the other they should pay more attention on the posts devoted to other users to understand the main characteristic of a product/service that attract consumers' attention. Hence, all these elements are able to affect the marketing strategies and the organizational process, as anticipated by previous studies [2] [8], for instance by considering the possibility to develop the role of expert of social networks and eWOM communications for deeply understanding consumers evaluations and perception, and proposing improving and corrections of current strategies. In this way, the firm would be ready to efficiently manage the large amount of information available online, and fast reply to consumers' changeable needs and preferences, as well as to predict the new trends.

Furthermore, the eWOM communication seems to be more useful for extracting knowledge on consumers' preferences than the standard questionnaire that firms would submit for directly asking consumers' opinion. In fact, one of the benefits of the eWOM is that it has the characteristics of informal communication able to solicit subjects' spontaneity and sincerity [17] [25] [26] [32]. This spontaneity is able to involve more people in discussions for proving different points of views and more information, by involving a huge number of active participants [14] [15] [16], with benefits for the reliability and validity of the achieved information. Through the our analysis of the ways which consumers use social network and contribute to evaluating firms' activity, the results might be considered a first step towards enabling online strategic learning with numerous, frequent and sparse consumers' information by the firms.

VI. FutureWorks

Future works could improve our findings, by employing quantitative research and Structural Equation Model analysis for testing the value of the relationships emerging in our study (consumers' knowledge of these media and their attitude to use the media for directly interacting with firms; and the knowledge of social networks and consumers' interest towards others' comments) and the effective impact on innovation process and retailing.

Due to the increasing importance of consumers' eWOM through Facebook from both a client and vendor point of view, future applications concerning retailing would explore the possibility to integrate the social networks like Facebook directly in the point of sale, by investigating to what extent this integration could influence the decision-making process and the subsequent purchasing behavior. Further research question will focus on to what extent eWOM and online interaction (through social networks) (i) will substitute the traditional face-to-face interactions in retail domain, (ii) will dramatically change the social experience linked to shopping activity, and (iii) will modify the traditional client-vendor relationship, in terms of consumers' requests of vendor opinion about a certain product.

References

[1] V. Corvello, and P. Migliarese, "Learning and knowledge and knowledge substitution: two approaches to knowledge acquisition in geographically distributed organizations", in the 10th World Multi-Conference on Systemics, Cybernetics and Informatics, vol. 6, pp. 260-265, 2006.

[2] F.J. Garrigos-Simon, R. Lapiedra Alcami, and T. Barbera Ribera, "Social networks and web 3.0: their impact on the management and marketing of organization", Management Decision, vol. 50 no. 10, pp. 1880-1890, 2012.

[3] L. Di Pietro, and E. Pantano, "An empirical investigation of social network infl uence on consumer purchasing decision: The case of Facebook", Journal of Direct, Data and Digital Marketing Practice, vol. 14 no. 1, pp. 18-29, 2012.

[4] T. Hogg, "Inferring preference correlations from social networks", Electronic Commerce Research and Applications, vol. 9 no. 1, pp. 29-37, 2009.

[5] O. Hinz, C. Schulze, and C. Takac, "New product adoption in social networks: Why direction matters", Journal of Business Research, in press.

[6] N. Archak, A. Ghose, and P. Ipeirotis, "'Show me the money!': Deriving the pricing power of product features by mining consumer reviews" , in the 13th ACM International Conference on Knowledge Discovery and Data Mining, pp. 56 – 65, 2007.

[7] S. Utz, P. Kerkhof, and J. van den Bos, "Consumers rule: how consumer reviews influence perceived trustworthiness of online stores", Electronic Commerce Research and Applications, vol. 11 no. 1, pp. 49-58, 2012.

[8] E. Pantano and V. Corvello, "The impact of experience on companies' reaction to negative comments on social networks", Journal of Direct, Data and Digital Marketing Practice, in press.

[9] C.M.K. Cheung, and D.R. Thadani D.R., "The impact of electronic word-of-mouth communication: a literature analysis and integrative model", Decision Support Systems, vol. 54 no. 1, pp. 461-470, 2012.

[10] Y.Y.Y. Chan, and E.W.T. Ngai, "Conceptualising electronic word of mouth activity: An input-process-output perspective", Marketing Intelligence & Planning, vol. 29 no. 5, pp. 488-516, 2011.

[11] J. Harris, P. Gupta, "'You should buy this one!'" The influence of online recommendations on product attitudes and choice confidence, International Journal of Electronic Marketing and Retailing, vol. 2 no. 2, pp. 176-189, 2008.

[12] J. Hauser, G.J. Tells, and A. Griffin, "Research on innovation: a review and agenda for Marketing Science", vol. 25 no. 6, pp. 687-717, 2006.

[13] J. Casillas, and L. Sanchez, "Knowledge extraction from fuzzy data for estimating consumer behavior models", in the IEEE International Conference on Fuzzy Systems, pp. 164-170, 2006.

[14] L.B. Jappesen, "User toolkits for innovation: consumers support each other", Journal of Product Innovation Management, vol. 22 no. 4, pp. 347-362, 2005.

[15] R. Greer, and D. Lei, "Collaborative innovation with customers: a review of the literature and suggestions for future research", International Journal of Management Reviews, vol. 14, pp. 63-84, 2012.

[16] J. Fuller, K. Hutter, and R. Fullant, "Why co-creation experience matters? Creative experience and its impact on the quantity and quality of creative contributions", R&D Managements, vol. 41 no. 3, pp.259-273, 2011.

[17] K. De Valck, van Bruggen G.H, and B. Wierenga, "Virtual communities: a marketing perspective", Decision Support Systems, vol. 47 no. 3, pp. 185-203, 2009.

[18] M. Cha, A. Mislove, and K.P. Gummadi, "A measurement-driven analysis of information propagation in the Flickr social network", in the 18th ACM World Wide Web Conference Committee, pp. 721-730, 2009.

[19] S. Tirunillai, and G.J. Tellis, "Does chatter really matter? Dynamics of user-generate content and stock performance", Marketing Science, vol. 31 no. 2, pp. 198-215, 2012.

[20] A. Messenger, and J. Whittle, "Recommendations based on user-generated comments in social media", in the IEEE International Conference on Privacy, Security, Risk and Trust and International Conference on Social Computing; pp. 505-508, 2011.

[21] N. Archak, A. Ghose, A., and P. Ipeirotis, "Deriving the pricing power of product features by mining consumer reviews", Management Science, vol. 57 no. 8, pp. 1485-1509, 2011.

[22] X. Dou, J.A. Walden, J.A., S. Lee, J.Y. and Lee, "Does source matter? Examining source effects in online product reviews", Computers in Human Behavior, vol. 28 no. 5, pp. 1555-1563, 2012.

[23] P. Cheol, W. Yao, Y. Ying, and R.K. You, "Factors Influencing eWOM Effects: Using Experience, Credibility, and Susceptibility", International Journal of Social Science and Humanity, vol. 1, no. 1, 2011.

[24] T.W. Gruen, T. Osmonbekov, and A.J. Czaplewski, "eWOM: the impact of customer-tocustomer online know-how exchange oncustomer value and loyalty", Journal of Business Research, vol. 59 no.4, 449–56, 2006.

[25] M.P. O'Mahony, and B. Smyth, B. (2010) "A classification-based review recommender", Knowledge-Based Systems, vol. 23, pp. 323-329, 2010.

[26] E. Agichtein, C. Castillo, D. Donato, A. Gionis, and G. Mishne, "Finding high-quality content in social media", in the ACM International Conference on Web Search and Web Data Mining, pp.183-194, 2008.

[27] J. Lee, D.Y. Park, and I. Han, "The effect of negative online consumer reviews on product attitude: An information processing view", Electronic Commerce Research and Applications, vol. 7, no. 3, 341-352, 2008.

[28] T. Hennig-Thurau, K.P. Gwinner, G. Walsh, and D.D. Gremler, "Electronic Word-of-Mouth via Consumer-Opinion Platforms: What motivates Consumers to Articulate themselves on the Internet?", Journal of Interactive Marketing, vol. 18 no.1, pp.38-52, 2004.

[29] S. Bambauer-Sachse, and S. Mangold, "Brand equity dilution through negative online word-of-mouth communication", Journal of Retailing and Consumer Services, vol. 18, pp. 38-45, 2011.

[30] C. Vasquez, "Complaints online: the case of TripAdvisor", Journal of Pragmatics, vol. 43, pp. 1707-1717, 2011.

[31] S. Sen, and D. Lerman, "An examination into negative consumer reviews on the web", Journal of Interactive Marketing, vol. 21 no. 4, pp. 76-94, 2007.

[32] D. Schmallegger, and D. Carson, "Blogs in tourism: Changing approaches to information exchange", Journal of Vacation Marketing, vol. 14, pp. 99-110, 2008.

[33] A. Munzel, B. Jahn, and W.H. Kunz, "The power of saying sorry-insights on customer service in new media online channels", in the 12th International Research Conference in Service Managements, 2012.

[34] S. Sofaer, "Qualitative research methods", International Journal for Quality in Health Care, vol. 14 no. 4, pp. 329-336, 2002.

For Your Eyes Only – Biometric Protection of PDF Documents

J. Siciarek[1], M. Smiatacz[1], and B. Wiszniewski[1]
[1]Dept. of Intelligent Interactive Systems, Faculty of ETI, Gdansk University of Technology, Gdansk, Poland

Abstract— *The paper introduces a concept of a digital document content encryption/decryption with facial biometric data coming from a legitimate user. Access to the document content is simple and straightforward, especially during collaborative work with mobile devices equipped with cameras. Various contexts of document exchange are presented with regard to the next generation pro-active digital documents proposed by authors. An important point is that documents developed in the project referred in the paper use common formats, it this particular case PDF.*

Keywords: Face recognition, biometric password, encryption

1. Introduction

Documents play a key role in any organized structure invented by human civilization, as they are both *information units* and *interface units* to collaborating people. This phenomenon is particularly common in knowledge based organizations, whose members, often called *knowledge workers*, cooperate by exchanging documents to make decisions, discover facts or accumulate knowledge.

The MENAID project [1] addresses these issues by approaching collaborative computing and virtual cooperation with next generation pro-active digital documents, which are *mobile*, *interactive*, *executable* and *intelligent*. Before going to the main theme of the paper let us refer to two basic concepts of such documents developed during the project, namely a *Mobile Interactive Document (MIND)* architecture of documents capable of traveling through Internet as autonomous agents, and an *Interactive Open Document Architecture (IODA)* enabling implementation of executable papers that may be freely transferred between digital libraries. By referring to MIND and IODA we can emphasize better the issue of protecting content from unauthorized access during various document exchange scenarios. An important point is that our architectures do not require any specific representation format for the document, as any content conformant to the MIME standard may be exchanged.

1.1 Mobile documents

Architecture of MIND is based on a simple combination of two popular Web concepts: automatic XML data binding with Java objects, and mobile agents. Data binding allows for converting units of information contained in document components into functional objects in a computer memory, augmented next with mobility to make them autonomous objects, capable of migrating in an open distributed system [2]. Owing to this, a static representation of an electronic document is transformed into a set of dynamic objects that can migrate to remote locations, and perform actions at these locations by interacting locally with their users and services (see Figure 1).

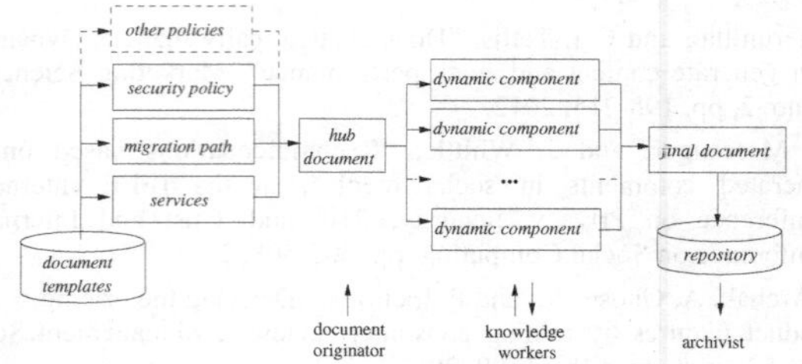

Fig. 1: Components of the MIND mobile document

Lifecycle of a MIND document is initiated by its *originator*, a worker who is responsible for designing a logical structure of a *hub document*, possibly by using a repository of *document templates*. Logical structure of the document includes in particular: a document *migration path*, and specification of *services* required by it during its journey through various locations of the collaborating workers' organization. Document *security policy* specifies access rights to various document parts between subsequent collaborators, indicated as participants of the workflow process defined by the document migration path.

Migration path is specified with a workflow definition language, in terms of *activities* to be performed by each respective worker upon document delivery, and *transitions* of documents to other workers. In our current implementation of MIND we utilize email messaging for document transitions. A lightweight email client, implemented by us for that purpose, can automatically retrieve documents attached to the email message from the receiving worker's mailbox, authenticate the worker, and make them executable objects by unmarshaling. Upon completion of one activity, the email client interprets a document migration path to determine the next activity and workers, serializes documents and sends them as email attachments.

Knowledge workers interact with dynamic components currently residing on their personal devices and contribute to their content when performing the required activity. Upon completion of the last activity specified by the migration path, document components return to their originator to be integrated into a final document and archived.

1.2 Executable papers

A key point about the IODA architecture [3] is that it enables paper executability without subscribing to any specific document format nor requiring implementation of document functionality in any particular programming language. It just provides a sort of a *spine* that binds common tools and services that already exist in a Web document ecosystem. A document spine is implemented as an XML file that simply specifies components of a multi-layered structure of digital objects (see Figure 2).

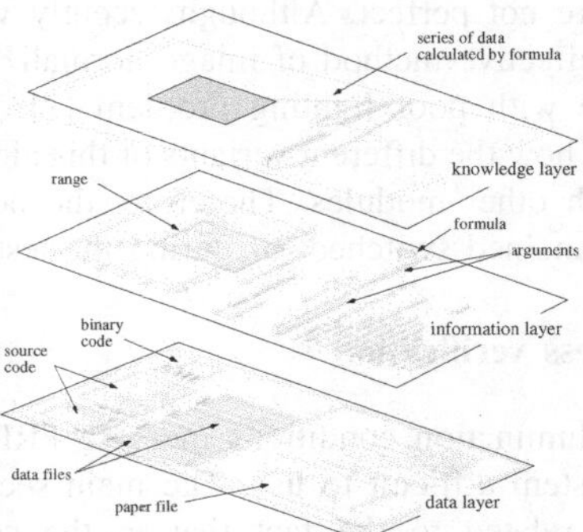

Fig. 2: Layers of the IODA executable paper

Functionality making IODA content executable may be implemented directly with standard notations used for providing functionality and interactivity of Web pages, from simple scripts, through Web- browser plug-ins available from third-party repositories, up to private or public Web services.

The base *data layer* contains a principal document in its native format, such as TIFF or JPEG for scanned analog documents, or PDF for born digital documents. Along with a principal document the data layer may contain data files, other associated documents, and services, like in the case of MIND documents. Association of documents, data and services is implicitly defined by patterns used to interpret a principal document fragment, and other components of the data layer. Interpretation patterns constitute the *information layer*. IODA does not impose any specific format to define these patterns. They are defined with metadata tags marking fragments of a principal document. Markings may take the form of a *point* (a character or a pixel), a *text range*, a rectangular *page area*, or a structure (a collection of any of the former). Tag's metadata associate each respective marking with a function (and if necessary with other objects of the data layer), which is executed upon receiving events generated by user actions. User actions performed by clicking on a marked document fragment may be any service specified by its related metadata. Services of the information layer combine respective data of the data layer to facilitate user interaction with marked fragments of IODA documents. However, user interaction scenarios, e.g. performed by reviewers, may require contexts of interpretation patterns implemented by the information layer. This is a task of the knowledge layer, which provides mechanisms for dynamic *annotations* and *links*. These operations are performed mostly by using a standard browser functionality.

2. Secure document delivery

Just until recently it was enough to protect an electronic document, stored in a server somewhere on the Web, by a security mechanisms built in the service granting access to the document content. But when documents are allowed to leave their safe habitat and interact with users after installing themselves on unfamiliar devices (as in the case of MIND or IODA documents described before) they are on their own – very often outside of a trusted (or even out of any) network, from which they might try to get support to protect themselves. One example might be calling authorization services of their home (originator's) server (see Figure 1). Mechanisms embedded in documents to protect access to their content against unauthorized users or tools must cope not only with the possible document theft, but also loosing an access device with the protected document. Certainly the latter is worse, as personal devices may have already a software installed that enables access to the protected document. On the other hand the protection mechanism should be easy to use and intrinsically related to the legitimate document user identity. Throughout the rest of this paper we will argue to base such mechanism on biometrics.

2.1 Biometric protection of data

There are at least two reasons for the increasing interest in biometric security solutions. First, a properly working biometric algorithm adds another security layer to the protected system, so brute force style password attack is less effective. Second, it can aid computers in improving their experience with users. A typical workstation is still blind today, so it keeps asking the user "is that you?". Once it is able to recognize the person in front of the screen, it may "feel safer" and stop bothering users with explicit identity checks.

2.1.1 Face recognition

From all biometric techniques the face recognition ones seem to be the best choice when it comes to securing access to the document content. Fingerprint readers are far less popular than cameras, identification by means of voice recognition could be cumbersome, and behavioral methods are less useful in this context. During our work on biometric security systems for mobile devices in the SART-2 project [4] we have developed a universal *Classification Framework* (CF) library [5], which can greatly simplify development and evaluation of any dedicated face recognition system. CF modules enable object localization, illumination normalization, feature extraction, classification, etc., and can be easily plugged into any security protection system, and reconfigured, if necessary. In consequence, we have been able to combine various algorithms into one face identification library; it exports just two methods: one for training the system, and another for performing the identification. One of such configured libraries was employed in the PDF protection system described in this paper.

Our face recognition engine, used during experiments described in section 2.3, performs object detection with the popular method proposed originally by Viola and Jones [6], and proceeds similarly to the algorithm described in [7], passing the cropped and histogram-normalized image to the two feature extraction pipelines; one of them calculates *Local Binary Patterns*, and another performs *Gabor filtering*. Each pipeline creates the secondary feature space by using *Kernel Linear Discriminant Analysis* (KLDA), and then applies the multi-modal minimal-distance classifier with cosine metrics to compute the final decision. Identity verification is based on a simple voting scheme: if both pipelines agree and provide the positive result, the user is allowed to access the file, otherwise the access attempt is rejected.

We decided to use the configuration described above because our preliminary experiments [4] indicated that it performs sufficiently well. However, we can easily change it in order to adapt the system to somewhat limited capabilities of mobile devices, or to adjust the size of the biometric data that must be attached to the document sent over the network.

Any biometric system can be characterized by two important parameters: the *false acceptance rate* (FAR) representing the probability that an impostor will be able to force the blockade, and the *false rejection rate* (FRR) indicating how often the legitimate user will not be recognized properly. Increasing the security level through the reduction of FAR inevitably leads to the lower satisfaction of genuine users, as the FRR gets higher automatically. For the application presented here we opt for security rather than comfort of use. However, our face recognition library offers the possibility of tuning the FAR/FRR ratio by changing a simple parameter. Tests performed during the SART-2 project (68 cycles, each involving more than 13000 images) indicated that the current configuration provides FAR of about 4% with the acceptable comfort level. Those results were obtained for images coming from CMU-PIE database [8], which is a challenging dataset. Experiments described in section 2.3 were more limited, but carried out in typical real-life conditions.

Although we are using the general *face recognition* term, the action performed by our biometric security system shall be called *identity verification*. This means that the user attempting to open the document declares some identity to the system, and the role of the latter is to check whether the acquired feature vector $\mathbf{x}$ extracted from his/her face image is *similar enough* to the stored template. Many algorithms, however, have been designed to perform a typical *recognition*, i.e., their goal is to identify the class (person) which is *most similar* to $\mathbf{x}$. In other words, recognition is about distinguishing between known persons – it is a multi-class problem. In the case of verification there is only one class; thus, in order to use KLDA, we have to create an artificial "negative" class representing "the rest of the world". We used 66 frontal images from CMU-PIE for that, but the influence of the content of the negative set on the system's performance will be a subject of our further research.

Many face recognition systems, including various commercial applications, work incorrectly when illumination conditions are not perfect. Although recently we have developed an effective method of image normalization that is able to cope with poor lighting problem [9], we are still investigating how the different variants of this algorithm may interfere with other modules. Therefore, the normalization procedure remained switched off during the tests.

2.1.2 Liveness verification

Inferior illumination conditions increase FRR and could make the system difficult to use. The main security threat, however, is related to the fact that in the case of face recognition biometric data can be obtained (or stolen) easily, e.g., from public Web pages. Any attacker may simply print the face image or even display it his/her smart-phone screen in front of the camera. This indicates that one of the most important elements of robust face recognition applications shall be the *liveness detection* module, capable of distinguishing between a real person and his/her photograph. To achieve such functionality, we have implemented an advanced eye-blinking detection mechanism combining the *Support Vector Machine* with *Conditional Random Fields* [10]. We have also proposed the special motion analysis procedure, based on the features extracted from the *optical flow field* [11]. Because we are currently working on a new version of the liveness detection algorithm, that module was not used during the tests described later in this paper.

2.1.3 Emotion identification

In the extreme case yet another type of attack is possible – a legitimate user might be forced by aggressors to appear in front of the camera to unlock the document content. Although little can be done under such circumstances, the possibility of applying some anomaly detection technique that would be able to detect the unusual behavior of the person is worth investigating. Emotion recognition based on face images has been studied for a long time [12], the related algorithms, however, are usually based on the analysis of very distinctive face expressions. The symptoms of the high stress level may be subtle and vary considerably from person to person. Moreover, acquisition of experimental data may be expected to be particularly difficult in this case.

2.2 Secure PDF documents

PDF is one of the most popular document formats. It enables presenting documents to the end user in the same form as on author/designer desktop – documents are easy to share via Internet, to display by widely available viewers, like Acrobat Reader, Evince, or Web browsers with a proper plug-in installed.

Protection of PDF documents requires two passwords. One is for *owners*, who may have unlimited access to the document content and can change its passwords and access permissions, and another is for *users*, authorized to open the document and perform operations according to the user access permissions specified in the special *encryption dictionary* embedded in the document [13]. Access permissions may involve modifying, copying or extracting text or graphics, adding and editing text in annotations or interactive form fields, and printing. Unfortunately, there is no mechanism to force developers of PDF tools to honor access permissions set in a PDF document. This, however, has nothing to do with cracking encrypted PDF documents, which can be protected quite well with the standard Adobe's encryption handler using symmetric encryption keys [13].

2.2.1 Standard PDF security handler

The strength of PDF encryption is determined by the combination of both: the length and complexity of a textual password invented by the document owner, and the length of the encryption key supported by the PDF version used. With increasing computing power of CPUs , and yet more radical of GPUs, the RC4 algorithm with a 40-bit key used by older PDF documents yields them today practically defenseless against brute force or dictionary attacks. Publicly available tools, like HashCat [14] for example, can find a 40-bit key, i.e. crack any password, regardless of its length and complexity (complete key-space used), in less than 24 hours. With longer encryption keys the situation gets better, so that for eight or more characters from a complete key-space calculation of MD5 passwords is still a matter of months.

Certainly, taking an advantage of the full length of 32 character passwords and 128-bit (PDF 1.6) or 256-bit (PDF 1.7) keys is a must for secure PDF documents. But even long, a password may be weak and easy to guess or steal, so it is important to aid users in inventing complex and long passwords, especially when they have to handle many documents at the same time. The solution should be automatically generated passwords that are hard to crack, but do not have to be memorized nor can be lost.

2.2.2 Biometric password

We propose to exploit the standard PDF password mechanism mentioned above. The idea, shown in Figure 3, is to provide a password generating application with a (training) set of photos of a legitimate user, from which a *biometric definition* DEF of him/her is derived and used to generate a textual password. The document can be encrypted then with a standard algorithm of level 2 or 3, as specified by the value of parameter V in a PDF document encryption dictionary mentioned before [13].

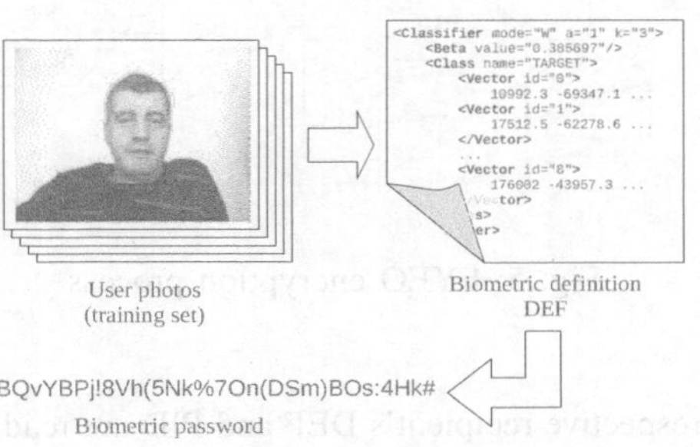

Fig. 3: Biometric password generation scheme

Upon receiving an encrypted document the user has just to face the camera of his/her computer or personal device. If the face in question matches the one required, the document can be decrypted. A dedicated piece of FYEO software to interpret biometric data can be attached to the document data layer – if implemented as an executable paper (see Figure 2), or plugged in a document browser – if implemented otherwise.

Prior to sending any FYEO protected document its potential recipient has to register at the *system training point*, shown in Figure 4. Each user is required to take a series of $n = 7, .., 25$ face shots for the training set. The set of images is processed by the *image to biometric data encoder*, which generates each respective user's face definition DEF in a form of a textual (XML) data file. Logical structure of that file is really simple, and may be seen in Figure 3; it consists of several `<Vector>` elements, each one containing a record of less than one hundred decimal floating point numbers. Upon creation, a DEF file is stored in a *biometric data database* and (optionally) personal user identifier PID is generated.

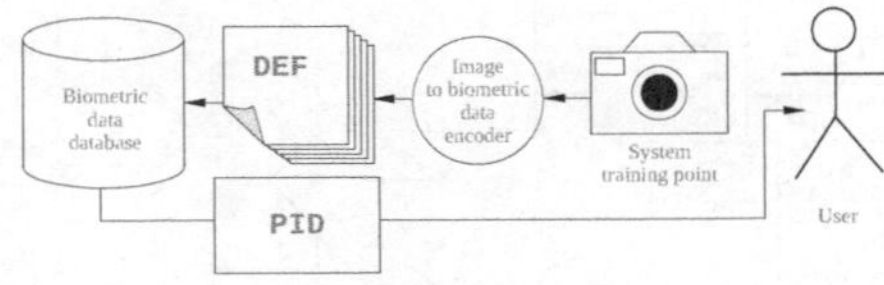

Fig. 4: FYEO Registration process

When a biometrically protected document is about to be sent to a registered user, the FYEO encryption process (shown in Figure 5) is started by the document originator, who picks the document from the *library of unsecured documents* (or simply creates a new one).

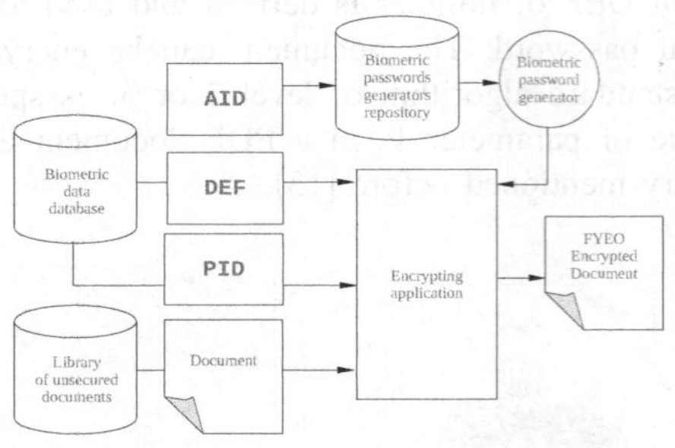

Fig. 5: FYEO encryption process

The respective recipient's DEF and PID are read from the *biometric data database*, and a specific password generation algorithm is chosen from the *biometric password generators repository*. A *biometric password generator* is an application that works in a plug-in mode, which enables usage of various algorithms – each one identified by its unique *algorithm identifier* AID. Given the size and diversity of the DEF file content, arbitrarily many password generation algorithms may be implemented and stored in the repository. Each time, however, only the algorithm whose status is currently set to *valid* (for example has not expired) may be chosen. The *encrypting application* encodes a document based on the password generated by the *biometric password generator* from the user's DEF data and (optionally) a personal identifier PID provided by the user. DEF and AID data may be added as PDF's internal objects or just appended to the document's file (what is the case of our prototype). After that the encrypted document may be delivered to any remote user as an email attachment or uploaded to the user's device.

The FYEO decryption process is performed on the client device, as shown in Figure 6.

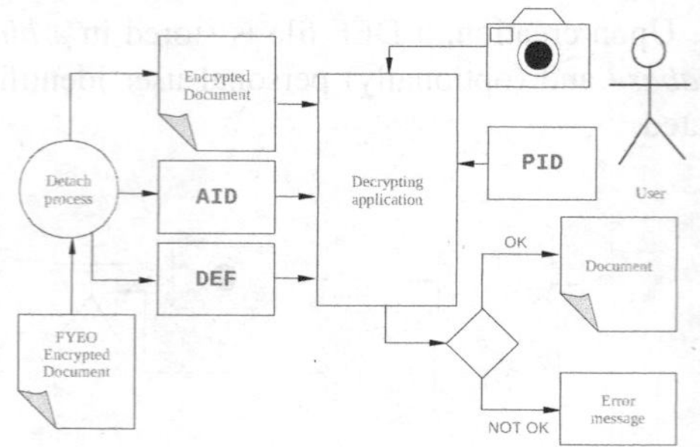

Fig. 6: FYEO decryption process (client device)

When the receiving user tries to open a document protected with a biometric password a *detach process* separates a biometric definition data DEF from the document, checks if a decoding plug-in with a proper AID is available and its state is valid. If these conditions are met the user is prompted to take a face shot. Thus obtained image is processed by the *decrypting application*, which compares data from the image with the biometric DEF definition separated from the received document. If the *biometric data classifier* embedded in the application decides that the image matches the received biometric definition, it calls its *biometric password generator* for the password to decrypt the encrypted PDF document. From now on it can be displayed with any PDF document viewer.

2.2.3 Combined biometric password and personal key

In order to make the authentication process more secure the FYEO encrypted document may ask the user for his/her personal PID key, assigned during the registration process shown in Figure 4. In such a case the key is passed to the *biometric password generator* shown in Figure 3, and used as an additional element in the encryption key generation process, in the fashion similar to the *salt* used in encryption processes.

2.3 Experiments

As mentioned before, exhaustive tests of the CF library have been performed during the SART-2 project to assess the optimal FAR/FRR ratio determining acceptable comfort levels of using the implemented algorithms in a general biometric application. Presenting them here is out of the scope of this paper. Instead we present results of several *ad hoc* experiments performed by us to demonstrate the possible attacks on the FYEO architecture. First we have prepared three training sets of photos shown in Figure 7.

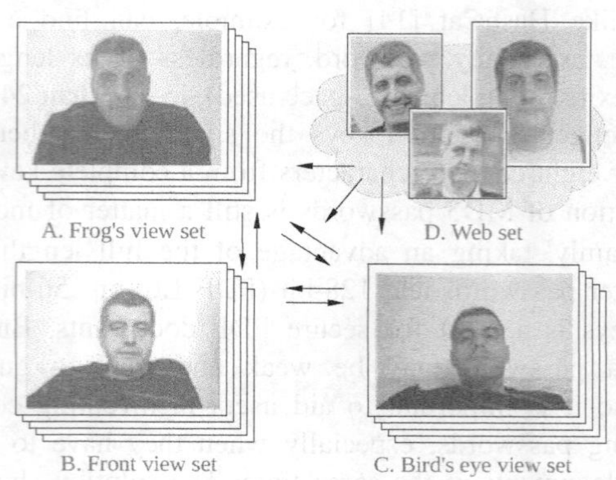

Fig. 7: Sets of photos used in experiments

They contain images of the same person, all recorded with the same camera built in the user's personal laptop; the respective sets of photos were taken when the person was standing and looking from above his laptop (A), sitting in front of it (B), and lying on his back and looking from below it (C). Photographs in respective sets A, B, and C were very similar, as they had been taken during a short period of time during a regular use of the laptop by that person.

Next, three DEF files have been generated (see Figure 4), each one for a specific subset of A, B and C; these subsets formed *training sets*. For each training set a 32-character password has been generated with randomly selected password generators using the complete key-space (see Figure 5):

```
A: 8Lt%5VmW6Sj%2To:AGpX0Rv$6Uj%0HtX
B: BQvYBPj!8Vh(5Nk%7On(DSm)BOs:4Hk#
C: 5Nj:4SvZ1Ul)DPh!6Li:EIg(ESs:5Or!
```

For testing purposes we have also collected set D of photographs of the same person, which we were able to find on the Web. Note that photographs in D contain images of the person in various contexts (inclined, diverted, smiling, sober, etc.), also that person's age varies.

The remaining photos from A, B, C (not used in training sets), and the Web set D photos were used as *testing sets*. For each tested combination (marked respectively in Figure 7 with arrows) only three photos of the sitting user have been *false accepted* by FYEO trained with photos of the standing user. This was due to the camera angle, because the user was holding a laptop on his knees, so when taking them the angle was sometimes more like the frog's view than the front view. Each time FYEO was trained with respective subsets of A, B, or C, the remaining photos from the same set used as the testing set, have been *true accepted*. Moreover all D photos have always been *false rejected* by FYEO, if trained respectively with A, B, or C.

Note that rejection of an image of the same person, as the one for which a biometric system has been trained, is in general considered an *error*. However, Web based photos used as input should be *rejected* by FYEO, no matter what person they present. Therefore photos for the training set must be carefully selected – enabling true accept for testing photos of the user which are close to the ones of the training set, and false reject for those which are not. Our experiments indicate that manipulating the camera angle is quite effective in providing that.

Having these results in mind consider the following attacks on FYEO.

2.3.1 Illegal interception

A document may be stolen or sent by mistake to an adversary, who does not know identity of its legitimate user, and is not aware of the FYEO protection. Most likely the attack would be applying *brute force* or *dictionary* methods on the password. The document is as safe as the password encrypted PDF document could be; given the fact that the password is full length and consisting of characters from the entire character plane, it would be rather unrealistic to crack it in any reasonable time (say less than hundreds of days).

2.3.2 Device theft

If the user's personal device is stolen, an adversary may know identity of the user, and most likely will be able to use the FYEO client code. In such a case an impostor may look for the identified user photos on the Web, as well as in local directories of the stolen device. False reject rates estimated in our experiments indicate that photos of the same person taken at arbitrary camera angles can be effectively distinguished by CF algorithms used by FYEO, from the training set of photos, taken at a specific angle (not known to the adversary).

2.3.3 Web-cam takeover

A more dangerous situation is when attackers can take over the user's web-cam, as photos taken by the latter may be close to the ones used for the training set. Getting access to the user's web-cam from outside is possible, as demonstrated in 2012 by the Weelsof virus targeting computer users in USA, Great Britain, Germany and Poland. This ransomeware, disguised as some fake law enforcement agency, displayed image of the user's face streamed from his/her connected web-cam as "recording" [15]. As a precaution FYEO users may be advised to take unusual positions, e.g. lying on back, when taking shots for the training set, and to remember what position to take when opening the document later. The attacker would not know for sure at what angle photos were created during a training session.

2.3.4 Direct assault

The user may be physically forced by the attacker to open the document by looking at the camera of his/her personal device. To prevent that some additional functionality may be implemented in the FYEO software, eg. a special mimic or gesture which upon detection would destroy the document or device. More subtle face expressions related to various emotional states of the user (fear, anger, pain, etc.), informing the system about any unusual situation, can be detected by some of our algorithms.

2.3.5 Hacked training point

Photos of the training set may be stolen if an adversary can get access to the FYEO system training point. Since it does not require any network connection, it should be off-line all the time, and the training photos destroyed as soon as DEF files are generated; they are not needed any longer and cannot be recovered from the DEF file content. One possibility is sabotage from inside the organization, e.g. unauthorized copying of files to the USB stick during the registration process, but this is the matter of a general security policy of the related organization using FYEO protected documents.

2.3.6 Hacked server

Finally the organization server (see Figure 5) may be attacked at several points:

- *Biometric data database* does not contain any useful data unless user PIDs are kept in open text instead of a digested format.
- *Library of unsecured documents* may contain confidential data and must be protected by the existing security mechanisms of the server. An alternative is to create a document on the fly right before encrypting and sending it out.
- *Biometric passwords generators repository* may be useful to hackers only if after forcing the server's security mechanisms they would know AIDs. For more demanding security levels, a special password generator may be created on the fly, instead of using one from the repository

3. Conclusions

The purpose of our work reported in this paper has not been improving or replacing the existing security mechanisms in PDF. Our choice to implement FYEO biometric protection for PDF has been motivated by the encryption mechanisms built directly in the PDF document content, rather then "enveloped" around the document file, e.g. as is the case of ZIP files. Any FYEO protected PDF document is protected to the extent provided by the security handler of the revision level specified in the encryption dictionary of the original PDF document.

We have approached the problem of PDF security from the perspective of automatic generation of passwords from facial biometric data. Our method enables generation of passwords that may be arbitrarily long and complex, using the complete key-space, which do not have to be memorized or written down by users. In fact our FYEO approach subscribes to the concept of exploiting hard AI problems for security purposes, stated formally by the inventors of CAPTCHA [16]. In their terminology, a program delivering photo i of the user attempting to access a protected document is *verifier* V, while the FYEO client side is *prover* P. P receives from V transformed image $t(i)$, and outputs label $\lambda(i)$, which in our case is a DEF file, identifying the user. Breaking in a document with a forged photo would require finding image transformation $i \rightarrow t(i)$, capable of making P to calculate DEF that can eventually lead to document opening. This is a hard AI problem belonging to the $\mathcal{P}2$ family defined formally in [16]. Owing to the modular structure of the CF library, new algorithms making the system more resistant to impostors are planned to be added, to further complicate the problem of finding transformation $t(i)$. They will include in the first place liveness verification and emotion detection, but in the future may also include detection of gestures combined with faces, or specific visual tokens incorporated in the image.

Further extensions of the FYEO scheme may combine biometric passwords with personal keys, either built in the personal device – a FYEO document may be then decrypted only on a device with a specific ID, or at specific geographical location identified by the user's device GPS receiver, and so on, or in a form of physical tokens – USB memory sticks or eID cards plugged-in the device prior to the FYEO document opening attempt.

Acknowledgment

This work was supported by the National Science Centre grants no. N N516 367936 and DEC1-2011/01/B/ST6/06500.

References

[1] MeNaID project home page, "Methods and tools of future document engineering." [Online]. Available: www.menaid.org.pl

[2] M. Godlewska and B. Wiszniewski, "Distributed MIND – a new processing model based on mobile interactive documents," in *Proc. 8th Int. Conf. PPAM 2009*, ser. LNCS, vol. 6068. Springer, 2010, pp. 244–249.

[3] J. Siciarek and B. Wiszniewski, "IODA - an interactive open document architecture," *Procedia CS*, vol. 4, pp. 668–677, 2011.

[4] SART-2 project home page, "Biometric security system for mobile workstations," 2012. [Online]. Available: http://sart2.eti.pg.gda.pl/

[5] M. Smiatacz and K. Przybycien, "A framework for training and testing of complex pattern recognition systems," in *Proc. IEEE Conf. on Signal and Image Processing Applications (ICSIPA)*, 2011, pp. 198–203.

[6] P. Viola and M. J. Jones, "Robust real-time face detection," *Int. J. Comp. Vision*, vol. 57, no. 2, pp. 137–154, 2004.

[7] X. Tan and B. Triggs, "Enhanced local texture feature sets for face recognition under difficult lighting conditions," *IEEE Trans. Image Processing*, vol. 19, no. 6, pp. 1635–1650, 2010.

[8] T. Sim, S. Baker, and M. Bsat, "The CMU pose, illumination, and expression (PIE) database," in *Proc. 5th Int. Conf. on Automatic Face and Gesture Recognition*, 2002, pp. 53–58.

[9] M. Smiatacz, "Image normalization method for face identification under difficult lighting conditions," in *Proc. 11th IEEE Int. Conf. on Information Sciences, Signal Processing and their Applications (ISSPA)*, 2012, pp. 204–209.

[10] M. Szwoch and P. Pieniążek, "Eye blink based detection of liveness in biometric authentication systems using conditional random fields," *LNCS*, vol. 7594, pp. 669–676, 2012.

[11] M. Smiatacz, "Liveness measurements using optical flow for biometric person authentication," *Metrology and Measurement Systems*, vol. 19, no. 2, pp. 257–268, 2012.

[12] G. Donato, M. S. Bartlett, J. C. Hager, P. Ekman, and T. J. Sejnowski, "Classifying facial actions," *IEEE Trans. Pattern Analysis and Machine Intelligence*, vol. 21, no. 10, pp. 974–989, 1999.

[13] *Document management – Portable document format – Part 1: PDF 1.7*, Adobe Systems Inc., 2008. [Online]. Available: http://www.adobe.com/devnet/pdf/pdf_reference.html

[14] J. Steube, "Hashcat – advanced password recovery," March 7, 2013. [Online]. Available: http://hashcat.net/hashcat/

[15] T. Meskauskas, "The FBI Federal Bureau of Investigation screen locker," July 16, 2012. [Online]. Available: http://www.pcrisk.com/removal-guides/6765-remove-the-fbi-federal-bureau-of-investigation-screen-locker

[16] L. V. Ahn, M. Blum, N. J. Hopper, and J. Langford, "CAPTCHA: using hard AI problems for security," in *Proc. 22nd Int. Conf. on Theory and Applications of Cryptographic Techniques EUROCRYPT'03*. Springer, 2003, pp. 294–311.

Exploring Chinese Users' Acceptance of Social Commerce Sites

Jia Shen
Department of Information Systems and Supply Chain Management
College of Business Administration
Rider University
Lawrenceville, NJ, USA

Abstract – *With its rapid economic growth and the largest number of Internet users worldwide, China and its vast online markets are of particular interests to companies globally. This paper describes a study of Chinese users' acceptance of an emerging E-commerce technology: social commerce websites. Leveraging the power of social networking technologies with online shopping, social commerce sites have emerged in recent years to address the fundamental nature of shopping as a social experience. Despite tremendous business interest and anticipated potential benefits, some central issues remain such as whether Chinese Internet users will adopt such websites and the factors that affect the adoption. This study extends the Technology Acceptance Model (TAM) with social factors such as social comparison, social presence, and enjoyment in the acceptance of social commerce websites. Results provide significant support of the extended model.*

Keywords: social commerce, social comparison, social presence, enjoyment, user acceptance

1 Introduction

As home to the world's largest Internet population, China is rapidly developing e-commerce systems, and is catching the attention of companies with global ambitions. By 2012, China had 538 million Internet users (www.internetworldstats.com), and the number of e-commerce shoppers is projected to grow into 329 million by 2015 [1]. The vast online market and its cultural background draw attention to study Chinese online consumers for unique opportunities.

Meanwhile, online social networking and social media technologies continue to gain recognition in China and worldwide. Seeking to tap into the potentials of these technologies for E-commerce, businesses are exploring ways to combine the power of social networking with online shopping for better service and new business opportunities. For example, there is an upward trend of merchants creating ads and retails pages on Facebook, with the intention of attracting online social network users and their friends [2]. Additionally, a new wave of start-up firms are developing text mining algorithms to track "social relationship data" between online users, that can be used to target behavior-oriented ads. However the evidence is still inconclusive that these are the best online platforms to increase sales using social networking.

Social commerce sites have emerged as a strong potential platform to combine online social networking with online shopping. Gathering people in an online place to exchange shopping ideas, social commerce sites offer features similar to social networking sites such as personal blog and profile webpage, with the addition of E-commerce tools and software to allow users to easily copy product pictures and post them on their web pages. Users can also post product recommendations, create wish lists, comment on items, and make purchases. The result is the creation of online social commerce communities. Examples of social commerce sites include Kaboodle.com, ShopStyle.com, ThisNext.com, and Wists.com, all launched between 2006 and 2007. In China, similar social commerce sites emerged around 2009, such as Taobao's Taojianghu (Tao World) section, Meilishuo (Beauty Legend), and Mogujie (Mushroom Street).

Social commerce aims at addressing the fundamental nature of shopping as a social experience. Despite tremendous business interest and anticipated potential benefits, some central questions remain. Will consumers adopt social commerce technology? What are the factors that lead to the adoption? Although technology adoption in general and e-commerce adoption in particular are both well studied, the specificity of social commerce clearly calls for further theoretical development. Such understanding will also better inform business managers who make strategic decisions regarding the integration of social networking and online commerce. Additionally, system designers will have important insight that may lead to improved functionality, design, and use of such systems. With China being the home to the world's largest online population and the second largest e-commerce shopper population (www.internetworldstats.com), the investigation of the social commerce platform in China bears more significance theoretically and practically.

2 Conceptual Background

To answer these questions, this research utilizes the Technology Acceptance Model (TAM) [3]. TAM has been recognized as one of the most powerful models in examining the acceptance of new IT. Adapted from the Theory of Reasoned Action (TRA) model, TAM posits that two beliefs – perceived ease of use (PEOU) and perceived usefulness (PU) - determine one's behavioral intention to use a technology. While the parsimony of TAM makes it easy to apply to a variety of situations, the leanness of the model is also considered as its key limitation. The model lacks the ability to help business managers or system designers to understand the factors that contribute to the adoption or abandonment of new IT. As a result, a number of studies have been conducted to examine additional antecedents to IT use (e.g., cultural dimensions [4]).

This study proposes three additional constructs as key antecedents to the adoption of social commerce sites: Tendency to Social Comparison, Social Presence, and Perceived Enjoyment. Social comparison is an essential social phenomenon where human beings compare themselves with others for self-evaluation and information seeking. Rooted in social science, the original theory of social comparison treated social comparison as a secondary choice when objective information to evaluate oneself is not available [5]. Subsequent research suggests that social comparison is a central feature of human social life [6]. In this study, tendency to social comparison is defined as the degree to which an individual tends to compare his or her opinions with others, and be influenced by others. Recent studies have found that individuals differ quite a bit in their tendency to compare themselves with others [6].

The second construct, Social Presence is defined as the extent to which a medium allows a user to experience others as being psychologically present [7]. Research has shown that increased sense of social presence can be achieved through stimulating the imagination of interaction with other humans (e.g., through socially rich text and picture content, personalized greetings, human audio and video, intelligent agents), or by providing means for actual interaction with other humans [8]. Technologies such as personalization, recommendation, and consumer reviews can enable the feeling of a place where people interact, thus increasing the social presence of websites [9]. Increased social presence can in turn affect other factors such as perceived usefulness of the website [10].

The third construct which is likely to affect social commerce website adoption is perceived enjoyment. Online shopping is a voluntary and hedonic activity, and users participate because they are intrinsically motivated. In studies of technology adoption, the concept of Perceived Enjoyment has been defined and measured as the extent to which the activity of using a specific system is perceived to be enjoyable in it's own right, aside from any performance consequences resulting from system use [11]. Studies have found perceived enjoyment to be a significant factor in adopting technologies for activities such as web browsing and instant messaging, including Chinese users [12].

3 Research Model and Hypotheses

Based on TAM and the three additional variables described above, a research model is proposed with five variables: Perceived Ease of Use (PEOU), Perceived Usefulness (PU), Tendency to Social Comparison, Social Presence, Perceived Enjoyment, and Behavioral Intention (BI) to use social commerce sites. Figure 1 shows the research model.

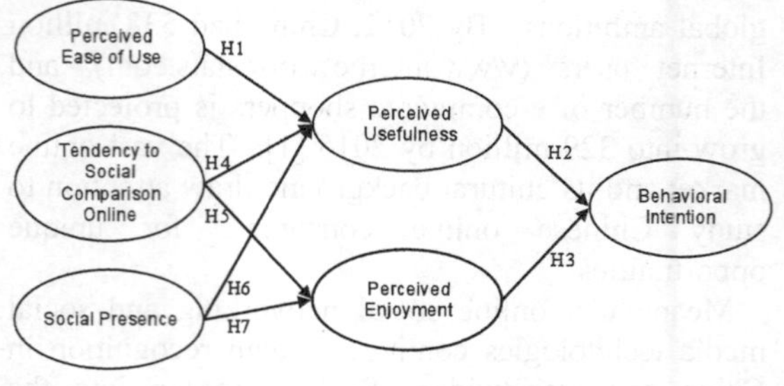

Figure 1: Research Model.

According to TAM, the hypothesized relationship among PEOU, PU, and BI are specified below:

- H1: Perceived Ease of Use will positively affect Perceived Usefulness of social commerce websites.
- H2: Perceived Usefulness will positively affect Behavioral Intention to use social commerce websites.

Incorporating flow theory and the results of subsequent studies of enjoyment and technology adoption [13], it is postulated that the more the users perceive the site to be enjoyable, the more likely they will adopt the site. Thus:

•H3. Perceived Enjoyment will positively affect Behavioral Intention to use social commerce websites.

Given the social nature of shopping, tendency to social comparison is postulated to have an impact in user's adoption of social commerce sites. Empirical studies of online shopping suggest that the provision of recommendations and consumer reviews increase the perceived usefulness of the website [9]. These findings are consistent with marketing research indicating that consumers are influenced by other consumers in their decision making process, such as information seeking, alternative evaluation, and choice [14]. Given the social nature of shopping and the features specific to social commerce websites, it is postulated that people who are more likely to compare and be influenced by others are more likely to find the social commerce sites useful (H4), and enjoyable (H5). Thus:

- H4: Tendency to Social Comparison will positively affect Perceived Usefulness of social commerce websites.
- H5: Tendency to Social Comparison will positively affect Perceived Enjoyment of social commerce websites.

Finally, based on studies of social presence and the adoption of e-commerce systems [10, 15], it is hypothesized that the stronger the social presence of the shopping site, the more useful (H6) and enjoyable users (H7) will perceive it to be. Thus:

- H6. Social Presence will positively affect Perceived Usefulness of social commerce websites.
- H7. Social Presence will positively affect Perceived Enjoyment of social commerce websites.

4 Data Collection

Data were collected through a survey conducted in Fall 2010 in China. The survey was given to undergraduate and graduate business students at a university in northeastern China. Subjects were instructed to use Taojianhu (Tao World), a social commerce site for the users of Taobao (www.taobao.com) – the largest e-commerce website in China. Taojianhu was chosen for this study given it was the leading social commerce site in China at the time of the research, with many features supporting social commerce activities. The site was developed by Taobao in 2009 to provide social networking functions to Taobao users, and was offered as an affiliate site at the time of the study in fall 2010. In May 2011, the website was redesigned to be part of MyTaobao function on the Taobao website (http://tech.sina.com.cn/i/2011-05-24/11005563438.shtml). Features on the social commerce site include friend contacts, updates, product ratings, discussions, and direct shopper-to-shopper interactions such as polls, "Sharing of treasure", "ask other shoppers", "help-me-choose", group shopping, as well as traditional E-commerce functions such as browsing by brand and searching. Subjects were asked to complete product search and shopping tasks by interacting with the site; then write up a short essay reflecting on the features provided on the website. The precise purpose of the study and the research model were neither discussed nor alluded to. Course credits were awarded for survey participation.

After completing the assignment, students were given the URL to participate in the online survey. In constructing the questionnaire, the PEOU, PU, and BI items were adapted from Davis [3]. Items for the Tendency to Social Comparison scale were adapted from Gibbons and Buunk [16] study. Perceived Enjoyment scale was adopted from Novak [13]. The Social Presence items were adapted from Gefen and Straub [10]. All items were measured on a seven-point scale ranging from strongly disagree (1) to strongly agree (7). All research documents were prepared in English and then translated into Chinese, and cross-examined to ensure consistency.

5 Data Analysis and Results

A total of 84 valid responses were collected from Chinese users. To examine the hypotheses and research model, the data were analyzed using Structural Equation Modeling (SEM) and SmartPLS software [17]. This approach allows simultaneous analysis of the measurement model (factors), and the structural model (path analysis), and has been widely used. In the measurement model, the reliability of the constructs as measured in the AVE and composite reliabilities of the different measures all exceed the recommended 0.70 level, indicating that the measures are robust. Tests on convergent validity and discriminant validity were conducted, and the results supported the measurement model. Analysis on the mean and standard deviation (SD) for each of the main constructs in the model reveal that subjects reported overall positive attitude towards the social commerce site, and found it easy to use, useful, enjoyable, and are likely to use it in their shopping tasks in the future. Details on the measurement model are not discussed due to space limitations.

Figure 2 shows the results of the structural model. The test yields results of path coefficients (β), which indicates the positive and negative relationships between the constructs, the strength of the relationships, and their statistical significance. The test also yields squared multiple correlations (R^2) values, which indicate the amount of variance of the dependent construct that can be explained by the independent constructs.

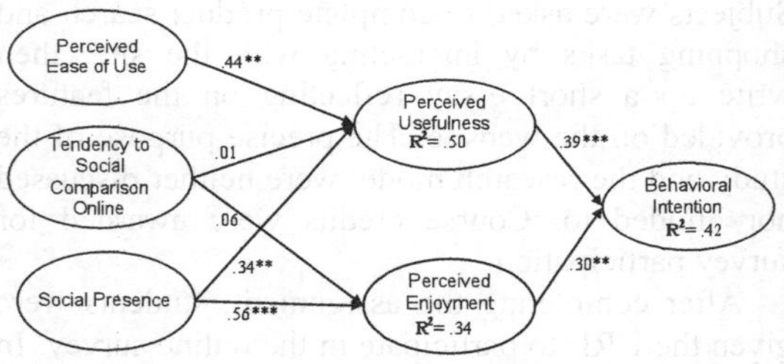

Figure 2: Research Model Results.

Overall, the China model accounts for 42% of variance in Behavioural Intention, 50% in Perceived Usefulness, and 34% in Perceived Enjoyment. Perceived Ease of Use is an antecedent to Perceived Usefulness (β= .44, $p<.01$). Perceived Usefulness has a strong effect on Behaviour Intention (β= .39, $p<.001$). Perceived Enjoyment also affects Behaviour Intention significantly (β=.30, $p<.01$). Social Comparison does not have a significant effect on Perceived Enjoyment or Perceived Usefulness. Social Presence has a strong effect on Perceived Enjoyment (β= .56, $p<.001$), and a modest one on Perceived Usefulness (β= .34, $p<.05$).

Thus hypotheses H1, H2, H3, H6, and H7 were supported. H4 and H5 were not supported.

6 Discussions

This study examined factors associated with Chinese users' intentions to use social commerce websites. The TAM antecedents are verified in the social commerce context: perceived ease of use and perceived usefulness are both significant factors affecting intentions to adopt social commerce websites. This study also reveals that perceived enjoyment is a significant antecedent to intentions. As the use of social media continues to grow among Internet users and consumers, our results strongly suggest that businesses should consider the potential power associated with integrating online social networking technologies with their e-commerce strategies in creating an easy-to-use, enjoyable, and useful shopping experience.

The results show that social presence significantly affects both perceived usefulness (with a coefficient of .34), and perceived enjoyment (with a coefficient of .56). This suggests that establishing the presence of other online shoppers and creating a sense of an online shopping community are critical in the adoption of such social commerce websites.

One interesting result is that tendency to social comparison does not affect perceived usefulness and perceived enjoyment directly. This result is worth further investigation in future studies from directions such as the impact of strength of social ties (weak ties vs. strong ties) as a moderating factor on the impact of tendency to social comparison.

In the open-ended questions, Chinese study participants reported that one of the main reasons they would adopt the website in future shopping activities was because of the social interactions with other shoppers online: "I would use it because it allows my friends to help me choose products and provide their inputs." "When I can't make up my mind, others can help me on this site." "It enables sharing of shopping experiences."

The social features of the website not only enable social interactions among web users, but can also serve other purposes such as making new discoveries of products online. "The most useful feature of the Taojianghua site is the ability to keep in touch with family and friends – so one's aware of their latest updates and shopping ideas;" "It combines shopping with social networking on one site;" "The sharing-of-treasures function allows me to make new discoveries"; "It allows me to share my shopping experiences with others; and vice versa – there are a lot of valuable advice offered on the site."

When asked about concerns that prevent them from using the site in the future, privacy concerns topped the list. "The registration process was too complicated, and required too much personal information". One unique feature in E-commerce website registration in China is the requirement to use a valid cell phone number for each account for verification purpose. Many felt it made the registration process long, and could lead to potential security breaches. "I am concerned about the information I provide may be used for other purposes." Additionally, authenticity of products for sale on the websites was another issue that some were concerned about. "I did not trust the quality of products on the site." This reflected a general concern of product quality which is a broader issue affecting commerce both online and offline in China in the rapid economic development stage.

7 Contributions and Future Research

This research is among the first to empirically examine the merging of social networking with E-commerce technologies for Chinese online consumers. Theoretically, this research contributes by extending the Technology Acceptance Model with factors extracted from social comparison theory, social presence, and enjoyment. The two additional factors: social presence and perceived enjoyment were significant in the model in addition to PEOU and PU.

Understanding consumer perceptions and intentions to use a social commerce website have direct management implications. A recent study on Chinese E-commerce development suggests that Chinese consumers are the most likely in the world to check for product recommendations on social networking sites [1]. Largely because of consumer wariness and distrust of merchants, forty percent of online consumers in China say they've read and posted reviews—more than double the rate in the United States. Conversely, only 19 percent of consumers in China go to official brand or manufacturer sites, compared with 41 to 60 percent in Japan, the United States, and the European Union [1]. This reinforces the findings in this study in terms of the potentials of social commerce sites in China.

From a practical perspective, the current research model suggests that in addition to focusing on ease of use and usefulness, the site should foster a sense of other online shoppers, and create enjoyment in the shopping process. The result can produce a greater likelihood that Chinese consumers will find the site useful, use the site, and increase product sales.

One possible direction for future research is to examine the type of online shopping tasks that are most suitable for social commerce websites. Will users prefer using social commerce sites than traditional E-commerce site for certain shopping activities, such as browsing or searching [18]? Will they prefer the site when they are more involved with the product, i.e., when the product is more relevant to them? Also, will the strength of the social ties affect users' use of such shopping sites, such as family and friends vs. other online shoppers? With the growing popularity of social media and E-commerce technology integration, research in this area is timely and important.

8 References

[1] J. Walters, Y. Kuo, W. Jap, and H. Hsu, "The World's Next E-commerce Superpower: Navigating China's Unique Online-Shopping Ecosystem," *The Boston consulting Group Report,* Novembe, 2011.

[2] S. E. Needleman, "Merchants Push Sales Through Social Media - Early Adopters Add Shopping-Cart Apps to Fan Pages to Sell Items," in *Wall Street Journal*, June 1 2010.

[3] F. D. Davis, "Perceived Usefulness, Perceived Ease of Use and User Acceptance of Information Technology," *MIS Quarterly,* vol. 13, pp. 319-340, 1989.

[4] E. Mao and P. Palvia, "Testing an extended model of IT acceptance in the Chinese cultural context," *ACM SIGMIS Database,* vol. 37, pp. 20-32, 2006.

[5] L. Festinger, "A Theory of Social Comparison Processes," *Human Relations,* vol. 7, pp. 117-140, 1954.

[6] A. P. Buunk and F. X. Gibbons, "Social comparison: The end of a theory and the emergence of a field," *Organizational Behavior and Human Decision Processes,* vol. 102, pp. 3-21, Jan 2007.

[7] J. Fulk, C. W. Steinfield, J. Schmitz, and J. G. Power, "A social information processing model of media use in organizations," *Communication Research,* vol. 14, pp. 529-552, 1987.

[8] K. Hassanein and M. Head, "Manipulating social presence through the web interface and

its impact on attitude towards online shopping," *International Journal of Human-Computer Studies,* vol. 65, pp. 689-708, 2007.

[9] N. Kumar and I. Benbasat, "The Influence of Recommendations and Consumer Reviews on Evaluations of Websites," *Information Systems Research,* vol. 17, pp. 425-439, Dec 2006.

[10] D. Gefen and D. Straub, "Managing User Trust in B2C e-Services," *E-Service Journal,* vol. 2, pp. 7-24, 2003.

[11] F. D. Davis and R. P. Bagozzi, "What Do Intention Scales Measure?," *The Journal of General Psychology,* vol. 119, pp. 391-407, 1992.

[12] Y. Lu, T. Zhou, and B. Wang, "Exploring Chinese Users' Acceptance of Instant Messaging Using the Theory of Planned Behavior, the Technology Acceptance Model, and the Flow Theory," *Computers in Human Behavior,* vol. 6, pp. 1-11, 2008.

[13] T. P. Novak, D. L. Hoffman, and Y.-F. Yung, "Measuring the Customer Experience in Online Environments: A Structural Modeling Approach," *Marketing Science,* vol. 19, pp. 22-42, 2000.

[14] H. H. Friedman and R. B. Fireworker, "The susceptibility of consumers to unseen group influence," *Journal of Social Psychology,* vol. 102, pp. 155-156, 1977.

[15] B. Suh and I. Han, "Effect of trust on customer acceptance of Internet banking," *Electronic Commerce Research and Applications,* vol. 1, pp. 247-263, Autumn-Winter 2002.

[16] F. X. Gibbons and B. P. Buunk, "Individual differences in social comparison: Development of a scale of social comparison orientation," *Journal of Personality and Social Psychology,* vol. 76, pp. 129-142, Jan 1999.

[17] C. M. Ringle, S. Wende, and A. Will, "SmartPLS", 2.0 (beta) ed Hamburg, Germany University of Hamburg 2005.

[18] W. Hong, J. Y. L. Thong, and K. Y. Tam, "The Effects of Information Format and Shopping Task on Consumers' Online Shopping Behavior: A Cognitive Fit Perspective," *Journal of Management Information Systems,* vol. 21, pp. 149-184, 2004.

The Dynamic Business Web Template Design and Implementation

Z. Wang[1,2], D. Sparks[1], and X. Zhang[2]
[1]Department of Math/CS, Virginia Wesleyan College, Norfolk, VA, USA
[2]College of Information Engineering, Taiyuan University of Technology, Taiyuan, Shanxi, China

Abstract - *The paper presents the design and implementation of the online Web template tool that allows people without any programming knowledge design and maintain the website contents. The project incorporates PHP code to create each page on the website and perform functions for the website, CSS code to create the style sheet for the website, and MySQL database to hold information for different parts of the website. The focus of this study is to create an easily navigated website that a small company can easily edit to incorporate their own information.*

Keywords: Dynamic Business Web, Web template tool, database information system, online system, PHP/MySQL

1 Introduction

In last decades, we have experienced the most profound changes in our daily life. It is so called the information age. Online information systems truly bring the "Digital Revolution" in our modern society [1]. The systems can be found in the forms of the airline reservation system, banking system, student registration system, etc. For a small business, construction of such a system may be a big cost. The importance of this study is to create a website for small businesses to create and edit their own website for their companies. The website is dynamic, meaning that the information on the website can be edited at any time by their staff, even after it is live. The project presents a website for small businesses that can be very personalized. It is owned by the businesses, not on a server from another company. The business owner can add or edit their website at anytime without having to hire a programmer. The paper is organized as follows. In the next section, system design is discussed, and a case study is presented in the third section. A conclusion is given in the last section.

2 System design

The goal of the project was to create a website for small business owners that is easily edited by someone with no programming or computer science knowledge. The best way to accomplish this goal was to use PHP coding and a MySQL database [2] [3]. The PHP code creates a user-friendly interface for editing the website and displays all the information onto the website. The MySQL database is used to store all the information for the website and stores the user names and passwords.

2.1 The Database Structure

The database consists of four tables, each with a different purpose. All the tables can be edited or updated through the PHP files. Below each table name, there will be a display of the descriptive summary for that table.

Table 1 *Business_Name* - stores the business name that can be retrieved for use on the website

Field	Type	Null	Key	Default	Extra
id	int(11)	YES		NULL	
name	varchar(100)	YES		NULL	

Table 2 *Pages* - stores the information for the pages

Field	Type	Null	Key	Default	Extra
id	int(11)	NO	PRI	NULL	auto_increment
menu_name	varchar(30)	NO		NULL	
position	int(3)	NO		NULL	
visible	tinyint(1)	NO		NULL	

Table 3 *Subjects* - stores the information for the subjects

Field	Type	Null	Key	Default	Extra
id	int(11)	NO	PRI	NULL	auto_increment
subject_id	int(11)	NO		NULL	
menu_name	varchar(30)	NO		NULL	
position	int(3)	NO		NULL	
visible	tinyint(1)	NO		NULL	
content	text	NO		NULL	

Table 4 *Users* - stores the usernames and passwords for users

Field	Type	Null	Key	Default	Extra
id	int(11)	NO	PRI	NULL	auto_increment
username	varchar(50)	NO		NULL	
hashed_password	varchar(40)	NO		NULL	

2.2 The Website Content

Type the title approximately 2.5 centimeters (1 inch) from the top of the first page and use 20 points type-font size in bold. Center the title (horizontally) on the page. Leave approximately 1 centimeter (0.4- inches) between the title and the name and address of yourself (and of your co-authors, if any.) Type name(s) and address(s) in 11 points and center them (horizontally) on the page. Note that authors are advised not to include their email addresses.

The following (Figure 1) flowchart describes the basic flow of the website.

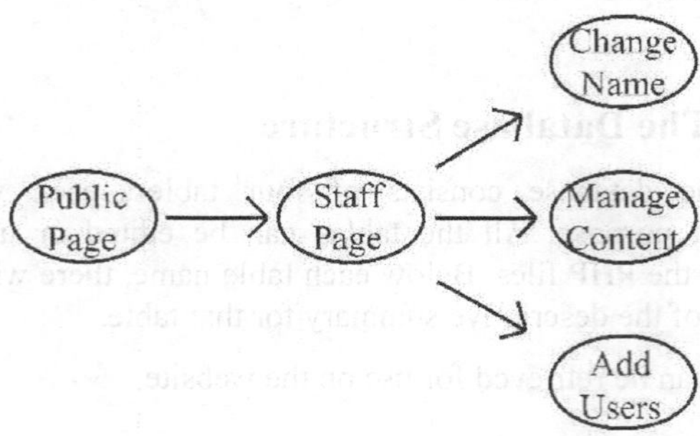

Figure 1 Flow char of the Website

When viewing the site, everyone starts at the public page. The public webpage can be multiple pages of information that the "staff" (administrator/s of the website) member has added through the staff area. The Staff Page can be accessed from the bottom of the public page through a link at the bottom. From the link, a user will be presented with a login page, displayed in Figure 2.

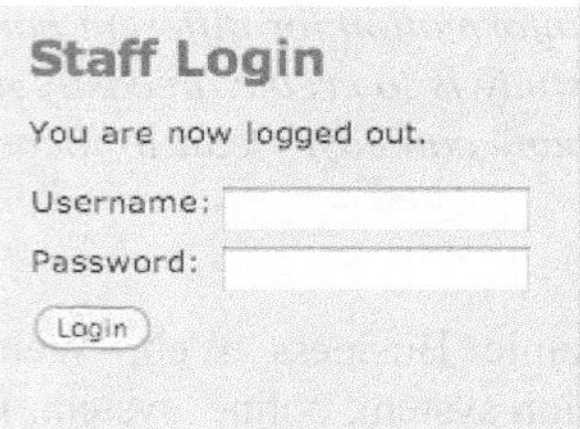

Figure 2 Login page

From this login area, a "staff" member can login to edit the website. Once the user has logged in, a session is started for the user. A session code (PHP) is used throughout the Staff Area to insure security, making sure no one can access this area without logging in first. After the username and password have been confirmed, the user is redirected to the Staff Menu. The following (Figure 3) is a display of the staff menu.

Staff Menu

Welcome to the staff area, users.

- Change Website Name
- Manage Website Content
- Add Staff User
- Logout

Figure 3 Staff menu page

From here, you can go to three different areas to edit the website. The first is "Change Website Name" and this allows the user to change the website name, which is displayed in the Title Bar of the website and the header of the actual website. The "Manage Website Content" area allows users to create, edit, and delete subjects and pages that will be viewed on the public website. Finally, the user can click the "Add Staff User" link. This area is for adding additional people to edit the content of the website

3 Case Study

There are total 23 PHP files in the system and a brief description is as follows.

content.php – the page that the user is redirected to when the "Manage Website Content" is clicked (link located in Staff Menu). Displays a link to all the current subjects/pages and also allows the user to create a new subject.

1)*create_name.php* – changes the name of the website in the Business_Name table and redirects to staff area.

2)*create_subject.php* – inserts the contents that is inserts the contents of the form into the subjects table then redirects to content.php

3)*delete_page.php* – deletes the page from the pages table and the website then redirect to content.php

4)*delete_subject.php* – deletes the subject from the subject table and the pages under that subject from the pages table then redirects to content.php

5)*edit_page.php* – presents a form to edit the content on a page then updates the changes in the page table.

6)*edit_subject.php* – presents a form to edit a subject then updates the changes to the subject table.

7)*index.php* – homepage/public page, display the content from all tables, except users, however no changes can be made.

8)*login.php* – displays a form to enter a username and password then checks the username and password with the users table, if they match, it starts a session and redirects to staff.php

9)*logout.php* – ends the session and redirects to index.php

10) *new_name.php* – displays a form to change then name of the website.

11) *new_page.php* – displays a form to create a new page.

12) *new_subject.php* – displays a form to create a new subject.

13) *new_user.php* – displays a form to add a new user.

14) *page_form.php* – displays a form for a page.

15) *staff.php* – displays the Staff Menu.

Seven of the .php files are used as includes for the websites:

16) *connection.php* – connects to the MySQL database.

```
<?php
require("constants.php");

$connection = mysql_connect(DB_SERVER,DB_USER,DB_PASS);
if (!$connection) {
    die("Database connection failed: " . mysql_error());
}

$db_select = mysql_select_db(DB_NAME,$connection);
if (!$db_select) {
    die("Database selection failed: " . mysql_error());
}
?>
```

Figure 4 The *connection.php* file

17) *constants.php* – constants that are used for the database connection.

18) *footer.php* – footer to be used for each page of the website.

19) *form_functions.php* – a list of functions that are used for forms in the website. Includes: check_required_fields, check_max_field_lengths, and display_errors.

20) *functions.php* – a list of functions that are used in many other PHP files. Includes:

a) mysql_prep (checks which PHP version)

b) redirect_to (used to switch to another page)

c) confirm_query (makes sure proposed query is valid)

d) get_all_subjects (collects all subjects from subjects table and returns all subjects)

e) get_pages_for_subject (collects pages from a subject and returns the pages)

f) get_subject_by_id (collects and returns a specific subject)

g) get_page_id (collects and returns a specific page)

h) get_default_page (gets the data for default page when a subject is selected in public view)

i) find_selected_page (gets the data for the page that is selected)

j) navigation (creates the navigation bar for the staff area)

k) public_navigation (creates the navigation bar for the public)

l) get_name (gets the business name from the Business_Name table)

21) *header.php* – header that is used for each page of the website.

22) *sessions.php* – starts session and confirms that the user is logged in.

```
<?php
    session_start();

    function logged_in() {
        return isset($_SESSION['user_id']);
    }

    function confirm_logged_in() {
        if (!logged_in()) {
            redirect_to("login.php");
        }
    }
?>
```

Figure 5 The *sessions.php* file

4 Conclusions

This paper introduce a business Website template system that was created a great way for a small business owner to have their own website, which they can easily edit without having to learn any computer languages. The use of PHP, CSS, and MySQL database were the right choice of languages to create a user-friendly site that would accomplish the goals of this project. The design and implementation strategy can be easily expanded in other online database applications.

5 References

[1] J. Ahigian and Z. Wang. "A low-cost online inventory database system" , Proceedings of the 2009 International Conference on E-Learning, E-Business, Enterprise Information Systems, & E-Government (EEE'09), 276-280, CSREA Press, 2009.

[2] D. Lash. "The Web wizard's guide to PHP", Prentice Hall, 2003.

[3] L. Ullman. "PHP and MySQL for Dynamic Web Sites". Peachpit Press, 2003.

An Online Database System for Card Stores

G. Johnson[1], Z. Wang[1,2], and X. Zhang[2]
[1]Department of Math/CS, Virginia Wesleyan College, Norfolk, VA, USA
[2]College of Information Engineering, Taiyuan University of Technology, Taiyuan, Shanxi, China

Abstract - *Purchasing cards can be a hassle at times. People always would like to buy product from local card stores; however, it is difficult for them to maintain an accurate card stock, as cards are coming and going at a constant rate. In attempts to promote keeping a constant database, an online store that can be used to purchase product and keep their inventories accurate. The purpose of this project was to create a reasonable database system that could be used by small card shops to maintain an online inventory that customers could view and that the shop would be able to easily edit and maintain. We use MySQL and PHP coding to implement the system.*

Keywords: Shopping store; card stores; database system; online information system; PHP/MySQL

1 Introduction

In the past decades, the online information technology has been one of the most interesting areas in the world [1]. But for small companies and institutions which represent the majority of the business activities, the studies of low-cost online database systems are very urgent and important. Even though there are some research reports in these fields [2][3], more methods of designs and implementations need to be explored. In this paper, we focus a few of the local stores that are interested in creating and maintaining an online database that already had a full list of all Magic: The Gathering cards in existence. After their inquiries, one of the local stores, ThetaTech, shared their findings. Robert Koon, owner of ThetaTech, stated that he found that only one company, Crystal Commerce, was the sole company that currently supplied any such database. Another company, StarCityGames, has a different database; however, it is a private database. Crystal Commerce requires a fairly reasonable upfront cost but also required an upkeep cost as well as a percentage of all online sales (Crystal Commerce). Robert mentioned that the pricing on the website was for a basic company, as they create an array of sites. Since Crystal Commerce would also be providing the Magic: The Gathering card database, the costs would be much higher. He explained that it would realistically take upwards of two years based on his average of sales to properly cover and see a true profit from the Crystal Commerce group site, due to the percentages they want from his online sales.

After this discussion, he was asked if another system were available at a more realistic price, would he consider buying it. He immediately said he would, as he doesn't like the interface of the system that is supplied by Crystal Commerce and it would be nice to have a more basic database, similar to StarCityGames. Ultimately, there is a want by companies to have a more simplistic system that could be used as either a basic database or an online sales system. The design of a Magic: The Gathering card database could take advantage of MySQL and PHP web coding to create a simple, yet efficient inventory system for these companies to use [4]. The paper is organized as follows. The system design methodology including the database structure and Web pages is presented in the second section. The case study for the whole system's content follows. The conclusion is given in the last section.

2 System Design

The purpose of this project was to create a reasonable database system that could be used by small card shops to maintain an online inventory that customers could view and that the shop would be able to easily edit and maintain. While this project could be completed with other methods, including simply adding links to spreadsheets on GoogleDocs or using HeidiSQL to create the database, the decision was made to use MySQL and PHP coding to design this site. For this project, the UNIX server at Virginia Wesleyan College, which had PHP and MySQL installed on it, was selected to create and display the system. This server and software would allow to properly store and code the site as needed. The project presents can easily be edited using HTML or CSS Stylesheets to visually enhance the site for each customer. The PHP is used to access and project the information from the MySQL tables onto the webpage, as well as for password security of the administration section.

2.1 The Database

The database consists of a single table, using an array of different columns. Only parts of the table can be edited or updated from the pHp files; however, new entries may be added from the PHP pages. Below is a screenshot of the table and information about each field type.

MagicList - This table stores all the data about the cards that is presented to the customer, shown in Table 1.

Table 1 The *MagicList* table

Field	Type	Null	Key	Default	Extra
Name	varchar(50)	YES		NULL	
ManaCost	varchar(15)	YES		NULL	
Rarity	varchar(5)	YES		NULL	
SetID	varchar(30)	YES		NULL	
CardCondition	varchar(5)	YES		NULL	
Price	double(7,2)	YES		NULL	
Stock	int(11)	YES		NULL	

Name - This field stores the name of each card. This is the first descriptive value used in differentiating cards.

ManaCost - This field stores the amount of Mana used to play the card in a game of Magic: The Gathering. This field is purely descriptive to assist the players.

Rarity - This field stores the rarity of the card. This is done with C being common, U being uncommon, R being rare, M being mythic rare, and L being a basic land.

SetID - This field stores the name of the set for each card. As some cards have an identical name, this field is used to differentiate one card from another, as it is possible for two cards to have the same name and different prices.

CardCondition: This field stores the value that represents the condition of the card. As card condition affects the value of each card. NM represents Near Mint or Mint condition, SP represents Slightly Played condition, MP stands for Moderately Played condition, and HP stands for Heavily Played condition. This is used to differentiate cards from the same set that should have different prices based on condition.

Price - This field stores the price of a particular card based on the information in the previous fields.

Stock - This field stores the quantity of the card that the store currently possesses.

2.2 The Website

When looking at this project, my website was developed to cover all the basic needs of the customer and the store. Here is a flowchart describing how the site actually works.

Figure 1 Login page

When everyone first reaches the website, they will begin at the main page. This is a public page used to give all users access to the public/non-password protected section of the site. In this public section, a person may log into the admin section, may search for a card, or may look at the entire inventory.

If a person attempts to log into the admin section, the password they enter is passed to via a PHP session. If they have entered the correct password, they will gain access to the admin section; however, if they entered the wrong password, they will be redirected to the log-in page to attempt again (Figure 2).

Figure 2 Failed to login message

Within the admin section, a user may also search for a card and see the entire inventory, as they can in the public section of the site. They may also do alterations to the price or stock of any particular card that is in the database. Finally, they may fill out a form and add more cards to the database. They are advised against adding entire sets of cards, as this will take a major amount of time. They may still do so, to save money if they feel it is worth their time.

3 Case Study

The overall content as well as example codes are introduced as follows. The System URL is: http://zwang.vwc.edu/~gcjohnson/CS489ProjectMain.html.

3.1 HTML Files

This project uses 4 HTML pages as part of the website.

a) *CS489ProjectMain.html* – This is the main page of the site and the page that links the user to any section they need access to.
b) *CS489ProjectPurpose.html* – This page was created as a source of explanation. It explains my entire reason for creating this particular project. The usefulness to the user is none and would be removed when presented to a customer.
c) *CS489ProjectSchedule.html* – This page was created as a source of explanation. It was used to display my tentative schedule for this particular project. The usefulness to the user is none and would be removed when presented to a customer.
d) *CS489AdminLog.html* – This is the page where the user enters the password to enter the Admin Section. This passes the entered value to a PHP file which starts the session for password protection.

3.2 PHP Files

This project's main driving force came from the usage of PHP code. Whether it was just for passing the session password, or for accessing the database created in MySQL, the PHP code gives the site many unique capabilities that not included in the spectrum of basic HTML coding. This project has 14 PHP pages.

a) *CS489AdminSection.php* - This is the main page of the admin portion of the site and the page that links the user to any section they need access to within the admin portion. The PHP is used to recheck the session stored password entry.
b) *CS489ProjectAdminSearch.php* – Form to input information user is searching for. This one is for the Admin section only.
c) *CS489ProjectAdminSearch2.php* – Page that publishes results of the user's search. This is for the Admin section only.
d) *CS489AdminLog.php* – This page receives the entry form CS489AdminLog.html and stores it into a new session. It then compares this stored entry with the site's private password. If the two match, it moves the user to CS489AdminSection.php; else it will redirect the user to return to the log-in page. Here is a section of code that shows this process.

```
<?php
    session_start();

    $pass = $_POST["pass"];
    $_SESSION['p'] = $pass;


    if($pass != "theta")
        print "Login fail! Go back to main page!
            <A HREF=CS489AdminLog.html>Go Back</A>";
    else
    {
?>
<script type="text/javascript">
<!--
        window.location = "CS489AdminSection.php"
//-->
</script>
<?php
    }
?>
```

e) *CS489ProjectAdminTable.php* – Displays the entire database to the Admin. Here is the code that accesses the MySQL table and displays it to the page.

```
$host = 'localhost';
$user = 'gcjohnson';
$passwd = 'cs480';
$database = 'gcjohnson';

$connect = mysql_connect($host, $user, $passwd);
$table_name = 'MagicList';

print "<P><CENTER>$table_name Data <P><HR>";

$query = "SELECT * FROM $table_name";
mysql_select_db($database);

$result_id = mysql_query($query, $connect);
if($result_id)
{
        print '<TABLE border=1>';
        print '<TH> Name <TH> ManaCost <TH> Rarity <TH> SetID
   <TH> CardCondition <TH> Price <TH> Stock';
        while($row = mysql_fetch_row($result_id))
        {
                print '<TR>';
                        foreach ($row as $field)
                                print "<TD>$field</TD>";
                print '</TR>';
        }
}
else
{    die ("Query=$query failed!");    }
mysql_close($connect);
```

f) *CS489ProjectPriceChange2.php* – Checks to make sure all fields that are required were filled in CS489ProjectPriceChange.php. If they were, it edits the price of the selected card from the database.

g) *CS489ProjectStockChange.php* – Form to input information for editing or updating the stock of a single card in the database.

h) *CS489ProjectStockChange2.php* – Checks to make sure all fields that are required were filled in CS489ProjectStockChange.php. If they were, it edits the stock count of the selected card from the database.

i) *CS489ProjectTable.php* – Displays the entire database to the general user. It returns each result as a link to a page that pertains to the particular item. For the purpose of this project, those pages were not written due to the volume of pages it would require.

j) *CS489ProjectCardSearch.php* – Form to input information user is searching for. This one is for the general section.

k) *CS489ProjectCardSearch2.php* – Page that publishes results of the user's search. This is for the general section.

l) *CS489ProjectNewCard.php* – Form to input information for a new card being added to the database.

m) *CS489ProjectNewCard2.php* – Checks to make sure all fields that are required were filled in CS489ProjectNewCard.php. If they were, it inserts the new card into the database.

n) *CS489ProjectPriceChange.php* – Form to input information for editing or updating the price of a single card in the database.

4 Conclusions

In conclusion, this project generated a basic database that could be used by local shops for their Magic: The Gathering inventory. In order to be completely useable by the shops, all the other sets would need to be input into the database and the stocks and prices properly updated. To accomplish the goal, MySQL and PHP provided the appropriate tools to compile and complete a basic database. With further study into MySQL and PHP, a much more complex database system can be created to generate greater uses for companies in need of online inventories.

5 References

[1] D. Weirich, and Z. Wang, The study of online cataloging information systems, *Proceedings of the 2008 International Conference on Parallel and Distributed Processing Techniques and Applications (PDPTA'08)*, 465-470, CSREA Press, 2008

[2] J. Ahigian and Z. Wang, A low-cost online inventory database system, *Proceedings of the 2009 International Conference on E-Learning, E-Business, Enterprise Information Systems, & E-Government (EEE'09)*, 276-280, CSREA Press, 2009

[3] P. Woodson and Z. J. Wang, A Shopping Store Online Information System, *Proceedings of the first International Conference on Computing, Measurement, Control, and Sensor Network*, 56-59, IEEE Computer Society, 2012

[4] D. Lash. *The Web wizard's guide to PHP*. Prentice Hall, 2003

SWEP Protocol and S-Wallet System - Mobile Payments using Near Field Communications

S. H. V. C. Silva, E. L. Flôres, G. A. Carrijo, A. C. P. Veiga, and M. B. P. Carneiro
Faculdade de Engenharia Elétrica, Universidade Federal de Uberlândia, Uberlândia, Minas Gerais, Brazil

Abstract — *This paper presents a system for mobile payments denominated S-Wallet using the technology of Near Field Communications (NFC) currently present in several smartphone devices. For this system, a protocol called SWEP was developed with encryption algorithms (RSA and 3DES). An application for the Android platform has been also developed in order to carry out performance tests and security. The protocol presented in this study proved to be adaptable to different situations of mobile payment. The S-Wallet system showed satisfactory results compared to other systems in the literature. The project carried out in this research can be used to maximize security, usability and efficiency of mobile payments.*

Keywords— Near Field Communications, Android, Mobile Payments Protocol, Mobile Payments, Mobile Wallet.

1 Introduction

Today, society has witnessed new forms of business relationship compared to methods of purchase and payment of the ninth century. The man has totally changed his way of interacting with society through the creation and popularization of the Internet occurred in 1994 [1]. After the introduction of security protocols [2] and technology such as Digital Subscriber Line (DSL) [3], the World Wide Web has been used continuously and in the year 2000 happened the "Internet Bubble" [4].

In the "Internet Bubble", many real-world companies whether they are telecom operators, financial institutions, or TV stations sponsored and invested in the creation and development of web portals for interacting with the Internet [5]. Emerged in this period the first e-commerce portals (e-commerce) [6], being performed by platforms such as web browser, or other types of devices that enable access to the worldwide web. The market began at this stage a reformulation, where the individual uses the means of payment such as credit cards or internet banking to make payments online.

In parallel to this novelty in the way of interaction between man and society, there was also an evolution of telecommunications technologies. The transmission of voice and data have evolved since the Global System for Mobile Communications (GSM) [7] and Code Division Multiple Access (CDMA) [8], to the 2G and 3G networks with High Speed Downlink Pocket Access Plus (HSPA+) [9] enabling rapid data transmission between cellular network, evolving to the current Long Term Evolution (LTE) [10]. The mobile phone has evolved from a mere device for voice communication between two people, or even groups of people, for a multifunction device with embedded operational system, now called "smartphone" [11].

Smart in the name and efficient in their functionality, the integration of an operational system to the smartphone enabled the reinvention of how humans deal with the internet, with media and with data. With the ability of just one touch of your fingers, you can have access to numerous applications within the Android platform (system created by Google) [12] or IOs platform (system developed by Apple) [13].

These applications enable the user interaction with social networks, reading of news feeds, magazines, and newspapers. The evolution of devices and mobile telecommunications networks enabled the human being to have control over your financial, social and professional life just by using a network-connected device.

In this environment of technological development, then we can mention the birth of a new mode of payment methods. With the wide penetration of smartphone on the market (today there are about 258 million mobile phones in Brazil, with 49 million of those using 3G data plan) [14] and the popularization of e-commerce ($11 billion is the expected total revenue for 2012) [15] thus arises the market for *e-wallets* [16] and *m-commerce* [17].

M-commerce is defined as mobile payment or m-payment, where the user makes the payments for purchases products, services, or accounts via cell phone or smartphone. This type of payment increases the speed of financial exchanges performed by the devices, enables retailers to customize the customer service and reduces costs for retailers and financial institutions. You can also consider the m-commerce as a subset of e-commerce, but with a real interaction between the user and the merchant, and virtual in how money is represented.

Define also e-wallets or Mobile Wallets as a software application to perform m-payment that is shipped in the smartphone with user details (possibly data from your bank account or credit card). This software allows you to make payments using this type of device. Users can integrate inside the smartphone various instruments of debit or credit in the same application.

The money that was previously used only by paper money and plastic cards with magnetic stripe or microchip, is now scanned. Therefore, large technology companies that perform payments like Google and Paypal, and financial institutions such as Mastercard and Visa are developing projects in the sector of mobile payments that is expected to grow to U.S. $ 172 billion in 2012 [18].

Mobile payments are divided into two types: remote mobile payments and mobile payments by proximity [19].

In remote mobile payment users log your transactions from anywhere, by sending Short Message Service (SMS) between the parties of using a platform Wireless Application Protocol (WAP). Transactions can be Person to Person (P2P) or Person to Business (P2B) [20].

The proximity mobile payment, known as contactless payment, occurs when a user has a phone with Near Field Communication technology (NFC). The technology boards a chip and antenna structure in the device hardware. This technology allows you to store user information and perform communication with readers in shops and retail establishments. To pay the user is required to bring the apparatus to a few centimeters from the reader and, through a wireless communication standard, the purchase is performed. This type of payment is studied in this paper, which is used NFC technology to develop a protocol that can provide secure financial transactions between two devices, good usability and user interaction.

This paper presents the development of a protocol for mobile payments in conjunction with an application for Android mobile platform, used to make payments with a smartphone. The purpose of this development is to define the communication between the protocol and application.

Based on the evolution of mobile payments mentioned in this paper, a system that integrates protocol and application was developed. This system was named Smart Wallet - S-Wallet. The goal of S-Wallet is to provide smartphone users a complete solution for P2P payments and POS (Point of Sale) payments.

The S-Wallet consists of a protocol for mobile payments called in this paper Smart Way for Easy Payments (SWEP). It also has an account in the cloud (cloud computing) [21] called S-Wallet Account, establishing contact between financial institutions and telecommunications companies to purchase credits and an application (App) for the Android platform.

This paper is structured as follows. Section 2 describes the NFC, Section 3 presents the technology used in the S-Wallet system and SWEP protocol and section 4 describes the App. The results obtained in the tests are presented in section 5. In section 6 a conclusion are made, and finally, section 7 shows the proposed future work.

2 NFC

The near field communication (NFC) is a radiofrequency technology, but it differs from others by its operating distance, which is typically 0-20cm between devices [22].

NFC is a technology that evolved from a combination of other Technologies for contactless identification and communication, which facilitates connectivity between electronic devices. It allows two-way interactions in a simple and safe way among electronic devices, allowing consumers to effect make safe contactless transactions, access digital content and connect devices with a single touch.

The purpose of NFC is to make communication between devices simpler. Just approaching them for this to occur, eliminating the need for any complex procedures. Because of the operating distance being short, this communication is inherently safe with respect to interception attempts. If you need to restrain this type of action, the routine security measures should be developed in the network protocol and / or application.

The NFC technology can be used mainly for two purposes:

• *Transmission of a small amount of data:* as the purpose is not to provide to the NFC great speeds, but a secure communication within walking distance, it is not suitable for the transmission of large volumes of data. Thus, data such as payment information, business cards, authentication, are best suited for transfers exclusively by NFC;

• *Initiator for secondary communication:* when recognizing two devices by simple approximation, the NFC can be used to initiate a secondary communication channel such as Bluetooth or Wi-Fi.

The NFC specification also states that this technology is compatible with Radiofrequency Identification devices (RFID), which operate on the same frequency and same modes of operation (especially passive) [23]. In this way many NFC enabled devices are able to emulate RFID cards or tags.

3 SWEP protocol

In this section, we define the members of SWEP protocol, as S-Wallet account as well as communications performed between different parts of the cycle of mobile payments. The SWEP protocol was developed in this work in order to provide security and convenience for purchases made with smartphone devices. These devices feature NFC technology, which allows to pay for purchases at retail stores or payments between customers (P2P). The use of this protocol requires the user to own a bank account, or a signature of operator plans or pre-paid to the transfer of funds to the S-Wallet account.

The S-Wallet system meets the needs of users such as security, usability and anonymity. With SWEP protocol, the information is encrypted, communication occurs through secure connections and the exchange of certificates. Moreover, this protocol is based on password authentication, facial or QR-Code for the registration confirmation and payment.

The participating entities of the payment cycle in the structure of S-Wallet are: Bank, Telecommunication Operator, Client Application, Retail (Shop), P2P Application, S-Wallet account. Figure 1 shows this structure interaction.

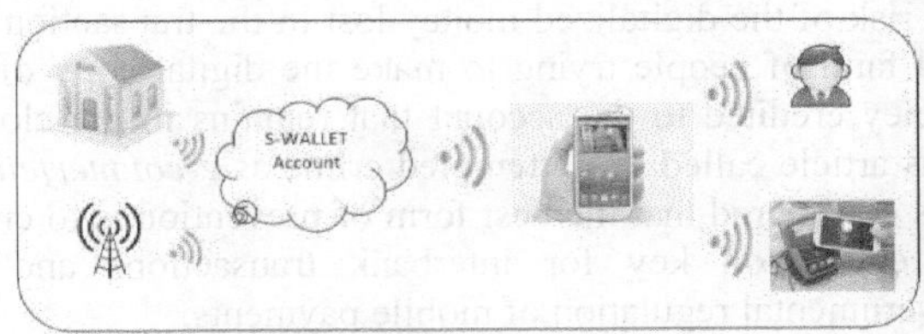

Figure 1 - Entities participating in the payment cycle of S-Wallet.

This article shows the communication between the S-Wallet Account, the Client Applications and P2P. However, this work is not intended to provide information about the communication between financial institutions and telecommunications to the S-Wallet, neither the possibility of payments between Customer and Retail.

The goal of S-Wallet Account is to keep in real-time all parties that interact during payment transactions integrated and with access to information relating to balance, credit, debt and transaction history. This account is stored in the cloud and can be accessed from any mobile device and personal computer. The credit authorizations received by the S-Wallet Account are transferred to the Client Application.

Client Application: it is the App installed on the client device that performs the operations of network communication, protocol and start making the payment. Moreover, App stores the data and information pertaining to the transaction.

P2P application: it is the App installed on the user's smartphone to make P2P payments. This App has the same purpose of the Client Application. The App behaves in two ways: *receiving and sending.* The first when it receives payments and the second when it performs payments.

The S-Wallet account remains stored in the cloud, where the customer can transfer amounts from your bank account or your operator account. Through this establishment of credits within the account, the user can make mobile payments. Here begins the first part of the protocol and the definition of *eNotas.*

eNotas: It can be defined as the creation of virtual money. Its structure consists of: an ID, a public key encryption, digital certificates, authentication, monetary value of the amount to be transferred, and a signature of the account. This signature is 128 bytes in size, and this structure is stored in a sequence of bytes (byte array), creating essentially one eNota of 170 bytes. The eNota is inserted into a data packet is encrypted and forwarded for P2P payments or POS.

3.1 SWEP Structure

One of the concerns regarding the development of the SWEP protocol in this work was related to the security of financial transactions between the entities of the S-Wallet system. This concern is inherent because, after the acquisition of credits by the user, P2P trade could be executed in *offline* mode. Therefore it is not possible to check all transactions.

It was also verified in this paper some risks such as: the risk of the digitalized money lost in the transaction and bad faith of people trying to make the digital copy of the money credited to the account that remains in the clouds. This article called this attempted crime as *e-counterfeiting*. It is considered that the best form of prevention is to create an encryption key for interbank transactions and the governmental regulation of mobile payments.

At the time of creation of S-Wallet Account, the user download to your personal computer an application of the S-Wallet account. On this account the user can manage their credit data, balances, history, and make new credit transfers. In this record, the user creates an ID linked to all your transfers.

The next step is to make the user download the S-Wallet App on your smartphone. This App is defined as a MIDlet, developed in Java ME for Android. This MIDlet protocol was implemented with SWEP to perform every communication between entities and with special functionalities.

During registration, at first, the connection between the S-Wallet Account and Client Application enables the exchange of digital certificates and public key of the account. The S-Wallet Account has a private key for authentication with users. The RSA key pair used to authenticate the client with other users and payment terminals is generated by the App. During startup, the ID of the user account and the public key (RSA) are registered with the S-Wallet account. This account sends to the client an authentication certificate linked to your ID. With the receipt of the user's public key, the S-Wallet (Account) also generates an X.509 certificate to the public key and sends it to the Client App.

In a second stage, the existing credit balance in the account can be used by the App for the creation of eNotas. These eNotas are coded and entered into a data packet (issuer) and are sent to another Client App (receiver). During reception of eNota, the smartphone receptor initiates the MIDlet, which decodes it, it extracts the data, and verifies the client certificate authentication. Users can manage their eNotas through S-Wallet App, allowing also managing the balance and history of transactions.

3.2 Structure of the cryptographic keys

The keys that are part of the SWEP protocol are respectively:

• The S-Wallet Account has two RSA key pairs: one for signature and another for encoding. The key signature is used to authenticate the exchange of credits between the account and Client App. We use this key also to generate certificates for POS terminals. The key pair encodings provides secure data communication between entities that are part of the process, and

• The App Client on the mobile user has a unique RSA key pair, which receives a certificate signed by the S-Wallet account. Using this certificate and the corresponding private key, the app can communicate securely and with other Apps and certified payment terminals. For practical reasons, this key pair is used to sign and encrypt.

3.3 Stages of SWEP

During the development of the SWEP protocol many interactions were thought among the entities of the payment flow. This article shows the interaction between two customers during the performance of a P2P payment.

As previously mentioned, the App of the receiver client behaves in a passive manner (smart card). Moreover, the App of the emitter client acts as an active device. This emitter simulates a smart card terminal, which initiates the communication security in S-Wallet account. This active mode is provided by the App (MIDlet). The MIDlet is the center of communication and coding of the entire payment flow.

Following the steps of the message flow and the stages of the SWEP protocol are defined for a P2P payment between customers using the S-wallet App:

1) The sender (App Client 1 - App-1) selects the App (MIDlet) to transfer monetary values to the receiver (Client 2 App - App-2). After identification (facial recognition or PIN) with the App, the user accesses your data panel, with the possibility of creating a eNota with a certain value to be transferred. It starts a request for communication between users. In that first handshake between the issuer App and the receiver App, there is an exchange of information regarding IDs and authentication certificates to ensure security of the connection and the information to be transmitted;

2) Once you have determined the amount to be transferred, we can define the value of the *eNota* of X$ (Dollars). Performs up the process of transferring the eNota from App-1 to App-2 using NFC. The MIDlets of these two clients interact through a secure channel to ensure effective connection between devices;

3) After the creation of eNota, App Receiver (Client App - 2 or App-2) generates a random X code and sends it to the issuer's App (App Client - 1 or App-1), along with the PKI certificate key-related to the MIDlet (and also to the receiver). This certificate contains the ID of the App-2 and its public key;

4) After receiving X and certificate, App-1 performs the following steps:

• Checks information on the certificate, extracts the ID from App-2 and its public key;

• Creates a random and symmetric session key (3DES) C1;

• The RSA encodes the C1 key with the public key of the App-2. Resulting in R1 response;

• Generates an ID for that session;

• The RSA encryption, digitally signs (X, session ID, Receiver ID, C1) with the RSA private key from App-1. The answer R2 consists in session ID and certificate information of App-1; and

• Send the answers R1 and R2 to the App-2.

5) After receiving (responses R1, R2), the App-2 performs the following steps:

• The RSA encryption decodes the response R1 with the private key of the App-2. Resulting in key C1;

• Store the session ID;

• Checks the certificate of App-1;

• Verifies the signature of the App-1in X, in the session ID, in the receiver ID and in the key C1;

• Calculates the key Message Authentication Code (MAC) C2 = SHA-1 (C1);

• Calculates a 3DES MAC in the session ID and in X, with the key C2, generating the response R3, and

• Sends the response R3 to App-1.

6) The App A-1 receives the response R3, verifies the MAC, performs a 3DES encryption of eNota under the key C1, resulting in message M1 and sends it to the App-2;

7) The App-2 decodes the message M1, stores and verifies eNota, calculates a 3DES MAC named of message M2 under the received eNota with the C2 key and sends it to the App-1;

8) When the App-1 receives the message M2, it checks the MAC, and if successful, the system delivers these and launches a data in the transaction history; and

9) After performing steps 1-8, App-2 can notify the user of the arrival of a new eNota.

There is at the SWEP protocol an assurance that the symmetric key C1 is generated by S-Wallet App. This key is signed with a certified key pair. Moreover, after the response R3, both applications Client 1 and 2 have the legitimacy of communication reliability. As the App-2 (receiver) correctly recovers the C1 key, this proves that it has the private key connected with your certificate. With this, the App-1 (issuer) shows the possession of the private key signing X, the session ID and the C1 key properly. Thus, it is established that X was received correctly, the session ID and the C1 key are unique and the message is destined to the App Client 2.

4 App S-Wallet

In the first stage of the S-Wallet system, the graphical user interface and layout of the application have not been developed. However, several tests were conducted of the functionality and usability of this system taking into account the reliability of the exchange of messages, the security in the execution and completion of the transaction.

The application of S-Wallet installed on user's mobile device behaves as a middleware. For better integration of all structures of this system, it was developed using the Android SDK platform based on Java.

The Fig. 2 shows the S-Wallet system structure.

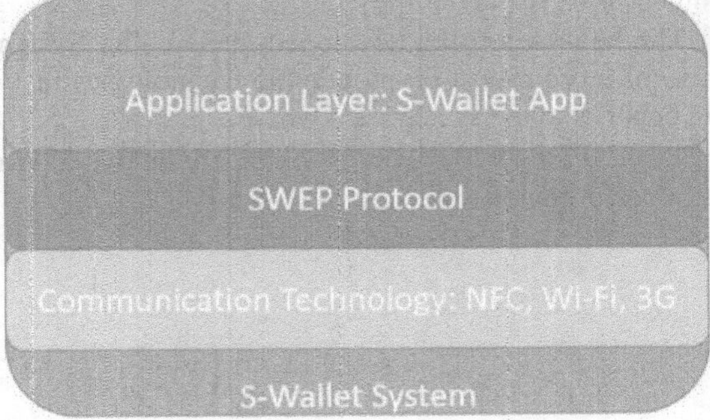

Figure 2 – S-Wallet system structure.

In the Application Layer exists the user interaction through S-Wallet App. All security operations and integration are performed by SWEP protocol. The main communication technology of the S-Wallet system is the NFC. This technology enables the exchange of information at close range.

The S-Wallet account is part of the system as a whole, but considering the blocks to be installed and initialized by the user's mobile device it remains at a higher level. Even interacting with all the system, that account remains stored in the cloud and it is not part of any system layer.

5 Results

This section describes the hardware equipment and software used in the development of the S-Wallet and tests performed to verify the performance, security and usability of the system.

For the simulation of a cloud service representing the S-Wallet Account, we used a Samsung Chronos NP700 notebook with Core i5, 6GB RAM, using Apache Tomcat. The Account was developed in Java using the Java Card Development Kit to facilitate integration with the Android application.

Because NFC is a technology being developed and its integration with mobile devices is still small, the final choice of device to be used was the device Galaxy S III with Cortex-A9 1.4 GHz Quad-core processor, 1 GB of RAM and Android OS, v4.0.4 (Ice Cream Sandwich).

The application for Android was developed in Java language using the Eclipse IDE and the Android SDK platform. The S-Wallet application was developed in a basic way in its design in order to test the communication protocol and the completion of an exchange of data between two devices with the application installed.

The first test was to verify the performance of the SWEP protocol. The goal of the S-Wallet system is to provide fast mobile payment and also security in data exchange. The implemented solution has presented 5 sec *overhead* in computational calculations related to encoding and decoding encryption.

Due to the use of a robust hardware like the Galaxy S III processor (Cortex-A9), the use of encodings and security signatures as RSA, 3DES and SHA-1 brought the expected performance to the S-Wallet system. This system has demonstrated safety and reliability in data exchange payments with virtual money.

The next step to be developed in S-Wallet System is the use of more robust cryptographic technologies that can bring benefits to the system as a whole.

Table 1 show the results obtained in the S-Wallet system performance test.

Table 1 - S-wallet system performance

System Activity	Time (ms)
Startup of the S-Wallet MIDlet	1.350
Authentication (Facial or PIN)	1.850
Select Type of Payment	210
P2P connection	770
Choice of the value of eNota	500
Sending eNota	3.570
Complete transaction / Receipt of completed transaction	3.680
TOTAL	**11.930**

It can be seen in Table 1 that the activity of the system that requires more time to be realized is the "Sending eNota" and data exchanged for the completion of the transaction. These two activities result in 7250 ms, being 3680 ms and 3570 respectively. This occurs due to the exchange of certificates and cryptographic keys. The total duration of the activities performed by the system S-Wallet was 11,930 ms.

Table 2 illustrates the results of performance of the cryptographic security system of the S-Wallet, taking into consideration the steps performed by the SWEP Protocol.

Table 2 – Performance of the cryptographic security system of s-wallet.

Encryption of S-Wallet	Time (ms)
Account Authentication S-Wallet/App	5.000
Exchange of certificates App-1 / App-2	1.520
RSA encryption (Step 4)	377
Coding RSA/3DES/SHA-1 (Step 5)	585
3DES encryption (Step 6)	150
3DES encryption (Step 7)	148
Final Authentication / Transaction Receipt	487
TOTAL	**8.267**

It can be observed in Table 2 that the total time of the cryptographic system of the S-Wallet account was 8267 ms.. When you increase the amount of data transferred, the calculation result of the transaction time of 10 eNotas from one smartphone to another was 14.8 seconds. Thus, when two clients are already authenticated, the time average of the data flow between the App-1 and App-2 is 1.48 sec per eNota.

Regardless of the number of eNotas used, there was an *"overhead"* of 4.8 sec. This value can be considered relatively large, taking into account the expectation of performance expected during the SWEP protocol development. This high *overhead* was due to encryption protocols used and the way the smartphone communicate with each other.

The majority of the time used for cryptographic coding was due to the asymmetric key operations (RSA). It can be seen from Table 2 that the total time used in coding RSA (RSA encryption (Step 4) + Coding RSA/3DES/SHA-1 (Step 5)) was 962 ms.. The overhead of using the RSA is another significant reason for the high time of the transaction for the S-Wallet System.

6 Conclusions

This paper presented a system for mobile payments called S-Wallet using NFC technology currently present in several smartphone devices. For this system, we developed a protocol named SWEP with encryption algorithms (RSA and 3DES) and certificate exchange between the parties to make a highly secure communication.

The protocol SWEP fulfilled the requirements of reliability, safety and speed in the financial transaction of sending the eNota. In order to perform the tests, the application for the Android platform was developed in a simple manner. The S-Wallet system proposed in this article uses the Android SDK based on JAVA.

The main advantage of S-Wallet system compared to systems currently developed is that the integration between the S-Wallet Account, the App and SWEP protocol provided more security and speed for the transaction of mobile payments.

At first the S-Wallet System user depends only on devices online to receive credit on your account. However during the continuity of transactions, everything else occur *offline*.

The efficiency of encryption keys of SWEP protocol enabled security and usability for the end user.

7 Future work

As future work we intend to develop a protocol with encryption keys such as AES and ECDSA. These keys can provide higher speed and higher performance for the S-Wallet.

The speed of the encryption system can be improved with the analysis and development of a code that is based on hybrid algorithms using symmetric and asymmetric keys.

Moreover, as future work, we will improve the user interface by developing a more interactive layout. You can with this layout test the system in the field, bringing the results that may be studied. These studies will allow us to compare the S-Wallet System with other existing technologies, helping to continually improve this system in future versions.

8 References

[1] T. J. Berners-Lee, R. Cailliau, J-F Groff, B. Pollermann, (1992) CERN, "World-Wide Web: An Information Infrastructure for High-Energy Physics", Proceedings published by World Scientific, Singapore, ed. D Perret-Gallix, 1992.

[2] E. Rescorla, (2000) “Http over tls”, RFC 2818.

[3] T. Starr, J. M. Cioffi, P. J. Silverman, “Understanding digital subscriber line technology”, 1999 - Prentice Hall.

[4] A. B. Perkins, M. C. Perkins, “The Internet bubble: the inside story on why it burst--and what you can do to profit now!”, 2001 – Harper business.

[5] J. M. Gallaugher, C. E. Downing, “Portal Combat: An Empirical Study of Competition in the Web Portal Industry”, Journal of Information Technology Management. Vol. 11, No. 1-2, 2000, pp. 13-24.

[6] E. Turban, J. K. Lee, D. King, T. P. Liang, and D. Turban. 2009. “Electronic Commerce 2010 (6th ed..)”. Prentice Hall Press, Upper Saddle River, NJ, USA.

[7] M. Mouly, Marie-Bernadette Pautet. 1992. “The GSM System for Mobile Communications”. Telecom Publishing.

[8] Andrew J. Viterbi. 1995. “CDMA: Principles of Spread Spectrum Communication”. Addison Wesley Longman Publishing Co., Inc., Redwood City, CA, USA.

[9] Harri Holma and Antti Toskala. 2006. “HSDPA/HSUPA for UMTS: High Speed Radio Access for Mobile Communications”. John Wiley & Sons.

[10] Stefania Sesia, Issam Toufik, and Matthew Baker. 2009. *Lte, the UMTS Long Term Evolution: From Theory to Practice*. Wiley Publishing.

[11] PC Magazine. (2011b). “Smartphone Definition from PC Magazine Encyclopedia. PC Magazine. Accessed on August 20th, 2012: http://www.pcmag.com/encyclopedia_term/0,2542,t=Smartphone&i=51537,00.asp

[12] Margaret Butler. 2011. Android: Changing the Mobile Landscape. *IEEE Pervasive Computing* 10, 1 (January 2011), 4-7.

[13] Sharon P. Hall and Eric Anderson. 2009. Operating systems for mobile computing. J. Comput. Small Coll. 25, 2 (December 2009), 64-71.

[14] TELECO – Inteligência em Telecomunicações – “3G: 3ª Geração de Celular no Brasil”. Avalable at: http://www.teleco.com.br/3g_brasil.asp. Data de acesso: 20/08/2012

[15] PLUS Consultoria em e-commerce – “E-commerce no Brasil”. Avalable at: http://www.plusecommerce.com.br/p/e-commerce-no-brasil.html. Data de acesso: 20/08/2012

[16] Gusev, Marjan. "E-Commerce A big step towards E-Bussiness". Institute of Informatics Faculty of National Sciences and Mathematics, University St .Cyril And Methodius”, 2011.

[17] Dahlberg, Tomi, et al. "Past, present and future of mobile payments research: A literature review." Electronic Commerce Research and Applications 7.2 (2008): 165-181.

[18] ABRAS – Associação Brasileira de Supermercados – “Tecnologia poderá impulsionar reinvenção do dinheiro”. Avalable at: http://www.abrasnet.com.br/clipping.php?area=5&clipping=31250. Data de acesso: 21/08/2012.

[19] Urbino, Natacha P., et al. "Mobile Payment: Uma visão geral." FaSCi-Tech1.3 (2012).

[20] Shy, Oz. "Person-to-person electronic funds transfers: recent developments and policy issues." FRB of Boston Public Policy Discussion Paper 10-1 (2010).

[21] Armbrust, Michael, et al. "A view of cloud computing." Communications of the ACM 53.4 (2010): 50-58.

[22] Fischer, Jeffrey. "NFC in cell phones: The new paradigm for an interactive world [Near-Field Communications]." Communications Magazine, IEEE 47.6 (2009): 22-28.

[23] Michahelles, Florian, et al. "Pervasive RFID and near field communication technology." Pervasive Computing, IEEE 6.3 (2007): 94-96.

Multidisciplinarity in Knowledge Transmision Management System (KTMS) evaluation.

Etienne Z. Gnimpieba, Douglas Jennewein, Luke Fuhrman, Carol M. Lushbough
Computer Science Department, University of South Dakota, 414 E. Clark St. Vermillion, SD 57069, USA,
{Etienne.gnimpieba; Doug.Jennewein; Luke.Fuhrman, Carol.Lushbough}@usd.edu

Corresponding author: Etienne.gnimpieba@usd.edu, +1 605 223 0383.

~o~

Abstract: Translational pluridisciplinary education has become a strong academic challenge in this century. The internet has proved its potential for creating online learning environments to support education. The development of the web based knowledge transmission management system (KTMS) faces many shortcoming, including lack of pedagogical consideration in the design of web-based learning Systems, lack of interoperability and shareable learning objects, and lack of interdisciplinary integration. These shortcomings are not easy to identify by common end users. Decision makers need formal indicators to guide their choice. This paper aim to provide a flexible criteria set for KTMS evaluation involving multidisciplinarity, sharability and collaborativity.

Keywords: knowledge, learning object, learning object repositories, evaluation criteria, education, multidisciplinary.

1. Introduction

Personalized e-commerce improves customer-relationship management (CRM) to provide better service by anticipating customer needs even if data are from different data source. This is because customer satisfaction is the most important focus in CRM systems design. Education aims is ensure that tools improve students' learning process. A Knowledge Transmision Management System (KTMS) is define to be a web portal or tool that provides resources for learning, teaching, training, or helping with executing work/problems. It can be a learning object repository (LOR), learning management system (LMS), courses management system (CMS), virtual learning environment (VLE), computer based training (CBT) portal or a simple website. Any Knowledge Transmission Management System (KTMS) must enable users to personalize their learning in order to adapt to changing business needs (career profile). These requirements expose many weaknesses of KTMS: interoperability, share ability, industry guidance for manageable system design, and pedagogical consideration in the design of web-based learning systems and multidisciplinary management [1]. Among other things, the transversality of certain disciplines such as bioinformatics does not facilitate the construction of a linear training profile, based on a set of pre-requisites of formal education discipline [2]. This feature is a weakness because it contradicts the need for specialization training and the increasing need for crossing disciplines (interdisciplinarity, pluridisciplinarity). But it may prove to be a strength in the construction of a flexible profile, including adaptability to a particular career profile.

We are witnessing a growing development of tools for managing the transmission of knowledge using computer engineering, called *computer-based teaching education* (CBTE). Users need to choose an appropriate tool; and to be able to evaluate the quality of the results obtained from using that tool. The existing evaluation criteria for KTMS tools are based on the specific needs of particular users or owners of these tools [3] [4] [5]. In addition, these criteria do not take into account the multidisciplinarity aspects of the new generation of academic disciplines (Bioinformatics, sociolinguistics, pharmacogenomics, nanotechnology, genetic toxicology, etc.) [6]. We propose new criteria to expand these KTMS evaluation criteria. Our approach is based on the use of communication evaluation tools and exigencies that relate to multidisciplinary.

2. Multidisciplinarity criteria for LORs evaluation

To make a decision as to the usefulness of a tool for managing the transmission of knowledge (KTMS), many objective and functional criteria are necessary. Our proposed criteria provide a 5 axis feature to measure a given KMS: pedagogy (P), technical (T), communication (C), interdisciplinarity (I), and other criteria related to the specific user context (O). Each criterion overall (P, T, C, I, O) can be detailed to refine the evaluation in a given axis, as with the technical criterion T (Figure 1).

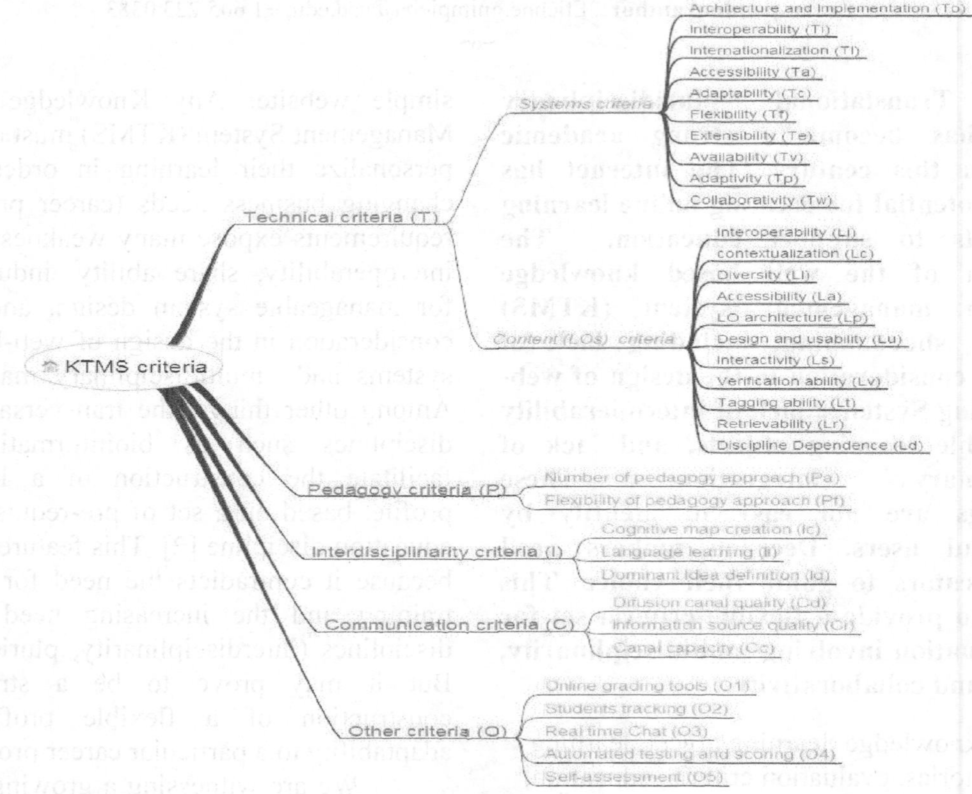

Figure 1: Overview concept map summarizing our multi-criteria set (5 global criteria and 34 detail criteria).

2.1. Pedagogy based criteria (P)

The evolution of pedagogical requirements of education, and the particularity of bioinformatics necessitates an adaptation of evaluation parameters in pedagogy [7][8]. We propose two criteria for KTMS pedagogy evaluation: the number of pedagogical approaches (Pa), and the flexibility of these approaches in the KTMS (Pf).

- Number of pedagogical approaches (Pa).

There are no standards in terms of pedagogical approach [9], but a few commonly used approaches are: competence-based teacher education (CBTE), humanistic-based teacher education (HBTE), problem based, team based, academic tradition, social efficiency tradition, developmentalist tradition, social reconstructionist tradition, writing for learn, etc. For efficiency (efficacy with optimal resources), knowledge transmission systems should allow the possibility to choose and combine several training pedagogical approaches. Pa describes the number of pedagogical approaches that can be used in the tool. Formally, we have:

$$Pa = [1 \ldots k] \qquad \text{(Eq.1)}$$

Where k is the maximum number of pedagogical approaches in the system.

- **Flexibility of the pedagogy approach (Pf)**

To use a single educational approach to efficiently transmit multi-disciplinary knowledge is difficult. An ability to change pedagogical approaches is important in a good KTMS. Pf criterion depends on the number of pedagogical approaches (Pa) described previously. Pf measure the ability of the KTMS, to use several pedagogical approaches simultaneously.

2.2. System and Content Technical criteria (T)

Content (Learning Objects, LOs) of KTMS (LORs, LMS, CMS, VLEs) do not yet possess international standards. [5] proposes a set of criteria by federation of seven main characteristics of (LOs). This criterion set can follow LOs in its life cycle (before, during and after, including in KTMS). These criteria cannot allow understanding of the multidisciplinary aspect of LO and KTMS. We propose two additional criteria to improve these limits: Ld (dependence between two or more disciplines for each given LOs), and Tc (collaborativity in the KTMS as ability to integrate collaboration, networking, sharing). We have 11 criteria for describing LOs (Table 1 grey background) and 10 criteria for KTMS design (Table 1 white background).

Table 1: BKTMS and content evaluation criteria description.
Table 1 shows the criteria for KTMS (LMS, LOR, VLE, etc) in grey background and their content (LOs) in white background, with collaborative and discipline dependence criteria Ld.

Criteria	Description	Code
Interoperability	Metadata accuracy, Compliance with the main import/export standards (IMS, SCORM, LOM, IMS).	Li
Contextualization	Is LO indivisible (atomic)? LO aggregation (granularity) level, Is LO modular? Does LO have a strong visual element?	Lc
Diversity / Internationalization	Is LO flexible (can be modified)? LO suitability for localisation LO internationalisation level, language.	Ll
Accessibility	Is LO designed for all? Compliance with accessibility standards (W3C).	La
LO architecture	Is LO architecture layered in order to separate data, presentation and application logics?	Lp
Design and usability	Aesthetics, Navigation, User-friendly interface, Information structuration, Personalization.	Lu
Interactivity	Member's contribution strategies.	Ls
Verification ability	Automatic verification of capability with known protocols.	Lv
Tagging ability	Automatic metadata generation or simplified metadata tagging.	Lt
Retrievability	User should be able to retrieve LO in different ways.	Lr
Discipline dependence	LO should depend on more than one discipline.	Ld
Overall architecture and implementation	Scalability,Modularity (of the architecture), Possibility of multiple installations on a single platform, Reasonable performance optimisations, Look and feel is configurable, Security, Modular authentication, Robustness and stability, Installation, dependencies and portability.	To
Interoperability	Integration is straightforward, VLE standard support.	Ti
Internationalization and localization	Localisable user interface, Localisation to relevant languages, Unicode text editing and storage, Time zones and date localization, Alternative language support.	Tl
Accessibility	Text only navigation support, Scalable fonts and graphics.	Ta
Adaptability	Facilities to customise for the educational institution's needs.	Tc
Flexibility	Personalisation aspects (facilities of each individual user to his/her own view of the platform).	Tf
Extensibility	Good programming style, Availability of a documented API.	Te
Availability	On licence, partialy open or open.	Tv
Adaptivity	all kinds of automatic adaptation to the individual user's needs, Personal annotations of LOs, Automatically adapted content.	Tp
Collaborativity	Ability to integrate collaborative work, networking, sharing.	Tw

- **Discipline dependency (Ld).**

This criterion measures the ability of each LO to interact with other disciplines, and especially different disciplines. As in all pluridisciplinary domains, the multidisciplinary course content depends on the specialty of the person who builds it. Thus bioinformatics courses vary as a function of the professor's specialty (biologist or computational scientist) [10]. Pevzner proposes a bioinformatics course characterization approach using game theory, the goal (success) being to find the best strategy for a bioinformatics problem solution. Starting from their own background (biology or computer science), users take supplemental courses (computer science or biology) to enhance skills. This perception helps us to define the dependency discipline criterion in KTMS. This ability can be "high (3), medium (2) or low (1)". We have:

$$Ld = [1\ 2\ 3] \quad \text{(Eq.2)}$$

Formal explanation of the Ld criterion:

Let P be a pluridisciplinary problem (with n disciplines d1 .. dn), where obtaining the solution S requires the skills set Sk1, Sk2, Sk3.

Assume that, for a given skill Ski, a user may have Low level (L or 1), Medium (M or 2), or High (H or 3). The resolution of the problem P requires at least M level on each used skill Sk1, Sk2 and Sk3.

Let (u1..un) represent n users whose backgrounds are respectively (d1..dp) in p disciplines. Let C1 represent a course which delivers skills Sk1, Sk4 in the discipline d1.

The Ld criterion for the course C1 (LO) will define its ability to allow users to include a course containing skills Sk2 and Sk3 helpful to the resolution of the problem P. This ability may be high, medium or low. $Ld = [1\ 2\ 3]$ by equation (Eq.2).

Example: in bioinformatics (n = 2, biology and computer science), P can be DNA sequence alignment with Sk1=Algorithm, Sk2 =BLAST tool used and Sk3 = sequencing DNA (Figure 2).

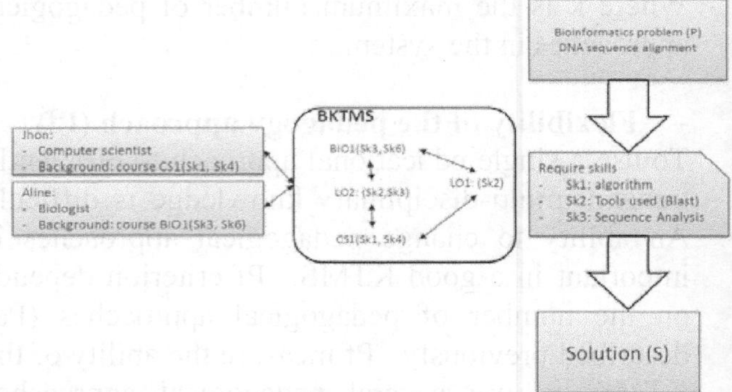

Figure 2: Example of bioinformatics discipline dependence Ld involved in 2 LOs (LO1, LO2) for a given KTMS.

Consider two users, John and Aline, with computer science and biology backgrounds respectively. Figure 2 shows the dependence that may exist in interdisciplinary training for Aline and John in this case.

- **Collaborativity (Tw).**

The development of pluridisciplinary programs like bioinformatics is accelerating, given translational science needs. Web technologies are changing with the involvement of users in system design as well as in the creation and management of massive data (Web3.0, web services, workflow). The interactivity, the connectivity, and the sharability become inherent in the performance of web-based systems like the KTMS. The Tw criterion measures the ability of the KTMS to facilitate collaboration, networking and sharing of resources.

2.2.1 Communication criteria (C)

Based on information theory, we propose in this paragraph a characterization of communication between users (student, teacher, etc) through the KTMS. Information from a sender to a receiver using communication channels (language, format, support material, software, etc.) is represented here in the KTMS. We have the broadcast or diffusion channel (Figure 3a), the multiple access channel (Figure 3b) and the multiple access broadcast channel. (Figure 3c).

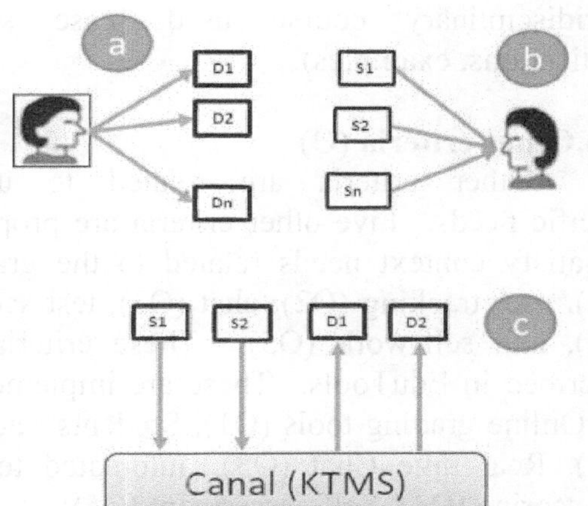

Figure 3: Communication channel types, broadcast (a), multiple access (b), multiple access broadcast (c).

KTMS functions can be modeled by a multiple access diffusion channel. Indeed, a KTMS can be represented as an intermediary between the source and destination in knowledge transmission. We study here how to improve the communication performances through those of KTMS which plays a preponderant role in knowledge efficient transfer. Like any communication channel, the performance is given by its capacity and its protocol (Jacquet et al. 2008). This corresponds to the possibility of a KTMS to meet all the needs of the user (the channel capacity), and to have a protocol that ensures the quality of transmission. The criteria proposed here are based on the Shanon theory for communication [11] and derivative works [12][13][14]. We have identified three criteria: Number of diffusion channels (Cd) (video, slide, image, animations, etc); Quality of information Sources (Ci); Channel capacity (Cc).
According to the previous cited works, we have:

$$C_m = max_X\left\{\left(h\left(T((X))\right) - h(T(X)/X)\right\}\right.$$
(Eq.3)

where
C_m is the channel maximal capacity
X is the information sent from the source
$T(X)$ is the information decoded by receptor (understand)
h is the entropy of X. Then h is the incertitude (error or probability) on the information received.
Since $h(X) \in [0..1]$, then, $C_m \in [0..1]$.
We describe then Cc as a characteristic function given by:

$$Cc(X) = \begin{cases} 8 \text{ if } Cm = 0 \\ 6 \text{ if } 0 < Cm \leq 0.5 \\ 3 \text{ if } 0.5 < Cm \leq 0.75 \\ 1 \text{ if } 0.75 < Cm \leq 1 \end{cases} \quad \text{(Eq.4)}$$

<u>Use explanation process:</u>

- The sender encodes the information X: C(X).
  Example: the teacher built the course resource (containing knowledge)
- The sender transmits C(X) (using the KTMS), and the receiver get Y=T(C(X))
- The receiver decodes the information Y: D(Y). There are errors if D(Y) is different from X. *(for example, the administrator or student gives a bad evaluation in return)*.

2.3. Interdisciplinarity based criteria (I)

Making changes in education requires a redefinition of the notion of academic discipline. It is problematic today to adjust some curricula to the old definition of academic discipline (e.g. math, physics, biology, english, etc.). One of the principal reasons for this difficulty is the intersection of disciplines (e.g. transdisciplinarity, interdisciplinarity, pluridisciplinarity). Here, it's important to mention the subtle difference between these X-disciplinarity (X=trans-, pluri-, inter-). As the prefix "trans" indicates, transdisciplinarity concerns that which is at once between the disciplines, across the different disciplines, and beyond all disciplines. Its goal is the understanding of the present world, of which one of the imperatives is the unity of knowledge. Pluridisciplinarity pertains to the study of research topics in several disciplines at the same time. Interdisciplinarity concerns the transfer of methods from one discipline to another. For example, a neuron in biology is used in mathematics and bioinformatics to build an algorithm [15]. This crossing aims to obtain programs that better reflect the societal and industrial innovations. Thus, the Interdisciplinary Criteria becomes a key feature in KTMS assessment.

The Biggs and Collis model (1982) was adapted to interdisciplinary programs by [6]. This model allows structuring of an interdisciplinary program at 3 levels. This view helps us to begin from the usual program structure (level 1), and integrate each additional discipline, using transitions for clarifying interactions between the disciplines involved. It also highlights the strength of the collaborative aspects of the disciplines of knowledge transmission.

The criteria proposed here measure the ability of a KTMS to integrate these three levels in design and content management. This amounts to measuring the multidisciplinary flexibility of the system. The three criteria are:

- **Pluridisciplinarity cognitive map creation (Ic).**

This criterion measures the ability of KTMS to create a specific cognitive map for pluridisciplinary cases (bioinformatics, pharmacogenomics, etc.).

- **Pluridisciplinarity learning language (Il).**

This criterion measures the ability of KTMS to manage a pluridisciplinary language interacting with languages of others disciplines (biology language + informatics language ≠ Bioinformatics language, Statistics + biology ≠ Biostatistics). Several dictionaries end glossaries are available for bioinformatics language ("Glossary of bioinformatics terms.," 2007;[17]. These references contain more than 1000 terms specific to bioinformatics or adapted for the bioinformatics context. It can be employed for the development of the bioinformatics knowledge transmission and learning language specification performance.

- **Dominant idea definition (Id).**

This criterion measures the ability of KTMS to help users in the identification and specification of the main topic in the pluridisciplinary course used (case study, applications, examples).

2.4.Other criteria (O)

Other criteria are related to user's specific needs. Five other criteria are proposed to satisfy context needs related to the grading (O1), user tracking (O2), chat (O3), test scoring (O4), and self-work (O5). These criteria are described in EduTools. These are implemented by: Online grading tools (O1), Students tracking (O2), Real time Chat (O3), automated testing and scoring (O4), Self-assessment (O5).

3.Conclusion

Faced with the KTMS evaluation issue, we proposed here a set of criteria that allow decision maker to measure the quality of a given KTMS. In our proposal, we focused on the weaknesses of existing criteria and the major limitations of internet-based KTMS. These weaknesses are multidisciplinarity, collaborativity and sharing that were integrated using communication tools.

The criteria set proposed is also flexible. This allows them to measure the qualitative and quantitative aspects of each feature. This work is far from covering all the needs of educators, but it still provides a preliminary step toward opening the door to a standardization of quality criteria for KTMS.

Terminologies

LOs: Learning Objects
LORs: Learning Object Repository
CBT: Computer Based Training
CMS: course management system
LMS: Learning Management System
KTMS: Knowledge Transmission Management System
BKTMS: Bioinformatics Knowledge Transmission Management System
SCORM: Sharable Content Object Reference Model
VLEs: Virtual learning environments
CBTE: competence-based teacher education,
HBTE: humanistic-based teacher education,
IMS: instructional management system
LOM: learning object model

7

Acknowledgments: The authors would like to thank Dr. Doug Goodman and Jerry Prentice for their helpful corrections on this work.

Funding: This work was made possible by SD-INBRE Grant # P20RR016479-09 from the National Center for Research Resources (NCRR), a component of the National Institutes of Health (NIH). Its contents are solely the responsibility of the authors and do not necessarily represent the official views of NCRR or NIH. NSF Grant IOS-1126481 Integrating the BioExtract Server with the iPlant Collaborative.

References

[1]T. Ishaya, “Interoperable Learning Objects Management,” *igi-global.com*.

[2]B. E. Goodman, “Targeting relevance: the challenges of interdisciplinary teaching and learning.,” *The Physiologist*, vol. 55, no. 1, pp. 1, 3–6, Feb. 2012.

[3]M. V Schneider, P. Walter, M.-C. Blatter, J. Watson, M. D. Brazas, K. Rother, A. Budd, A. Via, C. W. G. van Gelder, J. Jacob, P. Fernandes, T. H. Nyrönen, J. De Las Rivas, T. Blicher, R. C. Jimenez, J. Loveland, J. McDowall, P. Jones, B. W. Vaughan, R. Lopez, T. K. Attwood, and C. Brooksbank, “Bioinformatics Training Network (BTN): a community resource for bioinformatics trainers.,” *Briefings in bioinformatics*, vol. 13, no. 3, pp. 383–9, Nov. 2011.

[4]P. L. Blyth, “Window shopping.,” *Health facilities management*, vol. 13, no. 4, pp. 38, 40, 42, Apr. 2000.

[5]E. Kurilovas and V. D. E, “Multiple Criteria Comparative Evaluation of E-Learning Systems and Components,” vol. 20, no. 4, pp. 499–518, 2009.

[6]L. Ivanitskaya, D. Clark, G. Montgomery, and R. Primeau, “Interdisciplinary Learning : Process and Outcomes,” vol. 27, no. 2, pp. 95–112, 2002.

[7]S. Fatimah and M. Yassin, “Interdisciplinary Integration Through Problem-Based Learning with ICT in Pre- Service Teacher Education,” no. 2006, pp. 377–385, 2010.

[8]L. K. Michaelsen and M. Sweet, “Team-Based Learning,” *New Directions for Teaching and Learning*, vol. 2011, no. 128, pp. 41–51, 2011.

[9]F. Korthagen and J. Buitink, “What pedagogical approaches are there in teacher education?,” *kennisbasislerarenopleiders.nl*, 2006.

[10] P. a Pevzner, “Educating biologists in the 21st century: bioinformatics scientists versus bioinformatics technicians.,” *Bioinformatics (Oxford, England)*, vol. 20, no. 14, pp. 2159–61, Sep. 2004.

[11] C. E. Shannon and W. Weaver, *Mathematical Theory of Communication*, vol. 27, no. 1. University of Illinois Press, 1949, p. 125.

[12] P. Jacquet, B. Mans, and G. Rodolakis, *Information propagation speed in Delay Tolerant Networks: Analytic upper bounds*. 2008, pp. 6–10.

[13] W. Szpankowski, *Analytic algorithmics, combinatorics, and information theory*. Ieee, 2005, pp. 210–210.

[14] R. V. L. Hartley, “Transmission of Information,” *Bell System Technical Journal*, vol. 7, no. 3, pp. 535–563, 1928.

[15] K.-C. V. Nicolescu, Basarab, *Manifesto of Transdisciplinarity*. New York, New York, USA: State Univ of New York, 2002, p. 169.

[16] “Glossary of bioinformatics terms.,” *Current protocols in bioinformatics / editoral board, Andreas D. Baxevanis ... [et al.]*, vol. Appendix 2, p. Appendix 2, Jun. 2007.

[17] J. M. Hancock and M. J. Zvelebil, Eds., *Dictionary of Bioinformatics and Computational Biology*. Hoboken, NJ, USA: John Wiley & Sons, Inc., 2004.

SESSION

MANAGEMENT, TOOLS, WEB, INFORMATION EXTRACTION + APPLICATIONS AND STANDARDS

Chair(s)

TBA

A smart home for an active and independent old age in the elderly

Damiano Falcioni, Alberto Polzonetti, and Barbara Re
School of Science and Technology University of Camerino, Italy

Abstract – *In this paper we describe the project "Private Assisted House". The project is intended to contribute to the diffusion of a new culture of smart home concept, that is not strictly linked to domotics in its traditional meaning, by placing the home user at the centre of the technological solutions developed. We have discussed about the reference context and about objectives and goal of the project. Finally, important question about the eco-sustainability and domotic coherence are developed. In conclusion we referred to the SWOT analysis – a strategic planning instrument employed for the assessment of project Strengths, Weaknesses, Opportunities and Threats.*

Keywords: domotic , smart-objects, old people

1 Introduction

This project implements a model of "Private Assisted House – PAss" type service aimed at promoting an active old age for elderly people in their own home, i.e. the place where they can continue doing their usual activities, whether they live alone or with their family, by availing themselves of innovative services, based on user-friendly technological contents. The project is intended to contribute to the diffusion of a new culture of smart home concept, that is not strictly linked to domotics in its traditional meaning, by placing the home user at the centre of the technological solutions developed. [2]. The PAss model integrates the most advanced tele-assistance technologies and creates the cognitive, training and assistance support required for the actual diffusion of smart-objects, using the production capabilities of the factories of the Marche region of Italy, which are thus offered an interesting opportunity of positioning themselves in a potentially unlimited market both in terms of geographical and target customers [9]. Interventions are structured on different lines of action: their common objective is to build an eco-system able to sustain multiple usage scenarios and to guarantee a bidirectional contact, diversified according to need, between the elderly and the outside world. As a consequence, the house will have to adapt to the requirements of those living in it, also allowing the prevention of dangerous situations.

During its construction, a house can be designed ad hoc for an older person, or it can be adapted in a flexible way over the years to the life cycle of its occupants who, as they grow old, modify their living and 'usability' needs. This should drive the planning of non-invasive actions aimed at restructuring and adaptation; besides allowing the introduction of the instruments needed for domestic space automation and control, they could also improve energy sustainability.

The PAss model is therefore based on an integration platform to be designed and developed from scratch, able to integrate and coordinate domestic automation, tele-assistance solutions, and smart-objects in an adaptive way [11],[12]In fact, we will analyze in depth some smart–objects that have been specifically developed both in the medical and in the furniture components areas. As far as the medical area is concerned, smart-objects will enable the measurement of vital parameters such as cardiac and respiratory rate, temperature, activity, metabolic consumption, ECG waveforms, etc.

Furniture components will be the object of in-depth analysis specifically those for the bathroom and bedroom, considering that the former is the place where the higher percentage of falls occur whilst the latter is the place where the elderly spend the greatest part of their time. A representative, although not exhaustive, sample of smart-objects in the furniture area consists of chairs, beds, armchairs, sofas and drawers. In this sense, the distinctive element is given by a few innovative technical materials that in part belong to the nautical, furniture and construction industries, and among these textiles, metallic and plastic materials, and composite materials, that will be employed for the production of smart-objects and will be studied ad hoc to reduce some critical aspects of the manufactured objects, in particular when they are intended for older users. And finally, speaking about smart-objects, the role of the TV is crucial since this is the preferred instrument of communication for old people. The integration platform will be devised so as to take smart-objects into consideration in their widest multiplicity, without limiting potential future developments in domestic environment automation and control. Last but not least, the role of the platform is to create integration with the outside world (e.g. in the healthcare and social fields) guaranteeing compliance with hospital and domotics sector standards and offering the different stakeholders a dedicated view of the home, whilst respecting the privacy of the individual. [10]

2 The reference context

The project proposal is part of a European, national and, especially regional context of the Italian Marche, characterized by an increasing percentage of elderly people, the majority with limited independence and most likely tending to worsen and to chronic illness. According to recent demographic projections in Italy, in 2011 the over 65s accounted for 20.3% of the Italian population, whilst in 2020 they will make up 22.5% and by 2065 are estimated to reach the threshold of 32.6%. Even more important will be the increase of people over 80 years of age, which in the same periods will switch from 2.8% to 3.7% to 10% (source: www.demo.istat.it). It goes without saying that the prospects for longevity and an elderly but active population are rising quickly. In 2070, there will be a lot more grandparents than grandchildren. In such a scenario, Italy is one of the European countries with the highest ageing index in Europe. In a near future, this means exponential increase of the care, hospital and regional expense for the elderly. The progression of disability should also be taken seriously into consideration. The data estimated by CENSIS for 2010 – 2020 – 2040 show that disability, caused by ageing and by chronic degenerative diseases, is increasing in a significant and alarming way, 6.7% (about 4.1 million people in 2010) and 7.9% in 2020 (equal to 4.8 million people); this increase is bound to create heavy pressure on the demand for services.

The needs analysis shows a difference in ageing. This is particularly evident as regards disability. Since a univocal pattern for "elderly management" is lacking, it is more than ever necessary to identify the wide variety of needs and situations in order to provide a suitable offer of services and solutions possibly supported by technological platforms and smart-objects. There is a substantial difference in every individual between physical and psychological ageing. The level of disability an elderly person faces is the result of multiple factors that can be ascribed to a range of problems. These factors are unique to every individual on the basis of his/her genetic predispositions. When referring to an old person, we should consider his/her lifestyle, socio-economic and cultural level, household composition, etc.

This project intends to provide an appropriate response to elderly people's requirements and needs, starting from their diversities. The solutions we will introduce allow the emphasis to be placed on personalization and adaptability of these solutions. In this regard, the active involvement of elderly people, either in good health or with differing degrees of disability, both in the drafting phase of the project proposal and during the implementation of investment programs, allowed us to collect real first-hand needs and requirements. Besides, the opportunity of an independent life offered by PAss means an opening towards the outside world through one's home. This permits the presence of several care givers who contribute to the well-being of the elderly with different roles and competences. In this sense, the integration platform enables an opening towards the healthcare and welfare systems, voluntary associations, research facilities and, more broadly, towards all those subjects that actively contribute to improve the quality of life of the elderly and, consequently, of their relatives.

The PAss project aims to also take structural aspects into account from the viewpoint of diversity. In this regard, the key issues involve three different levels. The first one arises from the fact that interventions are mainly carried out on existing structures, which were sometimes built long ago. All the requirements imposed by the layout of unalterable walls, openings, fixtures have to be considered and dealt with. The second aspect concerns possible cohabitation with other people, either relatives or care givers. The last one regards the need for reversible (or easy to modify) interventions, due to possible variations in the elderly person's needs and the possibility of different arrangements being made for the old person as a result of the worsening of his/her conditions.

The above scenario clearly shows the increased demand for entirely new assistance services that are able to stimulate the market of the Marche region's industries and to re-qualify home assistance services [7]. Up to now, the hospitalization of a frail elderly person (e.g. for simple bronchitis) represents just a substitutive (and therefore improper) response for other less demanding services that could technically and professionally solve the problem in an effective way. The PAss model tends to reduce improper hospitalizations by trying to promote home assistance and rehabilitation care in someone's own residence. For this purpose, the combination of technical-scientific skills on offer in the territory of the Marche region is varied and identifiable in manufacturing, handicraft, services and research industries. Such a multiplicity is likewise recognizable in the project partnerships.

Although tele-assistance systems currently available in the market are quite sophisticated, they are only partially able to meet elderly users' requirements. The market offers dozens of more or less valid systems for vital parameters remote control or domotics [5] . However, up to now, there are no systems integrating vital and 'boundary' aspects, into which ambient and individual elements flow, to replicate routine functionalities and help users, guaranteeing them a quality of lifestyle that is constant over time, in spite of the deterioration of their functions. The implementation of such a system without doubt requires deep technological knowledge and integration capacity, but also the association of a strong experience in application. We can then state that the synergy between technology and experience applied in this field allows the opening of new scenarios of Ambient Assisted Living.

By extending the functionalities of tele-assistance solutions, the integration platform we intend to develop, will be able to meet user and outside world requirements in a flexible and adaptable way. In this regard, we intend to innovate the very concept of smart home, which will no longer be connected to domotics in a traditional way, but will address solutions to the elderly. The user has primary needs of functionality, but also of "sense of normality" in terms of living and moving in an environment that is monitored, but not transformed into a Big Brother set full of videocameras. The innovation consists in making the available technology compatible with home user needs and habits, without altering its architecture too much and avoiding dependence on a dedicated data processing centre that would make costs inapplicable in the market.

Current international research projects and the related living patterns employed are mainly oriented to the integration of new domotic-robotic technologies able to solve some of the users issues, since it is not always possible to carry out radical changes in the structure or in furniture elements and systems completing it, without bringing into question the existing morphological-functional characteristics. This implies that an essential aspect of DfA is neglected, i.e. the idea that a "for all" house should be designed for all people and not only for certain users categories such as elderly and disabled users.[13]

From the methodological viewpoint, the new project will be based on the international regulation ISO/DIS 13407 – Human Centred Design Processes for Interactive Systems. The direct consequence could be the passive acceptance of the restricting condition about the inclusion of house aids, very expensive and difficult to integrate as they are. They alter the aesthetic-functional aspects, in opposite trend vs. the expectations of users which are more and more sensible to high standards of domestic spaces architecture and design. For these reasons, the project is "user centred", it aims to integrate the three characterizing aspects of a smart object making them to interact: furniture, in which all main functions are grouped (bed, wardrobe, chairs, etc.) developed according to the reference target, multisensory and multimodal interaction system through the senses of touch (touch screen), voice (voice, gestures recognition) of user-friendly interfaces and use of daily metaphors, integration of innovative technologies able to recall information (augmented memory) and increase the surrounding environment vision (augmented reality) of remote data and information.
In this sense, smart-object will gain an innovation level mainly through the use of smart or functional materials, i.e. able to carry out some functions, sensible, i.e. able to be reactive, active or interactive to external stimuli. [1]

3 Objectives and goals

According to the objectives of the announcement, the PAss project intends to facilitate active and independent longevity in the elderly, whilst realizing the wish of most elderly people to grow old in their own home. This is the reason why the "Private Assisted House" type of assistance model, which is the basis of the project proposal, represents an answer to the heterogeneity of the psycho-physical and social conditions of the elderly, who may also possibly be disabled. Particular attention is addressed to inexpensiveness and usability of the solutions in order to ensure the maximum level of access. The same importance is given to the role of scalability, since the house is seen as the place that is able to change with the passage of time and to adapt itself to the requirements of the people who live in it. The attention given to energy requirements will be crucial, favoring smart-grid integration where the house is both a producer and a consumer of energy.

With reference to feasibility objectives, the "Private Assisted house" type of assistance model is characterized by a particular attention to diversities, while answering in a personalized manner to concrete requirements in terms of: safety, automation, prevention, and communication. This will be possible thanks to the intention, common to all the partners, to build an integration platform. This will allow a real integration of functionalities of domotics and smart-objects within the house in addition to enabling basic functionalities of tele-assistance solutions.

OR 1 – Build a heritage of knowledge,[8] directed at guiding assistance scenarios according to the "Private Assisted house" model. This will highlight a multitude of needs, while offering a useful reference to solve critical states, typical of such scenarios linked to assistance. To this end it is necessary to map the entities of analysis, among which we can list as examples the following: (i) psycho-physical and social conditions of the elderly person, (ii) the home environment in terms of structural and functional characteristics, (iii) the network of assistance where the elderly person is or can be placed, (iv) smart-objects, and sensoristics in general as a point of contact with the environment, (v) daily activities, better known as "activities of everyday life". A complexity emerges that is the result of the combination of various entities which nevertheless allow the creation of personalized assistance models, which are able to respond to the principle of a safe life at home, and thus identify possible behavioral patterns, precursors of a dangerous situation. The temporal dimension will be matter of study since life conditions, psycho-physical ones in particular, evolve continuously.

OR 2 – Design and develop an integration platform useful for the governance of the home. The integration platform PAss offers a horizontal dimension which allows the various vertical dimensions (smart-objects, environmental sensoristics, domotics, etc ...) to be enabled in a unitary and harmonized manner, and also permits a dialogue to be established with the external world in an adequate manner. Thanks to the governance level shown, the integration platform con easily be thought to answer for the scalability and interoperability of the solutions. In this sense we can imagine that applications will be the result of a dynamic integration of data and services which diverse suppliers (third party platforms) put at the disposal of the home through the integration platform. Tele-assistance platforms (UniCam and Aditech), are platforms which, even if with different aims, are dedicated to medical matters integrating certified devices according to standard 93/42. The monitoring platform of the home environment is nevertheless a platform integrating domotic sensors not typical of the medical field. The said platforms will be a kind of back-end, their duty will be to produce data that will be stored, aggregated, integrated, and shown from the integration platform with the purpose of synthetizing them and making them available to different kinds of users, answering to multiple scenarios of use. The management will be crucial of the normalized information and of its transformation useful in observing dangerous situations, and where necessary restoring stimuli and support to the elderly person. Not less important is the need to offer an integrated support of the information through the platform.

OR 3 – Identify, design, and develop a series of smart-objects. Smart-objects, produced within the partnership or acquired from the market, are classified in two macro-areas: medical and furnishings. With regard to the medical area this means ensuring the completeness of analyses with respect to basic vital parameters. With regard to pieces of furniture, smart objects will be part of the definition of a complex and flexible house model, designed as a system of smart items, addable and repeatable in standard modules. Such items will be suitable to realize any domestic living environment with an view to quality and complete accessibility, for a wide range of users. In particular, house spaces related to the bathroom, kitchen and bedroom will be studied in depth, since they are rooms in which an elderly person most needs an assisted inhabitable environment created through techology which is the least invasive possible, integrated inside the same smart-objects and with particular attention to ergonomy, user interface, and use of ecosustainable materials, evaluated by means of defining their cost of production in terms of energetic and environmental impact through the use of evaluation systems related to their life cycle (LCA). As regards materials, smart-objects to be introduced will respond to the needs of athermicity, water resistance, washability, recyclability and pleasantness of their materials. Of the utmost importance in this context is fire resistance, which is an issue common to all materials to be introduced into a house, in particular with regard to the difficulties involved in removing elderly or handicapped people.

OR 4 – Design and develop "in visible" and adaptable sensoristic solutions . The aim is to design and then develop sensoristic solutions to be placed within the house so as to ensure a continuous flow of information, useful for recognizing scenarios (activities-situations-events) originating within it. In this way, it is possible to observe changes in respect to usual behavior, which is often symptomatic of a worsening of psycho-physical health conditions. We intend to equip the areas of the house with the ability to perceive and classify the activities which the users carry out within. The main items of development are the infrastructure, i.e. the sensoristic component which is able to indirectly monitor activities and environmental conditions, without the use of devices to be worn like bracelets or tags, or which could violate privacy such as video cameras and the home processor, i.e. the application which analyzes and correlates data extracted by sensors in real time, recognizing the activities carried out within the rooms and revealing possible abnormalities in behavior or risk situations.

OR 5 – Promote a new culture which sees the PAss model like a pivot of a production capability in the Marche region's industries and in the definition of new professional positions whose main characteristic is to respond to multidisciplinary needs. By way of example we can mention the definition of a new designer role of house environments, who develops the personalization of single houses and who in interacting with the market is able to develop the personalization of single houses ensuring an appropriate integration of technological aids and care services.

4 Eco-sustainability and domotic coherence of the project

4.1 Impact of the project on the energy efficiency of the house environment to which it is addressed

The level of sustainability of the project will be identified through two different, but parallel phases, one addressed at determining environmental impact of the designed products, in terms of consumption of used energy (embodied energy) and of harmful emissions (Co2 pollution) verified by means of an environmental energy certificate , the other one addressed at determining energy efficiency in order to achieve the environmental comfort (hygrothermal, visual, acoustic, air quality) verified by the energy certificate as well as the acoustic and air purity certificates.

The determination of overall ecological environmental impact should take into account not only the use of natural, biocompatible, or recycled materials, which by themselves do not ensure the real sustainability of the product, but also the use of smart materials characterized for the most part, by their capability of self-configuration, self-monitoring, and self-healing which contribute, during their life cycle, to add efficiency, savings and optimization of available energy resources.

4.2 Impact of the project on active and passive safety of the home environment at which it is aimed.

The aim of equipping each area of the home with its own level of intelligence allowing it to "identify" activity and risk scenarios, allow a drive towards crucial enhancement both in active and passive safety of the home.

The enhancement of active safety is linked to the possibility of anticipating risk situations, on the one hand through indirect behavioral monitoring intended to evaluate the regularity of performance of "ordinary" daily activities; on the other hand through automatic recognition of a series of critical or anyway anomalous situations which allows particular operations of protection or alerting to be activated. Unlike standard security systems, in which sensors are used to identify risk situations which are already ongoing (e.g. presence of gas, smoke or flooding), PAss aims to create a preventive system, addressed at anticipating critical situations and realizing a series of implementations to avoid them. By way of example, the gas in the kitchen will be automatically isolated with a solenoid valve when no cooking activity is taking place, then automatically reactivated when use of the kitchen is needed; besides the presence of gas and smokes, the air quality (content of carbon dioxide, powders and carbon monoxide) will be monitored in order to manage automatic activation of ventilators, and possibly of alarms in case of dangerous mixtures. A time activated water flow restrictor will be used, which is activated in case of any use not in keeping with the activities carried out, etc.

Through indirect behavioral monitoring (without the use of sensors that have to be worn and visual sensors), it will be possible to observe dangerous conditions (e.g falls, the absence of activity signals during waking hours, etc.), but also identify inconsistent conditions (e.g. absences from the home that are not temporary but without any completion of connected operations, like the closing of windows or doors; performance of exceptionally fragmented activities that are not terminated) which may be indicators of confusional states or stress. Finally it will be possible to automate many repetitive actions which may be perceived as an intrusive duty in the use of different devices. By way of example, the automatic activation and deactivation of anti-intrusion security equipment will be possible, based on the actual waking hours of the user and of his/her position within the home.

4.3 Level of integration of the project with the basic domotic functions regarding the home environment at which it is aimed.

The PAss project, is aimed at equipping the areas of the house with an innovative level of smartness, thus primarily aiming not to require intensive learning or adaptation to the introduction of the technology itself.

From this viewpoint, PAss aims to test a set of technological "proxies", i.e. of interfaces towards standard domotic systems able to change their complexity and promote interoperability. An interface structure will be tested, in this direction, towards house systems (household appliances, plants and basic automation already available in general) which are able to translate commands and settings typically transmitted by means of remote controls, push-button panels or complex touch panels with multiple menus, into simple vocal commands or ones given through wireless systems, that are automatically contextualized.

We mean in other words to test command repeaters which acquire information from the completed activity and from the user position, simplifying operative complexity in a relevant way. By way of example, it will be possible to command the opening of a motorized shutter without having to specify the reason for which this information is acquired by the user position. Similarly, it will be possible to translate the main commands of a tv set into vocal commands or onto a single wireless device, or moreover, to lower the temperature or light in a particular area.

These proxies are an innovative way to realize interoperabilità, whose efficacy doesn't rely on a complex, even if desirable, standardization of communication among different domotic systems, but on the interposition between the user and technology of a smart "normalization" system, that is able to fill the communication gap.

4.4 Integration level with assistance functions

The PAss project takes into consideration some important aspects of the living conditions of the elderly [6], [4]. Among these aspects there is in particular the fact that only a small percentage have a broadband connection, whilst most of them use mobiles or landline phones. This state of digital divide is a symptom of the poor penetration of organized assistance services within the territory, which is also due to their high cost, when they are planned in a non structured way. In this sense, the PAss project intends to trial the integration of the same smart monitoring system, developed for the automation support activities, with organized assistance functions in order to considerably reduce their cost.

The experiment will be used to evaluate three main aspects. On the one hand the feasibility will be tested of remotely monitoring, as well as voluntary requests for help, also the state of health (monitoring of vital parameters through sensors connected to a network, such as a thermometer, stetho/phonendoscope, oximeter, etc.) and critical risk situations (e.g. falls, absence of activity signals during waking hours, markedly non consistent behaviors which are an indication of confusional states, presence of smoke or carbon monoxide, flooding), by automating their recognition and verification, whilst reducing the cost for surveillance. On the other hand the feasibility will be tested of connecting local networks of home and social services which allow implementation of efficient and economically sustainable daily assistance activities, such as identification and repair of faults, support in the supply of consumer products and medicines, support of organized mobility (with sharing of times and routes), support of waste disposal, etc.

Finally, a further aspect that will be tested is linked to mnemonic support in daily activities. Thanks to the smart system of behavioral analysis, it will be possible to recall, by means of reminders supported by multimedial appliances, possible lapses of memory such as the scheduled assumption of medicines, disposing of waste or simply any other customary activities. The same system could be trialed for connection to institutions (e.g. notes about formalities or deadlines), to services to citizens (e.g. notes about utilities, events), or simply for adjusting the rhythm of daily life in general.

4.5 Impact on the user

A possible and more natural use scenario refers to support of elderly-related activities. The elderly person could take advantage of the presence of the integration platform and therefore of uniform access across the different services available, thanks to sensors and devices placed in the home. In this context the characteristics of the suggested solution will make it possible to integrate new devices, including according to possible changes in the level of independence of the elderly person, possibly allowing him/her to be able to control the different aids and devices available at home remotely. In actual fact, the characteristics proper to the suggested solution will enable adaptation of the support to the elderly person with regard to peculiarities both of his/her conditions (with the introduction of particular sensors and aids), and with reference to the peculiarities of his/her housing context, i.e. an actual house or a condominium flat.

Moreover the elderly person could also be assisted by applications installed on the platform [3]. Such applications will monitor his/her actions and could support him/her in daily activities such as the assumption of medicines. The extendible nature of the suggested solution makes the realization feasible of any software application, which also integrates information retrieved from devices and sensors, in order to support the activities of the elderly.

By way of example we can refer to Mr John Smith, who lives independently with his family, until progressive ageing, the departure and absence of his children and the unfortunate death of his wife require the adaptation of his home in terms of monitoring. John's needs then change when, because of a critical time due to a car accident, he is no longer able to move around independently within his home. The need for monitoring evolves with regard to the need to introduce functions and services which are able to ensure mobility within and outside the home: The integration platform, and more generally the solutions suggested by the Pass project.

It is clear that the PAss project represents an occasion to test a course of self management of personal assistance, in order to enable the elderly person, affected by a more or less severe level of disability, to live in the same way as other people.

Particular attention is given to scenarios in terms of use in respect to external data users. There are at least three macro use scenarios identified.

The first one is the scenario in medical field. The users of this scenario could be, on the one hand, for example, hospitals, specialized centres, pharmacies, and general practice MDs, that is all the chain typical of the regional health system, whilst on the other hand the patient's home, residential homes, social centres, etc. The information given in this context requires a high level of precision as well as a high timeliness of communications. Context data from the field of domotics and smart-objects, which although useful in order to decode the situation as well as possible, are not at a high level of criticality.

The second use scenario is the one belonging to the social field. In this scenario the users could be relatives, assistance and welfare centres. The information given in this context represents summarizing data related to the state of the user or the elderly person. The information will be aggregated in a concise way, in order to allow an overall evaluation with respect to standard parameters of the user situation and allow the critical issues discovered in terms of alerts or notices to be picked up. The information will be correlated by other general monitoring information obtained from environmental sensors as well as from other smart-objects. The third use scenario belongs to the medical scientific research field. The users of this scenario could be researchers who intend to analyze the data supplied by the various medical and other sensors, to study, by way of example, possible correlations between pathologies and life style. The great entity of acquirable data, that may possibly be matched to a multitude of homes and elderly people are a real knowledge base from which data for further studies may be obtained.

5 Conclusions

During implementation of the project, the partners intend to analyze the following solutions. A new service pattern that is able to recognize and value the old person in his/her family environment, placing him/her at the centre of a network of people able to guarantee him/her innovative services, based on user-friendly technological content. The clear advantages are the postponement of loss of independence, improvement of physical and cognitive state, reduction of hospitalizations and an opportunity of providing the elderly with a more balanced medical and social standard. An integration platform that recognizes and values the differences in terms of elderly needs and conditions in integrating domotics, tele-assistance solutions and smart-objects. In this regard, we recognize a number of benefits connected to the co-ordinated management of technologies. One for all, the flexibility and scalability of solutions, but not less important are: (i) purchase cost effectiveness, (ii) abatement of management and maintenance costs, (iii) effective and efficient employment of resources, (iv) access to a wider range of solutions and configurations, etc.

A set of smart-objects able to combine design/ergonomics, intelligence and accessibility (in physical terms). The advantages are mainly related to enhancement of performance and technical quality of smart-objects once they have been integrated with the technological solutions provided. "Invisible" and adaptable sensoristic solutions which have the advantage of making the environment liveable and pleasant even though controlled.

However, the development of these solutions has some risks, during project implementation we will manage a number of problems as described hereinafter. In this regard, we referred to the SWOT analysis – a strategic planning instrument employed for the assessment of project Strengths, Weaknesses, Opportunities and Threats.

STRENGTHS	WEAKNESSES
▪ Potentially very wide market ▪ Mature technologies ▪ Partners skills and capabilities gained on site and combining qualifications collected through a years of experience ▪ Good research multidisciplinary base ▪ Varied and complementary partnership ▪ Consistency with political guidelines, at European, national and international level ▪ Proposal scalability and compliance with standards	▪ Uncertainties with regard to government grants in the field of assistance and low level of integration between public and private sectors ▪ Issues in terms of patenting ▪ Lack of dedicated knowledge networks and consequent low level of diffusion vs. actual potentialities

OPPORTUNITIES	THREATS
▪ Demographic change Increase of digital natives ▪ Development and diffusion of European programs in the reference areas	▪ Financial and political pressures ▪ Decline in terms of national addressing of the issue of assistance to old people ▪ Clinical resistance of patients ▪ Ethic and legal issues ▪ Limited integration of eHealth systems vs. real expectations regarding the adoption of electronic health records

6 References

[1] Addington, M., & Schodek, D. (2012). Smart materials and Technologies in Architecture. Routledge.

[2] Bertolino, A., De Angelis, G., Frantzen, L., & Polini, A. (2009). The plastic framework and tools for testing service-oriented applications. Software Engineering, 106-139.

[3] Cacciabue, P. C., Hjälmdahl, M., Luedtke, A., & Riccioli, C. (Eds.). (2011). Human Modelling in Assisted.

[4] Choomkasean, J., Mongkolnam, P., & Chan, J. H. (2012). Multimedia Delivery for Elderly People: A Conceptual Model. In Advances in Information Technology (pp. 58-69). Springer Berlin Heidelberg.

[5] Friedewald, M., & Da Costa, O. (2003). Science and technology roadmapping: Ambient intelligence in everyday life (AmI@ Life). Karlsruhe: Fraunhofer-Institut für System- und Innovationsforschung (FhG-ISI).

[6] GAYMU, J., & SPRINGER, S. (2010). Living conditions and life satisfaction of older Europeans living alone: A gender and cross-country analysis. Ageing and Society, 30(7), 1153.

[7] Glendinning, C., Halliwell, S., Jacobs, S., Rummery, K., & Tyrer, J. (2001). New kinds of care, new kinds of relationships: how purchasing services affects relationships in giving and receiving personal assistance. Health & Social Care in the Community, 8(3), 201-211.

[8] Kauppinen, T., Paakkarinen, P., Mäkelä, E., Kuittinen, H., Väätäinen, J., Hyvönen, E., ... & De Pablos, P. O. (2011). Geospatio-temporal semantic web for cultural heritage. Digital Culture and E-Tourism: Technologies, Applications and Management Approaches. IGI Global, Hershey, Pennsylvania.

[9] McCreadie, C., & Tinker, A. (2005). The acceptability of assistive technology to older people. Ageing and Society, 25(1), 91-110.

[10] Moonen, R. (2012). Designing ICT based services for intellectually disabled people.

[11] Siegemund, F. (2004). A context-aware communication platform for smart objects. Pervasive Computing, 69-86.Leslie Lamport. "LaTeX: A Document Preparation System". Addison-Wesley Publishing Company, 1986.

The Correlation of Speech and Hand Gestures for Multimodal Web Interaction

Jing Liu[1], **Manolya Kavakli**[2]
Department of Computing, Macquarie University, Sydney, NSW, Australia

Abstract - *With the development of Multimodal Interfaces (MMI) in Human Computer Interaction (HCI), there is an increasing interest at applying this technology to multimodal web interaction. Multimodal web interfaces can provide end-users with a natural, flexible and non-invasive interface that allow graphical, vocal and gestural interaction with web. Integration of speech and gestures in an MMI framework is now the focus of the researchers in this area. In order to combine speech and gestures in multimodal web interaction, it is essential to know the correlations between speech and associated gestures. This paper presents an empirical study aimed at studying the correlations between speech and hand gestures from a cognitive aspect. The methodology used in this paper is the video analysis to investigate the cognitive actions of speakers in the descriptions of objects using speech and hand gestures. The speakers' cognitive actions are analyzed using a cognitive scheme and protocol analysis method. Our initial findings suggest that speech is highly correlated with co-verbal hand gestures perceptually and semantically, regardless of the age, gender, background of the speakers, or the speed of speech and gesticulation.*

Keywords: multimodal web interaction, speech, co-verbal hand gestures, cognitive actions

1 Introduction

The Multimodal Interaction Activity is an initiative from W3C aiming to provide means to support multimodal interaction scenarios on the web. Multimodal interaction offers significant ease of use and benefits over uni-modal interaction from many aspects. Hands-free operation is needed in mobile devices with limited keyboards, as well as when a traditional desktop computer is unavailable to host the application user interface for controlling other devices. Multimodal web interaction is driven by the possibility in embedded and network-based speech processing for integrated multimodal web browsers. There is an exciting range of applications relevant to integrated multimodal web browsers. For instance, an ambient intelligent web interface is expected to add value to remote control of home entertainment systems. It can enable sensors, interactive screens, input devices for speech, gestures and tactile information to directly interact with each house and outdoor device. End-users with disability will also benefit from this technology [1][2]. VoiceXML is the W3C's standard XML format for specifying interactive voice dialogues between a human and a computer. It allows voice applications to be developed and deployed in an analogous way to HTML for visual applications [3]. With the emergence of MMI integrating speech and gestures [4][5], it is possible to combine these two input modes in web interfaces to get joint benefits. A system using personal robot as ubiquitous multimedia mobile web interfaces enable end-users to access web by speech and hand gestures [6]. The correlation of speech and hand gesture is crucial for integrating them in MMI as well as multimodal web browsers, since the architecture for MMI is time-sensitive for joint input.

2 Related work

A gesture is a form of non-verbal communication in which physical actions communicate particular messages, either in place of speech or together with speech. All speakers use gestures, although the typology of gesticulation may differ. They are tightly timed with speech [7]. Iconic gestures are found to precede the related speech within 2 seconds in [8]. Currently there are three different views about the relationship between speech and gestures. The first one points that speech and gestures are separately communicated [9]-[12]. According to this view, the primary role of gestures is to compensate for speech, when verbal communication is temporarily unavailable (e.g. coughing or hard to express by words). They argue that the process of gesture production has no effect on the process of speech production or the cognitive processes related to speech.

The second point of view is proposed initially by Robert Krauss [13][14]. It states that speech and gestures are linked reciprocally at a specific point during speech production. They point that the production of gestures is activated when speakers come across some difficulties in lexical retrieval. The activation of gestures in turn activates the lexical affiliate of that concept in mind, which results in articulating of the word successfully. According to this view, gestures are linked with speech only to the extent that it stimulates the activation of word retrieval in speech at a moment.

The third one articulated by David McNeill [7] argues that speech and gesture form an integrated system of communication. The links between speech and gesture are presented at the different levels of speech production (e.g. discourse, syntax, semantics and prosody). From this

Table I : Cognitive action categories

Category	Name	Description	Examples
Physical	D-action	Make depictions	Lines, circles, arrows, words
	L-action	Look at previous depictions	-
	M-action	Other physical actions	Move a pen, move elements, gesture
Perceptual	P-action	Attend to visual features of elements	Shapes, sizes, textures
		Attend to spatial relations among elements	Proximity, alignment, intersection
		Organize or compare elements	Grouping, similarity, contrast
Functional	F-action	Explore the issues of interactions between artifacts and people/nature	Functions, circulation of people, views, lighting conditions
		Consider psychological reactions of people	Fascination, motivation, cheerfulness
Conceptual	E-action	Make preferential and aesthetic evaluations	Like-dislike, good-bad, beautiful-ugly
	G-action	Set up goals	-
	K-action	Retrieve knowledge	-

standpoint, speech and gesture co-occur with one another during the same underlying thought process, even though the two modalities may capture and reflect different aspects of the common underlying cognitive process. The process of the productions of gesture and speech should therefore influence each other at any disrupted point.

There are actually already some neuropsychological and neurophysiologic evidence supporting the idea that speech and gesture share the same communicating system [15]. From the language aspect, some researchers hypothesize that language originate from an ancient system in which arm gestures is the communication tool [16]. Recently Corballis [17] propose that spoken language is developed as the repertoire of gestures gradually transferred from arm to mouth. From the gesture aspect, previous studies [7][12] show that pronouncing words and executing gestures with the same meaning are interacted and temporally coordinated. There is also evidence indicating that gesture has the impact on the utterance co-occurred. Kita also claims that gesture helps the speaker package information at an early stage of utterance production [18]. Conversely, gestures influence speech spectra of utterance produced simultaneously with the gestures [15].

In this paper, we are inspired by and expand the third view regarding the relationship between speech and gestures that they form a single communication system. Our hypothesis is that speech and co-occurring hand gestures are highly correlated to one another from cognitive aspect.

3 Types of gestures

According to [7], there are four main types of gesture regarding to their relationship to the concurrent speech. Deictic gestures mostly refer to actual entities and are used to specialize and locate in physical space. For example, imagine that you are communicating with a child and trying to tell him what the surroundings are. You normally say, 'Look, there is ... there' with a pointing gesture referring the object you mention. It may be hard for the child to recognize what you are talking about without the gesture. Iconic gestures mostly convey information about the outline of a picture of shape or object in space or the hands represent the shape or the object itself. These gestures are imagistically representational. Metaphoric gestures are also representational, but they are more associated with abstract ideas related to subjective notions, rather than the object itself. Beat gestures are small baton-like hand movements that serve to mark the speech pace normally. These gestures are not considered to convey any semantic information.

Among these four types, deictic gestures are probably the simplest gestures and beat gestures exhibit relatively little structural variation. Iconic gestures and metaphoric gestures are more complex than deictic and beat gestures with respect to both gesticulation and information they convey. Iconic gestures bear a close formal relationship to the semantic content of speech [19]. When we externalize imaginary environment of shapes and objects in our minds, it is a natural and intuitive way to use our hands as well as speech. Research has shown that the articulation of shapes and objects is performed using iconic gestures in both sign language and natural gestures [20]. This is also observed in our experiments. People used a variety of iconic gestures when they described the objects with tangible shapes.

4 Cognitive analysis

Cognitive analysis is the analysis of those properties of the objects that are accounted for in terms of cognitive concepts, such as various types of mental representation. It is to reveal the content what the speakers see, attend to, think of and retrieve from the memory by cognitive analysis of video/audio protocols. We used the content-oriented retrospective protocol analysis to investigate the cognitive actions of speakers. M. Suwa, T. Purcell, and J. Gero, [22] developed a coding scheme to code designers' cognitive actions. The scheme identifies various types of cognitive actions and reveals the structure of cognitive actions in designing process. We introduce the coding scheme briefly in the following part, before we illustrate how we used it in our experiments.

4.1 Coding scheme for cognitive actions

According to Suwa's coding scheme, cognitive actions of designers are classified into four information categories: physical, perceptual, functional and conceptual. Table I shows the detailed information about the four categories. M.

Table II : Codes of P-actions

Psg: discover a space as ground	Pfn: attend to the feature of a new depiction
Pfnp: attend to the feature of a new relation or Psg	Pfp: discover a new feature of an existing depiction, of Pcsg, or of Prsg
Prn: create or attend to a new relation between two new depictions or Psg	Prnp: create or attend to a new relation between a new depiction and an existing one
Prp: discover a spatial or organizational relation	Pcf: continually attend to a feature
Pcr: continually attend to a relation	Pcsg: continually attend to a space as ground
Prf: remember a feature of a depiction	Prr: remember a spatial or organizational relation
Prsg: remember a space as ground	Pipsr: implement a previously mentioned relation by giving new depictions or features

Table III : Codes of F-actions

Fnp: think of a function independently of depictions	Fre-i: re-interpretation
Fn: associate a new depiction, feature or relation with a new function	Fcp: continually think of a function independently of depictions
Fc: continually think of a function	Fr: remember a function
Frp: remember a function independently of depictions	Fi: implement a previously explored function by creating a new depiction, feature or relation

Suwa, T. Purcell, and J. Gero [22] claimed that these four categories are classified according to how it is processed by human cognition. Thus, physical actions correspond to sensory level at which incoming information is first processed sensorially. Then the incoming information is processed perceptually and semantically which are represented by perceptual actions, functional and conceptual actions respectively.

4.2 Codes of different actions

The coding scheme explored by Suwa etc. is based on the architectural designers' design activities. They detected a wide range of cognitive activities during the design session which is a complex task. The details about the procedures and coding can be found in [22][23]. In our experiments, what we are concerned is the correlation between speech and hand gestures. We therefore coded hand gestures as M-actions which represented by Mge. We expanded the Mge into four sub-classes: Mgei indicating iconic gestures, Mged corresponding to deictic gestures, Mgem for metaphoric gestures and also Mgeb for beat gestures. For the purpose of analysis, we will use G to represent gestures which include all M-actions. Perceptual and functional actions are also coded analyzing speakers' speech which is believed to reflect

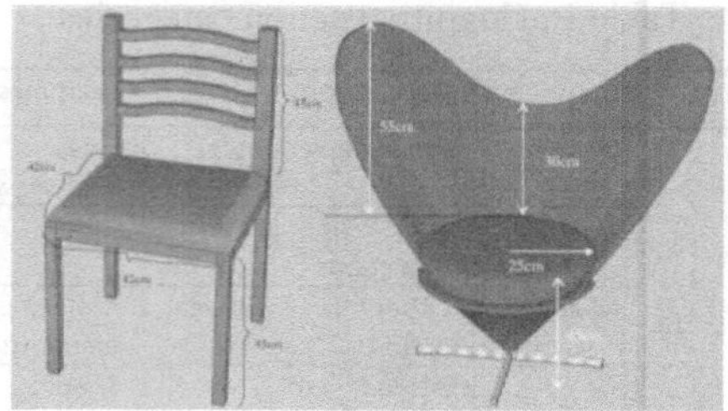

Figure 1. Classic chair (left) and Abstract chair (right)

cognitive thoughts in the speakers' mind. We rarely found conceptual actions in the protocols we captured. So, we only show the subcategories and codes of perceptual actions and functional actions in Table II and Table III. P-actions and F-actions are used to indicate perceptual actions and functional actions in the following.

5 Data and processiong

The hypothesis taken as a base for this study is that speech and co-verbal hand gestures are correlated with each other at the perceptual level as well as the semantic level. The correlation has nothing to do with the age, the gender and the background of the speakers, nor the speed of the speech and gesticulation. In order to explore the correlation between speech and co-verbal hand gestures we conducted our own experiments. In our experiments, the participants were required to describe two chairs (See Fig.1) with different structures, as if they are having a video conference with someone. Protocol analyses are carried out on the videos/audios we captured.

5.1 Corpus and data

This study is based on the analysis of a set of multimodal corpus collected by ourselves. 16 volunteers (aging from twenties to fifties, including 12 females and 4 males) were involved in the data collection for the experiment. They are from different cultural backgrounds but speak English in our experiment. The participants were required to describe two different types of chairs naturally to the camera. One is a traditional chair with a simple structure. Another one is designed with an abstract shape and structure, which is expected to trigger more gestures of. We gave 3D pictures about both chairs to the participants. They described the objects freely in front of a camera. The camera was placed in such a way that the hands and the upper body gestures could be recorded clearly. All their speech was recorded with the video camera using internal microphone. Finally, we obtained approximately 30 minutes of monologue object description data.

5.2 Coding process

Participants in the experiment were encouraged to use as many gestures as possible. The analysis is via two annotations tool: Anvil [24] for video annotation and Praat[25] for audio annotation.

5.2.1 Segmention

Segmentation is the first step of the coding process. There are different rules for segmentation. One rule is that protocols can be segmented by verbalization events (e.g. pauses, intonations and syntactic markers). But for cognitive segments, we divided the protocols based on cognitive actions which reflect the subject's intention. We identified a new segment when there is a change in the speakers' intention or the contents of their thoughts. For example, a participant may have said, "the seat of this chair is square… and then for the leg part ..."

The speaker changes his/her attention from the seat part to the leg part. That case we define the start point of a new segment as 'and then ...' consequently. A single segment can include one sentence or many.

5.2.2 Gesture coding

We first analyzed the videos and segmented the video footage while listening to the speech to ensure that we obtained the starting and ending frame of the segmentation. For gesture analysis of each segment, we recorded the gesture types (iconic, metaphoric, beat, deictic) corresponding to McNeill's classification.

We extracted gestures from the video protocols based on the ANVIL built-in gesture phase descriptions. In the description file, a gesture is divided into 7 phases: (Pre, Stroke, Hold, Beats, Recoil, Partial-retract, Retract)(quoted from help pages in ANVIL). In our analysis, gestures are represented only by 'stroke' phase, because the stroke phase is the most energetic part of a gesture movement and also the requisite part of a gesture. The movement for a gesture stroke was often apparent in the video frames as a blurring of the hands; the cessation of the blurring in one stroke movement was taken as the end of a gesture [26]. Other phases were not recorded since the beginnings of other phases for each gesture were subject to greater subjectivity and difficulty in identification.

5.2.3 Cognitive action coding

Coding of cognitive actions was finalized by speech analysis via the annotation tool Praat. By Praat, we were able to analyze the speech with the display of speech intensity contour. This is helpful in pinpointing the start and end point of a segment as well as the words related to the gestures. Praat also allows users to rehear any selected part of the audio (e.g. one segmentation) unlimited times to make the coding more reliable.

We illustrate a coding example for one segment as follows.

The following sentences were excerpted from one participant's description about the traditional chair: "*Then the back of the chair very much straights up from the back leg. There are four strips going across and each stripe is curved a little bit and arched like this*"

Table IV. Coding example for one segment

M-actions		F-actions		P-actions	
M_{gei}	straight up	F_n	back	P_{fp1}	straight up
M_{gei}	strips	F_c1	numerical info 4	P_{fp2}	square
M_{geb}	4	F_c2	stripes	P_{fp3}	curved
M_{gei}	curved			P_{cf}	arched
				P_{rp}	going across

The excerpted part was about the back of the chair. Before this segment the participant mentioned the legs and after it he talked about the seat of the chair.

Four gestures were detected while we coded this segment. The participant gestured when he said 'straight up', 'four, 'strips' and 'curved'.

According to the coding scheme described above, we coded the cognitive actions for this segment as shown in Table IV.

6 Results

Approximately 30 minutes of monologue object descriptions in our video footage were obtained for the total 16 participants. We used seconds as a time measure. A total of 1974.02 seconds (from 42.73 seconds to 365 seconds for different participants) of video footage captured for analysis. In total, 100 segments (from 2 segments to 13 segments for different participants) were coded after segmentation.

We examined the frequency with which gestures, perceptual actions and functional actions occurred throughout the object description process of speakers. For each participant, we calculated the total of occurrences of physical, perceptual and functional actions. Table V displays the occurrences of these three actions for different speakers. From the table we can see, we obtained 13 segments for the participant (P1) and only got 2 segments for P16. P1 gestured 55 times during the whole process while P13 only produced 8 gestures. We detected the maximum numbers of P-actions and F-actions for P1 (49 and 44) respectively and the minimum for P16 (only 5 and 7 respectively). The reason for the difference could be the degree of comfort in using English to talk or describe complexity. We had some participants who come from non-English speaking countries but were required to speak in English.

It can be seen from the table that in our experiments, P2 had 24 gestures produced which is less than P8's (32), but we detected 24 P-actions for her which is more than P8's (22). 17 F-actions were coded for P12 which is more than P5's (15), but we obtained 17 P-actions and 15 gestures for her which are both less than P5's (21 and 25). However, we still can observe that the whole trend of these three actions is quite close to one another. This can be clearly seen in Fig 2. From this figure we can see the lines representing gestures, P-actions and F-actions are very close to each other, even though they cross lines at some points.

We calculated the correlation coefficients between the number of segments and each type of actions throughout all

Table V. Numbers of actions for participants

P	Sum(Seg)	Sum(G)	Sum(P)	Sum(F)
P1	13	55	49	44
P2	9	24	24	15
P3	13	43	41	25
P4	4	19	16	10
P5	6	25	21	15
P6	6	16	17	17
P7	4	11	11	8
P8	7	32	22	29
P9	6	21	22	26
P10	8	18	21	17
P11	4	10	11	11
P12	5	15	17	17
P13	3	8	7	10
P14	6	16	12	17
P15	4	15	8	11
P16	2	11	5	7

participants. As can been seen from Table.VI, there are strong correlations between gestures and different types of cognitive actions. Gestures are strongly correlated with perceptual actions (0.9566) as well as functional actions (0.8834). In addition to this, the segments are also strongly correlated with gestures (0.9028) and perceptual actions (0.9549). However, we found that segments are not so strongly correlated with functional actions (0.7988).

As we introduced before, for the same task, different speakers finished the experiments at different times (shortest time: 42.73 seconds and longest time: 365 seconds). As mentioned before, the participants were from different backgrounds (e.g. some are Australian local speakers and some are Asian speakers). The age of these participants vary from twenties to fifties. The speed of their talking and gesticulation are also varying. However, the correlation coefficients are calculated without calculating the effects of these factors. We can now state that gestures are strongly correlated with perceptual actions and functional actions without considering any individual differences.

Now we may relate gestures to speech from the cognitive aspect. We believe that speech is the important and reliable reflection of speakers' cognitive thoughts. The definition of the coding scheme for cognitive actions implied that the perceptual processing of incoming information is indicated by perceptual actions. Functional actions can reflect the semantic processing of incoming information. Therefore, the information we extracted from speech can reflect speakers' cognitive actions at different levels. After analyzing the codes for gestures and cognitive actions, we found that speech and co-occurring hand gestures are correlated with one another perceptually as well as semantically. This relationship is neither affected by the age, the gender, the background of the speakers nor the speed of the speech and gesticulation.

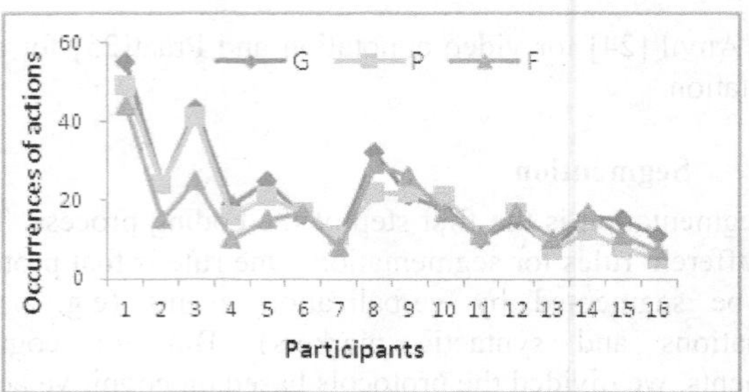

Figure 2. Occurrences of actions for participants

Table VI. Correlation coefficients

	G	P	F	Seg
G	1.000	0.9566	0.8834	0.9028
P	0.9566	1.000	0.8651	0.9549
F	0.8834	0.8651	1.000	0.7988
Seg	0.9028	0.9549	0.7988	1.000

7 Conclusion and future work

7.1 Conclusion

We started this paper in order to explore the correlation between speech and co-verbal hand gestures from the cognitive aspect for multimodal web interaction. The view of that speech and co-occurring hand gestures share the same communication system is not new. But a few researchers studied their relationship from the cognitive aspects by statistical analysis of cognitive. By making use of a coding scheme for designers' cognitive actions, we examined videos/audios of speakers which recorded speech and gesture information of speakers. We analyzed cognitive actions of speakers using the coding scheme and investigated the number of gestures and related P-actions and F-actions of various participants in our experiments. Our conclusion is that speech and hand gestures are strongly correlated, from the perceptual aspect as well as the semantic aspect. This was visible with the correlation coefficients of gestures and cognitive actions in participants (0.9566 for gestures and P-actions and 0.8834 for gestures and F-actions). There are already some researches which enable end-users to access web by speech. Considering that speech and hand gestures are highly correlated, we can expect a multimodal web which has web pages one can speak to and gesture at in future.

7.2 Limitations and future directions

We acknowledge that future work needs more samples. Future studies may need to work on the consistency of the annotations and codes. This was not possible to perform for this paper. Only one person was working on the annotation of gestures and the coding of cognitive actions. Further work can also address how to fuse gesture into multimodal web interaction.

8 Acknowledgement

This work was supported in part by the Australian Research Council Discovery grant DP0988088 to Manolya Kavakli, titled "A Gesture-Based Interface for Designing in Virtual Reality"

References

[1] González, Julia, Mercedes Macías, Roberto Rodríguez, and Fernando Sánchez. "Accessibility metrics of web pages for blind end-users." In Web Engineering, pp. 374-383. Springer Berlin Heidelberg, 2003.

[2] Knudsen, Lars Emil, and Harald Holone. "A multimodal approach to accessible web content on smartphones." In Computers Helping People with Special Needs, pp. 1-8. Springer Berlin Heidelberg, 2012.

[3] Larson, James A. "W3c speech interface languages: Voicexml [standards in a nutshell]." *Signal Processing Magazine, IEEE* 24.3 (2007): 126-131.

[4] Larson, James A. "W3c speech interface languages: Voicexml [standards in a nutshell]." *Signal Processing Magazine, IEEE* 24.3 (2007): 126-131.

[5] Wachs, Juan Pablo, Mathias Kölsch, Helman Stern, and Yael Edan." Vision-based hand-gesture applications." *Communications of the ACM* 54, no. 2 (2011): 60-71.

[6] Ruiz-del-Solar, Javier. "Personal robots as ubiquitous-multimedial-mobile web interfaces." In Web Conference, 2007. LA-WEB 2007. Latin American, pp. 120-127. IEEE, 2007.

[7] D. McNeill, Hand and Mind: What Gestures Reveal about Thought. Univ. Chicago Press, 1992.

[8] Liu, J. and Kavakli, M. "Temporal Relation between Speech and Co-verbal Iconic Gestures in Multimodal Interface Design", Retrieved April, 2012

[9] B. Butterworth and G. Beattie, "Gestures and silence as indicators of planning in speech," in Recent Advances in the Psychology of Language: Formal and Experimental Approaches, ed., 1978

[10] U. Hadar, "Two types of gesture and their role in speech production," Journal of Language and Social Psychology, vol. 8, no. 3-4, pp. 221–228, 1989.

[11] U. Hadar, D. Wenkert-Olenik, R. Krauss, and N. Soroker,"Gesture and the processing of speech: Neuropsychological evidence," Brain and language, vol. 62, no. 1, pp. 107–126,

[12] W. Levelt, G. Richardson, and W. La Heij, "Pointing and voicing in deictic expressions," Journal of Memory an Language, vol. 24, no. 2, pp. 133–164, 1985.

[13] R. Krauss, "Why do we gesture when we speak?" Current Directions in Psychological Science, vol. 7, no. 2, pp. 54–60, 1998.

[14] R. Krauss and U. Hadar, "The role of speech-related arm/hand gestures in word retrieval," Gesture, speech, and sign, pp. 93–116, 1999..

[15] P. Bernardis and M. Gentilucci, "Speech and gesture share the same communication system," Neuropsychologia, vol. 44, no. 2, pp. 178–190, 2006.

[16] D. Armstrong, W. Stokoe, and S. Wilcox, Gesture and the Nature of Language. Cambridge University Press, 1995.

[17] M. Corballis, From hand to mouth: The origins of language. Princeton University Press, 2003.

[18] S. Kita, "How representational gestures help speaking," Language and gesture, pp. 162–185, 2000.

[19] A. Erol, G. Bebis, M. Nicolescu, R. Boyle, and X. Twombly, Vision-based hand pose estimation: A review," Computer Vision and Image Understanding, vol. 108, no. 1, pp. 52–73, 2007.

[20] T. Marsh, "An iconic gesture is worth more than a thousand words," in Information Visualization, 1998. Proceedings. 1998 IEEE Conference on. IEEE, 1998, pp. 222–223.

[21] T. A. van Dijk. (2000) Cognitive discourse analysis. http://www.discourses.org/UnpublishedArticles/cogn-dis-anal.htm. University of Amsterdam.

[22] M. Suwa, T. Purcell, and J. Gero, "Macroscopic analysis of design processes based on a scheme for coding designers' cognitive actions," Design studies, vol. 19, no. 4, pp. 455–483, 1998.

[23] M. Suwa, J. Gero, and T. Purcell, "Analysis of cognitive processes of a designer as the foundation for support tools," in Artificial Intelligence in Design, vol. 98, 1998, pp. 229–248.

[24] M. Kipp. (2000-2012) The video annotation research tool. http://www.anvil-software.org/.

[25] P. Boersma and D. Weenink. The video annotation research tool. University of Amsterdam.

[26] Y. Yasinnik, M. Renwick, and S. Shattuck-Hufnagel, "The timing of speech-accompanying gestures with respect to prosody," Proceedings of Sound to Sense, MIT, 2004.

A Comparative Study of Multiple Social Network Sites Based on Google Analytics Data

S. M. Horng
Department of Business Administration
National Chengchi University, Taiwan (ROC)

Abstract
This study collects the data from four social network sites to study user behavior. Data are retrieved from their Google Analytics measures, including visits, percentage of new visits, bounce rate, average time on page, and average time on site. Through statistical analyses and in-depth interviews with the founders of the web services, several patterns from analyzing the measures are identified and categorized into two groups, visiting behavior and user behavior. Managerial implications are proposed and discussed based on the analyzed results and discussions with practitioners.
Keywords: Google Analytics, user behavior, social network sites

Introduction

The term "web 2.0" was first documented by O'Reilly (2005) and its impact on the internet has been studied widely. An important development of web 2.0 services is the increasing user-generated content on the Web, and the ability to combine parts of it to form new content. Three web 2.0 collaborative tools, Blogs, Mashups, and Wikis (Dearstyne, 2007), are predominantly important and have stimulated the development of internet-based social network sites (referred to as SNS throughout the remainder of the study). The key success factor of SNS is the high traffic flow representing higher fees for advertisements and better conditions for any e-commerce application. However, traffic flow is not the only indicator to be considered; other indicators such as average time spent on the site, average time spent on pages, et al., are also important to the long-term development of online services. This study worked with several web services to collect their Google Analytics measures and is directed at identifying an index performance model to the SNS. The results could provide online services guidelines on how to operate their web site and better predict the development of their online services.

Literature Review

According to Khoo et al. (2008), web metrics or web analytics record and analyze visitor traffic to and through a web site. Three common tools are identified. Frist, combinations of user panels and browser logging tools are used to track online user populations. Second, network traffic data are collected directly from ISP servers. Third, site-specific server log parsers or page tagging technologies are used to measure traffic through a particular site. Google analytics is categorized as the third tool. Of the three most popular web analytics software, Google Analytics, ClickTracks, and Coremetrics (Chafkin, 2006), Google Analytics is the only one among the three systems that is free of charge. Several studies have reported its applications in practice. A library developed several interactive tutorials that covered basic services, and used Google Analytics to record usage statistics and perform evaluations (Braender et al., 2009). A university created an interactive learning platform in which faculty and students could write and comment about emerging social issues surrounding the web. They also used Google Analytics to gather usage information (Betty, 2008). A company used website optimization provider SiteSpect in conjunction with Google Analytics to evaluate the quality of video distribution (Bannan, 2008). Plaza (2009) utilized data from Google Analytics to develop a tracking methodology for academics to analyze the effectiveness of visits, and found that return visits were the main engine for nurturing session length. These applications of Google Analytics from the literature focused on the performance of a single web service and improvement by benchmarking, while cross-websites analysis might provide information on a broader view of online services.

Methodology and Results

Identify case companies and Google Analytics measures for study

The data on Google Analytics are only available for those registering their sites on Google. Four companies based in Taiwan agreed to provide their Google Analytics data for this study. For confidential reasons, the companies in this study are represented as A, B, C, and D. The following is a brief description of them. Company A combines maps and blogs so that users can post articles on the location indicating where they live and interact with other users via this platform. Company B provides an online platform to collect articles on pre-defined topics. In addition to user-provided contents, articles on different sites can be tagged or recommended on this site so that users are able to read many high-quality articles devoted to a specific topic at a single site. Company C is an online service specifically for dining information. The user can search for restaurants based on several pre-defined topics such as menu, price, location, et al. In addition, opinions regarding a specific restaurant are also posted as important references for other users. The last one offers a free platform for student users, especially campus clubs, to interact on the site.

Table 1. Google Analytics measures used in this study and their definitions

Measure	Definition
Visit	The number of times your visitors visit to your site (individual sessions initiated by each of your visitors). If a user is inactive on your site for 30 minutes or more, any future activity will be attributed to a new session. Users that leave your site and return within 30 minutes will be counted as part of the original session.
BR	Bounce rate is the percentage of single-page visits or visits in which a person leaves your site from the entrance (landing) page. This metric is used to measure visit quality – a high bounce rate generally indicates that site entrance pages are not relevant to your visitors.
% NV	The number of new visits by individuals who have never been to the site before divided by the number of visits.
ATOP	Average time on page. Total time on site for all visits divided by the number of pages.
ATOS	Average time on site. Total time on site for all visits divided by the total number of visits.

Many measures are available on Google Analytics for retrieval. After discussing with the founders of the four online companies, 15 important variables were identified including Bounces, Bounce Rate, Entrances, Exits, percent of Exit, Visitors, New Visits, Percent of New Visits, Time on Page, Average Time on Page, Pageviews, The Number of Pages per Visit, Time on Site, Average Time on Site, and Visits. Since some of the variables are combinations of others or highly correlated with each other, the data are further reduced into five items in which their definitions from Google (2009) are shown in Table 1.

Data collection

Companies A, B, C, and D recorded data for 480, 1002, 615, and 335 days, respectively, during the period from 2006 to 2009. In order to analyze the sites only when they are well established, data with less than 1000 visits per day are further removed, resulting in 480, 857, 615, and 332 days. Since company A has its data recorded for members separately from non-members, a total of 6 cases are analyzed, including case A, case B, case C, case D, case A(m) for members, and case A(n) for non-members.

Data analysis

A focus group interview with the founders of these websites revealed that visit was the most important index. They also proposed several questions which became the research topics of this study. First, what is the relationship between visit and other indices and what are their managerial implications? Second, how can the abnormal records of daily visit be identified and what are their managerial implications? The issue of managerial implications arises for the second question because all of the companies experience a similar pattern in that the number of visits jumps significantly in periods of promotional events and then drop to normal levels several days later. It is difficult to evaluate the long-term effect of promotional events. To answer the first question, Pearson correlation coefficients are calculated for relationships between visit and the four other measures, BR, %NV, ATOP, and ATOS. Most of them are significant at 0.05 levels across the six cases. However, the correlation relationship might not be consistent over time. In order to identify the pairwise correlation relationship along a timeline, a moving window of 60 days is used to calculate the Pearson correlation coefficients over the data collection period. The moving window works as follows: The first coefficient is calculated based on day one to day 60; the second coefficient is based on day two to day 61; and so on. A data set of 200 days produces 141 Pearson correlation coefficients.

Figure 1 shows the correlation relationships between visit and the four other measures for case C. All of the four correlation coefficients fluctuate over time when observed individually and none of them show a consistent relationship. Using the data for the entire collection period to calculate one correlation coefficient might lead to a misinterpretation of the real relationship between them. The same fluctuating patterns were observed across all of the other five cases.

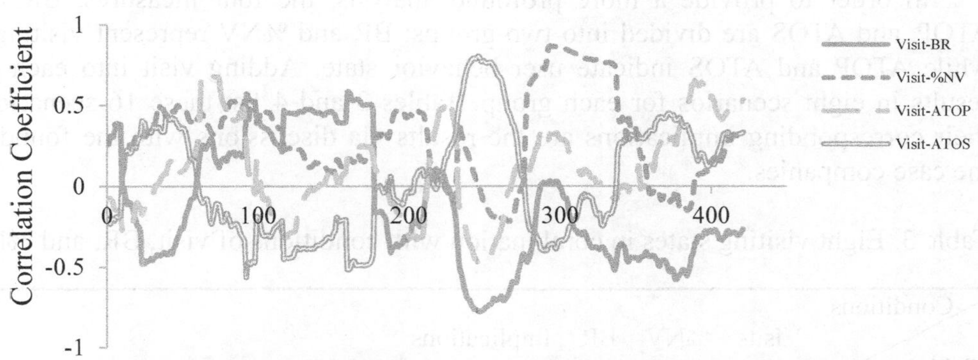

Fig. 1 Correlation coefficients of moving window between visit and four other measures over the data collection period for case C

With the sample size of 60, the *t* value of 2.39 is significant at 0.01, requiring correlation coefficients of larger than 0.3 or less than -0.3. The four correlation coefficient curves on Fig.1, except the one between visit and %NV, show both significantly positive and negative relationships. Table 2 illustrates the Pearson correlation coefficient results for the four relationships, visit vs. BR, visit vs. %NV, visit vs. ATOP, and visit vs. ATOS, across the six cases with or without (shadowed areas) the moving window calculations. It is interesting to note that only three relationships, visit vs. %NV for case C and A(m) and visit vs. BR for A(n) provide consistent results with or without the moving window calculations. Case A(m) represents only the members and a positive relationship between visit and %NV is intuitively illogical. However, several interviews with members of company A reveal that a certain portion of them remain inactive and become active only for special events. When users are inactive for a long time, they are defined by Google Analytics as new visitors. A negative relationship between visit and BR for non-members is expected. Many of the non-member users might visit the site through links from other sites or search results, and leave immediately when services offered on the site do not meet their expectations. The last consistent relationship is between visit and %NV for case C, indicating that it attracted many new users during the time when the data were collected.

Table 2. Pearson correlation coefficient results for the six cases

Relationship / Case	Visit-BR		Visit-%NV		Visit-ATOP		Visit-ATOS	
A	-	+/-	-	+/-		+/-	-	+/-
B	-	+/-	-	+/-		+/-	-	+/-
C		+/-	-	-	+	+/-	+	+/-
D	-	+/-	-	+/-		+/-		+/-
A(m)	-	+/-	+	+	+	+/-	+	+/-
A(n)	-	-	-	+/-	-	+/-	+	+/-

Notes:

- All of the results are based on the significant level of 0.01.
- Shadowed areas represent the results for which the correlation coefficients take the entire data set as a whole. "-" indicates a significantly negative relationship and "+" a significantly positive one. An empty cell represents an insignificant relationship.
- "+/-" indicates that the correlation coefficients of moving windows are both significantly positive and negative along the time frame for each case.

In order to provide a more profound analysis, the four measures, BR, %NV, ATOP, and ATOS are divided into two groups: BR and %NV represent visiting state while ATOP and ATOS indicate user behavior state. Adding visit into each group results in eight scenarios for each group. Tables 3 and 4 list these 16 scenarios and their corresponding implications are the results via discussions with the founders of the case companies.

Table 3. Eight visiting states in combination with conditions of visit, BR, and %NV

Visiting state \ Conditions	Visits	%NV	BR	Implications
1	+	+	+	A typical situation when the number of visits is increased by new users, some of whom are not interested in this site.
2	+	-	-	Attracts many loyal users.
3	+	+	-	Attracts many new users who are interested in this site.
4	+	-	+	Fewer new users and more loyal users who left the site after a short time.
5	-	-	-	Similar to the first scenario with decreased number of visits.
6	-	+	+	Higher portion of new users leave the site quickly, or the sudden drop of regular users causes a higher %NV.
7	-	-	+	Both the numbers of new or regular old users decrease and they stay on the site for short periods.
8	-	+	-	The portion of new visitors interested in this site increases and/or the portion of regular users decreases.

Notes: "+"and "-" represent significant increased and decreased value, respectively, in visit, %NV", or BR.

Table 4 Eight user behavior combinations among conditions of visit, BR, and %NV

User behavior \ Conditions	Visits	ATOP	ATOS	Implications
1	+	+	+	Increased users show great interest in this site.
2	+	+	-	Increased users show less interest in this site.
3	+	-	+	Increased users show great interest in certain pages.
4	+	-	-	Increased users quickly browse many pages on the site.
5	-	-	-	The site is dying.
6	-	-	+	Only loyal users visit and show greater interest in many pages.
7	-	+	-	Only loyal users visit and quickly browse many pages on the site.
8	-	+	+	Only loyal users visit and stay on certain pages for long periods of time.

Notes: "+"and "-" represent significant increased and decreased value, respectively, in visit, ATOP, or ATOS.

After examination of the data, Table 5 shows the combinations of visiting states and user behavior for the six cases. To identify the visiting and user behavior states each case belongs to, the significant correlation coefficients of moving windows between visit and the four measures, BR, %NV, ATOP, and ATOS are marked for further analysis. Next, only the visits at the marked period showing significant growing or dropping patterns are considered. Note that cases B and D have similar results. When visits increase as indicated by the visiting states of 1, 2, 3, or 4, user behavior 1, 2, or 4 can be seen in both of the cases, and user behavior 3 (ATOP decreases and ATOS increases) is never observed. When visits are down as indicated by visiting states 5, 6, 7, and 8, ATOP and ATOS both increase in cases B and D. It is speculated that the increasing number of visitors in both cases stay for long periods of time on several targeted pages related to their promotional events. On the other hand, loyal users continue visiting both of the sites when the number of total visits is down, resulting in higher ATOP and ATOS. When considering cases A and C, visiting states 1, 3, 5, and 7 are never found. That is, visits and %NV are negatively correlated. The founders indicated that their social communities attract a high rate of revisiting users as well as new visitors. In addition, as the visits drop, ATOP increases in case A and decreases in case C. The nature of company C, which provides an information-based web service, might explain this finding.

Table 5 Observed combinations of visiting states and user behavior states for the six cases

Case / Visiting state	A	A(m)	A(n)	B	C	D
1	-	4	-	2	-	2
2	1,2,4	-	2	1,2	1,2,3	1,2,4
3	-	-	-	1,2	-	1,4
4	2,4	2	1,4	4	1,2	-
5	-	8	6	-	-	6
6	7,8	-	-	8	5	8
7	-	-	-	8	-	8
8	7,8	6,8	8	8	5,6	8

Note: Except for the first column, the numbers represent user behavior states. Multiple numbers in one cell indicate more than one user behavior state is observed at that visiting state. The user behavior states are added in this table only when significant correlation coefficients are observed.

Companies A, B, and D focus on building up their virtual communities while company C's strategy is to provide information. Sites A, B, and D are defined as interaction-based websites and site C is an information-based website. The differences between these two types of websites can be stated as follows. As visits increase (visiting states 1, 2, 3, and 4), user behavior 3 is never found on site A, B, and D. User behavior 5 is not found when visits are down on sites A, B, and D. That is, user behavior 3 and 5 are the unique features of the users on site C.

After in-depth interviews with the founders of the case companies, positive and negative indicators for the visiting states are identified. Visiting state 3 is agreed by all to have the best indicator for the web operation. Visits increase and most of the new users are also interested in the services or contents of the site. However, one interviewee indicated that visiting states 2 and 4 do not necessarily signify failure of the site, but rather might also reflect healthy development of the online service under the condition of no promotional events. Visiting states 5 and 7 are considered as indicators of the end of the online services by all of the interviewees. One of the founders also considered visiting state 4 a warning sign that might result in failure in the long term.

In terms of user behavior, scenario 1 was unanimously deemed to signify the best condition. However, a rising ATOS is also important when longevity of the user is considered. Dependent on business models, user behavior scenarios 5 or 8 are indicators of the declining stage of a web site.

Conclusions and Future Work

This study collected Google Analytics data from four social network sites. Through a focus group interview with the founders of the web services, the five most important measures were identified. Correlation analysis was used to provide a foundation for the findings. Visits and its relationships with BR and %NV represent visiting states, and visits and its relationship with ATOP and ATOS signify user behavior. By combining the actual data analyses and in-depth interviews, the managerial implications for visiting states and user behavior are both identified. Although some of the results are case dependent, others are commonly applicable to all online services.

As indicated previously, identifying abnormal records of visits and studying this factor's managerial implication is the second issue proposed by website founders and is currently addressed by this study. In addition, the differences between members and non-members of case A are also an intriguing topic requiring further analysis.

References

Bannan, K. J. (2008). RADirect uses Web *analytics* to improve online video success. *B to B*, 93, 14.

Betty, P. (2008). Creation, management, and assessment of library screencasts: The Regis libraries animated tutorials project. *Journal of Library Administration*, 48, 295-315.

Braender, L. M., Kapp, C. M. & Years, J. (2009). Using web technology to teach students about their digital world. *Journal of Information Systems Education*, 20, 145-153.

Chafkin, M. (2006). Analyze This, Says Google. Inc., 28-30.

Dearstyne, B. W. (2007). Blogs, mashups, & wikis: Oh, My! Information Management Journal, 41, 25-33.

Google, *Google Analytics [computer software]*, 2009, http://www.google.com/analytics, accessed on 10/10/2009.

Khoo, M., Pagano, J., Washington, A. L., Recker, M., Palmer, B. & Donahue, R. A. (2008). Using web metrics to analyze digital libraries. *Proceedings of the 8th ACM/IEEE-CS Joint Conference on Digital Libraries*, 375-384.

Plaza, B. (2009). Monitoring web traffic source effectiveness with Google analytics: An experiment with time series, *Aslib Proceedings*, 61, 474-482.

WorldComp-EEE 13

Academic Research Quality E-Valuation: An Adaptive Hybrid Model based on Journal Rankings and Citing Methodologies

Evangelia A.E.C. Lipitakis[1] and Alexandra Lipitakis[2]
Kent Business School, University of Kent
Canterbury, Kent CT2 7PE, England
(1) eael2@kent.ac.uk (2) aial2@kent.ac.uk

Abstract *– The quality of the journal of the received citations of large sets of publications for evaluating the quality performance in the case of individual researchers, research groups and academic departments is an interesting research problem. An adaptive model incorporating and examining variables, such as the quality of journals of a set of publication as well as the cited and citing articles within the given set of publications is proposed. This hybrid bibliometric methodology can be used as an alternative methodology to citations counts. The proposed weighted citations are taken into account according to the quality of their publication outlet and the computational procedure is based on weighted parameters affected by the journal quality for the evaluation of the citing and cited papers.The proposed research quality evaluation (RQE) methodology can be considered as a quality performance evaluation approach by using efficient research journal quality ranking indicators and citing methodologies based on weighted parameters. The proposed research quality evaluation methodology by examining the number of citations of a publication as well as its source of publication, evaluates a set of publications by taking into account the following indicators: (i) the total number of publications (productivity), (ii) the number of citations a paper has received (impact) (iii) the quality of the journal that the citing article has been published in (citing quality factor), (iv) the number of cited papers of a publication (impact) and (v) the quality of the journal that the cited article has been published in (cited quality factor). The considered journal quality citing and cited indices are used in combination with predetermined evaluation weight parameters in order to produce an efficient research quality evaluation methodology.*

Contact Author: Evangelia Lipitakis, eael2@kent.ac.uk

Keywords: Advanced bibliometric indicators, business and management, citing and cited quality factors, journal quality citing index, journal quality ranking, research impact, research quality e-valuation, quantitative methods, weighted citations

1. Introduction

In the past decades considerable research efforts have been directed towards the areas of research quality evaluation methodologies, journal quality rankings, advanced bibliomeric indicators, e-business and management, and related applications (Todorov and Glanzel, 1988; Doyle and Arthurs, 1995; Garfield, 1999; Glanzel and Moed, 2002, Van Raan, 2003-2004; Hirsch, 2005; Moed, 2005; Nederhof, 2006; Mingers and Harzing, 2007; Truex et al., 2008; Molinary and Molinary, 2008; Mingers and Lipitakis, 2010; Lipitakis and Lipitakis, 2012; Mingers and Lipitakis, 2013). Various advanced bibliometric indicators can be used to efficiently measure the productivity and impact of research at several academic levels, such as at the level of individual researchers, research groups and university departments. The Leiden Methodology (Van Raan, 2003; Waltman et al., 2010 & 2011) which normalizes the citation rate of a set of publications for subject field and time, has been recently tested for the evaluation of research of three leading UK business schools in the area of Business, Economics and Management, (Mingers and Lipitakis, 2013).

Traditionally, citation based metrics have only considered the number of publications a paper has received and not the quality of the citations.

At this point we need to consider the following research question "In research quality performance evaluation, should we consider and treat all citations equally?" The purpose of our research is to consider the eventuality that all citations are not equal and that they differ in some way. Given that citations come from journals, so far all citations have been treated equally regardless of whether the citations have been received by papers that have been published in high quality journals or low quality journals. This practice does not consider that citations from top journals should, perhaps, count for more than citations from poor quality journals. One basic assumption of bibliometric analysis is that scientists with important and original material endeavour to publish their results vigorously in the open international journal literature. Although journal articles differ widely in importance, it has been noticed that authors in most cases seek to publish in the better and, if possible, the best journals (Glanzel, 1996; Hicks, 1999; Van Raan, 2004).

In this paper, a new research quality evaluation methodology that examines the number of *cited* and *citing* articles of a set of publication as well as their source of publication is introduced. More specifically, this new methodology evaluates a set of publications by taking into account the following indicators: (i) the total number of publications (productivity), (ii) the number of citations a paper has received (impact), (iii) the quality of the journal that the citing article has been published in (citing quality factor), (iv) the number of cited papers and (v) the quality of the journal that the cited paper has been published in (cited quality factor). The three first components have been recently proposed by Lipitakis (2013) as part of the Journal Quality Citing (JQC) methodology. The above described indicators based on the previous JQC methodology can be extended for the academic research quality performance assessment. The purpose of our proposed methodology is to weight citations according to the quality of their publication outlet. This methodology is based on weighted parameters affected by the journal quality for the evaluation of each given and received citation. If we assume that high quality journals publish significant and original scientific research then our proposed weighted citations methodology reflects both the productivity and impact of a set of publications in a given field.

2. Citation Methodologies and Journal Ranking Indicators: A Synoptic Literature Review

New methodologies for the evaluation of research quality performance are mainly focused on the efficient use of advanced bibliometric indicators and scientometric information (data), efficient adapted peer reviewing methods and certain hybrid methodologies for identifying excellent researchers of all types (Nederhof, 2006). Furthermore, new classes of hybrid methodologies incorporating both qualitative and quantitative advantageous elements are being developed. More specifically, certain quantitative elements are present in the class of qualitative methods, while qualitative elements appear also in the quantitative methods. The derivation of new and extended (modified) methodologies for measuring the research output quality of an individual researcher and/or a research unit in science and social sciences is a challenging research topic currently under investigation. Several bibliometric studies have focused more on the citation impact of a journal rather than that of the published research paper (Nederhof, 2006). Various recent studies have focused on new methods of assessing scholarly influence based on journal ranking indicators. For example, a recent study examined the use of the Hirsch-type indices for the evaluation of the scholarly influence of Information Systems (IS) researchers (Truex et al., 2008). Another study assessed the impact of a set of IS journals, publications and researchers using a weighted citations count on authors and institutions where a publication with less authors receives more weight than a pubication with more authors (Lowry et al., 2007a; Chua et al., 2002). The presentation of a method, using advanced statistical methods, is based on cumulative n^{th} citation distributions on a publications ranking classification scheme (Egghe, 2007a) has also been considered. Additionally, a study on the complementary Hirsch type index, the h_m, for the comparison of journals within the same subject field (Molinary and Molinary, 2008) has also been presented.

Several research studies measuring the perceived quality of journals have been presented. The use of citation analysis for the evaluation of the 17 most influential management journals in the area of management has been presented (Tahai and Meyer, 1999). The assessment of the relative quality of 30 academic journals in the area of International Business (IB) using two main approaches for journal quality evaluation; surveys and citation analysis, including bibliometric indicators such as the number of total citations, citations per publications and the impact factor has been considered (DuBois and Reeb, 2000). Two approaches for measuring the quality of 29 academic journals in the fields of economics and finance have been introduced; the use of the average age of the received citations and citation counts of the examined journals (McNulty and Boekeloo, 1999). In a recent research study four distinct classes for the classification of 15 "*quantifiable research assessment measurements*" (RAMs) for journal quality evaluation of 110 academic journals in the field of Statistics & Probability using the ISI subject category classification have been proposed, including journal quality measures such as the 2 year journal impact factor and several of its variations, the h-index, the H-STAR index, the Eigenfactor Index (EI), the Article Influence Index (AII), etc.

Calculations of the harmonic averages of the journal rankings, as an alternative journal quality measure, by allocating equal weights for all the proposed classes were also given (Chang and McAller, 2012). The evaluation of the 40 top cited journals in the fields of business, economics, finance and management using the so-called *"research assessment measurements"* (RAMs) and harmonic average of the rankings of the journal ranking indicator of the selected journals has been also presented (Chang et al., 2011). Furthermore, various quantitative studies proposing the use linear programming for determining and assigning weights within a set of journals in a given field have been presented for journal quality ranking (Tse, 2001; Horowitz, 2003; Mingers et al., 2007).

3. On the relationship of the Hybrid RQE method and the PageRank-Eigenfactor algorithms

A set of methodologies similar to the one presented in this chapter, called the Pagerank algorithm and the Eigenfactor Index has been presented. In the following we state certain similarities our proposed methodology has with the PageRank (Brin and Page, 1998) and Eigenfactor (Bergstrom et al., 2008; Davis, 2008) algorithmic mechanisms. The Pagerank algorithm (Brin and Page, 1998) is used by Google online search engine to assign weights in web pages depending on how heavily they have been used in order to measure their relative importance within a set i.e. the World Wide Web (www). A web page that has received many inbound links from other web pages in the given set, receives a high PageRank and is considered of significant importance. PageRank however, does not rank highly solely the number of inbound links. According to Page and Brin (1999), an incoming link from an important web page (i.e. www.yahoo.com) bares more significantly more weight than many inbound links of obscure web pages. The higher the PageRank of an inbound link, the more the weight it allocates to the recipient web page. Pagerank has been characterized as *"an attempt to see how good an approximation to importance* can be obtained just from the link structure." (Page and Brin, 1999, p.3). The same principles rule in the case of the Eigenfactor index; received citations from highly ranked journals carry more weight than received citations from average/lower ranked journals (Bergstrom, 2007; Bergstrom et al., 2008; Davis, 2008; Fersht, 2009).

The concept of the Pagerank algorithm can be adapted to any set of reciprocal interactive entities, in our case a set of publications where the inbound links can be identified as the received citations a paper receives (*citing* articles) and the outbound links can be identified as the referenced papers (*cited* articles).

The methodology presented in this chapter proposes a quantitative method (citation count) that incorporates the quality of the journals of the citing papers (weighted parameters) in a hybrid methodology, based on existing and novel research performance quality assessments. The term hybrid model here denotes the combined use of advanced bibliometric methodologies and journal quality ranking indicators in the modelling process.

4. An Adaptive Model for Evaluating the Research Quality Performance at individual researcher level

In this section we propose an adaptive model for the evaluation of the research quality performance based on citing and cited quality factors using journal ranking indicators. This generalized adaptive model can be used for evaluating the academic research quality performance at individual researcher level and can be extended for evaluating the research quality performance at research group level, department level and university level involving large scale data processing bibliometric indicators.

An Adaptive Research Quality Evaluation model for computing the total research work of an individual researcher using three level bibliometric indicators can be derived by the following modelling scheme:

$$TRQEI = \sum_{J=1}^{N} RQEI_J = W_{L1} \sum_{J=1}^{N} [\,(\varepsilon_{JP}{}^{J}\, JP_J)] + W_{L2} [\sum_{K=1}^{NCG(J)} (\varepsilon_{CG}{}^{K,J}\, CGP_{K,J})\,] + W_{L3} [\sum_{L=1}^{NCD(J)} \varepsilon_{CD}{}^{L,J}\, CDP_{L,J}], \quad (4.1)$$

where TRQEI is the total number of Research Quality Evaluation journals indicators of all the published papers of the considered individual researcher, RQEI indicator of each one paper of the N-publications of the researcher and

JP_J, J=1,2,…,N, is the number of published papers, with N the total number of publications of the researcher,

CGP_K, K=1,2,…,NCG, is the number of citing papers for each published paper, with NCG the number of citing papers.

CDP_L, L=1,2,…,NCD, is the number of cided papers in each publication, with NCD the number of cited papers,

The adaptive parameters ε_{JP} , ε_{CD} , ε_{CG} are affecting respectively the variables JP, CDP, CGP. The numerical real values of the adaptive parameters ε_{JP}, ε_{CD}, ε_{CG} can be selected from predetermined values corresponding to the chosen journal quality measure. In a recent study for the determination of an efficient journal quality measure as a weighted parameter for the evaluation of citing articles in the fields of business and management, a class of 8 journal ranking indicators including the 2 year impact factor, the 5 year impact factor, the h-index, the eigenfactor score, and the immediacy index has been considered (Lipitakis, 2013). The 8 journal ranking indicators have been tested in a dataset of more than 1,000 journals in the wider area of business and management using bibliometric indicators from the ISI Web of Science (WoS) online citation database. The results indicated the 5 year journal impact factor as the most efficient journal quality measure in the given subject areas. In our proposed methodology, in the case of the evaluation of a set of publications in the fields of business and management, the numerical values of the adaptive parameters ε_{JP}, ε_{CD}, ε_{CG} would be affected by the predetermined values of the impact factor 5 year in a given year and subject field (Lipitakis, 2013).

The three terms of the equation (4.1) correspond to three different levels of bibliometric factors, namely (L1) the published journal papers indicator, (L2) the citing papers indicators of each citing paper and (L3) the cited papers indicators of each paper. The weighed real parameters W_{L1}, W_{L2} and W_{L3} can be selected from predetermined values of tables with different scales (for example, $W_{L1} \in [0.0, 100.0]$, $W_{L2} \in [0.0, 10.0]$ and $W_{L3} \in [0.0, 2.0]$) and correspond to the levels L1 (productivity), L2 and L3 (impact).

Note that the selection of the cited papers in each publication is a matter of personal preference of the researcher depending on several factors, such as the direct relevance of the cited paper with the publication, the scientific status of the top researcher works, the publication outlet of the cited paper, the top academic foundation in which researcher is affiliated to etc.

The total number of Research Quality Evaluation Journals indicator TRQEI can be considered as a function of productivity and impact, i.e.

$$TRQEI = f\Big(\sum_{J=1}^{N} [(\varepsilon_{JP}{}^{J}\, JP_J)],\ \sum_{K=1}^{NCG(J)} (\varepsilon_{CG}{}^{K,J}\, CGP_{K,J})],\ CDF\Big), \qquad (4.2)$$

where the second term of the function in (4.2) is related to the Journal Quality Citing (JQC) indicator and CDF is the cited papers factor related to the research quality performance (Lipitakis, 2013). The JQC index calculates the weighted citations of a publication, based on weighted parameters affected by the journal quality for the evaluation of each given citation.

In the case that $W_{L1} = W_{L3} = 0.0$, the modelling scheme (4.1), leads to the following simplified (impact) function form

$$TRQEI^* = W_{L2}\,\Big[\sum_{K=1}^{NCG(J)} (\varepsilon_{CG}{}^{K,J}\, CGP_{K,J})\Big] = f\Big(\sum_{K=1}^{NCG(J)} (\varepsilon_{CG}{}^{K,J}\, CGP_{K,J})\Big). \qquad (4.3)$$

In the case of $W_{L1} = W_{L3} = 0.0$, TRQEI* becomes the Journal Quality Citing methodology (Lipitakis, 2013) which has been used for the assessment of the quality of the journal of the received citations of large sets of publications for the research quality performance evaluation in the case of an academic department or a researcher. Extensive numerical experimentation and statistical analysis of this model for the evaluation of the academic research output (journal articles) of three leading UK business schools in the fields of business, economics, management and O/R & management science using the 5 year journal impact factor as a journal quality ranking weighted parameter for the computation of weighted citations have been recently presented (Lipitakis, 2013). The obtained numerical results have indicated that this research quality methodology can be efficiently used in large scale academic research quality evaluation cases and that in the case of the Journal Quality Citing index produced similar results with to the UK RAE 2008 peer review assessment (Lipitakis, 2013).

The proposed adaptive hybrid model (4.1), a modified model of (4.3) that incorporates and examines more variables, such as the quality of the journals of the publications of the academic/researcher's research output, as well as publications and journals of the citing articles and cited references of the publications, includes also other publication types (such as books, conference papers, reports, working papers, etc.).

5. Conclusions

The quality of the journal of the cited and citing articles of a set of publications for evaluating the quality performance in the case of individual researchers is investigated. An adaptive model incorporating and examining variables, such as the quality of journals of the cited and citing articles within the set of publications is considered. This hybrid bibliometric methodology, as an alternative methodology to citations counts, examines the quality of the journals of the cited and citing articles that they have been published in and evaluates the quality of the received and given citations (citing and cited articles) in the set of publications. The considered journal quality citing and cited indices are used in combination with predetermined evaluation weight parameters in order to produce an efficient research quality evaluation methodology.

Some early obtained numerical results indicate that the new research quality evaluation methodology could be also used in large scale academic research quality cases and in the case of the Journal Citing Quality index which is a simplified form of our proposed model, there is a clear degree of concordance with the results of the UK RAE 2008 peer review exercise. The proposed adaptive hybrid RQE model can be considered as a quality performance evaluation approach by using efficient research journal quality ranking indicators and advanced bibliometric indicators based on weighted parameters.

References

BERGSTROM C. (2007): Eigenfactor: Measuring the value and prestige of scholarly journals, C&RL News 68, 314-316

BERGSTROM C., WEST J.D. and WISEMAN M.A. (2008): The Eigenfactor Metrics, The Journal of Neuroscience 28, 11433-11434

BRIN S. and PAGE L. (1998): The anatomy of a large-scale hypertextual Web search engine, Computer Networks and ISDN Systems 30, 107–117.

CHANG C.L. and MCALEER M. (2012): Ranking Journal Quality by Harmonic Mean of Ranks: An Application to ISI Statistics and Probability", Statistica Neerlandica, 67, 27-53.

CHANG C.L., MCALEER M. and OXLEY L. (2011): What Makes a Great Journal Great in Economics? The Singer Not The Song, Journal of Economic Surveys, 25, 326-361.

CHUA C., CAO L., COUSINS K. and STRAUB D. (2002): Measuring Researcher-Production in Information Systems, Journal of the Association of Information Systems 3, 145-215.

DAVIS P.M. (2008): Eigenfactor: Does the principle of repeated improvement result in better estimates than raw citation counts? Journal of the American Society for Information Science and Technology 59, 2186-2188

DOYLE J. and ARTHURS A. (1995): Judging the quality of research in business schools, Omega, International Journal of Management Science 23, 257–270.

DUBOIS F.L. and REEB D. (2000): Ranking the International Business Journals, Journal of International Business Studies, 31, 689-704.

EGGHE L. (2007): Probabilities for encountering genius, basic, ordinary or insignificant papers based on the cumulative nth citation distribution, Scientometrics 70, 167-181

FERSHT A. (2009): The most influential journals: Impact factor and Eigenfactor, Procs of the National Academy of Sciences of the U.S.A. 106, 6883-6884

GARFIELD E. (1999): Journal Impact Factor: A Brief Review, Canadian Medical Association Journal 161, 979-980

GLANZEL W. (1996): A bibliometric approach to social sciences, national research performance in 6 selected social science areas 1990-1992, Scientometrics 35, 291-307

GLANZEL W. and MOED H.F. (2002): Journal impact measures in bibliometric research, Scientometrics 53, 171-193

HICKS D. (1999): The Difficulty of Achieving Full Coverage of International Social Science Literature and the Bibliometric Consequences, Scientometrics 44 (2), 193-215

HIRSCH J. (2005): An index to quantify an individual's scientific research output, Proceedings of The National Academy of Sciences of the U.S.A., 102:46, 16569-16572

HOROWITZ I. (2003): Preference-neutral attribute weights in the journal-ranking problem, Journal of the Operational Research Society, 54, 452-457.

LIPITAKIS A. and LIPITAKIS E.A.E.C. (2012): On the e-valuation of certain e-business strategies on firm performance by adaptive algorithmic modeling: An alternative strategic managerial approach, Computer Technology and Application 3, 38-46

LIPITAKIS EV.A.E.C. (2013): The use of bibliometric methods in evaluation research performance in Business and Management: A study of three UK Business Schools, Doctoral Thesis, KBS, University of Kent, Canterbury, England

LOWRY P.B., KARUGA G.G. and RICHARDSON V.J. (2007): Assessing leading Institutions, Faculty and Articles in premier Information Systems Research Journals, Communications of the Association for Information Systems 20, 142-203

McNULTY, J. E. and BOEKELOO, J. (1999): Two Approaches to Measuring Journal Quality: Application to Finance Journals, Journal of Economics and Finance, 23, 30-38.

MINGERS J. and HARZING A.W. (2007): Ranking journals in business and management: a statistical analysis of the Harzing data set, European Journal of Information Systems 16, 303-316

MINGERS J. and LIPITAKIS EV. A.E.C. (2010): Counting the Citations: A Comparison of Web of Science and Google Scholar in the Field of Business and Management, Scientometrics 85, 613-625

MINGERS J. and LIPITAKIS EV. A.E.C. (2013): Evaluating a Department's Research: Testing the Leiden Methodology in Business and Management, Information Processing and Management 49, 587–595

MINGERS J. and WALSHAM G. (2010): Towards ethical information systems: The contribution of discourse ethics, MIS QUARTERLY 34 (4), 833-854

MINGERS J., WATSON K. and SCAPARRA P. (2009): Estimating business and management journal quality from the 2008 Research Assessment Exercise in the UK, Information Processing & Management, 48, 1078-1093

MOED H.F.: Citation Analysis in Research Evaluation, Dordrecht (Netherlands), Springer, 2005

MOLINARY J.F. and MOLINARY A. (2008): A new methodology for ranking scientific institutions, Scientometrics 75, 163-174

NEDERHOF A.J. (2006): Bibliometric monitoring of research performance in the social sciences and humanities, Scientometrics 66, 81-100.

PAGE L. and BRIN S. (1999): The PageRank Citation Ranking: Bringing Order to the Web, Technical Report, Stanford InfoLab [Online]. Availble at: http://ilpubs.stanford.edu:8090/422/ (Accessed 2013).

TAHAI A. and MEYER M.J. (1999): Revealed Preference Study of Management Journals' Direct Influences, Strategic Management Journal, 20, 279-296

TODOROV R. and GLANZEL W. (1988): Journal Citation Measures: A Concise Review, Journal of Information Science 14, 47-56

TRUEX III D.P., CUELLAR M.J. and TAKEDA H. (2008): Assessing scholarly influence: Proposing new metrics, ICIS 2008 Procs, 1-19

TSE A.C.B. (2001): Using mathematical programming to solve large ranking problems, Journal of the Operational Research Society, 52, 1144–1150.

VAN RAAN A.F.J. (2003): The use of bibliometric analysis in research performance assessment and monitoring of interdisciplinary scientific developments, Technology Assessment – Theory and Practice 1, 20–29.

VAN RAAN A.F.J. (2004): Measuring Science: Capita selecta of current main issues, in Moed-Glanzel (eds): Handbook of quantitative science and technology research group, Kluwer Academic, 19-50

WALTMAN L., ECK N.J., LEEUWEN T.N., VISSER M.S. and VAN RAAN A.F. (2010): Towards a new crown indicator: Some theoretical considerations, Journal of Informetrics5, 37-47

WALTMAN L., ECK N.J., LEEUWEN T.N., VISSER M.S. and VAN RAAN A.F. (2011): Towards a new crown indicator: An empirical analysis, Scientometrics 87, 467-481

Research and Design on Freely Oriented Crawler Engine

Xin He [1],Sheng Yang [2], Yunpeng Li [3], Biren Chen [4],and Jin-shuo Liu [5]
[12345]Computer School, Wuhan University, Wuhan, P. R. China

Abstract - *The crawler is an indispensable tool for today's numerous network applications, such as search engine, public opinion analysis. Although the intelligence and practicability of crawler have been improving, users pay too much attention to the configuration file for the reason that one configuration file can only be used in crawling and parsing one specific type of web pages. In order to solve this problem, we provide a design plan on crawler engine that is based on some basic technology like the regular expression matching. The designed crawler engine can generate configuration file automatically by a simple interaction with users, which may reduce the heavy burden on writing the configuration file .Also, it makes greatly attribute to improve the easy-to-use, the precision and recall of the crawler.*

Keywords: crawler, crawler engine, regular expression matching, search engine

1 Introduction

Web Crawler is a program that can crawl web pages automatically, it works as follows: firstly it starts from an initial set of URLs, called the seed, to obtain a URL. Then, it downloads the webpage, extracts all URLs from this page and adds these new URLs to the URL frontier. After that, another URL will be obtained from the frontier, and the crawler repeats the above-mentioned process until it reaches a certain standard that means the crawler can stop working. Broadly, crawler includes capturing and parsing web pages [1]. At present, web crawler as a significant access to get the web pages is widely applied to the search engines, public opinion analysis and etc.

Generally speaking, the configuration of the crawler needs to be customized according to the user's requirements of data source, such as the requirements of theme and spot. For a specific kind of web page structure, the crawler requires a corresponding written configuration file. Due to the users' limited knowledge to computer, the customization process frequently needs a professional programmer to complete. On the other hand, the web structure is so diverse and complex that the web crawler can't parse those pages that mismatch the configuration file, which restricts the crawler's precision and recall in a great degree. Furthermore, since users often change their requirements of information from the Internet, programmers have to revise, sometimes even rewrite, the configuration file. It is an urgent problem about how to reduce the programmers' heavy pressure on the frequent change of requirements.

In order to solve the question above, we consider a suitable design of a Crawler Engine as a driver to make crawlers to be more easy-to-use. This paper designs a crawler engine program that can crawl information in accordance with users' requirement, generate the configuration file automatically and drive the crawler to get the data from the web by simple interaction.

The paper is organized as followings: In section 1, we present the introduction of the relevant concept and problems of the Web Crawler. In section 2, the principle of crawler will be given. The section 3 is the detailed illustration of the principle of the crawler engine. The design of the crawler engine is shown in section 4. Lastly, we conclude the paper in section 5.

2 Background

The designed crawler engine acts on the Scalable Web Crawler. The Scalable Web Crawler [3] can expand the crawl range to the entire web from certain seed URLs, which mainly used for offering data to the portal site search engine and large web service provider.

The performance of Scalable Web Crawler is expected to be able to handle tens of thousands of pages per second. Also, it should cover as many important pages as possible and keep the latest version of them at the same time [3].

The architecture of Scalable Web Crawler is shown in the picture1 [4].The architecture is divided into 5 parts: the capturing module, the parsing module, link filter module, database and URL frontier [5].

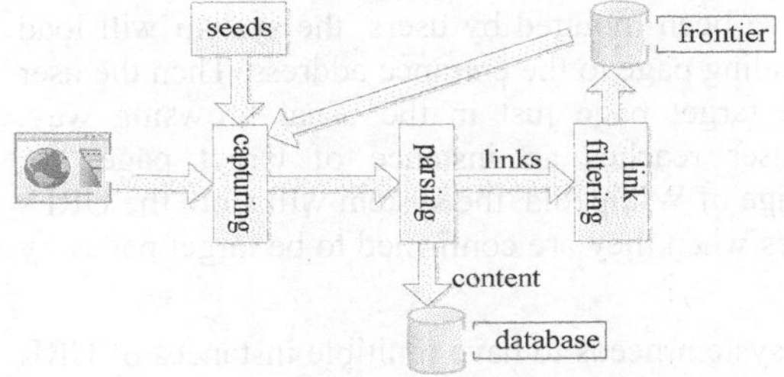

Picture 1 The architecture of Scalable Web Crawler

A typical workflow of crawler is as follows: firstly it crawls a specified web page according to the seed in the frontier. Next, after the web page has been downloaded, the parsing module extracts the useful content and stores them into the database. At the same time, the useless links like advertising links will be filtered out by the link filter module. Also, the link filter will remove the repeated links and links that have been crawled already according to a certain strategy. Finally, the frontier will store the links that wait to be crawled.

Moreover, there are two strategies known as breadth-first and depth-first for crawler to crawl pages. The breadth-first ordering is in accordance with traversal level to crawl pages, when all pages at the same level have been finished crawling, it continues crawling in a deeper level. On the other hand, the depth-first crawls don't crawl until reach a leaf-node of one hyperlink, and then returns to the previous link to choose another link to crawl [6].

The crawler engine to be realized acts as an intermediate layer between the user and crawler. For upper layer, it provides users with an easy-to-use interface; for lower layer, it is compatible with a specific crawler program. So, users can easily manipulate the crawler with the use of the crawler engine. The picture 2 describes the work level of the crawler engine. The crawler engine will lead to a more efficient of crawler service for users. So, the inconvenience that caused by the configuration file should be written by programmers can easily be avoided.

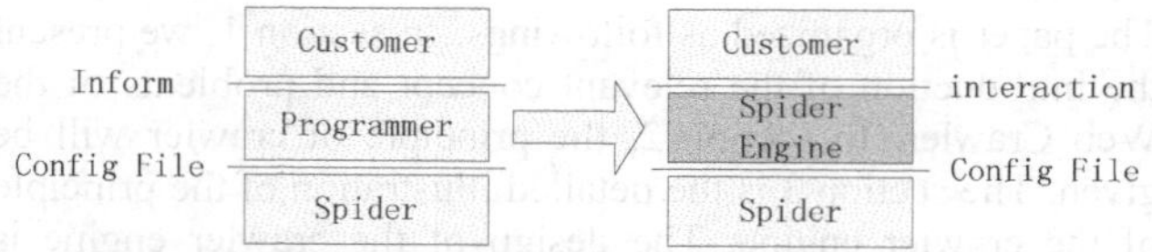

Picture 2 The work level of the crawler engine

3 Principle

The crawler engine is required to complete the configuration of crawler and drive the crawler to crawl webpages. Generally speaking, a full crawler working process consists of two parts, crawling and parsing. Crawling is to crawl pages from the Web, while parsing is expected to parse and classify the content of the page that has been crawled just before. To make this process successfully carried out, the crawler is needed to be informed the page spot and the position of the key information in the page, which provides the basis for the process of crawling and analyzing.

3.1 Crawling Locating

Most crawlers require the user to provide an entrance address, which is also required in our system. After the entrance addresses have been inputted by users, the system will load the corresponding page to the entrance address. Then the user can find the target page just in the usual browsing way. When the user reaches an instance of target page, for example a page of Wikipedia, the system will store the URLs of these pages when they are confirmed to be target pages by users.

Usually, the system needs to have multiple instances of URL to analyze. Generally speaking, the format of URL is as following:

protocol://hostname[:port]/path/page.xxx[?arg1=VALUE1 &arg2=VALUE2&...&argn=VALUEn]#fragment

In the formula above, hostname may include a few"." that are used to segment IP address or URL; path may frequently include one or more"/"; xxx is the suffix that indicate the webpage format, such as htm, html, asp, jsp, php and etc. var=VALUE is the webpage parameter (which may have multiple parameter assignment), and these assignments are separated by "&"; "#" is pieces of information that commonly used in locating anchor and etc. Since the URL stored by the system can be taken as a string, the system can make use of the regular expression quickly matching the text to handle URL matching problem.

It can be known from the analysis of URL format that there are obvious tokens, such as "/", ".", "?", "&", "=", "#". For these URLs obtained, we can use these tokens to cut them into some substrings, forming the following structure:

```
struct URLSeparator {
  String protocol;            // substring before "://"
  List<String> hostname;      // the substring separated by '.'
                              after"://" and before path
  long port;                  // the number after hostname
                              and :
  List<String> path;          // the substring separated by '/'
  String page;                // the substring after last '/',
                              e. g: index.asp
  struct EQU {                // the struct shows definition of
                              arguments in URL
    String arg;
    String value;
  };
  List<EQU> equations;        // argument list is after '?' and
                              before '#',which is often
                              separated by '&' and '='
  String fragment;            // the substring after '#'
};
```

The system records the format of URLs of pages labeled by users, parses these URLs according to the structure above, and compares the similarities and difference of each node of lists and element of structures in multiple URLs .After that, the system can get the common features of all kinds of page structures. For example:

For the entry page of Wikipedia, there are two instance of URL:

http://en.wikipedia.org/wiki/MediGene

http://en.wikipedia.org/wiki/Caleb_Simper

Through the above analysis, we can draw the conclusion that both the protocol and host name are same except for the page. We can design the target web pages' URL by making use of the regular expression matching. The regular expression to match the URL above is:

*^http://en.wikipedia.org/wiki/.**

In this way the crawler can choose the target page like entry page of Wikipedia successfully. Consequently, we can write this regular expression into the configuration file to inform the crawler of the format of target pages' URL.

3.2 Key Information Locating

Not only should the crawler crawl the content of target web page, but also it should extract the key information interested by users in the HTML code. In general, the location of the key information is always same for one typical type of web structure, for an instance, the title is always included in a particular type of label. Take two pages above for example:

```
<h1 id="firstHeading" class="firstHeading" lang="en">
  <span dir="auto">MediGene</span>
  <!--The other one is Caleb_simper above-->
</h1>
```

Generally, a HTML label should include label name, attributes, inner HTML, in which the label name, id, name are token as the significant attributes to mark the label. In the same way dealing with the URL, we can adopt the following structure to determine the key tag:

```
struct TagSpecifier{
    String target;              // identify the type of the target
    String tagName;             // the name of tag, e. g: p span h1
    String tagId;               // the attribute "id" of tag
    List<String> tagClass; // the attribute "class" of tag(may
                                have various classes)
    String tagName;             // the attribute "name" of tag
};
```

Common with the URLSeparator , the structure records the key label information. Take all the label information of different pages in the same type into account. For example, analyzing the structure above, we can provide the following method for the web parsing:

```
public String getTitle(){
  String innerHTML = $("h1 #firstHeading").html(); //using
jQuery
  grammar
  if (innerHTML is found)
    return innerHTML.replaceAll("<[^>]*?>", "");
       //get the string without tags (which is the key
information of the page)
  return "";        // miss
}
```

The parsing module calls the method, and then it can parse the HTML pages to get the content of the entry pages on the Wikipedia.

4 Design plan

The workflow of system is as follows: when we need to gather information from a specific type of web pages, the system should have four steps. Firstly, it calls for the user to provide some basic configuration, such as the entrance URL, the strategy chosen (breadth-first or depth-first) and so on; next, the system should download the target pages that include key information; thirdly, users are asked to provide the location of key information in those sample pages; finally, when the system obtains enough sample web pages of a specific type to analyze comprehensively, it can draft the needed configuration file automatically in order to drive the crawler to crawl web pages and write the consequence into database. The flowchart of the system is described in picture 3.

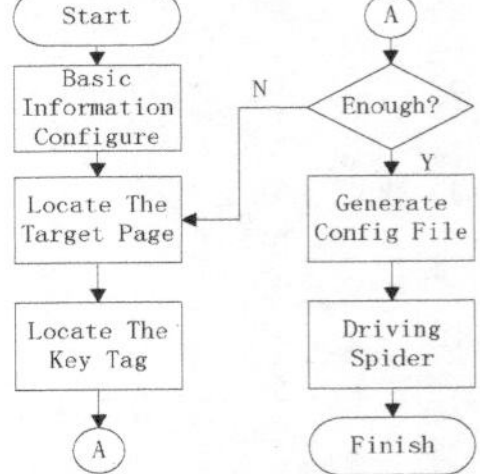

Picture 3 The flowchart of the crawler engine

The basic information configure module is required to offer the indispensable configure information such as the entrance address, crawling depth, breadth-first or depth-first strategy, the same page crawling time interval, the crawler process, etc.

Then, the system needs to complete the configuration of target web pages by interacting with users. The system loads the entry page, and then the user browses the webpage in the usual way and informs the system the target page including the key information. The users may continue to find several webpages with the same type and inform all of them to the system. Lastly, the system parses URLs of these webpages and forms the structured information above (URL separator), at the same time, it downloads these web pages for further use.

In the process of web pages selection, taking the cross-domain access restrictions of browsers and the security of the server into consideration, it is obvious that writing the code remotely is unrealistic and not permitted by law. In order to keep the system be friendly and accurate, we can modify the copy of the web pages on the Internet, which has been downloaded previously in the locating process. So, we add event listener and handler function to the copy. By this way, we can achieve the effect of getting HTML label of the key information by using the mouse to click on the pages. Adding following jQuery code to the copy:

```
$(document).ready(function(){
    $("*").click(function(){        // add onclick listener
      get    the    $(this).tagName,    $(this).attr("id"),
$(this).attr("class"), $(this).attr("name");
    });
  $("*").mouseover(function(){   // add onmouseover listener
      Use $(this).css() to change the style to sign up the
element
    });
  $("*").mouseout(function(){      //add onmouseout listener
      Use $(this).css() to reset the style to sign up the
element
    });
});
```

When mouse clicked, the system will be provided with an object that shows the element of what users have chosen. In general, the commonly used identifying attributes are id, class, span and so on. The system will record these identifying attributes, integrate identifying attributes of several web pages with the same structure and get the common features that can be used to crawl the similar web pages. In this way, when users clicking on the key information, the system can obtain its label to form the structured information above (Tag Specifier).

After collecting a certain amount structured data of URL and key information label, the system can start analyzing. The analyzing process is mainly to complete the retention of the same attribute values and the deletion of the difference. Eventually, forming a "matcher" formed in the same way with the regular expression, and it will be written in the configuration file for crawler processing.

After completing the configuration file, the system can drive the crawler to start crawling. Like most other crawlers, the crawler will start from the web pages of the entry URL, and use the configuration file to crawl URLs in the web pages to form the frontier. When web pages have been downloaded, the parsing module will spot the featured label defined in the configuration file, extract the "innerHTML" of a tag and remove all labels to get the plain text that only contains the key information. Ultimately, the above plain text will be stored into database. These data stored into the database can play a role in application such as search engine, public opinion analysis later.

It needs to be noted that the system is often based on a particular crawler for its corresponding configuration information. When replacing the crawler and the parsing module, the engine system needs to rebuild the interface with the crawler. Generally, the underlying interface changes don't have an effect on the interface between the system and the users. In this case, the system only needs to publish the corresponding engine update package. This approach is similar to the approach of three-mode with two-tier interface in the database.

5 Summary

The system is designed to solve the massive requirement to crawler configuration that caused by the diverse organization of the websites and the various structure of web pages.

The characteristic of the system is the configuration information can be collected and accessed automatically through a simple interactive way. At the same time, the system effectively reduces the dependence for programmers for website updating or other various reasons in the process of crawler work. By this way, our system not only reduces the cost of crawler system but also greatly facilitate users, which creates the possibility for the further promotion and use of crawlers.

The system can be furthermore applied to search engine, public opinion analysis and other application. With the promotion of an efficient and practical crawler engine, these applications can succeed in crawling the web pages conveniently and effectively, parse the web pages accurately and provide a higher quality service for the users.

6 References

[1] ZHOU De-mao,LI Zhou-jun.Survey of High-performance Web Crawler[J].Computer Science,2009,36(8)

[2] LI Sheng-Tao, YU Zhi-Hua, CHENG Xue-Qi BAI Shuo. A Survey on Web Crawling [J].Computer Science,2003,2

[3] Bing Liu. Web Data Mining [M].Tsinghua University Press

[4] Jiang Ke .Design and Implementation of the Focused Crawler System Based on Customized Domain Conceptions[D]. Xi An : Xidian University,2007

[5] Sun Li-wei，HE Guo—hui，WU Li — fa. Research on the Web Crawler [J]. Computer Knowledge and technology,2010(15)

[6] Tan Long-Yuan.Design and Implementation of Crawler Technology for Topics [D].Wuhan University of Technology,2009

[7] HU Jun-wei, QIN Yi — qing , ZHANG — Wei.Regular expression and its applications to web information extraction [J].Journal of Beijing Institute of Machinery

SESSION

POSTERS AND SHORT PAPERS

Chair(s)

TBA

Remote-Access Enhanced Laboratory for the Course Microprocessors and Systems

Jing Zhang, and Karthik Devarajan
Systems Engineering Dept., University of Arkansas at Little Rock, Little Rock, Arkansas, USA

Abstract - *Remote-access of computer systems can significantly enhance the laboratory for electrical engineering education. This paper presents our practice of remote-access of laboratory by using the remote desktop, one standard feature of Microsoft Windows and Virtual Private Network (VPN). The remote access has substantially enhanced the experiments of students in the course "microprocessors and systems".*

Keywords: e-learning, remote-access, microprocessors, systems, laboratory

1 Introduction

Remote Desktop is a feature of Microsoft Windows [1]. With Remote Desktop Connection, one can access a remote computer running Windows from another computer running Windows that is connected to the same network or to the Internet and use all of the computer's programs, files, and network resources of the remote computer. By using this feature we have developed the remote access of our laboratory for the course "microprocessors and systems", which has enhanced the experiments of students substantially.

2 Remote-Access Enhanced Laboratory

Microsoft Remote Desktop function mstsc.exe creates connections to a remote computer, which makes it possible for the remote access of the remote computer and all software installed in the remote computer. With this function, students with the remote-access permission of a desktop in the laboratory can access the desktop inside the laboratory through the campus network without entering the laboratory. From home computers, students can use VPN to set the connection between the home computers to campus network through internet and then, connect to the laboratory desktop with mstsc.exe. With Microsoft Remote Desktop and VPN, we developed the remote-access enhanced laboratory for the course "microprocessors and systems". The system is shown in Figure 1. The development of the remote access is to enhance the existing laboratory experiments by increasing the accessing time and flexibility.

The laboratory of microprocessors & systems as shown in Figure 1 consists of six workstations, in which one workstation was set in standby state. As shown in Figure 2, each workstation is equipped with a desktop computer, a video camera and two experimental systems: 1) 32-bit microcontroller TMS320F2812 from Texas Instruments and 2) 8-bit microcontroller C8051F380 from Silicon Labs. The microprocessor systems were connected to the desktop and operated with IDE (Integrated Development Environment) software (Code Composer Studio and Silicon Lab IDE) for development and debugging of programs. It supports up to 20 students each semester. Without remote-access, up to 4 students were assigned to one workstation and completed each experiment within two hours each week. The laboratory was open to students only when a teaching assistant is available. After the development of remote-access capability, students can access the experimental systems without such time restriction. Students with the remote-access permission completed the most experiments individually by sharing accessing time during a week, which significantly enhanced the experimental capability of the laboratory.

2.1 Lab Projects and Operation

The lab operation is designed to combine the traditional one with the remote-access features. During one semester, one lab project was assigned for each week. We keep one scheduled lab meeting time per week on Friday. Like the traditional lab course, the lab meeting time on Friday was two hours. Different from the traditional lab course, students were required to use more time during a week to complete each lab experimental project. Before the scheduled lab meeting session, they should use remote access to complete the programming and debugging of programs required for each project. They attended the meeting time mainly for experiments which they had to handle with the hardware circuit, for instance, pressing a button or using a probe of oscilloscope to measure the waveforms. Students were also required to submit the report after the two-hour session. The time-consuming activities for programming and debugging should be completed before the two-hour session by using remote access of the lab. Each student was required to complete the lab individually. In this way all students were given the same chance to complete a project during a week.

The experimental projects in Spring 2013 included:

Lab 01: Silicon Laboratories IDE

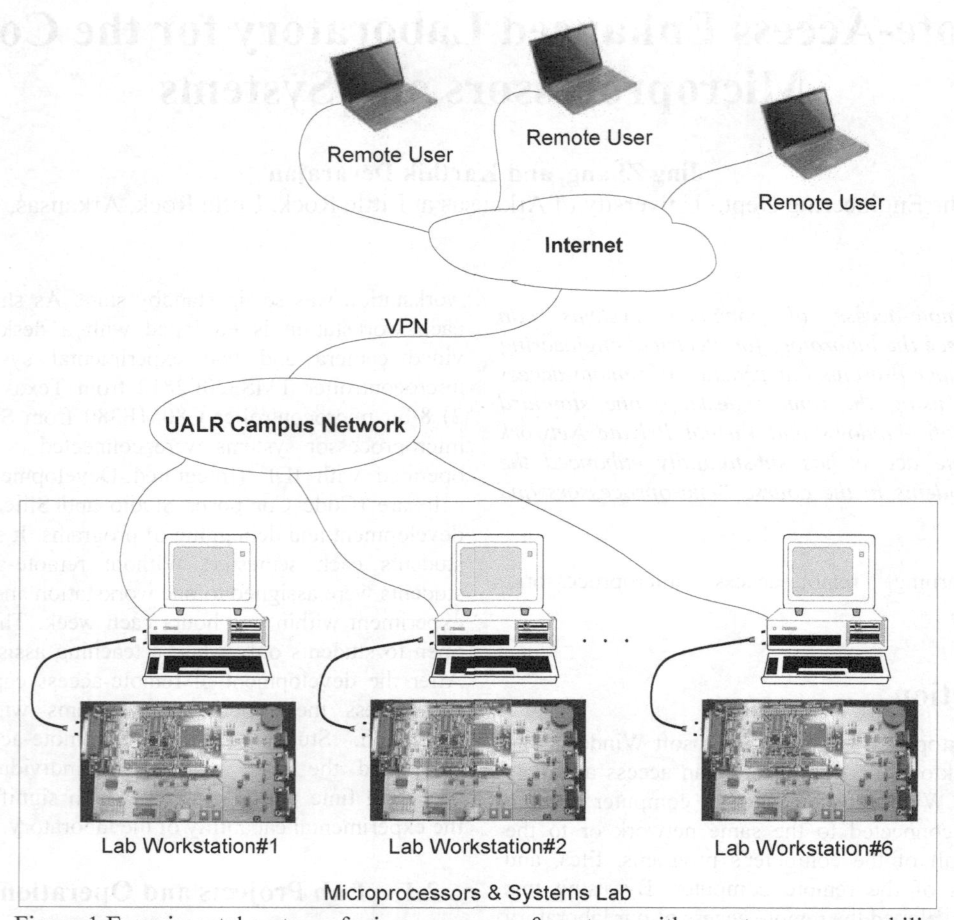

Figure 1 Experimental system of microprocessors & systems with remote-access capability

Lab 02: Instructions for Program Flow Control
Lab 03: 8051 Addressing Modes
Lab 04: 8051 Arithmetic and Logic Instructions
Lab 05: 8051 Program in C
Lab 06: C8051 Timer0 Program
Lab 07: C8051 Port I/O's Programming
Lab 08: C8051 Interrupt Programming
Lab 09: C8051 ADC Programming
Lab 10: C8051 UART0 Port Programming

The ten lab projects were designed for students to learn the fundamentals of microprocessors and systems and the procedure to develop the program for a microprocessor system.

2.2 Evaluation of Remote-Access Enhanced Laboratory

The remote-access enhanced laboratory was provided accompanying the course Microprocessors and Systems since Spring 2012. With the remote-access features the lab course for microprocessors and systems was significantly approved. With the five operating workstations we successfully provided the lab course for about 15 students each semester. Each workstation was shared by three students with the goal that each should complete each lab experimental project individually. It was impossible for the lab without remote-access feature. For the time consuming part of programming and debugging students could work without the time restriction anymore. They may flexibly choose the time to complete the most work for the experimental projects.

To evaluate the remote-access enhanced laboratory a survey about the usage of remote access of the laboratory was completed at the end of each semester since Spring 2012. The results were shown in Figure 3, in which the horizontal axis is the voting number of students. The survey covers two aspects: 1) how students used the remote access to complete lab experimental projects, and 2) whether students accepted the remote-access enhanced laboratory.

2.2.1 How to Use Remote-Access Enhanced Laboratory

Compared to a traditional laboratory, a remote-access enhanced laboratory provides students much more flexibilities to complete experimental projects. Students may choose

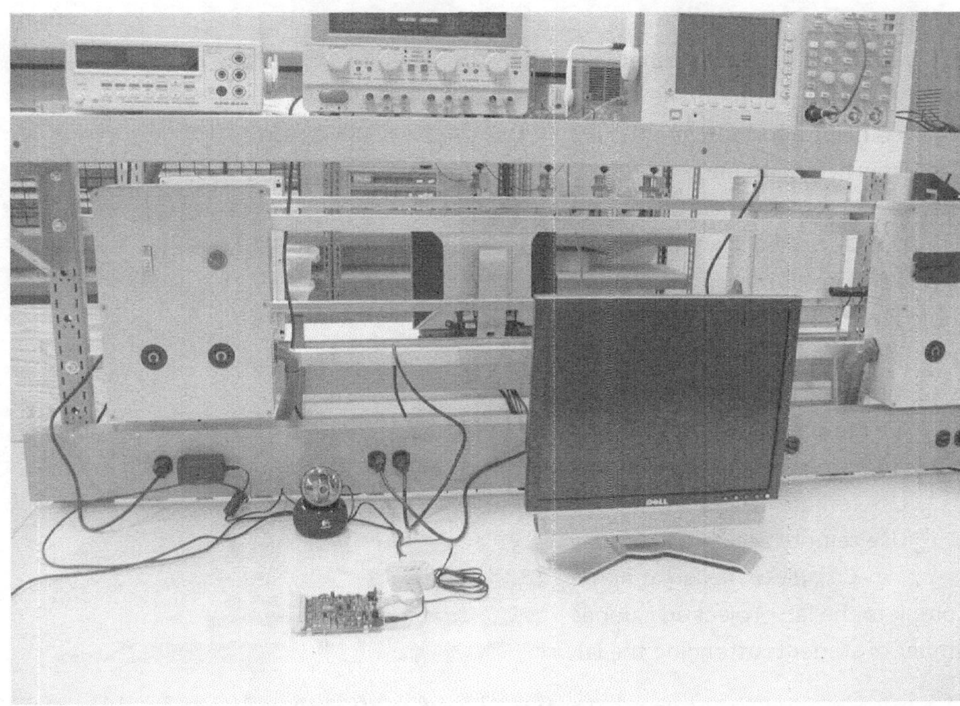

Figure 2 Workstation for the course Microprocessors and Systems Lab

different locations with different time schdules and spent different time to complete each experimental project. With the survey the way the students used the remote-access enhanced laboratory was investigated as following.

Location to use remote access: about 50% of students use the remote access from their home, which required to connect to the campus network with VPN. Other 50% of students use the remote access on the campus. One important reason for those students was the unstable performance of VPN for the network connection from home to the campus network.

The time schedule to use the remote access to complete an experimental project: almost all students used the remote access to complete a project on Wednesday and Thursday. Most students spent between one to two hours per week working with remote access. There were students who used the remote access more than three hours per week. Such students took the advantages of remote-access for developing their skill in programming. They developed additional programs besides the required ones for each project.

2.2.2 Acceptance of Remote-Access Enhanced Laboratory

The surveys show that the remote-access enhanced laboratory was well accepted by the students. Almost all students attending the course wished to use more remote access for their experimental projects. They also agreed that the remote access were helpful for them to complete experimental projects on time.

2.3 Future Improvements

The remote-access enhanced laboratory for the course "Microprocessors and Systems" was developed and operated since Spring 2012. The experience with two Spring semesters was helpful for the further improvement and development of remote-access enhanced laboratory, not only for the course "Microprocessors and Systems", but also for other laboratories. Current remote access was realized based on the existing function Remote Desktop of Microsoft Windows operating system and network communication tool VPN. Based on the experience of practical operation two important improvements are necessary.

2.3.1 Automatic scheduling and control of remote access

Current remote access of each workstation was assigned by the network administrator of the department. Three or four students were assigned to one workstation. The access schedule was orally developed among students assigned to one workstation. At one time only one student can access the workstation remotely. If he or she did not log out after the end of usage, other students could not log in and use the workstation. It is necessary to develop a tool to control the remote access in the future.

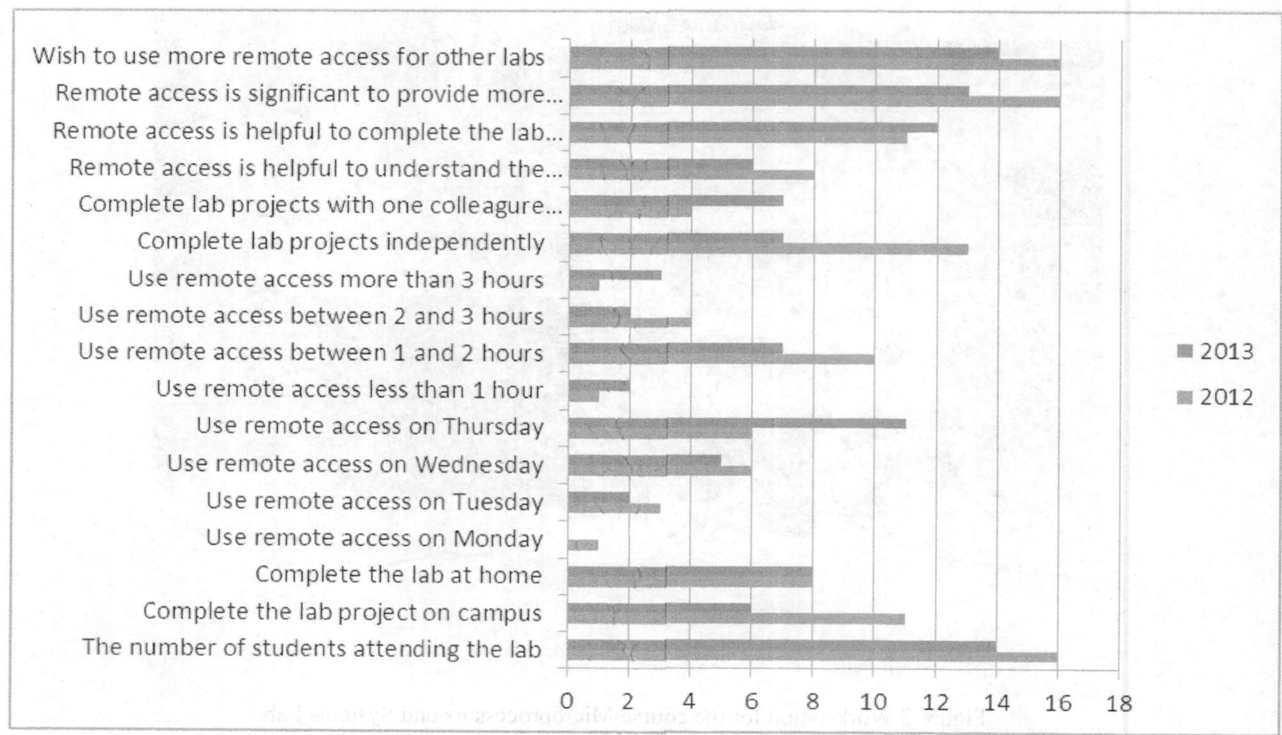

Figure 3 Survey about the application of remote-access enhanced laboratory

2.3.2 Usage of Workstations

Another improvement is to make all workstations shared by all students. Currently one workstation was assigned to only three or four students. The project files of each student were stored in the computer of the workstation, which restricted the students to use the same workstation during one semeseter. If a network storage is available for students to store their files, they may not be restricted to one special workstation. Instead they may use any workstation available in the laboratory, which should fully explore the capacitance of the available equipment.

3 Conclusions

After the practical operation of the remote-access enhanced laboratory for the course "Microprocessors and Systems", the instructor's experience and students' feedback have shown that the remote access can enhance a traditional laboratory substantially. Remote access will provide students the flexibility to complete experimental projects. With the remote access, students can complete each project individually with less time restriction.

4 References

[1] Microsoft "Remote Desktop Connection". http://windows.microsoft.com/en-us/windows7/products/features/remote-desktop-connection, 2013.

An English Listening Learning Framework based on the Learning Emotion

Yu-Chen Kuo and Tsu-Yang Wang
Department of Computer Science and Information Management
Soochow University, Taipei, Taiwan

Abstract - *In the context-aware learning, the learners interact with the learning environment to stimulate the learners' emotions. Learners will be immersed in the context-aware learning environment thus enhance their learning performance. Csikszentmihalyi discovered the learning emotion of the Flow Experience. Then, many other scholars found that, when learners involve in the Flow Experience during learning, they can improve learning efficiency. Therefore, the learning emotion such as the attention and the meditation may affect learners' learning performance. However, most of scholars had discussed the attention but not meditation. Hence we would like to design an English listening learning system based on the learning emotion. We observe learners' learning emotion during learning, and give them some aids when they're unconcentrated or anxious, help them to stay in a good learning emotion. We want to explore the affective the attention and the meditation on learning performance.*

Keywords: attention, brainwave, context-awareness learning, meditation, learning emotion

1 Introduction

In the traditional learning, each learner learned from the same textbook. But, each learner had his own learning emotion. Some learner was concentrating and some was loosing. Thus, there were only few learners can have good learning performance. The learning performance could be improved if we apply technology into learning.

1.1 Context-awareness learning

With the progress of information technology, e-learning has become a very popular research topic. Applying the information technology into learning, and providing many kinds of e-learning platform, such as notebooks or mobile devices, learners could learn by using these devices without teachers. Motiwalla used mobile device with wireless network to achieve mobile learning [1]. Learners could use the mobile device to learn through the wireless network anytime and anywhere. Thus, Ogata and Yano proposed the Context-Aware Support for Computer-Supported Ubiquitous Learning [2]. Kuo had mentioned that the purpose of the context-awareness was to make learners to interact with the environment [3]. By doing this, learners can make their learning impressive, and let their learning performance better.

1.2 Learning emotions

In 1975, Csikszentmihalyi, proposed the Flow Experience [4]. He observed some artists, athletes and professional chess player, and found out that when they are completely entered the concentrate mode and didn't feel any anxiety, their efficiency will totally be improved. Some scholar also found that the Flow Experience can improve learners' learning performance [5]. Thus, the learning emotions such as the attention and the meditation may affect learners' learning performance.

1.3 Research motivation

In the past, most of scholars had discussed the effect the attention but not meditation. Hence we design an English listening learning system by using NeuroSky MindSet to identify learners' attention and meditation [6][7]. We want to find out how's the attention and the meditation going during learning, to explore the affective of learning performance by the attention and the meditation.

2 Methods

We will use the NeuroSky MindSet to observe learners' brainwave while they're learning, and identify their attention and meditation. We will divide the learners into 3 groups. There are 2 experimental groups and 1 control group. One of the experimental groups will be aided by the system according to the attention, and the other experimental group will be aided by the system according to the meditation.

2.1 Experimental group for the attention

The process of the experimental group with the aid of attention is shown in Fig. 1. First, the learner will choose a chapter and start learning. Meanwhile, MindSet will start to identify the learner's attention. If the learner's attention fell behind the standard, the system will start to play the video of the chapter to help the learner to concentrate on the chapter. After 3 minutes, if the learner's attention is getting back, then the system will shut the video down; otherwise, system will further provide subtitles. Another 3 minutes later, if learner's attention is raised, then the system will stop providing anything; otherwise, the system will keep them all.

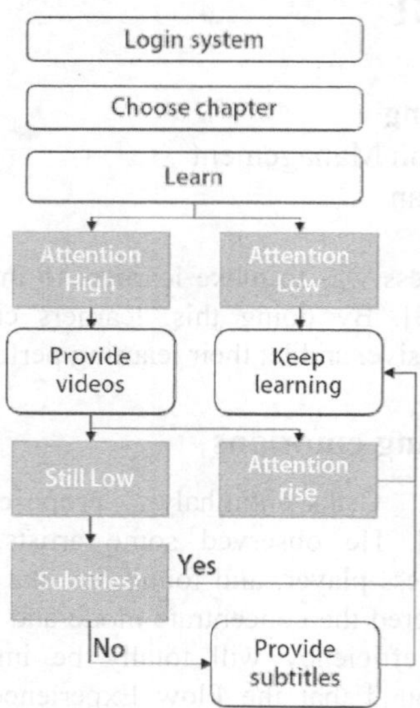

Fig 1. Process of the experimental group for the attention

2.2 Experimental group for the meditation

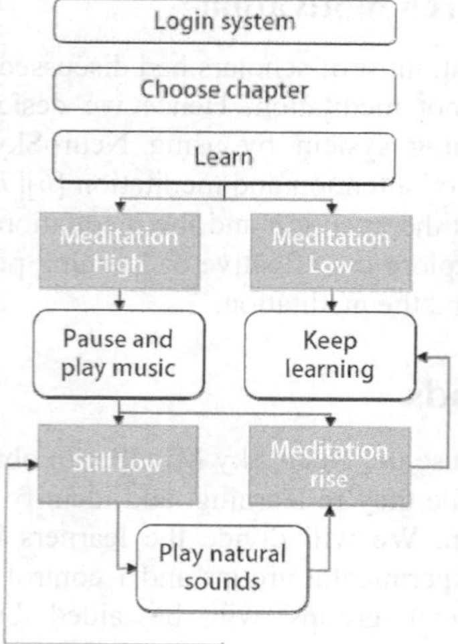

Fig 2. Process of the experimental group for the meditation

The process of the experimental group with the aid of meditation is shown in Fig. 2. In the beginning, as same as the other experimental group, the learner will choose a chapter and start learning. In the same time, MindSet will start identifying the learner's meditation. If the learner's meditation fell behind the standard, the system will pause the learning, and start playing some soft music to help the learner to relax. After 3 minutes, if the learner's meditation is getting back, then the system will shut the music down and back to the learning; otherwise, system will provide some relaxing natural sounds. Another 3 minute later, if learner's meditation is raised, then the system will stop providing anything and back to learning; otherwise, the system will keep playing the natural sounds, and try to help the learner.

3 Conclusions

We expect to be able to produce the following results through our experiment.

3.1 Learning emotion will effect the learners' learning performance

Through comparing the pretest and the posttest of learners on English listening ability, we expect learners in two experimental groups will improve their learning performance significantly by using our English listening learning system.

3.2 Attention and meditation are related

With the aid of our system, we expect learners in the experimental group for the attention will raise not only their attention but also their meditation. Similarly, learners in the experimental group for the meditation will raise both of their meditation and their attention too. We wish we could observe that the attention and the meditation are related, and they are both important to learning performance of English Listening.

4 References

[1] L.F. Motiwalla, "Mobile learning: a framework and evaluation," Computers & Education, 49 (3), pp. 581–596, 2007.

[2] H. Ogata and Y. Yano, "Context-Aware Support for Computer-Supported Ubiquitous Learning," Proceedings of the 2nd IEEE International Workshop on Wireless and Mobile Technologies in Education, pp. 27-34, 2004.

[3] Z. Y. Kuo, TELDAP e-Newsletter (Taiwan), 10-2, 2012, http://newsletter.teldap.tw/news/ProgramTourismContent.php ?nid=4395&lid=498

[4] M. Csikszentmihalyi, "Optimal experience in work and leisure." Journal of Personality and Social Psychology, 56(5), 815-822, 1975.

[5] L. A. Schenkel, "Optimal Educational Experiences and Their Relationship to Selof-concept and Flow in Adolescent high-ability and Gifted Learners." Unpublished doctoral dissertation, College of William and Mary, Williamsburg, Virginia, 2011.

[6] NeuroSky, Inc., "NeuroSky's eSense™ Meters and Detection of Mental State." 2009, http://www.neurosky.com/

[7] Katie Crowley, Aidan Sliney, Ian Pitt, Dave Murphy, "Evaluating a Brain-Computer Interface to Categorise Human Emotional Response." 10th IEEE International Conference on Advanced Learning Technologies, 276-278, 2010.

Enhancing Community and Program Delivery with Cohorts in a 100% Online Graduate Program in Applied Computer Science

Adel Abunawass and Edwin Rudolph
Department of Computer Science, University of West Georgia, Carrollton, Georgia, USA

Abstract - *This poster focuses on the advantages of a cohort matriculation model for a 100% online professional masters program in applied computer science. This program is designed to provide individuals with a bachelor's degree in any discipline the opportunity to gain skills and knowledge needed to retrain for a career in information technology. Among the pedagogical challenges in delivering this program include an ability to foster a sense of a community among online students that is integral to student success and retention, and prepare students to effectively work in groups and on team oriented projects when they are unable to engage each other face to face. Additionally, there are administrative challenges for a small academic department to efficiently recruit and admit new students and manage resources to support the program. This poster discusses our implementation of a cohort model as an effective way to help address these challenges.*

Keywords: Online education; cohorts; learning tools and strategies; e-learning design and methodologies; computer science curriculum

1 Background

The Master of Science in Applied Computer Science program offered by the University of West Georgia is a 100% online, professional, career oriented, two-year graduate program that specifically targets individuals with a bachelor's degree in any discipline seeking to retrain and acquire new knowledge and skills for a career in information technology. The curriculum focuses on software design and development, ancillary knowledge areas, with integration of professional practices and teamwork through two project experiences (one at the end of the first year, another after the second and final year). The program has been offered completely online since 2011 and currently enrolls approximately 30 students. The program is offered by a small, teaching-focused computer science department consisting of 9 faculty, 2 instructional/technical support staff, and 1 administrative assistant. Approximately 3 - 4 faculty are currently involved in delivering graduate courses each year. The department also offers an ABET accredited undergraduate program in computer science.

2 Cohort Model

One of the challenges in offering the program in a fully online format is how to help students to stay engaged and encourage retention when there is no face to face interaction and (as the program imposes no restriction on students' geographic location and for which the target population includes working professionals) little or no synchronous online class meetings. From a pedagogical standpoint, we felt that adopting a cohort matriculation model would provide the best means for establishing a sense of community among the students in the program and help to encourage them to stay engaged with their studies. The cohort is maintained through the program's prerequisite structure, which requires all students to follow exactly the same path to fulfilling curricular requirements. This model has the advantages of ensuring students progress through the program as a group and are familiar with each other as they are asked to interact and work together on various class assignments, projects, and discussions.

To establish the community aspect of the cohort, we ask students to participate in a few simple activities during their first semester in the program. First, as part of a mandatory asynchronous online orientation, the students create a brief video introduction of themselves and post it to a dedicated graduate students' "portal" web site within our Moodle learning management system. Then, as part of one the classes in their first semester, the students are asked to view several of the videos for other members of their cohort and respond to a couple of questions about each. Additionally, students may also be asked to introduce themselves in each class through an online discussion forum within Moodle. In this way, they gain a basic familiarity with their cohort classmates.

As the students continue in the program, the cohort community is reinforced through various group activities and projects. Interaction is facilitated through a variety of tools including cloud-based bug tracking, wiki, and revision control systems such as Bitbucket; our Moodle LMS; and Blackboard Collaborate Instant Messaging. As part of the first and second year project experiences, the first and second year cohorts are brought together as a team engaged in a semester-long software development project that provides an opportunity for the less experienced first year students to work directly with the more experienced second year students.

From an administrative perspective, using a cohort model helps our small department efficiently and effectively manage recruitment, admissions, and resource allocation for the program. We admit one cohort each year during the Fall semester; in this way we focus all of our recruitment and admission efforts for the year on the Fall semester rather than repeating and compressing the process every 4 months. From a resource allocation standpoint, requiring students to begin in the Fall and strongly encouraging them to complete the program in two years creates a predictable semester course schedule and expectations for faculty resource requirements.

Gesture Technology: An Innovative "Leap" for Workflow

Miguel Toimil[1], **Namchul Shin**[2], **and Alan Eisner**[3]
[1]Computer Science, Pace University, New York, NY USA
[2]Information Technology, Pace University, New York, NY, USA
[3]Management and Management Science, Pace University, New York, NY, USA

Abstract - *This research (in progress) aims to examine the use of gesture technology for business processes, more specifically how this technology improves workflow and productivity. The key questions we raise for this research are as follows: 1) What could gesture technology be used for in the business world? 2) What are practical uses for gesture technology? and 3) How could workers use gesture technology to improve workflow and productivity? In order to tackle these questions, we study an organization using gesture technology for its business operations and examine how the technology improves workflow and productivity. Research in this aspect of technology could reveal some interesting and useful insights for the use of gesture technology for business processes and the way it can bring operational benefits to businesses.*

Keywords: Gesture technology, business process, workflow, productivity

1 Introduction

Gesture technology has lately made significant advancements in recent years and increased its potentials for the business world as well as the practical world. Companies, such as Microsoft, Leap, and Sony, have created systems, which allow people to use gestures or movements in order to perform various functions. As this technology continues to evolve, it will allow users to do their jobs despite physical disabilities or increased distances. Architects would be able to use their hands to create blueprints in massive 3D models, giving a better image as to how buildings would look like with a capability to alter the plans with a simple movement of the wrist. The newcomer into the market is the "Leap Motion". This is a little device connecting to a computer, which allows fingers to perform the same functions as the keyboard and mouse. This particular device can be used to streamline business processes by allowing people to work more efficiently.

This research (in progress) aims to examine the use of gesture technology for business processes, more specifically how this technology improves workflow and productivity. The key questions we raise for this research are as follows: 1) What could gesture technology be used for in the business world? 2) What are practical uses for gesture technology? and 3) How could workers use gesture technology to improve workflow and productivity? In order to tackle these questions, we study an organization using gesture technology for its business operations and examine how the technology improves workflow and productivity. Research in this aspect of technology could reveal some interesting and useful insights for the use of gesture technology for business processes and the way it can bring operational benefits to businesses.

2 Gesture Technology

Worker productivity in the modern age has many factors to account for in addition to human capacity to work. Businesses have to account for technology used for daily business operations and how easy it is to use; if technology is complicated to navigate and use, employees' inputs and energy for productivity could be wasted since they would try to get it to work in their favor or figure out a way to make it easier to use. A majority of work can now be done from behind a computer screen, but even so, it is not as if technology has been completely optimized to suit ease of access and work. The keyboard and mouse has made an effect on workers and how quickly and effectively workers can accomplish their work. As you can imagine from the use of a laptop, however, it will require you to completely alter your posture to accommodate typing quicker, while sacrificing comfort and energy [1].

Gesture technology makes daily lives of workers easier by changing the way they control computers with semi-natural movement, allowing them to use basic gestures with their hands in order to perform certain functions. This technology has been implemented with touchpads and touchscreens in recent years, but even those mediums require some sort of physical connection with the technology to make them work. A device such as Leap Motion, however, (http://www.leapmotion.com) would allow someone to create a 3D model on a computer using their hands, manipulating the model as if it were clay in their hands, only without the mess (see Figure 1).

The device (about the size of iPod—see Figure 2) uses infrared cameras on the surface in order to detect and monitor 8 cubic feet of space around the camera. This allows people to control their computers without being subjected to having bad posture in using a keyboard and a mouse. This device is of course not meant to replace the keyboard and mouse by any means; it is meant to supplement the devices for those who feel uncomfortable using a keyboard and mouse due to posture or arthritis, or for those who just want to use a system that flows better with natural hand movement. This could be an improvement to workflow in many businesses because it would allow people to perform their tasks in a manner that will make them feel less tired due to the movement less artificial. If a function has a natural workflow to it, it will work a lot better than a forced attempt at the workflow. Computerized tasks using a keyboard and mouse could be done easier if you were just using your hands. Worker fatigue and morale are directly connected to how quickly and efficiently workers accomplish their work. If workers were given an alternative to a cramped workstation, by which they can accomplish their tasks easier based on a sort of free flow movement, they would work more efficiently and have a more positive work outlook and output [2].

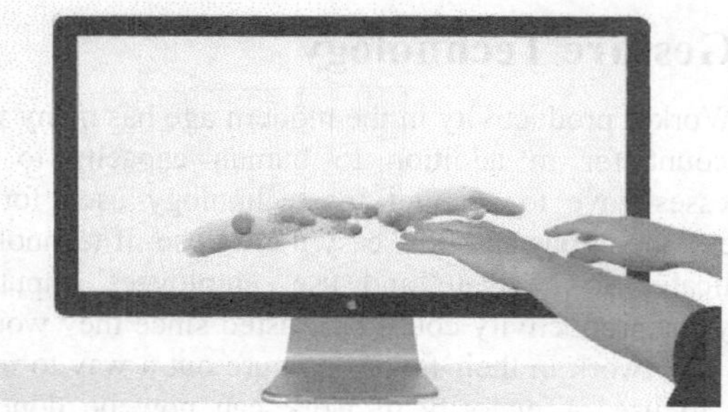

Figure 1: Leap Motion Gesture Technology

3 Impact of Gesture Technology on Workflow and Productivity

The Leap Motion device implementing gesture technology is new to the market. This device, however, has already been making strides in the business world. This device is clamored for a latest innovation in gesture control technology. Microsoft Kinect was one of many attempts to streamline workflow by gesture control for not only entertainment purposes but business purposes as well. Speculating that gesture technology makes a significant impact on workflow, this research (in progress) attempts to examine the potential of the technology for improvement in workflow: how gesture technology improves workflow and enables workers to perform better, e.g., increase productivity. We will study one or two organization(s) in depth to illustrate the way gesture technology can bring operational benefits to businesses.

Figure 2: Leap Motion Device

4 References

[1] Feathers, D.J., Rollings, K., and Hedge, A. "Alternative computer mouse designs: Performance, posture, and subjective evaluations for college students aged 18-25," Work: Journal of Prevention, Assessment and Rehabilitation, vol. 44, 115-122, 2013.

[2] Ng, H.C., Tao, D, and Or, C.K.L. "Age differences in computer input device use: A comparison of touchscreen, trackball, and mouse," Advances in Intelligent Systems and Computing, vol. 206, 1015-1024, 2013.

An Intelligent EFL Learning Platform for the Cultivation of Students' Autonomy

Yan Tian
School of Foreign Languages, Shanghai Jiao Tong University,
No. 800, Dongchuan Road, Minhang, Shanghai 200240, China

Abstract - *English language learners need individualized guidance and effective supervision in their autonomous learning. This paper reports a study on the use of an intelligent EFL learning platform by a group of students of English as a foreign language (EFL) in China. Via a methodology that included the survey questionnaires and open-ended oral interviews, the study examines learners' perceptions of the use of an intelligent EFL learning platform—the Website of Shanghai Jiao Tong University English Learning Center by a group of 80 Chinese college students learning English by themselves out of class.*

Keywords: intelligent, EFL, learning platform, cultivation, students' autonomy

1 Introduction

Learning a foreign language only in classroom is far from enough for non-English majors at colleges and universities. Autonomous learning out-of-class is of greater importance. Therefore, individual guidance and effective supervision should be provided to cultivate students' autonomy.

Theoretically speaking, as adult language learners, college students should be strongly self-motivated and self-disciplined in their English learning out of class. However, the fact is that many of them are at a loss what to learn besides their textbooks, let alone how to learn efficiently. Many of them used to make self-study plans for their out-of-class learning, but they usually ended up failing in carrying out the plan due to poor self-discipline as well as non-effective supervision.

In order to help Chinese college students to learn English out of class efficiently, an intelligent EFL learning platform (http://202.120.60.18) was developed for the cultivation of their autonomy. This platform is able to obtain the initial status of a learner by a "Learning Style Test", a "Motivation Test" and a series of "Proficiency Tests" of different language skills, such as listening tests, reading tests, writing tests and translation tests, with which the system would provide the learner with the overall recommendations of his/her online study plans and content arrangements. It is also able to automatically guide the learner to learning according to the results of his/her learning style, based on the "Learning Style Test", the "Motivation Test" and the Proficiency Tests, by intelligent management and classification of learning materials. In addition, it can present automatic feedback to learners by regular email reminders of the contents to be covered and tests to be taken before the deadlines. Furthermore, when students finish the online tests, it can instantly present their scores (both of objective questions and of subjective ones) as well as the key answers to them.

2 Rationales

Both the classroom learning and out-of-class learning of a foreign language form a complete learning process. For adult foreign language learners, out of-class learning is more important because well-planned and efficient autonomous learning leads to an ultimate success of foreign language learning.

However, autonomous language learning out-of-class requires individual guidance and effective supervision which can be done by an intelligent system. With the current technology of Artificial Intelligence and Natural Language Processing, the task of automatic supervision can be fulfilled at will.

3 Methodology

80 non-English majors from two natural English classes at Shanghai Jiao Tong University (SJTU) participated in the experiment. When these subjects entered SJTU in September 2012, they were asked to make their own out-of-class English leaning plan. Without any interference, they were asked to complete the questionnaire concerning the implementation of their self-study plan at the end of the first semester. Then, at the second semester which began in February 2013, they were asked to learn English out of class by log in the online intelligent EFL learning platform, as shown below.

Fig.1 The homepage of the intelligent EFL learning platform

At the end of the semester in June 2013, a survey questionnaire will be given to obtain the students' perceptions of the use of the learning platform. Open-ended oral interviews will also be given to collect the data.

Then a comparison will be made to draw the conclusion of the effectiveness of this intelligent EFL learning platform in guiding and supervising students' out-of-class English learning as well as the cultivating of students' autonomy.

4 References

[1] Bertin, J.C. & Narcy-Combes J.P. (2012). Tutoring at a Distance: Modeling as a Tool to Control Chaos, Computer Assisted Language Learning, 25(2):111-127.

[2] Esit, O. (2011). Your Verbal Zone: an Intelligent Computer-assisted Language Learning Program in Support of Turkish Learners' Vocabulary Learning, Computer Assisted Language Learning, 24(3):211-232.

[3] Lai, C. & Gu M. (2011). Self-regulated Out-of-class Language Learning with Technology, Computer Assisted Language Learning, 24(4):317-335.

[4] Amaral, L., Meurers, D. & Ziai, R. (2011). Analyzing Learner Language: Towards a Flexible Natural Language Processing Architecture for Intelligent Language Tutors, Computer Assisted Language Learning, 24(1):1-16.

[5] Arnold, N. & Ducate, L. (2011). Present and Future Promises of CALL: From Theory and Research to New Directions in Language Teaching. CALICO Monograph Series Volume5, 2nd Edition.

Foundation items: The 985 Research Project of the Center for Teaching and Learning Development of Shanghai Jiao Tong University; The Innovative Project of Social Science & Liberal Arts of Shanghai Jiao Tong University.

Acquisition of foreign language vocabulary in the context of consolidation models

D. Krusko[1]

[1]Department of Informatics, Siberian Federal University, Krasnoyarsk, Russia Federation

Abstract— *This paper reviews vocabulary learning evidence using concordance "standard model" of memory consolidation and a new approach, the "multiple memory trace" theory. Based on the findings of the experiment of the foreign language vocabulary learning with arbitrary time intervals between repetitions of training information and precise fixation of the measured parameters, a statistical analysis was conducted and identified statistical regularities of the vocabulary acquisition. This has been hypothesized by the influence of vocabulary item translation frequency for vocabulary memorizing. I reviewed the impact and opportunities of spacing repetitions used. In the experiment, two different techniques in the learning of vocabulary were used to adequately assess the strengths and weaknesses of each approach of memory consolidation. Overall, these findings indicate some discrepancies with standard model of memory consolidation, as well as the benefits of the approach is the combined use of both theories.*

Keywords: memory consolidation, multiple trace theory, vocabulary learning

1. Introduction

There are a number of attempts to describe the process of forgetting and remembering information through computation models. Each of the models is based on a theory of a consolidation of information in memory and includes a set of assumptions about the optimal construction of the educational process. This article examines the assumption that multiple trace theory more accurately describes the process of acquiring vocabulary and in particular, that the recall of information from memory has a greater impact on memorization than passive repetition.

Multiple trace theory (MTT) was formulated and formed from standard consolidation theory based on evidence of patients with retrograde amnesia and damage of brain regions [9]. The main points of controversy between theories are view on the process to recall the recent and remote memories (including the involvement in this process of the hippocampal complex) and the fact that MTT postulates that different types of memory are encoding, storage and retrieval in different ways, while the standard theory does not differentiate.

In particular, the standard consolidation theory assumed that hippocampal complex (HC) engages in the process of storing episodic and semantic memory only to the stabilization of the information in the memory (consolidation period) and further the information may be retrieval from neocortical circuits without HC. Survey data with retrograde amnesia show that memory loss is significantly different for autobiographical, episodic and semantic memories. If the memory loss from patients with temporal lobe lesions for the details of autobiographical memory spreads from several years, several decades to total loss of autobiographical events then episodic and semantic memory are relatively preserved [6].

Most studies on the vocabulary learning describes experiments about acquiring of a foreign language vocabulary that study participants had not studied previously. Study of the effect of an early studied information on the acquisition of a new information given little attention and the nature of this process is not clearly understood. MTT suggests that our memory about some episode or some item of the knowledge is a set of distributed and interconnected memory traces. Based on this, I put forward the hypothesis that in memorizing vocabulary items affects frequency of their translations in already studied language.

While most of the debate is on the role of hippocampus in the process of retrieving information from memory in order to support one or the other theory, almost no attention is paid to the functional features of both theories to practical use.

The purpose of this article is to statistically prove the standard consolidation theory and the multiple trace theory based on experimental data, the study of foreign language vocabulary. Quantify the impact of recall trials and passive study-only trials on memorization. The results can be used to change the approach to the study of foreign language vocabulary, and to refine the existing computational models of forgetting and remembering information.

2. The standard consolidation and multiple trace theories

Because multiple trace theory was formed from the standard consolidation theory due to the accumulation of contradictions, some points of view relating to the formation, maintenance and recovery of episodic memory are shared with the standard consolidation theory. The postulates of the theory put forward, which is reflected in this article. Common points in the two theories are [9].

- "The hippocampal complex rapidly (and obligatory) encodes all information that is attended or consciously apprehended. This process involves what is called short-term consolidation.
- This information is sparsely encoded in a distributed ensemble of hippocampal complex neurons".

Interpretation of these items can serve a partition of the memorizing process for at least two stages. During the first stage all information are encoded (it is not necessary that the various types of information are processed in the same way) before the subsequent preservation. Naturally it is expected that after the information is sparsely encoded in a distributed ensemble of neurons, it begins to have quite different characteristics in speed of forgetting and the probability of retrieval from a memory. This assumption is reflected in the working memory models [1], [2].

The following postulates of MTT are different from the standard consolidation theory [9].

- "Each re-activation of memory trace occurs in an altered neuronal and experiential context.
- Because the hippocampal complex obligatorily encodes all information that is attended, the re-activation of a memory trace results in the creation of a newly encoded hippocampal trace, which also is sparse and distributed.
- By virtue of indexing a similar set of neocortical neurons encoding the features of the information in the memory, each such trace shares some or all of the information about the initial information".

For example semantic information about the world as Grand Canyon located in Arizona, sushi is Japan food and etc, being acquired in some event during the consolidation process separated from the original event and stored independently.

In MTT, as a result of each successful retrieval of information for example in case exam will create new traces by replicating the recalled. If a memory has more than one trace, then the effect of all of them on memory retrieval is additive: any trace may cause retrieval, and the reliability of each trace action is independent of the number of traces. Therefore, failure in retrieval only occurs when all traces of a given memory fail. Recall of information in MTT is given a more important role in the process of remembering. At the same time the standard consolidation theory emphasizes the impact of rehearsal memorized information. With the amount of information rehearsals the strength of the information in memory increases and therefore it is less likely that this information will be forgotten.

On the basis of the postulates of MTT is reasonable to assume that the number of memory traces for vocabulary items with a high occurrence frequency will be more, than for rare vocabulary items. Accordingly the probability to create a stable trace of foreign language vocabulary item in the memory should be higher for items whose translation has a high occurrence frequency, than for rare vocabulary items.

3. The Experiment

I performed an experiment on studying the vocabulary of a foreign language to test both of the above theories. In this experiment, 15 participants learned a set of 80 Russian-English word pairs. Studying of the vocabulary occurred within two months on the principle of always available e-learning system. That is participants were able to use the system at any time convenient to them and they worked with the system as long as they wanted. During the whole training process, the e-learning system collected anonymous statistical information about the learning process, as all the participants were informed before the experiment.

This experiment accomplished several goals. First, it provided a collection of extensive statistical information about the process of foreign vocabulary learning by means of online e-learning system in an informal and free atmosphere. To eliminate the effect of different algorithms the choice of words for lessons and exams, all participants worked with the Rastrigin's adaptive model for education systems [10]. The choice of the model was based on prior results. In an earlier experiments this model showed one of the best results in comparison with the Bush-Mosteller, Krichevsky, Miller-McGill, Restla, Thurstone and Hull models [10]. A distinctive feature of Rastrigin's model is that it assumes, that the process of memorizing different vocabulary items is not the same. Some elements of vocabulary can be learned with less difficulty and faster than others.

Second, the experiment provided a statistical test of both theories. The results showed which of the theories is the most complete and accurate description of the process of acquiring vocabulary. These results are particularly important when choosing a theory for the construction of an adequate computational model that can be used in the process of foreign language teaching. Experiment results allow the incorporation of additional components in existing computational models. For instance in the design of e-learning vocabulary system difference between recall-or-restudy trials and study-only trials (both trials techniques described below) may be taken into account in constructing the learning process.

Third, experimental data allow to test hypothesis about impact the frequency of vocabulary item translation on the memorizing vocabulary items process.

Fourth, the experiments provides evidence that allows visualization, in order to survey the possible regularities and investigate the possible patterns and nomination of assumptions, which may also be included in computational model. This evidence helps to understand long-term memory process better, which will aid in both model and theory development.

4. Experiment Design

During the experiment to study the vocabulary, two different approaches to learning have been tested. The e-learning system was both combined for two different approaches to learning: study-only approach and recall-or restudy approach. Study-only trials or passive study is when vocabulary elements in turn with their translation are displayed to the student and the student decides her/himself how long he/she will look to a particular vocabulary element, and when to move on the next. The recall-or-restudy trials were conducted by the type of an examination for the elements shown earlier in study-only trials. The essence of these approaches is described below.

E-learning system shows Russian word to the participant in the upper left side of screen and the participant had to recall its meaning. The participant was asked:

"Do You know this word? Yes/Maybe/No"

If the participant was confident in his knowledge of the vocabulary item, the system goes to the next vocabulary element of the set for the exam.

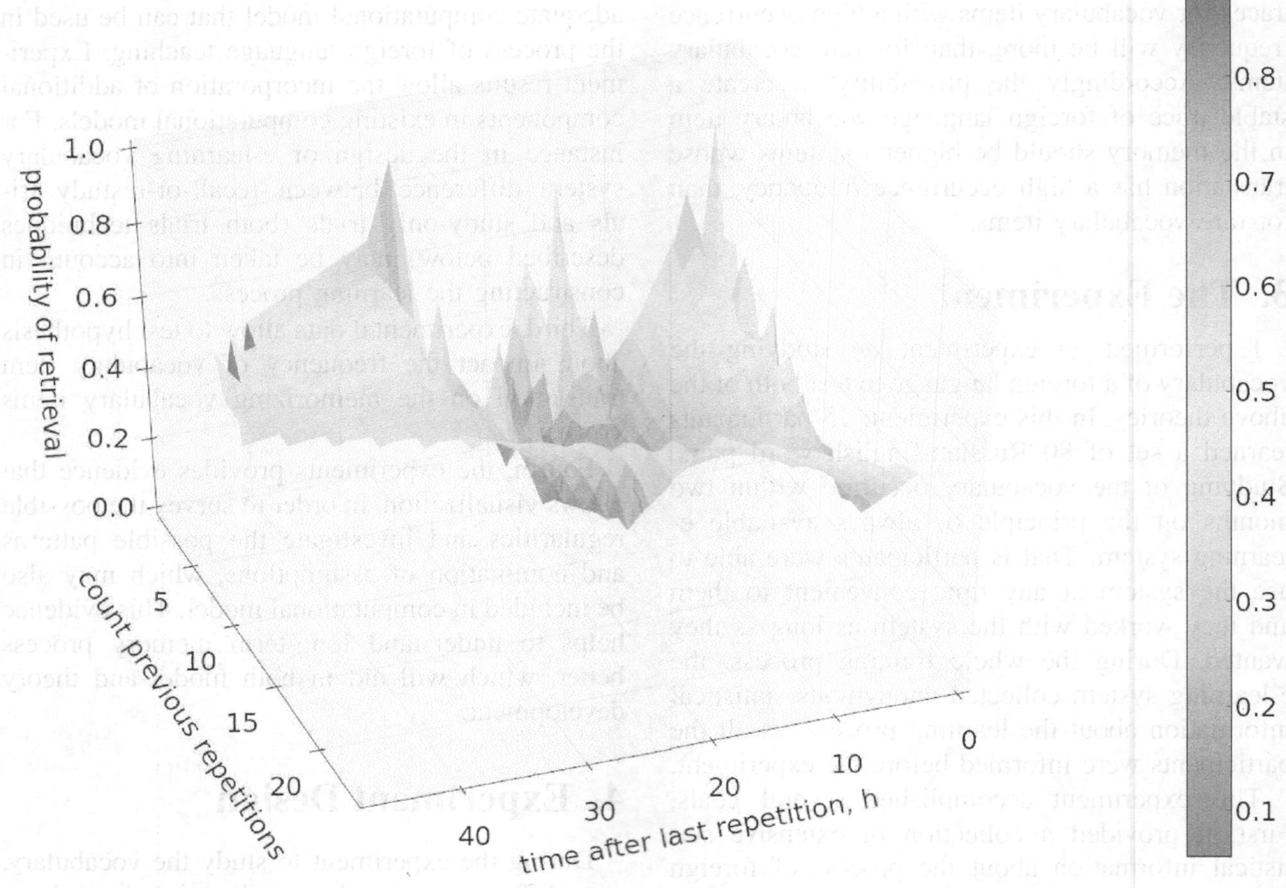

Fig. 1: Probability of vocabulary item retrieval

If the participant was not confident in his knowledge, he chose the *"Maybe"* element. In this case the vocabulary element was displayed with it's translation and the participant was again asked: *"Did you know it? Yes/No"*.

The answers of participants taking into account tips and time (accurate within 10 ms) were recorded. In order to validate the results, at end of the experiment, for each participant was conducted an examination on the entire list of words under the supervision of the experimenter. A participant had to tell translation of every vocabulary item to the experimenter. All experiment results of the participant that were untrue, that were untrue, were discarded and not included in the final selection for analysis.

The first presentation of each word was a study-only presentation of the pair. Each subsequent session consisted of two sets of words: one set for the recall-or-restudy trials and other for study-only trials. The number of elements in sets for each lesson are set individually at 1, .., 40 on uniform distribution law. Peculiarity of the Rastrigin's model that words for study-only and for examination are selected based on likelihood of how well the experiment participant knows a specific word (for each participant is calculated according to its specific features). First select those words, which are less likely to be known by the user.

The stimuli were 80 Russian-English word pairs. Russian words were chosen so that words frequencies for their translations were distributed in the uniform distribution law. The data about word frequency were not used in the computational model in this experiment and did not influence at words choice as with study-only and recall-or-restudy trials. Word frequency were used only in the analysis process. The source of word frequency data was taken the corpus of contemporary American English (ANC). Russian words were taken from the A.P. Chekhov's work of classical Russian literature. Word of the various parts of speech, of different lengths were selected for the experiment in their initial form (in the infinitive form for verbs). The main criteria for the choice of words was the requirements that the word should not originate from other languages, and that a set of words for the experiment must not contain paronymous words. As for the words translations that do not have an unambiguous translation were chosen to 3 English synonyms that best describes a word meaning in current context. Word pairs order of introduction and assignment to conditions was randomized individually for each participant. All study participants were students aged 25 to 33 and attended free of charge. There were 9 males and 6 females. All participants were fluent in English and have never learned Russian.

5. Results and Discussion

At the end of the experiment, after a preliminary analysis of the results, 9 participants data were selected. 5 were males and 4 were females. Some of the participants dropped out during the final exam for the reason that their previous answers did not correspond to the actual knowledge, other participants did not fulfill the exam. Our results are theoretically important because they strongly advocate which parameters of the learning process have an impact on the process of memorizing.

The method used conditional mutual information, which is reduction in the uncertainty between two random variables due to the knowledge of the third. For further processing the experimental data was aggregated by hours.

The conditional mutual information of random variables X and Y given Z is defined by:

$$I(X;Y \mid Z) = \sum_{z \in Z} p(z) \sum_{y \in Y} \sum_{x \in X} p(x,y \mid z) \cdot \log \left(\frac{p(x,y \mid z)}{p(x \mid z) \cdot p(y \mid z)} \right) \quad (1)$$

[8], [11].

For random variables X and Y were taken probability of success vocabulary element retrieval and count hours after last learning consistently. To find out which parameters influence mainly on the success of vocabulary element retrieval, a random variable Z was calculated alternatively with different variants. Obtained in the calculation results are shown in Table 1.

Table 1: Conditional mutual information

Z	$I(X;Y\|Z)$, bit
Count study-only trials	0.01
Count good answers on recall trials/Count recall trials	0.017
Count good answers on recall trials	0.03
Count recall trials	0.43
Count study-only + recall trials	1.85

The table shows that recall trials have a much greater impact than the study-only trail. The calculation results demonstrate the greatest impact on vocabulary item retrieval is the sum of the count study-only trials plus count recall trials.

To check the dependency between participants' answers, the number of hours since the last study, count study trials and count recall trials was performed in two-step procedure of the cluster analysis based on Bayesian Information Criterion (BIC). The results of the clustering procedure confirm evidence obtained with the conditional mutual information method. In Figure 2, it is seen that the number of recall trials has a greater impact than study trials. Another observation is that after some number of recall trials and study trials, an exam result in the short term becomes independent of the number of hours since the last the vocabulary item study.

To test the hypothesis that memorizing vocabulary items affects the frequency of their translations on the bases of the experimental data, the

Clusters

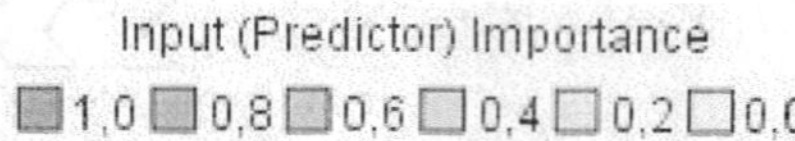

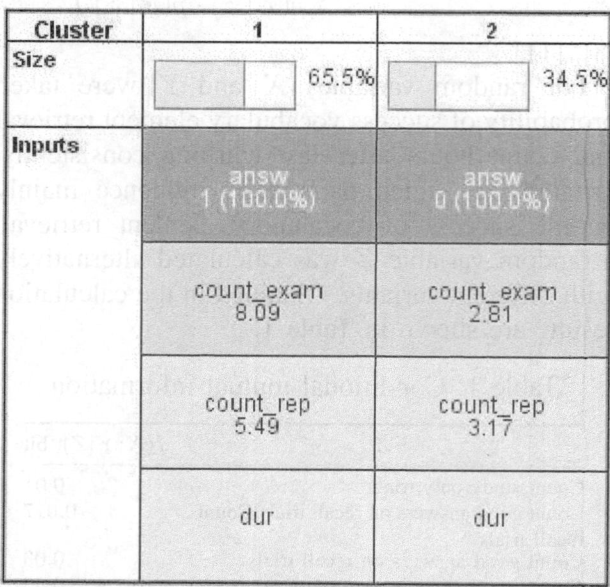

Fig. 2: Two step clusteranalyse. answ - answer (1- know, 0 - don't know), count_exam - count recall trials, count_rep - count study trials, dur - the number of hours since the last study

relationship between vocabulary item translation frequency and the ratio of the number of correct answers to the number of wrong answers in the recall-or-restudy trials was platted (see Figure 3). These evidences correspond to the hypothesis and show that participants make more correct answers for vocabulary items whose translation frequency is higher. A reduction of the correct answers ration at the end graphs (frequencies 16 and 38) may be associated with the mismatch interests of participants and a thematic of vocabulary items. To confirm the hypothesis it is necessary to conduct additional experiments with a large vocabulary and possibly thematic categorization of vocabulary items.

For the analysis of additional dependencies showed in Figure 1 relationships between the probability of success of vocabulary element retrieval,

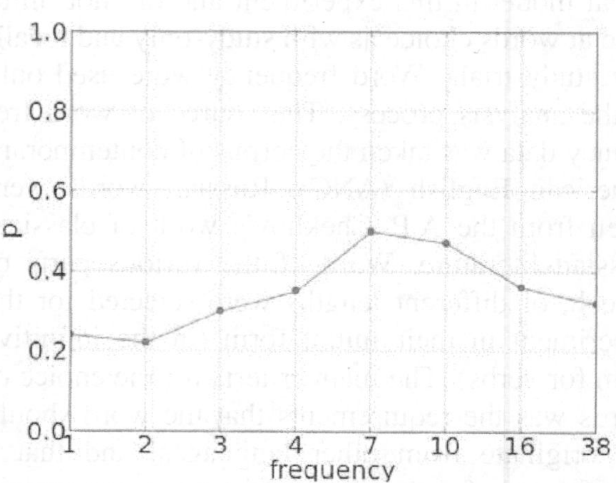

Fig. 3: Word frequency and the ratio (p) of the number of correct answers to the number of wrong answers

the number of hours since the last study (both study-only and recall-or-restudy) and the number of repetitions (the number of study-only element trials plus the number recall-or-restudy trials). For greater clarity, the data for visualization were limited by the number of repetitions to the value of 20. The probability of success of vocabulary element retrieval with the number of repetitions more than 20 tend to 1 independent of the number of hours since the last the vocabulary item study.

In Figure 1 it is seen in particular reducing the likelihood of the success of vocabulary element retrieval with some increase in the number of repetitions. These findings are consistent with the results of previous studies [3], [4]. In particular by comparing the experimental data in a verbal-learning paradigm with massed intervals and testing intervals was found that, spaced intervals are an advantage with respect to long-term memory[5]. Based on this findings the spacing effect was formulated. Further studies have found enhance in memory consolidation by distributed learning. Translating this effect on synaptic consolidation, it is assumed that mechanisms of the synaptic connections proliferation depends on intervals between memory reactivation. If the interval since the last memory reactivation is sufficient for the synthesis of proteins, long-term memory is strengthen [7].

In Figure 1 it is also observed to extremes-minimum (in the region of 10-12 hours and 19-21 hours) passing further to extremes-maxima. I assume that these extremes-peaks are associated with periods of sleep participants. Memory consolidation during the sleep has received considerable attention in the standard theory. Experts claim that, the interval of single night will greatly increase the strength of the memory and presented the possibility that the the power of recollection undergoes a process of ripening and maturing during the time which intervenes [12].

These findings confirm the effect that recall trials are more effective than study-only trials [5]. Previous studies investigating spaced trials also demonstrate enhance long-term memory in comparison with massed trials [7]. At the same time, research into the effectiveness of the combined approach recall or restudy and study-only with optimal intervals for spaced repetitions is the subject of further studies.

These evidences generally suggest that the MTT more accurately describes the process of acquiring vocabulary. However, according to these data are, the sharing of the two theories gives better results than the use of any of the theories separately.

Acknowledgment

The research was conducted with the support of the joint program DAAD and Ministry of Education and Science of the Russian Federation "Mikhail Lomonosov".

References

[1] R. C. Atkinson and R. M. Shiffrin, "Human memory: A proposed system and its control processes," *The psychology of learning and motivation: Advances in research and theory*, vol. 2, pp. 89–195, 1968.

[2] A. Baddeley, "Working memory: Looking back and looking forward," *Nature Reviews Neuroscience*, vol. 4, no. 10, pp. 829–839, 2003.

[3] B. H. Challis, "Spacing effects on cued-memory tests depend on level of processing," *Journal of Experimental Psychology: Learning, Memory, and Cognition*, vol. 19, pp. 389–396, 1993.

[4] L. J. Cuddy and L. L. Jacoby, "When forgetting helps memory: an analysis of repetition effects," *Journal of Verbal Learning and Verbal Behavior*, vol. 21, pp. 451–467, 1982.

[5] W. L. Cull, "Untangling the benefits of multiple study opportunities and repeated testing for cued recall," *Applied Cognitive Psychology*, vol. 14, pp. 215–235, 2000.

[6] T. Fujii, M. Moscovitch, and L. Nadel, "Memory consolidation, retrograde amnesia, and the temporal lobe," *Handbook of neuropsychology, 2nd edition*, vol. 4, 2000.

[7] L. Litman and L. Davachi, "Distributed learning enhances relational memory consolidation," *Learning & Memory*, vol. 15, no. 9, pp. 711–716, 2008.

[8] K. Makarychev *et al.*, "A new class of non-Shannon-type inequalities for entropies," *Communications in Information and Systems N2*, vol. 2, pp. 147–166, 2002.

[9] L. Nadel and M. Moscovitch, "Memory consolidation, retrograde amnesia and the hyppocampal complex," *Current Opinion in Neurobiology*, vol. 7, pp. 217–227, 1997.

[10] L. A. Rastrigin and R. H. Erenstein, *Adaptive learning with a student model*. Zinatne, Riga, 1988.

[11] R. Renner and U. Maurer, "About the mutual (conditional) information," 2005.

[12] L. R. Squire and P. Alvarez, "Retrograde amnesia and memory consolidation: a neurobiological perspective," *Current Opinion in Neurobiology*, vol. 5, pp. 169–177, 1995.

Understanding usage behaviors in social network service site -- A study using well-being model and self-determination theory

Nai-Ching Yeh and Judy Chuan-Chuan Lin*
Department of Information Management, National Taiwan University of Science and Technology, Taipei, Taiwan, R.O.C.
cherishyeh@gmail.com

Department of Computer Science and Information Management, Soochow University, Taipei, Taiwan, R.O.C.
jclin@csim.scu.edu.tw (* Corresponding Author)

***Abstract*— The purpose of this study is to explore the predictors of continuance intention towards social networking sites. Based on well-being model and self-determination theory, we proposed the effects of enjoyment, well-being, autonomy, relatedness, and competence on individuals' intention to continuously participate in social networking sites. Preliminary Data were collected from Facebook. Results showed the significant influences of well-being on enjoyment, while autonomy, relatedness, and competence are important factors stimulating individuals' well-being. The results also indicated that enjoyment, autonomy, relatedness, and competence are important factors stimulating individuals' continued intention in a social networking site, whereas well-being affects continuance intention mediating by enjoyment with indirect influence.**

Keywords—eWOM; SNS; well-being; self-determination theory

I. INTRODUCTION

Social media was seen as an effective channel to approach consumers for its ability to attract people's attention. This resulted in large-scale marketing spending in social media advertisement. As a well-known social networking site, Facebook enjoys a rapid uptake in numbers of users. According to statistics, its users have reached 835 million in March 2012 [8]. While Facebook has remarkable performance, it was confronted by the difficulty of retaining its users. For sustainability, social networking practitioners should strengthen users' continuance intention to keep users on the site, and further create maximum benefits of social influence in business.

The significances of well-being and enjoyment have been considered important in promoting IT usage. From a need perspective, prior studies have provide evidence that self-determination factors as essential needs should be satisfied to sublimate psychological growth and well-being [3], and persevere and perform better in activities [4] , [15]. In spite of well-being model and self-determination theory have significant impacts on individuals' behavior, the integrated conception of them seems scarce in online social networking. This study, thus, proposed an integrated model by combining well-being model and self-determination theory to predict participants' continuance intention in social networking sites.

II. RESEARCH MODEL AND HYPOTHESES

This research proposed enjoyment, well-being, and the three self-determination factors as constructs that have effects on individuals' continuance usage. Furthermore, well-being was seen as a predictor of enjoyment, while the three self-determination factors were seen as antecedents of well-being.

From motivational perspective, perceived enjoyment has been found to have significant impact on users' acceptance of technology in various contexts. In the hedonic-oriented online interactive environment, prior studies have shown that users' enjoyable experiences significantly stimulate their intention toward a specific system, especially voluntary usage. Researchers have also demonstrated that users' enjoyable experiences significantly affect their continued IT usage intention [9]. Accordingly, the following hypothesis was suggested:

【H1】Enjoyment is positively related to continuance intention towards a social networking website.

In prior research, Fehring et al. [5] have provided evidence that spiritual well-being is associated with positive moods states in elderly people. Moreover, Shin and Lyubomirsky [16] demonstrated that well-being was increased through intentional activities and further cultivates positive feelings. In connection with online contexts, enjoyment was representatively seen as positive affective response to individual experience that reflects generalized feelings such as pleasure, liking, and fun. While enjoyable experience was regarded as an important predictor of usage intention toward social networks, well-being was a trigger that can stimulate individual's enjoyable feeling. Moreover, well-being can be seen as a potential motivation that promotes individual's action [10]. In particular, Frey and Stutzer [6] deemed well-being as the core value and the final goal of economic activities. Along this point of view, numerous studies have shown the important role of well-being on promoting IT usage. Based on above noted, the current study emphasized the importance of well-being for enhancing enjoyment and usage intention in social networking sites, and proposed the following hypotheses:

【H2】Well-being is positively related to enjoyment in a social networking website.

【H3】Well-being is positively related to continuance intention towards a social networking website.

Based on Ryan and Deci's [14] point of view, Reis et al. [12] explored the hypothesis that emotional well-being may be understood in terms of the degree to which the three basic needs-autonomy, competence, and relatedness are satisfied in daily activity. With SDT approach, Burton et al. [2] showed that intrinsic self-regulation is an important predictor of psychological well-being outcomes in educational settings. Moreover, previous research supported the universality of SDT processes by assessing need satisfaction and well-being simultaneously [11]. As noted, this line of research asserted that satisfaction of basic psychological needs as the important predictors of well-being. These arguments lead to the following hypotheses:

【H4a】 Autonomy is positively related to well-being in a social networking website.

【H4b】 Relatedness is positively related to well-being in a social networking website.

【H4c】 Competence is positively related to well-being in a social networking website.

While SDT as a general theory of motivation that focused on psychological need satisfaction, researchers applied it to explore individuals' continuance intention of technology usage. Sørebø et al. [17] examined the effects of self-determination theory constructs in the context of teachers' utilization of e-learning technology. Roca and Gagne [13] also showed that applying SDT to e-learning in a work setting can be useful for predicting continuance intention. As a result of online social networking websites provide platform for social interaction, it seems reasonable to apply SDT into online social context. Therefore, the current research posited the following hypotheses:

【H5a】 Autonomy is positively related to continuance intention in a social networking website.

【H5b】 Relatedness is positively related to continuance intention in a social networking website.

【H5c】 Competence is positively related to continuance intention in a social networking website.

III. METHODOLOGY AND OUTCOME

The current study plans to employ an online survey to examine the research model and test the proposed hypotheses. Measurements of all the constructs were based from prior studies with slight modifications to fit the online social networking context by using five-point Likert scales, ranging from "strongly disagree" (1) to "strongly agree" (5). Enjoyment will be measured with 4-items adapted from Hassanein and Head's [7] research on online shopping. Well-being will be measured with the 5-items WHO (Five) Well-Being Index [1]. Items on the three self-determination factors (autonomy, relatedness, competence) will be based [17] and modified to assess individuals' basic need in terms of online social networking, in which, autonomy will be measured with 5-items, and relatedness will be measured with 8-items, while competence will be measured with 5-items. Continuance intention will be measured by 4-items adopted from online technology continued usage research [18].

The purpose of this proposal is to explore the power of social influence, and examine the possible factors affecting user's well-being and intention to WOM communication. The results are expected to provide better insights for the development as well as the management of a successful social media with great attraction and influence

IV. ACKNOWLEDGMENT

The authors would like to express their appreciation to National Science council of Republic of China for financially supporting this study under Contract Number NSC 99-2410-H-031-046-MY2 and NSC 101-2410-H-031-025-MY2 .

V. REFERENCE

[1] Awata, S., Bech, P., Koizumi, Y., Seki, T., Kuriyama, S., Hozawa, A. Ohmori, K., Nakaya, N., Matsuoka, H., & Tsuji, I. (2007). Validity and utility of the Japanese version of the WHO-Five Well-Being Index in the context of detecting suicidal ideation in elderly community residents. International Psychogeriatrics , 19(1), 77-88.

[2] Burton, K. D., Lydon, J. E., D'Alessandro, D. U., & Koestner, R. (2006). The differential effects of intrinsic and identified motivation on well-being and performance: Prospective, experimental, and implicit approaches to self-determination theory. Journal of Personality and Social Psychology, 91(4), 750-762.

[3] Chen, K. C., & Jang, S. J. (2010). Motivation in online learning: Testing a model of self-determination theory. Computers in Human Behavior, 26, 741-752.

[4] Deci, E. L., Ryan, R. M., Gagné, M., Leone, D. R., Usunov, J., & Kornazheva, B. P. (2001). Need satisfaction, motivation, and well-being in the work organizations of a former eastern bloc country: a cross-cultural study of self-determination. Personality and Social Psychology Bulletin, 27(8), 930–942.

[5] Fehring, R.J., Miller, J.F., & Shaw, C. (1997). Spiritual well-being, religiosity, hope, depression, and other mood states in elderly people coping with cancer. Oncology Nursing Forum, 24(4), 663-71.

[6] Frey, B. S., & Stutzer, A. (2002). What can economists learn from happiness research? Journal of Economic Literature, 40, 402-435.

[7] Hassanein, K., & Head, M. (2007). Manipulating perceived social presence through the web interface and its impact on attitude towards online shopping. International Journal of Human-Computer Studies, 65, 689-708.

[8] Internet World Stats (2012). FACEBOOK users in the world. http://www.internetworldstats.com/facebook.htm (accessed May 15, 2012).IPPF (2012). Understanding young people's right to decide: Why is it important to develop capacities for autonomous decision-making? International Planned Parenthood Federation.

[9] Kim, B. (2010). An empirical investigation of mobile data service continuance: Incorporating the theory of planned behavior into the expectation–confirmation model. Expert Systems with Applications, 32, 7033-7039.

[10] Layard, R. (2005). Happiness: Lessons from a New Science. New York: Penguin Press.

[11] Milyavskaya, M., & Koestner, R. (2011). Psychological needs, motivation, and well-being: A test of self-determination theory across multiple domains. Personality and Individual Differences, 50, 387-391.

[12] Reis, H. T., Sheldon, K. M., Gable, S. L., Roscoe, J., Ryan, R. M. (2000). Daily well-being- The role of autonomy, competence, and relatedness. Personality & Social Psychology Bulletin, 26, 419-435.

[13] Roca, J. C., & Gagne`, M. (2008). Understanding e-learning continuance intention in the workplace: A self-determination theory perspective. Computers in Human Behavior, 24, 1585-1604.

[14] Ryan, R. M., & Deci, E. L. (2000). Self-determination theory and the facilitation of intrinsic motivation, social development , and well-being. American Psychologist, 55(1), 68-78.

[15] Ryan, R. M., Rigby, C. S., & Przybylski, A. (2006). The motivational pull of video games: A self-determination theory approach. Motivation and Emotion, 30, 347–363.

[16] Shin, N.L., & Lyubomirsky, S. (2009). Enhancing well - being and alleviating depressive symptoms with positive psychology interventions: A practice-friendly meta-analysis. Journal of Clinical Psychology, 65(5), 467-487.

[17] Sørebø, Ø, Halvari, H., Gulli, V. F., Kristiansen, R. (2009). The role of self-determination theory in explaining teachers' motivation to continue to use e-learning technology. Computers & Education, 53, 1177-1187.

[18] Zhang, Y., Fang, Y., Wei, K.-K., & Chen, H. (2010). Exploring the role of psychological safety in promoting the intention to continue sharing knowledge in virtual communities. International Journal of Information Management, 30, 425-436

A systematic review of integration of ICT in science classrooms

Chiu-Liang Chen, Janet Mei-Chuen Lin, Yi-Jiun Wu, Yu-Wen Huang, & Rong-Ching Chen
Graduate Institute of Information and Computer Education, National Taiwan Normal University, Taiwan

Abstract – *In this study we conducted a systematic review of the literature on the integration of information and computer technologies (ICT) in science education in elementary and secondary schools. A total of 227 papers were selected for manual screening using a set of predefined inclusion criteria. The screening yielded 172 papers for data extraction and analysis. Data from each of these 172 papers were extracted with a template consisting of 16 items, including area, subject, topics, ICT tools used, purpose of the ICT tools, learning theory, teaching strategy, learning activities, skills required of the instructor to implement the integration, participants, data collected, research findings, etc. These data allowed us to analyze how ICT tools have been used to improve science teaching and, in particular, what novel learning activities, as opposed to traditional classroom teaching activities, have been made possible by integrating ICT in instruction, thus providing students with more effective ways of learning science.*

Keywords: ICT integration, systematic reviews, science education.

1. Introduction

As Light and Pillemer [1] pointed out, "the need for research synthesis can only be realized when one understands that in order for the gains of scholarship to be cumulative, there must be a link between the past and future research. Often the need for a new study is not as great as the need for the assimilation of already existing studies." Briner & Denyer [2] further stressed that "the emphasis on empirical contributions rather than reviews and syntheses has resulted in a voluminous, fragmented and contested field."

Information and communications technologies (ICT) tools have been used in classrooms around the world for many decades and much has been reported about how ICT has impacted teaching and learning. The purpose of this study is to synthesize research findings published between 2000 and 2012 on the use of ICT in science classrooms. We are particularly interested in investigating what novel learning activities, as opposed to traditional classroom teaching activities, have been made possible by integrating ICT in science instruction, thus providing students with more effective ways of learning science.

2. Method

A systematic review utilizes *organized*, *transparent*, and *replicable* procedures to comprehensively locate and synthesize individual studies, and draws conclusions about what we currently know and do not know about a given question or topic [2, 3]. The following subsections describe the major steps of the systematic review we conducted, including data collection, data extraction, and data synthesis.

2.1 Data Collection

The entire data collection process we performed is depicted in Figure 1. To search for articles that involved the use of ICT tools in education, published in English between 2000 and 2012, we began with identifying six databases for searching relevant articles: ACM Digital Library, EBSCOhost (Wilson Databases), Ed/ITLib, Education Journals (ProQuest), ERIC, and ISI Web of Knowledge. The search string used was: *(ICT OR technology OR computer OR system) AND (teach* OR learn* OR educat* OR instruct* OR pedagogi*).*

The initial search returned a total of 45,618 articles. The articles were managed with EndNote. For each article we recorded the title of the article, the journal where the article was published, the year and month of publication, the volume and issue numbers, names of the authors, and the abstract. After removing the duplicates and the articles from non-academic sources, as well as journals that were irrelevant to our topic, the number of articles was reduced to 14,524.

The 14,524 papers then were divided into three groups and screened manually by four researchers. Articles of Group 1 were examined by researchers A and B, Group 2 by researchers B and C, and Group 3 by researchers A and C. The examiners tried to decide if an article should be included for analysis based on the title and the abstract of the article; however, if that was not enough to make the decision, full text was read. Whenever two examiners of the same group disagreed about whether an article should be included, the fourth researcher helped to reconcile the disagreement. Manual screening of the three groups resulted in the removal of 12,785 articles. Only 1,739 articles were kept for further analysis. The overall inter-examiner agreement rate was 86.88%. Among the 1,739 articles, 227 were identified as related to science teaching.

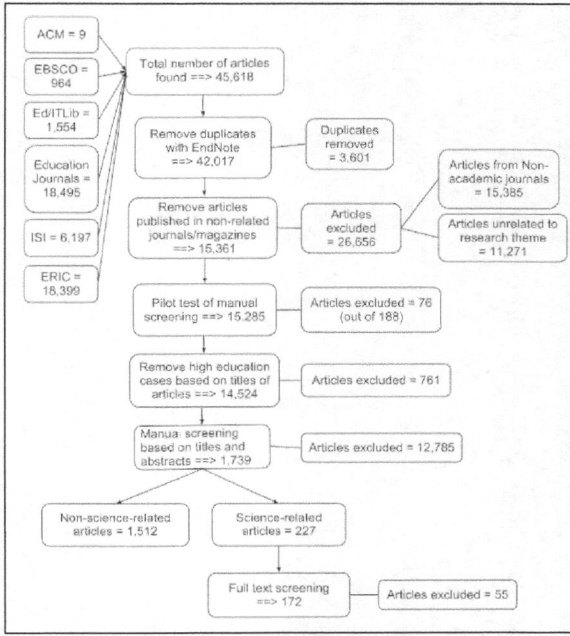

Figure 1. The data collection process

2.2 Data Extraction

Other than the information managed by EndNote about each paper, our data extraction template consisted of 16 items to record important data about each paper that was finally included for analysis: keywords, the research aim, research method, country, participants, data collected, research findings, content area, subject, topics, ICT tools used, purpose of the ICT tools, learning theory, teaching strategy, learning activities, and skills required of the instructor to implement the integration. We pilot tested the template against 30+ papers and modified the template as needed to ensure that a fairly standard and through examination of each paper can be conducted in a single reading.

Second-round manual screening was conducted along with data extraction using the following inclusion criteria:

(1) Only the subjects of natural sciences taught in elementary and secondary schools, including physics, chemistry, biology, and earth science, are to be included for analysis. (This criterion excluded teaching of computer science.)

(2) The ICT tools used in a study must manifest the use of digital and/or network functionalities in supporting learning. (This criterion excluded the cases in which ICT tools were used "superficially;" for example, using intelligent whiteboard only as a projector screen or using a portable computer as a sound recorder or digital camera.)

(3) The article must report one or more ICT-integration cases and each case has to satisfy the following conditions:

 (a) The case of ICT-integrated instruction reported must be class-based. (This criterion excluded instruction offered by summer/winter camps.) In addition, there must be clearly specified learning content.

 (b) The article must have a detailed description of learning activities, which includes explicit presence of a teacher to guide students through the activities, or implicit presence of teacher(s) embedded in the pre-organized learning materials and activities provided by a learning system/software. Furthermore, the learning activities must exhibit new ways of learning, as opposed to traditional classroom learning activities, and have positive impact on teaching and learning (for example, improved learning effectiveness, and/or enhanced interest in learning).

At the end of the second-round screening, 172 papers were retained and data were extracted from them.

2.3. Data Synthesis

We are currently in the process of analyzing the data extracted from the 172 papers. It is expected to be completed by the end of May. The findings will be available for reporting by the time EEE'13 takes place in July 2013.

3. Acknowledgement

This research was financially supported by Taiwan's National Science Council under Grant No. NSC 100-251-S-003-021-MY2.

4. References

[1] R.J. Light and D. Pillemer. Summing up: The Science of Reviewing Research. Cambridge, MA: Harvard University Press, 1984.

[2] R.B. Briner and D. Denyer, "Systematic review and evidence synthesis as a practice and scholarship tool." Handbook of Evidence-Based Management: Companies, Classrooms and Research. Oxford University Press. Retrieved April 10, 2013 from http://www.cebma.org/wp-content/uploads/Briner-Denyer-Systematic-Review-Evidence-Synthesis.pdf.

[3] J.H. Littell, J. Corcoran, and V.K. Pillai. Systematic Reviews and Meta-Analysis. New York: Oxford University Press, 2008.

SESSION

E-COMMERCE AND PRIVACY + EDUCATION AND LEARNING METHODS + KNOWLEDGE-BASED SYSTEMS

Chair(s)

Prof. Hamid Arabnia
University of Georgia

Meeting the E-Commerce Privacy Key Concept, A Conceptual Survey

Seyyed Mohammad Reza Farshchi*,1, Saber Mesgari2, Davud MohammadPur3
1Department of Mathematics, Applied Mathematics, FUM University, Tehran, Iran.
2Department of Electrical Engineering, Amirkabir University of Technology, Tehran, Iran.
3Department of Computer Engineering, University of Zanjan, Zanjan, Iran.
*Shiveex@Gmail.Com

Abstract- *User privacy protection is of the utmost importance. We show that privacy has been acknowledged as a human right that is beneficial not only to each individual but also to society as a whole. We describe privacy-related legislation and address criticism against privacy. We also summarize the existing approaches to protect privacy. We also show that currently deployed e-commerce protocols reveal to service providers user personal data such as user identity and billing information, as well as the product or services the user purchases. Such information is sensitive because, e.g., it may reveal the political views, religion, sexual orientation or health condition of the user. Frequently without user awareness, service providers gather that information to profile users in order to, e.g., offer a personalized service or discriminate them. Consequently, we study privacy-preserving e-commerce protocols. First, we categorize them as private purchase protocols, in which the service provider does not learn which items are bought by the user, and anonymous purchase protocols, in which the user identity is not disclosed to the service provider. And finally, we also summarize our work on anonymous purchase.*

Keywords: Privacy Protocol, Privacy, E-commerce.

1 Introduction

The progress of information and communication technologies (ICT) has eased the collection, storage and sharing of web user's personal information. When users search the web, engage in online transactions or utilize social networks, service providers collect and store personal information for various purposes, e.g., offering a personalized service, improving usability, or delivering targeted advertising. Personal information encompasses not only data such as identity, address and telephone number, but also any information that reveals users interests, thoughts and beliefs, such as the search terms employed in search engines.

The progress of profiling techniques has automated the analysis of user personal data. Service providers apply profiling techniques to the personal information gathered to classify users into categories of their interest. Afterwards, service providers make decisions on how to treat users depending on how they were profiled, which leads to user automatic discrimination. Moreover, users are frequently unaware of the fact that they are being profiled and the profiling algorithm employed is kept secret by service providers. Some definition was adopted directly from [1]. Privacy is key in the promotion of liberty, autonomy, self hood, human relations, and in furthering the existence of a free society [1]. In particular, it provides freedom from scrutiny, prejudice, pressure to conform, exploitation, and the judgment of others [2].

Some scholars have valued privacy as an individual right that protects the ability to control information about oneself [3]. Others have broadened the importance of privacy as a collective right required in a democratic society and key for political participation, human dignity and autonomy [4]. In a similar line, some studies highlight the close relation between privacy and intimacy [5], while others extend the need of privacy to any type of social relationship [6].

Furthermore, privacy is not only an individual interest but also a social value [7]. It is a common value in the sense that all individuals value some privacy, a public value because of its importance in a democratic political system, and a collective value because technology and market forces make it difficult for an individual to have privacy without everybody sharing a similar level of privacy [8].

E-commerce allows the buying and selling of products and services through communication networks. Currently deployed e-commerce protocols typically disclose user data to the service provider. Those user data consist of information required by the method of payment employed and the identity and number of products bought. The former normally encompasses contact details such as name, address, phone number or email address, financial details such as bank account or credit card number, and other personal data such as birth date or social security number. The latter may reveal user's interests and needs. Therefore, currently deployed e-commerce protocols disclose sensitive user data.

2 Privacy Model

The concept of privacy is frequently used in legal, political, philosophical and technical literature and multiple privacy definitions have been proposed. However, there exists no common definition since its meaning changes with the discipline in which it is used and even with the different viewpoints within a field of study. In fact, the concept of privacy differs depending on the context to which it is applied. Therefore, a common approach to define privacy considers several privacy categories [9].

- Body privacy relates to protection against body exposure and seeks to prevent intrusions into an individual's physical space or solitude. Compulsory medical treatments or collection of biometric data are within the scope of body privacy.

- Behavior privacy extends such protection to any aspect of an individual's behaviour, including thoughts, feelings and beliefs. Political affiliation, sexual preferences and religious practices are important aspects of behavior privacy.

- Organization privacy refers to groups, corporations or societies that wish to conceal their secrets or activities from other individuals or organizations.

- Communication privacy protects individuals' freedom to communicate among themselves without monitoring or interception by other individuals or organizations.

Data privacy is applied to the collection, storage and sharing of personal data, and is sometimes subdivided into types such as financial, location or medical privacy depending on the type of data.

As can be seen, such classifications are based on both the type of individual and the type of information that require privacy and the classification's categories overlap partially. Due to the progress of ICT, communication privacy and data privacy are nowadays closely linked and the term information privacy is employed to encompass both. We are interested in the protection of information privacy in the context of e-commerce transactions.

Although most scholars think that privacy is a valuable concept, there are some critical accounts on privacy. Thomson claims that privacy is a cluster of rights that overlaps already existing rights such as property and body security [10].

Similarly, Bork defends that privacy is encompassed by liberty or autonomy [11]. Posner argues that privacy is detrimental for economy because, by concealing information, it harms market efficiency, and that therefore privacy should only be protected when access to information would reduce its value [12].

2.1 Privacy vs. Usability

Security and privacy have often been sacrificed for the sake of usability. Protecting access to a computer with a password is a classic example [14]. Although everybody acknowledges that implementing some access control mechanism is needed from a security perspective, oftentimes password authentication is disabled for the sake of usability. In the physical world, however, hardly anyone is willing to leave his home door unlocked, despite the time costs and unforseen incidents (e.g. key losses) that locking and unlocking doors causes.

In the online world, security and privacy are also undermined to improve usability. Examples include banks that require easy-to-remember but insecure personal data for an ongoing debate on the need to trade-off security and privacy has been fostered by authorities that wish to deploy surveillance and other privacy invasive measures in order to prevent crime.

Authentication purposes [15], social networks that disclose the identities of registered users so that finding friends is easy, or e-commerce websites that offer a wide array of payment methods, some of them less secure or less privacy-preserving than others.

We think that security, privacy and usability are not conflicting requirements and thus the goal is to design secure and privacy-preserving systems that are usable. Usability not only benefits the users' experience but also improves the system's security and privacy. In particular, when users have a security role, usability plays a crucial role in avoiding security failures. For example, unusable systems that require users to have many passwords may lead to weak password choices or password reuse, which harms the system's security.

Additionally, to evaluate the usability of systems, research also focuses on experiment design and on conducting surveys and interviews to find out both how users perceive security and privacy in a system and their understanding of the system's operation [16].

2.2 Privacy vs. Profiling

Patterns and correlations in large amounts of users' personal data. Constructing user profiles encompasses defining the goals of the analysis, collecting the data to be analyzed, preparing the data by removing some user attributes, finding correlations and patterns on those data, and analyzing the results to eliminate irrelevant patterns.

The application of user profiles consists in classifying users according to the patterns found. User profile application gives feedback and also allows the refinement of constructed user profiles.

Profiling is a tool employed in many domains. In the financial sector, user profiling is employed, e.g., to detect fraud. In the human resources departments, it is used to evaluate the candidate's skills and behavior. In e-commerce, user profiles are used to classify customers into categories so as to predict their behaviour and allow for customer management.

2.3 Privacy vs. Transparency

Transparency, aka openness, refers to a set of policies and procedures that allows users to access, understand, use and audit information and activities held by an organization such as the government, a public society or a private company. In the case of governments, transparency is often regarded as a fundamental property for democracy since it ensures the right to be informed.

Public and private organizations can also benefit from transparency to improve user's confidence, insofar as transparency does not affect intellectual property or research activities.

We also regard transparency as a useful property that allows users to control organizations' activities and that helps to balance the power between users and organizations. However, recently, it has been advocated that users should also lean towards transparency [17]. For example, Facebook12 managers have claimed that ―more visibility makes us better people. More transparency should make for a more tolerant society in which people eventually accept that everybody sometimes does bad or embarrassing things‖. Generally, it is claimed that users would enjoy the same benefits that organizations obtain through transparency, i.e., generating trust and being more moral and effective.

However, we argue that user transparency would provoke a major power imbalance between users and organizations. User transparency means that users, who are the vulnerable parties, would give away all their information to organizations. If user transparency was implemented, organizations would control users totally.

In the context of privacy protection, transparency often refers to the set of policies and tools through which users can monitor how a service provider handles their personal data. It has been argued that, in so called ―smart environments‖, privacy protection via data disclosure minimization is not adequate because data knowledge is necessary to carry out smart functionalities, and that the goal should be shifted to providing transparency [18]. However, the claim that data knowledge is necessary to carry out smart functionalities is unsupported.

3 Demand and Threat to Privacy

Since old times, human beings have demanded privacy. Although privacy as a concept did not exist in some cultures and languages until recently, most cultures have recognized the individual's need to withhold certain facts or acts from The concept of privacy is frequently used in legal, political, philosophical society. For example, anthropologic studies [19] have shown that seclusion and restricted access to ceremonies were utilized to protect privacy. Some studies of animals even claim that privacy needs are not restricted to humans [20] and that wildlife documentaries threaten animals' right to privacy [5].

However, some studies show that users are either not aware of data being shared or not aware of the privacy implications of sharing personal data [4].

Other studies show that they are indeed concerned about personal data being collected [21] and that service provider's techniques to alleviate such concerns, such as privacy policies or privacy seals, are not well understood [22, 18]. Aside from that, citizens value privacy protection as a necessary countermeasure against surveillance and identity theft.

- Surveillance. Surveillance can be defined as the process of monitoring the communications and actions of one or more individuals.13 Personal surveillance refers to the case in which only one individual is investigated, while mass surveillance affects a large group. The purpose of the latter is commonly to identify individuals from the group that possess some characteristic.

Surveillance can be carried out via a wide array of techniques. Physical surveillance involves listening and watching, possibly remotely in terms of space and time. Communication surveillance involves intercepting or eavesdropping an individual's communications.

We are particularly interested in data surveillance, which employs users personal data stored in remote servers. Nowadays, data surveillance is effective thanks to the great amount of personal data collected by service providers. Additionally, it is cheaper than other forms of surveillance because it can be automated. Techniques that allow such automation include profiling and matching records of the same user in different servers.

- Identity Theft. Identity theft consists in pretending to be another person by using that person's identity. Usually, identity theft is used to gain access to resources or benefits. Nowadays, identity theft is a real threat to users whose personal data is stored remotely. Unfortunately, data breaches are not infrequent and stolen personal data can be used to impersonate someone else.

As can be seen, privacy protection techniques that seek to minimize the amount of personal data disclosed to service providers are useful to prevent both surveillance and identity theft. Privacy protection is thus necessary to mitigate users' privacy concerns and to favor their participation in the information society.

3.1 E-commerce Protocols

Currently deployed e-commerce protocols do not protect user privacy. The security properties they usually provide are communication security, i.e., data is exchanged in an encrypted manner to prevent eavesdropping, authentication between buyer and merchant and non-repudiation. Therefore, buyers are authenticated and they disclose which items they buy to the vendor.

Typically, e-commerce protocols consist of a purchase phase in which users select the product they want to buy and reveal this information to the service providers, a payment phase in which users pay to service providers in order to buy the selected products, and a delivery phase in which the buyer receives digital goods or a receipt that allows them to claim delivery of the purchased products.

A wide array of payment methods is nowadays available: credit cards, Paypal, billing to mobile phones and landlines, cash on delivery, cheques, debit cards, electronic money (e.g. bitcoin), gift cards, postal money order, wire transfer and invoices. Currently, credits cards represent more than ninety per cent of online payments in the US, while PayPal is the fastest growing payment method with more than 100 million active users worldwide. Therefore, we are going to focus our analysis on those payment methods.

In the mid-1990s, payment protocols based on credit cards employed the SSL protocol to secure communications. Such payment protocols disclosed user personal and financial data to service providers. In the late 1990s, credit card companies promoted the use of Secure Electronic Transaction (SET), a set of security protocols that allowed using the existing payment card infrastructure in the Internet. From a privacy perspective, the main feature of SET is that it avoided the disclosure of user financial information to the service provider.

Instead, this information was communicated to the service provider encrypted with the public key of the bank, which received it from service providers and verified it. However, SET was not successful because of its deployment costs and because it required user's to employ a user public key certified by the bank.

Currently, most credit card companies employ 3-D secure, a protocol that employs TLS (the successor of SSL) for the sake of communication security and adds an authentication step. When buyers enter the payment phase, they are redirected from the e-commerce web site to a card issuing bank web site to authorize the transaction. Typically, a password-based authentication method is employed, in which the password is tied to the card. The password is not communicated to the service provider, which reduces the risks derived from security breaches in the service provider domain. To prevent such security breaches, credit card companies enforce the deployment of the Payment Card Industry Data Security Standard (PCI DSS) in the service provider domain. In the next paragraph, we say some tips about the desirable properties of E-commerce protocols.

One of the main properties an e-commerce protocol should provide is fairness. Fairness ensures that either service provider receives a payment and user receives the product, or both of them receive nothing. In the case of digital goods, copyright protection is needed to avoid illegal distribution. Authors in [32] give an overview of copyright protection protocols. Access control is used for two purposes. First, it is required to ensure that only entitled users can purchase. Second, it ensures that only users that have purchased a service can access it. Profiling techniques are employed to provide personalized services.

3.2 Private Purchase

Oblivious transfer (OT) was proposed in [23]. Traditionally, security in OT was analyzed in a half-simulation model where simulation security is required against an adversarial receiver, but just stand-alone privacy is required against an adversarial sender. This notion was showed to admit practical attacks against receiver's security [24]. Author at [7], as well as subsequent works [5], present efficient adaptive OT schemes in a full-simulation model. However, these works are not universally composable secure.

An adaptive universally composable secure OT scheme was proposed [25]. They utilize the approach of assisted decryption used in [26, 11], where the sender sends to the receiver a collection of ciphertexts and in each transfer phase helps the receiver to decrypt one of them. As pointed out in [27], this approach allows for transfer phases with constant computational and communication complexity, and it is suitable to ensure that the sender does not change the messages in each transfer phase, which are important properties for constructing a private purchase protocol based on OT. In contrast, in other non-adaptive UC-secure OT schemes [28, 10], in each transfer phase the receiver hands a set of keys to the sender, who sends back a collection of ciphertexts such that the receiver is able to decrypt only one of them.

The first Priced Oblivious Transfer (POT) scheme [1], as well as subsequent works [2], analyzes security in the half-simulation model. In [8], it is explained why these protocols fail even under sequential composition and a practical attack is shown.

POT is a concrete instantiation of oblivious transfer with access control protocols. Access control mechanisms for OT proposed so far can roughly be divided into two groups: those that do not preserve user anonymity and those that preserve it.

In the first group, conditional oblivious transfer schemes [13, 20], in which a sender with input x and a receiver with input y interact in such a way that a transfer is completed only when $q(x, y) = 1$ for some public predicate $q(\cdot, \cdot)$, are non-adaptive and employ the half-simulation model. On the other hand, security of both the non-adaptive [1, 29] and the adaptive [11] Generalized Oblivious Transfer schemes proposed so far, which can be instantiated as non-adaptive and adaptive POT schemes respectively, depends on the underlying OT scheme utilized to implement them, but these solutions are rather inefficient.

In the second group, we find solutions that employ anonymous credentials. Author in [2] propose a scheme in which access control policies are described by a state graph, such that each state allows access to a subset of the records. In the initialization phase, the database records are encrypted on input an index from 1 to N. Additionally, each user obtains a credential that binds her to a state in the graph. To access a record, the user proves possession of her credential and proves that the index of the record is included in the subset of indices defined by her state. Each access to the database determines a transition from one state to another, which depends on the record accessed. The user obtains a new credential that binds her to her new state. Access control is enforced by limiting the possible transitions between states.

This scheme has the nice properties that it can be applied to different OT schemes and that it permits changing the policies without needing to rerun the initialization phase of the OT scheme. However, as noted by Camenisch et al. [28], the scheme is inefficient for two reasons. First, users must obtain a new credential each time they access the database. Second, a large class of access control policies cannot be efficiently expressed via state graphs.

In next section, we introduce some protocols that allow a user, on input meter readings from a meter and a tariff policy from the service provider, to compute the fee to be paid, to reveal the fee to the service provider and to prove to the service provider that such fee is correct without disclosing any information on the meter readings. We have considered two types of meters: tamper-resistant and non-tamper-resistant. For additional reading you can refer to [1, 35].

In fact, the meter outputs signed readings which are used by the user to prove correctness of the fee calculation. In the other word, the proof of correctness of the fee calculation that is sent by the user to the service provider does not suffice because such calculation could be done on input fake meter readings. In this case, the service provider must perform extra checks to ensure correctness of the fee calculation.

4 Anonymous Billings Protocol

Several protocols propose the anonymization of meter readings and the aggregation of meter readings of a group of users to protect user privacy [5, 7]. The NIST privacy subgroup [15] suggests anonymizing traces of readings, as proposed by author at [9], but also warns of the ease of re-identification. These proposals, however, do not explain how the service provider, after receiving anonymized or aggregated meter readings, can bill users.

4.1 Access Control

We briefly review our work on access control protocols. Both protocols provide users with anonymity. Additionally, the first protocol, based on oblivious transfer, allows the implementation of anonymous and private purchases simultaneously, as in [18].

Access control based on anonymous credentials allows users to prove to a service provider in a privacy-friendly manner that they possess the credentials required to access a resource. To achieve perfect privacy, the information that service providers can learn from the access control protocol should in principle be just one bit, which indicates whether a user should be granted access. However, existing anonymous credential schemes reveal additional information to the service provider such as the identity of the credential issuer, the credential type, and constraints on the attributes of the credential that reveal more than the access decision itself. In addition, the efficiency of selective attribute disclosure is not optimal incidental, accidental or deliberate leakages of information resulting from disclosing the final bill. We show that by adding some, in the long run small, amount of noise it is possible to offer strong privacy guarantees on what an adversary can infer from the final bill. We use new techniques for differential privacy that could be more widely applicable. Second, we attempt to minimize the cost of privacy through a cryptographic oblivious billing mechanism. The true cost of service provision is tracked across billing periods, but not revealed to the service provider, which can only verify the deposited funds cover costs.

This allows customers to determine the levels of privacy they require and even get a rebate for the additional funds they used to protect their privacy.

5 Conclusions

We have explained why privacy is necessary and why it should be protected. We have also shown that currently deployed e-commerce and consumption billing protocols do not protect user privacy. We have focused on protocols that allow users to buy digital goods and to pay their utility consumption bills without disclosing to the service provider the items that they buy or the consumption measurements. We have also survey some tips about protocols that provide users with anonymity.

Some approaches can be combined into a single protocol that provides private and anonymous purchases simultaneously. Additionally, we have described how to provide those protocols with fairness and copyright protection.

6 References

[1] Alfredo Rial, Privacy-Preserving E-Commerce Protocols, Phd Thesis, 2013.

[2] A.L. Allen. Uneasy access: Privacy for women in a free society. Rowman & Littlefield Pub Incorporated, 1988.

[3] Ross Anderson and Shailendra Fuloria. On the security economics of electricity metering. In The Ninth Workshop on the Economics of Information Security, 2010.

[4] Benny Applebaum, Yuval Ishai, and Eyal Kushilevitz. From secrecy to soundness: Efficient verification via secure computation. In Samson Abramsky, Cyril Gavoille, Claude Kirchner, Friedhelm Meyer auf der Heide, and Paul G. Spirakis, editors, ICALP (1), volume 6198 of Lecture Notes in Computer Science, pages 152–163. Springer, 2010.

[5] N. Asokan, Victor Shoup, and Michael Waidner. Optimistic fair exchange of digital signatures (extended abstract). In EUROCRYPT, pages 591–606, 1998.

[6] Man Ho Au, Willy Susilo, and Yi Mu. Constant-size dynamic k-taa. In Roberto De Prisco and Moti Yung, editors, SCN, volume 4116 of Lecture Notes in Computer Science, pages 111–125. Springer, 2006.

[7] Gildas Avoine and Serge Vaudenay. Optimistic fair exchange based on publicly verifiable secret sharing. In Huaxiong Wang, Josef Pieprzyk, and Vijay Varadharajan, editors, ACISP, volume 3108 of Lecture Notes in Computer Science, pages 74–85. Springer, 2004.

[8] Josep Balasch, Bart Preneel, Alfredo Rial, Marijn Scheir, and Ingrid Verbauwhede. Anonymous E-Cash for Resource Constrained Devices. Cosic internal report, 2012.

[9] Josep Balasch, Alfredo Rial, Carmela Troncoso, Bart Preneel, Ingrid Verbauwhede, Christophe Geuens, KU Leuven, and Sint-Michielsstraat ICRI. Pretp: Privacy-preserving electronic toll pricing. In Usenix Security, volume 10, 2010.

[10] Feng Bao, Robert H. Deng, and Wenbo Mao. Efficient and practical fair exchange protocols with off-line ttp. In IEEE Symposium on Security and Privacy, pages 77–85. IEEE Computer Society, 1998.

[11] Mauro Barni and Franco Bartolini. Watermarking Systems Engineering: Enabling Digital Assets Security and Other Applications. CRC Press, 1 edition, February 2004.

[12] Leonard E. Baum and Ted Petrie. Statistical Inference for Probabilistic Functions of Finite State Markov Chains. The Annals of Mathematical Statistics, 37(6):1554–1563, 1966.

[13] M. Belenkiy, M. Chase, M. Kohlweiss, and A. Lysyanskaya. P-signatures and noninteractive anonymous credentials. In R. Canetti, editor, TCC, volume 4948 of Lecture Notes in Computer Science, pages 356–374. Springer, 2008.

[14] Mira Belenkiy, Melissa Chase, Markulf Kohlweiss, and Anna Lysyanskaya.Compact e-cash and simulatable vrfs revisited. Cryptology ePrint Archive, Report 2009/107, 2009. http://eprint.iacr.org/.

[15] Mihir Bellare and Oded Goldreich. On defining proofs of knowledge. In Ernest F. Brickell, editor, CRYPTO '92, volume 740, pages 390–420. Springer-Verlag, 1992.

[16] Mihir Bellare and Phillip Rogaway. Random oracles are practical: A paradigm for designing efficient protocols. In First ACM Conference on Computer and Communication Security, pages 62–73. Association for Computing Machinery, 1993.

[17] Siavosh Benabbas, Rosario Gennaro, and Yevgeniy Vahlis. Verifiable delegation of computation over large datasets. Cryptology ePrint Archive, Report 2011/132, 2011. http://eprint.iacr.org/.

[18] Paola Benassi. Truste: an online privacy seal program. Communications of the ACM, 42(2):56–59, 1999.

[19] Oliver Berthold, Hannes Federrath, and Marit Köhntopp. Project —anonymity and unobservability in the internetl. In CFP '00: Proceedings of the tenth conference on Computers, freedom and privacy, pages 57–65, New York, NY, USA, 2000. ACM.

[20] Ian F. Blake and Vladimir Kolesnikov. Strong conditional oblivious transfer and computing on intervals. In In Advances in Cryptology -ASIACRYPT 2004, pages 515–529. Springer, 2004.

[21] Dan Boneh, Craig Gentry, Ben Lynn, and Hovav Shacham. Aggregate and verifiably encrypted signatures from bilinear maps. In Eli Biham, editor, EUROCRYPT, volume 2656 of Lecture Notes in Computer Science, pages 416–432. Springer, 2003.

[22] R.H. Bork. The tempting of America: the political seduction of the law. Free Press, 1990.

[23] X. Boyen and B. Waters. Full-domain subgroup hiding and constant-size group signatures. In T. Okamoto and X. Wang, editors, Public Key Cryptography, volume 4450 of Lecture Notes in Computer Science, pages 1–15. Springer, 2007.

[24] Stefan Brands. Untraceable off-line cash in wallets with observers (extended abstract). In Douglas R. Stinson, editor, CRYPTO, volume 773 of Lecture Notes in Computer Science, pages 302–318. Springer, 1993.

[25] Stefan Brands. Rapid demonstration of linear relations connected by boolean operators. In Walter Fumy, editor, Advances in Cryptology —EUROCRYPT '97, volume 1233 of LNCS, pages 318–333. Springer Verlag, 1997.

[26] Alex Braunstein, Laura Granka, and Jessica Staddon. Indirect content privacy surveys: measuring privacy without asking about it. In Proceedings of the Seventh Symposium on Usable Privacy and Security, page 15. ACM, 2011.

[27] Leo Breiman. Random forests. Machine Learning, 45(1):5–32, 2001.

[28] J. Camenisch and M. Stadler. Efficient group signature schemes for large groups. In Burt Kaliski, editor, CRYPTO '97, volume 1296 of LNCS, pages 410–424. Springer Verlag, 1997.

[29] Jan Camenisch. Group Signature Schemes and Payment Systems Based on the Discrete Logarithm Problem. PhD thesis, ETH Zürich, 1998.

[30] Jan Camenisch, Rafik Chaabouni, and Abhi Shelat. Efficient protocols for set membership and range proofs. In Josef Pieprzyk, editor, ASIACRYPT, volume 5350 of Lecture Notes in Computer Science, pages 234–252. Springer, 2008.

[31] Jan Camenisch, Maria Dubovitskaya, and Gregory Neven. Oblivious transfer with access control. In Ehab Al-Shaer, Somesh Jha, and Angelos D. Keromytis, editors, ACM Conference on Computer and Communications Security, pages 131–140. ACM, 2009.

[32] Jan Camenisch, Maria Dubovitskaya, and Gregory Neven. Unlinkable priced oblivious transfer with rechargeable wallets. In Radu Sion, editor, Financial Cryptography and Data Security, volume 6052 of Lecture Notes in Computer Science, pages 66–81. Springer Berlin Heidelberg, 2010.

[33] William Aiello, Yuval Ishai, and Omer Reingold. Priced oblivious transfer: How to sell digital goods. In Pfitzmann [103], pages 119–135.

[34] Alfredo Rial and G. Danezis, Privacy-Preserving Smart Metering, WPES 2011.

[35] Alfredo Rial and G. Danezis, Privacy-Preserving Smart Metering. In Information Security Solutions Europe, 2012, Brussels, Belgium.

Course Management Systems:

Basic Improvements To Course Management Systems Through Modern Design Techniques

Jeff Brandon, Mark Beilfuss, Cameron Henige, Rolando Casipit, Kyle Head, Tom Lagona, Rodger Lee

Department of Computer Science, Central Michigan University, Mount Pleasant, Michigan, U.S.A

Abstract

Schools rely heavily on web technologies such as Blackboard to improve the learning experience of students. Blackboard exists as a tool for instructors to publish information and give students easy access to it. One of the most important features of Blackboard is giving instructors the ability to assign quizzes to students to complete over the Internet. Unfortunately there are some obvious flaws with translating a traditionally paper-based activity to the web which can lead to teaching professionals preferring paper examinations over entirely digital assignments and activities. Web based assignments can also facilitate and environment that allows students to cheat by looking up answers available online, some question types simply aren't easy to represent with existing web technologies, and the current systems can be difficult to navigate due to lack of a consistent layout across classrooms. Because of these issues many instructors are wary of investing in a technology that has the potential to have a positive impact on student experience and the environment. We see these problems which cause a reluctance to adopt these systems into classrooms and teaching curriculum as a stumbling block that can be overcome. Taking into account user feedback and an analysis of known shortcomings with the current systems we have formulated and designed a system that attempts to rectify these problems. We have integrated various methods such as dynamically generated questions and cheat detection into our solution to make it more appealing to those in the education industry. Our results show that many of the concerns raised by instructors can indeed be solved with the creative application of web technologies. We have also found that there are some issues such as access and uptime, which in general can't be solved completely without elaborate and expensive processes.

1. Introduction

A course management system shouldn't be about how feature rich the environment is. There should be a focus on how accessible the features are because student engagement is increased when the instructor uses a CMS to promote self-discovery of course material.[1] This self-discovery of material greatly increases knowledge retention opposed to other methods of teaching such as lecturing. A grade book system and a system for creating tests would be the pillars of said system for teachers. These two systems should be able to interact, with one another seamlessly. The quiz system should allow an instructor the ability to create an array of questions with types such as text response, multiple choice, matching, and more to reflect the style of question he or she would ask on a pencil and paper style exam. Not only should the application for quiz making be robust, but easy and intuitive to use. The simpler the application is to understand and operate, the more an end user will return to use the system again in the future. Through various on campus interviews we have found that teachers and students said that their main problem with systems like Blackboard was that it was not easy to use. The grade book systems did not provide enough relevant data to keeping track of grades and quizzes limited educators in the questions they could ask by only allowing a small set of question types.

In this paper we will discuss how our web-based grading and quiz systems, key components in any course management system, are an improvement over current products such as the Blackboard system. With a focus on user experience our application will be able to provide a better end result while still efficiently accomplishing its stated purpose. Throughout development we will be using various design techniques and testing solutions that will be expanded on in sections three and four including the basics of our system. For now the course management system will consist of only a grade book and a quiz creation system. We believe that through a more intuitive user interface, teaching aids such as Blackboard can be used more effectively in higher education, both by teachers and students.

In section two we will go into more detail about how the grading and quiz applications function. In addition to a more detailed description of the product we will discuss other web-based software solutions, such as Blackboard, and define what a course management system is. We will review user testimony of the two products which we used as a guideline for our current software solution. Finally a brief discussion of our approach will be given before a more thorough explanation in the later sections is laid out.

2. Background and Related Works

First we must define what we mean when we talk about a web based educational system. A course management suite, or CMS as it will be referred to throughout the rest of this document, is a fundamental part of web based education. A CMS consists of tools to view and manage grades for the educator to use. It also provides a window into the students personal grades for the student and it should be a place where online assignments may be completed with relative ease and without limitations. This system is available online and has three general user types: instructors, students, and admins.

The CMS should also be thought of as an extension of the classroom where learning can occur rather than a means to submit homework. The learning that takes place in a CMS is called Web-Based Learning. Badrul H. Khan is the author of the book *Web-Based Instruction,* in which he states, "A [Web Based Instruction] learning environment should include many resources, support collaboration, implement web based activities as part of the learning framework, and support both novices and experts".[2] Based on this one of our main goals within this project is to design a user interface that is both easy to learn but does not slow down the more adept user. A web based instruction or WBI should also allow for courses to be taught entirely online or be used as a supplement to a traditional classroom setting. An immediate benefit of WBI is the paper saved by proctoring exams and quizzes without using any paper.

Education is still a field where there are plenty of opportunities for software development; especially for web-based systems. The most high profile types of web systems are course management systems and include educational management systems like Blackboard, WebCT, and LearningSpace among others. These programs provide a wide array of services meant for both educators and students alike. Even though they have functionality ranging from grade books to quiz systems, there is still room for improvement in the ways they are implemented and how they are accessed within the management system itself. Although course management systems offer a wide range of tools, faculty primarily use the "static" tools for storing syllabi and class materials, making announcements, and handling administrative tasks [3]. Since these programs have become so ingrained in the education experience, why do most users find the experience of using them for quizzes so undesirable? We want to know so that a better system for web learning can be designed and implemented to improve the learning of students and the educational abilities of teachers at all levels of education with a web based exam and grade system that is intuitive and pleasurable to use.

Historically, course management systems are rigid, clunky, programs that take months of training to use to their full potential because all of the features offered are either hard to navigate to or find. On the tools entry for Blackboard there are over 15 different options to choose from including: a grade book, announcements, a discussion board, a glossary of terms, and many more items used less frequently. While all of these are helpful features or provide useful information it is overwhelming for the typical user who only needs to access one feature at any given time. A professor at the University of Wisconsin River Falls stated "I started using the CMS so I could have online quizzing capability. I have been disappointed with its limited functionality and inflexibility."[3] This resentment for the online quiz system is something that can be avoided with some improvements. The quiz systems implemented by most course management systems are typically limited to asking certain types of questions that may not be appropriate for all courses. In the case of mathematics it is incredibly difficult to ask a quiz question that allows for showing the steps a student took to reach their answer. This can be very relevant to offering partial credit when a student answers incorrectly but did the majority of the given task correctly. To take Blackboard for an example, it only allows a single correct answer to their quiz questions and many educators like to implement questions that ask the student to mark several correct answers from a list of a few options. By adding these features to the quiz system we hope to make user generated quizzes more commonplace in the class room without sacrificing the freedoms associated with the pencil and paper style examination.

One of the nicest features of a course management system is the interoperability between the different features. A student can take a quiz on Blackboard, and once they are finished they would be able to check their scores instantly; a teacher requires assuming no further grading. This instant feedback allows the student to review material, and compare their scores with the class average while seeing exactly what they might not understand fully and need to work on; thus driving better focus in the course. This also is an important reason the quiz system should be incorporated into the rest of a CMS so that grades can be immediately recorded without additional human transcribing. Blackboard also gives students and teachers access to supplemental materials that would be difficult to access otherwise. On the Central Michigan University web page about why to use Blackboard one of the reasons listed is that "a growing number of textbook publishers are making materials and test item pools available for use in Bb."[3] This means students have more access to the materials they need to succeed along with other course materials their professors may have uploaded to the course page. This ever increasing amount of available information helps make it easier than ever to provide a valuable CMS to educators and students eager to save time and effort using a well-designed system.

3. Application Techniques

The implementation of our project was done in a software engineering environment. First our idea for our quiz and grade system was solidified. After this we began to design models for how the data will be displayed and accessed to various user types which were also designed in this phase. When we had a fair understanding of how we wanted to store and display our data we began to design our user interface, the database and the tables it would contain, and decided on which tools we were going to use to accomplish this. Once this was agreed upon and planned, we were ready to begin our implementation of a web based quiz system that was both easy to use and understand.

Our implementation of a course management system runs on the .net framework, and will be hosted on Microsoft Server. It uses server-side scripting to retrieve and format the data, as well as client-side scripting to display the formatting. The interface of the application will have a common theme that will be established on the homepage of the application; a simple and user-friendly system for use in the classroom. This will provide the user with a sense of familiarity with the system almost instantly because access to each feature is readily available from the landing page via an easy to interpret panel system. The panel system makes used of meaningful images with labels to make navigation as streamlined as possible. The interface will use only components that are necessary to the pages functioning to avoid cluttering the "real estate" available to the page. The pages will have dynamically generated content depending on the task that needs to be accomplished. This task will take into account a number of factors starting with the user type, then considering the courses the user is a member of, and finally the specific quiz or exam the user wishes to observe. The webpage will be displayed using the HTML format, and it will be stylized with CSS. The questions and grades are stored in a database and are retrieved using SQL based on the user and the courses they are currently enrolled in. When a student attempts to access either part of the system, the server will create the page using C#, and user will be directed to the student page. This will have options to either view grades or take a quiz or test if any of their course instructors have assigned them. When a teacher attempts to access either part of the system, they will be directed to the teacher page. This page will have options to edit grades in the case of an error, or create a quiz or test assignment. When an admin accesses either part of the system, they will be directed to the admin page. This will be more oriented towards viewing the database information rather than a "form" style page. They will be able to edit anything they need to weather it is question modification or score updating, the admin will be able to correct any errors experienced by teachers and students. All types of users will be required to log in before information will be presented to them. This is a standard security procedure and is very important because student specific score information is sensitive and should not be made available to the public domain without the express consent of the student. Therefore these login settings are necessary and achieve the desired level of security without adding too much hassle for each end user. The authentication is done through Active Directory. There will also be a FAQ section to provide help for any issues that may arise. It will answer questions as well as show a step-by-step guide through the entire process of creating a quiz or taking one.

Quizzes will be created in a very basic way, to begin creating a quiz all that is required from the user is a name for the quiz and a course for which the quiz is designed. With this, a quiz is inserted into the database where it is assigned a unique identifier that will be used to retrieve the information about that quiz. After the quiz is created the user can add questions to the quiz one at a time by first selecting a question type and then entering the user prompt for the question. From here it will be necessary to add any other information required by the question, for instance, a multiple choice question would require the user to enter in at least two choices for the quiz taker to choose from. There is no limit to how many options may be added but there must at least be two. During this phase the quiz creator is also asked to mark the correct answer(s) to the given question so that automatic grading can occur when students finish their quiz or exam. One other important aspect to question creation is that the user can specify a point value to each question as they create it to provide weight to questions that matter more to the students fundamental understanding of the topic at hand. A default value of ten points per question is set to begin with otherwise. After all questions are added, the total point value for the quiz is determined and displayed accordingly. Admin and educator users can also view a sample quiz to make sure that the information that they desired to convey is displayed properly. If any mistakes should occur, they can be edited and fixed with ease. After the quiz is successfully completed the educator can set a date for the quiz to be due by, and also a date that determines when the assignment should become visible to the students enrolled in the course for which the assignment was designed. This concludes our basic implementations of quiz creation, initialization, and storage for our projects CMS.

4. Empirical Studies

After speaking with professors that use Blackboard at Central Michigan University and reviewing the opinions expressed by Glenda Morgan in her study, we have determined a few features that should make our system a better experience for users with a teaching background. One of our key goals for the system is that it will not experience visible downtime. This was one of the biggest issues that we have found with Blackboard. The fact that Blackboard is such an important system means that it should not be offline ever, and if it is, should be down for as short a time period as possible. Each time a server goes down, it will result in inaccessible assignment pages, and the chance increases that a student will not be able to complete an assignment before the scheduled due date. This can create issues for teachers as well when students ask for extensions on assignments because they couldn't complete them at due to the unexpected down time they could not plan for. This hassle is one aspect of online education management systems we hope we can bypass to make the web education experience more smooth and enjoyable for all parties involved. In higher education students are working on assignments at all hours of the day and will need to access a course management system like Blackboard at a moments notice. We will use high quality equipment to ensure that there are minimal outages, and take advantage of modern technology to achieve a high level of service. This will be one of the most difficult aspects to perfect because there are several variables we cannot control that could lead to server downtime but we hope to mitigate these chances by allocating resources mindfully and otherwise managing our resources well.

We have also found that students have taken issue when a quiz or test becomes interrupted; the student is locked out and cannot complete the test due to connectivity problems on the server side of operations. This can be very frustrating to students because it is as if their time limit on the exam is unexpectedly cut short when they become locked out due to connection failure. Since quizzes are typically already open internet, we will be more lax with the security of the student, meaning that if their connection gets interrupted, we can just let them continue where they left off, rather than going through the hassle of proving that the network failed. Teachers have also had issues in the past with the limitations of the types of questions they can include in a quiz or test. Our system allows for a wide variety of question types. We will allow for multiple choice, short answer, images, and even videos. Using these forms of media will provide a much better system than the one currently in place because it provides greater flexibility to educators enabling them to ask types of questions impossible to provide in paper, like a video prompt.

Teachers will also need to have a very straight-forward grade input system to make their lives easy. It needs to have every student on the same page, and should not require the teacher to "load" a page in order to change the grades of a different student. Current systems only view the grades of one student at a time and we hope our multi-student view system can make entering grades much faster for teachers and professors who will use our system. We believe that making the grading system easy for teachers is an important step in designing a successful CMS because without accurate grade information, the statistics that we wish to display will not be accurate. By making the grade entering process simple and quick we foster a web environment that will be able to display useful information to teachers and students alike so long as the important data entry is completed. These statistics are an important form of feedback for both teachers and students. Teachers can see class averages over time and for specific assignments with a few button clicks. Students can track their progress in the course throughout the semester and easily calculate what grades they may need on future assignments so that they can earn their desired course grade. We hope that this system can help end the lack of information that leads to students guessing at their current class standings at the end of semesters. We also wish to display to the student how their score compares to the class average for specific assignments or for the course as a whole.

We have also had many complaints about the sharp edges of Blackboard. Our system will use more streamlined layouts, and will still convey the school colors for a more aesthetically pleasing appearance. Our goal will be to implement asynchronous javascript and xml or Ajax to help resolve this issue while providing a more dynamic grading experience. This would also allow for a student viewing their grades to see their grade entered in real time as the professor enters it without having to refresh the page. Another issue students seem to have is with understanding the completion status of their grades due to a complex system used by Blackboard. There is also the issue of granting extra credit to assignments which, in Blackboard, is not supported well so workarounds are implemented by educators that leave students with less than accurate results. This is because each teacher that implements an extra credit system is not uniform and often does not convey their extra credit system easily to the student that wants to calculate his or her grade accurately. Our system will use clear and concise language to display the status of a grade. We will also exclude the extra "fluff" implemented by the current generation of course management systems. There are currently very vague words being used as well as extra columns that we do not find necessary. These are unnecessary and will be left out of the initial grades display and will be located in an advanced statistics section for grade viewing. Overall, the system should be very intuitive even for non tech-savvy people, and should easily be a much simpler and reliable system than the system currently in place. In addition to personal grades we want it to be easy for educators to compare individual scores with the course average without additional calculations on their behalf. This way educators and students can accurately gauge performance on both an individual level and at the class level. This is important to teachers who want to create a class average of say seventy percent so they can determine the curve they want to apply to students grades and for educators who wish to gauge how well their material is getting across to their pupils. This self-assessment tool should help educators refine their methods further into what methods of teaching work best for specific course material. Also this growth helps the teachers become better at their work, and will improve the learning environment both inside and outside the classroom.

When implementing our design we faced some limitations. One obstacle we faced was trying to find a server to host our website. Because we could not find one for more permanent use, we hosted our pages locally to run a working prototype of our design. We were successfully able to add users to our system that could design quizzes relatively easily just as we had hoped for. We also had limited availability of the tools we desired to work with in the class computer lab so when we did host our project, only a small subset of group members were available to view the end result and the demos we wished to show had to be pre-recorded.

5. Other Considerations

Current course management systems are confusing for the educators who do not have much background in using technology, specifically web applications. Some educators are hesitant to use course management systems because they can have a steep learning curve for them to create quizzes without having taken training courses or calling assistance from university technical support. With our new course management systems quiz creator, the user interface is easy to use and understand. The quiz creator is developed to be a simple step by step process that will not slow down a more advanced user, but will also facilitate learning the system for the novice user. We want our system to be easy to learn but we do not want a "hand holding" process to get in the way of experienced users because if the creation system itself slows down the user, it will cause a reluctance to return to the program after the required skills to create assignments have been acquired.

The system is very intuitive even for new users of the system because it is designed with non-tech savvy people in mind by hiding the unnecessary materials in the quiz creator and exam pages. This way the average user has the basic commands and features laid out before them without the clutter and confusion of the current generation of course management systems. Buttons are clearly labeled so the user can go directly to where they want to go and use the added functions, as the user deems necessary. This made the system simple to navigate and user-friendly without sacrificing too much in terms of functionality. Aside from simplicity, the new course management system saves time over the existing Blackboard system by utilizing features that are easy to operate, automatically saving changes made to quizzes (i.e. answering questions, creating questions, etc.) and the grade book periodically, and by being optimized for use in todays high speed world. The entire process is fairly stream lined because it is designed to focus on one step at a time. This is advantageous for many reasons. It minimizes end user confusion and maximizes time spent actually producing new content for quiz or exam assignments. It also helps the web pages for quiz creation small which speed up load times. If the system is too slow or unresponsive for too long it can leave a sour taste in a user's mouth which may lead them to shy away from online course management suites in the future, which is the last thing we want to do.

Online cheating is another one of the problems with the current course management systems like Blackboard, where a teacher cannot assure the integrity of test result. This problem is addressed with the new Course management system. Once the quiz or exam is started, the browser is locked with the test questionnaire and the examinee cannot open tabs other than those that are part of the current exam. This system will prevent students to search answers from online sources, thus online cheating is avoided without the need of third party applications. There are other methods of cheating that students could potentially perpetrate that are beyond the control of this system, but they are the same methods that could be used to cheat on a traditional pencil and paper examination that educators know to look for already so this we view as a non issue.

6. Conclusion

The problem with present Blackboard like course management system quiz implementations is that users can create quizzes and examinations, but they are limited to a specific format that yields undesirable examinations. Because of this, not every department at an educational institution can benefit fully from the system. Questions that are shoehorned into said format can also lead to confusion among students, thus leading to more time spent making corrections. Based on interviews from various teachers, some seldom use the Blackboard system because they are not comfortable to use it, while others do not use Blackboard to conduct examination because of its lack of functions that they need.

The process of implementing our system has been a valuable software engineering experience for everyone involved. It provided us with valuable insights into what a project feels like to work on within the phases of a development cycle. We look forward to being able to apply this information in the future on other software engineering and development projects. By carrying out this implementation of a quiz system we believe that we are all stronger developers than before we designed our project. A CMS was a fitting project for us because we had experience working with them as students in the past and our group experience featured knowledge of developing web pages. We also experienced time limitations at the end of the semester that resulted in product that could benefit from the addition of a few features we did not have time to fully implement.

By using our modern course management system, Teachers are able to create quizzes, assignments, and exams with broader functions that are not available with present course management systems, such as mathematical equation symbols and the ability to upload multimedia directly into questions. The system also handles the various interruptions that can happen during an exam letting the users start from where they left off by using auto save features. These features save users a plethora of time that may have otherwise been spent ironing out problems with connectivity or reentering answers that were not saved. Students can view their grade right after the examination as well as view scores with the class average, after any weighting, as well as any other operations that may be applied to a student's grade, provided that the assignment was in a format that lends itself to automated grading like multiple choice exams or matching questions. Even if the entire exam is not made up of these types of questions, a grade for the portion of the assignment that was made up of them can be calculated and returned to the user at the time of exam completion. This means that any exam that uses a combination of question styles that can automatically be graded with question styles that do require grading will be inherently faster to grade for teachers. The questions left to grade will be the more difficult styles to grade like short answer, and essay questions, but that is to be expected. Even by just grading the simpler question styles, the time spent by educators grading should be reduced by a factor proportional to the number of easy to grade questions they place on their examinations.

The result of using a cleaner, simpler system is clear. A user-friendly interface, easy to use, anxiety free for students, will increase the students and teachers interest in using the system. The integrity of the course is maintained via a competent security system and the current problems of the users are addressed accordingly. Through further revisions of our system, we will continue to design a product that is not focused on having a feature for every occasion, but making the course management system a fully integrated piece of the modern classroom.

References

1. Carmean, C., & Haefner, J. (2002). Mind over matter: Transforming course management systems into effective learning environments. *EDUCAUSE Review*, *37*(6), 26-34. Retrieved from http://net.educause.edu/ir/library/pdf/erm0261.pdf

2. Kahn, Badrul H, (1997). Web-Based Instruction. Educational Technology Publications Inc., Eaglewood Cliffs New Jersey.

3. Morgan, G. (2003). *Faculty use of course management systems*. (Vol. 2). Boulder, Colorado: EDUCAUSE. Retrieved from http://net.educause.edu/ir/library/pdf/ers0302/rs/ers0302w.pdf

4. *Why use Blackboard?*. (n.d.). Retrieved from http://www.cmich.edu/academics/off_campus_online/Bb_CMU/Pages/Why_use_Blackboard.aspx

Content Development for Distance Education in Advanced University Mathematics Using Mizar

Takaya IDO[1], Hiroyuki OKAZAKI[1], Hiroshi YAMAZAKI[1], Pauline Naomi KAWAMOTO[1], Katsumi WASAKI[1], and Yasunari SHIDAMA[1]
[1]Shinshu University, 4-17-1 Wakasato Nagano-city, Nagano 380-8553, Japan

Abstract— *The Mizar project focuses on the formalization of mathematical theorems and their proofs using a formal descriptive language. It is an international joint project concerning the construction of a library system that will make automatic verification possible by a computer. The purpose of this study is to develops contents for distance education programs in advanced university mathematics using Mizar, and here we report on the current situation of this study.*

Keywords: Formal Verification, Mizar, Euclidean Algorithm

1. Introduction

When teaching mathematical content to students who have varying levels of knowledge and understanding, making the material perfectly understandable without lapses in logic can be exceedingly difficult. This is not simply limited to the topic of logic algorithms covered in the present study. Even if an extensive textbook were to be used, a student would still need to make an effort to "read between the lines," and a teacher would need to teach in accordance with the student's level of understanding. In addition, to confirm and consolidate that understanding, in all likelihood, it would also be necessary for the students solve some part2.1 of a proof problem and completely describe the logical steps taken. Is it truly possible for teachers to explain the material in the text to each student individually, correct and edit solutions submitted by all students, and follow up according to instructions until the student's answers are complete? As a solution to these issues, we have been researching and developing a system of teaching materials that uses the formal mathematical descriptive language of the Mizar processing system to support teachers.[1][1] Mizar is an international joint project in which current work includes using formal mathematical descriptive language to provide formal descriptions of present mathematical theorems and their proofs, thereby forming a system of automatic checking via a computer and creating a library.[2] The authors are participants in this project, and the system of teaching materials introduced in this study is being developed using the achievements of Mizar as a resource. We developed the formalized library on the Euclidean algorithm;[3] it is also recorded in the Mizar Project Library and is publically available at

http://mizar.uwb.edu.pl/version /current/html/ntalgo_1.html

These libraries store complete documentation of every single result and proof and link all necessary theorems to the mathematical system of axioms from which they are derived. They are presented as self-complete libraries that use formal mathematical descriptive language and have no need for outside referencing. Upon clicking the "proof" button on the webpage, every line of the proof is displayed. Furthermore, links for the definitions of all theorems and terminology used in each library are included, so that by continually linking back to definitions, one can return back to the axiom system of set theory. The Mizar system is based on Tarski-Grothendieck (TG) set theory and first-order predicate logic. Using a formal descriptive language based on this, Mizar documents formal proofs of theorems and automatically detects mistakes in a proof by using a processing system known as the Mizar Proof Checker. Our current research aims to set up a system of teaching materials that will integrate both the libraries and proof checker with a general-use CMS system.(CMS system + Mizar)[4][5][6] A group of students used this system. We present the data and discuss the lessons learned.

2. MANUSCRIPT PREPARATION

In the process of developing the teaching materials, it is necessary to have a text where all contents of the teaching materials are formally described, their validity is expressed as mathematical propositions, and descriptions of complete proofs are provided. The full formal developed in this study are available at http://mizar.uwb.edu.pl/version/current/html/ntalgo_1.html . Because of presentational constraints, from this point on, please refer to the above URL for details whenever "reference webpage" is mentioned. As mentioned in the Introduction, when clicking on the "proof" button on the webpage, one can read the complete proof. Furthermore, links are included for all terminology and current theorems used in the library. In this section, we provide an overview of how this works.[7][8] The Euclidean algorithm is a well-known algorithm where, given two arbitrary integers a and b, the greatest common divisor is obtained through repeated calculation. An example implementation in Python is shown, as Code 2-1. There are many ways to express this algorithm

Table 1: Code 2-1

```
def gcd(a, b):
  Return the greatest common
  divisor of 2 integers a and b
  a, b = abs(a), abs(b)
  while b:
  a, b = b, a % b
  return a
```

in formal mathematical descriptive language. A simple way is to use the given integers a, b- to be exact, their absolute values abs (a) and abs (b),respectively- as initial values and then express them in terms of two successive constructive procedures, shown below, in the form of progressions of natural numbers.(Mizar Code 2-2) The equal to sign (=)

Table 2: Mizar Code 2-2

```
A . 0 = abs a
B . 0 = abs b
A . (i + 1) = B . i
B . (i + 1) = (A . i) mod (B . i)
( for all natural number i )
```

is a symbol literally expressing that the terms on both sides of the sign are equal to each other, unlike in the C programming language, where the value of the variable on the right replaces that of the variable on the left. Thus, in the process of finding the greatest common divisor of a, b, we took the operating variables temporarily used to keep the results in memory and expressed them as progressions with subscripts that indicate the number of times the calculations are successively repeated. Furthermore, to express the stopping conditions for the aforementioned algorithm, as well as express what equates to the return value of the function (e.g., in a programming language) obtained when the stopping conditions are satisfied, we introduced the set of all subscripts "i" of the number progression B satisfying the stopping conditions, in other words, B. i = 0 (Mizar Code 2-3) and minimum natural number belonging to this subset of

Table 3: Mizar Code 2-3

```
{ i where i is natural number
such that B.i = 0}
```

natural numbers (Mizar Code 2-4) giving it the value "A.i0."

Table 4: Mizar Code 2-4

```
i0= min { i where i is natural
number such that B.i = 0}
```

Here i0 is the first subscript- the natural number indicating the number of times the algorithm is repeated- to satisfy the stopping conditions. Below is the formal expression using Mizar language, which expresses the process for obtaining the greatest common divisor of a, b using the method mentioned above, by defining it as the functional application ALGO_GCD (a, b). Reference Mizar Code 2-5. INT and NAT, respectively, are expressions for all integers

Table 5: Mizar Code 2-5

```
definition
let a, b be Element of INT ;
func ALGO_GCD (a,b)
-> Element of NAT means
ex A, B being sequence of NAT st
( A . 0 = abs a \& B . 0 = abs b
\& ( for i being Element of NAT holds
( A . (i + 1) = B . i \& B . (i + 1)
= (A . i) mod (B . i) ) )
\& it = A . (min* { i
where i is Element of
   NAT : B . i = 0 }));
existence (WEB page reference)
uniqueness (WEB page reference)
end;
```

and natural numbers. "st" is an abbreviation for "such that." The English pronoun "it" is a natural number, and represents ALGO_GCD (a, b) itself (in other words, what equates to the return value of the function in a programming language). For the above definition to be mathematically valid, the natural number "it" satisfying the description above needs to exist and also needs to be uniquely identified in relation to a, b; Mizar calls these conditions "existence" and "uniqueness," respectively. In the formally described definition including the proofs which show that both can be established is necessary. This enables us to deductively prove that the computation algorithm is feasible for any given integers a, b, which always stops and gives some value as a return value. This alone, however, is not sufficient to inductively prove the validity of the above algorithm; the fact that ALGO_GCD (a, b), defined in relation to given arbitrary integers a, b, actually gives us the greatest common divisor of a, b is asserted below as a proposition and is proven. Reference ALGO_GCD.

Table 6: ALGO_GCD

```
theorem
for a, b being Element of INT holds
ALGO_GCD (a,b) = a gcd b
proof (WEB page reference)
end;
```

3. Teaching Materials and Practice Problems

As stated in Section 1 and explained in Section 2, the formal descriptions in http://mizar.uwb.edu.pl/version /current/html/ntalgo_1.html

are, similar to the definitions and theorems already in the Mizar library, a self-complete text without the need of outside references. Each theorem includes a complete proof. For any referenced or applied theorems, definitions, or terminology, links are posted to the reference source and the system of axioms in set theory can eventually be reached by following these links. We developed a textual commentary on this formalized account of the Euclidean algorithm as teaching material. This text commentary is stored in the general-use course management system Moodle. We highlight the substantial sections of this commentary below.

3.1 Feasibility of the Computational Algorithm

Given integers a, b, to show that the computational algorithm is always feasible, proving the existence, as well as uniqueness in relation to a, b, of natural number "it" as the return value of the function appearing in the formal definition Mizar Code 2-5 is necessary. For this, showing that the natural number progressions A and B satisfying the recurrence formula (2-2 reposted) can always be constructed from the

Table 7: Mizar Code 2-2

```
A . 0 = abs a
B . 0 = abs b
A . (i + 1) = B . i
B . (i + 1) = (A . i) mod (B . i)
( for all  natural number i )
```

given integers a, b is first necessary. The natural number progressions A, B are functions to themselves from the set of all natural numbers NAT, and the possibility of constructing A, B depends on the proof of existence of A, B by recursive functions based on the recurrence formula Mizar Code 2-2. To prove the existence of recursive functions, an existence theorem of functions, based on set theory axioms, is used. In the teaching materials, this is formalized using the scheme provided below, which corresponds to the recurrence formula Mizar Code 2-2 and general recursive definitions stored in the Mizar library. Reference Mizar Code RECDEF_2:sch 2. In the teaching materials, a detailed explanation is provided, mainly using the following lemma. (Mizar Code 3-1) For practice problems, to reinforce understanding of the recursive concept, a proof and description problem is given on the existence theorem of the number progression satisfying the recurrence formula that defines the Fibonacci sequence.

http://cai2.cs.shinshu-u.ac.jp/mizar /moodle/mod/mizar/view.php?id=787

3.2 Stopping of the Computational Algorithm

In addition to showing the possibility of constructing (or the existence of) the natural number progressions A, B that

Table 8: Mizar Code RECDEF_2:sch 2

```
scheme :: RECDEF_2:sch 2
DoubleChoiceRec{
F1() -> non empty set ,
F2() -> non empty set ,
F3() -> Element of F1(),
F4() -> Element of F2(),
P1[ set , set , set , set , set ] } :
ex f being Function of NAT,F1()
ex g being Function of NAT,F2() st
( f . 0 = F3() \& g . 0 = F4()
\& ( for n being Element of NAT holds
P1[n,f . n,g . n,f . (n + 1),
  g . (n + 1)]))
provided
A1: for n being Element of NAT
for x being Element of F1()
for y being Element of F2()
ex x1 being Element of F1()
ex y1 being Element of F2()
st P1[n,x,y,x1,y1]
```

Table 9: Mizar Code 3-1

```
for a, b being Element of
INT ex A, B being sequence of NAT st
( A . 0 = abs a \& B . 0 = abs b
\& ( for i being Element of NAT holds
( A . (i + 1) = B . i \& B . (i + 1)
= (A . i) mod (B . i) ) ) )
```

satisfy the recurrence formula Mizar Code 2-2, it also needs to be shown that the repeated calculation algorithm stops at a finite number of iterations. For this, the existence of the set of all subscripts "i" of the natural number progression B satisfying the stopping condition B.i = 0 (2-3 reposted), as

Table 10: Mizar Code 2-3

```
{ i where i is natural number
 such that B.i = 0}
```

well as the existence of a minimum natural number belonging to this subset of natural numbers (2-4 reposted), must

Table 11: Mizar Code 2-4

```
i0= min{ i where i is natural number such that B.i = 0}
```

be shown. For this, the well-known theorem "a minimum element exists for a non-empty set of natural numbers" is used. In addition, in terms of the existence itself of the set Mizar Code 2-3, there is a formal proof based on the axiom schema of separation in set theory. To show that this set is not empty, we use proof by contradiction and begin with the assumption that a natural number "i," which gives B.i = 0, does not exist. It is then shown that the natural number progressions A, B from the recurrence formula Mizar Code 2-2 are decreasing progressions, and as a result, A.i and B.i must have been negative values; thus, contradicting the fact that A.i and B.i are natural numbers. In the teaching material, this section is explained using the following lemma, (Mizar Code 3-2) and the meaning of proof by contradiction is also discussed. For practice problems, we provided fill-in-the-blank questions based on the description of this proof and a proof by contradiction proof problem involving a proposition related to simple set operations.

Table 12: Mizar Code 3-2

```
for a, b being Element of INT
for A, B being sequence
of NAT st A.0
= abs a \& B.0
= abs b \&
( for i being Element of NAT holds
(A . (i + 1) = B . i \& B . (i + 1)
= (A . i) mod (B . i))) holds
{ i where i is Element of NAT :
B . i = 0 } is
non empty Subset of NAT
```

http://cai2.cs.shinshu-u.ac.jp/mizar /moodle/mod/mizar/view.php?id=792

3.3 Uniqueness of the Return Value in Relation to a, b

Under the formal definition Mizar Code 2-5, the uniqueness of natural number "it" (the return value of function ALGO_GCD (a, b)) in relation to a, b, comes down to its uniqueness in relation to initial values A.0 = abs (a) and B.0 = abs (b) of the natural number progressions A and B satisfying the recurrence formula Mizar Code 2-2. For this, it must be proven that the two pairs of natural number progressions A, B1 and A2, B2, both satisfying the same initial conditions

```
A1.0= abs( a), B1.0= abs(b),
A2.0= abs( a), B2.0= abs(b),
```

and having been constructed by the recurrence formula Mizar Code 2-2, are consistent as functions to themselves from the set of all natural numbers NAT- in other words, as functions, they must satisfy verbatims A1 = A2 and B1 = B2. To this end, it must be shown that the verbatims A1.i = A2.i and B1.i = B2.i hold for any arbitrary natural number "i" and that mathematical induction is used in relation to "i." There are a number of mathematical induction schemes stored in the Mizar library, and in the teaching material presented here, we used the following Mizar Code 3-3 In the teaching material, commentary is provided on this section, which includes a number of different forms of mathematical induction. As practice problems, we provided a fill-in-the-blank problem based on the proof in this section, and, to ensure that students become more familiar with mathematical induction proofs, we also provided a proof problem involving progressions of natural numbers, with the proposition shown here: Figure 2

Table 13: Mizar Code 3-3

```
scheme
NatInd{ P1[ Nat] } :
for k being Nat holds P1[k]
provided
A1: P1[ 0 ] and
A2: for k being Nat st P1[k]
holds P1[k + 1]
```

http://cai2.cs.shinshu-u.ac.jp/mizar /moodle/mod/mizar/view.php?id=784

The students are asked to fill in a section of the proof in the blank space. The system performs a check, and students can continue studying by themselves until no errors remain.

3.4 Proving that the Return Value, ALGO_GCD (a, b), Provides the Greatest Common Divisor of a, b

As previously mentioned, to deductively prove the validity of the algorithm, it needs to be proven that ALGO_GCD (a, b), defined in terms of the given arbitrary integers, actually gives the greatest common divisor of a, b; for this, a proof is provided with the proposition shown below. (Mizar Code NATLGO 1:2) The greatest common factor "a gcd b" of a, b is defined in the Mizar library as follows : (Mizar Code a gcd d) "Nat" and "Integer" are the variable forms of natural numbers and integers, respectively. The pronoun "it" represents "a gcd b" itself (as previously noted) and equates to the return value of the function in programming language. In addition, the predicate "x divides y," defined in terms of integers x, y, is defined as follows. (Mizar Code x divides y) To prove "ALGO_GCD (a, b) = a gcd b" of the theorem above, it first needs to be shown that

Table 14: Mizar Code NATLGO_1:2

```
theorem
for a, b being Element of INT holds
ALGO_GCD (a,b) = a gcd b
```

Table 15: Mizar Code a gcd d

```
definition
let a, b be Integer;
func a gcd b -> Nat means
( it divides a \& it divides b \&
( for m being Integer st m divides a
\& m divides b holds m divides it ));
existence
uniqueness
commutativity ;
end;
```

```
A.i gcd B.i = A.(i+1) gcd B.(i+1)
```

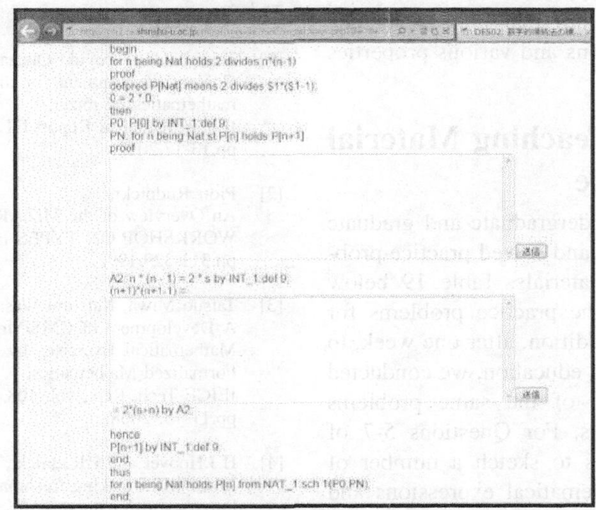

Fig. 1: An example from the teaching material

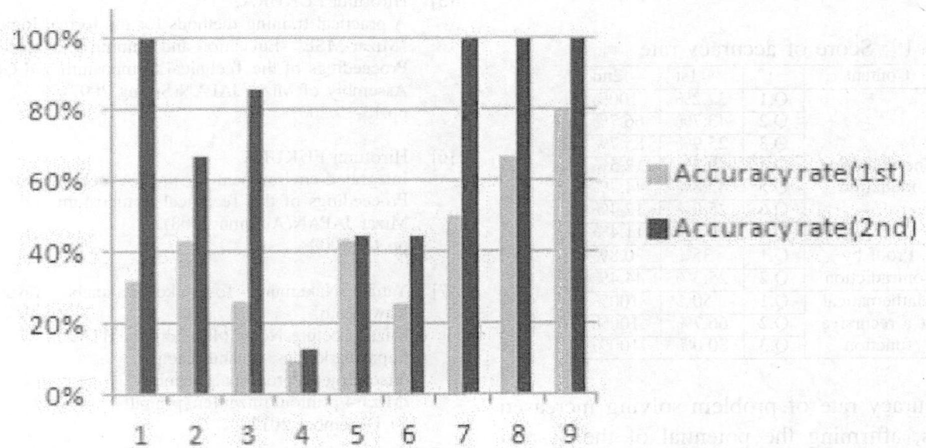

Fig. 2: score of accuracy rate

Table 16: Mizar Code x divides y

```
definition
let i1, i2 be Integer;
pred i1 divides i2 means
ex i3 being Integer st i2 = i1 * i3;
reflexivity
end;
```

holds for any arbitrary "i" of the natural number progressions A, B, obtained by the recurrence formula Mizar Code 2-2. It then needs to be shown that because of this,

```
A.0 gcd B.0 = A.i gcd B.i
```

holds, and finally, when the stopping condition B.i = 0 is satisfied,

```
A.i gcd B.i = A.i gcd 0 = A.i
```

holds. For this, we use (Mizar Code NAT_D:28) stored in

Table 17: Mizar Code NAT_D:28

```
theorem :: NAT_D:28
for m, n being Nat st m > 0 holds
n gcd m = m gcd (n mod m)
```

the library, and the lemma (Mizar Code 3-4) along with

Table 18: Mizar Code 3-4

```
LM6: for a being Element of
NAT holds a gcd 0 = a
```

mathematical induction. For this section, teaching materials are still being created, and we are planning to include commentary on both mod operations and various properties of the gcd.

4. Evaluation of the Teaching Material and Tasks for the Future

As a trial, approximately 20 undergraduate and graduate computer science students studied and solved practice problems from the above teaching materials. Table 19 below outlines the topic and score of the practice problems for each subsection in Section 3. In addition, after one week, to verify whether there is an effect on education, we conducted a second experiment with some of the same problems but different values as parameters. For Questions 5-7 of subsection 3.1, we asked students to sketch a number of simple proofs using regular mathematical expressions and in the second experiment, the questions required knowledge of how to express proof lines in the Mizar language. Fig.3 shows that the accuracy rate of problem solving increased for most questions, affirming the potential of the system as an effective educational tool. For the proof-sketching questions(3.1:5-7), students had some trouble translating mathematical knowledge into the Mizar language, indicating the need for a longer introductory training period for learning Mizar expressions. As mentioned in Section 1, the novelty of this teaching material lies in the fact that a formal mathematical language and a processing system are used to help students write their proofs and a computer is used to automate the explanation of mistakes in an attempted proof. The formal descriptive language used in the teaching materials and practice problems of this study are for students who are majoring in computer science or related fields, who are already familiar with programming languages, should not have any trouble. However, for the student who is relatively unfamiliar with programming languages, continued efforts are needed to lessen the burden of learning the formal language, so that they can focus on understanding and mastering content. In the future, considering measures such as replacing the terminology of formal descriptions with Japanese language might be worth.

Table 19: Score of accuracy rate

Section	Content		1st	2nd
3.1	The definition induction	Q.1	32.2%	100%
		Q.2	43.7%	66.7%
		Q.3	25.9%	85.7%
		Q.4	9.3%	12.5%
		Q.5	42.8%	44.4%
		Q.6	25.0%	17.4%
		Q.7	26.1%	11.4%
3.2	Proof by contradiction	Q.1	35%	30.8%
		Q.2	25.3%	44.4%
3.3	Mathematical of a recursive function	Q.1	50%	100%
		Q.2	66.7%	100%
		Q.3	80.0%	100%

References

[1] Takaya Ido, Hiroyuki Okazaki, Hiroshi Yamazaki, Yasunari shidama, Content development for distance education for advance university mathematics by mizar, IEICE Technical Report ET2012-55 (2012-11), pp.13-17,2012.

[2] Piotr Rudnicki, An Overview of the MIZAR Project, WORKSHOP ON TYPES FOR PROOFS AND PROGRAMS, pp.311-329,1992.

[3] Tatsuo Miwa, Katsumi Wasaki, Noboru Endo, Yasunari Shidama, A Development of CMS/Moodle Assignment Module for Interactive Mathematical Exercises by using Mizar Proof Checking System in Formalized Mathematics, IEICE Tech. Rep., vol. 108, no. 247, ET2008-41, pp.11-16, 2008.

[4] H.J.Hoover and P.Rudnicki, Mizar MSE:making freshman logic formal, http://www.cs.ualberta.ca/p̃iotr/Mizar-MSE/leaflet.ps, 1992.

[5] Hirofumi FUKURA, A practical training methods for the formal logic with proof checker "Mizar-MSE" -Education and training that uses "baby Mizar"-, Proceedings of the Technical Symposium and General Assembly of Mizar JAPAN(Spring 2007), pp.13-19,2007.

[6] Hirofumi FUKURA, Integrated environment for proof checker Mizar-MSE, Proceedings of the Technical Symposium and General Assembly of Mizar JAPAN(Autumn 2008), pp.1-9,2008.

[7] Yatuka Nakamura, Toshihiko Watanabe, Yasushi Tanaka, Pauline Kawamoto, Mizar Lecture Notes (4th Edition, HTML), http://markun.cs.shinshu-u.ac.jp /kiso/projects/proofchecker/mizar /Mizar4/printout/mizar4en_prn.pdf 14 December 2012.

[8] V. Shoup, A Computational Introduction to Number Theory and Algebra, http://www.shoup.net/ntb/ 14 December 2012.

The application of web-tracking method for research of local government units' websites utility

Kesra Nermend, Barbara Wasikowska, and Ammar Shihab
Faculty of Economic and administration, Szczecin University, Szczecin, Poland

Abstract - One of the basic qualities of the region's development Is an information technology, where is the information technology playing essential and vital role in the development of the region. Especially at this time the information technology, it is making progress be developed in the field of Internet and information society, which is makes governments trying hard to improve the interface of electronic Web Pages and makes it suitable for future requirements. As yet, however, there is no constant standard in local government interfaces of the sort used by investment companies to attract investors, customers and other companies. On the other side, the interfaces of local governments do not meet the following requirements. We have analyzed the information of Polish local government web sites because we did not find the ideal qualities required, and that satisfy the requirements of successful websites in the world. The essential goal of this study, is developing Polish local government websites to be more adequate, efficient and Usability for the foreign investor in Poland. The study also aims is extracting a good quality and characteristics from websites to be circulated to the other websites.

Keywords: local government website, web-tracking, information architecture, Usability website, knowledge-base

1 Introduction

The goal of the following protocol is to provide methodological recommendations of optimize Polish local government websites dedicated to foreigner investors in the Polish cities. The study focuses on analyzing and improving the usability usually carried out in relation to commercial online systems such as electronic trading systems, social websites, e-banking or tourist systems. This Study is testing a service facility of Polish local government websites in terms of economic usability for foreigners visiting Poland for tourism, investment and business. The model of structured content focused on improving the information architecture and usability testing. The proposed method allows the selection of the optimal procedure in the local governments in order to achieve an adequate range of information and content provide adequately to the users' needs. The range of design includes the organizational process, navigation project and outlining search systems that would assist the user with obtaining information. The role of study is to help decision-makers to identification of specific website quality lacks. One of the problems of Polish local government websites involved with localization and language selection, which can bear upon the usability of a website. For example, we observed that some city websites have much more information in the Polish language than in English, and increase frustration for foreigner users. In addition, some websites use textual translation engines, which gives results in limited and weak translations.

Previous research has also shown that a user may become frustrated when page-load times exceed 8 to 10 seconds without feedback.

Another problem involves user behavior in different cultures. Some foreigners users have extensive internet experience and some have less, and their interests seriously. French people have different interests from people from the U.S., for example, and both have different interests from Middle Eastern people.

- In the use of multivariate methods analysis, Comparative studies Internet service facility in researching gives us ready to perform the scheduling of the local government websites in terms of usefulness of information for foreigners visiting the Polish local government web site.
- The use of web tracking method in the knowledge base integrated with a web browser can Opportunities and to identify and assess the quality of service information website.

Link methods of analysis multivariate and measurement data allows the development of information structures, which can be more efficient and enhance the interface of Polish local government websites.

Designing complex internet systems requires consideration of a set of functional aspects. Utility, which identified as an attribute specifying the ease of using interactive devices and applications, is becoming increasingly influential. Local government websites usually have different specification and objectives. A study conducted in this area is not as widely implemented as in commercial systems. Recently available publications have exhibited new dedicated research which focuses on systems of certain cities or regions. They can be a decisive factor for foreigners choosing a holiday destination, businessmen looking for investment locations or potential students choosing the place of their future education. Building information infrastructure based on well developed networks and shared database are the contemporary need and prerogative of public institutions. Consequently, The optimization and evaluate procedures in the Polish local Government website and quality of interfaces of cities in order to achieve an adequate range of available information and content relevant to the user's needs. As methods by which citizens can influence the extent of government failure at the local government level, both exit and voice have various limitations [6]. In the last few years, There still does not exist a consensus about how to evaluate the results of the investments in e-government projects. Because the fact that isn't all the results of the e-government innovation processes. On the other hand, the complexity itself of the concept of e-government makes it difficult to define an evaluation system that can be applied to all the areas covered by that concept (e-Democracy, e-Administration, e-Services) [4]. Joint development of the Internet is the process of interaction by a group of local governments cooperating. This process enables citizens to track and trace the status of the interface and access to the site and evaluate the application the modification on the site. [5]. The difference between a website with no visitors from the search engines and a website that is full of visitors from the search engines is optimal. Search Engine Optimization is the difference between loss and profit on the Internet in the local government website. [2]

2. Evaluating website local government:

Web site optimization focuses on how "computer programs" at Google and the other search engines will perceive your website with the goal of getting them to recommend (rankings) your website to as many people as possible who are searching for keywords relating to your products and services.

2.1 Website Design:

For most businesses, the best choice is a combination of both worlds. The website should be well optimized to get search engines and recommend websites. At the same time, the website needs to be well designed to convert "visitors" to buyers.

How to tell a Good Website Optimizer from a Bad Website Optimizer?

There is a few uncomplicated questions make it easy to differentiate between a good and poor website optimizer.

We have seen far too many people lose time, money and sometimes their dreams, because they hired a website company that failed to market their products and services successfully [3]. For years, many people assumed that websites were like magic because they saw the commercials and heard stories of people building websites and getting rich. Many people assumed when create a good website would be soon have lots of new clients wanting to buy your products and services.

The truth is that websites are not magic. A good website that attracts new clients from Google and the other search engines can make your company a substantial profit. On the other hand, a poor website was like putting your advertisement in last year's phone book after everyone has already thrown it in the trash.

3. Methodology:

3.1 Data Collect:

This Study is testing a service facility of Polish local government websites in terms of economic usability for foreigners visiting Poland for tourism, investment and business. The modeling and optimization of the structural content focused on improving the information architecture and usability testing. We Determined the main and sub-main factor in Polish local government websites for collecting data information. Given the limited analysis-oriented research which would also determine some standards for local governmental websites, the methodology proposed for this study is a comparative analysis. This method enables identification of model sites and specifying indicators of multidimensional-input evaluation from the point of usability and information access. In order to evaluate city websites, each of them should be assigned to certain variables that are necessary to determine their suitability. The variables should be selected in a way that would reflect the strengths and weaknesses of the chosen approach. The usefulness of the website to the visitors not residing in a given city has been considered into account. This could be tourists, potential investors, students, etc. The aims of the research is to comparative analysis of websites in selected Polish cities and performing their ranking by means of aggregative vector measurement.

The study involved the analysis of 20 cities, where the information published on the websites available in two languages: Polish, and English. Nine categories have defined, each of them classified into subgroups:

1. Education (kindergartens, elementary schools, middle schools, high schools, colleges, exchanging text books)
2. Tourism and tourist attractions (mountains, rivers, marine areas, forests, monuments, recreational areas, museums)
3. Hotels (4-5 star, 1-3 star hotels, guest houses, motels, youth hostels)
4. Restaurants (pubs and clubs, bars, cafés, casinos, restaurants)
5. Transportation (airports, parking lots, buses, taxi, airport, parking, trams, trains, railway, ticket Price)
6. Accommodation

7. Investments (investment offer, investment services, locations, information about investments, Investment incentives, IT, news and publications)
8. Health (medical hotline, pharmacies, first aid, dentists, English-speaking doctors, emergency Service)
9. Business (commerce Chamber, Business Center Club, economic zones, the city offers, conferences, business and marketing, information and publications)

Within each category, points on a scale of 0 .. 9 awarded, depending on the accessibility of information (By using arithmetic mean value). In this way, we have nine indicators has obtained. The comparative analysis of Polish city websites of aggregative vector measurement has been used.

We began by collecting data from Polish local government websites using 9 factors (education, tourism, investment, health, hotels, restaurants, accommodations, transportation, business). All factors subdivided into different properties ; for example, we have 7 categories related to investment that mean sub-factor (investment offers, investor service, location of investment, information about investment, investment incentives, IT, news and publications). We used a range from 0 to 9 to grade these categories, depending on how much information is available and how long it takes to access. Note that we extracted all information for two languages, Polish and English. All information collected in 2012.

The role of methodology is to help decision-makers to identify the determinants shortfalls in website quality. We created an electronic questionnaire system that finds and stores all user navigation (links Used), and recognizes the web page type using web tracking and a custom-built knowledge base. The system also records all answers with times for each question and stores all of them into a database for analysis.

Table (1): Shows collected data information for the main category in an English language website

Cites	Education	Tourism	Hotel	Restaurant	Transports	Accommodations	Investment	Healthy	Business
Poznan	0	9	9	9	9	5	7	0	0
Szczecin	2	5	9	9	0	0	4	0	0
Warsaw	0	3	2	9	3	2	0	2	5
Krakow	0	2	9	9	9	6	0	9	5
Wroclaw	0	0	0	0	0	0	0	0	0
Gdansk	0	9	9	9	9	9	5	0	5
Lodz	0	2	9	0	9	9	6	9	6
Bydgoszcz	0	5	0	0	1	1	5	5	5
Lublin	0	6	9	0	0	9	5	0	5
Katowice	0	7	0	0	6	0	9	0	9
Bialystok	6	5	0	0	0	0	3	0	3
Gdynia	0	3	0	0	0	0	3	0	0
Czestochowa	0	2	9	0	0	9	0	0	0
Sosnowiec	0	0	0	0	0	0	0	0	0
Radom	0	2	7	9	0	9	7	0	0
Kielce	0	3	6	0	0	6	4	0	4
Gliwice	2	2	4	9	0	4	5	0	0
Torun	2	0	9	9	0	9	2	0	0
Bytom	0	0	0	0	0	0	7	0	0
Zabrze	0	0	0	0	0	0	0	0	0

Table (2): Shows collected data information for the main category in a Polish language website.

Cites	Education	Tourism	Hotel	Restaurant	Transports	Accommodation	Investment	Healthy	Business
Poznan	9	7	9	9	9	9	9	7	5
Szczecin	4	7	8	5	0	0	9	0	0
Warsaw	9	7	4	9	0	4	0	4	2
Krakow	9	6	0	5	9	3	4	0	3
Wroclaw	8	3	9	5	9	9	0	7	8
Gdansk	8	6	9	0	8	9	9	3	5
Lodz	7	3	9	8	6	9	9	5	4
Bydgoszcz	9	3	9	0	7	9	4	5	6
Lublin	0	5	9	0	0	9	8	0	9
Katowice	9	3	4	0	0	4	9	0	3
Bialystok	9	6	4	7	8	4	3	5	2
Gdynia	6	3	0	0	8	0	7	0	0
Czestochowa	8	2	9	0	9	9	6	7	1
Sosnowiec	9	1	3	3	4	3	9	1	1
Radom	9	1	8	8	8	8	7	5	1

Kielce	8	3	5	0	5	5	4	3	6
Gliwice	9	9	4	9	4	4	4	3	5
Torun	1	5	9	9	1	9	8	0	5
Bytom	9	0	0	0	0	0	6	3	0
Zabrze	0	0	3	3	5	3	1	7	4

When we distinguish between (table 1) and (table 2) is clear to find that information in Polish language have much more information than English language. This is mean that local governments do not have an interest in an English language website .

3.2 Primary Questionnaire Form:

After creating 11 questions for three factors of interest (investment, business, tourism), The primary questionnaire form has been tested on people of various cultures in several countries (China, Malaysia, USA, UAE, Iraq, etc.). We selected 5 questions for each factor using a Laggard scale of 1 to 5 and input them into an electronic questionnaire system. The system had built by VB.net.

3.3 Web-tracking and Knowledge base system:

A typical test procedure for the construction of such a measuring method consists of five stages: (1) selection, (2) elimination and (3) normalization of variables, (4) determining the pattern and anti-pattern and (5) synthetic vector measurement. Elaborate model of user test by using electronic questionnaire system. We selected 8 cities for foreign and Polish users using the K-mean method and the Matlab code program. This method will give's Four groups of a city's website.

The system involved in working on knowledge base to recognize the web page type begin the process before the user do answer for each question. We selected three factors (investment, business and tourism) and built a database of keywords and root words for each factor. The system compares the words on a given webpage with the database to classify the web page as one of the three types.

During the user exam, the system stores all navigation browsing for the user (user imprint) into a database, answers the questions (yes/no), time taken to answer, quality of answers (0–9), usability, friendliness, design, name of cities, the number of characters in the last web page accessed, number of links followed, webpage type, and date of registration entry.

PROPOSED SOLUTION STRUCTURE SYNTHETIC VECTOR MEASURE (1)

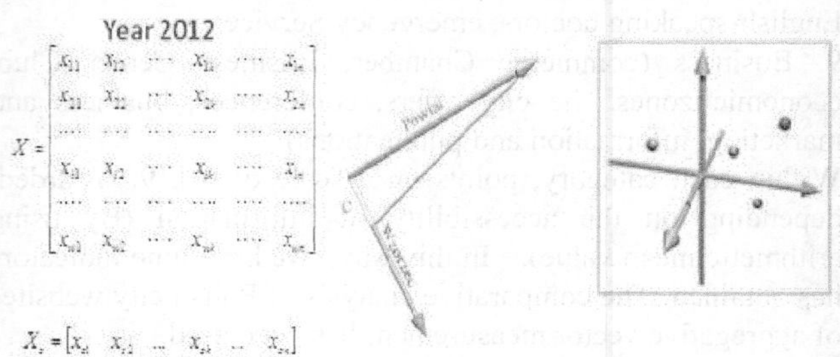

Fig(1): SHOWS PROPOSED SOLUTIONS DESIGN VECTOR MEASURE SYNTHETIC (1)

PROPOSED SOLUTIONS DESIGN VECTOR MEASURE SYNTHETIC (2)

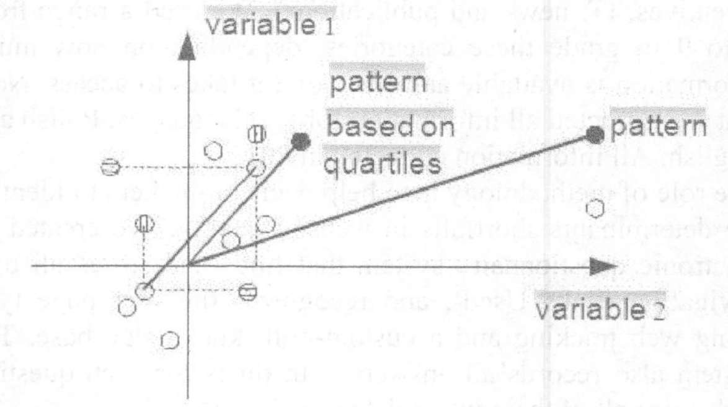

Fig(2): SHOWS PROPOSED SOLUTIONS DESIGN VECTOR MEASURE SYNTHETIC (2).

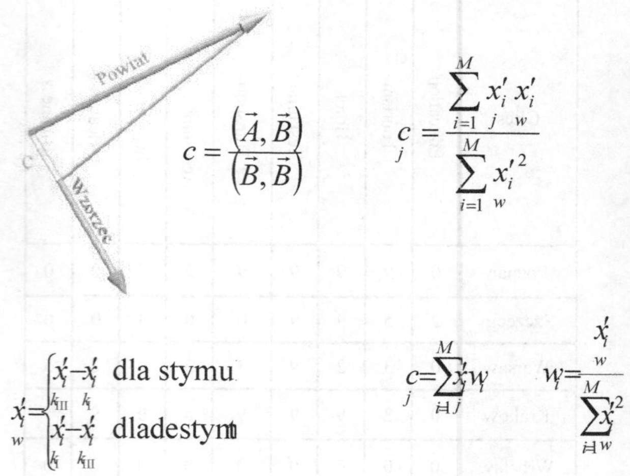

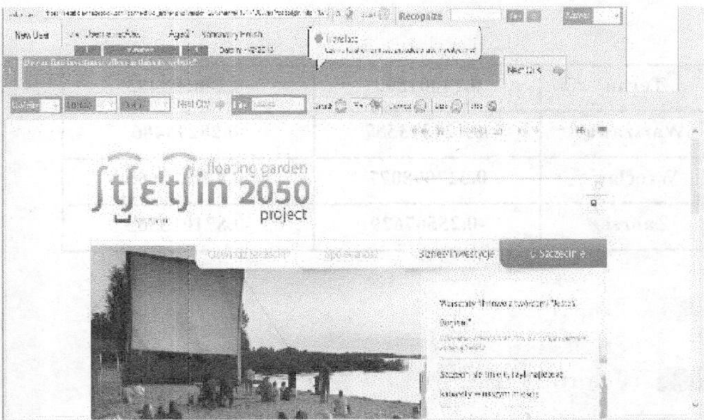

fig(3): shows the implicit explorer worked and allows us to browse inside the electronic questionnaire system. More than 100 users of different cultures participated in the trial of the system.

The system involved in working on the knowledge base to recognize the web page type begin the process before the user do answer for each question. We selected three factors (investment, business and tourism) and built a database of keywords and root words for each factor. The system compares the words on a given webpage with the database to classify the web page as one of the three types.

During the user exam, the system stores all navigation browsing for the user (user imprint) into a database, answers the questions (yes/no), time taken to answer, quality of answers (0–9), usability, friendliness, design, name of cities, the number of characters in the last web page accessed, number of links followed, webpage type, and date of registration entry.

The following data is output by the system for analysis:

1. Username, age, nationality and date of initial registration
2. The name of a city represented by the website in question
3. Answers to questions (yes/no)
4. Breadth of information and ease of access, rated from 0 to 9 (0 = bad, 9 = excellent)
5. Number and name of links visited during the experiment time while the electronic questionnaire was active (user imprint)
6. Time has taken to answer each question
7. Number of characters on the last page viewed before answering
8. Web page types (investment, business, tourism)
9. Web site usability, friendliness and design, as evaluated by the user, also on a 0– 9 scale

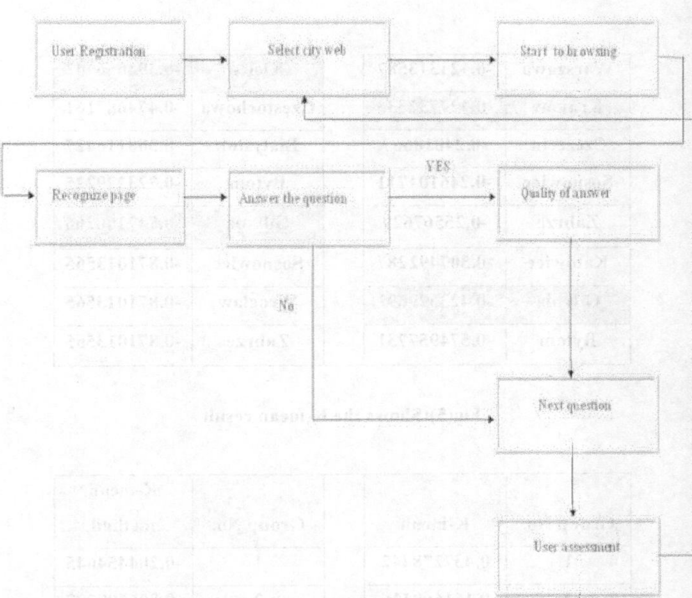

Fig (4) : Shows Diagram of the electronic questionnaire system .

8 cities have been selected during test by foreign and Polish Users for analyzing, four Cities selected by using K-mean method and used Matlab code program to find city rank selection. This method divided into four Groups depending on the neighbors rank of this city's website.

K-mean provided 4 city from 4 groups, and we added additional 4 city because k-mean is not giving Szczecin and Warsaw in it. The suggestion is to added two cities to make more accurate in optimal result table (3,4) shows the rankings of cities with selection.

Table (3,4): Shows cities rank selection in two different language English and Polish.

Polish Language

cities	City rank
Poznań	0.627918795
Łódź	0.356818455
Wrocław	0.327098077
Gdańsk	0.256504776
Radom	0.228583174
Bydgoszcz	0.157219013
Częstochowa	0.154811287
Gliwice	0.137088899
Toruń	0.11001893
Białystok	0.087457734
Lublin	-0.033613078
Kielce	-0.112845762

English Language

cities	City Rank
Gdansk	0.300890218
Łódź	0.254301204
Kraków	0.246476613
Poznan	0.151361403
Radom	-0.158444048
Lublin	-0.170852858
Katowice	-0.190982279
Toruń	-0.248599483
Warszawa	-0.28296486
Szczecin	-0.294884339
Gliwice	-0.342692366
Bydgoszcz	-0.361186167

Warszawa	-0.121313587	Kielce	-0.394656442
Kraków	-0.127732333	Częstochowa	-0.474687161
Szczecin	-0.24010667	Białystok	-0.580116427
Sosnowiec	-0.246101711	Bytom	-0.723229225
Zabrze	-0.25567629	Gdynia	-0.747166266
Katowice	-0.307492287	Sosnowiec	-0.871013565
Gdynia	-0.423679691	Wrocław	-0.871013565
Bytom	-0.574957731	Zabrze	-0.871013565

Fig(5):Shows the K-mean result

Group No.	K-mean	Group No.	K-mean method
1	0.437278442	1	-0.204454645
2	0.161669116	2	-0.806687237
3	-0.399318711	3	-0.400667713
4	-0.180610215	4	0.20575736

1	Łódź	1	Katowice
2	Bydgoszcz	2	Gdynia
3	Gdynia	3	Kielce
4	Kraków	4	Krakow

Table (6):Shows cities selected in the web-tracking system

Cities	Web Polish Language	Web English Language
Białystok	0.087457734	-0.580116427
Bydgoszcz	0.157219013	-0.361186167
Bytom	-0.574957731	-0.723229225
Częstochowa	0.154811287	-0.474687161
Gdańsk	0.256504776	0.300890218
Gdynia	-0.423679691	-0.747166266
Gliwice	0.137088899	-0.342692366
Katowice	-0.307492287	-0.190982279
Kielce	-0.112845762	-0.394656442
Kraków	-0.127732333	0.246476613
Łódź	0.356818455	0.254301204
Lublin	-0.033613078	-0.170852858
Poznań	0.627918795	0.151361403
Radom	0.228583174	-0.158444048
Sosnowiec	-0.246101711	-0.871013565
Szczecin	-0.24010667	-0.294884339
Toruń	0.11001893	-0.248599483
Warszawa	-0.121313587	-0.28296486
Wrocław	0.327098077	-0.871013565
Zabrze	-0.25567629	-0.871013565

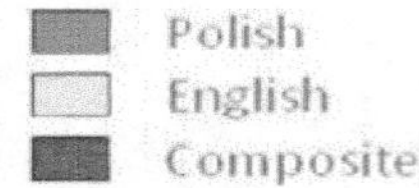

4. Empirical study

Table (7): Shows the values of variables assigned to websites of Polish city in the Polish language.

Towns	Education	Tour ism	Hotels	Restaurants	Transport	Accommodations	Investments	Health	Business
Białystok	9	6	4	7	8	4	3	5	2
Bydgoszcz	9	3	9	0	7	9	4	5	6
Bytom	9	0	0	0	0	0	6	3	0
Częstochowa	8	2	9	0	9	9	6	7	1
Gdańsk	8	6	9	0	8	9	9	3	5
Gdynia	6	3	0	0	8	0	7	0	0
Gliwice	9	9	4	9	4	4	4	3	5
Katowice	9	3	4	0	0	4	9	0	3
Kielce	8	3	5	0	5	5	4	3	6
Kraków	9	6	0	5	9	3	4	0	3
Łódź	7	3	9	8	6	9	9	5	4
Lublin	0	5	9	0	0	9	8	0	9
Poznań	9	7	9	9	9	9	9	7	5
Radom	9	1	8	8	8	8	7	5	1
Sosnowiec	9	1	3	3	4	3	9	1	1
Szczecin	4	7	8	5	0	0	9	0	0
Toruń	1	5	9	9	1	9	8	0	5
Warszawa	9	7	4	9	0	4	0	4	2
Wrocław	8	3	9	5	9	9	0	7	8
Zabrze	0	0	3	3	5	3	1	7	4

When creating a pattern and anti-pattern all the variables were taken as stimulants. Table (7) shows the value of measurement for individual cities. The city of Poznan has the best website. It is clear that the value of measurement for this website significantly varies from all the others. The pieces of information in the examined categories were available on this site. Therefore, this website can be considered exemplary. The two subsequent cities characterized by a much smaller value of measurement, but their sites are similar to each other. The worst websites are those of Bytom and Gdynia. This is mainly due to lack of information in most of the categories. Similar calculations were made for WebPages in English. Table number (8) shows the values of indicators for individual cities. Table (8). The Values of variables for websites in English.

Towns	Education	Tourism	Hotels	Restaurants	Transport	Accommodation	Investments	Health	Business
Białystok	6	5	0	0	0	0	3	0	3
Bydgoszcz	0	5	0	0	1	1	5	5	5
Bytom	0	0	0	0	0	0	7	0	0
Częstochowa	0	2	9	0	0	9	0	0	0
Gdańsk	0	9	9	9	9	9	5	0	5
Gdynia	0	3	0	0	0	0	3	0	0
Gliwice	2	2	4	9	0	4	5	0	0
Katowice	0	7	0	0	6	0	9	0	9
Kielce	0	3	6	0	0	6	4	0	4
Kraków	0	2	9	9	9	6	0	9	5
Łódź	0	2	9	0	9	9	6	9	6
Lublin	0	6	9	0	0	9	5	0	5
Poznań	0	9	9	9	9	5	7	0	0
Radom	0	2	7	9	0	9	7	0	0
Sosnowiec	0	0	0	0	0	0	0	0	0
Szczecin	2	5	9	9	0	0	4	0	0
Toruń	2	0	9	9	0	9	2	0	0
Warszawa	0	3	2	9	3	2	0	2	5
Wrocław	0	0	0	0	0	0	0	0	0
Zabrze	0	0	0	0	0	0	0	0	0

While standardizing, the average value and standard deviation calculated for the websites in the Polish language consider to represent the average value and standard deviation. Similarly, the adopted pattern was the same pattern as the pattern for the websites in Polish language. Thus, the measure in both studies can be related to each other. The results of calculations presented in Table 3,4. It is clear that most cities do not pay close attention to the English versions of their websites. The value of measurement for the website of Poznan, the best in the previous list almost reached zero. In the previous table, the website of Poznan would be placed among average websites. Wroclaw, along with Zabrze fell from third to the last place on the ranking list. This results from the lack of information from the analyzed categories in English. Unique page is that of the city of Gdansk since the value of measurement for the English version of this website is higher than that of its Polish counterpart. This reveals a huge effort of the rulers of this city to attract foreign tourists.

5. Conclusion

The article presented a comparative analysis of selected websites of Polish cities in three languages: Polish, English and German. The analysis was based on a synthetic vector measure. In some cases, the analyzed websites of the cities turned out to be insufficient, especially when it comes to foreign languages. A lot of cities did not publish any useful piece of information for foreigners (in the analyzed categories). Along with which one would expect a large number of foreign tourists. Such research could enable developing a standardized website for the local government unit. Positively influence the position and perception of Polish cities in relation to other cities around the world.

6. Bibliography

[1]. Aczel A., D. (2000) Statystyka w zarządzaniu, Warszawa, PWN.

[2]. Andrew Sears and Julie A. Jacko. (2007). The Human-Computer Interaction Handbook: Fundamentals, Evolving Technologies, and Emerging Applications (2nd ed.). CRC Press

[3]. Kesra Nermend, Jarosław Jankowski, Ammar Shihab,"Comparative study of the quality of the international version of municipal websites in Poland". Published in Journal related to the Congress of the young IT scientists ISM in selected issues of applied information ISBN: 978-83-7518-530-0, University of Szczecin, Poland 2012, Chapter 8, Page 137-156.

[4]. Becker H., Carey C., Acm sigchi curricula for human-computer interaction. http://sigchi.org, 1994.

[5]. Carlos Flavian1, Raquel Gurrea2, Carlos Orus, A heuristic evaluation of websites design for achieving the web successional

[6]. Carstens, Deborah S. and Patterson, Pauline (2005): Usability Testing of Travel Websites. In Journal of Usability Studies, 1 (1) pp. 47-61.

[7]. Costin PRIBEANU, Ruxandra-Dora MARINESCU, Dragoş Daniel IORDACHE, Maria Gheorghe-MOISII, Exploring the Usability of Municipal Web Sites: A Comparison Based on Expert Evaluation Results from Four Case Studies, Informatica Economică vol. 14, no. 4/2010.

[8]. D.D. Iordache, R.D. Marinescu, M. Gheorghe-Moisii, C. Pribeanu, "A case study in formative evaluation of a local administration web site", Revista Română de Interacţiune Om-Calculator, 3, (spe- cial issue RoCHI 2010), pp. 39-56, 2010.

[9]. Doug Fox, Shiva Naidu, Usability Evaluation of Three Social Networking Sites,Usability News (2009)Volume: 11, Issue: 1, Pages: 1-11.

[10]. E.C. Law, M.C. Lárusdóttir, M. Norgaard, (Eds), *Downstream Utility 2007: The Good, the Bad, and the Utterly Useless Usability Evaluation Feedback.* Toulouse, France, November 6th 2007. IRIT Press - Toulouse.

[11]. E.T. Hvannberg, E.L.C. Law, M.C. Larusdotir, "Heuristic Evaluation: Comparing ways of finding an reporting usability problems", *Interacting with Computers*, 19, pp.255-240, 2007.

[12]. G. Cockton, A. Woolrych, "Understanding inspection methods: lessons from an assessment of heuristic evaluation" Blandford, A., Vanderdonckt, J., Gray, P.D. (Eds.), *Proceedings of People and Computers XV*. Springer-Verlag, 2001, 171–182.

[13]. Galitz W.O., The Essential Guide to User Interface Design: And Introduction to GUI Design Principles and Techniques, Wiley Publishing Inc., Indianapolis 2007.

[14]. HELLWIG Z. (1968) Zastosowanie metody taksonomicznej do typologicznego podziału krajów ze względu na poziom ich rozwoju oraz zasoby i strukturę wykwalifikowanych kadr, Przegląd Statystyczny, nr 4.

[15]. International Organization for Standarization. International standards. http://www.iso.org

[16]. Ivory, M., Sinha, R., and Hearst, M. Empirically Validated Web Page Design Metrics in *CHI 2001, ACM Conference on Human Factors in Computing Systems, CHI Letters 3(1)*, 2001

[17]. J. Nielsen, *Usability Engineering*. Academic Press, New York, 1993.

[18]. Jakob Nielsen, Hoa Loranger. Prioritizing Web Usability. New Riders, 2006.

[19]. KOLENDA M. (2006) *Taksonomia numeryczna. Klasyfikacja, porządkowanie i analiza obiektów wielocechowych*. Wrocław, Wydawnictwo Akademii Ekonomicznej im. Oskara Langego we Wrocławiu.

[20]. KUKUŁA, K. (2000) *Metoda unitaryzacji zerowanej*. Warszawa, PWN.

[21]. M. Theofanos, W. Quesenbery, "Towards the Design of Effective Formative Test Reports", In *Journal of Usability Studies,* vol 1, no. 1, 2005, pp. 27-45.

[22]. Mark Pearrow. Funkcjonalnosc stron internetowych. Helion, 2006.

[23]. Mohammad Mannan and P. C. van Oorschot. 2008. Security and usability: the gap in real-world online banking. In Proceedings of the 2007 Workshop on New Security Paradigms (NSPW '07). ACM, New York, NY, USA, 1-14.

[24]. Morville P., Rosenfeld L., Information Architecture for the World Wide Web, O'Reilly, Sebastopol 2006.

[25]. Morville, P. & Rosenfeld, L. (2006). Information Architecture for the World Wide Web: Designing Large-Scale Web Sites, 3rd Edition. Sebastopol, CA: O'Reilly & Associates, Inc.

[26]. Nermend K. (2006) A synthetic measure of sea environment pollution, Polish Journal of Environmetal Studies, Vol. 15 no 4b 2006 s. 127-129.

[27]. Nermend K. (2007) Taxonomic Vector Measure of Region Development (TWMRR). Polish Journal of Environmental Studies, no. 4A.

[28]. Nermend K. (2008) Rachunek wektorowy w analizie rozwoju regionalnego. Szczecin, Wydawnictwo Naukowe Uniwersytetu Szczecińskiego

[29]. Nermend K. (2008) Zastosowanie rzutu wektora do budowy miernika syntetycznego. Przegląd Statystyczny, no. 3.

[30]. Nermend K. (2009) Vector Calculus in Regional Development Analysis, Series: Contributions to Economics, Springer.

[31]. Nielsen J., Loranger H., Prioritizing Web Usability, New Riders, Berkeley 2006

[32]. ONTI, Contents, Available at: http://www.sgp.gov.ar/contenidos/onti/onti.html

[33]. Steve Krug. Nie każ mi myśleć. O życiowym podejściu do funkcjonalności stron internetowych. Helion, Gliwice, 2006.

[34]. Steve Krug. Nie każ mi myśleć. O życiowym

podejściu do funkcjonalności stron internetowych. Helion, Gliwice, 2006.

[35]. Vredenburg, K., Mao, J.-Y., Smith, P. W., & Carey, T. (2002). A survey of user-centered design practice. Proceedings of CHI 2002, 471-478. New York, NY: ACM.

[36]. Younghwa Lee and Kenneth A. Kozar. 2009. Designing usable online stores: A landscape preference perspective. Inf. Manage. 46, 1 (January 2009), 31-41.

[37]. Zimmerman Donald E., Akerelrea Carol A., Usability Testing: An Evaluation Process for Internet Communications, John Wiley & Sons, Inc., The Internet Encyclopedia, 2004

Towards Open Distance and Electronic Learning (OdeL)

Mmafani Serote[1], Mokateko Mathimbi[1] and Munienge Mbodila[2]
[1]School of Computing, University of South Africa, Mukleuneuck Ridge, South Africa
[2]Department of Computer Science, Science foundation Unit, University of Venda, Thohoyandou, South Africa

Abstract - *In the past decade, learning has moved from classrooms and print-based to involve more technology use such as online platforms, mobile devices and Social media. There has been recent widespread use of mobile devices to support learning activities in a bid to keep up with the said future of learning as electronic learning. This research draws from the question of whether media influence learning, and tried to establish if teaching information technology in open distance using electronic media influences learning. Education is viewed as a social practice and therefore online learning environments are expected to support the learning process during social interactions following the social learning theory. Mobile and electronic learning (e-Learning) are fast becoming the new panache in learning. Learners utilize their mobile phones to connect with other learners and to network. In computer mediated communication, learners can work with media like e-mails, short message service (SMS), Facebook, twitter, etc. Generally learners have been noted to use their mobile phones as learning devices to access teaching material located on the module website and also to communicate with the fellow learners on the module, creating focus groups on social networks for live message exchange and content sharing. This study will be a qualitative research and will concentrate on learning using e-learning content such as discussion forums and podcasts as teaching tools to facilitate the learning process.*

Keywords: *Computer Mediated Communication, Learning, Social Media, e-Learning, OdeL, Social Learning, ODLP*

1 Introduction

The process of teaching and learning has progressively moved from classroom and paper mode of delivery to online platforms and mobile devices, particularly towards Social media (Carter 1996). Many researches as asked the question, "Do media influence learning?" This is the question on which this research is based. The research tries to address this question. The use of social media for learning has moved learning to mobile devices and smart phones as most of these have internet browsing capabilities and social networking applications. Lan & Si 2010 comment on the advantage of using these mobile devices for learning purposes by suggesting that because of the mobile devices' portability and availability, they are therefore able to speed up communication and message delivery and subsequently contribute by positively influencing learning.

Chen et al. 2008 support this view by reporting that learners with smart phones and mobile devices were recorded to have logged into the academic reminder system double the number of times as the ones with desktops and laptops. With the widespread use of mobile devices for learning comes a new era, the electronic-learning (e-learning) or learning on the go era. McLoughlin & Lee (in Dabbagh & Kitsantas 2012:3) reflected this phenomenon in yet another way when they noted that learning on demand is becoming a modern society lifestyle type; which suggests that flexibility and mobility in learning are becoming a need for the day to day functioning of society. This growing need for online learning requires for higher education institutions to use technology and media in the delivery of distance learning content. Learners in distance learning institutions no longer want to wait for the post office mail to receive their study content, they now require it on the go; as and when it becomes available. They also require this content to be accessible wherever they are and give rise to the need for e-learning. This is aligned with the views of (Harasim 2002; Swan & Shea 2005) that learning is a social process, which brings about the need for on demand and online delivery of study content.

2 Overview of online (electronic) teaching and learning

E-learning has been defined as the use of information technology tools for learning. This includes formal and informal learning. Cross as well as Selwyn (in Dabbagh & Kitsantas 2012:3) define the concept of formal and informal learning. They assert that formal learning is well structured and driven by institutions such as schools, whereas informal learning is dependent on the learner and obtained in their interactions and experiences and is driven by their areas of interest. E-learning was used for informal learning during the Web 1.0 period however; it has gained popularity into the formal learning space with the introduction of Web 2.0 technologies. Cormode & Krishnamurthy (in Greenhow et al. 2009:1) explain that there was an introduction of the "first-generation web" or "Web 1.0", ten years ago and it was welcomed as the latest and greatest education and communication resource as compared to the older information and teaching resources such as books, overhead transparency and classroom lectures. Greenhow et al. went on to point out the introduction of the "web 2.0" technology in the twenty first century. The web 2 was then adapted as the new and better tool as the successor of web 1. This was due to the technical nature of web 1 and the relative usability of "web 2.0" tools. Dabbagh & Kitsantas 2012, report on social media as a network of diverse communication tools with a focus on social aspects of the internet for sharing ideas and working together to reach common goals. It is this aspect of social media that allows for mobile devices to be used for teaching and learning because social media is accessible on most mobile devices.

According to the findings of prior research as documented by (Lan & Sie 2010), the use of mobile devices to support learning activities has been reported to be beneficial because it encourages learner-to-learner interaction, the same interaction which was reported by (Moore & Kearsley 2005) to be motivating and stimulating for learners. A view supported by (Richardson & Swan 2003) as they have asserted that this interaction is critical in learning. Due to the idea that education is viewed as a social practice, and learners often use mobile devices for social networking per the social learning theory, it follows that mobile devices should be capable of being used as learning tools to support online learning. The social learning theory further perceives learning to take place during social interactions in a community with similar interests (Wenger, 2000). Therefore by virtue of social networks and discussion forums being social environments, learning should take place in this platform as well.

Barron (in Greenhow et al. 2009:121) and Dabbagh & Kitsantas 2012 present similar concepts referred to as a learning ecology and the personal learning environments respectively. A learning ecology is based on the view that individuals are presented with and are active in many online settings, they create their own learning contexts in and across these settings; these individuals also engage in interest driven activities which serve as permeable contextual boundaries. The learning ecology can become self-sustainable given sufficient time, flexibility and the necessary resources. According to McGloughlin (in n Dabbagh & Kitsantas 2012:4), personal learning environments can help integrate formal (classroom) and informal (social) learning in the context of higher education, by creating personal and social learning contexts to support learner-centered education systems that use rich online media. Daft & Lengel (in Connell et al. 2001:118) define media richness as:

"The ability of information to change understanding within a time interval. Communication transactions that can overcome different frames of reference or clarify ambiguous issues to change understanding in a timely manner are considered rich. Communications that require a long time to enable understanding or that cannot overcome different perspectives are lower in richness. In a sense, richness pertains to the learning capacity of a communication". Media richness depends on four factors, response time, how fast can the responses be; multiple cues, whether the media can convey voice, tone and presence; language variety, meanings that can be used from language symbols; and personal focus, customization by users to their own preferences (Connell et al. 2001). Media are classified in descending richness as follows:

- Facet-face (FTF);
- video, telephone;
- computer-mediated communication (CMC);
- addressed written communication;
- unaddressed written communication and
- formal numeric text

Therefore after FTF, video and telephone, CMC is the next richest media to use for communication. This implies that using CMC for teaching should be an improvement on FTF, video and telephone. For the rich media to be effective in teaching and learning it has to convey the physical presence of the communicating participants; and this is the medium's social presence (Connell et al. 2001). This is the fundamental principle of the social presence theory.

3 Overview of the Open distance electronic learning (ODeL)

In a bid to stay ahead of the game, distance educators find themselves trying out many technologies to enhance or improve the learner learning experience and facilitate their course work. They often find themselves utilizing a variety of media which can get overwhelming as the different technologies might require a variety of different skills (Carter 1996). Lee et al. 2004 have advised that there should be careful selection of user friendly tools as part of institutional strategies for e-learning. They also recommend that educators are trained on how to use the selected tools and they also have reflection sessions to discuss areas of concern. There are high- end course management platforms or systems such as Blackboard, Moodle, and Sakai, which might come with a golden price tag and could require some technical configurations and installation processes; which could be disadvantageous for non-technical educators and learners, if they do not have the required skill. This further implies that those without the required skill will not make optimum use of the tools' functionality. Greenhow et al. 2009, came to the conclusion that it is no longer feasible for anyone to be literate in every available online technology. They further pointed out that digital literacy includes knowing which technologies are fit for the user's intended purpose, knowing when to use these technologies, when to use them, how and which functions to use. Cao And Hong 2011 reiterate this view and summarize the basics for social media utilization in teaching by proposing factors affecting social media utilization as individual readiness and literacy, external pressure, expected benefits, perceived risks of using social media.

There are also low-end content management tools such as discussion forums or pages, chat rooms, blogs and social networking sites. These are said to be low end as they are often free, easy to use and easily accessible to the educators and learners. Snow & Sampson 2010, provide a list of such content management platforms and tools. For this research the chosen media are:

- Discussion forums;
- SMS (Short Message Services);
- E-mail; and
- Telephone

The e-learning content has been made available in an information technology module taught in an open distance mode of delivery. The participation and progress of the learners will be recorded and compared to the previous year where e-learning was not used. The results will be reported on and used to determine the impact of the e-learning initiative. To determine if social media had an influence on learning, the Media richness theory and the Social Presence theory will be used in the data gathering process. In the module's discussion forum, the learners discuss the module content and help each other by addressing each other's questions and comments regarding the module. The SMSs are used to remind learners of important dates and events. For example a reminder to book for their practical exam, or to alert them of an important announcement that has been posted on the online notice board, which must be read. The telephone is used by learners who phone in wit queries. E-mails are used to communicate announcements, details regarding the module content and administrative details. They are also used by learners to send their queries. Maximum allowed number of pages is seven for Regular Research Papers (RRP) and Regular Research Reports (RRR); four for Short Research Papers (SRP); and two for Posters (PST).

4 The impact of media on learning

Based on the work of Cf. Redecker et al. (2010) Study conducted by the Institute for Prospective Technological Studies (IPTS) indicates that social media can improve teaching and learning opportunities in Europe as noted the figure below.

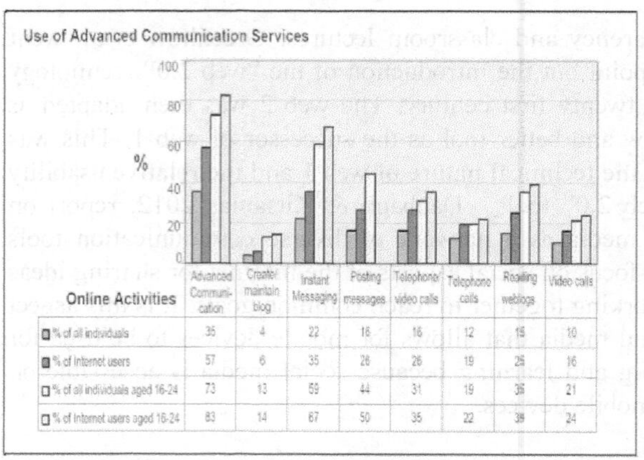

Online Activities	Advanced Communi-cation	Create/ maintain blog	Instant Messaging	Posting messages	Telephone/ video calls	Telephone calls	Reading weblogs	Video calls
% of all individuals	35	4	22	16	16	12	15	10
% of Internet users	57	6	35	26	26	19	25	16
% of all individuals aged 16-24	73	13	59	44	31	19	36	21
% of Internet users aged 16-24	83	14	67	50	35	22	39	24

Figure1: Use of Advanced Communication Services

The impact on learner education is the main emphasis in the literature of this study. Some benefits were noted by Kamel Boulos and Wheeler (in Carter 2006:32) when they reported that "Social media encourages more user interaction, collaboration, and participation". Vie (in Carter 2006:33) emphasizes that learning informally through Social Media increases opportunities for learner engagement and in formal learning settings.

5 Conclusion

Learner satisfaction and learning outcomes are related. Other researchers in this area support that informal learning that takes place at home to enrich formal learning. Social media supports and promote learning, fast and easy through dynamic and flexible teamwork with other learners. This study aims to confirm that rich media results in better performance of learners.

6 References

[1] Cao,Y. and Hong,P. (2011) Antecedents and consequences of social media utilization in college teaching: a proposed model with mixed-methods investigation, On the Horizon, Vol. 19 No: 4, pp 297 – 306

[2] Carter, V. (1996) Do media influence learning? Revisiting the debate in the context of distance education, Open Learning, The Journal of Open, Distance and e-Learning, Vol. 11, No.1, pp 31-40

[3] Connell, J.B., Mendelsohn, G.A., Robins, R.W. and Canny, J. (2008) Effects of Communication Medium on Interpersonal Perceptions: Don't Hang Up on the Telephone Yet! , Paper presented at the 2001 International ACM SIGGROUP Conference on Supporting Group Work, Boulder, Colorado, USA, pp 117-124

[4] Dabbagh, N. and Kitsantas, A. (2012) Personal Learning Environments, social media, and self-regulated learning: A natural formula for connecting formal and informal learning, Internet and Higher Education, Vol. 15, pp 3–8

[5] Dalsgaard, C.(2006) Social software: E-learning beyond learning management systems , Institute of Information and Media Studies, University of Aarhus, Denmark, online [http://www.imv.au.dk]

[6] Greenhow, C., Robelia, B. and Hughes,J.E. Greenhow, C., Robelia, B., & Hughes, J.E. (2009) Research on Learning and Teaching with Web 2.0: Bridging Conversations, Educational Researcher, Vol38, No.4, 280-283

[7] Harasim, L. (2002) What makes online learning communities successful? The role of collaborative learning in social and intellectual development

[8] Lan, Y.F., and Sie, S. (2010) Using RSS to support mobile learning based on media richness theory, Computers and Education, Vol. 55, pp 723 – 732

[9] Lee, C.S., Tan, D.T.H, and Goh, W.S. (2004) The Next Generation of E-Learning: strategies for media rich online teaching and engaged learning , Journal of Distance Education Technologies, Vol. 2, No 4, pp 1-17

[10] Redecker, C., Ala-Mutka, K and Punie, Y. (2010) Study conducted by the Institute for Prospective Technological Studies (IPTS) on Learning in Europe 2.0 POLICY BRIEF, Joint Research Centre: Institute for Prospective Technological Studies, pp 1-17

[11] Richardson, J. C., & Swan, K. (2003). Examining social presence in online courses in relation to learners' perceived learning and satisfaction. Journal of Asynchronous Learning Networks, 7(1), 68-88.

[12] Snow, E. and Sampson, P. (2010) Course Platforms for Teaching Online, Teaching Geoscience Online - A Workshop for Digital Faculty, University of South Florida, University of Texas, University of Michigan, [online] http://serc.carleton.edu/NAGTWorkshops/online/platforms.html accessed 20 December 2012.

[13] Swan, K & Shea, P. (2005). The development of virtual learning communities. In. S. R. Hiltz & R. Goldman, Asynchronous Learning Networks: The Research Frontier. New York: Hampton Press, 239-260.

[14] Wenger, E. (2000) Communities of Practice and Social Learning Systems, Sage, London, vol. 7, No. 2, pp 225-246

Interactive Social Distance Learning Environment

Maram A. Alshareef
Educational Diploma Program, King Abdulaziz University,
Kingdom of Saudi Arabia, P.O. Box 80254, Jeddah 21589.
aralshareef@kau.edu.sa,

***Abstract*— this paper presents a results of a study conducted for student enrolled in communication skills course in King Abdulazize University, Saudi Arabia. The study is to evaluate the success of an interactive social learning environment. A survey was offered to students in classes who used Twitter in order to identify areas where the survey aim succeeded. The survey results proved that the posts in twits in Twitter were the areas of greatest concern.**

***Index* Distance Learning Environment, Twitter, Web 2.0, Social Learning, Student Satisfaction.**

I. INTRODUCTION

These days, students forced educational institutions to move from traditional teaching methods to social learning. Higher Education students are integrating ICT completely in their everyday life and call for educational institutions to support their digital learning styles. In addition, instructors are increasingly taking up social computing applications in their work and free time. Different types of collaborative content applications, such as Facebook, Twitter, Blogs and Wikis, are used by people of all ages, supporting the collaborative creation and sharing of knowledge between young and old, students and experts, inside and outside organizations and educational institutions. This paper focuses on using Twitter as an interactive social learning environment.

The study conducted in King Abdulaziz University Students to present the impact of using Twitter to identify areas where the survey aims succeeded. The survey results proved that the posts in Twitter among students were the areas of greatest concern.

As a result, traditional teaching and learning methods in educational institutions should be adapted to provide accommodation the learning needs of the new generation of digital native students and instructors. Recently, Web 2.0 concepts have started to open new doors for more effective learning and have the potential to overcome many of the limitations of traditional learning models. Social computing tools in Web 2.0 [7] have a potential to support both, students in higher education institutions and instructors updating their skills in new ways. In this paper, we show in which way the Web 2.0 tools [7], under development at the King Abdul Aziz University , puts crucial success factors for Web 2.0 enhanced learning into practice, applying well known concepts like social learning.

In this study, we use Twitters as tools of social interactive distance learning. By browsing the nominated noble works and the comments made by peers as well as instructors on students' blogs, students are empowered to stimulate new ideas different from each other. Survey results show that students who took the lab courses are satisfied with turning in lab results through blog posting, getting instructor's in-class interactions, piracy reduction, and social learning.

Socially outgoing users aim for more involvement in ongoing interactions by making use of the rules and procedures in the Twitter. They tend to specialize in one usage procedure (such as answering questions or greeting newcomers). Understanding the influence that socially outgoing learners have on the success of social interaction in a learning context helps the adoption and adaptation of Web 2.0 services [7] for learning environments.

II. RELATED WORK

Web 2.0 technologies are potentially playing a key role in the context of learning and knowledge transfer by transforming the information society into a knowledge society [1]. Research on the prospective role of Web 2.0 services in supporting social interaction with educational merits is being recently explored by several scholars, including [5]. The social interactions supported by Web 2.0 services are characterized by power laws and log normal distributions which generally imply that only a small percentage of participants remain active above the threshold required for the interaction's continuance and development [1].

A blog is a website comprising blog posts, or content written by the blogger, which are typically organized into categories and sorted in reverse chronological order [Wright 2006].

By methods and techniques of Twitter analysis, researchers can study how information flows through network ties, how people acquire information and resources, and how cleavages and coalitions operate. Therefore, in addition to studying on whole networks, researchers are also interest in discovering densely-knit clusters or cliques and looking for cohesive subgroups [12].

Picking up the valuable pieces of information from the blogs that we follow would often require tiresome reading, unless somehow we are informed about the relevance of an item [9]. While technology is important, keeping in touch with social science will be just as important. Twitter analysis [10] helps identify the structural features of a computer supported collaborative learning group or community and the relevance that we are looking for. In addition, learning from peers [6] or so-called social learning has arguably become a noticeable subject regarding participation, learning activities and knowledge construction in computer-supported collaborative learning in higher education. In this paper, quantitative analysis will be conducted to examine the effects of social learning of educational blogs in the classroom settings.

It further concludes that blogging has the potential to be a transformational technology for teaching and learning. Oravec [8] observed that the blog has many dimensions that are suited to students' 'unique voices', empowering them, and encouraging them to become more critically analytical in their thinking. A number of universities round the world have commenced with the use of blogging tools. However, it is found that few of the blogs in education are used in-class. Dailey [2] considers that the biggest advantage of blogs has more to do with something we always have too little of in the classroom—time. Blogging gives back to our students something that many of us often lack—the time to think. Many blogs are, in fact, used as tools to keep students engaged in the learning situations, either solitary or social, when they are not in class.

This paper, quantitative analysis will be conducted to examine the effects of social learning of educational blogs in the classroom settings.

III. METHODOLOGY

Using data from a 200-student course on communication skills at a King Abdul Aziz university, we empirically tested how impacts into students' performance twitter. A study was performed for students enrolled in two sections of the course. The survey was conducted on-line using electronic questionnaires at Deanship of distance learning King Abdulaziz University. The representation of respondents by gender was 140 girls and 60 boys. The questionnaire was designed to measure the performance of the Twitter variables on the student collaboration. Following the work of [4] and [11], advice relations could be administered to acquire a more trustworthy measure of the advice network.

This research is based as the following hypothesis: Twitter performance will be positively related to the student's satisfaction. Accordingly the above hypothesis can be consisted from the following sub questioners:

- H1.1: Twitter using Twitter provide a satisfying learning experience.
- H1.2: Using Twitter I found this class is more satisfying than most other classes.
- H1.3; Using Twitter, I found this class is an interesting one
- H1.4: Class via Using Twitter gives me flexibility for extracurricular
- H1.5: Class via Using Twitter gives me flexibility for study time
- H1.6: I am feeling to getting a good education through Using Twitter.
- H1.7: The technology of Using Twitter associated with Class is easy to use
- H1.8: Using Twitter, It is easy to get feedback.

The survey included numerous scales to evaluate the constructs of interest. For that, the scales were measured using a 7-point Likert type scale anchored with the statements "Strongly Disagree" = 1, "Strongly Agree" = 7, and "Neutral" as the mid-point.

IV. RESULTS AND DISCUSSIONS

The result was analyzed and tested using LISREL [3]. Table 1 shows the results with Factor loading.

A shown in the following tables and figures, a t-test was used to explain the value of the results of 8 questions and gives the respondents on level of satisfaction with the Twitter. It is clear that there is significant effect for Twitter satisfaction with $p < .011$. Students in this study are generally satisfied with course online via Twitter learning. As shown in T-value, the students find that the Twitter tools, I found this class is an interesting class.

Table 1 Results of Factor loading

Q	Item	Factor Loading
Q1	Twitter using Twitter provide a satisfying learning experience.	0.912
Q2	Using Twitter I found this class is more satisfying than most other classes.	0.961
Q3	Using Twitter, I found this class is an interesting one	0.921
Q4	Class via Using Twitter gives me flexibility for extracurricular	0.936
Q5	Class via Using Twitter gives me flexibility for study time	0.903
Q6	I am feeling to getting a good education through Using Twitter	0.917
Q7	The technology of Using Twitter associated with Class is easy to use	0.951
Q8	Using Twitter, It is easy to get feedback	0.944

As shown in table 1 and Figure 1, most of students strongly agree that "Using Twitter I found this class is more satisfying than most other classes" with highest factor loading 0.961. And agree that "Class via Using Twitter gives me flexibility for study time" with lowest factor loading 0.903.

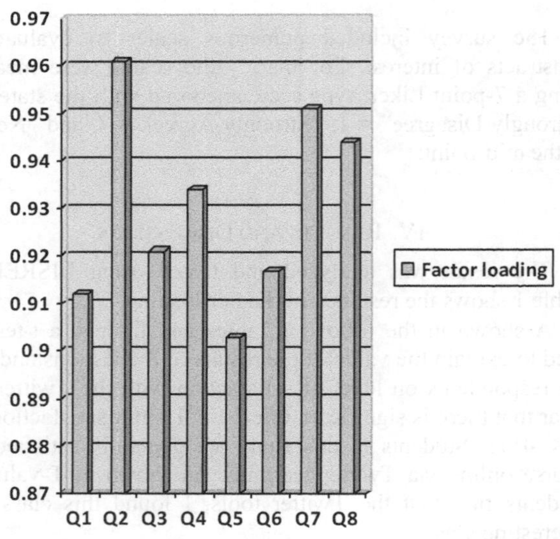

Figure 1 Results of Factor loading

Student found that Class via Twitter gives them flexibility for study time with factor loading 0.936. As shown in figure 2, they also found that the technology of Twitter associated with Class is easy to use with 18.01. Figure 2 shows that the best results get from Q3 and Q8, therefore, they found that Class via Twitter gives students flexibility for extracurricular and they are feeling to getting a good education. Table 2 and Figure 2 shows also that Q3 reflect a best question where students found that using Twitter the class is an interesting one with 21.05 T-value.

Table 2. T-Value Results

Q	Item	T-value
Q1	Twitter using Twitter provide a satisfying learning experience.	17.71
Q2	Using Twitter I found this class is more satisfying than most other classes.	19.18
Q3	Using Twitter, I found this class is an interesting one	21.05
Q4	Class via Using Twitter gives me flexibility for extracurricular	19.01
Q5	Class via Using Twitter gives me flexibility for study time	18.03
Q6	I am feeling to getting a good education through Using Twitter	19.01
Q7	The technology of Using Twitter associated with Class is easy to use	18.01
Q8	Using Twitter, It is easy to get feedback	19.71

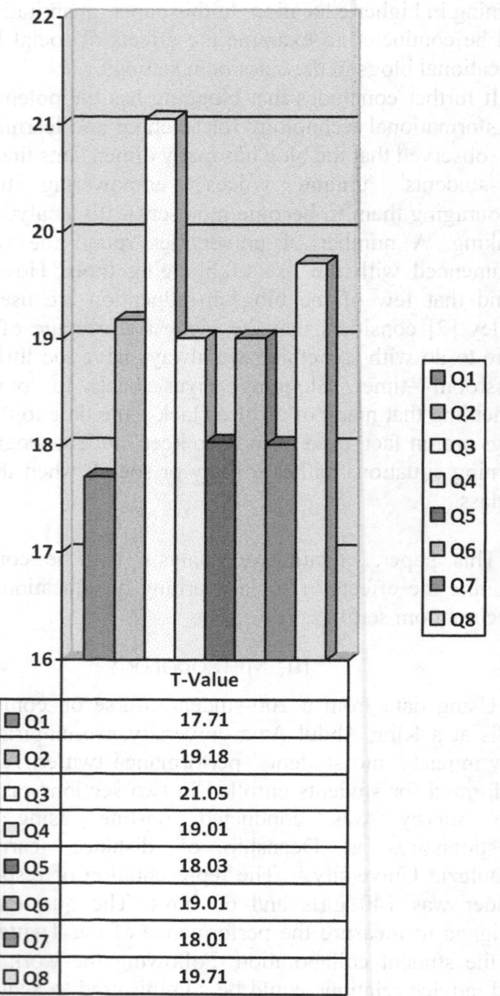

Figure 2. T-Value Results

In table 3, Student found that Twitter using Twitter provide a satisfying learning experience with P-value 0.015. They also found that the technology of Twitter associated with Class is easy to use with 0.018. Figure 3 shows that the best results get from Q7 and Q8, therefore, they found that the technology of Using Twitter associated with Class is easy to use and they are feeling to getting a good education. Table 2 and Figure 2 shows also that Q3 reflect a lowest P-value where students found that using Twitter the class is an interesting one with 0.11 P-value

Table 3. P-Value results

Q	Item	P-value
Q1	Twitter using Twitter provide a satisfying learning experience.	.015
Q2	Using Twitter I found this class is more satisfying than most other classes.	.016
Q3	Using Twitter, I found this class is an interesting one	.011
Q4	Class via Using Twitter gives me flexibility for extracurricular	.015
Q5	Class via Using Twitter gives me flexibility for study time	.017
Q6	I am feeling to getting a good education through Using Twitter	.019
Q7	The technology of Using Twitter associated with Class is easy to use	.018
Q8	Using Twitter, It is easy to get feedback	.017

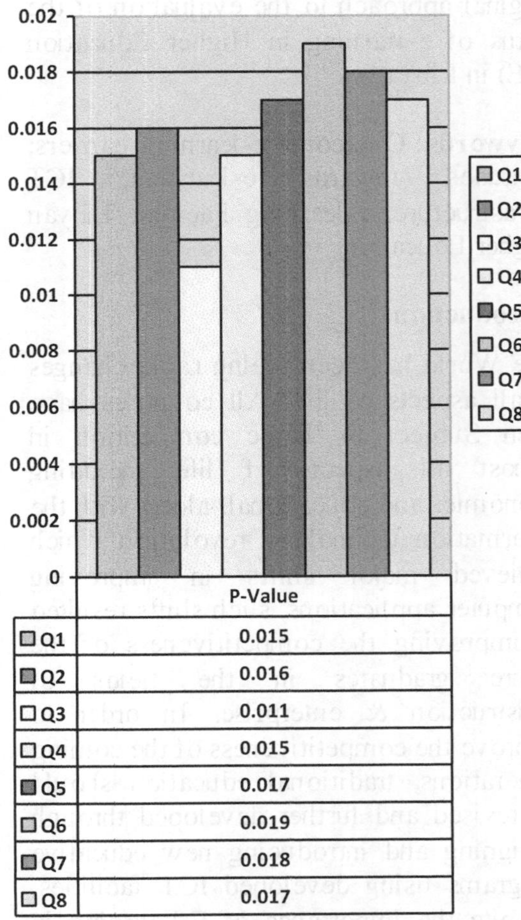

Figure 3P-Value Results

V. Conclusions

As results, we can see the significant come from using Twitters with traditional class. This study raised some important issues in the using of Twitter technology and proved that the ease of use of the technology how to meet students' needs for communication. In addition, this paper shows that the Twitter played a major role in student satisfaction with the online course. These results also suggest that we should be evaluating Twitter technology use and understanding in our classrooms in King Abdulaziz University.

VI. References

[1] P. Anderson, "What is Web 2.0? Ideas, technologies and implications for education" JISC Technical Report, 2007, Retrieved 23rd January, 2008, from http://www.jisc.ac.uk/media/documents/techwatch/tsw0701b.pdf

[2] John Dailey, Blogging for learning: Now everyone has something to say. Feedback, Joe Misiewicz Editor. Broadcast Educators Association. 2006.

[3] Stephen O'Hear, "Seconds Out, Round Two," The Guardian, November 15, 2005,

[4] Arnaud Leene, "Web 2.0 Checklist 2.0," MicroContent Musings, July 21, 2005,

[5] B. Nardi, D. Schiano, M. Gumbrecht, and L. Swartz, "Why We Blog" Communications of the Association for Computing Machinery. December 2004, pp. 41-46.

[6] Newman, Mark "The Structure and Function of Complex Networks". SIAM Review 45: 167-256. 2003.

[7] Tim O'Reilly, "What Is Web 2.0," September 30,2005,

[8] Jo Ann Oravec, "Bookmarking the World: Weblog Applications in Education", Journal of Adolescent & Adult Literacy, 45(7), Apr 2002, p616-21.

[9] Carrington, Peter J., John Scott and Stanley Wasserman (Eds.). Models and Methods in Twitter Analysis. New York: Cambridge University Press. 2005.

[10] Breiger, Ronald L. "The Analysis of Twitters." Pp. 505-526 in Handbook of Data Analysis, edited by Melissa Hardy and Alan Bryman. London: Sage Publications. 2004.

[11] Pedro A. Willging. Using Twitter Analysis Techniques to Examine Online Interactions. US-China Education Review, 2005.2(9).

[12] Jeremy Wright, Blog Marketing, McGraw-Hill, 2006.

Overcoming the barriers to implement electronic learning in Higher education (HE)

Dr. Nasreddin B. ElZoghbi ,
E-Mail: " nzoghobi@yahoo.com "
University of Tripoli Faculty of Science
Computer Science Dept. P.O.Box 13270
Tripoli Libya

Sir. Abdulbasit S. Khashkhush
"A.S.Khashkhush@edu.salford.ac.uk "
Salford University,
great Manchester M5 4WT,
UK.

Abstract

Technological innovations have not only brought benefits to business, but to Higher Education, worldwide. Colleges and universities are using E-learning to make learning more accessible and efficient. This paper assessed the attitudes of staff member towards challenges to embracing e-learning. However, Libya is a very wide State and the distribution of the population is concentrated in certain & specified areas make the academic education sometimes difficult either due to distance from the educational centres or due to lack of time or due to handicapped body or others. E-Learning system enables students of all ages and abilities the chance to learn anywhere, at any time and at their own pace. This paper aims to shed light on the role of e-Learning in the Libyan Education System and how it can be improved as well as discussing in general the effectiveness of this system in Libyan higher education by focusing on the factors that affect the up take of this system in Libya. Nevertheless, in this paper the semi-structured interviews with the senior leaders within two universities had been used to identify the factors that affect e-Learning. The paper concludes that at present "e-Learning" does not apply. Nevertheless this is not to say that it cannot be achieved in the future. It suggests that e-Learning requires a minimum technological plat form. However, this paper focuses on two public universities (University of Tripoli and the Al-Zawia University, and hence the generalisation of the findings outside of these universities cannot be validated. However, the paper's findings appear to be intuitively general sable beyond the subject topic.

This paper can support capacity building in e-Learning systems in Libya by the identification of needs, which is an important initial stage in any capacity building programme. Overall This is an original approach to the evaluation of the status of e-learning in Higher Education (HE) in Libya.

Keywords: Overcome e-learning barriers; Attitudes towards e-learning, ICT infrastructure, e-learning Factors, Libyan Higher Education,

Introduction:

The World has been seeing rapid changes in all aspects of life. All countries have been Subject to fierce competition in almost all aspects of life including economic, and educational, along with the information technology revolution which achieved major shifts in improving computer applications, such shifts resulted in improving the competitiveness of the future graduates in the fields of construction & enterprise. In order to improve the competitiveness of the coming generations, traditional education should be revised and further developed through designing and introducing new educative programs using developed ICT facilities. Despite the importance of E-Learning in Higher Education (HE) and human development in Libya, implementation of E-learning is facing a number of challenges in Libyan universities. Those challenges can be summarized as follows:

Leadership; ICT infrastructure; Finance; Culture; Instructors & learners; Lack of Strategy; and Technical expertise. Regardless of these challenges the future is optimistic, offering innovative and advanced opportunities to implement e-learning.

The E-learning program, if established in Libya, will help to solve the problems resulting from a shortage of traditional education institutions that hold an increasing number of students who wish to study at university providing them with a chance to learn and promote scientific cooperation and research in order to reach every individual in the community. E-learning would also provide education for those who missed such opportunities and give provide them with knowledge of technological developments to continue in other areas of technical development.

Definition of E-learning:

There is a wide range of definitions for E-learning. E-learning offers opportunities to learn anywhere without being in a lecture theatre (Yieke, 2005); E-learning is defined as learning facilitated and supported through the use of information and communications technology. E-learning is no longer simply associated with distance or remote learning, but forms part of a conscious choice of the best and most appropriate ways of promoting effective learning. Khan (2000) defines that E-learning encompasses web-based learning (WBL); internet-based training (IBT); advanced distributing learning (ADL); and online learning (OL). More simply, E-learning can be thought of as anything that incorporates technology with interactivity to support learning, training and communication among groups and between individuals. Basically, technology has given us the opportunity to learn anywhere, anytime, and at our own pace. Additionally E-learning is using technology to deliver learning and training programs (Knowledge passed through the internet, network, or standalone computer). Therefore it is any technology-mediated learning using computers whether from a distance or in a classroom setting(Nicholas Croft 2010).

Higher Education context in Libya:

Libya is an Arab country located in Northern Africa and it covers a land area about 1,759,540 sq km. The capital of Libya is Tripoli and the main language spoken is Arabic. Italian and English languages are widely understood in the major cities of Libya. The total population of Libya is approximately 5.5 million, of which 1.7 million are students; over 270,000 of whom study at the tertiary level (Clark, 2004). El-Hawat (2003) reported that in the academic year 1975/76 the number of university students was estimated to be 13,418. This number has increased to more than 200,000 of which about an additional 65,000 students enrolled in the higher technical and vocational sector. The consequence of this rapid increase in the number of students in HE in Libya has resulted in an increase in the number of institutions providing HE. The university sector in Libya started in the early 1950s with the establishment of the “Libyan University”. It has campuses in Benghazi and Tripoli and it has grown over the years to incorporate Faculties of Arts and Education; Faculty of Science; Faculty of Economics and Faculty of Commerce, Law, and Agriculture.

Libya has a history of sending university students abroad. In 1978, more than 3,000 students were studying in the United States alone. However, by 2002 those figure had dropped to just 33 as a result of sanctions imposed in 1986, which restricted travel to the United States by Libyan nationals. According to the British Council (British

Council Press Release, 2003) the United Kingdom signed a cultural agreement with Libya at the end of 2003 which is expected to result in an increase in the number of Libyan students studying in the UK. Officials from the British Council estimate that there were more than 3000 Libyan students enrolled at British institutions of higher and further education in 2004; of those, 90 percent are said to be on Libyan government scholarships. (Clark, 2004).

Methodology

This study was conducted during the period from August to September 2009. Involving two main universities in Libya, University of Tripoli and the Al-Zawia University. Each university was visited by the author, conducting face to face Semi-structured interviews. Observation and the collection of supporting documentation will also be utilized for triangulation purposes. The numbers of interviewees in the two case study organisations were 16 in case study "A" and 15 in case study "B", Table (1).

Table 1. Interviewee groups from the two case study organisations:

Position of the interviewees	Referred in the findings	Case Study "A"	Case Study "B"	Total each level
Dean of the Faculty, Registrar and Administrative manager	Senior Leader (SL)	3/3 "One from each level";	3/3 "One from each level";	6;
Heads of Academic Departments	Heads of Academic Departments (HODs)	6/12;	6/9;	12;
Staff member	Academic staff and administrations' office (STM)	7;	6;	13;
Total each cases	---	16.	15	31

Analysis of attitudes towards major challenges in applying E-learning:

In this paper, the attitudes of staff members were identified through data collection. How these attitudes would affect the implementation of E-learning is as follows:

Leadership support:

The transition from traditional delivery methods to the implementation of E-learning environments inevitably involves the management of change (Betts, 1998). The need for support from an organization's leaders in order to begin and maintain any new approach to learning is addressed in the works of Abdelraheem (2006) and McPherson and Nunes (2006). Moreover, Liaw et al. (2007) went further by stating "instructors' leadership is a crucial factor to affect learners' attitudes to implement E-learning". If leadership fails to understand currently emerging futuristic technologies and their potential to develop a vision and strategy to support and enhance learning, acceptance of E-learning will be slow if not impossible (Minton, 2000).

From the viewpoint of the interviewees commitment and support by the leadership is one of the most important factors. The adoption of a new way of doing business or of a new technology is unlikely to succeed if it does not have widespread organizational support, and especially if it does not have acceptance from the leadership. The project that has considerable support gives the people who are working on implementing the project more confidence that the project will proceed to a successful conclusion. This study concluded, after analysis, that leadership support is an important factor for e-learning implementation in the Libyan Higher Education.

This study concluded that SL support is important for all e-learning implementation stages. Furthermore, HOD and STM can play a major role in the implementation of e-learning initiatives. The positive commitment, enthusiasm and support from all three levels for the implementation of e-learning are crucial for both Faculties and Universities to deal effectively and efficiently with new concepts, processes and/or technologies. This factor has been reported by many authors (among them Nunes (2006). Participants from the two categories (HOD and STM) have acknowledged that previous projects had been successful when supported by a senior leader.

The author saw in both cases that there was a lack of knowledge among a few on the SL level generally on e-learning concepts, which makes e-learning less effective if implemented. Therefore, this study suggests that in order to gain support and acceptance from senior leaders, it is crucial for them to understand the issue and what it can provide for higher education. Moreover, they need to know what the project requires and how to implement it.

Technological infrastructure:

Lack of public awareness on ICT and weak data communications infrastructures are two of the main factors affecting E-learning (Karmakar and Wahid, 2007). An organization that wants to implement E-learning should attain at least the minimum hardware requirements and the software required. The hardware part of E-learning includes the physical equipment that must be present to supply E-learning, e.g., servers and networks (O'Neill et al., 2003; Ettinger et al., 2006). O'Neill et al. (2003) suggested that the success of the technological infrastructure also has implications for the success of virtual learning; malfunctioning hardware or software can both be barriers which can cause frustration and affect the learning process. Valentine (2002) agreed with O'Neill et al. that hardware and tool malfunctions can be greatly detrimental to the effectiveness of E-learning.

Another important factor covered within this paper is the required technology infrastructure to implement E-learning in Libyan higher education. The data from the interviews revealed that interviewees in Case "A" (with a reasonably established infrastructure) were willing to implement E-learning initiatives; while interviewees in Case "B" (which lacked appropriate infrastructure) wanted to participate in the implementation of E-learning initiatives. To be successful such a programme needs to have an infrastructure that is capable of supporting and enabling the execution of E-learning. . (Croft N. 2011).

Therefore, this paper suggests that the Higher Education in Libya needs to have in place good quality technology in all universities. At the moment in terms of technology there is a dissimilarity between the two case studies; for example, Case Study "B" has shortages of computers e despite the fact that they have a plan to fully computerize the university as a part of their effort to develop a technological culture which encourages and promotes the use of technology in day-to-day activities and tasks.

The requirement for this technological infrastructure was identified by respondents as an important part of their work, and as a basic need to launch E-learning programmes. The study data showed that Case Study "A" enjoyed the best technological infrastructure capability, while Case Study "B" showed the lowest standard of technological infrastructure, but the author expects the level of technology use among Libyan Staff member will increase in coming years, as the plan is to provide the university in Case Study "B" with computers and sufficient technology.

Funds:

The consideration of the initial cost as well as the continuing costs of installing, maintaining, using and upgrading technology, and the human capital costs to support E-learning, is very important (Valentine, 2002). Marengo and Marengo (2005) demonstrated that the costs of technological infrastructure include digital content costs, maintenance costs, content hosting costs, hardware and software costs and costs of E-learning staff. Staff costs include tutoring costs, administration and management costs and Expert in Multimedia Technology (ETM) costs. In addition, Marengo and Marengo (2005) stated that, in cases where the hardware and software supplied by the faculty to circulate the contents (software, document, etc..) are not sufficient, the E-learning evaluation needs to take into account the cost of items, such as the purchase of a server and its relative software. The lack of money can be problematical for the implementation of E-learning particularly with the continuous labour costs of instructors (Cho and Berge, 2002; James-Gordon et al., 2003; Berge and Muilenburg, 2006).

The majority (87.5%, 14) of the interviewees agreed that the university has enough financial resources to cover the expenses and technical requirements of adopting and providing E-learning (Figure1). The author found in the interviews that this factor was not of significance to the interviewees. They confirmed that the entire funding for any project comes from a single source; that the government is based on political decision-taking and thus if the universities decide to adopt E-learning, there would be no problem in funding. Only one STM from Case Study "A" responded 'don't know about the availability' in answer to this particular question.

Most of the interviewees stated if they wanted to request anything the university is able to afford it. One senior leader from Case Study "A" and another one in the same position in Case Study "B" reported that if a decision is taken on the adoption and implementation of any project, such as E-learning for example, it will be passed together with a budget from the finance sector and that a decision on E-learning implementation must come from the General People's Committee of HE. The author agrees that this is the system in Libya in all public sectors.

The author concluded that funding is not a significant factor in Libya because if a decision is taken to implement E-learning, funding will be approved by the government, and thus in Libya it is a different scenario to that stated in the literature where other sources say that it is possible that E-learning could be undertaken either by the government or by private investment or by partnership.

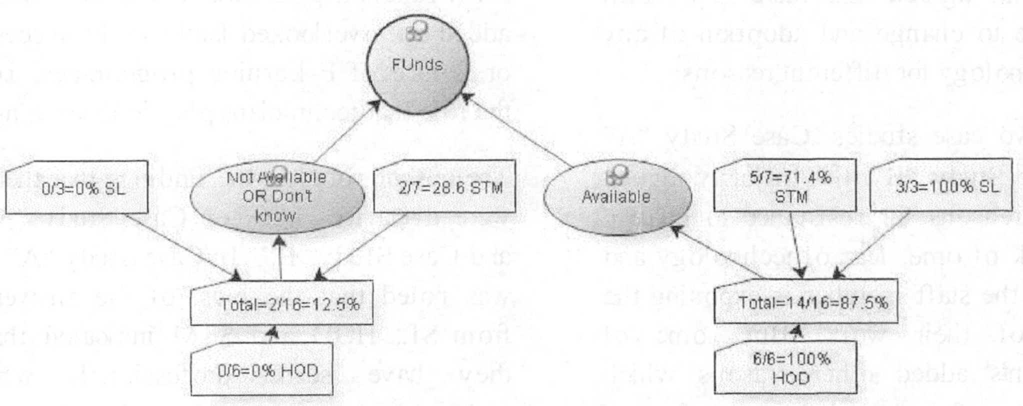

Figure1 Case Study "A": Number of respondents who confirmed that funding could be made available.

Resistance to changes:

Resistance to change is one of the important factors affecting the implementation of E-learning (Minton, 2000; Cho and Berge, 2002; Berge and Muilenburg, 2006; Ettinger et al., 2006). This resistance to change in some countries is usually because of the high percentage of illiteracy in those countries (Karmakar and Wahid, 2007). Moreover, Habibu (2003) stated that resistance to change is one of the factors that should be considered when implementing E-learning. It relates particularly to non-technical issues which includes academic staff, administrators, and/or managers. This resistance can be divided into three main reasons: fear of ICT; lack of time to design, develop and maintain support for online classes' materials, and fear of exposing the quality of work. Lecturers are one of the major factors that contribute to the success of E-learning. For lecturers, implementation of E-learning programmes represents a change in teaching style and materials. The precise nature of the change is difficult to quantify (O'Neill et al., 2003). O'Neill et al. (2003) stressed that human resources should be committed to the project at an early stage and lecturers should be selected based on their attitude towards technology. According to Liaw et al. (2007) personal attitude is a major factor affecting usage of IT. . (Croft N. 2011).

Understanding a user's attitudes toward E-learning facilities is important for the creation of appropriate E-learning environments for teaching and learning.

The acceptance and implementation of electronic learning involves altering human behaviour and activities. The majority of the respondents (81.3%) agreed that there is a natural resistance to change for different reasons. The senior leaders believed that their Heads of Department and their staff members resisted change because they fear using technology; because they lack time to design on-line teaching materials; and because E-learning might expose the quality of their work and may lead to a reduction in jobs.

Resistance to change and staff culture are important factors affecting the implementation of E-learning The implementation of electronic learning involves changing individual behaviour and activities and the majority of the respondents agreed that there is a usual resistance to change and adoption of any new technology for different reasons.

In the two case studies, Case Study "A" and Case Study "B", the majority agreed that the reasons for resistance to change are a lack of time, fear of technology and fear that the staff member is exposing the quality of their work. But some of respondents added other reasons which were: fear of losing their jobs, fear of using the English language and time pressures on their work load.

Staff education/training:

One of the most challenging factors for STM and universities around the world is technology and the need for continuous training for keeping up-to-date with advanced technology.

Staff education and knowledge is another important factor for the successful adoption of E-learning systems, University staff members need to be aware of the need to continue learning and to utilise IT technological infrastructures to acquire and manage knowledge. Training to use E-learning systems will ensure that they can utilise the full potential and capabilities offered by ICT tools. If universities provided staff with adequate and quality training to facilitate the use of technology and E-learning systems then staff would, in all probability, find E-learning systems easy to use. It is important that universities promote and educate staff to use E-learning systems rather than forcing them to do so.

Technical expertise:

Lack of personal technological expertise in solving technical problems is one of the main factors affecting an E-learning programme (O'Neill et al., 2003; Berge and Muilenburg, 2006). Valentine (2002) added one overlooked factor in the success or failure of E-learning programmes, i.e. the role that technicians play in E-learning.

The author noted in the findings that there were disparities between Case Study "A" and Case Study "B". In Case Study "A" it was noted that the most of the answers from SL, HOD and STM indicated that they have some professionals who undertake the maintenance of equipment (for example, computers) and that they also have some expertise in programming, multimedia technology and experts in information technology, and project management. In Case Study "B" most of the answers from the interviewees indicated that there was a shortage of such professionals who can maintain equipment such as hardware and multimedia technology; there was also a shortage of specialists in software programming such as project management and information systems.

Strategy:

From the literature and the findings, the setting up of a strategy was found to be an important factor for the implementation of E-learning in the Libyan case studies.

This study concluded that the strategy has not only to be directed from the leadership, it also has to be established within each faculty to enable all participants/staff to work towards realizing the goals and objectives of such a programme and to ensure that work is undertaken towards achieving the essential goal of implementing E-learning.

The findings revealed that a strategy for the implementation of E-learning in Libya was non-existent. This was supported by SL, HOD and STM in Case Study "A" and

HOD and STM from Case Study "B". One of the STMs stated that the technology was available and the adoption of E-learning should be a part of the University strategy.

Therefore, this study suggests that Higher Education in Libya needs to have a comprehensive and clear strategic plan to implement E-learning programmes, and the author believes that postgraduate programmes with their fewer students could be used as a pilot for E-learning systems after an E-learning strategy has been introduced.

Overcoming factors that affect the initiation of E-learning in Libyan HEIs:

Overcoming the factors that prevent the implementation of E-learning programmes in Libya is very important to Libyan HE, because the country needs to develop its HE universities and education system to reach everybody in the rural areas and to face an increasing demand for higher education and a growing number of students. Therefore, it should take urgent steps to overcome these factors.

Firstly, as this study suggests in the discussion on strategy, ministry of Higher Education in Libya needs to have a complete strategy plan to implement E-learning programmes with specificguiding principles to follow in E-learning development, and should submit a draft to the universities on an E-learning strategy, so that they can commence preliminary steps to implement E-learning and encourage strategic projects in Libya HE. The strategy should encompass project management and educational objectives; technology infrastructure, training and usage support; comprehensive E-learning-related training programmes and a strategy for technical support and maintenance. (Croft N. 2011)

Another point is equality in the technical infrastructure in all Libyan HE universities and faculties. This is very important as it will enable them to share information, collaborate, and allow staff to gain knowledge and skills by technology. They should all have a good infrastructure as the researcher noted that there was a notable difference between the two case studies: Case Study A had a good infrastructure and Case Study B had a lack of infrastructure and in Case Study B many of the interviewees acknowledged the need to launch a technology infrastructure as a prerequisite for the implementation of E-learning initiatives.

Moreover, HE should organize seminars and workshops, lectures and conferences about the value and benefits of E-learning to increase the overall awareness of a technology culture and the fact that it should be launched at all levels in the HE universities.

The implementation of E-learning should be understood well in advance and awareness by staff in Libyan HE universities must be raised by staff attending lectures (there was a lack of attendance at such events in Case A), seminars and conferences. All this must take place in order to raise the awareness of electronic culture (Case Study B) within the STM to allow for the application of electronic learning, because currently the STM culture, especially within the older generations, hinders the implementation of E-learning.

Furthermore, Libyan HE should establish an independent training department to unify the training strategy in order to implement such a programme and to determine training objectives, needs & types, to provide quality training, and to select targeted individuals and the quality of trainees for E-learning.

The training department should also respond to the training needs of each HE university with particular regard to E-learning and should implement a clear plan for training in order to increase the capacity and development of staff knowledge and skills.

The training should include technology especially training on computer skills, introduce ICDL and the internet and it should include training on the English language. Additionally if the STM gained more knowledge, skills, and experience of technology and became more ICT literate, then they would be more prepared to use such programmes.

The ICDL exists to assist individuals in performing their work and duties by using computers and to perform the required tasks. The ICDL system encompasses seven training units: the basic concepts of information technology; using a computer and managing files; word processing; spreadsheets; databases; presentations, and information and communications. ICDL courses will provide trainees with a solid foundation of basic skills to help them use computer skills efficiently and with full confidence especially for the older generation STM. New computers users and staff with a poor knowledge of the English language can use the Arabic version of ICDL.

In addition, there is a need to utilise training taken abroad if it is not available in Libya in order to increase the effectiveness of STM in the use of technology and to increase their technical skills so that they can be technically qualified.

As a result, training should have a strategy which should be addressed early on with other strategies and should encourage STM through a motivation and reward system.

A further point which should help overcome resistance to change is a reward system which is likely to increase energy, creativity, provide complete and better services and improve productivity from STM to help in the implementation of E-learning. Also this reward system should be aligned to motivate staff performance that is consistent with the universities' strategy, to attract and retain people with the skills and knowledge required to conform with the HE strategic goals, and to create a supportive culture and structure. (Nicholas Croft 2010)

Conclusion:

The implementation of E-learning can create enormous changes within a Libyan HE university, so it can expect to face factors such as resistance to change as the institution changes the way instructors teach, managers manage, and reforms are undertaken of the current work process by changing boring routine work, eliminating bureaucracy, and improving transparency.

The factors affecting the implementation of E-learning should be well understood in advance and increasing awareness by the staff in Libyan HE universities must be raised by staff members attending lectures, seminars and conferences. The failure of Libyan HE Institutions to accept and develop a vision and strategy to understand the current emerging advanced technologies will seriously undermine any potential to implement the E-learning process. As a result, training should have a strategy which should be addressed early alongside other strategies and should encourage STM through a motivation and reward system. E-learning requires a minimum technological platform which includes necessary hardware, adequate telecommunication capabilities and access to software. Lecturers should be selected based on their experience, potential and outlook toward new technology. Experts in multimedia technology have to support teachers in the activities of organization and management and, to some extent, the development of E-learning courses as well. The implementation of E-learning programmes represents a change in teaching style and materials.

This paper has contributed to the discussion how Overcoming factors that affect the initiation of E-learning in Libyan HE.

References:

Abdelraheem, A., Y., (2006) "The implementation of E-learning in the Arab University: Challenges and opportunities". In Proceeding of APRU DLI Tokyo, Japan.

Berge, Z., and Muilenburg, L., Y., (2006) "Barriers to distance Education: Perceptions of K-12 Educators". Retrieved September 21 2007 from: http://www.emoderators.com/barriers/barriersK12.html.

Betts, K., S., (1998) "An Institutional Overview: Factors Influencing Faculty Participation in Distance Education in Postsecondary Education in the United States: An Institutional Study". Online Journal of Distance Learning Administration, Vol. 1 No. 3. Retrieved November 28, 2007 from: http://www.westga.edu/%7Edistance/betts13.html.

British Council Press Release. 18 Dec. 2003. "British Council Signs Major Agreement With Libya."

Cho, S., K., and Berge, Z., (2002) "Overcoming Barriers to Distance Training and Education" Journal of USDLA Vol. 16(1). Retrieved September 21 2007 from:

http://www.emoderators.com/barriers/cho.html.

Clark, N., (2004) "World Education News and Views" available at:

http://www.wes.org/ewenr/PF/04Jul/PFP/practical.htm 02/05/2007

Croft, N. , Dalton, A. and Grant, M. (2011) Overcoming isolation in distance learning: Building a learning community through time, space and sector. Working Paper. Higher Education Academy Centre for Education in the Built Environment (CEBE).

El-Hawat, A., (2004) "African Higher Education: An International Reference Handbook" (Damtew Teferra and Philip. G. Altbach, eds., Indiana University Press, 2003), pp. 391-402.

Ettinger, A., Holton, V., and Blass, E., (2006) "E-learning experience: Key questions to ask when considering implementing E-learning" Industrial and Commercial Training. Vol. 38, No. 3, PP. 143-147.

Habibu, A., (2003) "E-learning Challenges In Africa Case Study Uganda, Institute of Computer Science Makerere University Uganda" Retrieved August, 30, 2007 from: http://www.google.co.uk/search?q=introuction+to+%22E-learning+challenges.

James-Gordon, Y., Young, A., and Bal, J., (2003) "External environment forces affecting E-learning providers" Marketing Intelligence & Planning. Vol. 21, No. 3, PP. 168-172

Karmakar, C., K., Wahid, CM., M., (2007) "Prospects Of E-learning in the context of current ICT Infrastructure of Bangladesh" Retrieved November 05,2007 from: http://www.codewitz.net/papers/MMT_83-89_FullPaper_Wahid_Karmakar.pdf.

Khan, B., H., (2000) "A framework for web-based learning". Englewood Cliffs, NJ: Educational Technology Publications.

Liaw, S., Huang, H., and Chen, G., (2007) "Surveying instructor and learner attitudes toward E-learning". Computer & Education, No. 49, 1066-1080.

McPherson, M., and Nunes, M., B. (2006) "Organisational issues for E-learning Critical success factors as identified by HE practitioners". International Journal of Educational Management, Vol. 20, No. 7, pp.542-558.

Marengo, A., and Marengo, V., (2005) "measuring the Economic Benefits of E-learning: A Proposal for New Index for Academic Environments". Journal of Information Technology, Vol. 4, PP.329-346.

Minton, M., C., (2000) "Is Your Organization Ready for E-learning?" Communication Project Magazine. Vol. 3.1, available at: http://www.comproj.com/Minton.htm.

Nicholas Croft, Alice Dalton, and Marcus Grant: (2010) Overcoming Isolation in Distance Learning: Building a Learning Community through Time and Space. Journal for Education in the Built Environment **5**(1).

O'Neill, K., Singh, G., and O'Donoghue, J., (2004) "Implementing eLearning Programmes for Higher Education: A Review of the Literature" Journal of Information Technology Education. Vol. 3, PP. 313-323.

Valentine, D., (2002) "Distance Learning: Promises, Problem, and Possibilities" Online Journal of Distance Learning Administration, Vol. V No. III. Retrieved December 22, 2007 from http://www.westga.edu/~distance/ojdla/fall53/valentine53.html.

Yieke, F., A., (2005), "Toward Alternatives in Higher Education: The Benefits and Challenges of E-learning in Africa", CODESRIA Bulletin No. 3&4, PP. 73-75

Improving Student Success Rate With Online Homework

Larry Wang, Zhu Cao
Mathematics Department, Southern Polytechnic State University, Marietta, GA, USA

Abstract - *The aim of this paper is to demonstrate how online homework improves student success rates in PreCalculus and Calculus I courses. WeBWorK, provided by the Mathematical Association of America, was adopted as the online homework system. In the spring of 2013, the system was implemented in two classes, one section of PreCalculus and one section of Calculus I. As a result, the pass rates of both sections with WeBWorK were well above other sections without WeBWorK (about 17% higher). This paper also shows how the WeBWorK system was used.*

Keywords: Online grading, WeBWorK, pass rate.

1 Introduction

As one of the core areas in college, Math often becomes a hurdle for students. The pass rate in this subject shows that math courses can hinder students' success in college endeavors. Currently, the pass rates in most sections of College Algebra, PreCalculus, and Calculus I at our institution are very low (around 60%). The cause of failure is partially due to the lack of interaction between teachers and students. With oversized classes (usually 30 or more students in a class), the instructor does not have enough time to grade homework. Some students do not work on suggested homework problems at all. Consequently, these students do poorly on the tests. They feel frustrated and lose their interest in the subject. An online homework system can help improve this situation. An online homework system will help make up for the lack of interaction between teachers and students. Students will likely do their homework online because many of them are used to and prefer a technological environment. If students complete their homework, they will come to class prepared and ready to participate in discussion. As a result, students will be motivated to learn and will be able to succeed in the course. The following two tables show the dramatic increases in pass rates with the WeBWorK system.

2 WeBWorK

WeBWorK is an open-source online homework system for math and science courses. It is supported by the Mathematical Association of America and the National Science Foundation and comes with a National Problem Library (NPL) of over 20,000 homework problems. Problems in the NPL target most lower division undergraduate math courses and some advanced courses. Supported courses include college algebra, discrete mathematics, probability and statistics, single and multivariable calculus, differential equations, linear algebra, and complex analysis. Over 300 colleges, universities, and high schools have successfully used WeBWorK. Unlike other commercial online homework softwares, WeBWork is free to students. It is also easier to manage and popularize the system. WeBWorK provides the tools needed to assign and grade homework easily. Students can do their homework from anywhere and at any time as long as they can access the internet. The assignments do not have to be completed all at once. They can also be printed out and worked on by students. Students receive feedback immediately after they submit their answers. They can keep trying until they get the correct answer or reach a limit of tries set by the instructor. The instant feedback either gives immediate gratification for correct answers or drives students to work hard in trying again: in both scenarios the student is more engaged in the homework. After the due date, students can view the solutions to the problems. WeBWorK offers students a personalized, interactive learning environment, where they can learn at their own pace and measure their own progress. In addition, WeBWorK provides different sets of problems for different students. This feature allows students to work together, yet still figure out how to solve the problems independently. Thus the common problem of academic dishonesty is avoided while still allowing students to work together.

3 Implementation

In the spring of 2013, WeBWorK was adopted in one section of PreCalculus and one section of Calculus I offered at Southern Polytechnic State University. Students were assigned homework through WeBWorK once every two weeks. Each of the assignments consisted of 10-20 questions with multiple parts and a due date. They were given four or five tries for each problem, depending on the difficulty of the problem. Usually, they were given one week to work on each assignment. During the weeks in which there was no WeBWorK homework, traditional homework was assigned. The homework contributed to about 15% of the final course grade. Students still took the regular quizzes, tests, and a comprehensive final exam for 85% of the course grade. Figure 1 shows a list of courses at SPSU supported by WeBWorK.

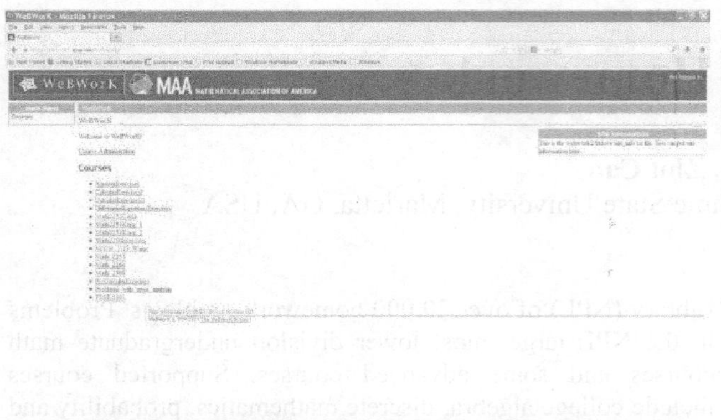

Figure 1: List of courses

Students click the course to enter the system with a username and password. Figure 2 shows the window for a student to enter his/her username and password.

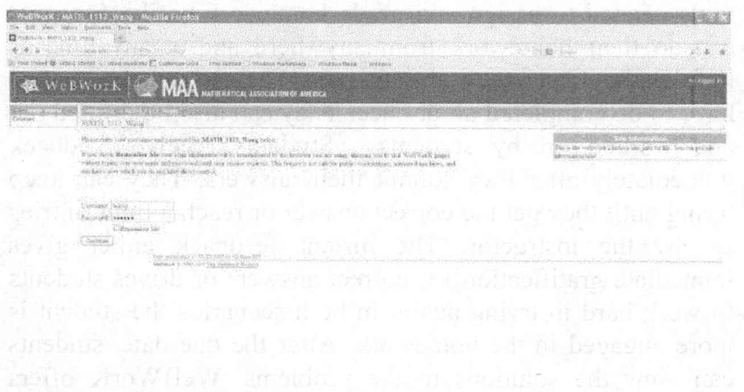

Figure 2: Login page

As shown in Figure 3, once students log into the system, they are shown a list of assignments.

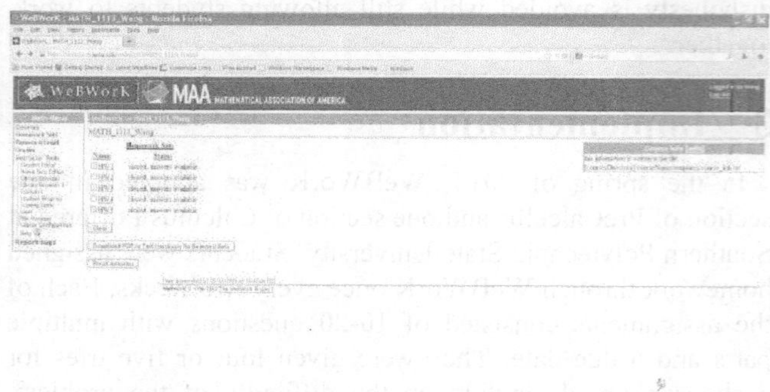

Figure 3: List of homework assignments

After students click the appropriate assignment, a collection of problems will be displayed for students to work on. Figure 4 shows what the problems look like.

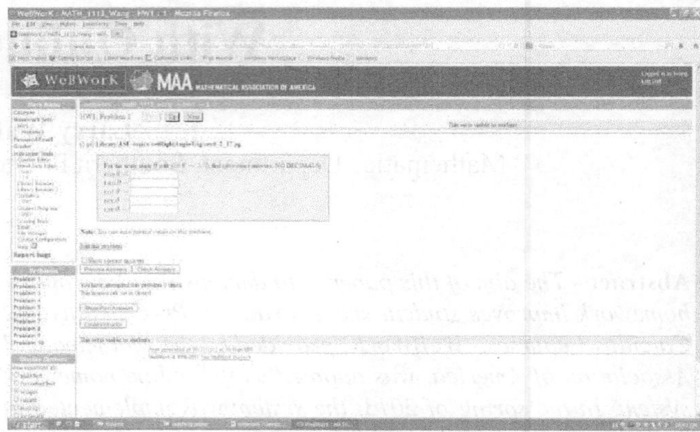

Figure 4: Problem page

After students work on the problems, they enter their answers in the boxes provided for each part of the problem.

Immediately, they can check whether the inputted answers are correct or not. They can keep trying until they reach the limit of four or five times.

4 Effects of WeBWorK

At the end of the spring of 2013, the pass rate in PreCalculus enhanced by WeBWorK was 17% higher than the pass rate in PreCalculus classes without WeBWorK. The percentage of A's and B's also increased by 27%. (See Table I).

The pass rate in the Calculus I class enhanced by WeBWorK was also 17% higher than the pass rate in Calculus I classes without WeBWorK. The percentage of A's and B's increased by 21%. (See Table II).

Compared with the sections in which WeBWorK was not used, the pass rate of those with WeBWorK was significantly higher, and the retention rate increased. Here are two tables that show the detailed effects:

Table I: Comparison on pass rates in PreCalculus.

	A	B	C	D	F	Pass Rate
With WW	26%	31%	14%	6%	11%	77%
Without WW	13%	17%	21%	9%	25%	60%

Table II: Comparison on pass rates in Calculus I.

	A	B	C	D	F	Pass Rate
With WW	30%	15%	20%	5%	10%	70%
Without WW	11%	13%	17%	12%	27%	53%

The tables show that WeBWorK improves students' performances in these classes. It was found that more students were motivated to work on their homework with WeBWorK. They prefer working with computers because students in the digital age are used to learning via technology. They like the instant response to their answers, and the option to correct wrong answers without any penalty. In this manner, students learn through their mistakes and are able to understand the problem fully. A survey conducted at the end of the spring of 2013 reflected students' positive feedback on the WeBWorK system. Here are four questions from the survey.

1. Between the traditional homework and the online homework from WeBWorK, do you like WeBWorK better?
2. Does WeBWorK help you learn in this course?
3. Do you agree that WeBWorK has more strengths than weaknesses?
4. Would you recommend others to use WeBWorK?

We summarized the responses in the following table III.

Table III: Survey result

	1	2	3	4
Yes	85%	89%	73%	82%
No	15%	11%	27%	18%

5 Conclusion and Future Work

The use of WeBWorK has significantly improved students' success rates. Both the pass rate and the students' response to survey questions support the positive effect of using WeBWorK. The results consistently showed a direct correlation between required use of WeBWorK for homework assignments and higher success rates.

We would like to further analyze the impact of using WeBWorK on subsequent courses. The pass rate of students taking Calculus II who came out of a redesigned Calculus I course with WeBWorK will be compared with the overall pass rate of all sections of Calculus II. Other plans for the future include using even more of the tools offered by WeBWorK (e.g., item analysis) to further increase student success rates.

6 Acknowledgements

We would like to thank Southern Polytechnic State University for providing us with a minigrant during the project. We also would like to thank Dr. Shangrong Deng for his help setting up the websites for the classes.

7 References

[1] Thomasenia Lott Adams. "Technology Makes a Difference in Community College Mathematics Teaching", Community College Journal of Research and Practice, 1997.

[2] E. Johnson and K. Green. "Promoting Mathematical Communication and Community via Blackboard"; Rimus: Problems, Research, and Issues in Mathematics, Undergraduate Education, Vol. XVII, No.4, October-December, 2007.

[3] C. Spitznagel. "Teaching Mathematical Writing Electronically", Proceedings of the 18th Annual International Conference on Technology in Collegiate Mathematic, March, 2006.

[4] Teresa Thiei and M. Brown. "Addressing the Crisis in College Mathematics: Designing Course for Student Success", Change: The Magazine of Higher Learning, 2008.

[5] http://WeBWorK.maa.org/intro.html.

Information Transfer Model in Hotel Chain Management

Niran Chawla
Computer and Engineering Management
Assumption University
Bangkok, Thailand
nirancl@gmail.com

Montri Wiboonrat*
College of Graduate Study in Management
Khon Kaen University
Bangkok, Thailand
montwi@kku.ac.th

Abstract *–In the modern world the main focus of hotel competition is not only between different hotel services but also information facility to customers. As the satisfaction of the value customer is of utmost importance for the successfulness of the whole value chain, effective management of information and process transfer is crucial. The challenge of reduced operating costs while increasing customer's satisfaction is the new challenge for doing hotel business. This research question derived from real case study with budget hotel chains, B2 hotel with 18 branches. In-depth interview with owner and 30% of hotel staffs were conducted to understand the existing problems, limitations, and exceed operation costs of information technology service management that deployed in 18 hotel branches. The study aims to highlight the feature of the concept of information transfer model (ITM) and hotel information chain management (HICM) in hotel management. The results of the research provide a model of how the HICM can improve hotel process management, reduce operations costs, and increase customer satisfactions.*

Keywords: Hotel information chain management, information transfer model, hotel chain management, information chain management.

1 Introduction

Globalization and increasingly competitive markets has driven both local and international hotels to develop their standards to ensure that they are ahead or at least keeping pace with their competitors. Technological changes and organizational improvements are important for effective integration of information chains. Many hotels, especially small and medium hotel (SMH), have not deployed IT to increase more customer expectation and completive advantage. However, in the 21st century, IT investment in hotel industry has increased drastically. Emerging of electronic transactions over Internet is stimulated the competition among online received and access information from hotel industries. Online information application has been generally deployed throughout hospitality industry. The hotel technology infrastructure must support advanced customer service applications, which provide front-desk staff with the tools and capabilities that they need to anticipate customer needs and deliver excellent services. Hotel information chain management (HICM) supports to increase management efficiency [4], to help the hotel operate profitably in spite of rising utility, labor, medical, and other operational costs [2].

According to [1] research, conducted in the U.S.A. in year 2008, there are three main instances in which hotel management considers IT to be particularly beneficial to the hotel workplace: (1) the increase in customer satisfaction, (2) employee efficiency, and (3) increasing revenue. It is notable that hotel management holds no strong belief that IT can be used as a tool for lowering expenses or improving the efficiency of their back office systems. More than half of the respondents considered IT an asset for enhancing the customer experiences [3].

The hotel business challenge is how to design a cost effective communication infrastructure that delivers advanced customer services and helps hotel staffs exceed customer expectation and to build customer loyalty. In order to improve the IT criteria of the Thailand Hotels Standard (THS), this research intends to determine the level of knowledge of currently available information technology (IT) systems, to gauge hotelier's understanding of future IT requirements in the hotel industry that can benefit hotel management professionals, and gain an understanding of the IT requirements of the hotel industry in the near future.

This research was developed a conceptual model of HICM that how hotel business process can be used to analyze the existing processes and help in renovation and integration of those processes, with a special emphasis on an inter-organizational level. It particularizes how IT and smart card (e-Money) technology would help such hotels to reduce total implementation costs by shortening develop period; minimize risk to construction for new branch hotel project by using stable and standard open platform; provide real time services to client at anytime, anywhere, and anyone; create competitive advantage among budget hotel chains [8][9]; easy to interface and connect with any other hotel chain; secure the foundation of HICM model in order to overseas expansion.

2 Information chain management

Communication technologies in the 21st century are changing the ways we live forever. Information chain management (ICM) is a portal of interchange information of each party. In this research, ICM is acting as centralized portal for all hotel breaches to access, update, exchange, and distribute their latest customer information or any requirement. Hotel stakeholders can keep connected via internet for any information, anytime, and anyplace, as illustrated in Figure 1. ICM is working on the top layer of IT system infrastructure. The basis of IT system infrastructure consists of a heterogeneous set of IT devices; a set of supported activities; a set of network communication systems; and some computing application systems the devices may rely on in order to carry out their business objectives.

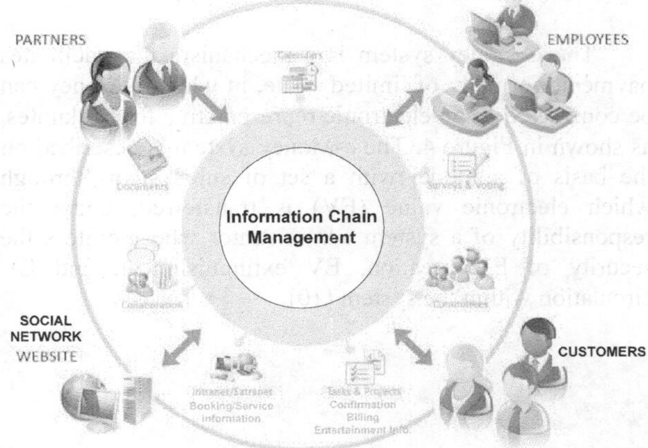

Figure 1. Information chain management

3 Research methodology

With the objective of analyzing the limitations of hotel information management (HIM) in the hospitality industry in Thailand, a case study, B2 hotel chain group in Thailand, was conducted to cover a budget hotel chain group to understand how the hospitality industry can solve the problems of the disintegration of information from the various deployment business applications. This research endeavored to answer proposed problems, interpretations, through the systematic analysis and synthesis of primary and secondary data. Primary data collection were performed through in-depth interview 180 employees, three level of hotel's employees: management (40), back office (70), and front office (70), of 18 hotels from three star hotel chain and 50 MBA students from operations management class subject to the new HIM for the year 2020 hotel management. Hotel management structure and existing IT systems were examined expose to total cost of ownership (TCO). Secondary data were investigated and analysis from the existing research papers after the year 2001, hotel standards and best practice guidelines. The new emerging technologies of IT which applies through hotel service management are the main topic of this research conditional on impact to; customer satisfactions; faster, better, and cheaper; supporting staff operations; reduce operation costs; supporting management decision; and creating new ideas of the 2020 hotel management system.

The research portrayed an interpretative approach from technology trend and service expectations from a group of stakeholder, including managers, IT directors, employees, and customers.

3.1 Examination of existing IT systems

B2 hotel is defined a budget hotel chain and characterized as medium size hotel around 80-150 rooms. Right now, they have more than 18 hotel chain operations in many provinces of Thailand. During year 2005-2010, B2 have only 4 hotels operations which investment of each hotel in fix costs of IT infrastructure system is around $10,000 USD and $16,700 USD for hotel software management license (lifetime agreement with $1,670 USD MA per year), and around $15,000 USD for security systems. The total fix investment of IT infrastructure and HIM is around $41,700 USD per hotel while the variable costs of operation will be $1,670 USD for maintenance agreement (MA) per year, and IT staffs $13,670 USD, and facility operations $10,000 USD. The total variable costs of IT infrastructure and ITSM is around $25,340 USD per year. During 2011-2012, B2 have built 15 hotels for investment and operations. The investment for IT infrastructure and HIM was under the same condition of fix costs and available costs.

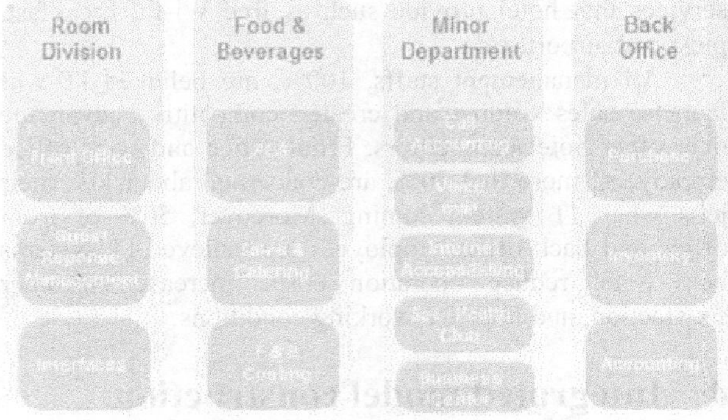

Figure 2. Silo information of hotel managemt by each department

In 2006, B2 have problems with information intergration and distribution among department. Each information is created and keep in their own department. It will take more time to transfer, by manual, from one to the others. Figure 2 is described the silo information management in each department of fron office and back office before applying to HICM within the same year.

3.2 Existing of software collabolation

The character of legacy hotel management is used many software working together or software collaboration. Since each software requirement and deployment was happened not the same time but they need to work together for exchange information. The problems are each software need coding gateway to transfer data in and out from their data based; or it needs third party software working as middle tool for transferring information. Moreover, each software relies on difference software companies which they cannot work together very well subject to conflict of interests [7], as demonstrated in Figure 3.

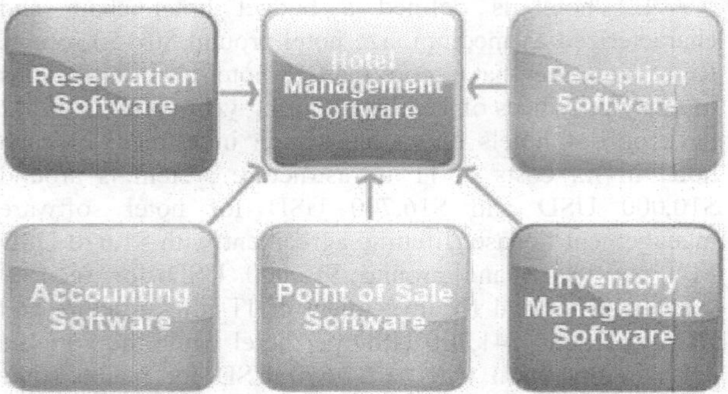

Figure 3. Software collaboration in hotel managemt

3.3 Survey results

The result from MBA student group shown 60% they need to know the hotel first by website, who's comments, price per night, location; 40% would like to know payment systems and must be online; 30% would like to know services that hotel provide such as free Wi-Fi, breakfast, pickup at airport, etc.

All management staffs, 100%, are believed IT will increase sales volume and created competitive advantage over other hotel competitors. Front office and back office employees, more that 70%, are concerned about loss their jobs when IT system coming. Moreover, 50% of front office and back office employees are believed IT systems help hotel reduce operation costs, increase customer satisfaction, and improve working conditions.

4 Integrated model construction

This new model was constructed and modified from the past 10 years hotel history investigation by personal in-depth interviews, group discusssion, and benchmarking amoung 3 star hotels. Synthesis by the rule of the best inclass of 3 star hotel strategies, the best strategy from each hotel were assimilated through ITM to construct and integrate information processes. Refer to hotel chain strategy of 3 star hotels, if the hotel strategic plans to enhance the operational productivities. The hotel can adopt ITM in three directions. First, the process control of food and beverage department, IT equipments such as point of sales (POS) are necessitated to deploy. Second, the deployment of inroom IT and function room embeded equipment is required. Third, online information and booking are needed to broad and wide advertising on website by supporting from local and international agency and social network. When the aim of hotel strategy is to improve the customer satisfaction and operation productivity, it is potential to deploy IT equipment and HIM software in two level approaches. First, infrastrucuture level is working to facilitate information transform for all transactions and communications amoung hotels, agencies, customers, supplier, and regulators. Second, software level is supporting in human interaction (GUI) among hotels, agencies, customers, supplier, and regulators through web applications and/or social network applications.

4.1 Smartcard system (e-Money)

The e-Money system is a mechanism that facilitates payment, normally of limited value, in which e-Money can be considered as an electronic representative for banknotes, as shown in Figure 4. The e-Money system is described on the basis of a model with a set of sub-systems through which electronic value (EV) is transferred, under the responsibility of a system administrator who monitors the security of EV creation, EV extinguishment, and EV circulation within the system [10].

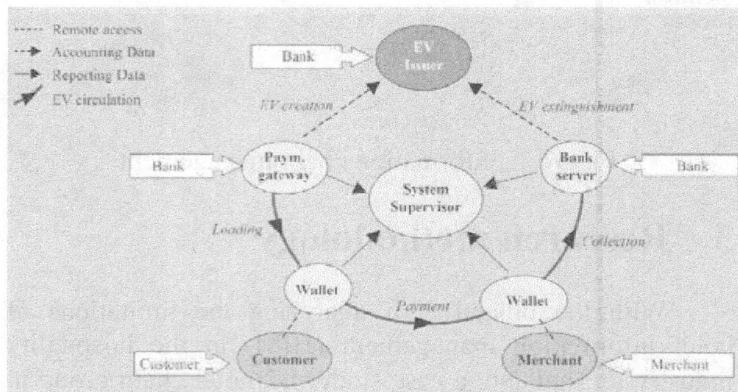

Figure 4. Functions of e-Money system managment

e-Money has multi-application loading platforms, and multi-industry applications accomplished via banking IC card, guarantees the industry card financial risk avoiding and fulfills the special business requirements in the industry. As a special consuming group, campus is a typical application for the banking IC card developed in multiply industries. The benefit functions of e-Money are not only applying to customers but also to hotel employees.

1. Convenience: e-purse in the card can be used for various purchase environments, very convenient.
2. Contactless card, easy payment
3. Integrate banking function, citizen card and campus card etc. into one-card, the card can be used in campus, public transport, micro payment, purchase, utility service.
4. Customize design and application down load
5. Adopt up-dated financial standards and be compatible other industries standards

Hotel e-Service management solution design, illustrated in Figure 5, purposes a guideline of system integration among emerging technologies such as ITM, HIM, HICM, e-Money, CRM, etc.

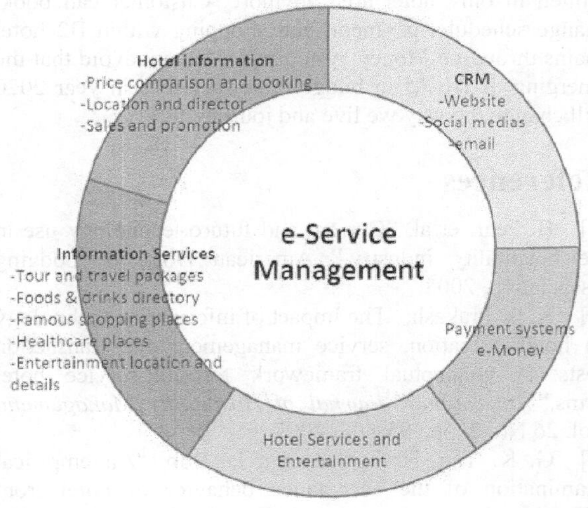

Figure 5. Functions of e-Service management

1. Using the e-Money to establish the hotel chain one-card application, recharge the card via EV and transfer machine.
2. Hotel chain: provide application identifier (AID) and master control key (leaded in by mother card or plaintext) for the hotel group one-card system, the application file of hotel system defines e-purse, identification etc. functions; achieve the e-money transferred to hotel e-purse, accomplish transaction verification and hotel funds settlement.
3. Hotel e-Card check-in: the cryptographic key system of hotel check-in application platform creates application keys via the master control key offered by hotel chain; the hotel application platform issues the e-Card on top of e-Money for the and creates sub-applications and one-card system files structure under the hotel management system, installs relevant operating keys and fulfills the check-in e-Card.
4. Customer: transfer the e-money or e-deposit book amount in the banking card into the e-purse of campus card via self-service transfer machine, and accomplish purchases, time& attendance, access controlling etc via the terminals inside the campus.

4.2 Information transfer model (ITM)

ITM is working as a core value of HICM. Since researches were working on MBA student group regarding what are the information that you need before and during on travel and hotel staff group regarding what are the popular questions from customers. The Figure 6 is described all possible functions of e-Service managemnt of HICM model before, during, and after service management lifecycle. Each function needs to work on ITM as portal of exchange data through information from custormer information to service process and business intelligence (BI) for management decision.

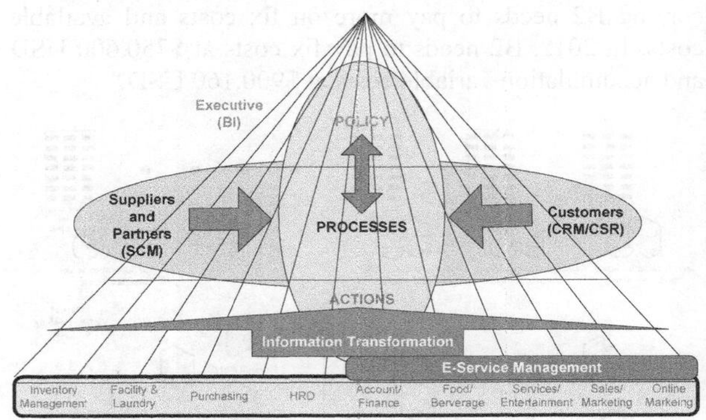

Figure 6. Functions of HICM model

There are three concern points from management level. First, the investment on software license, B2 needs to pay $16,700 USD each time for open new hotel and 10% or $1,670 USD of software MA each year. Second, each software hotel is running on stand alone mode. They are not desing for centelized management. Third, thery are not open for third party to intergrate new features or upgrade any applications. Therefore, after 2013, the new solution of HICM is purposed. The new solution is shown in Figure 7. The intergration technologies and applications of online booking, e-Money for check-in and payment for rooms and services, ubiquitous customer access, and centralized management. These new solution needs $333,400 USD for hardware and infrastructure, $66,700 USD for lifetime software license and centralized management.

ITM provides internet and transactions throughout HICM network service and entertainment areas by high speed wireless (Wi-Fi, 2.4 GHz, 802.11n, at data rate 100Mbits/s.) which customers can take pleasure in surfing internet for information, entertainment, and businesses. All expenses are integrated through e-Money account and cut-off after check out. Safety level of e-Money amount can set by smartcard holder to charging terminal. e-Money card can activate as key card to access room, private lounge, or coupon breakfast. Moreover, e-Money can apply throughout 18 branches of B2 hotel chain with the same services and quality. Forward marketing and promotion can be done to member account likes cash back to e-Money directly every time they purchase to B2 services and entertainment. Moreover, social network and e-mail is the IT channels to get direct to member about Thai's festivals or special events. These are the ways to keep customer in touch everyone, every time, and everywhere with cheaper transaction.

Decentralized IT management was applied since the beginning of B2 operation in 2006. Each B2 hotel has unique IT infrastructure because the sizing of each B2 hotel is not the same room number, layout design, and room decoration. Every B2 hotel has the same platform of software hotel management system one time deployment for lifetime operation fix rate at $16,700 USD and $1,670 USD each year management free. Each year of new hotels coming B2 needs to pay more on fix costs and available costs. In 2012, B2 needs to pay fix costs at $750,600 USD and accumulation variable costs at $900,160 USD.

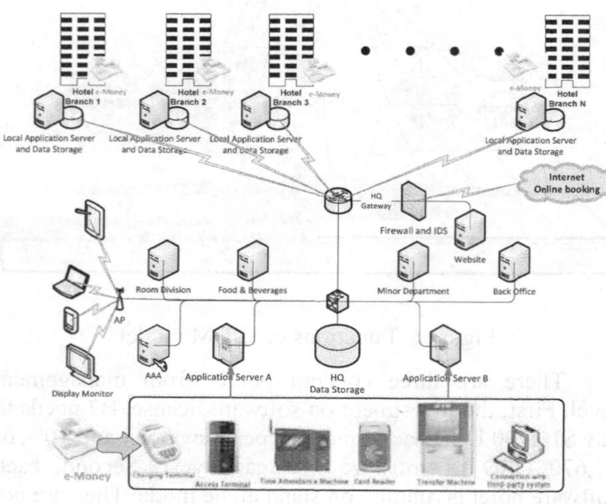

Figure 7. B2 branches inter-communicatoin of HICM

The new centralized HICM needs to resolve fix costs and operation costs, new customer services, tracking customer's behavior, and central management system. IT System and IT infrastructure analysis has been made and conducted proposal according project feasibility study. The result comes up with positive return on investment (ROI). The second part of analysis illustrated after cut –over old system, fix costs of hardware and software license need to pay only one time for lifetime operation at $455,000 USD, this investment include e-Money and HICM systems, with around $45,000 USD for annual operation costs at maximum 30 hotels. Moreover, the capability system of e-Money cards can provide up to 10,000,000 card holders. The forecasting ROI in condition of B2 build 3-4 hotels per year within year 2017 the new e-Money and HICM systems will break even.

5 Conclusions

Emerging of HICM in hotel management is reinforcement mechanism to sustain hospitality industry. Many hotels are change the way human doing business to IT doing business. The research results shown new centralized HICM helps reduce long-term investment in hardware infrastructure and yearly operation costs. Moreover, it is not only created new market services for customers such as e-Money but also improve hotel operation efficiency. Information network is not longer limited in only hotel area anymore. Customer can book, change schedule, payment, and shopping within B2 hotel chains through e-Money systems. We cannot avoid that the emerging of HICM in budget hotel services in year 2020 will change the way we live and journey forever.

References

[1] B. Pearl et al, "Current and future technology use in the hospitality industry," American Hotel & Lodging Association, 2008.

[2] K. C. Prakash, "The impact of information technology on hotel operation, service management and transaction costs: A conceptual framework for full-service hotel firms," *Interational Journal of Hospitality Management*, Vol. 26 No. 2, pp.395-408, 2007.

[3] G. K. Tae, H. L. Jae, and L. Rob, "An empirical examination of the acceptance behavior of hotel front office systems: An extended technology acceptance model," *Tourism Management*, Vol. 29, No. 3, pp. 500-513, 2008.

[4] A. Akarapong and K. Mingsarn, "The change in managerial efficiency of hotels in Chiang mai, Thailand," *Thammasat Economic Journal*, Vol.27, No.3, 2009.

[5] M. Kitamura, "Using ubiquitous networks to create new services based on the commercial and public infrastructure," Nomura Research Institute, Ltd., NRI paper No. 54, 2002.

[6] S. Sirirak and N. Islam, "Relationship between information and communication technology (ICT) adoption and hotel productivity: An empirical study of the hotels in Phuket, Thailand," Technology Management for Global Economic Growth (PICMET), pp. 1-9, 18-22 July 2010.

[7] MAiS, Fidelity Banquet & Event Management System, MAiS Informaton System INC., www.fidelity-mais.com, 2013.

[8] L. Yonghan and X. Yang, "A study of competitive advantage on services package-based economy hotel: 7 Days Inn as a case," International Conference on Management and Services Science (MASS), pp.1-4, 2011.

[9] A. Berislav, "Competitive advantages of the adoption and use of technological systems in hospitality marketing: The case study of Croatia," The 6th Intenational Conference Symposium on Parallel Computing in Electrical Engineering, pp.139-144, 2011.

[10] European Central Bank, Electronic Money System Security Objectives: According to the common criteria methodology, May 2003.

A Framework for Enabling Incidental Learning on the Web

Hongxue (Harris) Wang
School of Computing and Information Systems
Athabasca University
Alberta, Canada

Abstract

Incidental learning is learning something without intent, which usually happens at the time that is not dedicated to learn that thing. Examples of such time include work, game play and activities for leisure. In today's life of many people, a lot of time is spent on the surfing the Web. Should incidental learning be effectively implemented for individuals using the Web, it would make learning more effective for many. This can be especially true for adult learners since they most likely have less time dedicated to learning, or don't have any dedicated time for learning at all. In this paper we present a framework for enabling incidental learning on the Web. The framework identify six key elements for incidental learning on the web, describe a general process of incidental learning, two types of incidental learning and nine scenarios of incidental learning on the web. Finally, the framework prescribes a list of theories and essential technologies that are important for enabling incidental learning on the web.

Keywords: *incidental learning, informal learning, web-based learning, e-learning*

Introduction

Incidental learning is learning without intent, which happens at the time that is not dedicated to learn what is learned through the incidental learning session [1]. In today's society, we are given at least two advantages in developing and implementing enabling technologies and systems for incidental learning on the Web. The first one is that many individuals are spending a lot of time on the Web. This would make incidental learning on the web be able to occur more often. Imagine that such an "incident" could occur only once a year or even only once a lifetime, it might be enough to trigger a scientific invention for a well-prepared scientist, but wouldn't be enough for someone to learn substantially on a subject. As such, it makes more sense now for us to develop enabling technologies and systems for incidental learning on the web because more and more people will benefit from the technologies and systems more often. The second advantage we are given is the unprecedented availability on the world-wide web of knowledge of almost all subjects. This greatly ensures the feasibility of the research and development of technologies and systems in terms of source of knowledge and information. Because the information and knowledge needed to feed the learners on the Web is widely available, a software or intelligent agent should be able to collect the particular knowledge and information especially for an individual based on his/her overall learning goals and feed the individual in a way without his or her notice. As such, the enabling technologies and systems developed from this research could be used to learn knowledge in various topics and subjects!

In brief, the theories, technologies and systems developed from this research are intended to make incidental learning happen to learners while they are browsing the web; to make incidental learning on the web serve at least one of the learning goals the learners may have at the time; and to make incidental learning on the web more effective.

Significance and Contributions of the Research

Incidental learning brings at least two benefits to learners. One is that it effectively utilizes the times or tiny fractions of time that are not designated for learning; the second is that people will be able to learn with a pleasure but without pressure. They would be much happier to learn with less or no stress. Imagining that you could learn something effectively for a purpose or purposes while you are browsing the Web for pleasure, and imagining that people, such as our students, could build their knowledge and skills to satisfy the requirements of a course or courses while you are working or playing with the Web, isn't it wonderful and very significant in education and research?

The benefits can be more obvious for students taking online courses or other distance learning courses. As we know, most of these students are part-time as they often have other business to do other than completing courses. They cannot afford to take leave to study in traditional universities in the classroom, and they don't usually have a big trunk of their time to spend on a course study. However, they do spend time on the web for various reasons and purposes. If enabling technologies and systems are available for incidental learning on the web, it will help these learners greatly, because these students will be able to utilize fractions of their time to learn while they are working, playing or doing other things. The framework presented in this paper is intended to set a firm step towards the enabling technologies and systems.

Key elements of incidental learning

For a system that helps learners to realize incidental learning on the web, some key elements are needed:

1. Learner's capability of learning – this is the very basic requirement for incidental learning, or any learning to occur. An agent system designed for enabling incidental learning on the web must do its best to know what the learner is capable of learning. A learner may be capable of learning X but not Y. it won't help the learner to keep firing up incidental learning sessions that teach the learner something he or she is incapable of.
2. Learner's desire to learn -- without any desire to learn, no learning can be effective. The desire can be fostered gradually through certain enabling technologies. This may be the hardest part for an agent to do – to know whether the learner has the desire to learn at a specific time. The information may be gathered during the time learner is browsing the web, or after two or three tries of firing up an incidental learning session – when the learner has simply ignored. In any case, it is important for the agent system to know if the learner has the desire to learn at a given time; otherwise it would definitely be an annoying thing to the learner to keep firing up one incidental learning session after another.
3. Learning goals of the leaner – what topics and subjects the learner is interested in, at what level the learner is in a particular area or topic.
4. Triggers to fire up an incidental learning session – the system needs to be fired up at the right time while the learner is on the web. The triggers should be within the web document the learner is reading, together with the learner's motion such as mouse click.

5. Available learning content – the system must be able to get the right learning content to form a learning session for the learner. The content can be in a learning object repository, or mined from the web on the fly.
6. An effective incidental learning session – the session must be well controlled and properly sized in terms of both content and duration.

These key elements must be fully considered in the design and development of enabling technologies and systems for incidental learning on the web.

General process of incidental learning on the web

Incidental learning may happen consciously or unconsciously. In the former case, the learning session happens incidentally while the learning is doing something else, but during the session, the learner consciously knows she or he is in the learning session, and knows what he is supposed to learn. With consciousness, the learner could be more motivated during the session, and the learning should be more effective.

In the latter case, not only does the learning session, if it can be called a learning session, occur incidentally, the learner doesn't even know he or she is in a learning session, and what she or he is learning either.

For some learners, learning with a clear purpose or consciously should be more effective, while for learners who are really tired of learning certain things in certain area, incidental learning unconsciously should be more effective too.

While the learners may learn consciously or unconsciously, the agent system enabling incidental learning on the web must know what a particular learner is supposed to learn in a specific learning session. Hence, the process of incidental learning on the web can be generally depicted as follows:

1. Identify the point of interest within the context of what the learner is doing, or browsing in the case of web-based incidental learning;
2. Further develop the point of interest into a specific learning objective or objectives which are part of the learner's learning goals at the time;
3. Form a small learning session with content dynamically generated from the web or learning object repositories, and bring the learner into the learning session;
4. Present the learning session to the learner and/or bring the learner into the learning session;
5. Closing the session once the learner is done, or has left the session, and book keeping the learning session.

Types of Incidental Learning and Scenarios on the Web

The unique feature of incidental learning is that learning occurred incidentally in the view of the learner. Although the occurrence of learning may seem to be random (that's why incidental learning is also called random learning), the knowledge and skills acquired through it don't need to be random, especially when the incidental learning session is enabled by an intelligent agent system. That is to say, the learning outcome can be either expected or unexpected by the learner. We then have the following two types of incidental learning:

1. incidental learning from which something expected has been learned, we use letter E to refer to such learning, use letter E with a subscript to refer a learning goal that may consists of small gradients of learning goals or knowledge, denoted by letter e with or with a subscript.
2. incidental learning from which something unexpected has been learned, we use letter U to refer to such learning, use letter U with a subscript to refer a learning goal that may consists of small gradients of learning goals or knowledge, denoted by letter u with or with a subscript.

Let E={E1, E2, …, Em} represent the learning goals identified for a particular learner at a given time, and each Ei={ei1, ei2, …, eik}, where each eij represents a small learning goal or knowledge gradient; we further let U={U1, U2, …, Um} represent the learning goals identified for a particular learner at a given time, and each Ui={ui1, ui2, …, uik}, where each uij represents a small learning goal or knowledge gradient, we then may have the following different scenarios of incidental learning on the web:

1. incidental learning towards a consistent learning goal expected for the learner

In this scenario, the learner is going through several incidental-learning sessions fed by the agent, and all the knowledge gradients covered by the incidental learning sessions serve the same learning goal. After each incidental learning session, the learner will go back to his or her non-learning web browsing;

2. Incidental learning spread several learning goals, but all expected for the learner

In this scenario, the learner is going through several incidental-learning sessions fed by the agent, but the knowledge gradients covered by the incidental learning sessions serve the several different learning goals. After each incidental learning session, the learner will go back to his or her non-learning web browsing;

3. One incidental learning after another serves the same learning goal

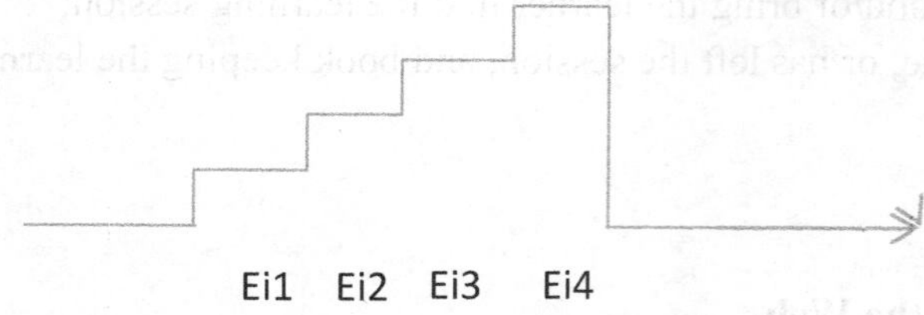

In this scenario, the learner is going through one incidental-learning session after another fed by the agent, and all the knowledge gradients covered by the incidental learning sessions serve the same learning goal.

After going through several incidental learning sessions, the learner then goes back to his or her non-learning web browsing;

4. One incidental learning after another serves different learning goals

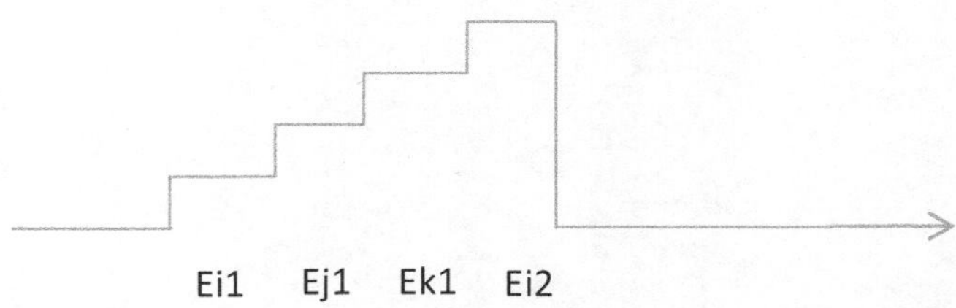

In this scenario, the learner is going through one incidental-learning session after another fed by the agent, but the knowledge gradients covered by the incidental learning sessions serve different learning goals. After going through several incidental learning sessions, the learner then goes back to his or her non-learning web browsing;

5. incidental learning towards a consistent learning goal unexpected for the learner

In this scenario, the learner is going through several incidental-learning sessions fed by the agent, and all the knowledge gradients covered by the incidental learning sessions serve the same learning goal. After each incidental learning session, the learner will go back to his or her non-learning web browsing;

6. Incidental learning spread several learning goals, but all unexpected for the learner

In this scenario, the learner is going through several incidental-learning sessions fed by the agent, but the knowledge gradients covered by the incidental learning sessions serve the several different learning goals. After each incidental learning session, the learner will go back to his or her non-learning web browsing;

7. One incidental learning after another serves for a mix of expected and unexpected learning goals

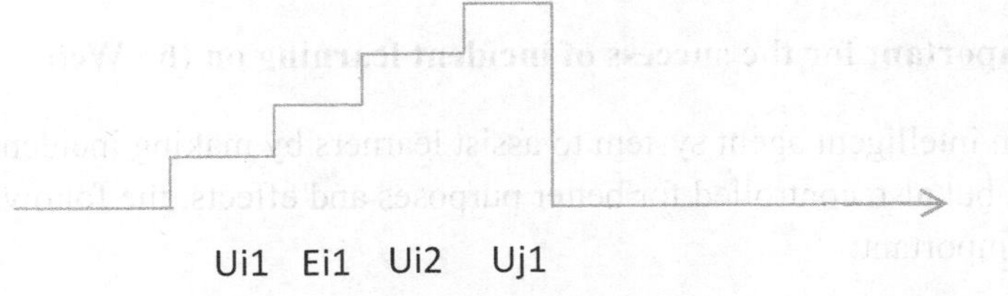

In this scenario, the learner is going through one incidental-learning session after another fed by the agent, and knowledge gradients covered by the incidental learning sessions serve a mix of different learning

expected or unexpected goals. After going through several incidental learning sessions, the learner then goes back to his or her non-learning web browsing;

8. One incidental learning after another but serves one expected learning goals and one unexpected learning goal

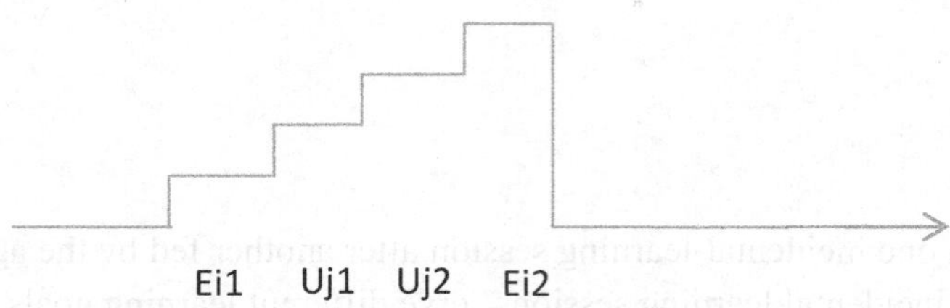

In this scenario, the learner is going through one incidental-learning session after another fed by the agent, and the knowledge gradients covered by the incidental learning sessions consistently serve one expected learning goal and one unexpected learning goal. After going through several incidental learning sessions, the learner then goes back to his or her non-learning web browsing;

9. Incidental learning spread several expected and unexpected learning goals

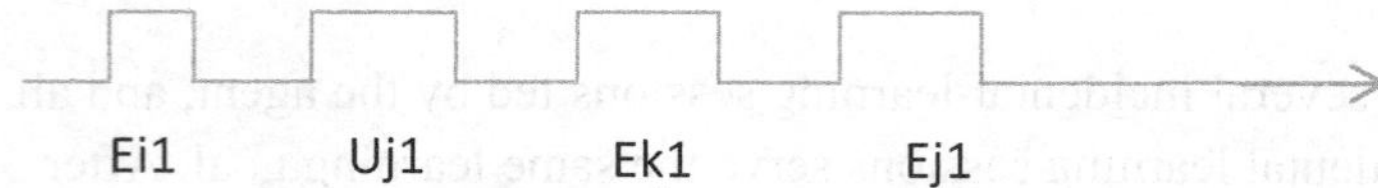

In this scenario, the learner is going through several incidental-learning sessions fed by the agent, and the knowledge gradients covered by the incidental learning sessions serve several different expected and unexpected learning goals. After each incidental learning session, the learner will go back to his or her non-learning web browsing.

The nine scenarios discussed above is not an exhausted list of all possible scenarios. In real cases without control, some learners may jump from one 'incidental learning session' from another across many different topics and subjects, while some may more likely stay with one topic or one subject. What this research is intended to do, however, is to implement a software agent which is able to assist learners and make incidental learning on the web for better results, and to better serve the learning goals of the learner.

Theories and enabling technologies important for the success of incident learning on the Web

To successfully design and implement an intelligent agent system to assist learners by making incidental learning on the web not only happening, but also controlled for better purposes and effects, the following theoretical and technical areas are very important:

1. Learner modeling for their personality and learning style. This is important for the intelligent agent in order to form and render right incidental learning sessions to the learner, to ensure the learning sessions are not only accepted but also welcome by the learner;

2. Learning and building learning goals for the learner. The main purpose of intelligent agent system is to not only make incidental learning on the web happen, but also happen to serve the learner's learning goals. Therefore, knowing what the learning goals are is very important.
3. Data/web mining to build incidental learning session dynamically. The system should be able to discover and select the best fit learning objects or material to form an incidental learning session whenever a trigger for a learning session is identified for the learner. Therefore, it is important for the agent system to do data mining on the web.
4. Doing effective learning analytics for adjust and fine-tune the learner models for better incidental learning sessions. Each incidental learning session should be evaluated after it's over, and the learner actions and performance during the sessions should be analyzed.
5. Intelligent agent technologies. While the proposed framework and the theories and technologies listed above are important for developing an intelligent agent for enabling incidental learning on the web, agent theories and technologies developed over the last few decades by researchers and practitioners in computing and AI community in particular are definitely a great asset for the success.

The above may not have covered all the important theories and technologies for designing and developing an intelligent agent for enabling incidental learning on the Web, but they do form a core or base for anyone to do further research and development in this direction.

Discussions

We presented in this paper a framework for enabling incidental learning on the Web. In the framework we have identified some key elements for enabling incidental learning on the web. These key elements are important for the design and implementation of any agent system for enabling incidental learning on the web.

We further discussed the general process of incidental learning on the web, two types of incidental learning, as well as several scenarios of web-based incidental learning. These are all parts of the entire framework on which intelligent system can be built to enable web-based incidental learning.

References

1. Baskett, H. K. M., Workplace Factors Which Enhance Self-directed Learning, a report of a project on self-directed learning in the workplace, a paper presented to the Seventh International Symposium on Self-Directed Learning, West Palm Beach, Florida, January 21-23, 1993. Available online at http://www.eric.ed.gov/PDFS/ED359354.pdf
2. Baylor, A.L. Perceived disorientation and incidental learning in a Web-based environment: Internal and external factors J of Educational Multimedia and Hypermedia Vol. 10/3 227-251:2001
3. Elley, W.B. (Dez 2005), [http//cela.albany.edu/reports/inpraise/main.html In praise of incidental learning: Lessons from some empirical findings on lan guage acquisition: 1997]
4. Kerka, Sandra 2000, Trends and Issues 2000 Alert No.18, Incidental learning
5. Marsick, V.J. & KJ Watkins (2001). Informal and incidental learning, new directions for adult and continuing education 89 25-34.
6. Mayer, R.E., Heiser, J. & Lonn,S. (2001). Cognitive constraints on multimedia learning: when presenting more material results in less understanding. Journal´of educational psychology, 93 pp.187-198
7. Schank, Roger, C. & Ch. Cleary (1995). Engines for Education, Lawrence Erlbaum Ass. Publishers Hillsdale NJ, pp. 95-105 (Incidental learning chapter).

e-Toogle: Education Platform for Cyber-Physical Environments

The 2013 International Conference on e-Learning, e-Business, Enterprise Information Systems, and e-Government (EEE'13)

Rafael Penna dos Santos* (rapennas@gmail.com), Greyce N. Schroeder (sgreyce@gmail.com), Ricardo N. Rodrigues (ricardonagel@gmail.com), Silvia S. C. Botelho (silviacb.botelho@gmail.com), Marcos Amaral (marcosamaralrg@gmail.com)
Center for Computational Science
Federal University of Rio Grande, FURG
Av. Itália km 8 Bairro Carreiros
96203-900
Rio Grande, RS, Brazil

***Abstract* — A Cyber-Physical Systems (or CPS) is a system that combines and coordinates physical and computational elements. The CPS incorporates the ability to act in the physical world with the intelligence of cyber world to add new features to real-world physical systems [1]. Among the various fields of activity of the CPS, can cite security systems, robotics, education, among others. Educational environments are characterized by being favorable places for the introduction of technologies aimed to facilitate the interaction/mediation between subjects and learning's objects. In this paper, we propose an technological architecture for education, where we identify the main constituents of a cyber-physical learning environment, and their interconnections. The e-Toggle platform is proposed as an implementation for this architecture. It is characterized as being a CPS focused in education and it uses ROS (Robot Operating System) for communication between the real devices and the virtual world.**

Keywords— Cyber-Physical Systems; CPS; Internet of Things; e-Learning;

I. Introduction

In recent years, technological advances are leading to new relationships between individuals and between these and technologies. New environments, digitally supported emerge, allowing different agents (real, virtual) interact in a way before unimaginable to the society. In this new technological landscape arise new theories, methodologies, techniques and tools that come from different areas related to human computer interface.

In this paradigm, different objects, equipped with embedded computing, can interact with each other, sensing and adapting to the environment in a transparent manner, making the human-computer interaction simpler.

Researches in the area called Internet of Things(IoT) [3], in accordance with the ideas of ubiquitous computing, seek to define models for the interconnection of any "thing" (objects, computers, animals, people, etc.) in a network, similar to the devices today already interconnected through Internet. Some of these models are the EPCglobal [4] and the UID architecture [5]. Although there are initiatives in order to create a standard for IoT such as UID Center [6], there is no set standard for this type of system.

More recently, a more specific line of research has emerged, coining the term Cyber-Physical Systems (CPS). A CPS is a system that combines and coordinates physical and computational elements. The CPS integrates the ability to act in the physical world and the intelligence from cyber (virtual) world, adding new resources to real world systems [1]. Among the field of activity of CPS, emerging research areas include security systems, sensors and actuators research, Internet of Things, medical applications, robotics, education, among others.

Research on Cyber-Physical Systems with focus on education is recent and scarce. Some works, like [7] and [8] indicate education as a promising application field for CPSs, but do not present results in this area.

The aim of this paper is to propose an educational technology architecture, where the components of physical and virtual environments become boosters learning. Therefore, it is presented a platform called e-Toggle, which is characterized by being a CPS oriented education.

This paper is organized as follows: first, the research methodology is introduced; then, a discussion about the relationship between education and technology is presented; on chapter 4, a new Cyber-Physical System with focus on educational applications, called e-Toogle, is proposed; on chapter 5, some case studies are presented to validate the proposal; finally, conclusion and future work are presented.

II. Research Methodology

A. Search and choice procedures

The focus on this work is on CPS's related with the Internet of Things (IoT) and with applications on education. Other CPS's research lines, such as security, energy and sensors networks are not discussed in this article. The emphasis of this review is on an empirical search instead of non-empirical explanations.

The empirical search for references was carried out in two phases. On the first phase, we searched for articles on Google Scholar, crossing the keywords Cyber-Physical Systems with keywords Internet of Things and education. On the second phase, we conducted a new search on some citations of papers from first phase. The search on Google Scholar was considered sufficient as it contemplates all major electronic databases.

In may 2013, our search returned 221 papers. After reading the abstracts, 30 were selected for further analysis. These 30 papers were divided in four categories as described in the next section.

B. Data Analysis

The review of these works follows guidelines established by [9], who stated that the purpose of a survey is to summarize the accumulated knowledge base on the topic of interest and highlight issues yet to investigate. Our data analysis proceeded as follows.

Every article found and selected in the empirical search has been read. The categories were not pre-determined before reviewing, but emerged from data instead. Using the constant comparative method [10], the first articles was read and its contents was observed to form a categorization attempt according to the research topic. The results of the first paper were noted. The following article was then selected and read. Its content was matched with the firs article. If it was similar, it was put in the same category as the first one (together with its specificity) and the third article was processed. Otherwise, the second content represented the first entry in a new research category. This process was repeated until all 30 articles have been read and examined. It should be noted that it is possible that a single article produces more than one research category.

C. Search results

We identify four main research categories: (a) System Project, Architecture and Modeling, (b) Survey papers, (c) Frameworks and (d) Applications.

Category 1: System Project, Architecture and Modeling

This category covers a wide range of articles, since it comprises all those which involve the steps of design, architecture and modeling of cyber-physical systems. This section presents only the main works.

[11] presents a research on developing a REST-style architecture for CPS. It is proposed a way to solve the requirements of CPS architecture through RESTful principles.

In [12], a concept lattice-based event model for CPS is introduced. Under this model, a CPS event is uniformly represented by three components: event type, its internal attributes, and its external attributes. The internal and external attributes together characterize the type, spatio-temporal properties of the event as well as the components that observe it. A set of event composition rules are defined where the CPS event composition is based on a CPS concept lattice. A real-life smart home example is used to illustrate the proposed event model.

In [13], a new seven layer sensor modeling approach is presented. The proposed architecture enables one to describe a sensor right from its physical properties to end functionality; where it defines the sensor services to talk with end applications.

Finally, [14] focuses on the challenges of modeling cyber-physical systems that arise from the intrinsic heterogeneity, concurrency, and sensitivity to timing of such systems. It uses a portion of an aircraft vehicle management systems (VMS), specifically the fuel management subsystem, to illustrate the challenges and then discusses technologies that at least partially address the challenges.

Category 2: Survey articles

Similarly to the previous one, this category also covers a wide range of articles, because it is composed of all those articles intended to produce a bibliographic review. This section also present only the main survey articles found in the empirical search.

One of the major references in the case of CPS surveys is “Cyber-Physical Systems: A New Frontier” [15]. This article first reviews some of the challenges and promises of CPS, followed by an articulation of some specific challenges and promises that are more closely related to the Sensor Networks, Ubiquitous and Trustworthy Computing.

[7] presents a future vision for cyber-physical systems and identifies some specific grand challenges, beyond research and educational challenges that must be addressed. It also discusses the resulting societal and economic impact of such advances in CPS.

At [16] the features of CPSs are described, and the research progresses are summarized from different perspectives such as energy control, secure control, transmission and management, control technique, system resource allocation, and model-based software design. After, the research challenges and some suggestions for future work are in brief outlined.

Yet, other important works on CPS surveys deserve to be mentioned as: Advances in Cyber-Physical Systems Research [17], and Cyber-Physical Systems: Close Encounters Between Two Parallel Worlds [Point of View] [8];

Category 3: Frameworks

Several frameworks for different applications appeared in our empirical search. The ones related with the subject of this article are briefly described below.

[18] presents a novel framework, based on CPS concept, for a networked interactive home based intelligent motor rehabilitation system to facilitate functional recovery post-stroke. Patients use proper rehabilitation appliances to conduct continuous, repetitive rehabilitation trainings while wireless sensor networks (WSN) collect data related to the patients' functional activities. Within this framework, it is expected that important information

and resources can be utilized in the rehabilitation stages more efficiently for an individual subject.

[19] involves the design and development of a prototyping platform and open design framework for a semi-autonomous wheelchair to realize a human-in-the-loop cyber physical system (HiLCPS) as an assisting technology. The system is designed to assist physically locked-in individuals in navigating indoor environments through the use of modular sensor, communication, and control designs. This enables the user to share control with the wheelchair and allows the system to operate semi-autonomously with a human in the loop.

In [20], a functional design of an interactive Cyber-Physical System (CPS) for people with disabilities and frail elderly people is introduced as an effective method of proactive service in smart space. In this article, the scenario-based functional design of CPS has been motivated by open issues, concepts, and framework architecture for resolving inter space interaction issues caused by changes in users' location and environment which is one of key issues in adjusting and re-setting smart environments for the target population.

Category 4: Applications

The last category includes studies related to applications utilizing CPSs as basic architecture for the development of specific scenarios. This category has two sub categories as main applications of interest: Persons with Disabilities and Education.

Category 4.1: People with Disability

A common theme that appeared in the searches under the category applications, was related to applications involving systems for people with disabilities. Among the major works, stand out systems for motor rehabilitation after stroke [18], for Semi-Autonomous Wheelchair Navigation [19] and for people with disability and frail elderly people [20].

Category 4.2: Education

The search of this empirical study showed that the use of Cyber-Physical Systems for educational purposes is very new and scarce. Some works like [7] and [8] identify education as one of the promising fields of application for CPSs, but do not focus or present results in this area. Thus, to complete this research, we have searched for articles that use similar concepts to CPS in education, even if does not present nomenclature and references for this type of system.

In [21] the author documents real-world experiences of innovators in higher education who have redesigned spaces for learning and teaching, including physical, virtual, formal, informal, blended, flexible, and time sensitive factors.

The reference [22] proposes a research model that examines the determinants of student learning satisfaction in a blended e-learning system (BELS) environment, based on social cognitive theory. The empirical findings indicate that computer self-efficacy, performance expectations, system functionality, content feature, interaction, and learning climate are the primary determinants of student learning satisfaction with BELS. Interaction has a significant effect on learning climate.

Yet [23] aimed to investigate the effect of experimenting with physical manipulative (PM), virtual manipulative (VM), and a blended combination of PM and VM on undergraduate students' understanding of concepts in the domain of Light and Color. Results revealed that the use of a blended combination of PM and VM enhanced students' conceptual understanding in the domain of Light and Color more than the use of PM or VM alone.

Last, [24] explores blending virtual and physical learning environments to enhance the experience of first year by immersing students into university culture through social and academic interaction between peers. The social network Facebook is used in parallel with the classroom to assess student performance.

III. Education and Technology

The fast speed on which new technological devices are introduced creates new necessities and imposes different modes of interaction. Some technological artifacts, like analog and digital photography, movie pictures, television, computers and videogames are technological resources developed with different ends and that have been improved along the years, contributing more intensely to construct what today we call digital culture.

In this new technological reality our brain is filed with images, movements and sounds, conducting a new mode of learning the world. The computer (which began been developed on 1946) has become an essential tool for any sector of society: throughout the web, millions of people have access to information, education and entertainment.

Furthermore, social relationship networks like Facebook, constitute a way of interaction characterized by the sharing of information and knowledge previously nonexistent among humans. For this extensive use of technology, the effects of changes arising from developments in the sector are being increasingly perceived in contemporary society.

The presence of so-called Information and Communication Technologies (ICTs) in Education is providing new ways of teaching and learning, where there are new ways to serve and access a large volume of information and knowledge [25].

Virtual learning environments (VLEs), according to [26] are computer systems that allow integrate different media, languages and resources, present information, develop interactions; perform and socialize productions, regardless of time and space for each participant. With the spread of the world wide web, education gains new perspectives. In this context, VLE are being used for distance learning, teleconferencing and scientific events [27].

In recent years, Cyber-Physical Systems (CPS) have emerged and, shyly, permeated work related to learning environments. These systems intend to integrate objects from the physical world and information systems, making interconnections as well as the sharing of information. Among the various fields of activity of the CPS, it can be cited education as the most promising. Thus, it has started to emerge the first Virtual-Physical Learning Environments.

All this progress in information technology and communication meets the theories of Piaget. For him, the behavior of living beings is not innate, neither the result of conditioning, and yes, the behavior is built on an interaction between the environment and the individual. This epistemological theory is characterized as interactional. The intelligence of the individual, as an adaptation to new situations, therefore, is related to the complexity of the individual interaction with the environment [2]. In other words, the more complex this interaction, the more "intelligent" is the individual. We realize that there are technological tools nowadays that offer such ease of interaction between subjects and the means that surround them, are others available content or learning objects differentiated.

Thus, we see that the CPS's can provide a computational model which can provide an interaction between subjects and media, more natural, at any time, by anyone and in different places, playing as catalyst role for a new education.

IV. E-TOOGLE PLATFORM

The e-Toogle platform is proposed as an implementation of a technological architecture for education applications. It is a CPS targeted on education. It uses ROS (Robot Operating System) for communication between real devices and the virtual world. Moreover, it uses Blender 3D rendering software as object visualization tool and Moodle as virtual-real learning environment.

The e-Toogle is a version of Toogle platform specially projected for education purposes.

The Toogle platform is composed by several objects that can be grouped on the following categories:

- Real elements with no processing, perception or actuation capacity, referred in this work as "things".
- Computational nodes with processing capacity.
- Graphical and simulation technologies with virtual representation capacity.
- Communication technologies capable of integrating different elements.

The Toogle system has been developed as a cyber-physical environments editor and navigator. Through Toogle, one can create any simulation scenario with 3D visualization and configure sensors and actuators on the lowest level for this scenario. With this environment, we have a relationship between the virtual and real world, which allows real objects to execute tasks, while simultaneously simulating them in the Toogle virtual environment. The opposite is also possible: simulate tasks in the virtual environment and forward the simulation parameters for real objects.

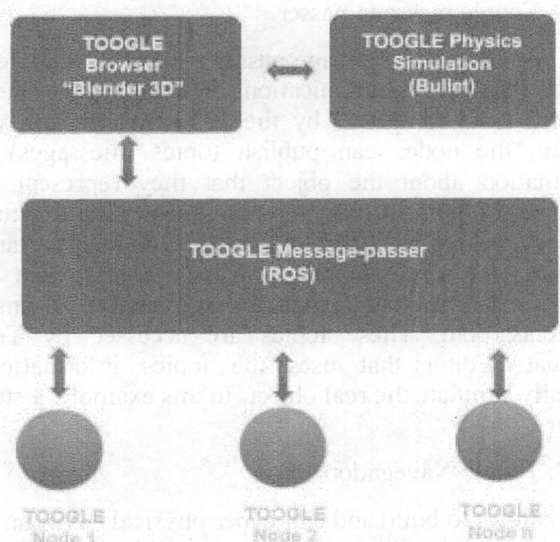

Figura 1. Toogle's Architecture

Figure 1 shows the modules that compose the system architecture. This modules are described below, but for a better understanding, we first describe the two main systems used to create Toogle.

ROS: is the Robot Operating System consisting of process (called nodes). These processes can run in different machines. The nodes use two types of communication to send messages to the system: the first is synchronous and is called service; the second is asynchronous, where topics are published on nodes.

Blender: the Blender development tool offers tridimensional graphical resources for object visualization and information representation. Blender has been adopted as visualization tool for ubiquitous environments due its open source and multi-platform characteristics. Moreover it supports stereoscopy, multiprojection and physics simulation.

A. Toogle Nodes

The system nodes are a representation of all objects perceived by the system. These objects can have its own processing capacity (like robots, computers and cell phones) or have no processing capacity (objects, vehicles, people). The CPS nodes represent physical and virtual objects within the system. The node configuration is saved in a xml file hosted in the network server. In this file, it is possible to configure the attributes of each node. In execution time, the attributes of each node can be modified by information received from sensors that are connected with them. Depending on the node processing capacity, actuators can be activated to control and supervise the function of nodes in the system.

The nodes can be created directly in Blender or imported from other pieces of software. The system allows the importing of several types of files. The 3D models can be rendered directly in Blender by a procedural technique that generates high resolution images without the necessity of importing external images.

B. Toogle message/passer

The Toggle message-passer is the middleware responsible for communication between nodes and the system. It is composed by the ROS system. In Toogle system, the nodes can publish topics (messages) with information about the object that they represent. This messages contain information about sensors and actuators that will be used by Toogle Navigator/Editor. For example, a topic can represent the position of a student in a classroom or the state (activated/deactivated) of a sensor in this classroom. These topics are accessed by Toogle Navigator/Editor that uses the topics information to virtually simulate the real object. In this example, a student avatar.

C. Toogle Navegador/Editor

It allows to build and edit cyber physical environments, providing navigability and interaction with the information provided by nodes. The Toogle editor allows creating, editing, biding and removing information within a given scenario. An analogy with internet pages can be drawn: a hypertext consists of an aggregate of information and their connections while the hyper-environments (physical-virtual environments) consists of an aggregate of "things" on a given scenario and their connections. Therefore, the editor is able to create and represent the different pieces of information provided by the nodes and making connections / links between them. For each hyper-environment it is possible to create and add new objects, track them, add pre-existing objects, insert sensors and actuators for these objects and enable its connections with other objects. In addition, the editor allows the visualization of messages exchange between objects. Figure 2 shows the Toogle Editor/Navigator.

The Toogle navigator allows the access and visualization of information that has been created in Toogle Editor. It is a tridimensional scenario visualizer, where a replica of a real world scenario can be seen, according to the connections created in editor. The Toogle Navigator/Editor uses the Blender developing tool to create, edit and visualize the tridimensional scenarios. An interface for multiprojection in a CAVE visualization environment is also available. This interface allows an immersive visualization of objects and information from Toogle.

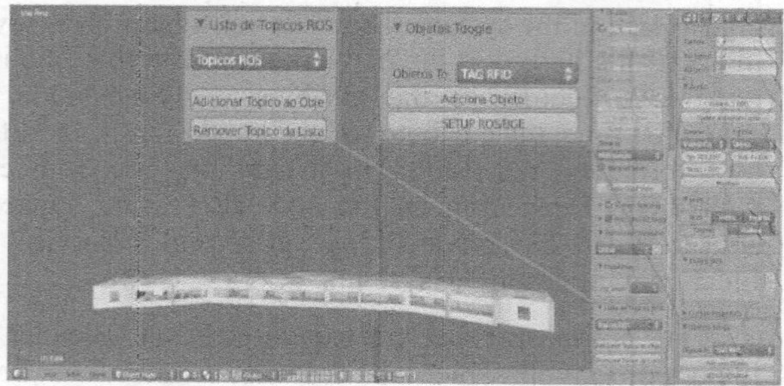

Figura 2. Toogle Editor/Navegador

The advent of HTML5 has enabled the development of tools for 2D/3D visualization for Web browsers without the need to use plugins. Thus, it was possible to build visualization and interaction Toggle realtime accessed remotely by the user. For this we have two main components: the server-side and client-side. On the server side we have the middleware ROS, it is integrated to the WebSocket server through the Java Script library "ROS BRIGDE". The middleware responsible for communication between server and client sides is the WebSocket (that is a feature provided by Html5). On the client side, we have the web browser with its java script libraries, web socket, responsible for communication, and libraries responsible for rendering the scene and their interactions.

D. Toogle Physics Simulation

This module is responsible for physical simulations, allowing realism and high performance computation. It uses Bullet open source library, which uses OpenGL for real time rendering. It has mechanisms for collision detection and rigid body dynamics. The physical simulator makes it possible to simulate objects that can fall, roll and collide with other objects, all with a very realistic appearance. Aspects of scene lighting make use of GLSL and Pixel Shaders techniques.

E. Education Module

As the e-Toogle is a version of Toogle platform designed for education, the last module we present is the Education one. The e-Toogle has an unique module for learning applications, with different pre-existing objects available, as described below:

- Moodle – The platform allows web pages to be incorpored as textures for objects in the scenario. This is possible mainly because Toogle Navigator is implemented using HTML 5 standard. Thus this module enables the insertion of Moodle black boards, where a rectangular object, with panel style, displays the contents of a registered course in Moodle. The course can be chosen according the object configuration.

- Attendance book – Virtual object associated with real sensors to detect the presence of students in the classroom and record their attendance. As the student enters the classroom carrying a RFID tag, he is detected by a RFID reader. This reader sends (through the message/passer module) the student ID to the system, which logs into the student's Moodle account, and register the student in the cyber physical environment.

- Virtual-Physical Blackboard – this object can be inserted wherever we want the virtual environment presents the contents simultaneously with the contents shown in classroom. Once the e-Toogle is installed on teacher's computer and this object is inserted in the scenario, the content displayed in classroom will be simultaneously presented in the virtual blackboard. If the teacher goes to the next slide in a presentation in classroom, the virtual environment will also reflect this change.

- Course calendar – object that contains class calendar, exams schedule, assignments due date, etc.

- Message tool – provides communication between students' avatars in the virtual environment. This tool is integrated with Moodle messaging system, which records all exchanged messages.

V. Case study: Computational algorithms class using e-Toogle

This case study is a prototype of a physical-virtual course with e-Toogle. The prototype was developed according to the steps described below:

Step 1: 3D modeling of physical building: we use the Toogle Editor to create a 3D model of the Center for Computational Science building at Federal University of Rio Grande (FURG). This building has classrooms, teachers offices, labs and bathrooms. The modeling is still a prototype, and several improvements ought to be made. Greater attention was given to classrooms explored in this case study.(Figure 3).

Figure 3. Modelo 3D do prédio do C3 - Sala de Aula

Step 2: Physical adequation (sensors and actuators): The classroom used in this case study was prepared. A computer with e-Toogle has been installed and RFID readers where connected to this computer. The RFID equipment undertaken was: reader L-RX201 and active tag DOMINO L-TG100, shown in Figure 4.

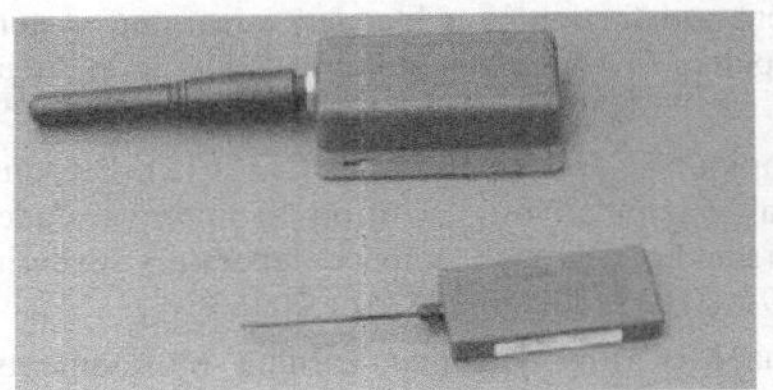

Figure 4. RFID reader and active tag

Step 3: Communication: This step consists on providing data communication from sensors to Toogle plataform, through Toogle Message/passer, which uses middleware (ROS). The library used for integration was ros.h. This communication can be better understood through the use of the object Attendance Book, which uses RFID technology to record student attendance. The communication between the RFID reader and the Toggle platform was over serial port and used the library boost-asio. The communication is done with the software sending the command to the reader to start reading the tags. The tag detected by the reader (attached to the student) is sent to the program that interprets the data received through the serial port, and publishes, on a topic of ROS, the desired data (tagsLidas topic). The data sent by the detection can be, for example, signal intensity, the tag ID, the reader ID. In our experiment, only the detected tag ID is published. Figure 8 shows the topic "tagsLidas" listing the codes of detected tags.

Step 4: Toogle-Editor: The hyper-environment was created using the Toogle-Editor. A virtual scenario was modeled, biding the information from sensors and virtual objects. The Toogle-Editor interface is shown in Figure 5.

Figure 5. Toogle Navigator/Editor

Step 5: Toogle-Navigator: the last step performed was to run the Toogle-Navigator. It enables the access to information related to hyper environment through a 3D environment. The presence of an element or its absence can be noticed through the radio frequency reader. In other words, the RFID reader emits Radio Frequency and if the label attached to the student is close enough to this reader it will produce a response signal. By detecting the signal sent by the reader, the tag sends its unique ID to the reader, wich, introduces into the system Toggle (step 3). The Toogle system manages the information and makes the updating of information in the virtual 3D environment in real time, in this case, putting the avatar corresponding to the student in the specific classroom. When running the Toogle-Navigator, the objects that were associated with the corresponding code tags (step 4) will simulate the presence of the student in the virtual environment, inserting the avatars when the reader reader detect the approach of the relevant tag (Figure 5). This is possible because the object "attendance book" has a function capable of receiving the topic of ROS with the tags's code read and identify which object (one of the nodes tags) has the property with the same code, placing, at this moment, the avatar in the correct environment. Finally, it can be viewed in figure 5 the objects Moodle and Virtual-Physical Blackboard, both from Education module, in the environment while the user navigates through it.

VI. Conclusion and Future Works

It was presented in this paper, a platform called e-Toggle, version of the Toogle platform designed for education. It was proposed as an implementation of an educational and technological architecture, being characterized by a CPS using the ROS for communication between the real and virtual world. Software Blender 3D was used as viewer for the system objects. Finally, Moodle was presented as a virtual-real environment for learning in this platform.

The architecture of e-Toggle was presented with 5 modules: Toggle Nodes, Toggle message / passer, Toggle Browser / Editor, Toggle physical simulator and Education Module. Finally, we presented a use case to validate the platform and use the results as feedback.

As future work, we intend to improve the education module, enabling new virtual/physical objects to be developed. It is important to emphasize that the focus from the present moment, where the platform is implemented and tested, becomes the creation of learning objects that provide greater interaction among individuals and the environment, providing an environment that, according to Piaget, provides learning of higher quality.

We also aim, at a second moment, the deployment of the prototype in some courses offered at the Center for Computational Sciences at Federal University of Rio Grande, so that new actual tests can be made, and the results can be used to determine new platform requirements.

Finally, it is also the intention of this work to create a Non-Restrictive Module, where the focus will be the development of objects that seek to minimize the restrictions of space-time, sensory and performance found by people with needs or not, at the educational environments.

REFERENCES

[1] Shunqing Yan, Yongxin Zhu, Qiannan Zhang, Qin Wang, Ming Ni, Guangwei Xie, "A Case Study of CPNS Intelligence: Provenance Reasoning over Tracing Cross Contamination in Food Supply Chain," 2012 32nd International Conference on Distributed Computing Systems Workshops, pp. 330-335, 2012 32nd International Conference on Distributed Computing Systems Workshops, 2012.

[2] Jean Piaget, "A Epistemologia Genética e a Pesquisa Psicológica". Rio de Janeiro: Freitas Bastos, 1974.

[3] E. Zouganeli and I. Svinnset, "Connected objects and the internet of things x2014; a paradigm shift," in Photonics in Switching, 2009. PS '09. International Conference on, 2009, pp. 1–4.

[4] Y. Huang and G. Li, "Descriptive models for /internet of things," in Intelligent Control and Information Processing (ICICIP), 2010 International Conference on, 2010, pp. 483–486.

[5] N. Koshizuka and K. Sakamura, "Ubiquitous id: Standards for ubiquitous computing and the internet of things," Pervasive Computing, IEEE, vol. 9, no. 4, pp. 98 –101, october-december 2010.

[6] uID Center, "http://www.uidcenter.org/," Apr 2011.

[7] Ragunathan (Raj) Rajkumar, Insup Lee, Lui Sha, and John Stankovic. 2010. Cyber-physical systems: the next computing revolution. In Proceedings of the 47th Design Automation Conference (DAC '10). ACM, New York, NY, USA, 731-736. DOI=10.1145/1837274.1837461 http://doi.acm.org/10.1145/1837274.1837461.

[8] Poovendran, R., "Cyber–Physical Systems: Close Encounters Between Two Parallel Worlds [Point of View]," Proceedings of the IEEE , vol.98, no.8, pp.1363,1366, Aug. 2010.

[9] Creswell, J. (1994). Research design qualitative and quantitative approaches. Thousand Oaks: Sage Publications..

[10] Lincoln, Y. S., & Guba, E. G. (1985). Naturalistic inquiry. Beverly Hills, CA: Sage Publications..

[11] Qiang Li, Weijun Qin, Bing Han, Ruicong Wang, Limin Sun. A case study on REST-style architecture for cyber-physical systems: Restful smart gateway. Comput. Sci. Inf. Syst 01/2011; 8:1317-1329. pp.1317-1329.

[12] Ying Tan, Mehmet C. Vuran, Steve Goddard, Yue Yu, Miao Song, and Shangping Ren. 2010. A concept lattice-based event model for Cyber-Physical Systems. In Proceedings of the 1st ACM/IEEE International Conference on Cyber-Physical Systems (ICCPS '10). ACM, New York, NY, USA, 50-60.

[13] Chattopadhyay, D.; Dasgupta, R., "A novel comprehensive sensor model for cyber physical system: Interoperability for heterogeneous sensor," Sensing Technology (ICST), 2012 Sixth International Conference on , vol., no., pp.179,183, 18-21 Dec. 2012

[14] Derler, Patricia and Lee, Edward A. and Sangiovanni-Vincentelli, Alberto L. Addressing Modeling Challenges in Cyber-Physical Systems. UCB/EECS-2011-17.

[15] Lui Sha; Gopalakrishnan, S.; Xue Liu; Qixin Wang, "Cyber-Physical Systems: A New Frontier," Sensor Networks, Ubiquitous and Trustworthy Computing, 2008. SUTC '08. IEEE International Conference on , vol., no., pp.1,9, 11-13 June 2008.

[16] Jianhua Shi; Jiafu Wan; Hehua Yan; Hui Suo, "A survey of Cyber-Physical Systems," Wireless Communications and Signal Processing (WCSP), 2011 International Conference on , vol., no., pp.1,6, 9-11 Nov. 2011 doi: 10.1109/WCSP.2011.6096958.

[17] Advances in Cyber-Physical Systems Research. Jiafu Wan, Hehua Yan, Hui Suo, Fang Li. TIIS 01/2011; 5:1891-1908. pp.1891-1908.

[18] Xuan Ma, Xikai Tu, Jian Huang, and Jiping He. 2011. A cyber-physical system based framework for motor rehabilitation after stroke. In Proceedings of the 1st International Conference on Wireless Technologies for Humanitarian Relief (ACWR '11). ACM, New York, NY, USA, 285-290.

[19] Ross Desmond, Matt Dickerman, James Fleming.. Human-in-the-Loop Cyber Physical Systems: Modular Designs for Semi-Autonomous Wheelchair Navigation.

[20] Shinyoung Lim, Lawrence Chung, Oakyoung Han, and Jae-Hyun Kim. 2011. An interactive cyber-physical system (CPS) for people with disability and frail elderly people. In Proceedings of the 5th International Conference on Ubiquitous Information Management and Communication (ICUIMC '11). ACM, New York, NY, USA, , Article 113 , 8 pages.

[21] Mike Keppell, Kay Souter, Matthew Riddle. Physical and Virtual Learning Spaces in Higher Education: Concepts for the Modern Learning Environment. 2011.

[22] Jen-Her Wu, Robert D. Tennyson, Tzyh-Lih Hsia, A study of student satisfaction in a blended e-learning system environment, Computers & Education, Volume 55, Issue 1, August 2010, Pages 155-164, ISSN 0360-1315, 10.1016/j.compedu.2009.12.012.

[23] Olympiou, G. and Zacharia, Z. C. (2012), Blending physical and virtual manipulatives: An effort to improve students' conceptual understanding through science laboratory experimentation. Sci. Ed., 96: 21–47. doi: 10.1002/sce.20463

[24] Joshua McCarthy. Blended learning environments: Using social networking sites to enhance the first year experience .Australasian Journal of Educational Technology 2010, 26(6), 729-740.

[25] Caparróz, A.S.C. & Lopes, M.C.P. 2008. Desafios e perspectivas em ambientes virtuais de aprendizagem: inter-relações, formação tecnológica e prática docente. Educação Formação e Tecnologias, (1), 50-58.

[26] Almeida, M.E.B. 2003. Educação a distância na internet: abordagens e contribuições dos ambientes digitais de aprendizagem. Educação e Pesquisa, (29), 327-340.

[27] Tarouco, L.M.R.; Konrath, M.L.P.; Carvalho, M.J.S.; Ávila, B.G. 2006. Formação de professores para produção e uso de objetos de aprendizagem. Revista Novas Tecnologias na Educação, (4), 1-10.

Learning Online: The Role of Attitudes Towards Online Communication

Nicola Marsden
IT Department, Heilbronn University, Heilbronn, Germany

Abstract – *In educating students to professionally deal with remote collaboration, educators are faced with attitudinal structures – both their own and their students – with might have an influence on their actual online behavior. In an exploratory factor analysis three factors which represent different attitudes found towards online communication were identified. In this paper these three dimensions are presented and future research based on these findings is outlined.*

Keywords: attitudes, factor analysis, online collaboration, computer-mediated communication

1 Introduction

Attitudes towards online communication can influence the approach a person takes towards working and learning online. For educators, this is relevant from several perspectives: (1) most learning today involves some extend of online communication, (2) preparing the students to effectively communicate online is a key competence students have to acquire, (3) students' attitudes might be homogeneous or they might differ from one another in their approaches and this is relevant for the approach taking to teaching them, (4) teachers' own attitudes need to be reflected and might be similar or dissimilar to their students' attitudes.

Thus researching the attitudinal structure people have towards online communication can help to improve learning and preparing students for communicating in their future work environment. Yet only few studies have focused on attitudes towards online communication and learning (Hammoud, Love & Brinkman, 2008; Korkmaz, 2012; Ku, Tseng & Akarasriworn, 2013). One reason to consider attitudes is that although the relationship between attitudes and actions is difficult, there is a connection and attitudes and resulting actions may lead to self-fulfilling prophecies (cf. Walther & Bazarova, 2007) – as a result one could argue that in understanding choice of media, mode of communication, preferences in collaboration platforms etc. attitudes should be taken into consideration.

Attitudes towards online communication reflect the approaches taken by scientific theories to a certain extend (Götz & Marsden, 2010). In an exploratory factor analysis (Marsden, 2013) three different approaches were identified based on Walther and Parks (2002): The first factor represents a focus on deficits of online communication, the second one a focus on social cues in online communication, and the third one a focus on the hyperpersonal options of online communication.

2 Attitudinal Structure Regarding Online Communication

The factors identified as dimensions of attitudes towards online communication (Marsden, 2013) can be described as follows:

Deficit Approach

People who take this approach focus on deficits of online communication and the necessity to make the right choice of media. The loss of (social) information is considered crucial and face to face has a decisive lead over online communication that can not be replicated. Thus it is important to choose an appropriate mode of communication for the task at hand and watch out for different things online and face to face.

Looking at scientific theories which are based on this approach on finds the notion that there has to be a match between information richness and media richness (Daft &

Lengel, 1986; Daft, Lengel, & Trevino, 1987). The basic assumption is that people choose a medium according to the cues they need. Some types of messages might be conveyed more efficiently in one medium than in another – thus it is important to match the message and the medium. A cue system or bandwidth is taken as a causal property: As bandwidth gets lower, certain aspects of communication are assumed to change. These differences include a decline in civility, coordination, empathy, and friendliness. There is assumed to be an optimal match between the message equivocality or uncertainty and the chosen media such that efficiency and effectiveness is optimal.

Social Cues Approach

Individuals taking this approach focus on relationships to others: The basic assumption is that – online or offline – people will find appropriate ways to socialize, and that online communication offers many options to build up positive relationships with others – the idea that communication via mail or online has many disadvantages is rejected.

Scientific theories based on this approach focus on the fact that online communication brings in new cues which are not available in face to face communication – thus offering more or other ways to communicate. For example, communicators can exchange social information through timing (e.g. night versus day time) or style (spelling, signature, emoticons etc.) of verbal messages online. This line of research has shown that the absence of certain cues can enhance communication arguing that cues present in face to face interaction might actually have negative effects: Physical appearance can lead to the attribution of a multitude of qualities via the halo effect, markers of taste, age, habitus, signs of out-group-membership etc can lead to a biased perception. Thus the absence of cues in online communication can, under certain circumstances, forge stronger group identities than face to face interaction (Spears and Lea, 1992, 1994). Based on the theories of social identity and self-categorization (e.g., Turner, Hogg, Oakes, Reicher, & Wetherell, 1987) individuals are conceptualized to have multiple layers of self that become relevant depending on which social identity is salient. When personal identities are salient, the person behaves according to the norms, beliefs and standards which correspond to his or her unique identity. When social identities are salient, the behavior is based on the norms of the group with which one is identified. This process is enhanced by online communication that lacks multimedia cues and renders the partners visually anonymous: Under conditions of visual anonymity, people act in ways more normative to the salient group (Postmes, Spears, & Lea, 1998; Spears & Lea, 1992). When pictures or videos are added, these effects diminish: Individuating information conveyed through physical appearance leads to the individuals being evaluated independently and with less group bias (Lea & Spears, 1995; Lea, Spears, & de Groot, 2001). Based on this approach, online communication makes group memberships and social identity more salient and promotes greater group identification.

Cues Bent and Twisted Approach

People with this approach hold attitudes which focus on the new chances and advantages of online communication: Face to face communication is considered as something that can actually be negative and online communication is taken to offer possibilities for communication which are even better than face to face communication and can actually improve communication.

A related scientific theory to this approach is Walther's (1996) hyperpersonal theory. It argues that online communication can be even more personal that face to face communication („hyperpersonal"), because in an asynchronous online setting, sender, receiver, channel, and feedback can work together to promote more socially desirable levels of interaction than face to face communication (Walther, 1996): In online communication, individualizing cues such as appearance, which are necessarily available in face to face interaction are not readily available. The cues available can be manipulated by the sender to customize his or her self-presentation. In asynchronous interactions, the sender can mindfully compose the message, edit and review the content before sending it to the receiver. The focus of all cognitive resources can be on the message construction and the cognitive load can be divided over a longer time than in face to face communication. In combination with these identity optimizing effects, the receiver tends to formulate idealized perceptions of the sender, interpreting the information available in terms of a common identity with the sender. Thus a positive feedback loop can lead to an interaction which is more positive than a face to face interaction might have been.

3 Future Research

Based on the finding that these different approaches have been identified as dimensions in an exploratory factor analysis future research should a.) confirm the attitudinal structure and b.) study the practical implications this attitudes have for learning and working online. Therefore, the development of a scale is planned which allows for an objective, valid, and reliable measure of the three approaches. Then hypotheses regarding affective, cognitive and behavioral components of these attitudes will be derived and tested.

4 References

Daft, R. L., & Lengel, R. H. (1986). Organizational information requirements, media richness, and structural determinants. *Management Science*, Vol. 32, pp. 554–571.

Daft, R. L., Lengel, R. H., & Trevino, L. K. (1987). Message equivocality, media selection, and manager performance: Implications for information systems. *MIS Quarterly*, Vol. 11, pp. 355–368.

Götz, K. & Marsden, N. (2010). *Soziale Interaktionen im Netz.* In: R. Holten & D. Nittel (Eds.): Theorie und Empirie von E-Learning. Einsatzchancen in Hochschule und Weiterbildung. Bielefeld: Bertelsmann, pp. 81-94.

Hammoud, L.; Love, S.; Brinkman, W.-P. (2008). The affect of lecturers' attitude on students' use of an online learning environment. ECCE '08: Proceedings of the 15th European conference on Cognitive ergonomics.

Korkmaz, Ö. (2012). A validity and reliability study of the Online Cooperative Learning Attitude Scale (OCLAS). Computers & Education, Vol. 59, Issue 4, pp. 1162-1169.
Ku, H.-Y.; Tseng, H. W.; Akarasriworn, C. (2013). Computers in Human Behavior. Vol. 29 Issue 3, pp. 922-929.

Lea, M., & Spears, R. (1995). Love at first byte? Building personal relationships over computer networks. In J. T. Wood & S. Duck (Eds.), *Under-studied relationships: Off the beaten track.* Thousand Oaks, CA: Sage, pp. 197-233.

Lea, M., Spears, R., & de Groot, D. (2001). Knowing me, knowing you: Anonymity effects on social identity processes within groups. *Personality & Social Psychology Bulletin*, Vol. 27, pp. 526–537.

Marsden, N. (2013). Attitudes towards Online Communication: An Exploratory Factor Analysis. In: Proceeding of SIGMIS-CPR'13, May 30–June 1, 2013, Cincinnati, Ohio, USA.

Postmes, T., Spears, R., & Lea, M. (1998). Breaching or building social boundaries? SIDE effects of computer-mediated communication. *Communication Research*, Vol. 25, pp. 689–715.

Spears, R., & Lea, M. (1992). Social influence and the influence of the 'social' in computer-mediated communication. In M. Lea (Ed.), *Contexts of computer-mediated communication.* New York, NY: Harvester Wheatsheaf, pp. 30–65.

Spears, R., & Lea, M. (1994). Panacea or panopticum? The hidden power of computer-mediated communication. *Communication Research*, 21, 427–459.

Turner, J. C., Hogg, M. A., Oakes, P. J., Reicher, S. D., & Wetherell, M. S. (1987). *Rediscovering the social group: A self-categorization theory.* Oxford, UK: Blackwell.

Walther, J. B. (1996) Computer-Mediated Communication: Impersonal, Interpersonal, and Hyperpersonal Interaction. *Communication Research*, Vol. 23, pp. 3-43.

Walther, J. B. & Bazarova, N. N. (2007), Misattribution in Virtual Groups: The Effects of Member Distribution on Self-Serving Bias and Partner Blame. *Human Communication Research*, Vol. 33, pp. 1-26.

Walther, J. B. & Parks, M. R. (2002). Cues filtered out, cues filtered in computer-mediated communication and relationships. In M. L. Knapp & J. A. Daly (Eds.), *Handbook of interpersonal communication* (3rd edition). Thousand Oaks, CA: Sage, pp. 529-563.